Radical INDECISION

Radical INDECISION

Barthes,

Blanchot,

Derrida,

and the Future of Criticism

LESLIE HILL

University of Notre Dame Press

Notre Dame, Indiana

Manufactured in the United States of America

Library of Congress Cataloging-in-Publication Data

Hill, Leslie, 1949–
Radical indecision : Barthes, Blanchot, Derrida, and the future of
criticism / Leslie Hill.
    p.   cm.
Includes bibliographical references and index.
ISBN-13: 978-0-268-03107-7 (pbk. : alk. paper)
ISBN-10: 0-268-03107-x (pbk. : alk. paper)
1. Criticism—History—20th century. 2. Criticism (Philosophy)
3. Literature—Philosophy. 4. Literature—History and
criticism—Theory, etc. 5. Philosophy, French—20th century.
6. Barthes, Roland—Criticism and interpretation.
7. Blanchot, Maurice—Criticism and interpretation.
8. Derrida, Jacques—Criticism and interpretation.   I. Title.
PN94.H56   2009
801'.950904—dc22

                                                        2009041713

The complaint is sometimes made that criticism is no longer capable of judging. But why is this? It is not criticism which out of sheer laziness cannot be bothered to evaluate, but the novel or poem that eschews evaluation because what it seeks is to affirm itself in isolation from all value. And in so far as criticism belongs more intimately to the life of the work, it experiences the work as something that cannot be evaluated, apprehending it as the depth, but also the absence of depth, that escapes each and every system of values, being prior to whatever has value and disqualifying in advance any assertion that would take hold of it to invest it with value. In this sense, criticism—literature—in my view is part of one of the most challenging yet important tasks of our time, unfolding in a movement that is necessarily undecided: the task of preserving and releasing thought from the notion of value, and consequently opening history to that which within history is already moving beyond all forms of value and readying itself for a wholly different—and still unpredictable—kind of affirmation.

Maurice Blanchot, "Qu'en est-il de la critique?"

(The Task of Criticism Today)

CONTENTS

Acknowledgements

I should like to thank the numerous friends, colleagues, and students who, often without realising, have contributed to this book in many different ways. I am particularly indebted to Kevin Hart for his encouragement and generosity, to Andrew Benjamin for his unfailing support, to Christophe Bident for his friendship, to Barbara Hanrahan for her belief in this project, and to Linda Paterson who first asked the question. Juliet, Melanie, Mig, and Susie also helped in more ways than I have space to mention. I am also grateful to the University of Warwick and to the Arts and Humanities Research Council (AHRC) for the provision of study leave that enabled me to complete what became a significantly longer book than I first envisaged. But such is the fate, I eventually learned, that befalls anyone who, gambling on the future, dallies with indecision.

Portions of this book have appeared elsewhere, and I am grateful for permission to use them again here. Part of chapter 1 was published as "'Affirmation without precedent': Maurice Blanchot and Criticism Today," in *After Blanchot: Literature, Philosophy, Criticism*, ed. Leslie Hill, Brian Nelson, and Dimitris Vardoulakis (Newark: University of Delaware Press, 2005); and passages from chapter 3 were incorporated into my "'Distrust of Poetry': Levinas, Blanchot, Celan," *MLN* 120, no. 5 (Winter 2005): 986–1008, copyright © The Johns Hopkins University Press, reprinted with permission.

PREFACE

For literary critics these are the very best of times—and the worst of times. The reach of criticism knows few bounds, and there is little that resists its ever greater expansion. What was once a narrow canon of consecrated works has become a whole Babelian library, a vast audio-visual archive, a proliferating digital complex. Detective fiction, unpublished masterpieces, pulp romance, oral narrative, soap operas, forgotten memoirs, cartoons, fragmentary epics, blockbuster movies, private letters, intimate journals, abandoned or rejected poems, laundry lists, and juvenilia: all these, and more, now have their official commentators, charged with the mission of finding cultural value in the hitherto most unlikely or unpromising places, identifying what is true in this or that text, its context, history, and situation, and promoting or demoting it accordingly in order to give it its rightful place in the universal pantheon.

There is no doubt that this evolution, which shows criticism engaging with the vital needs of the present, should be applauded. But it is only part of a much larger story. For the growth of academic criticism, together with the professionalisation which is one of its most characteristic defining features, has been accompanied in recent decades by an increasing reliance on a sequence of more or less easily defensible interpretative commonplaces embodied in a series of more or less established critical methodologies. Such developments are inevitable, and few are the readers who would want it otherwise. But as one rival approach follows upon the heels of another in the marketplace of ideas, it is sometimes as though criticism in the end is little more than a matter of applying more or less intelligently, more or less reductively, this or that new set of theoretical norms which it has become necessary to invoke in order to lend proper legitimacy to the act of criticism itself. As the net of possible approaches has widened, it has become less a case of inquiring into the purpose of criticism, more one of finding ever more compelling ways of extending its authority over texts, writings, and signatures.

Those who regret this state of affairs sometimes conclude that if criticism is moribund, it is because literary theory has all but killed it, and it is then an easy step to yearn for earlier times when it fell to a social and intellectual elite to set the cultural agenda and determine the value of artistic production and the values it was held to embody. Those days, however, are long gone, not least because in many cases the values in whose name judgements were made have themselves become threadbare, the casualties of interpretative obscurantism and the violence of history, the victims of an economic system in which nothing has value, but everything its price. And even when criticism has acknowledged its loss of belief in past values, it has often been simply to respond to the present as merely a reverse image of what prevailed in the past, thereby remaining all the more dependent on receding norms, or in the face of such changes to opt instead for objective description, forgetting that descriptive criteria are themselves only an expression of inherited values in disguise, or in the end to envisage replacing older verities with newer, better ones, omitting to consider the implications of the very possibility of any such substitution. This too is one of the sources of the malaise affecting criticism today. Even as it finds itself unable to subscribe wholeheartedly to the values of the past, so it is often unable to renounce them either. But the fact is, so long as it is subordinated, directly or indirectly, to the task of attributing value or values to the work, however credible, consensual, or admirable the ethical, moral, or political imperatives expressed in this way, criticism cannot be other than negative, reductive, and normative, radically jeopardising not only its ability to address the future of the work it takes as its object but also its chances of responding to its own possible or impossible future.

How, then, is criticism to answer this predicament? There is no return to past values that, in the end, does not culminate in prejudice, dogma, or simply nostalgia, and it is plainly not enough to reverse past norms or replace them with contemporary-sounding alternatives, for in either case the only outcome is complacency, not to say leaden conformism. And there can be no question of renouncing literary theory, which would be tantamount to a refusal to think. No, for this book, the only viable future for criticism is for it to turn aside from value and values in order to respond to its own occasion, not as a kind of dutiful obedience to prior authority, but as a singular, unpredictable event that does not coincide with itself, but reaches beyond the present to affirm a futurity that, like literature or writing, is never graspable in itself, but comes upon the reader only as a promise of the other.

Contrary to what is sometimes claimed, no longer to remain in thrall to value and values is not to yield to nihilism. As far as this book is concerned, it is quite possibly the exact opposite. For it should be remembered that, for a century or more, writing has shown little interest in inherited or established truths, and, even when it has endeavoured to impose itself through its militant appeal to ethico-political values, it has often proven strangely inadequate to the task of furthering those claims. And as humankind's own future, and the planet it inhabits, has become endangered, for reasons not unrelated to the desire to impose, extract, or recover value at any cost, so it has become ever more essential, rather than to subordinate writing to the tribunal of past values, to affirm writing's enduring disobedience to those values: not in the name of aesthetic autonomy, which is only another value in disguise, but in the name of the future in so far as it exceeds normative regulation. And here, for this book, lie the task and responsibility of what would call itself criticism: the chance of an encounter with the other, the unfamiliar, the alien, the strange, that, exceeding the past and the present, comes from the future, and is not convertible into an object of value.

This challenge is not, however, a new one. It has accompanied literary criticism since its beginnings in the closing years of the eighteenth century. For any activity which sees its task as deciding or deciding upon the future must first of all face the spectre of that which resists decision, without which there would be no need for criticism, and no possibility of its existence. The future of criticism hinges therefore on its responsiveness to the radical indecision which inhabits and traverses it as a condition of possibility and impossibility alike. It is not surprising, then, that the work of three of the most acutely inventive writers on literature in French or in any other language in the second half of the twentieth century, Roland Barthes, Maurice Blanchot, and Jacques Derrida, should be in the form of a lengthy engagement with the demand

and necessity of indecision, as announced by such names as the neuter, the neutral, or the undecidable. Too often in the past, however, indecision has been dismissed by commentators as a moment of negativity, a sign of weakness, or a lack of moral conviction in the face of difficult ethical or political dilemmas. Not so for this book. Here, indecision is anything but a negative predicament. Prior to all certainty, it is a singular and affirmative response to the singular writing of others.

Literature, it is often argued, by embodying value and values, provides an example: of human possibility, timeless significance, cultural worth. But what is an example, and how to be certain that it says anything at all—other than about itself: itself as same, in so far as it manifests itself, but also itself as other, in so far as it is always in excess of what it seems?

Chapter One

Instantiations

I

For example

> Fine art [*Die schöne Kunst*] shows its superiority precisely in this, that it describes things beautifully [*schön*] that in nature we would dislike or find ugly [*Dinge, die in der Natur häßlich oder mißfällig sein würden*]. The Furies, diseases, devastations of war, and so on are all harmful [*Schädlichkeiten*]; and yet they can be described, or even presented in a painting, very beautifully. There is only one kind of ugliness [*Häßlichkeit*] that cannot be presented in conformity with nature [*der Natur gemäß*] without obliterating all aesthetic liking [*ohne alles ästhetische Wohlgefallen zu Grunde zu richten*] and hence artistic beauty [*Kunstschönheit*]: that ugliness that arouses *disgust* [*Ekel*; Kant's emphasis]. For in that strange sensation, which rests on nothing but imagination [*Einbildung*], the object is presented as if it insisted, as it were, on our enjoying it even though that is just what we are forcefully resisting [*gleichsam, als ob er sich zum Genusse aufdränge, wider den wir doch mit Gewalt streben*]; and hence the artistic presentation of the object [*die künstliche Vorstellung des Gegenstandes*] is no longer distinguished in our sensation from the nature of this object itself, so that it cannot possibly be considered beautiful.
>
> Immanuel Kant, *Critique of Judgement*[1]

This I am happy to inform you is the reversed metamorphosis. The Laurel into Daphne. The old thing where it always was, back again. As when a man, having found at last what he sought, a woman, for example, or a friend, loses it or realizes what it is. And yet it is useless not to seek, not to want, for when you cease to seek you start to find, and when you cease to want, then life begins to ram her fish and chips down your gullet until you puke, and then the puke down your gullet until you puke the puke, and then the puked puke until you begin to like it.

Samuel Beckett, Watt[2]

One "thing" alone is inassimilable. It thus forms the transcendental of the transcendental, the untranscendentalisable, the unidealisable, and that is: that which is disgusting [*le dégoûtant;* what Kant calls *Ekel*]. . . . It is no longer a case of one of those negative values, or ugly or harmful objects which art may represent and thereby idealise. That which is absolutely excluded [*Cet exclu absolu*] does not even allow itself to be accorded the status of an object of negative pleasure or of ugliness redeemed by representation. It is unrepresentable. And at the same time unnamable in its singularity [*innommable dans sa singularité*].

Jacques Derrida, "Economimesis"[3]

Let me begin, then, with an example.

In the late 1940s a middle-aged French woman by the name of Suzanne Deschevaux-Dumesnil, an accomplished pianist with an enthusiasm for literature and theatre, was tirelessly hawking round the offices of various French publishers a series of manuscripts written in French by her partner, an Irishman by origin, who before the war, in Dublin and London, had established a minor reputation as a prose-writer, novelist, and sometime book reviewer, and at the time was eking out a living in Paris as a translator and occasional art critic. But despite the support of influential figures such as Max-Pol Fouchet and Tristan Tzara (who had been instrumental in obtaining publication in French of an earlier novel), Suzanne encountered rejection after rejection. It is hard to say how many times the work was turned down. Some have said it was dozens; others have identified at least six established publishers who declared themselves unimpressed.

This failure to find a publisher probably came as no surprise to those involved. Already some ten years earlier, a previous novel written in English had also been rejected several times over; and even as Suzanne was devoting her energies to the French manuscripts, a further novel, also written in English, was unsuccessfully doing the rounds on the other side of the Channel; by April 1953, according to the author, it too had been turned down by "a good score of London publishers." But finally one of the manuscripts Suzanne was struggling to place found its way into the hands of a young, twenty-six-year-old publisher by the name of Jérôme Lindon, who two years earlier had taken over as head of the wartime, formerly clandestine publishing house, the éditions de Minuit. Lindon decided to take the typescript home with him during his lunch break, started reading it in the Paris métro, and was soon convulsed in hoots of laughter. The very next day he resolved to accept for publication both the novel he was reading and its two sequels, and signed a contract with Suzanne. The date was 15 November 1950.[4]

The rest, of course, is history. For the title of that first all-but-unpublishable novel, as readers will have realised, was *Molloy,* and the name of its little-known expatriate author, Samuel Beckett—that self-same novelist, prose-writer, dramatist, and poet who, less than twenty years later, in autumn 1969, by an extraordinary reversal or reverse (not to say catastrophe, reportedly Suzanne's verdict on the matter), found himself not only the recipient of the Nobel Prize for literature and the object of the extensive consecration that comes with such awards but also the focal point of one of the most successful international critical industries of modern times, which, then and since, has seen the academic and other comment devoted to the author's writings proliferate seemingly without end.

But in the late 1940s and early 1950s all this lay in the future. At the time, it was no doubt legitimate for French publishers to ask themselves: who was this foreigner who had opted to write in French and, far from concealing his national origins, perversely flaunted them by giving his novel the unmistakeably Irish, far from French-sounding name of *Molloy?* Who wrote so tastelessly, among other things, about masturbation, ejaculation, and horses' rumps?[5] Whose characteristic gesture was one of "fatigue and disgust," as neatly worded in the Addenda to *Watt,* Beckett's last novel written in English, eventually published in Paris in 1953 by Maurice Girodias's controversial and—to some—disreputable Olympia Press? And whose nihilistic assault on inherited values, indeed on language itself, seemed beyond all bounds? "The absurdity of the world and the meaninglessness of our condition are conveyed in an absurd and deliberately insignificant fashion," wrote Maurice Nadeau—an influential admirer—apropos of *Molloy* in April 1951, and concluded as follows: "never did anybody dare so openly to insult everything which man holds to be certain, up to and including the very language on which he could at least rely to scream his doubt and despair."[6]

But to whom did the name Samuel Beckett refer? Early in 1947, in the unpublished *Eleutheria*, written shortly before embarking on *Molloy*, Beckett had provided a kind of prospective answer of his own, with self-conscious but typically self-lacerating humour, by having the character of the Spectator denounce, in the play's own words, the author of the "rubbish"—or "navet," literally a turnip—that Beckett at that very moment was busily writing. (Other more grotesque parts, it may be remembered, were written for characters called Krap, Piouk, and Skunk.) Garbling the author's foreign-sounding name, but politely invoking it nonetheless, the Spectator went on: "Beckett (*il dit: 'Béquet'*) Samuel, Béquet, Béquet, ça doit être un juif groenlandais mâtiné d'Auvergnat," "a cross between a Jew from Greenland and a peasant from the Auvergne," as Barbara Wright's translation ably puts it.[7] The self-portrait was no doubt designed to be protective as much as it was provocative. Either way, it was a measure of Beckett's unapologetic perception of his cultural outlandishness, that state beyond reassuring linguistic, national, or even aesthetic affiliation, to which, in the years that followed, he was to remain rigorously faithful, by declining for instance to give interviews to explain or explicate his work, or otherwise give it any public profile beyond that which was affirmed in and by the writing itself. The textual signature, so to speak, was enough; and it was all. As Beckett wrote in 1954, celebrating the work of his friend Jack Yeats, "l'artiste qui joue son être est de nulle part. Et il n'a pas de frères," "the artist who stakes his being is from nowhere, has no kith."[8]

It is perhaps hardly surprising, then, that Beckett did not at first enjoy significant commercial success with his French works. True, in later years he was to save Minuit (and Lindon) from financial crisis more than once. Initial sales were, however, modest. The French translation of *Murphy*, published in 1947, had not done well either, selling only four (four!) copies in its first year, and the failure of that first book in French explained why the publisher Pierre Bordas, offered *Molloy* in 1948, turned down the manuscript. Six years after publication, as James Knowlson reports, there were still 2,750 unsold copies of *Murphy* (in French), which Lindon was able to buy up and reissue under the Minuit imprint.[9] Early sales of *Molloy* were similarly disappointing. In its first year of trading, which would typically be the most successful period, especially in the case of a relatively unknown author, the book sold some 694 copies. If anything, sales were probably aided by a number of generally favourable reviews by prominent critics such as Maurice Nadeau, Jean Blanzat, Bernard Pingaud, Georges Bataille, and Jean Pouillon.[10] *Malone meurt* (*Malone Dies*), for its part, published later the same year, to less explicit critical acclaim, managed to sell only 241 copies. *L'Innommable* (*The Unnamable*), coming out in July 1953, several months after the controversy surrounding the first run of *En attendant Godot* (*Waiting for Godot*), fared somewhat better, achieving sales of 476.[11]

More than half a century after *Molloy*, *Malone meurt*, and *L'Innommable* were written, it is hard to imagine how these novels once seemed beyond the pale of what was publishable, worthy at best of marginal attention on the part of a select few. It seems almost superfluous to say this now, but in the course of the 1950s and 1960s, and perhaps even more so since, a remarkable transformation came about, totally redefining Beckett's status as a literary figure. As I write, all his works, virtually without exception, enjoy the unrivalled status of modern classics. They are the subject of close and devoted attention, and figure in countless university curricula throughout the world. Performances of his plays are staged, revived, and regularly reviewed as integral parts of the established repertoire. Far from the work being almost unpublishable, there is now a ready audience, on the evidence of the author's name alone, for almost everything in existence that Beckett wrote: draft manuscripts, abandoned works, notebooks, translations, correspondence, and marginal doodles. And this is not just a French or an English-language phenomenon, for Beckett's audience counts a multitude of different readers in many diverse languages, all eager to discover what new information or knowledge critics or editors may have to impart.

No longer a recalcitrant or barbarous outsider, then, Beckett today stands by common consent at the very heart of modern literary culture. As such, he is one of a select but oddly revealing band of writers—

including such strange bedfellows as Sade, Proust, Joyce, Kafka, or Sacher-Masoch—whose names do not merely denote bodies of work, but have spawned adjectives whose application extends far beyond the confines of those actual texts. "Beckettian" in this sense no longer means purely and simply whatever pertains to the author's work. It has come to identify an entire disposition, a philosophy, a worldview, an attitude to language, a way of feeling, thinking, talking, to which the only plausible response today appears to be one of knowing familiarity: "Ah, yes . . . " Beckett's reputation today, it would seem, has always already preceded the work; and even before reading occurs or a performance takes place, audiences believe they know what to expect. In other words, Beckett's work has ceased to be a singular, enigmatic, barely recognisable event. Instead, like some established rhetorical paradigm, it has come to exemplify a host of assumptions, conventions, judgements, or adjudications which now follow Beckett's name wherever it appears, providing readers with a series of ready-made evaluative frames or interpretative strategies from which they can select at will. And the list of off-the-peg readings made available to new or aspiring readers is a long one, with Beckett serving variously but persistently as an instantiation (in no particular order) of modernism, postmodernism, classicism, stoicism, scepticism, quietism, existentialism, absurdism, humanism, anti-humanism, pessimism, optimism, poststructuralism, nihilism, Irishism—and many others besides.

Admittedly, this metamorphosis in the status of Beckett's work is not unprecedented in the reception of literary works. Any process of canon formation necessarily implies changes, shifts, or upheavals by which previously unread or unreadable texts are discovered in hindsight, according to this or that critical perspective, to merit a place at the centre of literary or artistic culture. The reverse occurs too, when established, even celebrated works, justly or unjustly, depending on the point of view of critics, suddenly find themselves relegated to the periphery. Reception takes time; expectations are modified; fashions change. Critical judgements are subject to numerous contingencies, vagaries, or disagreements. All this is the stuff of literary critical debate, its everyday reality, and its life's blood. In this sense, there is nothing out of the ordinary in Beckett's change in fortune. It was nevertheless dramatic, partly because of the speed with which, in less than twenty years, the work travelled from margin to centre, from the barbarous to the familiar, the unpublishable to the canonic, the unreadable to the always already read, partly too because of the overwhelming critical unanimity with which the transformation occurred.

A case in a thousand, perhaps. But who today would risk ridicule by protesting about the offensive tastelessness of Beckett's writing?

Something, then, between 1947 and 1969, must have happened.

What happened, I shall argue, has to do with the possibility and impossibility of critical evaluation itself, with the comic inconsistency, the erratic uncertainty, and the necessary blindness that, as Beckett's writing testifies, betray the imprint of the irregular, the unpredictable, and the incalculable: in other words, the future.

To evaluate any literary work is to refer a judgement, whether positive or negative, to some implicit or explicit rule, norm, belief, or prejudice. It is to seek to justify or legitimate a given response to a text by appealing to a value—that is, some established measure by which each singular item might be converted into some general equivalent that would allow it to be compared, in principle, with each and every other item in the system —which the given object of judgement may then be thought to confirm, either positively or negatively, by illustration or default. In the process, the individual case is judged according to the extent to which it can be held to endorse, embody, and exemplify a given value. It becomes valuable or valid to the extent it can be portrayed as an instantiation of the rule it is thought to illustrate; and what counts, henceforth, is less the singularity of the case than the value it is considered to be promoting, defending, or threatening.

Two difficulties are immediately apparent, which have a clear bearing on the reception of Beckett's writing from 1950 onwards.

The first has to do with the account that evaluative criticism takes of those writings that resist, disobey, or flout the explicit or implicit rule according to which evaluation is being carried out. Various responses are possible. First, a critic may simply refuse to read what he or she has been reading, by abandoning reading altogether, or failing to read while apparently still doing so. Second, a critic can roundly condemn what she or he is evaluating because it fails to endorse the norms being applied. Or, thirdly, with more apparent generosity or tolerance, a critic can agree to judge the object of criticism allegedly on its merits, but to do so only in negative terms, on the basis of what the artwork is not, as a rejection, transgression, or critique of a still binding norm.

In Beckett's case, there is little doubt that all three strategies have been employed at one time or another. Today, the third is probably the most common. It reflects the inability of evaluative criticism to respond in affirmative fashion to that which is new, innovative, or unprecedented: that writing which, in whatever way, is resistant to the horizon of expectation deployed by the norm according to which evaluation is being performed. This may seem to be a criterion that has only limited relevance: how many works, one might ask, are genuinely innovative? This is to miss the point. For any text, before it becomes an object of evaluation for criticism, is a novelty: an unexpected event, the character or quality of which cannot be decided, at least for the moment, and possibly for considerably longer. This, of course, is how and why evaluation is possible at all, and why some think it necessary. For if the character or quality of the event were decided in advance, there would be no reason to evaluate it, nor any means to do so, and one would probably conclude that it was not an event at all. But if this resistance of the event to evaluation makes evaluation both possible and necessary, it also makes it inevitable that the act of evaluation will not meet its goal and reach any definitive conclusion. If evaluation is dependent on the unpredictability of the event, without which it cannot even occur, then it follows that the event's resistance to evaluation cannot wither away in the face of judgement. The challenge of the one to the other remains. Whatever the judgement proffered by a critic, the possibility always exists for that evaluation to be inappropriate or inadequate, or for it to be mistaken on any number of grounds, as a result of which it is always likely to be contested today or tomorrow by some other act of evaluation claiming for itself the same degree of entitlement or legitimacy as the first.

Evaluation, then, is never final; by its nature it can only ever be provisional. To be what it is and remain faithful to its vocation, at times seduced, at times rejected, at times acknowledged, at times ignored, it has to contend with that which resists its reductive ambitions. What resists is the incalculable, and the incalculable is what escapes the imposition of value, contests its authority, challenges its legitimacy and possibility. If it is to occur at all, it seems, critical evaluation is condemned to fail. It stumbles over its own final impossibility. For it can only address the incalculable by treating it as what it is not, that is, by refusing to read. Rather than responding to the singularity of the textual event it is allegedly evaluating, it remains trapped within an economy founded on identity, familiarity, or repetition, for which each and every new case is the duplicate or double of another that has always already been submitted to calculation. All of which explains, as traditional commentators are only too keen to remind their readers, why critical evaluation is by nature a conservative, conformist act, whose decisions are informed first of all by precedent, established standards, and pre-existing ideology, that is, by those very values it insists on applying.

It is perhaps not surprising, then, that having been initially ignored or condemned by critics, Beckett's work today is largely read in negative terms: either as testimony to the impending failure, disintegration, or collapse of (post)modern(ist) culture, or, alternatively, as a subverting, undermining, dismantling, overturning, or mocking of established certitudes or verities. This negativity, in turn, is but the obverse of the normative positivity of value or values. It is essentially a dialectical trait; and such is the irresistible power of the dialectic that it is an easy step "magically," in Hegel's famous phrase, to convert these negative readings into positive ones: anti-humanism into humanism, despair into hope, corrosive humour into stoic cheerfulness, bodily grotesques into models of mindful perseverance, with Beckett's work being used now to rehabilitate the very values—human dignity, say—it was previously seen so doggedly to be attacking.

In situations such as these, criticism's main priority, if only for its own survival, is to assert its authority, its ability to decide on the value (or lack of value) of a given text. If so, it is apparent that any act of critical judgement, to the extent that it is a judgement, while it may believe itself genuinely to be committed to a certain conception of justice, will always run the risk of perpetrating or perpetuating injustice. All judgement, even a judgement that seeks to legitimate itself by appealing to universal values, implies the possibility of misjudgement, however defined, just as the claim to dispense justice must always carry with it the risk of committing an injustice. It cannot be said with certainty, of course, that any reader or critic of Beckett, whatever his or her conviction of remaining just in respect of Beckett's writing, has ever avoided these pitfalls, and the fact that they are by definition ineluctable perhaps

explains why so many early publishers or readers, not to mention subsequent audiences, found it so hard to rise to the challenge of Beckett's
writing and do so in affirmative manner: that is, to read what was
written.

For that was and remains the pressing question for any reader confronting Beckett's writing, either for the first time or for the last: how to
read, that is, how to accommodate within the established parameters of
literary judgement a body of writing in which the gesture, theme, or
fantasy of expulsion (oral, nasal, and anal) is endowed with such uncompromising violence, a body in whose name Beckett's writing, faithful in
this respect at least to Kant's prescription, forces itself upon its sometimes reluctant readers, demanding they enjoy what is on offer, to the
point where the reader of *Watt,* say, is enjoined in Arsene's memorable
words to "puke the puke, and then the puked puke until you begin to
like it"—all the while continuing, like Arsene the well-named, to snort
"down the snout—haw!—so," as *Watt* puts it some pages later, not to
mention the future narrator of the second part of *Molloy* who, in similar
vein, likens his fate (inviting the reader to consider his or her own position on the matter) to that of "la merde qui attend la chasse d'eau," "the
turd waiting for the flush."[12] And if it is not possible to salvage such
assertions for artistic representation and the pure judgements of taste it
requires, as Kant thought necessary, how then to respond to the irresistible demand that Beckett's writing makes of the reader, including
that reader who might indeed want to resist the very reading that is forcing her or him to resist? Is it ever certain, it might then be asked, that
Beckett's work is readable at all?

The grotesque scatological charge that runs through Beckett's writing, and caused such offence to legal authorities in Dublin, Paris, and
London, reveals more than a jejune desire to shock complacent middle-
class audiences, the Church, or other would-be arbiters of taste. It is a
symptom of the bodily materiality and irreducible contingency of the
texts themselves, a sign of their recalcitrant objection to the idealising,
sublimating, essentialising movement of traditional aesthetics. For
while the Beckettian body is everywhere to be found in the thematic
content of *Molloy,* say, it exceeds that thematic horizon too, inscribing
itself within the consonantal and vocal texture of the writing not as a
source of meaning but as a singular textual signature or imprint. For it
is hardly by chance that Bécquet, Samuel, this Greenland Jew or peas-

ant from the Auvergne, in turning to a language not that of his mother or of his father, should not only rewrite his own name—should we pronounce it **bekIt** or **bekEt**, and should we say **mclwa** or **mclOI?**—but also provide himself in so doing with a series of prosthetic crutches or *béquilles* (B-E-K), not to say a bicycle (*bicyclette* [B-K-ETT], never the more common *vélo*), to help figure his exemplary (dis)embodiment within the language of the other, this otherness that is language itself, which is never mine.[13]

This insistent presence of the body in Beckett's writing raises an acute question of readability. For it is never certain what reading entails. What qualifications, diplomas, or certificates does it require? By what authority does it occur? Moreover, reading, in the same way as writing, is not an operation that it is easy or even possible to delimit. For one thing, it always already incorporates its own opposite. Just as declaring something unreadable or refusing to read is itself a decision taken by a reader who has already begun to read, so it is entirely possible to continue reading a text without reading it. Distraction, in a word, enables and disables reading at one and the same time. What one reader cannot put down, another cannot pick up. What is all too legible for one is unreadable for another. And so on. Not to read, then, is just as much a mode of reading as reading itself. It could always be argued, then, that the negative reaction of publishers to Beckett's work in the early phase of its reception was paradoxically somehow more adequate—if any reading can ever be deemed adequate—to the recalcitrant singularity of Beckett's writing than the response of those for whom the author's work was subsequently an object of cultural consecration. That Beckett himself may also have believed this, as early as 1950, is what lies behind the fact that, instead of celebrating the signature of his contract with Minuit, Beckett was moved to express his unhappiness "at the realization," recalls Jérôme Lindon, "that the publication of *Molloy* would lead to our bankruptcy."[14]

Beckett, however, was soon proved wrong; and within ten or twenty years the trickle of reviews that greeted *Molloy* had turned into a veritable flood of books, articles, and Ph.D. dissertations. True, the discipline of Beckett Studies—the term itself is a recognition of the massive institutional response to the author's work—boasts many impressive achievements, and it would be a foolish reader who would want to do without the scrupulous or informative work of critics and researchers too numerous to mention, as a result of whose efforts more is known today than was ever thought possible at one stage about the personal, familial, intellectual, social, historical, or material circumstances in which Beckett's work was produced. But even devoted students of Beckett would have to concede that much published criticism about the writer makes little claim upon the reader, not because commentators are insufficiently discriminating or because they discriminate too much, but because they necessarily always run the risk of falling victim to the infantile disorder of all literary criticism—which may be the fate of all criticism in general—which, in the guise of enabling access to the text, is to domesticate and normalise it, to reduce it to the horizon of expectation of the already known. So was this second period in Beckett reception fundamentally different from the first? Yes. But also: no. For rejection and consecration alike are haunted, as is all reading, by the failure to read, by anxiety in the face of the barbarous singularity of Beckett's writing, its own deep-seated refusal to allow itself to be read, as Derrida puts it, glossing Kant, notwithstanding the efforts of a generation and more of literary critics, as an object of negative pleasure or ugliness finally redeemed by representation.

The critical recuperation of Beckett was not without its costs. Just as it was dominated, to debilitating effect, by the negativity of its judgements, so its interpretations of the author soon became circular. Specific texts became plausible instantiations of Beckett's so-called worldview, the only evidence for which, not surprisingly, was to be found in those very texts themselves. As an all-embracing, unifying vision was ascribed to the author, on the evidence of the work itself, so that vision was used to explicate the works. The singularity of the body was unjustly effaced. Whence, among others, the belief held by numerous critics, especially early ones, that the voice or discourse or narrator or character holding forth in Beckett's texts, whether they be full-length narratives, short narratives, narrative fragments, or plays, was somehow the same self-present consciousness or persona. And whence too the equally strange conviction that the many discontinuities, discordances, inconsistencies, or aporetic doublings that may be observed in Beckett's trilogy might ultimately all give way to some final statement about the truth of being.[15]

Admittedly, it is sometimes wondered why Beckett became the subject of such an enormous critical industry. Does the fact that it was possible at all express some fatal complicity between Beckett's work and academic criticism? Did Beckett's professed distaste for scholarly learning conceal a greater degree of indebtedness to it, and a covert or unacknowledged reliance on that shadowy figure whom Estragon vituperated, "with finality," as the stage directions have it, as "Crritic"?[16] Beckett's own familiarity with literary and artistic tradition was of course extensive, and no doubt the many vestigial traces left in the work by that knowledge played a key role in attracting the attentions of academic readers. Beckett was also fortunate—or is it unfortunate?—to be active as a writer at a time when the institutions demanding and supplying literary critical discourse, that is, the media and the university system, underwent massive transformation and expansion, bringing about that strange professionalisation of literary critical activity that is such a salient feature of recent decades. Perhaps, rather than saying anything noteworthy about Beckett, the amount of work written on the writer may simply be seen as an oblique tribute to higher education policy in Europe, the United States, or the rest of the world.

But the reasons behind the prodigious development of Beckett Studies are not just historical or contextual. They have to do with the fundamental make-up of literature and literary criticism in general. For just as nothing is more real than nothing, in the famous words of one of Beckett's own favourite philosophers, so nothing stimulates reading more than unreadability. But unreadability, as I have suggested, is not some external threat to reading; it is more like its very condition of possibility, in which case the sheer volume of commentary provoked by Beckett's writing, rather than testifying to any implicit reliance upon literary criticism on the part of the work, may rather be said to exist in inverse proportion to its readability. In other words, it is precisely because Beckett's work resists reading that so many readers have found themselves in the position of attempting to overcome that resistance, even though it would then have to be acknowledged that to succeed in such a task would be not only undesirable but impossible too, since to do so would mean there was no longer anything left to read. Happily, unhappily, then, the rain continues to beat on the windows. Or, after all, perhaps not. But who can ever decide?

This quandary reveals something telling about the possibility or impossibility of literary criticism, which is this: while being ostensibly dedicated to making decisions concerning the value or lack of value of texts, their truthfulness or lack of truthfulness, or about the validity of this interpretation or that, criticism is most clearly exercised by what cannot be resolved. Who will say whether it was raining or not? In what world, at what time, to what purport? Nobody can answer, least of all the text of *Molloy*, its author, its reader, or its critic. And even if the narrator's doubts about the weather somehow achieve exemplary status in the novel, encapsulating what some might venture to call its paradigmatically sceptical postmodernist relationship to meaning, it is still far from clear what it is in the novel that is thereby exemplified or instantiated. For examples too are by their nature always double. They are both privileged in themselves and yet necessarily without distinctive qualities. They refer beyond themselves to all members of the class to which they are held to belong merely as one—indifferent—instance among others. But in so doing they necessarily also refer to themselves, thereby acquiring superior status as a result of which they are more than what they are, and are thus quite unlike all other members in their class, from which they now differ in so far as they have precisely become exemplary. Infinitely substitutable according to one criterion, they are radically irreplaceable according to another. Some examples, it seems, are better than others. In which case, what is it they exemplify? All other members of the class to which they are thought to belong, or merely themselves as sole members of the class of exemplary objects? It may be that it reassures the lecturer, say, to address *Molloy* as a novel belonging to this or that class of (post)modern novel, but this does not necessarily enable readers, here and now, to approach the singular text that is *Molloy*, except in so far as the novel is no longer addressed as the contingent work it is, whatever that may be, but only as an example of something else, which it is not.

A similar paradox inhabits *L'Innommable*. For here is a novel, text, narrative, monologue—already these appellations require a moot decision that cannot be referred to higher authority—whose very title speaks simultaneously, duplicitously, of both the possibility and impossibility of naming. Names, it is implied, are possible; yet somehow not in the case of whatever in this instance is thought to require a name. How may this contradiction be resolved? Is it a case of unnamability in general, which would imply that all names are impossible, or is it that in this particular instance no name can be found? Or as far as *L'Innommable* is concerned, is it not that both propositions are equally valid, suggesting not only that names are simultaneously possible and impossible but also that *L'Innommable* itself is both a name and not a name? It should be remembered here that the title of the book is itself nowhere explicated in the text of *L'Innommable,* which, in French at least, carefully refrains from marking its grammatical gender, which could be any one of two, even three possibilities. On the evidence of the text, then, it is impossible to decide whether the title refers to some entity that is male or female, masculine, feminine, or neuter, human or non-human, animal, vegetable, or mineral, or even any entity at all. There is no guarantee, therefore, following the possible analogy with *Molloy* or *Malone meurt* (assuming it can be said with certainty what those titles mean), that *L'Innommable* can be taken to be the name of some first-person narrator-hero. But to the extent that Beckett's title cannot but evoke all these available possibilities, several of which are mutually incompatible, it would follow that the title of *L'Innommable,* being in excess of these interpretative decisions, says more (or less) than all of them put together. It nevertheless remains, in itself and in its own right, a name—if only the nameless name of Beckett's writing. In *L'Innommable* itself, it survives, then, as a mere ghost, present only to the extent it is absent, a place-holder always about to be imminently replaced, a finite trace implying its own infinite erasure, a word that is also not a word, divorced from any given language but only in so far as it is synonymous with the giving (or taking) of language as such.

What holds for naming also applies here to examples. Like all named individuals, as the present discussion indicates, *L'Innommable,* that is, the text that goes by that name, may be deemed exemplary; this much is already implied in the title it gives itself, which cannot *not* function as a name and, by that token, as the name of an example or for an example, even as an exemplary name. *L'Innommable,* then, is perhaps an exemplary novel. But what may it be thought to exemplify, other than this infinite demand for a name, a demand that, by necessity, cannot ever be fulfilled? If *L'Innommable* has exemplary status, then, it is only in so far as it simultaneously carries a name and bears witness to the absence of that name. *L'Innommable* no doubt offers itself as a possible example, but as it does so, cannot *not* challenge that very possibility, and thus throw its own putative status as an example into doubt—in exemplary manner. Beckett's novel, then, asks to be read, in exemplary manner, as an exemplary text that resists the possibility of exemplification. As this spiral unfolds, it becomes apparent that what is at work here is not some essentialising dialectic of presentation, whereby what counts is the degree to which universality inhabits the particular only to the extent the latter is emptied of all inessential material, bodily, or idiomatic contingency, but something much more convoluted, by virtue of which it is the idiomatic singularity, the body, and the materiality of Beckett's writing—"matière, matière, tripotée sans cesse en vain," "matter, matter, pawed and pummelled endlessly in vain,"[17] says the text of *L'Innommable*—that resists and refuses sublimation, incorporation, and generalisation, enacting a movement more akin to what Derrida, in later texts, describes as a kind of textual auto-immune response, one that is prompted by survival, and necessary for it to occur, but which in this case is equally, and for the same reason, bent on destruction or dissolution.[18] Each coming becomes a going, every step forwards a step backwards. So whether *L'Innommable* is an example or not, and, if the former, of what it may then be an example— these are questions that remain hanging as questions, but to which no satisfactory answer can ever be given, because exemplary status is never guaranteed, and because wherever it is inscribed, it is immediately effaced too.

The demand for a name and the realisation that no name is possible collide in this way in Beckett's text, and endure, the one alongside the other, without prospect of resolution. Extremes meet. Aporia looms. "La recherche du moyen de faire cesser les choses, taire sa voix, est ce qui permet au discours de se poursuivre"; "The search for the means to put an end to things, an end to speech, is what enables the discourse to continue."[19] In any case, whatever the reader decides, or fails to decide, is of little importance as far as the text is concerned. Writing itself is the best and only available response to the infinite and interminable demand to which, without hope of success, it endeavours to respond. All that a reader can do in such circumstances is to persist in reading: without end. Read this text, in other words, says *L'Innommable*, but in reading this text, read also that which remains unreadable. Read these words, but read too that which is silently spaced out within these words and resists all words. Honour the name, but honour also the namelessness which, making the name both possible and impossible, exceeds all names, like some supernumerary phantom, overwriting each name as it occurs with the spectral trace of another. "Je le savais, nous serions cent qu'il nous faudrait être cent et un," the reader learns: "I knew it, there might be a hundred of us and we'd still lack the hundred and first."[20] Not the One, then: but always n + 1, the more-than-one, the no-longer-one, the multiple, and yet another . . .

The prescription is double, but without opposition or synthesis. As Maurice Blanchot later puts it, translating into his own idiom the demand of writing, of reading, and of that strange reading of writing doubled by the writing of reading, called literary criticism: "name the possible, respond to the impossible."[21]

What Beckett's writing asks of its reader or readers, then, as Blanchot's words suggest, without it being apparent that any reader can supply it without necessarily betraying the writing, is not judgement, in conformity with this or that law, value, principle, or rule, but something more demanding still: justice. True enough, as Derrida indicates, justice and the law are inseparable; the one implies the other, and to seek the one at some stage involves appealing (suspiciously, critically, responsibly) to the other. But the relationship is far from determinable with ease; and there is also radical incompatibility: between justice, on the one hand, writes Derrida, which is "infinite, incalculable, resistant to any rule, foreign to symmetry, heterogeneous and heterotopic," and the exercise of justice as right, legitimacy, or legality, which functions necessarily as a "stabilisable, statutory and calculable set-up [*dispositif*]," a "system of regulated and coded prescriptions."[22] The dissymmetry is irreducible. A text like *L'Innommable* belongs to a given language, but only to desist from that language according to the idiomatic singularity that makes it what it is. It may appeal, then, to the reader's judgement, but does it recognise the audience's authority? Do reader and writer even speak the same tongue? Do books such as those of Beckett, asks Blanchot, even want to be read?[23] And if they are read, in spite of themselves, so to speak, what is it that they require: the authoritative verdict of a critic, gathering up the text as an example, referring judgement to pre-existing, established criteria, or the convulsive laughter of Jérôme Lindon, his sudden trepidation at letting slip the loose typescript sheets of *Molloy* in the lift while changing trains at the La Motte-Piquet-Grenelle métro station in November 1950? If justice, as Jean-François Lyotard suggests, is inseparable from a feeling of discordance, maladjustment, or lack of fit, then, it may be, as Gilles Deleuze was wont to insist, that the only truly affirmative response to Beckett is to laugh silently, with the text, at the text, like the text: without resolution, in infinite discord.

Now, it is often argued, with strong ideological conviction, that evaluation is one of the abiding duties of all literary criticism. To promote and defend cultural, aesthetic, moral, human, or political values, it is claimed, is what literary criticism does; and if it fails in that endeavour, it may be said to fall short of its purpose and function. A powerful doxa has it, too, that evaluation corresponds to a fundamental human imperative. "[E]valuations," contends, for instance, Barbara Herrnstein Smith, "are not discrete acts or episodes punctuating experience but indistinguishable from the very processes of acting and experiencing themselves. In other words, for a responsive creature, to exist is to evaluate."[24] True enough, there are arguably few, if any, aspects of human life that do not have the potential to fall subject to evaluative decisions. But this is not to say that the economy of value, having universal validity and authority, is without limits, borders, or exteriority. For if this were to be the case, it is hard to see how value could be conferred at all. If everything already had value, it would mean, paradoxically, that nothing had value, but would have been assimilated in prescriptive manner to an all-consuming, totalising economy reducing every act or experience to the status of an item of exchange. Evaluation, in other words, can only occur in so far as it encounters resistance, not only in the sense that another might evaluate a given object differently, but more importantly in the sense that, in every object of evaluation, something remains which is irreducible to its positing or positioning as such. To decide from the outset that an event or experience is an object of evaluation is a circular gesture: it serves merely to endow the economy of value with oppressive self-evidence, and paradoxically to render all critical decisions redundant.

Herrnstein Smith is, of course, not alone in asserting the imperious necessity of values and evaluation. Steven Connor, whom readers will also know as an astute commentator of Beckett, begins his own response to the issue of cultural value by announcing a similarly bold principle. "The necessity of value," he argues, "is in this sense more like the necessity of breathing than, say, the necessity of earning one's living. There are ways of continuing to exist as a human being without the latter, but not without the former."[25] Here too the implications are prescriptive. On the one hand, by contrasting the necessity of breathing and the requirement to earn one's daily bread, Connor carefully separates the existential from the economic. But no sooner is the distinction advanced than, under the rubric of the "necessity of value," the economic is reintroduced into the existential realm of what, after Benjamin and Agamben, may be called: "bare life."[26] In other words, even as he suggests the existential has priority over the economic, Connor also implies that the existential too cannot *not* be subject to the economy of value. It is nothing other than the continuation of the value economy by other means. The realm of value undergoes a strange internal division: there are abstract values on the one side and more properly economic values on the other, belief systems on the one and weekly wages on the other. But how easy a matter is it to split off (moral, ethical, political) values from those (material) values as a result of which, by exchanging my labour for food and shelter, directly or indirectly, I am able to survive, to the point of being able to subscribe, as it were, to a set of given cultural values? In what sense are the former more necessary than the latter? I may not live on bread alone, but is it possible to live without bread at all? Connor claims there are ways of remaining human without meeting economic necessities; this can only imply that humanity finds its proper vocation in the pursuit of those so-called higher, cultural, or spiritual accomplishments that are the preserve of any "human being." Would that this were true! It arguably falls far short, however, of what seems to be the case from the perspective of, say, Beckett's writing. For as one of the trilogy's narrators tartly puts it: "A qui n'a rien il est interdit de ne pas aimer la merde." "To him who has nothing," says the translation, with a perhaps less compelling sense of repulsion, "it is forbidden not to relish filth."[27] Is this injunction—having no alternative but to find excrement tasteful, and relish what is repugnant—an existential or an economic one? Does it accord in either case with the presumption that (cultural) values are more necessary than (bodily) needs?

Evaluation, moreover, on this submission, proceeds towards its goal without interruption. It has no limits, no outside. "The non-evaluative or value-free," Connor confidently declares, "will always be a particular suburb of the domain of value, never a space outside it."[28] Here too agreement is possible up to a point. Evaluative criticism operates according to a powerful dialectic, and it is true that what is presented as free of value can often easily be shown to embody all kinds of value-laden assumptions, in just the same way, as reception of Beckett's work testifies, that what is claimed now to be empty of value, by magical sleight of hand, can turn into an exemplary embodiment of the highest values possible. But like any closed economy, this dialectic of value is deeply teleological. It is characterised by a resourceful sense of its own predetermined certainty, as a result of which it is always already in possession of what it takes to be its proper destiny. If so, instead of confronting the decisions that it claims are inescapable, it would seem rather to fall into the trap of referring them backwards in time to a tribunal that has always already made up its mind. And this is clear, I think, in Connor's notion that value, as he puts it, has the status of a kind of immanent transcendence. Connor explains:

> The necessity of value is thus endlessly to value and revalue our values themselves. But it is absurd to think of this imperative as coming from outside ourselves, even if its force is to evict us from our complacent tenure of that first-person plural. The paradoxical structure of value as immanent transcendence is what enables and requires us to recognize that it is only in the absolute putting of the "we" at risk that we realise the possibilities of our humanity. Neither side of the paradox, the side of risk or the side of realization, is definitive, or can diminish the necessity of the other.[29]

But while this description attributes to the dialectic of value a welcome sense of contradiction, it is soon apparent the concessions it makes are only provisional. The risks admitted here seem to have always already been recuperated within what Connor, in humanistic vein, describes as the economy of human possibility, in which case the first-person plural invoked with such warmth can never *absolutely* be put in doubt, since to do so would require that the self-evident value and values of what is "human" be set aside or at least deferred. The "absolute putting of the 'we' at risk" is in this respect anything but absolute: it is another name for humanism, the belief in the masterful transcendence of human possibility, which is what Blanchot and others, in a different but related context, describe quite simply as: nihilism.[30]

A decision has necessarily already been taken, then, as to the purpose and destination of the dialectic of value. In this sense, the scare quotes surrounding "we" are an inadequate safeguard. At any event, they cannot deflect the crucial question as to the identity of this "we." Who are "we": the cultured university elite? the technologically advanced West? factory workers in China? the inhabitants of Tuvalu? the numerous victims of state-sponsored genocide? our own future offspring? "We," it seems, always already know that the risks undergone by "us" will contribute to the realisation (?) of our (?) humanity: but who *are* we, "we," or "'we,'" whose possibilities have here become the measure of all future cultural, intellectual, material development? The negativity allowed here, then, is only a moment in the teleological realisation of values and valuation, in whose service it stands. The circle of value as immanent transcendence is a closed circuit. As such, it falls short of the goals it claims for itself; for without resistance and exteriority, without the radical risk that values themselves have no value at all, and are always already traversed by impossibility, indeterminacy, and indecision, the dialectic of value will only ever consist in repeating the same dogmatic credo. In the end, if values are to have any value, it is imperative that both values and value be suspended, set aside, and interrupted, if only for the duration of an act of decision; if not, the ascribing of value and the appeal to values become little more than an application of moralistic or ideological dogma. Indeed, if there were no exteriority to value and values, as Connor maintains, it is hard to see how it might be possible to reach the very decisions the critic defends with such authority and eloquence.

This book, then, here, now, at this very moment, protests.

In the nameless name of that which, being neither real nor realisable, escapes possibility, is unprecedented and incalculable, and thus belongs—does not *belong*—to the future: "On. Say on. Be said on. Somehow on. Till nohow on. Said nohow on."[31]

There is admittedly little doubt that literary criticism is saturated with ideological values of one kind or another. It would be foolish to argue otherwise. But this is not to say that literature or writing is reducible without remainder to the instantiation of such values. Indeed, the reverse is more likely to be the case. For criticism's different professions of faith in the inescapability and value of value and values beg numerous questions. It is presupposed for instance that the thing, if it is a thing, called literature can be delimited clearly, that it can therefore be constituted as an object, to be consumed by a reading subject in possession of appropriate, verifiable, or consensual protocols of interpretation, and attributable with confidence to a responsible (or irresponsible) authorial entity, namable as such, and implicitly or explicitly expressing itself according to established, identifiable channels of communication. The assumption too is that what commands literature, dominating it internally as well as externally, is meaning, for it is only within the horizon of meaning that the value or otherwise of any work may be determined. It is also taken for granted that criticism itself is in a position of authority over the literary object it has itself instituted. But by what authority is that position of authority itself guaranteed?

At every stage of the literary critical process, true enough, decisions have to be made; but these are decisions that, if they are to be taken at all, are inevitably haunted—as a condition of both possibility and impossibility—by indecision: indecisiveness, uncertainty, impossibility. Indecision in this sense is not liberal evasiveness. It is necessary difference, interruption, distance. "Indecision [*l'indécision*]," writes Blanchot, "is what brings nearer together [*rapproche*] near and far [*proche et lointain*]: both unsituated, unsituatable, never given in one place or time, but each according to its own distance [*son propre écart*] in time and place."[32] Literature, writing, before it becomes an object for critical evaluation, is always already something other: an indiscernible, irreducible, indeterminable, infinitely differentiated event, occurring not as a self-present certainty but more as an erasure, a distancing without distance, a questioning or opening without return.

The pressing question, then, is not the question of value, how a text may come to be exchanged for what it is not, but that of the singularity of the event, how a text (if it exists) interrupts the economy of the same governing the imposition of literary value and values, and, responding to the outside, comes to occur at all.

How, then, to respond to the unpredictability of an event, to speak to it, and address it?

An event, argues Lyotard, before it is something, in so far as it ever becomes something, is an interruption, which formulates itself initially, perhaps, purely as a question, a question without corresponding answer, in terms such as these: is it an event, is it happening, does it happen, is it coming, or, as Lyotard phrases it: *Arrive-t-il?* The answer, necessarily, it seems, according to the demands of time, is always in the affirmative: yes, it is coming; as such, however, as a coming that is only ever on the brink of coming, it remains perpetually in suspense, undecided, even though—or precisely because—the question of the event, posed by the event, as such, is the addressee of all phrases or sentences (in Lyotard's sense of the term). "This [i.e., the *Arrive-t-il?* or *Is It Happening?*]," Lyotard explains, "is what is appealed to by the phrases which occur. And, of course, he or she [i.e., the sender, perhaps the author of *Le Différend*] will never know whether or not the phrases have reached their destination. And this is something the sender must not know, that is the hypothesis. He or she knows only that this not knowing is the ultimate resistance the event [*l'événement*] can put up against the economic accounting of time [*l'usage comptable:* i.e., the reduction of time to units for the use—so to speak—of accountants]."[33]

There are, of course, numerous different ways of understanding the event, and many are the thinkers and artists in the course of the twentieth century who have sought to address the implications of an understanding of the event for art, literature, thought in general. The task is essential, yet infinite. For the event, by its very elusiveness, is precisely what resists calculation, the value or meaning of which cannot be decided in advance. Though it may be thought to *do* before it *is* (albeit, as Blanchot puts it, do without doing, simultaneously gathered and dispersed by the futural imminence that is the only temporality of the event), an event is irreducible to any performative speech act in the usual sense, if only because all genuine performatives (naming ships, performing weddings, making promises) only function within a specifically coded and regulated horizon. The event, however, breaches any such horizon of expectation. Can one in that case even say what it is? "Dire l'événement, est-ce possible?" "to speak the event, is that possible?" Derrida asks or is asked.[34] He replies: yes; and replies: no. Yes, because to say yes to the event and to the question of the event is the only possible response to the event, if it exists; no, because to say what the event is is an impossibility, if only because the event, as it arrives, if it arrives, in order for it to arrive, necessarily breaches the horizon of expectation, disrupts any economy founded on the (re)circulation of the same, which is to say any economy of value as such, and suspends my power to decide or my possibility of doing so, which is not to say the event belongs to the fullness of any presence, for it must, says Derrida, be iterable, that is, repeatable, in its irreducible singularity, which is another name for its repeatability, not as itself, that is, but as that which always differs from itself. Which is why, writes Lyotard, the event never occurs now. Events require a decision from us, but the time for decision is always too soon or too late.[35]

The event, as it occurs, if it occurs, argues Derrida, calls forth an affirmation in response. But this is not an affirmation that doubles a negation and is thus assimilable to it by dialectical conversion, in the same way that the dialectic of value transforms, say, a negation of value into a value-laden assertion, but an affirmation that interrupts time, says yes to the question itself, and yes to the possibility-impossibility of the event, that which comes or arrives. The event is not a familiar or comforting occurrence. What it brings may signify my ruin, dereliction, or abandonment; it may be even the instant of my death. This much can never be known or decided in advance, which is why any event, if it comes, always belongs to the future, not the future as deferred present, but the future as that which is incalculable, innovative, unforeseen, which can thus only ever be affirmed in a movement that precedes all positivity and all negation, both of which it traverses, enables and disables.[36] The event, adds Blanchot, entertains with literary narrative a strange futural relationship beyond actuality or effectiveness, that of a promise without prospect of success or failure, which it is *neither* possible to keep *nor* not to keep. For it exists in time only to the extent that it is also irreducible to time. Its fate is undecided: and undecidable. As Blanchot comments, with a passing nod to Heidegger:

> Always still to come [*encore à venir*], always already past, always
> present in a beginning so abrupt that it takes your breath away,
> even while it unfolds in the guise of a return and perpetual rebe-
> ginning . . . , such is the event that narrative seeks to approach.
> Such an event disrupts temporal relationships, but still affirms

time, that is, a particular way for time to occur, a time that belongs to narrative and introduces itself into the narrator's experience of duration in such a way as to transform it, a time of metamorphosis in which, in an imaginary simultaneity and in the form of the space that art seeks to realise, the different temporal ecstasies coincide.[37]

"It is as though there is a distance in time [*un écart de temps*], like a distance in place [*un écart de lieu*]," Blanchot explains elsewhere, "belonging neither to time nor to place. In this distance, we will come to write [*dans cet écart, nous en viendrons à écrire*, i.e., in the future]."[38] Writing gives us a different relation to time, then, but that time will never be made present, and writing's gift never given except in its very refusal. "Ma vie, ma vie," says one of Beckett's two (or more) narrators in *Molloy*, "tantôt j'en parle comme d'une chose finie, tantôt comme d'une plaisanterie qui dure encore, et j'ai tort, car elle est finie et elle dure à la fois, mais par quel temps du verbe exprimer cela?" "My life, my life, now I speak of it as something over, now as of a joke which still goes on, and it is neither, for at the same time it is over and it goes on, and is there any tense for that?"[39]

Whatever it may be possible to say is affirmed in and by the name "Beckett," then, before becoming an investment opportunity, a career move, or an industry, is necessarily if implausibly: an event. Indeed it is remarkable, amidst all else that has been written on Beckett, to see how, in recent French philosophy, in Foucault, Lyotard, Blanchot, Derrida, and, more explicitly still, in Deleuze or Badiou, Beckett's writing has proved deeply attractive—but at times secretly resistant too—to the effort to think the event, which has been one of the most persistent preoccupations of philosophy, literature, thought during the past fifty years.[40]

But if to write is not to communicate values and the value of values, why, then, bother to write? The question is a good one. And in March 1985 it was asked of Beckett, alongside 399 other established authors, by a team of journalists from the French newspaper *Libération*. "Pourquoi écrivez-vous?" they inquired; "why do you write?" Beckett's reply was terse, pointed and to the point, but without subject and without verb, as though to imply that what distinguished the act of writing was

that it was not an act, nor was it attributable to any intentional or responsible agent. "Bon qu'à ça," he wrote, meaning: "good for that
alone," "good for nothing else," "no good for anything else," "no good
at anything else," "hopeless at everything else," "hopefully only any
good at this."[41] Good or no good? Competent or incompetent? Hopeless
or hopeful? Positive or negative? Both or neither? And who or what? For
the terms of Beckett's answer were not poles in a dialectic, but the trace,
in the neuter, of an oscillation, a movement to and fro, a coming-and-
going: an inscribing and effacing of language that, in mocking the alternative while citing or reciting it, neutralises and displaces it, not however
to claim a place of safety from language and its self-inverting syntax, but
more radically, in much-quoted but nonetheless exacting words, to
"submit wholly to the incoercible absence of relation, in the absence of
terms."[42]

Beckett's reply, then, while submitting to the question, also rebuffed
it. To an impertinent query it responded with an impertinent affirmation; and, in so doing, silently inscribed the consonants pointing in the
direction of a signature or monogram: B–K–S, like Belacqua Shuah,
perhaps, or Béquet, Samuel, speaking, as it were, with the accent of a
Greenland Jew or an Irish peasant from the Auvergne.

II

Exemplary judgements

> But we think of the *beautiful* [*Schönen*] as having a *necessary* reference to
> liking [*eine notwendige Beziehung auf das Wohlgefallen*]. This necessity is of
> a special kind. It is not a theoretical objective necessity, allowing us to
> cognize a priori that everyone *will feel* this liking for the object I call
> beautiful. Nor is it a practical objective necessity, where, through concepts
> of a pure rational will that serves freely acting human beings as a rule [*zur
> Regel dient*], this liking is the necessary consequence of an objective law
> and means nothing other than that one absolutely (without any further
> aim) ought to act in a certain way. Rather, as a necessity that is thought
> in an aesthetic judgement, it can only be called *exemplary* [*exemplarisch*],
> i.e., a necessity of the assent of *everyone* to a judgement that is regarded as

an example of a universal rule that we are unable to state [*d. i. eine Notwendigkeit der Beistimmung aller zu einem Urteil, was wie Beispiel einer allgemeinen Regel, die man nicht angeben kann, angesehen wird*]. Since an aesthetic judgement is not an objective and cognitive one, this necessity cannot be derived from determinate concepts and hence is not apodeictic. Still less can it be inferred from the universality of experience (from a thorough agreement among judgements [*Einhelligkeit der Urteile*] about the beauty of a certain object). For not only would experience hardly furnish a sufficient amount of evidence for this, but a concept of the necessity of these judgements cannot be based on empirical judgements.

Immanuel Kant, *Critique of Judgement*[43]

There is no such thing as painting. There are only pictures, which, not being sausages, are neither good nor bad. All that can be said about them is that they are a more or less faithful translation of a series of meaningless, mysterious impulses towards the image [*qu'ils traduisent, avec plus ou moins de pertes, d'absurdes et mystérieuses poussées vers l'image*], and a more or less adequate response to dim inner tensions [*plus ou moins adéquats vis-à-vis d'obscures tensions internes*]. As for deciding how adequate a response, this isn't something you can say, since you aren't under the skin of whoever was stretched out on the easel [*dans la peau du tendu*]. The painter hasn't a clue most of the time anyway. In any case the coefficient is uninteresting. Profit and loss are all the same in the economy of art, where the unspoken is the light of the said, and every presence an absence. All you will ever know about a picture is how much you like it (and at a pinch why, if you're interested). But that is something you probably won't ever know either, unless you go deaf and forget everything you ever learnt [*oublier vos lettres*].

Samuel Beckett, "La Peinture des van Velde"[44]

Kant's *Critique of Judgement* (or *Judgement-Power*), this "epilogue to modernity and prologue to honourable postmodernity," as Lyotard calls it in *Le Différend*, tells what has often been taken to be a familiar story.[45] The challenge it poses to the specificity and authority of aesthetic judgements is nevertheless far-reaching. For what it more potently serves to underwrite is the imperious unavoidability of indecision: not quiescence or acquiescence, passivity or indifference, in the usual sense of such words, but on the contrary the realisation that it is impossible to have done with critical or other decisions, which continue to haunt the critical event long after it thinks it has done with deciding, as its simultaneous condition of possibility *and* impossibility, as that which makes decisions necessary and ineluctable, but also ensures that they can never be taken by the simple application of a rule and that therefore they can never be finally decided as such. So while Kant may be credited with a supremely powerful account of the possibility and necessity of universalising critical judgements and decisions, it can more surely be acknowledged that his thinking also manifests the very impossibility of attaining the goal which his demonstration aims to reach.

Let me start from the beginning. Any pure judgement of taste, Kant writes, must clearly be differentiated not only from the enjoyment that is a function of idiosyncratic personal inclination or preference but also from the pleasure taken in that which, being an object of the will, is found to be desirable because it corresponds to what is morally good or useful. Both unmediated sensuous pleasure and the liking for that which, under the tutelage of reason, is found to be ethically valuable are necessarily subject, each in their different ways, sensual here, abstract there, to criteria of interest, and only those judgements that display exemplary disinterestedness, Kant famously argues, may be deemed properly aesthetic. Interest—meaning any kind of economic or ideological stake or any presumption on behalf of the matter being judged— is incompatible with pure aesthetic judgement as such, which it can serve only to throw into doubt, corrupt, and thus disqualify. It is necessary, therefore, to be detached: interested enough to take pleasure in a presentation, perhaps, but at the same time essentially disinterested; all judgements of taste "must involve a claim to subjective universality [*ein Anspruch auf subjektive Allgemeinheit*]."[46] "Everyone has to admit," Kant explains, "that if a judgement about beauty is mingled with the least interest [*das mindeste Interesse*] then it is very partial [*parteilich*] and not a pure judgement of taste. In order to act as judge in matters of taste, we must not be in the least biased in favour of the thing's existence but must be wholly indifferent about it."[47] But how to separate, many readers have since asked, pleasure from interest? If what is at stake is pleasure or unpleasure, how can this be stripped of interest? And what guarantee is there, given its use in two different registers, sensible here, abstract there, that there is a single, reliable concept of interest as such? What interest of its own does Kant's discourse have in maintaining the requirement of aesthetic disinterest? Does not disinterest come inevitably to be haunted by its own interestedness?

But as these distinctions are put in place, precarious though they may be, a discriminating hierarchy or hierarchy of discriminations gradually unfolds, from the merely agreeable to the beautiful and to the good. Kant explains:

> We call agreeable [*angenehm*] what gratifies [*vergnügt*] us, beautiful what we just like [*bloß gefällt*], good what we esteem [*geschätzt*] or endorse [*gebilligt*], i.e. that to which we attribute an objective value [*objektiver Wert*]. Agreeableness [*Annehmlichkeit*] holds even for non-rational animals [*vernunftlose Tiere*]; beauty only for human beings, i.e. beings who are animal and yet rational [*tierische, aber doch vernünftige Wesen*], though it is not enough that they be rational (e.g. spirits) but they must be animal as well; the good, however, holds for every rational being as such [*für jedes vernünftige Wesen überhaupt*].[48]

Alongside the merely agreeable (on the one hand) and the good (on the other), that which is beautiful occupies what is in every respect an intermediary, transitional place. It exists, so to speak, on the cusp: interested enough to be a source of pleasure or unpleasure, not interested enough to be unduly swayed by inappropriate self-interest; too rational to be merely animal, too animal to be purely rational. It marks a limit, so to speak, between the materiality of the sensible, fit for animals deprived of reason, and the spiritual abstractions of the supersensible, accessible only to rational beings as such. But while inscribing that limit, it also blurs and suspends it, for if the separation between the agreeable and the good were absolute, then the beautiful would no longer be possible at all. That it is possible after all implies that the sensible and the supersensible in Kant somewhere come together, mingle, and are conjoined. But this only serves to accentuate the question of the enigmatic double affiliation of the beautiful; and it is nowhere clear in Kant's careful tabulation of their shared and distinct traits where exactly the limit may be said to pass or, for that matter, fail to pass between that which is the object of sensuous (animal, bestial, barbarous, or barbaric) gratification and that which is the cause of rational (human, ethical, cultured, enlightened) respect, even though the determination of that limit may be thought to be essential if the distinction between the agreeable and the good that underpins Kant's exposition of the beautiful is to be secured.

This tripartite articulation of the agreeable, the beautiful, and the good is, of course, merely one instance among many of Kant's analytical, critical strategy. It nevertheless demonstrates to what extent everything in the third *Critique* that relates to the presence or absence of beauty, the possibility (or not) of pure aesthetic judgements of taste, and much else besides, has principally to do, as Derrida among others has argued, with the inscribing and effacing of limits, the adjusting and removing of frames, that is, with the possibility of determination as such, together with the spectral threat of indeterminacy that seems destined always to return to problematise the task of thinking itself.[49] In this context, it is worth recalling Kant's declared reaction of disgust (*Ekel*), cited at the beginning of this chapter and framing the present discussion, so to speak, when faced with that which, by failing to redeem ugliness or the spectacle of human suffering for artistic effect, could not do other than to provoke disgust in the consumer or viewer. Kant's complaint was that in such cases there was inadequate differentiation between the artistic representation and the object it purported to represent, such that a viewer might no longer be able to discriminate between "the artistic presentation of the object" and "the nature of this object itself," and would thus be repelled by the latter in a way that would not have been the case had proper differentiation been maintained.

So far, so circular. For if art is inseparable from the frame that surrounds the artistic representation, if the purpose of art is to differentiate securely between representation and represented, and if beauty is the name given to pure aesthetic judgement, then it no doubt follows that any artwork that is not adequately framed in this way, and is not sufficiently differentiated from what it represents, does not merit the name of art and cannot be judged beautiful. But this analysis begs many questions. For how to tell the difference between that which is enclosed within a frame and that which displays an absence of frame? Do not both cases exemplify the possibility of a frame, and is not the second in that case already an instance of the first? Is the frame a part of what it frames, asks Derrida, or apart from it? If the former, how may it be removed from the picture; and if the latter, how may it be possible for it to serve as a frame at all? Which is to say that the specificity of the aesthetic object or artwork, if it exists, lies not in any identity it may have with itself but in its ever-shifting and uncertain boundaries.

It will be remembered that Kant's entire project in the *Critique of Judgement* was to find the philosophical means of crossing "an immense gulf [*eine unübersehbare Kluft:* i.e., a divide or abyss allowing no totalising vision]," namely the chasm separating the sensible from the supersensible, the domain of the concept of nature from the domain of freedom—not that there can be any question of the gap ever being simply abolished.⁵⁰ Judgement, *Urteilskraft*, in the third *Critique*, operating as the mediating link (*Mittelglied*) between reason and the understanding, is what provides the much-needed articulation between them. That articulation itself, as Derrida has powerfully argued, is in the abyssal form of an analogy, according to which it is supposed, Kant explains, that judgement "too may contain a priori, if not a legislation of its own [*eine eigene Gesetzgebung*], then at least a principle of its own [*ihr eigenes Prinzip*], perhaps a merely subjective one, by which to search for laws. Even though such a principle would lack a realm of objects [*Feld der Gegenstände*] as its own domain [*Gebiet*], it might still have some territory [*Boden*]; and this territory might be of such a character that none but this very principle might hold in it."⁵¹ Judgement, then, while having no specific object or objects of its own, over which it might wield conceptual or legislative authority, would nevertheless seem to have an area of competence and expertise. But what, then, is the proper task of judgement as such? Does it consist simply (though there is arguably nothing simple about it) in saying what it does, in order to do what it says? If so, it would explain why the third *Critique* is constrained constantly to mime its own conditions of possibility, to dramatise its own theoretical necessity by performing a theoretical operation which is none other than that of its own groundless regrounding. Which is no doubt what gives the third *Critique* at one and the same time both its power and imponderability, its trenchant decisiveness and its troubling indecision.

From the outset, Kant had further distinguished between determinative and reflective judgements. "Judgement [*Urteilskraft*] in general," he writes, "is the ability to think the particular [*das Besondere*] as contained under the universal [*dem Allgemeinen*]. If the universal (the rule, principle, law) is given, then judgement, which subsumes the particular under it, is *determinative* [*bestimmend*] (even though in its role as transcendental judgement it states a priori the conditions that must be met for subsumption under that universal to be possible). But if only the particular is given and judgement has to find the universal for it, then this power is merely *reflective* [*reflektierend*]."[52] Aesthetic judgements, Kant adds, belong to the second of these differentiated types; and, in articulating the specific tasks facing aesthetic judgement, he takes great care throughout to restrict its proper territory or area of competence along these lines. He does this by clearly differentiating aesthetic judgement, on the one hand, from conceptual cognition and, on the other, from those ethical imperatives that can only be grounded in an appeal to an idea of reason. Aesthetic judgements, Kant insists, do not, and cannot, deal in what is true or false, right or wrong, and whenever they claim to do so, they are guilty of exceeding their proper area of authority. This might seem to have the effect of subordinating reflective judgement, like some junior partner in the critical enterprise, to conceptual or ethical decisions taken elsewhere, and thereby enclose the aesthetic within an autarkic space of self-identity, with no opening onto the outside. The result, however, is precisely the reverse, as notably Lyotard argues in a number of articles and papers addressing this very issue in the third *Critique*. For Lyotard, the effect of Kant's insistence on the incompatibility of distinct genres of discourse (as Lyotard prefers to call them), and the irreducibility of transcendental argument to aesthetic judgement or ethical imperative, was rather to affirm the radical responsiveness of reflective, aesthetic judgement to that which, no longer falling subject to conceptual understanding or ethical pronouncement, is of the order of the untheorised, untheorisable, and unpredictable event. Aesthetic judgement does not presume to legislate; it considers, says Kant, "the character of the object only by holding it up to our feeling of pleasure and displeasure."[53]

There is an important lesson here. For as modern literary criticism has often discovered, sometimes to its cost, and to the intense frustration of at least some of its practitioners, theoretical, conceptual constructions addressing the essential nature of texts or textuality, however elaborate or well founded, though they may sometimes be mistaken for aesthetic judgements, do not coincide with them or guarantee them, nor do they provide readers with criteria with which to arbitrate upon the claims of the aesthetic. And the same is true of moral imperatives, whatever their good intentions or however much consensual agreement they may inspire. Artworks do give rise to intense moral debate on the part of some readers; but this does not imply the aesthetic itself has anything to do with moral norms, or that the moral or other implications of an artwork can ever be confidently determined. It is rather the opposite that is the case, since artworks can only inspire discussion by resisting the consensus within which the meanings ascribed to them may be deployed, in support of this or that ideological position, that is to say, by taking their place, which is also a non-place, within the dissensus that divides the aesthetic from the moral or moralistic.

As the logic of Kantian reflective judgement implies, aesthetic judgement faces a strange dilemma. It has at its disposal neither transcendental concepts nor moral imperatives, but merely examples of what today might be termed: best practice. Any aesthetic judgement, writes Kant, is only ever an instance or instantiation of the universal (or would-be universal) rule in whose name it judges, but that rule is itself never properly available, as Kant argues, since it cannot be derived from conceptual cognition nor established on the basis of the universality of experience. It is destined to be singular, which is not to say that for Kant it is in any sense solipsistic. Judgements do not belong to objects, but to subjective experience, and artworks themselves are only ever instantiations of something that cannot be made present (such as "art" or "literature," perhaps), which, if it exists at all, is largely indeterminate, and whose constitutive borders are entirely uncertain. Art begins and ends with nature, which is to say it hardly begins or ends at all. In such circumstances, as Lyotard puts it, rather than abandoning aesthetic judgement, or subsuming its object under conceptual, theoretical knowledge, or subordinating it to the ethical perspectives of practical reason, it becomes urgent to invent a rule for the case under discussion. But as that discussion proceeds—and it is hard to imagine that what modern literature knows as literary criticism is otherwise possible—it becomes plain that the promised reconciliation between the singular and the universal can never be anchored in anything other than the contingency of a constantly deferred encounter. The rule itself necessarily remains indeterminate. Examples exist, then, as I have suggested, and as this book will itself testify on many occasions, but it is never certain what it is they may be said to exemplify or instantiate. The only examples that may be treated as examples, it seems, turn out primarily to be examples only of themselves. Which is to say that, rather than providing a bridge between a given text and a universal rule or principle, all examples do is to display their own irreducible singularity as always more than what they can ever be taken to be.

There is no a priori concept of that which is beautiful. But the beautiful is universally liked. After the description of aesthetic judgement as being necessarily without interest, this is the second moment in Kant's analytic of the beautiful. Any judgement of beauty might therefore seem to rest ultimately on a necessarily undecidable claim. But Kant has no interest in reverting to sceptical relativism. His purpose is rather to discover unity in the potentially discouraging multiplicity of aesthetic judgements, and to this end proceeds to examine the question of causality in respect of the object of aesthetic judgement. The purpose, then, is to find purpose where it seems that none can be properly deduced or established. If art has a purpose, Kant argues, it must have to do with the feelings of pleasure (or displeasure) it elicits. But these cannot be made the object of conceptual understanding. Art, it seems, has a purpose, and must therefore be purposeful; but that purpose cannot be properly determined by conceptual means.

Kant's response to this dilemma is famously in the form of a compromise, if not a veritable paradox. "Beauty [*Schönheit*]," he writes, "is an object's form of purposiveness [*Form der Zweckmäßigkeit eines Gegenstandes*] insofar as it [i.e., beauty] is perceived in the object without the presentation of a purpose [*ohne Vorstellung eines Zwecks*]."[54] Something, that is, beauty, which is a form of purposiveness, is therefore perceived in an object, but without the purpose itself being presented. The division between purpose and purposiveness is absolutely crucial; but where does it pass? In a footnote immediately following, by way of example and counter-example, aiming to specify that separation but at the same time prolonging its difficulties, Kant goes on to cite, first, a stone utensil, taken from an ancient burial mound which, though self-evidently purposeful, because man-made, corresponds to no known purpose, yet for all that is not seen as beautiful, though it may on reflection be viewed as an artwork; and second, a tulip, "on the other hand [*hingegen*]," taken from nature, that "is considered beautiful, because in our perception of it we encounter a certain purposiveness [*eine gewisse Zweckmäßigkeit*] that, given how we are judging the flower [*so, wie wir sie beurteilen*], we do not refer to any purpose whatever [*auf gar keinen Zweck bezogen wird*]." No doubt the former, the tool, still has some memory of the purpose to which it was once put, whereas the tulip is without any such lingering reminder (or remainder). Or so it would seem. Again, all is a matter of framing, of separating like from like, dividing the one from the other even when they seem to invite the same response, always running the risk that the separation and divorce of purposiveness from purpose will be less of a clean break than anticipated. As Derrida comments:

> But in order for the cut [*la coupure:* i.e., the division of purposiveness from purpose] to appear—and it can still do so only along its edging [*selon sa bordure*]—the interrupted finality must show itself, both as finality and as interrupted—as edging [*bordure*]. Finality alone is not beautiful, nor is the absence *of* goal [*l'absence de but*], which we must distinguish here from the absence *of the* goal [*l'absence du but*]. It is finality-without-end which is *said to be* beautiful (*said to be* being here, as we have seen, the essential thing). So it is the *without* [*le sans*] that counts for beauty; neither the finality nor the end, neither the goal which is lacking nor the lacking of any goal, but the edging in *sans* of the pure cut, the *sans* of the finality-*sans*-end [*la bordure en sans de la coupure pure, le sans de la finalité-sans-fin*].[55]

The essential part in Kant's formulation, then, says Derrida, is *sans*, without: that which is both an inscription and an effacement, without negativity—what might perhaps be called a trace: supplementarity, parergonality (from *parergon*, a frame), says Derrida.[56] Resistance, slippage, indecision. What Blanchot (rather than Barthes) might address, or was already addressing, as the *neutre*, the neuter or neutral, that which withdraws but also retraces.

Naturally enough, there is a fourth moment in Kant's analytic of the beautiful. This concludes as follows: "Beautiful is what without concept [*ohne Begriff*] is cognized [*erkannt*] as the object of necessary liking."[57] But in what does such necessity consist? Judgements of beauty, in Kant, as seen earlier, since this was where Kant began, are not expressions of personal preference or private inclination. If they were, Kant's project would collapse into an empirical catalogue of likes and dislikes. It is essential therefore that judgements contain within them, as one of their conditions of possibility, a claim as to their universal validity. Importantly, that claim is not grounded in fact but in the necessary appeal it makes to what Kant here calls *Gemeinsinn,* meaning: shared sense, shared sensibility or feeling, shared responsiveness, even. "Common sense," says Pluhar; "sens commun," suggests Jean-René Ladmiral in his standard French version.[58] A means must be found, in other words, to bridge the gap between the subjective and the objective. Kant's argument runs as follows:

> Whenever we make a judgement declaring something to be beautiful, we permit no one to hold a different opinion, even though we base our judgement only on our feeling [*Gefühl*] rather than on concepts [*Begriffe*]; hence we regard this underlying feeling as a common rather than as a private feeling [*nicht als Privatgefühl sondern als ein gemeinschaftliches*]. But if we are to use this common sense [*Gemeinsinn*] in such a way, we cannot base it on experience; for it seeks to justify us in making judgements that contain an ought [*ein Sollen*]: it does not say that everyone *will* agree [*übereinstimmen werde*] with my judgement, but that everyone *ought* to [*solle*]. Hence the common sense, of whose judgement I am at that point offering my judgement of taste as an example [*Beispiel*], attributing to it *exemplary* validity [*exemplarische Gültigkeit*] on that account, is a mere ideal standard [*eine bloße idealische Norm*]. With this standard presupposed, we could rightly turn a judgement that agreed with it, as well as the liking that is expressed in it for some object, into a rule [*Regel*] for everyone. For although the principle is only subjective, it would still be assumed as subjectively universal [*für subjektiv-allgemein angenommen*] (an idea necessary for everyone); and so it could, like an objective prin-

ciple, demand universal assent insofar as agreement [*Einhellig-keit*] among different judging persons [*verschiedener Urteilenden*] is concerned, provided only we were certain [*wenn man nur sicher wäre*] that we had subsumed under it correctly [*richtig*].[59]

As elsewhere, it is hard to decide here whether Kant is doing anything other than simply addressing, in abyssal fashion, the conditions of possibility of his own discourse. Facing the necessity of articulating philosophically the transition between singular and universal, private and communal, Kant has recourse performatively, so to speak, to the idea of a necessity according to which the singularity of judgement may be brought into harmony with a rule, on the basis of which the necessity of a normative, subjective-universal principle may then be established. Does this resolve the argument, or merely displace and repeat an aporia? Much might be said of course about the status of the norm that Kant invokes here. Is it to be taken sociologically, as this passage in part seems to imply, or should it be taken transcendentally, as Kant elsewhere insists, notably in §31 of the third *Critique?* Does the appeal to an ethical imperative in Kant's analysis of *Gemeinsinn* imply a retreat from the specificity of aesthetic judgement defended with such rigour elsewhere? The implications of Kant's apparent uncertainty on these crucial points are important. They raise the question of the status of Kant's entire discourse on aesthetic judgement, which finds itself hanging in suspense.[60] Some readers have taken Kant's hesitation as an indication that judgements of taste, in the last resort, are conformist ones, which simply mirror prevailing social conventions; others, however, including most notably, in recent decades, Jean-François Lyotard, have vigorously argued the opposite, in order precisely to resist the threatened collapse of Kant's thinking into culturalist sociology or relativism.[61]

One aspect nevertheless remains clear. It is that the promised encounter between the singular and the universal, between the feeling that is mine and the common sense that belongs to the collectivity, however necessary it is deemed to be, whether as prior condition or as cultural expectation, cannot be guaranteed in fact ever to take place. As Lyotard insists, it is admittedly supposed by Kant not as given fact but as a "mere ideal standard." And the supposition is this: in proposing my singular judgement, I am necessarily putting it foward as a judgement that *ought* to secure universal assent, though there is no guarantee that it *will* do so. At the very moment it is advanced, albeit on the basis of my own feeling (*Gefühl*), my judgement, on Kant's submission, is always already in principle (though not necessarily in reality) an example of common sense, which is what allows me to claim exemplary, universal status for it. Much here is of course taken for granted, as Kant is aware: an assumption concerning (good) taste, a shared language, a common principle of translation, thanks to which the incommensurability of singular and general may yet be overcome, even as it is respected. But if the claim succeeds (and nothing guarantees that it will, just as nothing guarantees the requirement that my judgement have universal appeal either), then a rule may be derived from it, commanding universal assent—just so long, adds Kant, further hedging his bets, as the relationship between example and rule in this convoluted operation can be deemed to be properly construed, and the example correctly subsumed, according (it would appear) to determinative and not reflective judgement. True, there is a tribunal, whose role it is to arbitrate finally on such matters, which is the ultimate harmonisation, presupposed by Kant, between nature and human freedom. But this reconciliation, as Kant is the first to acknowledge, cannot be grounded in conceptual understanding; it has the status of a supersensible idea, which, necessarily, here and now, cannot be made present, and remains infinitely deferred, available only as a final supposition on the part of reason, as that supersensible substrate the function of which is precisely to harmonise the supersensible, nature, cognition, freedom, and the moral law.

But in the meantime, as far as judgement is concerned, everything hinges, not for the first time, on the status of the example as a mediating link, bridge, or transition between the universal and the singular and thus on the enigmatic decision, nowhere explictly affirmed as such, that accords such incontrovertible exemplarity to this judgement which is mine alone, and which on the basis of feeling I propose as necessary.

But how does an example of judgement acquire this privilege? Are all judgements exemplary, or is there a difference, for instance, between an example chosen at random and an example that is deemed to have the status of a model, between *Beispiel* and *Exemplar*, say, though these terms seem barely differentiated; and if so, how is that difference decided, and how may it be enforced? Are some examples good and others bad? If so, how to tell which is which? Are there specific qualifications that entitle or authorise me to present my feeling not merely as one empirical example among many, evidence perhaps of lingering idiosyncratic agreeableness, but as something that is in principle, if not in reality, binding upon others, and thus exemplary in the sense of constituting an a priori judgement, that is, having priority over other, merely empirical declarations of pleasure or displeasure, and worthy and demanding of approval by common sense? If it is crucial for the relation between example and rule to be correct, *richtig*, as Kant rules, who is it that will judge—*richten*—this to be the case?

The question, then, is this: how may I learn to exercise my judgement correctly, that is, according to the rules?

The issue is one that Kant considers in detail. It would be wrong, he avers, to abandon one's judgement simply to conform to the view of others. "Taste," he says, "lays claim merely to autonomy [*Autonomie*]; but to make other people's judgements [*fremde Urteile*] the basis determining one's own would be heteronomy [*Heteronomie*]."[62] How, then, to acquire autonomy? Not by applying conceptual understanding, since there is no a priori concept of beauty; nor by rejecting the judgements of others in order to "start from nothing but the crude disposition given to each of us by nature [*von der rohen Anlage seines Naturells anfangen*]"; no, only by following the example—that is, the model or precedent—supplied by others. The analogy, says Kant, is with ethical judgements. He explains:

> In religion, everyone must surely find the rule [*Regel*] for his conduct within himself, since he is also the one who remains responsible for his conduct and cannot put the blame for his offences on others on the grounds that they were his teachers and predecessors; yet even here an example [*Beispiel*] of virtue and holiness will always accomplish more than any universal precepts [*allgemeine Vorschriften*] we have received from priests or philosophers, or for that matter found within ourselves. Such an example, set for us in history, does not make dispensable the autonomy of virtue that arises from our own and original (a

priori) idea of morality [*Idee der Sittlichkeit*], nor does it transform this idea into a mechanism of imitation [*Mechanism der Nachahmung*]. *Following* by reference to a precedent [*Nachfolge, die sich auf einen Vorgang bezieht*], rather than imitating [*nicht Nachahmung*], is the right [*rechte*] term for any influence that products of an exemplary [*exemplarischen*] author may have on others; and this means no more than drawing on the same sources from which the predecessor himself drew, and learning from him only how to go about doing so. Among all our abilities and talents, taste is precisely what stands most in need of examples [*Beispiele*] regarding what has enjoyed the longest-lasting approval in the course of cultural progress [*im Fortgange der Kultur*], in order that it will not become uncouth [*ungeschlacht:* barbaric] again and relapse into the crudeness [*Rohigkeit:* rawness, brutality] of its first attempts; and taste needs this because its judgement cannot be determined by concepts and precepts.[63]

Autonomy, then, must be properly acquired. In order to render exemplary judgements I must begin by learning from example. In order to learn from example, no doubt, I have to learn to judge the example and examples of others. It is necessary therefore to learn to judge examples. But how to learn to judge examples? Only, it seems, by learning to judge examples. The logic of the example is rigorously inescapable, yet radically aporetic; it provides for the possibility of passage from barbarism to culture but submits that possibility to a vicious circle of infinite regress. In considering examples, says Kant, it is moreover essential to learn to distinguish between *Nachfolge* and *Nachahmung*, between properly following the example and mechanically imitating it, between a conformity with precedent that produces autonomy and one that is mired in heteronomy.[64] Yet how is this distinction to be maintained? Once again, it seems, only by example . . . Circularity or paralysis beckons. There can be no judgement without rules of judgement, but those rules, it seems, can only be given by means of examples, which are themselves necessarily subject to judgement. Judgement—knowing which example fits the case, what rule to apply, whether, how, and when to apply it, or when to suspend it—requires judgement.

Pure aesthetic judgements of taste, Kant maintains, are nevertheless possible. But only, it seems, on condition of being assigned a strangely shifting territory, full of underground gulfs and chasms, whose borders and boundaries are certainly essential, but also essentially uncertain, without doubt necessary, but also necessarily in doubt: where pleasure or unpleasure rules, separated from itself by an absolute absence of interest; where, without any possible appeal to an a priori concept of the beautiful, beauty nevertheless lays claim to universal assent; where beauty is attributed not to the object of beauty but— perception without perception—to a subjective response to the purposiveness without purpose of the object; and, in spite of all, where what is beautiful is the object of a necessary liking, albeit a liking it is necessary to acquire on the basis of just precedents that are more than *just* precedents. Quality, quantity, relation, modality. Such, says Derrida, is the ill-adjusted frame. But is it not the fate of any frame, he argues, never quite to fit what it is designed to enclose? There is no picture without the possibility of a frame; but that frame is never without being forced into place: an excess or residue always remains, protruding or leaving a gap to be repaired by yet another frame, and another, without term.

But then, as though the self-identity of the beautiful were not already sufficiently compromised, there is a *coup de théâtre*, leading to another difficult transition. The curtain comes down on the analytic of the beautiful; but it does so only to rise again immediately after, displaying a rather different spectacle, that of the sublime: fearsome and terrifying, formless and unlimited, a ruin, so to speak, countering all perception of purposiveness by dint of its counterpurposive form, its incommensurability and violence, an object not of positive but negative pleasure.[65] As the aesthetic turns aside from itself in this way, evoking in the spectator not the possibility or necessity of a judgement of taste but the power of the imagination, the power, that is, to step beyond the sensible world of beauty to entertain the intimidating possibility of the supersensible, under whose sway the sublime is held by Kant to unfold.

The questions that arise are many. Is Kant's account of the sublime, this "mere appendix [*bloßen Anhang*] to our aesthetic judging of the purposiveness of nature,"[66] the exception that proves or confirms the rule, or the example that defies and disables it? Is this supplementary analytic to be read as proof of the limitlessness of the aesthetic or of a disaster befalling the aesthetic as such? If the analogy famously put forward by Kant is with Moses' second commandment, to the effect that you (but who is addressed in these terms?) shall not make graven images, does this imply that the sublime is irretrievably subject to divine law, or that, by (not) displaying the law as that which cannot be made present, by dint of its appeal to the boundless potential of human freedom, it is able to contest or contravene that law, even as it stands—and by the fact of standing—before or alongside it? But this is perhaps the ambiguity of the sublime: overwhelming the beautiful, as it does, both conceptually and performatively, it speaks most powerfully or violently of the incommensurable, dissymmetrical, and irreconcilable—of the many relations without relation between concept and reason, the sensible and the supersensible, positive and negative pleasure, the aesthetic and the ethico-practical.

So many enigmas, then, requiring decision but also resisting it, giving rise to so many unresolvable aporetic dilemmas.

But none of these difficulties is accidental, contingent, or susceptible of remedy. Each bears witness to the aporetics of judgement as such, the inability of judgement, if judgement is to occur at all, to be finished with judgement, to be done with itself, and to reach the term it sets itself, which is also to say: its incapacity to take decisions, even when it is imperative to do so, without the lingering evidence, memory, or prospect of irreducible indecision.

The aporetics of judgement, Derrida suggests, are at least three in kind or number.[67] Each turns on the logic of exemplication and the status of the example within exemplification. At stake is the strange relation—both mutual implication and mutual resistance—that binds and unbinds the singular to the universal and vice versa. For while the singular necessarily implies the universal, without which it would not itself even be thinkable, it is also the case that the universal necessarily destroys the singular. To exist at all the singular must resist the universal to which it owes its definition. The same applies to the universal itself. For it is hard to understand how a universal rule might be said to obtain if it were unable to instantiate itself, even though, by doing so, it may run the risk of unravelling entirely. Is this to say the relationship between the singular and the universal should be construed according to a dialectic that might successfully mediate between both poles of the argument? To do so would be to fail the singular again. From the point of view of the dialectic, as Hegel famously explains in the opening pages of the *Phenomenology of Spirit,* the singular in itself is impossible; it is only thinkable at all as a result of the mediating universality of language.[68] Which is to say, of course, that justice, to the extent that it concerns the singular, that is, this case, and no other, here and now, would itself no longer be possible, which in turn implies that the universality of the law has at least been suspended, if not destroyed entirely.

Derrida in turn explores the implications of this logic by way of a series of examples. The first, he explains, concerns the relationship between a decision and the rule in whose name it is made. For justice to be done, as Kant argues, judgements must be freely enacted; they require the autonomy of the judge. But equally no judge should act capriciously; any verdict given, if it is to be just, must be legitimised by reference to a pre-existing universal rule. It is nevertheless essential, if injustice is to be avoided, for that rule to be reassessed, reviewed, reinvented, here and now, in respect of the singular case being examined, even if this may mean disregarding, contradicting, or modifying the law itself: in the cause of justice. The universal rule must be respected, but so must the singular case too. If not, injustice will follow. The law must be enacted, but also suspended. To do what is just, a decision is bound *simply to apply the law,* yet not *simply to apply the law.* The room left between the two sides or branches of this double imperative is exiguous in the extreme, and consists in perhaps no more than the difference in emphasis or tone between two synonymous formulations, between an application that is rigorously consistent and one that is consistently rigid: between the same and the same. That space must nevertheless be traversed by any decision claiming to act in the name of justice, which may disregard it—on the grounds that the law is the law, and values are values, without possible exception, or alternatively by ignoring the law entirely—only at a cost, the cost of justice itself. It is essential therefore to distinguish between legality, understood as conformity with the law and the cultural or social values embodied in a given legal system, and justice, which is inseparable from the law, yet always singular, therefore never purely present as such. The dissymmetry between the law and justice is irreducible, which is why it cannot be overcome by any appeal to dialectics. All judgement is enjoined to remain within the difficult and inhospitable space of an irreconcilable double bind, and it is imperative, in the name of justice itself, that the relation of non-relation between law and justice be respected, maintained, and affirmed as such, not mediated by any unifying dialectic. It is necessary to pass judgement, but impossible to pass beyond it. Judgement, in other words, is properly aporetic, from the Greek *a-poros*, meaning: absence of passage, impossibility of exit.

Justice is never achieved once and for all. Doubts always remain. Injustice is always possible. If so, all decisions, however just they appear, will continue to be haunted by the possibility of their injustice. But it would be wrong to lament this situation, or view Derrida's analysis as an exercise in pragmatic or liberal scepticism, or worse.[69] For at least two reasons. First, the indecision or undecidability that is inseparable from the possibility of justice (which is simultaneously and necessarily always the possibility of injustice) is not an obstacle to justice. It is a condition of possibility of justice. Without indecision or undecidability, there would be nothing to decide. Decisions, in order to be what they are at all, are necessarily traversed by numerous risks, possibilities of failure, uncertainties, and irresolvable conundrums, and it is plain that these are never entirely dispatched once a decision is reached. They continue to haunt the decision as a kind of spectral memory. In doing so, they speak of an unfulfilled, still unanswered, and perhaps unanswerable demand for justice. Precisely because justice is never purely present, never absolutely guaranteed by a decision, it appeals to us, writes Derrida, not only as a demand but also a promise, indissociable from an idea of the infinite perfectibility of justice, and therefore points to the future, a future that will never be present, and reaches far beyond what is graspable, calculable, or predictable. As Derrida explains:

> It is already apparent from this second aporia . . . that, if every presumption that justice may be determined with certainty in the present is indeed under deconstruction, it is on the basis of an infinite "idea of justice," infinite because irreducible, and irreducible because due to the other, prior to any contract, because justice is a *coming* [*parce qu'elle est venue*], the coming of the other

as a singularity that is always other. Impervious as it is to all scepticism, as one might put it in Pascalian terms, this "idea of justice" appears indestructible in its affirmative character, in the demand it makes for a gift without exchange, without circulation, without acknowledgement, without economic circularity, without calculation or rules, without reason or theoretical rationality in the sense of some regulatory control. Which is why it is sometimes viewed as (or accused of being) a kind of madness.[70]

Justice, then, says Derrida, cannot be contained within the circular economy of a dialectic of value. Nor can it be bound by any horizon of expectation or certainty, or made an object of temporal calculation. Justice demands a decision, here, now, and without delay. It cannot be deferred except at the cost of turning into its very opposite. The moment for decision is, by definition, never the right one. As far as the decision itself is concerned, it is always either too late—because the injustice to which it is a response has already endured too long—or too soon—because it is not yet certain what justice demands. This strange temporality, where time, so to speak, can no longer coincide with itself, is what gives justice the structure—structure without structure—of an event. This event is not present to itself. It comes or arrives as a kind of impossible possibility. The keyword here—and readers may remember that, on the evidence of Tom Driver, it was Beckett's keyword too—is the word: perhaps, "peut-être." *Perhaps:* hope and doubt, risk and danger, imminence and retreat, futurity without future, politics without end. Decisively exploiting the dissymmetry that exists in French between the future as *avenir,* that is, *à-venir,* from the Latin *venire,* to come, and meaning: that which will come (perhaps) as event (or e-vent), and the future as *futur,* from the Latin *esse,* to be, and meaning: that which will *be* as a deferred modification of present being, Derrida puts it as follows. Justice, he says,

perhaps has a future [*un avenir*], indeed [*justement*], in the sense of a time to come [*un à-venir*] that should be rigorously distinguished from the future [*futur*], in the sense of that which will be. The future that will be [*le futur*] forfeits the opening [*l'ouverture:* opening or openness], the coming [*venue*] of the other (who comes), without which there is no justice; and the future that will be [*le futur*] can always reproduce the present, announce or present itself as a future present in the modified form of the present. Justice is still *to come* [*à venir*], it *has* still to come [*elle a à venir*], it *is* to come [*est à-venir*], it is what deploys the very dimension of events irreducibly to come. It will always have it, this future to come [*à-venir*], and will always have had it. *Perhaps* this is why justice, insofar as it is not merely a juridical or political concept, opens up in and for the future still to come [*à l'avenir*] the transformation, recasting, or refounding of law [*droit*] and politics.⁷¹

Perhaps: the inescapable demand and irreducible indecision which speak in the word are not such that they should be resisted. Indeed, as Derrida suggests, the word *perhaps* is itself a sign of resistance which should be affirmed. Importantly, as Derrida emphasises, this is not in itself an ethico-moral requirement, and spills far beyond the practical horizon of what can be determined, in Kantian mode, as corresponding to any such category. Moreover, it is part of the structure of the event itself not to be an object of acceptance or rejection, approval or disapproval, right or wrong, not least, as Lyotard was found to argue earlier, because the event always already precedes the act of evaluation that seeks to say what the event means or is worth. The event itself, in its perpetual imminence, has in this sense always already taken place.⁷² It can perhaps therefore only be affirmed. This is not as yet to decide what it means; it is to prolong the questioning of the event before it has become a question.

But what, it may be asked, is the relationship between justice and literary criticism? Justice surely deals with living people, individuals or populations in history, not with texts: with South Africa, Rwanda, Northern Ireland, Iraq, the Shoah, not the rambling narrative voice of *L'Innommable*. But is it altogether certain where the one ends and the other begins? Life is sometimes defined as that which is capable of death; in this sense it is readily apparent to all who are alive that living is but a slow detour towards that end. And no sooner does a living being come to know this, than she or he has to face the realisation that dying is impossible. Dying, says Blanchot, is an event not within my power, and whenever it occurs it has the uncanny effect of removing from me once more the very possibility of dying. Death, then, inhabits life as a condition both of possibility and of impossibility, a limit without limit that determines life's margins while placing at its centre a meagre yet unspeakable enigma. This may seem quite different from what does or does not occur in literature, but writing in general, presupposing as it does not only my absence but the possibility of my death too, shares the same relationship to death as life itself. If it is right to seek justice for humans, and arguably also for those who are no longer human, or are still to become human, as well as those who are not recognised as human at all, and whose interests are not necessarily compatible with human possibility, it follows perhaps that it is right to seek justice for literary texts, which is not to say that in respect of any of these examples, which are more than examples, is it at all assured in advance what the demand for justice might require. But this uncertainty is of the essence; and in the pages that follow it will be one of my tasks to explore further how it may be possible for that most ancient and tired of discourses, literary criticism itself, to respond affirmatively to the question of justice.

True enough, it might also seem that aesthetic decisions, unlike those taken by legal or illegal tribunals, are rarely followed by real effects, but this is to assume too quickly that literature, with criticism at its side, is an autonomous practice, cut off from the law, and the social and political struggles it silently records. For it should be remembered, as Derrida is among the first to insist, that the historical and more-than-historical institution of literature *as* an institution is barely thinkable without the intervention of the law. At any event, how is it possible to be sure that reading or writing, both acts that involve making decisions, are without effects in the so-called real world? Even if this were so, and it were possible to establish as much to the satisfaction of common sense, would this not in its own right be a remarkable effect, akin to the self-effacing or self-displacing criteria explored by Kant: the effect without effect of that which has no effect? The question and questions therefore remain: both the strangely undecidable ground occupied by what is called literature and the irreducibility of that territory to conceptual knowledge or to ethico-moral imperatives. Literature, according to Blanchot—Kant's most rigorous commentator, suggests Jean-Luc Nancy[73]—is without concept, borders, purpose, or end. It is to that extent inessential, but for essential reasons; the only legislation to which it is subject is its own "essential inessentiality."

But how to respond to literature's essential inessentiality? In other words, how to approach literature, if it exists, with justice? Not by engaging with it in the manner of that lingering encounter of contemplative subject with fetishised object known as aestheticisation or the aesthetic; not by extracting from the work a ready-made generality or universality, a world-view or authorial vision; not by treating it as an object of commodified cultural exchange; not by evaluating it according to its conformity or lack of conformity with this or that existing moral, ideological, or other doctrinal discourse; but, more simply, perhaps more dangerously or problematically, to risk exposing reading to the demand for justice that, both in the work and beyond it, as something both readable and unreadable, deployed in words, in silence, and in secret, continues to speak in the immeasurable singularity of writing, in the uncertain knowledge that no risk, by definition, can be other than limitless, and in the realisation that there can be no prospect of justice without the possibility of injustice. Reading too, after all, is an event, involving risks and challenges that often exceed the powers of the reader, which is why it is both more and less than an act of evaluation. More simply, more provocatively, it is the site of an unusually exacting imperative: to read— that is, not only that which can be made subject to a decision that appeals, perhaps in vain, to value and values, but also that which, in and beyond any text, is resistant to any standard of evaluation at all.

The fact is, reading is never simple. For while literature is perpetually suffused with meanings and values, it remains irreducible to them. Its relationship to meaning, politics, the world, is oblique, indirect, always at a distance, yet without this distance being measured, stabilised, or kept in check, and the most important lessons that literature hands down to its readers derive from literature's own sceptical suspension of value, its deployment of an excess that can only ever be affirmed without necessarily ever being recuperated. Literature may address universality, but it is also irremediably and irrepressibly singular, merely a trace or vestige of itself, never an object of calculation. "It is through reverence," writes Blanchot, "by that which prolongs, maintains, and consecrates it (the idolatry that comes from naming [*propre à un nom*]) that the work [*l'œuvre*], always already in ruins, is objectified [*se fige*] or is merely added to the long list of cultural good works [*aux bonnes œuvres de la culture*]."[74] From which it follows that to treat writing as an object of cultural or moral value is to indulge in an act of piety or conformism always liable to be treated with scorn by literature itself.

This, then, is the argument which this book seeks to explore. The issues at stake could not be greater. For if literature, if criticism has a future, it is only in so far as it has the chance of outliving the institution-alisation that has become inseparable from its existence, but which, even as it allows it to flourish (since without these institutions criticism is barely likely to exist at all), also threatens its possible survival—into the future.

III

Affirmation without precedent

> There can be no understanding without prejudgement, and it would
> be contrary to the very sense of understanding to make it artificially free
> of all "prejudice." However, by that very token, it is essential to remain
> constantly vigilant and, while scrutinising a text, allow oneself to be
> scrutinised by it in turn.
>
> Maurice Blanchot, "Je juge votre questionnaire . . . "[75]

"Qu'en est-il de la critique?" "How do things stand with literary criticism?" This was the title, with echoes of both Mallarmé and Heidegger, under which, in spring 1959, alongside other prominent French critics at the time (Jean Starobinski, Jean-Pierre Faye, and Lucien Goldmann), Maurice Blanchot replied to a questionnaire from the editors (Edgar Morin, Kostas Axelos, and Jean Duvignaud) of the neo-Marxist quarterly, *Arguments*.[76] Blanchot's response, put forward on the basis of having to deal on a daily basis with some of the most challenging texts of the post-war years, was characteristically incisive.

Literary criticism, the writer argued, mindful of his own increasingly anomalous position on the margins of the one and outside the sphere of the other, is an activity that takes place at the uncertain and sometimes problematic intersection between two separate but equally powerful institutions: the world of journalism—what today would be called the media—with its dynamic but largely ephemeral interest in day-to-day events, and academia or the university, with its sedate but more durable commitment to verifiable knowledge.[77] To be active as a critic, Blanchot continued, was to derive legitimacy and authority from one or the other, sometimes both, of these complementary yet competing bodies. In this sense, he concluded, criticism had less to do with literature itself—assuming such a thing to exist—than with the political aspirations of the media or the academy and the ambitions of such institutions to exploit artistic production for their own purposes, which they did (and do) by translating art or literature into a discourse whose main function, explicitly or implicitly, was to legitimate a set of cultural, political, or ideological positions. Which is why literary criticism, as its history attests, ultimately reveals more about its own assumptions and values and the state of society embodied in them than about the literature it professes to take as its object. Claiming to speak to literature, it more often ends up merely talking about itself.

There remains, however, an underlying paradox. Despite their status as centres of discursive power, Blanchot observes, the institutions of literary criticism derive their prestige finally not from the persuasiveness of their own acts but from something much less assured, at the limit of their authority, upon which they are nevertheless dependent for their survival: "literature" itself. In a word, criticism needs "literature" far more than "literature" needs criticism. This secondariness or belatedness of criticism is one of its distinguishing features, and its dependency or contingency one of its most essential traits. Criticism is always circumstantial. Even when it adopts an air of knowing superiority over the object it claims to evaluate, criticism can never take precedence over the singularity of the case it endeavours to address. By a strange reversal, the would-be universality of aesthetic judgements finds itself reliant here on the recalcitrant materiality of texts to which its verdicts are meant confidently to be applied. The result, as both the media and the university are aware, is that literary criticism comes to exist in an odd twilight world, halfway between seriousness and frivolity, professionalism and amateurism, hovering uncertainly between description and prescription, and where what comes first are not criticism's own arguments or truth claims but the ignorance or unruliness of that upon which it claims to legislate. As Blanchot explains:

The language of criticism has this strange characteristic that the more it realises, develops, and asserts itself, the more it must efface itself; eventually, it breaks down. Not only does it not impose itself, attentive as it is to the requirement that it should not take the place of its object; it accomplishes and achieves its end only when it disappears. And this movement of disappearance is not the simple discretion of the servant who, having finished his tasks for the day and tidied the house, then withdraws: it is the very sense of its accomplishment which means that, in realising itself, it disappears.[78]

Thus Blanchot in 1959. True enough, over the past fifty years, much has happened. In particular, in response to developments in disciplines such as anthropology, linguistics, philosophy, psychoanalysis, and sociology, enormous strides have been made in providing literary criticism with better and more rigorous theoretical foundations and guaranteeing the professionalism of its procedures and the coherence of its methodology. The effects of these changes are plain to see in any modern university syllabus. The impressionism and obscurantism that characterised literary criticism in a previous epoch are increasingly subject to challenge. But perhaps most startling of all about this invasion of literary criticism by so many eclectic and hybrid discourses, each having its origin and specificity elsewhere —and I refer here to everything that makes up the strange multi-headed monster ubiquitously described as Literary Theory— is the short-lived fragility of each and every theoretical discourse that in recent years has been set to work defining "literature." No sooner does one way of addressing the so-called literary text gain currency, it seems, than it is immediately superseded by another. Competitiveness is the order of the day. Confusion may sometimes result; but more often the outcome is radical imponderability. But this is arguably not the fault of theoretical discourse; it rather derives from the problematic character of the so-called object of criticism itself.

Literature, it appears, is possessed of a kind of spectral indeterminacy, which allows it to be traversed by this or that critical methodology, even as it mutely slips away. Critical fashions pass; so-called literary texts obstinately remain; but, more importantly, so does the question of literature: what it is (if anything), where it starts or ends, what should be done with it. It could even be argued that what has most notably been achieved by the current proliferation of theoretical, or pre-, post-, post-post-, or anti-theoretical accounts of literature, rather than a conceptually more rigorous understanding of the thing we call literature, is an awareness of the mysterious unfindability—not to be confused with ethereal transcendence—of criticism's obscure object of desire: that is, literature, which cannot be presented or made present "as such," and which exists (if at all) only as a non-finite collection of examples primarily exemplifying themselves. This is perhaps not surprising. Already Kant, as we have seen, in considering the possibility of aesthetic judgements of the sort that might be addressed to literature, was obliged to do so in enigmatically self-cancelling and aporetic terms: as pleasure without interest, a perception of purposiveness without purpose in the artwork, appealing to a moment of necessary universalisation that remained however without guarantee or confirmation. Far from being self-identical, then, the object of aesthetic judgement, on this evidence, displays an extraordinary degree of instability—and inevitably so, since without such mutability on the part of its putative object, the theoretical revolution that is such a feature of recent decades would barely have occurred at all. Today, however, no less than in 1959, notwithstanding the radical changes in critical thinking that have occurred over the past half century, one troubling, impertinent fact still remains, as many a critic can attest, irrespective of whether he or she writes as an academic or a journalist. It is that criticism's existence is inseparable from a sense that it is always already on the brink of erasure. It is by nature redundant and expendable. It lives and dies with the works that prompt it, rarely outlasting the historical conjuncture to which it belongs. Far from embodying indispensable truth, it is continually threatened by worrying irrelevance.

This instant disposability of so much literary criticism, Blanchot goes on to argue, is not mere circumstance. It says something about the structure of the literary work itself. For it is apparent that any literary work, in order properly to exist at all, requires a future reader, without whom it would remain empty and inert. And if reading is a necessary feature of any work, perhaps even to the point of founding the work *as* a work, as Walter Benjamin suggests, the same arguably also goes for literary criticism. It too is inseparable from the work *as* a work. After all, a critic, in the first instance, is little more than a reader, albeit a reader of a peculiar kind, as Blanchot puts it, whose relationship to the work is doubly mediated: through both the reading of a writing and the writing of that reading. Criticism begins, in other words, with reading: by responding to the implicit appeal made by the work (or, better perhaps, the promise of the work-to-be) to the contingent, always future reader dormant in each and every one of us.

This act of reading, Blanchot explains, is both more dutiful and less inhibited than might first appear. For if the intervention of a reader is required for the work fully to be what it is, the work may be said not only to imply the reader, but to obligate him or her, who cannot *not* respond to what he or she is reading, since reading is already by way of being that response. To read, in this sense, is always to be indebted to the work. But the nature of this debt is enigmatic. The work does not instruct the reader how to read. On the contrary, while the reader's involvement is a necessary moment in the unfolding of the work, it is also, as far as the work is concerned, quite superfluous. The work itself cares little about how it is read, or even if it is read at all. This insouciance can often be bewildering. No sooner is the reader called upon to respond than he or she is told that response is unnecessary, redundant, or indifferent. No sooner is the reader put in the work's debt, then, than he or she is released from that debt; the obligation to the work is cancelled, and submissive constraint gives way to untrammelled freedom. "Read the text!" students are urged. "But how?" "Any way you like, but make sure you read it all!"

Admittedly, a reader can respond to this double bind of necessity and irrelevance, obligation and redundancy, by retreating into admiring or disapproving silence. This is the prerogative of any reader. The critic, however, who has decided to write about his or her reading, enjoys no such luxury; by definition, she or he is enjoined to address the work. But in what way? Minimally, taking on the role of mediator, a critic might endeavour merely to repeat the work. But it is soon apparent, as Borges shows in his famous story, "Pierre Menard, Author of the *Quixote*," that any such fidelity to the text is impossible, since any repetition, however rigorous, always adds to what it is repeating a hair's-breadth displacement, which is the effect of repetition itself. Exact repetition is impossible; to repeat is always already to transform.[79] Once the critic begins addressing the work, then, it is always to say something in response to the work which is not said by the work. This is the task of the critic; indeed there can be no other. It implies no originality on the part of the critic, is rather a function of the critic's supernumerary existence as a reader both internal and external to the work.

Here too there is ambivalence. The work, we know, is complete in itself; and nothing can be added or subtracted from the work without altering it fundamentally. But the work is also incomplete; for without the evidence of such incompletion, it would not be available to any critic to speak about the work in a way not always already anticipated by the work. Which is also to say the work is necessarily inhabited by an enigmatic silence or secret, a withholding of language that says both everything and nothing, and which the critic, warming to the task, is enjoined to translate into words of his or her own (and it is at this stage that academic or journalistic discourse intervenes, if it has not done so already, to channel, inflect, or appropriate the critic's speaking or provide the critic's reading with institutional, ideological, or methodological legitimacy). Whatever a critic's response—enthusiastic, hostile, or indifferent—and whatever the discursive context of the critical act—praise or polemic, demonstration or analysis—it will never be possible for criticism to overcome the incompletion that is an irreducible feature of the work. Criticism can never speak in place of the work, nor can it put an end to the work's own garrulous silence. Which is why criticism, in order to exist at all, is condemned to remain forever provisional: undecided—enjoined to decide, that is, but granted no power of decision over the work.

The critical relation, then, is the site of a strange inconsistency. The intervention of the critic is necessary, yet superfluous; the critic must respond to the work, but that response is in vain; the critic's task is to translate the work, but all criticism uncovers is evidence of the work's untranslatability. These paradoxes are revealing. For what criticism makes apparent in the work, embodied in the work's endless potential for commentary and interpretation, is not the self-identity of its object—as an example or instance of literature or literariness, that concept which in the hands of the Russian Formalists may be thought to found the possibility of modern literary theory as such—but what Blanchot in 1959 described as the work's essential non-coincidence with itself, "sa non-coïncidence essentielle avec elle-même," the effect of which, he adds, is to make the work itself perpetually "possible-impossible." The work is finite, yet also infinite. It is readable, yet essentially unreadable.[80] True enough, criticism has always known this, since it holds the secret to criticism's own longevity. For if it were possible once and for all to exhaust the text to which criticism endeavours to respond, this would spell the end not only for the work but for criticism too. It may be that the task of the critic is to decide upon the meanings and value of literary works, but what criticism encounters in the work, by necessity, is its own failure to decide once and for all. Criticism, then, may be a discourse that seeks to impose the self-evidence of its judgements; but it is also, at the same time, a discourse that harbours within itself the necessity of its own impotence.

The fact is, Blanchot argues, the literary work always already eludes the finality of judgement. An abiding duplicity separates the artwork from itself. Writing, for Blanchot, obeys at least two masters, which is to say it properly serves the interests of neither. The writer explains the workings—or, better, the *unworkings*—of this strange logic in a famous six-page chapter from *L'Espace littéraire*, first published in June 1953, entitled "Le Regard d'Orphée," "The Gaze of Orpheus."[81] It is towards this section in the book that Blanchot directs his reader's attention as towards the ever mobile secret centre of his inquiry. The Orpheus story is of course familiar to readers of literature—of Virgil, Ovid, Rilke, Cocteau, numerous others—as one of writing's most enduring self-images or tales of origin. Orpheus, the poet, is given permission by the gods to descend to the underworld in order to retrieve his loved one, Eurydice, who is more properly dead, and lead her back into the light of day, in return for which he must promise not to look back—"or else," says Ovid, "the gift would fail."[82] Like countless earlier commentators, Blanchot uses the story as a fable dealing with the achievement—and cost— of poetic inspiration. But Blanchot's retelling of the story is not simple. It lays bare a dual, dissymmetrical logic. On the one hand, he says, art speaks of loss, and therefore of the possibility of redemption. It records grievous absence, but, as it does so, it transfigures the object of mourning by substituting for it an image that retains the essential features of the absentee. Art, then, saves from death and represents light's victory over dark. True enough, success is indirect, since what is salvaged is not the object of desire itself but an intangible representation of it. But such obliqueness is inescapable; it is the price paid for the hubris of the work, which otherwise would not survive, and which, since it does survive, is able thereby to preserve both loved one and poet, who are remembered, in their absence, in the work.

But this familiar story conceals a more compelling, more properly subterranean plot. Orpheus' purpose in descending to the underworld, Blanchot points out, was not in fact to produce a work at all. More simply, more radically, it was in order to see Eurydice again—not an image of Eurydice, but Eurydice herself, as she is (or *is* not) in death: irretrievable, invisible, impossible, and irreducibly other. This, Blanchot insists, is the more powerful injunction: not to produce the work, but to travel to the limit of the visible in order to see what precisely cannot be seen. The act of mourning or poetic retrieval is traversed by a ghostly presence it can neither grasp nor renounce. And this is why, according to Blanchot, despite agreeing to avert his eyes, Orpheus nevertheless looks again, at which point Eurydice is lost twice over. Death is therefore double. From the perspective of the work, Orpheus' impatient transgression is an act of madness, carelessness, and irresponsibility. But that betrayal is merely a response to a more exacting requirement. As Blanchot explains:

> [A]ssuredly, by turning round to gaze at Eurydice, Orpheus ruins the work, the work immediately unravels, and Eurydice returns once more to the shadows; and as Orpheus looks on, the essence of night is no longer what is essential. He thus betrays the work, and Eurydice, and the night. But *not* to turn around to gaze at Eurydice would be no less a betrayal, no less an infidelity to the immeasurable, careless force of his movement, which does not want Eurydice in her daytime truth and everyday attraction, but wants her in her nocturnal obscurity, in her remoteness, with her body closed and face locked away, wants to see her not when she is visible, but when she is invisible, not as the intimacy of a familiar life, but as the strangeness of that which excludes all intimacy, and wants, not to restore her to life, but to have living in her the plenitude of her death.[83]

Orphic impatience, here, is not the opposite of patience; it is its hyperbolic intensification. "True patience," comments Blanchot, "does not exclude impatience, it is its intimate core: impatience suffered and endured without end. Orpheus' impatience is therefore also a fitting gesture [*un mouvement juste:* a just movement or impulse]: it marks the beginning of what will become his own passion, his greatest patience, his infinite lingering in death."[84]

If Orpheus breaks his promise not to look upon Eurydice, it is in order to fulfil another promise, that of his undying passion for Eurydice. But Eurydice is doubly dead, and, though each promise is affirmed without reserve, neither of them can in fact be kept. The work is sacrificed on the altar of its own dissolution. This entails, however, no covert resurrection. The promise of the work cannot be realised; it is this after all that seals its status as a promise. Promises cannot be made present; they belong to the future. Despite appearances to the contrary, then, there is no dialectic at work here, or rather the dialectic of the artwork that Blanchot presents is itself more properly—*im*properly—unhinged by something that exceeds it. It is, so to speak, paralysed, suspended, neither realised nor destroyed, and the fate of the poet, in Blanchot's retelling, is strongly reminiscent of the impasse confronted by the Kafka of *L'Espace littéraire,* who finds himself, says Blanchot, in the position of Abraham—who, in sacrificing Isaac to God, is at the selfsame time seemingly compelled to sacrifice God's own possible, terrestrial future.[85] The choice, then, is no choice, and the apparent alternative without issue or possibility of resolution. Time cannot progress, but stands still, returning forever as a question, according to a logic of non-identical repetition.

The work may be all, then, but for the poet it is still not enough. "The work is everything for Orpheus," says Blanchot, "—except for the desired look into whose depths it plummets, such that only in that look is the work able to go beyond itself, reach back to its origin, and be consecrated in impossibility."[86] So though the work is an act of deliberation, which must begin and end, it can do so only by abdicating its extremity, which remains unfathomable; yet that extremity, which is nowhere explicit, is what gives the work its singular appeal, and Orpheus' poem relies for its existence on something it cannot therefore embody. The work resists elucidation. It alludes to a secret which cannot be divulged by the work, but which nevertheless lies within the work at an intangible distance from the work, as a kind of secret without secret, simultaneously veiled yet unveiled, and in itself irreducible to any disclosure or disclosing of truth, visible or invisible.

It might be said that to uncover this absent secret of the work's singularity is criticism's task. But though it constitutes (and dissolves) the work as such, the secret remains forever inaccessible. Like "literature" itself, it is not an object, indeed it hardly exists at all, which is why criticism's lot is constantly to pursue it while never grasping it. At this point in Blanchot's text it is no doubt telling that, in drawing on myth, fable, or allegory, the critic is driven to blur the boundary between fiction and criticism in his own writing. As Blanchot makes plain in the prefatory note from *L'Espace littéraire* identifying the importance of Orpheus' gaze in his exposition, the pages recounting Orpheus' story themselves necessarily gesture towards something of which they cannot speak directly.

This is proof of the fact that the Orpheus legend for Blanchot is not simply a convenient crux on which to hang a theory of literature or literary creativity, but that the writer's retelling of the story actively partakes in the problematic it describes. In other words, Blanchot's own Orpheus story is an abyssal reflection of that which it is describing, and it is as though as a result the critical essay that is *L'Espace littéraire* is also possessed of a secret it cannot reveal or make present, not because Blanchot's text has somehow acquired prophetic status, but because simply, and without any kind of privilege, the text the reader is reading, irrespective of whether the text offers itself as criticism or as fiction, *is* that secret itself in its absolute withdrawal from presence and as an ever futural event. Which is to say that criticism here finds itself in exactly the same predicament as the literature about which it once claimed to say so much. In its indispensable inadequacy, criticism shares ultimately in literature's enigma and incompletion. Criticism is no pedestrian insult to literature—no, more radically than that, it is an extension of literature (if it exists) by other means, a vacuous yet unavoidable replication of what it once sought to transform into its own proper object, and which in its turn wreaks on its offspring its own final, paradoxical vengeance, which is to transform literary criticism into a minor branch of imaginative literature. For in the end, the fate of criticism, Blanchot says, is merely to display the radical yet demanding void that, if such exists, lies at the heart of literature itself.

Is this to say that criticism—not as external legislation, but immanent possibility—is a necessary culmination of the work? This, it may be remembered, was how Benjamin in 1920 sought to explicate the critical thinking of the Jena Romantics. For Friedrich Schlegel and Novalis, Benjamin wrote, "criticism, in its central intent, is not a judgement [*Beurteilung*] of the work, but both the fulfilment [*Vollendung*], completion [*Ergänzung*] and systematisation of the work, and its dissolution in the absolute." "The problem of immanent criticism," Benjamin added, "loses its paradoxical character in the Romantic definition of the concept, according to which criticism does not mean judging the work, since if it did so it would be nonsensical to announce a criterion immanent in the work. Criticism is rather a reflection [*Reflexion*] of the work, one that of course can only bring to fruition the germ immanent within it."[87] Elsewhere, Benjamin argued, it was the pure criticisability or *Kritisierbarkeit* of the work that, for the Romantics, constituted the work as such: "So long as a work is criticisable [*kritisierbar*], then it is an art work [*Kunstwerk*]; otherwise not. . . ."[88] What was implied here, of course, was the status of the artwork as a provisional stage in a spiralling process of infinite reflection culminating in the absolute Idea. In this respect, as Daniel Payot suggests, the criterion of criticisability, for Benjamin, was proof of the necessity of a progressive movement of aesthetic transcendence. "In other words," Payot explains, "the particular work, constitutively and in essence, is a form that is 'sublatable' ['*relevable*']: it is what it is—unity, completeness, solidity—and maintains itself as a work only in so far as within it empirical (contingent) form may be dissolved ('consumed') into the sphere of absolute form. A sublation of this type [*une telle relève*] is not something that affects finished form [*la forme achevée*] after the event: the possibility of sublation is much rather the condition, the transcendental ground of the work's own completeness [*complétude*]. The work is a work only to the extent that, by its very constitution, it has always already received the status of a consumable form: its very completeness is nothing other than what might be termed its 'sublatability' ['*relevabilité*']."[89]

In Blanchot, however, there is little trace of any such ambitions of transcendence. On the contrary, the upward movement of infinite reflection as articulated by the Romantics remains decisively blocked by the persistent and infinitely retrocessive movement not of the Idea but of what, with Levinas, Blanchot addresses as the *il y a:* that always prior affirmation that escapes negation, is irreducible to being or non-being, cannot be absorbed into truth or (for Blanchot at any rate) become the basis for any transcendence whatsoever. "Above all," writes Blanchot in *L'Écriture du désastre*, "the *there is* [*l'il y a*], as neuter [*en tant que neutre*], defies the question relating to it: if challenged, it ironically absorbs the challenge, which has no power over it. Even if it allows itself to be overcome, it does so because defeat is what is improperly proper to it [*est sa convenance inconvenante*], just as bad infinity [*le mauvais infini*] in its perpetual repetition determines it as true to the extent that it (falsely) imitates transcendence and thus exposes [*dénonce*] its essential ambiguity and the impossibility of subordinating that ambiguity to what is either true or just."[90]

The neuter, then, in Blanchot, this movement of simultaneous inscription and effacement, withdrawal and supplementation, which the writer describes elsewhere as what makes literature possible and yet impossible at the same time, interrupts decisively, by dint of its irreducible indecision, all forms of aesthetic transcendence. Literary criticism and literature alike are returned to the endless finitude that is their shared predicament. For if literary criticism is an institution without justification or purpose, other than that of asserting its own fragile authority, then, it is because this is already true of literature. Literature too is bound to disappearance. Its only essence, says Blanchot, lies in its essential non-essentiality, its lack of self-presence, identity, or worth. Literature is flummery. For the institutions of literary criticism, this is a troubling diagnosis. It suggests that, far from validating those values for which critics and readers display such voracious appetite, "literature" just as often treats them with disrespect, scepticism, or indifference.

This, at any rate, Blanchot argues, is what the history of modern literature shows. Time and again, literature has fallen short of the many worthwhile causes it was once thought to be promoting. Even in those cases where, seemingly for the very best of reasons, literature undertook to intervene politically—the canonic example, in France, during the 1940s and 1950s, was the committed literature of Sartre, de Beauvoir, and others—there too writing had the disquieting effect of undermining the very positions it was meant to protect. The decisiveness of action, as each of Sartre's novelistic or theatrical protagonists belatedly discovers, is always dissipated by the indecisiveness of words, those very words that Sartre, later in his literary career, in a reversal whose irony was not lost on the author, was minded to renounce by writing a book entitled precisely: *Les Mots* (*Words*). Sartre's ambition may have been to overcome the unruly awkwardness of writing and its failure to endorse the writer's ethico-political project by appealing to the dialectic of "qui perd gagne," "loser wins," but there was little guarantee, as Sartre was aware, that even his own words would prove so compliant as to allow themselves to be contained by philosophy.

"The situation is clearer now," Blanchot observed in 1945, referring to Sartre's (then, and since, unfinished) tetralogy of committed novels, *Les Chemins de la liberté* (*Paths of Freedom*), "the novel has nothing to fear from a didactic proposition [*une thèse*], provided the proposition is willing to be nothing without the novel. For the novel has its own rules of behaviour [*sa morale propre*]: ambiguity and equivocation. It has its own reality, which is the power to discover the world in the unreal and imaginary. And, finally, it has its own truth, which obliges it to assert nothing without seeking to take it back, and to allow nothing to succeed without first preparing its failure, so that every didactic proposition that triumphs in a novel immediately ceases to be true."[91] Bataille says something similar in an essay on Emily Brontë. Literature, he writes, is not civic duty; it is precarious, abyssal exposure to what lies at the edge of human experience. "Being inorganic," he writes, "it is irresponsible. Nothing rests upon it. It can say anything [*Elle peut tout dire*]."[92] Which does not exclude, it must be said, the enigmatic possibility or even necessity, notwithstanding (or, more accurately, precisely because of) the absence of any legislative authority competent to decide where responsibility here either begins or ends, that to write might also imply having to take responsibility for literature's very irresponsibility, or, as Blanchot puts it in *Le Pas au-delà*, without specifying whether this is an impossible injunction or an unanswerable question: "[to] assume responsibility [*répondre*: i.e., to be responsible and to take responsibility, responsibility therefore as both state and act, and in that sense a disposition, so to speak, that precedes both state and act] for that which escapes responsibility."[93] But for what else, one might respond, is it possible to assume responsibility, if not for that for which we are *not* responsible? Responsibility in this sense is no longer a form of moral ownership of one's actions or those of another: it is the extremity of the impossible itself.

But faced with the radical disobedience of the putative object of his or her concerns, how is a critic to respond? As for most things, there would appear to be always at least two choices. The first is straightforward enough. Whether by preference, moral or political conviction, or sheer laziness, it is no doubt possible to read so as to allow the object of reading to confirm, either positively or negatively, the reader's prejudices—those prejudices which, as Blanchot concedes, are an indispensable part of any act of understanding. As all readers know, it can be sometimes intensely pleasurable, after a moment's trembling hesitation, to rediscover familiar convictions in this way; whole literary genres, such as melodrama, thrive on these effects. But at some point any reader must stop, either because, for whatever reason, he or she simply abandons the act of reading or because, excessively challenged or affronted by the work, the reader refuses to continue reading, and passes to something less taxing or less offensive. On occasion, to cease reading in this way can no doubt seem—quite plausibly often is—a responsible course of action: in the face of repugnant propaganda, pornography, or massproduced kitsch. But in the end, all reading encounters a limit; it is bound to define itself therefore not simply in terms of what it can or will read but also in terms of what it cannot or will not read. If so, a second option stands facing the reader, who, instead of giving up, once he or she reaches the limit of the readable, may attempt instead to carry on, and expose his or her experience of reading to the promise or threat of the unreadable, thereby endeavouring to measure up to the demands of the text, which may mean relinquishing, at least provisionally, the assumptions that are among readers' most cherished possessions, in order to respond more scrupulously, in more affirmative vein, to what is written in a text or, more importantly, like Orpheus in search of Eurydice, attend to that—a silent demand, a hidden secret, or a ghostly presence—which remains unread, unreadable, even unwritten, within the work or beyond it.

At this stage it is apparent that the choice facing the reader—to read or not to read?—is less of an alternative than it might seem. For to cease reading, for whatever reason, is itself already an act of reading and decided upon while reading, just as any act of reading is itself always a confrontation with what cannot be read. In either case, reading is haunted by the spectre of the unreadable. That spectre is a necessary one. Without the prospect of the unreadable, no reading would be able to delimit its own task or purpose, and it would have no object to which to apply itself. Reading and unreadability, Derrida observes, are not in opposition. It is rather that the one is the condition of possibility— impossibility—of the other.[94] It is well known that readers often skip passages they believe they have already read. To read at all, it may be argued, is to encounter the unfamiliarity, the strangeness, the otherness of the unreadable. In other words, to read is by necessity to strain towards the point at which its own possibility is put into crisis. When this happens, as it eventually must, it becomes apparent that to read is not simply to scrutinise an object, it is also to be scrutinised by that object in turn; it is no longer to circumscribe the object of reading within an interpretative horizon grounded in familiarity, but to suspend that interpretative horizon by treating it in its turn as an object of reading. At this extreme point, in the name of justice itself, all critical decision-making has to be deferred, and the values underpinning decisions put into abeyance, without there being any guarantee that any decision will finally be made, or the values in question rehabilitated or reasserted, though there are circumstances too where justice may itself demand the reader cease reading so as not to lend legitimacy, for instance, to what is being read.

All this, Blanchot repeats, does not arise as a consequence of the superior value of literature or the aesthetic with respect to other modes of discourse. It is simply because "literature" is not the self-identical, aesthetic object criticism assumes it to be but a kind of corrosive vacancy that resists all positing and positioning. And this is also why "literature," however much the institutions of literary criticism may wish to claim otherwise, is not in itself a source of value or values, and why to read is to be exposed to an essential inessentiality that can only ever be affirmed in its very weakness. As Blanchot writes:

> [I]t is precisely the essence of literature to escape any determination of its essence, any assertion which might stabilise it or even turn it into a reality: literature is never given, but remains always

to be rediscovered or reinvented. It is not even certain that the word literature, or art, corresponds to anything real, or possible, or important.

And he goes on:

> Whoever affirms literature in itself affirms nothing. Whoever seeks it seeks only that which slips away; whoever finds it finds only what falls short of literature or, even worse, what lies beyond it. This is why, in the end, it is non-literature that each book pursues as the essence of what it loves and yearns passionately to discover.[95]

Writing, then, for Blanchot, is far from the autonomous activity as which it is sometimes portrayed. For at least three reasons: first, because it is subject to no legislation, external or internal, that it does not contest, if only because its very possibility necessarily precedes the drafting of any statute: "writing," Blanchot notes in *L'Entretien infini*, recalling Moses' broken tablets, "in this respect, is the greatest violence, since it transgresses the Law, all law, and its own law";[96] second, because, being essentially inessential, it has no self-identity which might be the basis for autonomy; and third, because it is not yet at all clear in what sense, if any, writing for Blanchot is an activity, a making or doing, whose objects (if they exist) belong to the practical world of means and ends.

Blanchot's purpose in all this is not to bind the fate of literature and criticism to nihilism, as impatient commentators have sometimes assumed. On the contrary, literature for Blanchot is inseparable, in its simultaneous possibility and impossibility, from the question that literature itself becomes for Hölderlin, Sade, Mallarmé, Kafka, Woolf, Artaud, Beckett, Celan, Duras, numerous others too. It is not premised therefore on the realisation or belief, in Nietzsche's famous charge, frequently cited by Heidegger as a key diagnosis (and symptom) of technological modernity itself, "that the highest values are being devalued ['*Daß die obersten Werte sich entwerten*']."[97] Indeed, writes Blanchot in 1973, referring perhaps indifferently to writing, literature, or the *neutre*, "he [*il*: he or it] is too lacking in scepticism to entertain hope [*trop peu sceptique pour espérer*]. He does not hope enough to stop at nihilism [*Il n'espère pas assez pour s'arrêter au nihilisme*]. The unknown without hope."[98] But nor is literature for Blanchot grounded in the notion that art's uncertainty, its forfeiting of self-evident legitimacy, ought primarily to be understood as an indictment of modern capitalist society, mirrored in a culture industry that grants art autonomy the better to enslave it, severing its time-honoured bond with the social world, with the result that art's role can henceforth only be one of unreconciled but melancholy negativity. This, it will be remembered, was the point of departure of Adorno's *Aesthetic Theory*, which precisely begins with the philosopher's dismay at the essential self-questioning—judged here to have taken on the air of an unquestioned article of faith—which art in the modern era has become. "It is everywhere assumed to be the case today that nothing concerning art can be assumed any longer to be the case," writes Adorno, "neither in itself, nor its relation to the whole, nor even its right to exist." So far so good, at least up to a point, Blanchot might rejoin; but Adorno continues in rather different vein: "The loss of what could be done without reflexion or unproblematically has not been compensated for by the open infinitude of new possibility that reflection confronts. In many respects, expansion appears as contraction."[99]

For Blanchot, however, and crucially so, literature is not bounded by philosophical horizons of this kind, whether ontological or sociological, deriving from the history of Being or the dialectics of history. Indeed, the philosophical (and more than philosophical) importance of literature—of Hölderlin and Mallarmé, among others—according to Blanchot, lies precisely in the extent to which, while set within the philosophical horizon, it necessarily also, by the appeal it makes to words, punctuates or disperses that horizon. This is why from 1960 onwards Blanchot was increasingly drawn to address literature under the rubric of what he terms "a change of epoch [*un changement d'époque*]." The suggestion was not simply that literature had somehow entered into a fresh periodisation or new epoch (from the Greek *epokhè*, meaning: a stoppage, or station, the position of a planet, or a fixed point of time), a claim which, relying simultaneously on saturnine certainty and terrestrial uncertainty, is at best aporetic (which has not prevented it, in recent years, from giving rise to an inordinate amount of inconsequential debate among literary critics concerning the differences between so-called modernity and postmodernity, not to mention so-called post-postmodernity, when it is plain to see the one is merely the repetition of the other—not as tragedy but as farce). More importantly, the implication was that literature was henceforth thinkable only according to its suspension (from the same Greek word, *epokhè*, meaning: suspension of judgement). And as Blanchot later suggests in *L'Écriture du désastre*, in a bold, elliptical double invocation—not to say conflation—of Athens and Jerusalem, *epokhè* may also be taken to name that decisively unde-cidable interruption which opens the possibility of messianic time: this always future and—in its very certainty—forever uncertain epoch that will always be deferred, even though the time to which it belongs is nec-essarily always: now, here, today, in this forever impending instant of my dying.[100]

The story that literature tells, then, in so far as it is a story at all, is not one of dispiriting decline, but of interruption, withdrawal, differ-ence: not the past, but the future, not the historial forgetting of Being nor the negativity of the dialectic, but radical openness. So if it is true, for instance, as Blanchot suggests in 1963 apropos of Louis-René Des Forêts's short novel, *Le Bavard,* that such a work, like some of its con-temporaries, is traversed by what he calls "an almost infinite nihilism," it is essential to read in these words a trembling doubt, an erasure even, as signalled by the peculiarity of an adverbial modifier (for what is an infinity that is not entirely itself?), and to set this re-marking of infinity alongside the desolate, ravishing joy that such emptiness, according to Blanchot, implies.[101] To say that literature asserts nothing, then, is not to fall prey to the lure of a substantified absence. Far more radically, it is to bind literature to a more essential kind of affirmation, no longer dependent on the authoritative imposition of value or values, and belonging therefore not to the certainties of the past but to the unpre-dictable demands of the future.

But what kind of future is at stake here? Futurity is not futuristic imagining, and responsiveness to the future is not prediction or predi-cation; to affirm the future is to affirm exposure to that which is without name, without example, and cannot be evaluated in advance—but with-out which justice itself cannot be affirmed in its turn. It is a decision that decides on behalf of undecidability. And this is what is essentially at issue in Blanchot's own critical account of literature, writing, poetry. Writing, he says, glossing the poems of René Char in 1953, and invoking Heraclitus' description of the impersonal, anonymous speaking of the oracle at Delphi, consists neither in saying nor concealing but in pointing, giving a sign:

> The language in which the origin speaks is essentially prophetic. This does not mean that it dictates future events, it means that it does not base itself on something which already is, either on a currently held truth, or solely on language which has already been spoken or verified. It announces, because it begins. It *points* towards the future, because it does not yet speak, and is language of the future to the extent that it is like a future language which is always ahead of itself, having its meaning and legitimacy only before it, which is to say that it is fundamentally without justification.[102]

There is nothing sure or self-evident about Char's poetry. The affirmation it demands or requires of reader or writer cannot be reduced to any given discursive position. In this respect there is nothing assertive about affirmation as Blanchot formulates it. It is, so to speak, neither positive nor negative. Like the *il y a* or the neuter in Blanchot, it both precedes and exceeds the dialectic of yes or no, even as it may manifest itself as a yes: a yes to the unpredictable, futural otherness of the event, as betokened by the singular injunction "viens," "come," addressed to a thought that may be a person, or to a person that may be a thought, which falls at the end of *L'Arrêt de mort*.[103] Affirmation in this context takes on a strangely singular and irreducible intensity. It leaves intact neither the who, nor the what, nor the how of reading: neither the putative reading subject, nor the supposed aesthetic object, nor the recourse to any pre-established critical method. It implies an interpretative decision, but one that is necessarily exposed at every stage to radical indecision. Reading here becomes an enigmatic event, therefore, which can no longer be simply configured as the encounter between a conscious, responsible subject and a stable object according to a regulated process of understanding.

This is not to say that affirmation in Blanchot's sense is not selective. But the differences within texts or between texts at stake here escape any proper aesthetic or moral codification; they imply no normative evaluation or canonic legislation. Writing, however, is not arbitrary. Whether as literature or criticism, it falls subject to an imperative that does not rely on any essential determination. As Blanchot formulates it, writing obeys a strangely fragile injunction, which is neither moral nor aesthetic, which may perhaps be addressed least inadequately by the term: ethical (though Blanchot, like Derrida, is not always convinced the ethical can be securely differentiated from moral dogma). In any case, it owes nothing to the aesthetic or the moral in any delimited sense, not least because any such injunction cannot be unified or reduced to any logic of unity such as ethics or morality strive to reach. Indeed it is an imperative without imperative that is radically suspicious of all forms of (aesthetic, moral, political) transcendence. Affirmation in Blanchot, in other words, affirms nothing outside itself: it challenges myth, aestheticism, moral authority, any kind of established political order, all homogeneity or unity, which it withdraws and effaces. It speaks not as renewed assertiveness, nor as a desire to impose a fresh set of values, be they viewed by some as heroically or dangerously transgressive.

Much rather what affirmation in Blanchot affirms, by way of the *neutre,* is a withdrawal from positionality, a movement of indecision always in excess of the unity of the one, forever dedicated to the otherness of the other, that which is perpetually other than any other.[104] For if indecision hesitates, it is not because it is unable to select the one rather than the other, rather because it refuses the necessity of that choice. "'Which of the two?'" asks a voice in *Le Pas au-delà.* "'—Neither the one nor the other, the other, the other,'" comes the answer.[105] Indecision, then, does not constitute itself as a gesture founded in negativity but as a fragile response to plurality, as a more radical form of affirmation than that which binds itself to asserting the same or its double. "What might be thought to respond or correspond to the neuter," says Blanchot, "is the fragility of what is already in the process of breaking [*la fragilité de ce qui déjà se brise*]: a passion more passive than anything else that may be said to be passive [*plus passive que tout ce qu'il y aurait de passif*: it is worth emphasising Blanchot's recourse, albeit in the conditional, to the *il y a*], a yes that has said yes [*oui qui a dit oui*] prior to all affirmation, as though the passage of dying had always already passed, preceding all consent."[106] Radical indecision in Blanchot, then, is not embarrassed uncertainty, quiescence, or quietism but critically decisive: it intervenes, incisively, to affirm that which is other, and always other than other.

Affirmation without precedent: this, then, was Blanchot's conclusion in 1959. Invoking critical indecision on his part did not of course imply any retreat from the decisions history or politics demanded. On the contrary, to affirm, he insisted, was necessarily always to distinguish, always to make choices; and, speaking of the future challenges of literature and criticism in *Arguments,* Blanchot was acutely mindful of the political struggles in which he himself had a part (against de Gaulle's undemocratic return to power in France in 1958 and France's continuing colonial war in Algeria, a war which it is well known the French Republic was never willing to name as such), and which were all the while occurring at—and accordingly within—literary criticism's own gates. "[C]riticism—literature—in my view," he wrote,

> is part of one of the most challenging yet important tasks of our time, unfolding in a movement that is necessarily undecided: the task of preserving and releasing thought from the notion of value, and consequently opening history to that which within history is already moving beyond all forms of value and readying itself for a wholly different—and still unpredictable—kind of affirmation.[107]

And in a passage excised from subsequent versions, but whose political implications at the time were hard to miss, Blanchot went on:

> Of what, then, does the literary work speak when it rejects all evaluation? Why do we feel ourselves bound by it to the concern for anonymous existence, to being as a neutral and impersonal power, excluding all distinct interest, all determined speech, and calling on the violent equality of becoming? And, if indeed this is the direction it opens up for us, is it not strange that we should then be led to rediscover, in the most superficial kind of criticism,

that which in journalistic form is part of the murmur of everyday experience [*la rumeur quotidienne*] and of life outside [*la vie du dehors*], the just continuation [*le prolongement juste*] of the movement of profound indeterminacy that seeks to communicate in the creation of the work in order to affirm in the work the future of communication and communication as future?[108]

Criticism today, Blanchot suggested, by dint of its necessity and impossibility, is faced with an exacting challenge: either of reasserting, after all, those moral, political, and aesthetic values that are under threat from the joyful—or is it pernicious?—scepticism of a literature which fails to validate them; or else of embarking on the more difficult course of affirming the otherness (beyond presence, identity, or sense) of an act of language no longer authorised by morality or truth, and thus no longer subject to a logic of identity or a dialectic of completion. Numerous are the critics, journalists and academics alike, who, sensitive to the urgency of the moral, the political, or the ethical, have preferred the former of these paths; but many too, often in silence, and not without hesitation, sometimes even with reluctance, are the writers and readers who have sought to meet the challenge synonymous with the second. The alternative, one might say, still remains; and there hangs, for Blanchot—and dare I say it? for the author of these lines—the future prospects of any critical writing on literature at all.

This, then, is what Blanchot's example—example without example— offers. In the pages that follow, in reading and rereading the work of Barthes, Blanchot, and Derrida, in their protracted engagement with some of the most difficult and unreadable of so-called literary texts, my purpose will be to pursue the implications of Blanchot's words in order to ask myself two questions that are of crucial concern to all who read and are driven to write about their reading: what is the future that lies *in* literary criticism? and what might be said to be the future *of* literary criticism?

Chapter Two

ROLAND BARTHES

From Ideology to Event

I

A case in point

> *To persist [S'entêter]* means to affirm the Irreducible in literature, that
> which, in literature, resists and survives the typecast languages *[discours
> typés]* surrounding it: philosophy, science, psychology; to act as though it
> were incomparable and immortal. A writer—by which I mean not
> someone who fulfils a function, or is the servant of an art, but the subject
> of a practice—needs the persistence *[l'entêtement]* of the lookout standing
> at the crossroads where all other languages meet, in a *trivial [triviale]*
> position compared to the purity of those doctrines *(trivialis,* according to
> etymology, is the epithet that characterises the prostitute waiting at the
> three-way fork in the road). All in all, to persist *[s'entêter]* means to
> maintain in spite of everything the force of drift and expectation *[d'une
> dérive et d'une attente].* And it is precisely because it persists that writing
> is given to constant displacement *[entraînée à se déplacer].*
>
> Roland Barthes, *Leçon*[1]

Few critics displayed with the economy or intensity of Roland Barthes
the contradictions and impasses, revisions and hesitations, shifts and
detours that mark the history of literary theory and criticism during the
second half of the twentieth century. From the early 1950s till his

untimely death in 1980, Barthes came to embody, one after the other, sometimes even simultaneously, a multiplicity of divergent and seemingly irreconcilable approaches to texts, literary and non-literary alike, ranging from a phenomenologically or existentially inspired thematicism to a proto-Marxian, at times explicitly Marxist commitment to ideological demystification, a protracted engagement with the concepts and methodology of Saussurean linguistics, an eclectic dalliance with sociology, anthropology, and psychoanalysis, the affirmation of textual plurality as a criterion of value, a rehabilitation of textual pleasure as an object of inquiry—all of which coexisted throughout with a deep-seated suspicion of ideological and other stereotypes, a restless distrust of political, interpretative, metalinguistic, even theoretical authority, a willingness at timely as well as untimely moments to defend the literary and artistic avant-garde, outweighed only by an equally uncompromising devotion to a favoured body of both established and neglected classics, and an acute sensitivity to textual forms in general, whose boundaries Barthes in his own writing was constantly exploring, deploying a mobile repertoire of styles and idioms that went from polemical intervention to theoretical excursus, from critical diagnosis to expressions of appreciation, from aphoristic fragment to oblique autobiographical exposure.[2]

Over a thirty-year period Barthes not only brought to literary and cultural criticism a fresh language of understanding, analysis, and commentary, he also supplied it with a new set of objects, spanning both popular culture and high art, from photography to fashion, food to film, myth to music, classical rhetoric to contemporary journalism. In the process, he placed at the centre of critical debate, in France and elsewhere, a distinctive set of theoretical and other concerns, each of which received from Barthes a characteristically decisive formulation: writing, *écriture*, as that which, irreducible to the opposition between form and content, reconciled the autonomy of the one with the historicity of the other; the social stereotype or myth, by which petty-bourgeois ideology infiltrated itself as incontrovertible self-evidence into the language of everyday life; the idea of a science of literary (and other) signs, which, by explaining the process of signification itself and the diversity of interpretation to which a text gave rise, might disqualify the dogmatism, obscurantism, and impressionism of traditional literary criticism; the practice of reading and writing as productive activities upon which it might be possible to base an affirmative politics or ethics; the multiplicity of the body as that which, exceeding signification, was inscribed within writing as resistance, recalcitrance, and risk; textuality itself as a paradoxical domain in which what prevailed was the signifier without the signified, structuration without structure, the novelistic without the novel, and where meaning itself was perpetually disappointed, interrupted, suspended, and returned to that which, in his first book in 1953 and one of the last lecture series he held at the Collège de France in 1977, thus framing the history of his dealings with the literary, Barthes addressed as the zero degree of writing or the neutrality of the neuter.[3]

As this prospectus suggests, Barthes was adept throughout his career at reinventing and reformulating his thinking, largely in response to an ever-changing sequence of socio-political, ideological, discursive, or theoretical conjunctures, with the result that, though Barthes would often pass through similar places, he always managed to approach them from an unfamiliar direction in order, then, to depart elsewhere. The writer's own favoured image for this perpetual movement, backwards as well as forwards, borrowed from Vico by way of both illustration and proof, was that of the spiral. Everything returned, he often remarked, but not necessarily in the same place, nor with the same effects or consequences. But this sometimes bewildering mobility was not without its price, and Barthes's distaste for stereotypical predictability, particularly in the latter phase of his career, was far from universally admired. For some, the writer's chameleon-like willingness to abandon one set of intellectual concerns for another, and to pass without pause, so to speak, from political engagement to scientific neutrality to amoral hedonism, was merely evidence that he was something less than a rigorous or consistent thinker and that what counted most of all in his intellectual development were subjective or humoral factors that he was wilfully wont to indulge: boredom, impatience, sensuality, disenchantment, longing.

This was an interpretation that in later years Barthes himself was not always minded to refute, if only because of the intellectual freedom it afforded him, and he had little hesitation in wryly listing, twice over, in *Roland Barthes par Roland Barthes*, the numerous ambitiously titled books he had once, or perhaps even still, planned to write, but had

postponed, in most cases *sine die*.[4] Gestures such as these were calculated to hold at bay the dominant stereotype of the critic as legislator, an
incontrovertible source of truth and knowledge (though there was
always the risk that the effect would be precisely the reverse, and that,
in drawing attention to his shortcomings, Barthes would reinforce the
image of his own authority, leaving commentators with little else to do
than to explicate his texts by repeating them). At any event, the figure of
Barthes that has tended to predominate in discussion of his work since
his death is not that of an incisive or rigorous theorist, the author of
numerous innovative methodological strategies and promoter of countless new conceptual moves, who imposed himself as such on his contemporaries, but that of the always covert or would-be autobiographer,
aspiring novelist, retiring aesthete, analyst of subjectivity, epicurean
moralist, utopian dreamer, or even postmodern lifestyle consultant.

True enough, these snapshots of Barthes's activities are not necessarily inaccurate ones. Some form an integral part of the writer's own
self-image or self-portrait. However, at a time when, for a variety of
reasons—the problematic status of its object, its rampant professionalisation, the apparent saturation of the field by an array of competing,
prescriptive methodologies—literary criticism is tempted to rely on
seemingly self-validating moral, political, aesthetic, or conceptual certainties, it has also become urgent to resist the image of Barthes as
indulgent self-commentator, and not to allow the stereotypes listed
above to obscure our understanding of the exacting internal logic of
Barthes's complex intellectual itinerary. For it may be argued with equal
if not greater plausibility that each of Barthes's notorious shifts in
emphasis or direction, rather than a result of idiosyncratic affective or
psychological factors, was prompted in fact by a series of fundamental
theoretical challenges. What readers today should perhaps therefore be
invited to consider in Barthes's writing is not its alleged playfulness but
rather its persistence and its precision, the concerted, sustained, and
rigorously uncompromising way in which it grapples with the possibilities and demands of literary criticism at the close of the twentieth
and shortly before the dawn of the twenty-first century.

What is primarily at stake here, then, is not the subjective idiosyncrasy of Barthes's critical writing but its theoretical necessity. For us
today, Barthes should be less eccentric exception than instructive ex-

ample. Admittedly, there is nothing straightforward about such exemplarity, as I have argued, and it is noticeable that one of Barthes's earliest gestures in *Mythologies* in 1957 was to challenge the implications of that naturalising rhetoric of exemplification, attributed by the writer to the petty bourgeoisie, that might, for instance, transform an apparently contingent, mundane photograph of a black African soldier dutifully saluting the French Republican flag on the cover of *Paris-Match* into a covert illustration and justification of the normality and universality of French colonial rule.[5] But examples can be disruptive too, as Barthes's analysis of that very photograph implied, eventually turning it, in the eyes of his numerous readers, into a potent emblem of the demythologising project in which Barthes was engaged.[6] Indeed, all examples, even if they are presented as mere illustrations of a general rule, by dint of the exceptional status conferred upon them by that very gesture, always risk becoming the very opposite of what they were at the outset. From being obedient servants, as Flaubert was to show in *Bouvard et Pécuchet*, they turn into ironic upstarts.[7] For as well as serving to endorse norms, examples are also manifestations of what exceeds those norms: no longer the gregarious one-among-the-many that can take the place of all others but the singular one-apart-from-the-many that, in the guise of that which is unique, incomparable, and monstrous, proves irreducible to any rule whatsoever.

If that which is exemplary is what occurs at the limit, as Barthes sometimes suggests, then it is also because what occurs at the limit is simultaneously without example. The paradox is revealing. It provides a clue to the challenge of reading Barthes's writing: its method and its madness, its power and its passion, its persistence and its errancy.

II

Into the wilderness

> History never guarantees victory pure and simple of one thing over its
> enemy: it always presents us, in the process of its unfolding, with
> outcomes impossible to imagine and syntheses impossible to predict.
> The mythologist is not even in the position of Moses, and cannot glimpse

the Promised Land. For the mythologist, the positivity of tomorrow is entirely hidden by the negativity of today; the value of his endeavour can only be assumed as an act of destruction: the one and the other coincide entirely, and nothing else remains [*rien ne dépasse*]. This subjective sense of history, for which the potent germ of the future *is nothing other* than the most radical apocalypse of the present, Saint-Just once summed up with a strange remark: "What constitutes the Republic," he wrote, "is the total destruction of its opposite." This should not, I think, be taken in the trivial sense of: "Something has to be cleared away before it can be rebuilt." The copula has an exhaustive meaning: there is, for a person such as this, a subjective night of history, where the future becomes essential, an essential destruction of the past [*où l'avenir se fait essence, destruction essentielle du passé*].

Roland Barthes, Mythologies[8]

The interests of Barthes during the early phase of his career were numerous and distinctive: contemporary writing, unfashionable literary classics, the theatre, music, film, strip-tease, wrestling, politics, clothes, motor-cars, the Tour de France, Greta Garbo, Einstein, much else besides. Running through his account of all these various objects or events, Barthes suggests, functioning at one and the same time as methodological principle, ideological touchstone, and Archimedean lever, but deriving more from Sartrean existentialism than Lévi-Straussian anthropology, was the opposition between Nature and Culture: between myth and history, mystification and politics, irresponsibility and responsibility, language as an expression of timeless essences and language as social act, theatre as hysterical display and theatre as historical intervention, signification as gelatinous or glutinous adhesion and signification as interruption, and so on. "In short," he put it in the original 1957 preface to *Mythologies*, "in the story that is told about life today, I was pained to see how Nature and History were merged at every moment, and I wanted to pin down, in the decorative show of *that-which-goes-without-saying* [*de ce-qui-va-de-soi*], the ideological abuse I found to be concealed within it."[9] "This is the key principle behind myth," he wrote; "it transforms history into nature."[10]

"If there is such a thing as a 'healthy' state of language," Barthes explained, "it is based on the arbitrary nature of the sign. What is nauseating [*l'écœurant*] about myth is its recourse to false nature, its *surfeit* of meaningful forms, just like those objects which obscure their functionality with a veneer of naturalness."[11] Myth, Barthes went on, was the unmistakeable hallmark of bourgeois ideology; "in a word," he argued, "in contemporary bourgeois society, the passage from the real to the ideological can be defined as the passage from anti-nature [*anti-physis*] to pseudo-nature [*pseudo-physis*]."[12] "A conjuring trick has taken place," he said, "turning reality inside out, emptying it of all history and filling it with nature, removing human significance from things so as to make them signify human insignificance. The function of myth is to empty reality of itself: it is, literally, a permanent draining away, a haemorrhage, or, if you will, an evaporation, in short, a perceptible absence."[13] And if myth was simply bourgeois ideology under another name, it followed that the working class, at least in so far as it was the subject of revolutionary change, was not a purveyor of myths; and rather like Sartre, who claimed, for much the same teleological, if unhappily counterintuitive reasons, that the working class was free by definition of all anti-semitism, so Barthes, adopting the same neo-Marxist perspective, thought the workers unlikely to be taken in by petty-bourgeois myth. "There is therefore one kind of language," he concluded, "that is not mythical, the language of those who are producers [*de l'homme producteur*]: wherever people speak to transform the real and not to preserve it within an image, wherever people bind their language to the making of things, metalanguage reverts to being an object-language, and myth is impossible. This is why language that is properly revolutionary cannot be mythical."[14]

As these instances show, Barthes's analysis proceeds by way of a series of dissymmetrical binary oppositions. For if the contrast between nature and history is what best enables the mythologist to understand bourgeois ideology, it is not because bourgeois representations are truly more natural than others. It is because they are a pseudo-nature: a sham, a deception, a charade, which it is the task and duty of the analyst to unmask, both in the name of signs and on behalf of the audience of progressive, but perhaps unwitting consumers. The aims and objectives of Barthesian demythologisation in its early manifestations are not theoretical in any impartial sense, then, but fiercely and avowedly polemical. The main enemy, Barthes still felt able to write in the 1970 preface to *Mythologies*, endowing the word with a characteristically emphatic capital letter, was middle-class normality and normativity: "la Norme bourgeoise."[15] But if Barthes's method was inseparable from sarcasm, he cheerfully conceded in 1957, it was because sarcasm, in current circumstances, was the condition of truth.[16] Admittedly, *Mythologies* offered more than invective. It was no longer a matter of trading one would-be progressive set of representations for a discredited reactionary one, as continued to be the case with ideological polemic elsewhere in France at the time, notably in the conformist backwaters of official Marxism. But Barthes's more important ambition was a radical reformulation of the relationship between language, meaning, history, politics, and ideology; and there is little doubt that it was this explicit political agenda, allied with a challenging new critical rhetoric, that won Barthes admiration and hostility alike from his readers at the time.

The longevity of many of the articles collected in *Mythologies*, more than fifty years after they first began appearing in *Les Lettres nouvelles*, is impressive. It is proof of the extent to which Barthes, writing sporadically on a monthly basis in response to this or that topical issue, was nevertheless able to develop a powerful critical and theoretical tool, one that in turn would help launch many other kinds of politically engaged inquiry into the relationship between ideology, the media, and the apparently self-evident representations of everyday life. But this is not to say that Barthes's underlying project was not without theoretical problems of its own; admittedly, these are not exclusive to *Mythologies*, and were already more markedly in evidence in Barthes's first book, *Le Degré zéro de l'écriture* (*Writing Degree Zero*) of 1953, which also brought him notoriety, and which the writer in 1957, displaying an unsuspected cogency of purpose not readily apparent from the dispersed nature of his output, described "all told [*à tout prendre*]" as already offering a "mythology of literary language."[17] *Le Degré zéro* in its own way was already a considerable achievement, and a book that articulated in prophetic fashion many of the critical and theoretical issues that were at the heart of all Barthes's future writing on literary texts. But by that very token, it was symptomatic of the abiding contradictions within literary criticism itself, which Barthes would endeavour to address, but only at the risk of considerably jeopardising the coherence of his own position.

The internal difficulties in Barthes's so-called mythology of literary language set out in *Le Degré zéro* had to do with three main sets of issues.

First, however much Barthes chose elsewhere to impugn the repressive character of bourgeois or petty-bourgeois ideological norms, which found expression according to Barthes in a chronically blinkered inability to imagine otherness,[18] the analysis the writer himself presented in *Le Degré zéro* was itself irretrievably, albeit unapologetically, prescriptive. Barthes's problems in this regard began from the outset, with the famous three-fold division of the literary work into language [*langue*], style [*style*], and writing [*écriture*]. In this cleverly refashioned trivium, which owed more than a little to Barthes's familiarity with classical rhetoric, emphasis fell unambiguously on the third of the author's conceptual protagonists, with the writer's own considerable powers of persuasion, in what is a compelling if at times almost theatrical rhetorical performance, being directed towards that end. However, in order to promote his lead performer, to articulate writing, *écriture*, as that concept which alone enables proper account to be taken of the relationship between literary form, authorial choice, and historical responsibility, Barthes was obliged to force both language and style, these two supporting players, into the wings, with unpredictable consequences. Their status, as a result, became ambiguous, uncertain, speculative, and self-contradictory—and empirically questionable.

Language, *langue*, Barthes began by arguing, was "like a natural environment [*comme une Nature*]," which is to say that it was simultaneously both natural (since that is how it appeared) and unnatural (since only something that is *not* natural can in fact resemble nature), which is also to say that it was straightforwardly neither (since something that is both natural and unnatural cannot be simply the one or the other). It was, he added, like heaven and earth joined together, "a familiar habitat"; however, it was also "a social object by definition." In language, what was given to the writer, Barthes explained, was "the whole of History," "complete and unified in the manner of a natural environment [*à la manière d'une Nature*]."[19] These are problematic assertions, even from Barthes's own perspective. For how to distinguish that which seems natural from that which is historical? Where does the divide pass within this contrasting pair of terms, each of which seems already to imply or incorporate the other? Is what Barthes compares to Nature, to adopt the terms he uses in *Mythologies*, not already in fact a pseudo-nature, not to say an anti-nature? If so, is not Barthes's own formulation a symptom of the tenaciously naturalising tendency of bourgeois ideology he was so committed to dismantling? Something of the same ambiguity attaches to what *Le Degré zéro* calls style. Style too, Barthes claims, is primarily natural in origin, having its roots in a writer's private, affective, bodily existence. It corresponds to what he describes, using a formula that may already be judged a contradiction in terms, "self-sufficient language [*un langage autarcique*]"; "what [style] refers to," he explains, "is at the level of biology or time past, not History [*au niveau d'une biologie ou d'un passé, non d'une Histoire*]," from which it follows that Barthes already knows, distinct from contingent temporality, what it is that properly constitutes history as an essential, meaningful project. That history is, of course, writing: history as writing and writing as history.[20] Barthes's conception of history, in other words, was entirely circular.

In the opening pages of *Le Degré zéro*, Barthes's main concern is to set the scene: to prepare an entrance. The star of the show is *écriture*: choice, decision, gesture, reflection, mediation, intervention—what Barthes, appealing to history as an object of purposeful responsibility and commitment, goes on to call "the morality of form [*la morale de la forme*]."[21] Writing, then, is fully historical, which is no doubt why, by contrast, language and style, in the Barthesian trivium, are demoted to the status of extras, with walk-on, non-speaking parts. At the beginning of *Le Degré zéro*, their status was uncertain. But once *écriture* takes up its position centre stage, there is no longer room for such hesitation. Summing up the argument so far, Barthes resorts to a brutal simplification. "In both cases," he writes, referring to language and to style, "we are indeed dealing with some natural environment [*une Nature*], that is, a familiar set of codified gestures [*un gestuaire familier*], where the role of energy is functional [*d'ordre opératoire*], serving at times to enumerate, at others to convert, but never to judge or to signify a choice."[22]

Choices, however, like privileges, always imply exclusions; and what Barthes in his own presentation is forced to exclude or at any rate repress, in order to turn the spotlight on *écriture*, is the complex relationship between history and language, understood in this case not as speech or writing but as socio-political institution, and the similarly vast relationship between writing, style, and what Barthes would soon affirm as one of the chief mobilising concepts in his work: the body. These are issues that would interest Barthes in subsequent texts; but as far as *Le Degré zéro* was concerned, those developments belonged to the future. Their necessity, however, was already apparent in Barthes's failure to question his own rhetorical and theoretical assumptions. How else, one might ask, was it possible for the writer to take as a preliminary condition or prerequisite for the very possibility of *écriture* that lengthy historical process by which the French language, like others across Europe and elsewhere, came to be constructed, imposed, and defended as the embodiment of French nationhood?[23] Similarly, how else might he dismiss the whole of literature before 1650 as incapable of *écriture* because still engaged in the difficult separation of nature from culture, "in the task of understanding Nature and not of expressing human essence"?[24] How else could Barthes conclude that, between the catholic churchman and mystic François Fénelon (1651–1715) and the inspector of historical monuments Prosper Mérimée (1803–70), between these two noteworthy but minor literary figures, separated by a century and more of turbulent political, social, and ideological events, the differences lay solely "in phenomena of language and accidents of style," withdrawn by definition from the history of writing as such?[25] And how else might a critic of literature, so soon after the Liberation, when poets had lived, suffered, and died in the name of freedom, nevertheless affirm that the whole of modern poetry, from Rimbaud to René Char, was merely a dalliance with the closure of Nature, a turning aside from history and society as such?[26]

Polemic is no doubt a two-edged sword; and to overcome an enemy can sometimes lead to Pyrrhic victory. Barthes's project, at least in part, was to attack a certain literary establishment, and this he did with remarkable effectiveness. At the same time, it is undeniable that Barthes's fashioning of the concept of *écriture* was at a cost, and that the conceptual framework set in place in *Le Degré zéro* is vulnerable at important moments to the charge of being dogmatic, reductive, or simply arbitrary. These difficulties are not only methodological ones; they also affect Barthes's whole account of literary and political history, which is unashamedly teleological. In itself this is not surprising; it merely confirms the extent to which Barthes in the early 1950s remained reliant on the Marxist or neo-Marxist model of historical progress to be found in the otherwise deeply antagonistic work of Sartre and Lukács (the second of whom Barthes had probably never read, though he most likely had indirect knowledge of the chief burden of Lukács's work). For despite their many differences, what Sartre and Lukács had in common was the proposition that the crucial turning point in French if not European literary (and social) history was the abortive revolution of 1848, resulting in the catastrophic failure of the progressive bourgeoisie to assume political power, which, at least on a simplistic reading of Marxist dialectics, would have led in due course to workers' revolution, as the regrettably short-lived rebellion of the Paris Commune in 1870–71, at least for some observers, served to testify.[27]

But in 1851 and 1852, France's middle classes chose instead to abandon the Republic and embrace the imperialist regime of Napoleon III, and thus go backwards in history. Marx's own riposte has achieved proverbial status. "Hegel remarks somewhere," he famously wrote, "that all great world historical events or characters always repeat themselves. He omitted to add: the first time as tragedy, the second time as farce."[28] History, then, in 1848, diverting into a blind alley, missed its appointed rendezvous; and what ensued, as Lukács and Sartre agree, as far as literature was concerned, was a story of marginalisation and withdrawal, represented emblematically in the figure of Flaubert, whose only dealings with the public sphere were conducted in a spirit of vitriolic denunciation and disengagement, and in whose work literature's political responsibilities were replaced by narcissistic aestheticism. And if Flaubert was problematic, so later naturalist writers, such as Zola, Maupassant, or Huysmans, were even less worthy of recommendation. On Lukács's part, the step that next followed was an unremitting, often violent repudiation of all forms of literary modernism, accused and found guilty of failing to engage with the historical or political process. A novel such as Beckett's *Molloy*, the critic wrote in 1958, speaking still on behalf of Soviet-era humanism, depicted "the deepest pathological degradation of man in the vegetative existence of an idiot," and in Beckett's work as a whole, as in much twentieth-century avant-garde art in general, what was to be found, Lukács contended, was overt glorification of "the pathological, the perverse, and the idiot-like, as the typical form of the 'condition humaine.'"[29] In his own pronouncements on the historical responsibilities of nineteenth- and twentieth-century writers, Sartre was more nuanced; but he too remained deeply suspicious of the ideological elitism of literary modernism. As far as *En attendant Godot* was concerned, he told Bernard Dort, although he admired the play, he deemed its pessimism, as he called it, essentially apolitical and reactionary. "All *Godot*'s themes," he explained, "are bourgeois themes: solitude, despair, clichés, incommunicability, they are all the product of the inner solitude of the bourgeoisie."[30] Between Lukács and Sartre the differences of language were considerable. A shared position remained, however, which was that literary modernism, in the end, amounted to little more than petty-bourgeois nihilism writ large.

In several significant ways, Barthes in *Le Degré zéro* turns aside from this reductive scenario. The novels of Flaubert, for instance, which occupy an important transitional place in Barthes's historical narrative too, are evidence of a very different crisis in the latter half of the nineteenth century, in which, rather than testifying passively to history's tragic loss of direction, the novel began instead actively to challenge both the intelligibility of history and the alleged transparency of bourgeois language. Flaubert's status thereby changed: he no longer did service as the typically irresponsible petty-bourgeois aesthete; he was now the paradigm of the ironic modern novelist whose fate was to be the mythologist of his own society. It was not for nothing, therefore, that, in *Le Degré zéro*, in *Mythologies*, and in many subsequent texts, Barthes emphasised the critical impact of this "flaubertisation" of literary discourse. For what Flaubert brought to the novel according to Barthes was not a gesture of depoliticisation but a different kind of critical immersion within language. "Between the third-person narrative as found in Balzac and that used by Flaubert," he observed, "there is a world of difference (that of 1848): History, on the one side, with its bitter lesson, but its coherence and confidence, reflecting the triumph of an order; on the other, art, which, to escape its divided consciousness, either satirises convention to excess, or tries to destroy it in anger. Modernity begins with the search for a Literature that is impossible."[31]

Though literary modernity was in every sense a more affirmative event for Barthes than for Lukács or Sartre, it continued nevertheless to be the site of a painful separation from History, an eloquent symptom of the unhappy consciousness of the modern writer as such. So while it is true that Barthes both identifies and thematises, to welcome effect, as an inescapable condition of literary modernity itself, that "multiplication of writings" by which no single dominant, ideological myth of language might be seen to prevail over others, leaving the texts of Flaubert, Mallarmé, Rimbaud, Surrealism, Queneau, Sartre, Blanchot, and Camus—the names are those cited by Barthes—to jostle for attention on an equal basis, each remaining incomparable and irreducible to all others, he did this with noticeable reluctance, and, in the end, only to describe it as an impasse: a cul-de-sac without future. The multiplication of writings was merely another sign of writerly alienation. "Every time the writer writes down a knot of tangled words [*trace un complexe de mots*]," Barthes concluded, "the very existence of Literature itself is called into question; what modernity gives us to read in the plurality of its writings is the impasse of its own History."[32] True enough, if literature faced an impasse, it was because it still yearned to be reconciled with History. Barthes knew this; and while he took care to offer his readers sight of this alternative prospectus, which only radical social change would bring about, he said, he was also conscious as a result that for the time being and perhaps for some time longer it might only be addressed as a futural fantasy: as utopia.

Utopia was not now, it was by definition no place at all; and it is clear that, between Barthes's unsatisfied dream of reconciliation between history and writing and his diagnosis of the aesthetic and political closure affecting writing as such, there was no contradiction. The two narratives belonged together—but only as the dual burden of the horizon of negativity bequeathed to him by the teleological Marxism to which Barthes in 1953, like numerous others, by conviction, conformism, or even sheer desperation, continued to cling. No wonder that Maurice Blanchot, reviewing *Le Degré zéro* for *La Nouvelle Nouvelle Revue française* later that year, while generally sympathetic, demurred at the apparent timidity of the book's prognosis. For if criticism at the present time were to be more than a mere acknowledgement of the empirical fact of the multiplication of writings, as the momentum of Barthes's argument required, then it was necessary to think writing not as a series of normative, responsible or irresponsible subjective choices within a given socio-historical context, as *Le Degré zéro* suggested, betraying its debt no doubt to Sartre's *Qu'est-ce que la littérature?*, but as a more radical experience of dispersion, exteriority, and non-identity. As Blanchot pointed out, revising Barthes's conclusions:

> Literature is not more diverse than in previous times, it is perhaps more monotonous, in the same way that night-time [*la nuit*] may be deemed more monotonous than daylight [*le jour*]. It is not separated from itself [*désunie*] because supposedly more subject to whim on the part of those who write, or because, beyond genre, rules, and traditions, it gives free rein to any number of unruly experiments. The diversity, originality, and anarchy of these endeavours are not what turn literature into a world dispersed [*un monde dispersé*]. We need to find a different formulation, and say: the experience of literature is exposure to dispersion itself [*l'épreuve même de la dispersion*], the approach to that which escapes unity, and the experience of that which is without shared understanding, agreement, or right—error [*l'erreur*] and the outside [*le dehors*], the ungraspable and the irregular.[33]

But here lay the third difficulty in Barthes's account. In many ways, it was the most telling and troubling of all, because it had to do with the question of the critic's own position within the conceptual shadow play he had so carefully mounted. For on the one hand Barthes's essay was nothing if not an intervention into contemporary debates on the aesthetic and ideological future of literature; indeed, more than once, in the years that followed, he would for that reason take up cudgels on behalf of this or that innovator or experimental writer, from Robbe-Grillet to Sollers, Pierre Guyotat to Renaud Camus, to defend them against ideologically motivated critical attack. But on the other hand, as far as *Le Degré zéro* was concerned, the position of the critic was largely one of disenchantment or melancholy, hedged in by negativity or fantasy, by History's impasse or its utopian reverse. Notwithstanding its conceptual novelty, then, nostalgia was the book's secret theme. Well might Blanchot suggest in 1959, in a moderately generous reworking of his 1953 review, that *Le Degré zéro de l'écriture* was one of only a few works in which "the future of literature [*l'avenir des lettres*] was inscribed," it was nevertheless hard to gauge from the book itself towards what kind of future it was pointing.[34]

This was not just a problem for *Le Degré zéro. Mythologies* soon came to much the same conclusion. There too the mythologist was left in difficult straits: not even cast as Moses, with no Promised Land even on the horizon. The work of the mythologist was no doubt important, worthwhile, and responsible, but for Barthes after 1957 it quickly exhausted itself, overcome by its own unrelieved negativity. By 1971, Barthes ruefully conceded, everyone had started to become his or her own mythologist, with implications that were not entirely happy ones.[35] For while this showed that it was still necessary to debunk petty-bourgeois representations of everyday life, it also pointed to something more problematic: not only was the discourse of the mythologist dependent for its survival on the very things it detested, but it ran the risk of simply turning into another conformist, normative ideology, queasily reminiscent of those it sought to overturn. The demystification of mythology had spawned its own mythology of demystification. It was also increasingly apparent that ideological demystification still entertained a nostalgic belief in the possibility of that which petty-bourgeois myth claimed to be, but was patently not: an innocently uncompromised, denotative naming of the world that would state things as they were, without mythical gloss or distortion.

What was clear to Barthes at any event, from the perspective of the mid- to late 1960s, was that the agenda of 1957 belonged to the past, not only because there was no point in repeating what had already been done, but also because the work of the mythologist had become locked in a vicious circle by which the attempt to overcome the pseudo-nature of petty-bourgeois representations had served merely to replace one conformist ideology with another. By 1970, then, the ideological criticism articulated and defended by the writer a decade and a half before seemed finally to have consumed itself, prompting Barthes, when asked to preface a new edition of *Mythologies,* to suggest instead that it was time semiology gave way to something much more violent, disruptive, and apocalyptic, capable of measuring up, so to speak, to the radical immeasurability of the future, and which he proposed calling semi-clastics [*semioclastie*].[36] As far as the 1950s were concerned, Barthes was right: from the point of view of the mythologist, there was no future, merely a mystified past and a disenchanted present.

III

A ghost in the machine

> To stop these discursive systems [*systèmes parlés*] from being distressing or uncomfortable, there is no other way than to inhabit one of them. Otherwise: *what about me, me, where am I in all of this?*
>
> Roland Barthes, *Le Plaisir du texte*[37]

The difficulties encountered by Barthes in *Le Degré zéro* were far from gratuitous or accidental. They were a consequence of the prescriptive nature of all ideological criticism in general. For the task such criticism gives itself is essentially one of translation. Its ambition is to intervene with the force of its own superior knowledge, to replace false consciousness with objective truth, and to identify within a given text the familiarity of the already known. Truth, as determined by the interpreter, features as both premiss and conclusion, and what is discovered at the end is already taken for granted at the beginning. All progress is therefore circular, and although ideological criticism may function importantly as a form of political resistance, there also necessarily comes a point, as Barthes was quick to realise, when it merely becomes tautological and falls victim to repetition and redundancy. "Racine is simply Racine," Barthes famously wrote in *Mythologies*, guying with the help of this particularly leaden example the unthinking reflex of much established criticism in its eulogising of one of France's most prestigious national monuments.[38] The remark summed up, in Barthes's view, the circular rhetoric of perpetual self-evidence characteristic not only of bourgeois or petty-bourgeois ideology, but of all ideology as such, which was one reason he later suggested abandoning the Marxist term "dominant ideology" on the grounds that it was simply a pleonasm. "For what is ideology?" he asked. "The idea *in so far as it dominates*."[39] If so, the problems affecting reception of Racine were even more pervasive than Barthes in 1957 cared to suggest. For what they implied was that, what-ever its political orientation, any criticism content with seeking in the text persuasive evidence for its own ideological beliefs, opinions, or val-ues, would only ever encounter its own reflection or mirror image. Like the ideology it sought to unmask, it was afflicted with a debilitating in-ability to respond to the other. Its perspectives were entirely negative. Ideological criticism, in a word, had no future.

Theoretically, historically, critically, then, to the extent that it aspired to make a decisive ideological intervention, *Le Degré zéro de l'écriture* was a decidedly problematic text.

But there was also a ghost in the machine, a phantom in the cup-board, a spanner in the works.

For alongside the conventionally normative, teleological, and nega-tive implications of Barthes's analysis, there was an anomaly: the con-cept, figure, or thing described as the zero degree itself. First, though it supplies the book with its title, the zero degree of writing is oddly mar-ginal to it. True enough, Barthes glosses the expression in his introduc-tion, but does so almost in passing, using it as an alternative name for neutrality or the neuter; and it is only in the last quarter of the book, for little more than a page, in the chapter entitled "Writing and Silence," that the term achieves any kind of conceptual prominence, only to with-draw again, before making a final bow in the closing pages.[40] As a result, *Le Degré zéro de l'écriture* has in fact surprisingly little to say . . . about the zero degree of writing. This eccentric relationship of conceptual frame to textual content may be explained by the genesis of the book, which began at the instigation of Maurice Nadeau as a series of discrete ar-ticles for *Combat* before turning into a volume in its own right.[41] But as far as readers are concerned, the fact is that the concept of the zero degree, rather than being properly introduced, described, and debated on the Barthesian theoretical stage, is mainly asked to contribute a brief cameo, to make a kind of guest appearance while having its main role elsewhere: in this case, in the linguistics of Viggo Brøndal, encountered by Barthes in 1947.

It could be argued in return, as Barthes himself hints in explaining the borrowing from Brøndal, that the motif of the zero degree in *Le Degré zéro* itself is less concept than figure, less of a rigorous theoretical formulation than a useful illustration or metaphor. If so, the zero degree may be thought to appear not as itself, but in disguise, as a kind of understudy for the figure of what elsewhere, both at the beginning and the end of the book, using an adjective rather than a noun, Barthes calls neuter or neutral [*neutre*]. It is at any rate in these terms that the zero degree is explained by Barthes: "we know," he says, "that certain linguists posit the existence of a third, neuter, or zero term [*un troisième terme, terme neutre ou terme-zéro*] in-between the two poles of a given opposition."[42] This formulation serves, however, only to exacerbate the anomalous status of the zero degree, which proves irreducible to the crucial opposition between History and Nature that Barthes develops and defends in the course of the book. The zero degree, he writes, is neither subjunctive nor imperative, but purely indicative; it belongs to a mode of language that is basic, transparent, and external to all literature; it stands at a distance from the world and its meanings, innocent and uncompromised. As these motifs suggest, the zero degree is a kind of nature. But equally, it is nothing of the sort. It is entirely a function of the writer's situation in society, the reader is told, a sign or indication of his or her responsibility, and bears the weight of a calculated ideological decision. It is a fully historical act. Is, then, the zero degree natural or unnatural, historical or ahistorical? True enough, this ambiguous account of the zero degree is consistent with Barthes's description of the neuter and for much the same reasons. Except—that what follows from this is that, instead of confirming or reinforcing the opposition between Nature and History which is, after all, Barthes's major theoretical proposition in *Le Degré zéro* (not to mention *Mythologies*), the zero degree now serves to interrupt, suspend, if not indeed contradict it altogether. For how is it possible for any writing, on Barthes's own submission, to escape the imperious burden of historical choice?

The answer is not long in coming. It is that the zero degree of writing is but a flicker of virtuality, midway between an anticipated event and a lost opportunity, which no sooner appears as a possibility than it disappears as an impossibility. This is a further reason why the zero degree appears to be something of an aberration. For though it serves as both prologue and epilogue to Barthes's conceptual drama, the thing itself, the zero degree as aesthetic project, is nevertheless a conspicuous failure, a false prospectus, a curtain-raiser that opens on to a bare and empty stage. As Barthes explains, in famously prophetic tones:

Every writer who comes into the world puts Literature on trial; but if Literature is found guilty, it is always granted a reprieve, which it uses to win back the writer; however much the writer creates a language that is free, it is sent back as a manufactured object, for luxury is never innocent: and it is this language, rendered stale and dead by the surging mass of the many who cannot speak it, that the writer must continue to employ. There is therefore an impasse in writing, which is the impasse of society itself: writers today are well aware of it: for them, the search for a non-style, or for an oral style, for a zero degree or spoken degree of writing, is nothing but the anticipation of an absolutely homogeneous state of society; for many of them realise that there can be no universal language without the concrete, and no longer mystical or nominal, universality of civil society.[43]

Here, then, the impasse that is the failure of political convergence between history and text and the utopia that is the fantasy of reconciliation serve in the end to cancel each other out. But not before something else had intervened, to accentuate the indecision and indecisiveness of that future, captured in the brevity and fragility of that critical interval in which the zero degree of writing, if only for a moment, for the blink of an eye, so to speak, somehow appeared possible yet impossible, as a chance within history as well as outside it, hesitant, uncertain, unreconciled. This in turn suggests two things. First, as Barthes knows from Brøndal, in so far as the zero degree is not merely one marked position among all other such positions, but also the unmarked position that is indicative of the possibility of an infinite number of marked positions, so the interval, interruption, or hiatus enacted by the zero degree—belonging neither to nature nor to history or equally to nature and history both, reinscribing and exceeding that opposition as such—is absolutely essential if language is to function and meaning take place at all. And second, what is therefore addressed in Barthes's text by the anomalous status of the zero degree, even though it may undermine Barthes's whole conceptual edifice, is the chance of writing in the future: as the secret hope of that which in nature most resists nature and in history most resists history.

The degree zero of writing may not be what *Le Degré zéro de l'ecriture* is about, but it is what enables Barthes's text to become what it is. For it is the name Barthes's writing gives itself, in the necessary absence of any external ideological authority, when it is brought to affirm its own future possibility as indecision: not as ideology but as event. In so far as writing is an historical object, the interruption of history to which the zero degree aspires is problematic, as Barthes readily acknowledges. But it is also inescapable, in so far as it is what makes Barthes's commentary on history possible, for like any metahistorical intervention Barthes's writing necessarily belongs at one and the same time to the historical tale it is telling and yet to some other dimension forcibly withdrawn from that history. It is in this respect symptomatic that all the writers named by Barthes in *Le Degré zéro* as the proponents of *écriture blanche*, whose writing bears witness to the exteriority and impossibility of the zero degree—Albert Camus, Jean Cayrol, Raymond Queneau, and Maurice Blanchot—were authors on whom Barthes had recently written, on whom he was planning to write, on whom he no doubt intended to write in future, or on whom he would postpone writing for several years.[44] The names Barthes supplies are not arbitrary ones; but nor do they correspond to a set of paradigmatic examples. They embody a series of challenges or promises, possibilities or impossibilities of reading and writing, belonging not only to the certain, uncertain future of Barthes's own writing, but to writing in general in so far as the challenge of the future was what was at stake within it.

As though to confirm this reciprocity between writing and the future, Barthes's initial cast of names comprising mainly prose-writers was soon joined by another name, arguably more important to Barthes than all the others put together, belonging to an author whose place was primarily in the theatre, and who, had he not existed, it would probably have been necessary for Barthes to invent: Bertolt Brecht.

Brecht was not an indifferent figure. In France at the time, he was a major ideological point of reference, and by the mid-1950s had begun to represent a radical alternative to what was often perceived as the apolitical absurdism of the plays of Ionesco, Beckett, Genet, sometimes Adamov. Barthes's own enthusiasm for Brechtian theatre was part of a larger project and closely related to his involvement, alongside Bernard Dort, Robert Voisin, and others, with the journal *Théâtre populaire*. The key turning point for Barthes, as for many like-minded contemporaries, were the two Paris visits made by the Berliner Ensemble in 1954 and 1955, which gave him the opportunity of seeing Brecht's own productions of *Mutter Courage und ihre Kinder* (*Mother Courage*), *Die Mutter* (*The Mother*), and *Der Kaukasische Kreidekreis* (*The Causasian Chalk Circle*). In an early review of the first of these plays, published in the left-wing weekly *France-Observateur,* Barthes set out the reasons for Brecht's significance.[45] Between the aesthetically accomplished but politically vacuous bourgeois theatre of the time and the politically progressive but aesthetically dour alternative theatre, Barthes argued, Brecht represented a radical third way, which made it possible to reconcile two separate forces, often seen, mistakenly in Barthes's view, as contradictory: formal innovation and political responsibility. Crucial too, for Barthes, in the complex dialectic of Brechtian dramaturgy, where it operated as a mediating element, integrating the aesthetic with the political, and the political with the aesthetic, was the role of pleasure: understood primarily not as the enjoyment of what is familiar, recognisable, and normative, but surprise at that which is different, disruptive, and disorientating. "Brecht," wrote Barthes, addressing his words as much to his own writing perhaps, "has found a way out of the impasse, by achieving an authentic synthesis between the rigour of political intent (in the loftiest sense of the word) and the total freedom of the stage."[46]

The crucial point for Barthes, paradoxically, was that Brechtian theatre, he put it in March 1958, was "not in any sense political theatre, in the narrow sense of the term, nor a theatre of propaganda, nor a theatre that might be thought to call for militant action." "It is essentially," he added, "a theatre of reflection, consciousness, and lucidity, a theatre of questioning."[47] Brechtian theatre, he explained, is a "subjective, psychoanalytic, apocalyptic theatre of demystification."[48] "In Brecht," he continued, in a more sustained account of epic theatre written some years later, "as in great realist painting, the tableau has a fundamental rather than ancillary narrative function; visuality is saturated with understanding, and is meaningful in its own right. A Brechtian tableau is almost like a tableau vivant; like narrative painting, it presents a suspended gesture [*un geste suspendu*], caught in virtually timeless manner [*éternisé virtuellement*] at its most fragile and intense moment of signification (what might be called its *numen,* in memory of the ancient gesture by which the gods either refused a destiny or acquiesced in it); whence its realism, since realism is only ever understanding the real [*une intelligence du réel*]."[49] Brechtian theatre, in other words, was a theatre of judgement and decision, with little if anything to do with the rule of politics as obedience to prior authority or conformity with established dogma, meaning, or value. It did not supply uncritical political answers, then, but asked political questions, which it suspended at the moment of crisis, giving theatrical form to a moment of decision frozen and immobilised at the extreme point where decision was necessary, but where the necessity of decision had not yet begun to preclude the possibility of alternative outcomes, where the decision had not yet and would not ever in fact take place at all. So, if Brecht pointed beyond the impasse in which the end of *Le Degré zéro de l'écriture* left the critic, it was not because Brecht found a more compelling way of imposing ideological or political decisions; it was because Brecht's theatre of decision, by that very token, was also, simultaneously and without possibility of resolution, a theatre of indecision.

In July 1955, during the company's second visit to Paris, Barthes also had the opportunity of attending the Berliner Ensemble production of Brecht's *Causasian Chalk Circle* at the Théâtre Sarah-Bernhardt.[50] Initially written in exile, and one of Brecht's most distinctive later works, the play weaves together at least three complementary and overlapping narrative threads: first, there is the story of two Soviet collective farms in the Causasus, framing the play as a whole, and turning on the proper use of an area of land, whether it should be restored to its traditional use as pasture or given over to more modern farming methods; second, there is the story of the kitchen maid Grusche, forced by a combination of trying circumstances and her own good nature to foster the governor's infant son, abandoned by his egotistical biological mother in her flight from the city after her husband's overthrow and execution, and who —Grusche—to protect the boy, not only risks her own life but compromises her future marital happiness too; and, lastly, there is the story of the scribe Azdak, come to denounce himself for inadvertently giving refuge to the grand-duke and allowing him to escape, but who, by a strange reversal, is pressed into service as a judge, and, after another round of counter-revolutionary upheaval, is finally entrusted with the task of deciding whether Grusche should be deemed the rightful mother of the governor's child and awarded parental responsibility or whether the child should be returned to his natural mother, who, by this stage, because of the wealth recently inherited by her son, views him mainly as a way of reclaiming her own privileged social position.

Nature and history meet, then, and it is necessary to decide. On one level, decision is hardly difficult; Azdak, like the Caucasian peasants in the frame story, takes the view that the future is more important than the past, becoming more essential than being, and tradition less compelling than social usefulness, so just as the valley is given over to those who will make best use of it, so Grusche is deemed the better mother, since it is she who has acted more like a mother than the child's actual, biological parent. Brecht's political point, which Barthes applauds, is unambiguous enough; it is simply that history has priority over nature, and that the bad new days, as Brecht once put it, should be allowed to prevail over the good old ones. More provocative and challenging, however, is the way in which Azdak, Brecht's apparent mouthpiece, reaches decisions in the play. For Azdak is no militant revolutionary, no representative of moral orthodoxy, no repository of superior wisdom, and bears little resemblance, if any, to the enlightened prince of old who would intervene at the end of a play to reward the virtuous, punish the wicked, and restore order. Instead, Azdak is frequently drunk, vulgar, corrupt, unreliable, irrational, and capricious. True, the responsibility for rendering justice is one that circumstances have thrust upon him. But many of his decisions are motivated not by any attempt to adhere to the law but by the desire simply, at times brutally, to reverse established precedent. In part this is Brecht's point. Being arbitrary in dispensing justice reveals that justice, in such a society, is itself arbitrary; and Azdak's inappropriate behaviour serves merely to demystify the law, which, unmasked, is shown to be an expression of the class society it serves. As one of the attendant ironshirts remarks, comically enough, when Adzak is appointed to his position: "Judges always were rogues; let rogues now be judges."[51] Barthes agreed. "In an unjust society," he wrote, summarising the play, "where formal law is mere hypocrisy in the service of the powerful, only a judge who is a rogue can render justice that is just."[52]

Two wrongs, then, in such circumstances, can make a right, and an upstart judge making arbitrary decisions is just as likely to achieve justice as a privileged member of the ruling class applying established statute. But this symmetry is deceptive. More is at stake here than a satirical inversion of prevailing bourgeois custom and practice. First, what Azdak's intervention suggests is that the law, being an imperfect product of history, is necessarily subject to challenge. It can always be disobeyed, reformed, revoked. All legal decisions carried out in the name of the law, then, whatever their purported legitimacy, and how-ever much they may seek to ground themselves by referring to the extant body of the law, are always contestable. But while the law itself is finite, justice, for its part, is infinite, and can never be achieved with total certainty. It is true that the legal machine enforces its authority by declaring its decisions final, but this is only because the law is secretly aware that the process over which it presides is in principle endless, and can be brought to a—premature—conclusion not by an appeal to jus-tice, but only by recourse to the power of the state, of which the law after all is merely the embodiment. What Azdak's purposeful inconsistency reveals, comically and polemically, is that justice is never possible with-out there being a real and potent threat of injustice.

This inconsistency at the heart of all decision-making introduces a further complex irony. The fact is, Azdak's quixotic methods may be irregular, but as Brecht's play demonstrates, they just as often bring about justice as they perpetrate injustice. Not for nothing is his two-year period of office remembered by the play's narrator as "a brief / golden age almost of justice [*einer kurzen / Goldenen Zeit beinah der Gerechtig-keit*]."[53] Paradoxically, it is only when the legal machine is divorced from itself, that is, both maintained and suspended, as it is in the figure of Azdak, for little more than a temporary hiatus or interregnum, that jus-tice, in the play, at least some of the time, may be said to occur. Justice and injustice are not easily disentangled. Each accompanies the other as its uncertain, always contestable and problematic shadow, in the same way that Azdak by his actions, for the time that is his, derides the law of the land by making it at one and the same time both worse and better than it is. In the end, and this is another of the play's critical iro-nies, it is not in the sometimes brutally (and comically) expeditious ver-dicts Azdak returns that his legacy lies, so to speak, but in the realisation by the audience that within every decision what should be affirmed is not the decision itself, which always has the capacity to be partial, inco-herent, and unjust, but the radical necessity of indecision that precedes,

traverses, survives, and exceeds it, for it is the possibility of always deciding otherwise, Brecht and Barthes both insist, that makes justice possible at all, even though or precisely because the authority of the law
may be radically threatened in the process.

At any event, as far as Barthes and Brecht were concerned, it was
never a question of replacing one law with another, but rather of exacerbating within theatre in particular and within writing in general that
undecidable moment when judgement hesitates, and where justice and
injustice truly hang in the balance. And though in later years Barthes's
ostensible interest in Brecht appeared to wane, he was still willing on
occasion to reiterate the Azdak principle, citing it again, for instance, in
the short-lived weekly column he wrote between December 1978 and
March 1979 for *Le Nouvel Observateur*.[54] And there is little doubt too that
the memory of Azdak had some bearing on Barthes's own relation to
the law, prompting him in the direction of many scandalous, improper,
untimely, seemingly perverse decisions of his own, as for instance,
from the mid-1960s onwards, his return to some of those very texts—by
Balzac, Zola, or Chateaubriand—which, a decade and a half before,
seemed hopelessly compromised by history. During this latter period of
his career, in which ideology featured increasingly in his writing as
a bête noire to be attacked at every opportunity, Barthes nevertheless
sought to remain faithful to that theatre of apocalyptic suspension that
in the 1950s had found such persuasive embodiment in Brecht. And it
was this, paradoxically, rather than any retreat from the political as
such, that was instrumental in transforming Barthes's relationship with
literary criticism, which became very different from what it had been in
Le Degré zéro de l'écriture. For it was now no longer a matter of reducing
a text to its repressive ideology and revealing its complicity with oppression, but of releasing the text itself from repression, thereby affirming
the power of literature to challenge those conformist ideologies that
sought to turn it into a mere continuation of themselves by other means.
Such was the circularity of ideology, with each counterposition being
foreshadowed and absorbed in advance by what it aimed to overturn,
that it was possible to intervene, Barthes argued, only by resorting to the
most indirect of methods. This new tactic, not as far removed from
Mythologies as it might appear, Barthes famously described in 1971 as
follows:

To act as though it were possible to speak innocently against ideology is to continue in the belief that language is merely the neutral instrument of prevailing opinion. But in reality today there is
no place in language that stands outside bourgeois ideology: our
language comes from that ideology, returns to it, remains enclosed within it. The only possible rejoinder is neither confrontation nor destruction, but only theft: to fragment the ancient text
of culture, science, literature, and disseminate its traits by using
language in unrecognisable ways, in much the same fashion as
one disguises stolen goods. . . . The social intervention of a text
(which does not necessarily take place at the moment when the
text appears) is not measurable by the composition of its audience, nor by the accuracy of the economico-social reflection inscribed within it or launched in the direction of those sociologists
eager to pick it up, but rather by the violence that allows it to *exceed [excéder]* those laws devised by society, ideology, or philosophy
in order to remain consistent with themselves in a splendid act of
historical understanding. This excess has a name: writing.[55]

Though these lines continue to bear witness to Barthes's enduring
debt to Brechtian *Verfremdung,* which might itself be plausibly described
as an expropriation of language (it involved among other things showing characters and situations on stage that were not represented as
themselves but cited, insisted Brecht, as part of an always contestable
set of social circumstances), the writer's love affair with Brecht had a
strangely sobering aftermath. In 1965, looking back at his work throughout the preceding decade on behalf of the theatre (and its possible-
impossible future), Barthes paid tribute to Brecht not for confirming
his belief in the theatre (which till then had been one of the abiding
sources of pleasure in the critic's professional and personal life) but for
provoking instead a radical loss of faith in it. Brecht, for Barthes, had
somehow brought a chapter to a close, by both exemplifying and articulating something that, in Barthes's own view, was increasingly incompatible with theatre in France, and likely to remain so. That something,
surprisingly, was not politics or the political, at least not explicitly. It
was what, referring to Brecht's theatre, Barthes chose to call, provocatively enough, *sa distinction,* its distinction.[56] What the critic meant by

this was not the conformity of Brechtian theatre to some prior moral, ethical, ideological, or other code but the force of difference, interruption, or suspension enacted by Brechtian dramaturgy, the jolt it delivered, Barthes later put it, by separating the sign from its effect.[57] Barthes's apparent loss of interest in the theatrical stage was in this respect less an abandonment than a displacement; for what was increasingly at issue for the critic was not the socio-political institution of the theatre but, by another spiral of transformation still powerfully shaped by the engagement with Brecht, the performative theatricality of a theoretical and critical discourse that, renouncing its militant appeal to ideological norms, was now able to turn to the disruptive, outlandish, singular event of text and criticism alike.

"Beneath the rule, find the exception," recommended Brecht, in the closing words of his play *Die Außnahme und die Regel* (*The Exception and the Rule*).[58] Boldly realigned by Barthes, put forward less as an indictment of capitalist exploitation than as an acerbic assertion of the power of disobedience and non-conformism, the phrase was one of the writer's favourite watchwords, which he used to underline the urgency of resisting simultaneously both the violence of ideology and the violence of counter-ideology, the violence of discourse and the violence of counter-discourse, in the endeavour to exhaust what he viewed increasingly as the specular, circular relationship between power and its critique. If critique itself turned into a rule, as was necessarily and inevitably the case, Barthes insisted, then it was little better than what it aimed to overturn. "Opposition (the blade of value)," he suggested in *Le Plaisir du texte*, "does not pass necessarily between established, named contraries (materialism and idealism, reformism and revolution, etc), but *always and everywhere* between *the exception and the rule*. The rule itself is abuse, and the exception ecstatic pleasure [*jouissance*]. For instance, at certain moments it is possible to argue in favour of the *exception* of the Mystics. Anything is preferable to the rule (generality, stereotype, idiolect: language as consistency)."[59]

Brechtian *distinction*, then, for Barthes, interrupting all ideological certainty and the repetitiveness of its stereotyped discourse, offered the possibility of another language, less prescriptive and less dogmatic, and therefore more attuned to the risk, both threat and chance, of the future.

Questions, however, remained. What was the place of criticism, where to draw the line, how to make a difference, when to decide?

IV

Evaluation without values

> Never underestimate the force of *suspension* of pleasure: which is a
> veritable *epoché*, a halt [*un arrêt*] that puts a stop in the distance to all
> accepted values (accepted by oneself). Pleasure is a *neuter* (the most
> perverse form of the demonic).
>
> Roland Barthes, *Le Plaisir du texte*[60]

Barthes's response, drawing once again on the legacy of ancient rhetoric, was to redescribe the field: to separate, articulate, and tabulate. So it was in 1966, in *Critique et vérité* (*Criticism and Truth*), replying to the invective of Raymond Picard and others (to whom he objected, with ample justification, that what they sought to do was simply to impose as universal, natural norms their own undeclared positivism and wilful blindness to the symbolic density of the literary text), that Barthes went on to propose a fresh set of methodological bearings. Science, criticism, reading, *science, critique, lecture:* these were the key coordinates in a reinvigorated, yet still hierarchical trivium.

Beyond the polemical context of the exchange with Picard, Barthes's more demanding purpose in *Critique et vérité* was to endeavour to resolve the tension within his own thinking between prescription and description, between an enduring commitment to critical but largely negative ideological norms and a responsiveness to that which was unpredictable, inventive, and interruptive in writing. Throughout the 1950s and early 1960s, as suggested earlier, Barthes was able simultaneously to affirm the future possibilities of writing and to hold that writing had reached an historical impasse only by positing some utopian moment when writing and history would somehow become reconciled. To what extent this prospect belonged to fantasy was arguably a moot point. For many other questions had also begun to arise. How to respond to meaning while also suspending it, how then to discriminate between different critical strategies, how to respond affirmatively to that which was new, how to be responsible without being repressive? These were some of the issues Barthes urgently needed to address.

He did so initially by ingeniously redistributing the tasks of criticism between the transcendental and the empirical. In the first category Barthes placed theory, science, in the form of a putative, future science of literature, the purpose of which ("if it ever exists [*si elle existe un jour*]," Barthes added, cautiously and providentially, in the light of subsequent debates) would be to specify literature's conditions of possibility of meaning: that is, not what a text may be thought or made to signify, but the underlying, transcendental structure of literariness (*literaturnost,* as the Russian Formalists had called it) that made possible all the particular meanings, both past and future, that might conceivably be attributed to a work by an individual critic or reader. "In a word," wrote Barthes, "its object will no longer be the full meanings [*les sens pleins*] of the art work, but on the contrary the empty meaning [*sens vide*] that sustains them all."[61] Methodologically, Barthes went on, such a science would be indebted to linguistics, from whom it would borrow, by analogy, its principal conceptual resources. As he explained:

> The science of literature will thus have as its object, not why this or that meaning should be accepted, nor even why it may have been accepted in the past (a question for the historian), but why it is *acceptable* [*acceptable*], not according to philological rules governing the letter of the text, but the linguistic rules governing the symbolic [*le symbole*]. Here, at the level of a science of discourse, the task is the same as that undertaken by recent linguistics, which is to describe the *grammaticality* of sentences, not their meaning [*sens*]. In parallel manner, the aim will be to describe the *acceptability* of works of art, not their meaning. The total number of possible meanings will not be classified according to some unchanging order, but rather like the evidence left behind by some vast "operational" capacity [*une immense disposition "opérante"*] (i.e. whose purpose is to produce artworks), scaled up from the individual author to society as a whole. Human beings have, perhaps, corresponding to the *faculty for language* postu-

lated by Humboldt and Chomsky, a *faculty for literature* [*une faculté de littérature*], a potential for speaking [*une énergie de parole*], quite unrelated to so-called "genius," and made up not of personal inspiration or desire, but of rules accumulated at a level far removed from that of the author.[62]

If this was the science of literature, as proposed, promised, or imagined by Barthes in 1966, criticism, for its part, according to this new programme of rights and responsibilities, was allocated a very different role. It had none of the legislative power or status of science; its function was more limited, localised, and specific, its purpose being to elaborate as exhaustively as possible one or other of the meanings implied or permitted by the underlying structure of the literary artwork. This did not mean, for Barthes, that criticism might behave in random or arbitrary manner. On the contrary, it too was subject to rules: rules, however, that were not immediately dependent on some external, normative authority, but which were entirely immanent to the work and the act of criticism. Criticism's task, then, was not to judge a text according to standards of moral correctness, ideological soundness, or external truth, but to translate, restate, and reaffirm the work in an exhaustive, theoretically informed, internally consistent manner. What the critic had to do, in other words, according to Barthes (and few today would disagree), was to address the whole of the work, take account of relevant contemporary theoretical findings, and put forward an interpretation that was internally consistent. Criticism, however, was not all; there was a third role in Barthes's scenario, scripted for the reader. But just as between science and criticism, theorist and commentator, there was an unbridgeable divide, so too, between the critic and the reader, this traditional poor relation, there was another veritable gulf, that of writing. Reading was what happened without writing; the reader was entirely innocent of the disruptive implications of writing. Desire alone was what sustained the reader, whose contribution to Barthes's repertoire was more nearly that of the grin on the Cheshire cat. "To read," Barthes wrote, "is to desire the work, to want to be the work, to refuse to shadow the work with any words other than the work's own words: the only commentary that might be produced by a pure reader, without the reader turning into a critic, is pastiche."[63]

As readers of Barthes will know, the methodological grid set out in *Critique et vérité* did not survive for long. The conceptual difficulties created by Barthes's tripartite division of labours were many and far-reaching. First, in order to put in place the speculative concept of a transcendental faculty for literature, as Barthes called it, it was necessary to find some means of extrapolating, on the basis of a bewildering range of historically contingent phenomena, what it was that might be thought reliably to constitute the transhistorical essence of literature as such. The move was an ambitious but brutally reductive one.[64] For the purpose of analysis, each literary text had to become an example or illustration, without remainder, of the rules governing it, which was already to fall foul of the self-deconstructive logic of exemplarity itself; and if the theorist were to admit partial defeat in this project, it would serve merely to confirm that the object of the proposed science of literature lacked stability, homogeneity, or coherence, as subsequent theorists, not to mention Barthes himself, were to realise, in order to concentrate their efforts not on detailing the essence of literature, assuming it to exist at all, but on narrative discourse, say, which, being both internal and external to literature, had entirely different status. At any event, like all transcendental enterprises, the work of the literary theorist could not be other than normative, as *Critique et vérité* implicitly conceded when it proposed, taking its lead from Chomsky, to adopt as reliable proof of the literary the criterion of acceptability, which raises many more questions than it answers: acceptable to whom, each reader will ask, at what time, in what place, in what circumstances, on what grounds? Rather than an essential determination of literature as such, a vicious circle ensues: what is deemed the object of theory is that which is acceptable as literary only in so far as it is acceptable as literary, which is at best a question, Barthes might otherwise say, for the historian or sociologist.

The transcendental theory of the kind Barthes proposed, though it offers itself modestly as a descriptive project, was also inevitably a prescriptive one, and it is striking, for instance, how, throughout *Critique et vérité,* by presumption rather than proof, literature is held to be not only autonomous and self-identical, but synonymous with the production of meaning(s). But not only did Barthes's science of literature find itself impossibly suspended in this way between the proliferation of the empirical and the inaccessibility of the transcendental, it also lacked a methodology. The only conceptual framework available to it relied on an analogy, which was uncertain enough in itself, between the essence of literature (if it existed) and the workings of language, and there was no compelling evidence that the fields of literary production and natural language might be collapsed together in this way. In any case, since the conditions of possibility of literature were, by definition, unavailable to experience, the fact is that the only access to the transcendental field of literariness had to be obtained by way of an individual text of which it might be assumed (but on what grounds?) that it was acceptable as literary, with the result that the rigorous divide between the transcendental and the empirical required by Barthes was no sooner established than effaced. In the end, it was hardly surprising that Barthes's science of literature mutated almost immediately into a reworked version of ancient rhetoric, as the subsequent evolution of narratology, in the work of Todorov, Genette, and numerous others, amply confirms.

The science of literature was not the only casualty of *Critique et vérité*. For criticism too, on the 1966 definition, the outlook was problematic. True, it did enjoy a less subordinate position to theoretical inquiry than Barthes's exposition suggested, since it was only by considering the interpretative acts of the critic that the theorist would be in a position to instantiate the empty meaning, the *sens vide*, it was the task of theory to identify. But the critic whose responsibility was limited to applying immanent interpretative rules to the artwork had another cause for concern; it was that, here too, criticism became blinkered and circular, always having to ignore the recalcitrant detail that resisted the critic's hermeneutic efforts, only ever destined to find in the artwork the interpretative moves it had put there itself. Barthes had implied as much some years earlier, in a 1963 piece entitled "Qu'est-ce que la critique? [What Is Criticism?]," where, somewhat mischievously, he had recourse to the very same example of leaden self-evidence that he had used to sardonic effect in *Mythologies* in order to make the point, on this occasion, that "critical discourse itself . . . is never anything other than tautological." "It consists in the end," he went on, "in stating belatedly [*avec retard*], albeit placing itself squarely within this belatedness [*ce retard*], that Racine is Racine, and Proust Proust; the 'proof' of criticism, if one exists, depends on the capacity not to *uncover* [*découvrir*] the work under scrutiny, but to *cover* [*couvrir*] it as completely as possible in its own language."[65] Admittedly, there was a difference, in the all-important delay, postponement, or deferral that occurred between one language and the next; nevertheless, it seemed both thematic and ideological criticism and the petty-bourgeois imagination that Barthes had so successfully lambasted in *Mythologies* were again victim to the same myopia, in that neither was able to imagine otherness without reducing it to a reflection in a mirror. This convergence between Barthes's skit on petty-bourgeois language and his characterisation of literary criticism is both instructive and chastening; for it shows how difficult it is for even allegedly non-ideological literary criticism to reach out towards the future to respond to the unpredictable event of writing, and embrace the "utopian idea," as Barthes went on to call it, placing his gloss for safe keeping within a parenthesis, "of a culture still to come [*à venir*], arising from a *radical, unprecedented, unforeseeable* revolution [*une révolution radicale, inouïe, imprévisible*], of which the author of these lines knows only that he, like Moses, will not enter it."[66]

The internal difficulties apparent within *Critique et vérité* did not however remain unanswered. Indeed, within two or three years, Barthes began defending a critical strategy that was very different, not to say the exact opposite of that advanced in 1966. Indeed, it is almost as though *Critique et vérité* served its author less to explicate his project than to exorcise it, less to lay a firm foundation for future work than to push it to the limit, where it promptly collapsed. At any event, everything the book had endeavoured to sideline or repress—reading, pleasure, the singularity of writing—quickly returned centre stage, and Barthes was soon found spelling out a new critical dispensation, which began, not with transcendental theory, nor with the multiple protocols of immanent meaning, but with an act of reading understood as a desiring encounter with the text, in which the first move was not to ask after meanings, whether fully-fledged or vacant, but to decide: to decide what kind of event was at stake in the encounter, and to decide how to address the text according to the logic of that event. To this need for an inaugural decision, on which everything else would turn, Barthes gave a knowing, perhaps ironic name: evaluation. And, famously, this was how the opening pages of *S/Z* put that concept of evaluation to work:

It is sometimes said that the asceticism of some Buddhists makes it possible for them to see the whole world in a single bean. This is what many early analysts of narrative would have liked, to be able to view the stories in the world (which are legion) within a single structure: what we shall do, they all thought, is to extract from each tale its model, then turn these models into a grand narrative structure, which we shall then be able to apply (for purposes of verification) to any narrative at all. The task was a daunting one (*"Science with patience, the torment is certain"*), and ultimately undesirable, for what in the process was lost was the difference of the text. Difference in this sense is not, of course, some replete, irreducible quality (as a mythic view of literary creation has it), it is not what designates the individuality of each text, and names, signs, countersigns, or closes it; it is, on the contrary, a difference that is never still, that is always connected to the infinity [*l'infini*] of texts, languages, and systems: a difference of which each text is the obverse. A choice must therefore be made [*il faut donc choisir*]: either to place all texts within the shuttling motion of a demonstration, giving them all equal status in the eyes of in-different science, forcing them back, inductively, to that Copy from which they will then be deduced; or to restore each text, not to its individuality, but its interplay [*son jeu*], returning it, even before anything is said about it, to the infinite paradigm of difference, and subjecting it from the outset to a founding typology [*une typologie fondatrice*] or evaluation. How then to posit the value of a text? How to establish an initial typology? The evaluation founding all texts cannot come from science, for science does not evaluate, nor from ideology, for the ideological (i.e. moral, aesthetic, political, alethic) value of a text is a representational value, not a productive one (ideology "reflects," it does not produce [*ne travaille pas*]). Our evaluation [*Notre évaluation*] can only be bound to a practice [*une pratique*], and this practice is the practice of writing. There is [*Il y a*], on the one hand, that which it is possible to write, and, on the other, that which it is no longer possible to write: that which is an integral part of the practice of the writer and that which has gone from it: what are the texts I would consent to write (or re-write), to desire, and to propose [*avancer*] as a force in the world that is mine? What evaluation finds is this: what may be written today (or re-written): the *writable* [*le scriptible*]. Why is the writable our value? Because what is at stake in literary work (in literature as work) is to make the reader no longer a consumer, but a producer of text. Our literature is characterised by the unremitting divorce, enshrined within the institution of literature, between the producer and the user of the text, between its owner and its client, author and reader, as a result of which the reader is immersed in a kind of idleness, intransitivity, or, in a word, *seriousness:* instead of being fully involved [*au lieu de jouer lui-même*], of acceding to the delights [*l'enchantement*] of the signifier and the exquisite enjoyment [*volupté*] of writing, the reader is allowed only the meagre freedom of either accepting or rejecting the text: reading here is merely a *referendum*. Opposite the writable text, then, is its countervalue, its negative, reactive value: that which can be read, but not written: the *readable* [*le lisible*]. We deem all readable texts classic texts.[67]

These are, to many readers, familiar, resonant words, and it is hard to underestimate their influence on the subsequent development of literary theory and the post-history of French structuralism (not to be confused with that phantom journalistic entity, to which Barthes never laid claim, called poststructuralism). Their logic is nevertheless complex, shifting, even tortuous, as Barthes sets about preparing the ground for what is arguably his most incisive contribution to literary criticism. His initial gesture, as is well known, was to relinquish the scientific approach that had held such appeal a few years before, and abandon the theory of literariness, like some ancient pipe-dream, to those analysts who still had faith in the dialectic of the universal and the particular, the model and the copy, according to which the latter is only ever intelligible as a result of the mediating power of the former and only available for scrutiny as a contingent instantiation of it. But renouncing the logic of exemplification, Barthes now had to find an alternative starting point, which he did, paradoxically enough, by relaunching the appeal to exemplification, formulated not as an essentialising gesture but as the need for a founding typology. Between the one and the other, though, there was a crucial difference which had to do with the constitutive, legislative power of Barthes's proposed typology.

If this typology was to fulfil the task entrusted to it, and properly found Barthes's project, it was essential, as Barthes rightly indicates, for it to be autonomous of all previous typologies, whether borrowed from science or any one of the ideological, political, moral, or other discourses that circulate within or around so-called literary texts. Simply to apply a previously existing typology would not in itself found anything; indeed, *Critique et vérité* had already demonstrated the problems that were liable to arise when critical concepts were simply imported from elsewhere. The founding typology which Barthes required, as the preamble to *S/Z* testifies, had therefore to be grounded on a decision, a choice, that, by its intervention, was capable of creating a specific, autonomous typology appropriate to the task in hand. This is why Barthes stages this foundational moment in *S/Z* as a deliberate act of evaluation. Evaluation, here, however, cannot be in the form of a judgement or pronouncement content with merely applying established values, for the reasons Barthes gives; it can only occur as an unprecedented act of affirmation that is in itself creative of value. Crucial to this formulation, largely borrowed from Nietzsche, is an essential, yet (as Barthes later conceded) precarious distinction: between the gregariousness of cultural exchange values (in the plural), to be rejected and set aside, and the differential quality of textual use value (in the singular), to be advanced and defended as a force in the world.[68]

This distinction is a necessary one as far as Barthes's discourse is concerned. But its fragility reveals an important and unavoidable paradox. For if evaluation is to occur as a founding event, as Barthes proposes, it is necessarily also the case that all values, including not only the value of values but the value of value too, can and must themselves be interrupted, suspended, if only for an instant, for the brief interval of an intervention, and put in abeyance. All evaluative decisions, if they are to evaluate anything, are required first to hesitate before going on to deliberate; without such deferral, evaluation is merely the peremptory, authoritarian, formulaic application of an existing norm. That this opening gesture necessarily constitutes both an interruption and a detour is apparent from Barthes's own digressive exordium. Indeed, before *S/Z* can itself properly begin, it is necessary for Barthes to preface his decision with an account of its prehistory and context. The need for evaluation itself must be evaluated. Infinite regress looms. As I have already argued, evaluation, to the extent that it occurs as a decision and an event, is always premised on prior indecision, on the necessary and lingering undecidability of the case, which, coming before anything else that may be said about the text, Barthes explains, cannot be erased or expunged. Indecision not only precedes evaluation; it also renders it perpetually provisional. Evaluation in Barthes's sense, then, though it claims to owe everything only to itself, is paradoxically never an original, founding act; it is always separated from itself, deferred and divided, always therefore a transvaluation, which, as such, contains at least two distinct moments: a pause and a gesture, an effacement and an inscription, an interval and an act.

Barthes begins, then, by hesitating. But hesitation is never enough, and like Azdak, this other sometimes impatient, sometimes dilatory seeker after pleasure, Barthes is required to respond, and to provide at least a temporary solution to the dilemma of making a start, in the certain knowledge that what will be decided cannot be other than uncertain: that it may not be effective, for instance, or may prove unconvincing to his assembled audience of friends and students, or may even perpetrate an injustice. Whatever evaluative criterion is proposed, whatever the decision reached, neither will be exhaustive. Grounds for challenge, dissent, or appeal will always remain. A choice, however, here, now, must be made. In other words, in the absence of any universal norms to which obedience can confidently be given, the critic has to improvise—which is what Barthes does, by ushering on to the discursive stage a pair of familiar-unfamiliar terms, which are recast and redefined in the process, as though their status were more properly that of neologisms, like so many other words in Barthes's signature lexicon. Importantly, although Barthes's opening appeal is to a single founding affirmation, formulated initially in terms of that which—he asserts—it is possible today to write or rewrite, it is apparent this is no stable, self-identical criterion. On the contrary, no sooner does Barthes articulate his affirmative stance than it splits into two dissymmetrical claims: the *scriptible,* on the one hand, and, on the other, different from it, while also deferring to it, its negative, reactive, dialectical doublet, the *lisible.* Two forces, two values, two economies, then, are put in play, neither of which is entirely separate from the other, but neither of which is entirely reducible to the other. The relationship between the twin faces of Barthes's founding act of evaluation is itself both certain and uncertain, distinct and indistinct, decisive and indecisive; and it is the ongoing double act between Barthes's two textual performers that provides the critic with the opportunity of articulating a new legislative textual order, one in which there are always at least two possible positions, the *lisible* and the *scriptible*, but where those positions themselves are shifting and dynamic enough to elude the trap of tautological repetition that so bedevils the critical act for Barthes once the commitment is made to merely applying the ideological norms, assumptions, and beliefs that presided over criticism's inception.

Crucial to this distinction between *scriptible* and *lisible*, between what today can be written or rewritten and what on the other hand can only be read, according to Barthes, is the present tense or presence of writing, unfolding now, before the writer, as an unfinished event. This is what makes it possible to discriminate between (on the one hand) a textual product without production, which is how the *lisible* is defined, and the reason why it can only be read, and (on the other) textual production without product, which is how Barthes describes the *scriptible* and why, paradoxically, there is little in fact to be said about it. "The writable text [*le texte scriptible*]," he tells the reader, "is a perpetual present, which no language *of consequence* can touch (for it would transform it, fatally, into something past); the writable text is *ourselves in the process of writing* [*nous en train d'écrire*]."[69] Writing as practice, production, performance: this, then, is the pivot on which all else turns. But if the writable text is not an object, who then is responsible for it, and who can speak on its behalf? Such questions are in a sense inappropriate. They are not in any case susceptible to any answer. For writing, in the performative sense of the word, according to Barthes, has no regularity or identity other than its own exteriority or excess, does not give rise to such finite objects as may be found in libraries, in bookshops, or on computer disks, and is subject to no authority other than itself. But if the practice of writing is so profoundly transgressive, what makes it possible for Barthes the textual critic or commentator to appeal to its legislative power, its force of decision, in order to found a typology? What is it, conversely, that entitles him to present mere reading (in much the same way as in *Critique et vérité*) as an impoverished, sub-altern, or submissive relationship to textuality, able only to say yes or no, as though writing itself were any different? In other words, when Barthes endeavours to lay down the law, what is the source and extent of his authority? And if it is true, as Barthes contends elsewhere, that the author of a text is more effect than cause, more actor than propri-etor, more textual figure than biographical entity, who or what is in fact responsible for taking decisions in Barthes's text? To all these ques-tions, no doubt, the answer is the same: writing itself. Circularity again beckons: aporia, infinite regress, lack of foundation.

Questions such as these are never confronted directly in *S/Z* itself. But they exert discreet but perceptible pressure on Barthes's text. They account for instance for at least one curious feature of the theoretical preamble to *S/Z*, which I have cited above at some length: the slip-pages, in Barthes's exposition, from one personal pronoun to another. First, the reader is treated to the dismal spectacle of those benighted proponents of narrative grammar who still believe in grand theory, to whom Barthes begins by attributing an appropriately confident and ambitious first-person plural ("we"), only for it to disappear into a dis-missive third-person ("they"), as Barthes distances himself from the project. Some lines later, a second, distinct, but indeterminate first-person plural takes over: a "we" whose defining feature is now its—our?—responsibility for an act of evaluation. "Our evaluation [*Notre évaluation*]," writes Barthes, not pausing to explicate the range or import of this unspecified first-person plural. Who are we? Who is Barthes's text addressing? For whom does it speak? For us who are free spirits, hedonists, and aesthetes? For us moderns who are the children of the future, belong to no country, and join only in the secret wisdom of the gay science, as Nietzsche once famously put it? For those among us who are literary critics and professional commentators? For Barthes's friends and members of his seminar, to whom the material composing *S/Z* was first delivered, and to whom the book is dedicated? Or solely for us, Roland Barthes, as the royal *we* of standard French academic usage plausibly suggests, but which Barthes later denounces in a radio interview as a distastefully regal form of self-infatuation?[70] We, Bar-thes's readers, whoever we are, are no doubt potentially all these things, and many more to boot, but equally we are not necessarily any of them, and it is telling that, when it falls to the writer, by way of exemplification, to dramatise this critical first-person plural, after a brief dalliance with a neutral, apodictic third person ("there is"), he reverts to the first-person singular, admittedly an ambiguous one, in part generic, universal, or theatrical, but in part irreducibly specific and personal: "what are the texts," asks Barthes, speaking in principle for every reader, but incontrovertibly in the first instance only for himself, that "*I* would consent to write (or re-write), to desire, and to propose as a force in the world that is *mine*" (*my* emphasis, LH).

The reasons for this uncertainty of address are not hard to find. On the one hand, it is no doubt true that, on good pedagogical grounds, and because of the unorthodox, even dissident character of the general argument put forward in *S/Z*, Barthes was concerned to be an enabling presence, and to avoid appearing unduly magisterial. But Barthes—that is, Barthes's writing or text—also had another, less visible motivation. It is that in order to supply his appeal to value (rather than values) with a coherent theoretical foundation, Barthes must reach beyond the solipsistic domain of idiosyncratic tastes or desires in order to claim for his own, singular aesthetic response some necessary universal validity. Were Barthes not to do so, or fail in doing so, as Kant had already explained in the third *Critique*, Barthesian theory or criticism would risk turning into little more than a list of personal likes and dislikes of mere anecdotal interest to the reader and quite incapable of founding any typology at all. At the same time, while it was imperative for Barthes's critical discourse that some theoretical bridge be constructed between the singularity of the critic's desire and the universal address of critical discourse, between the performer and his audience, so to speak, Barthes himself was well aware—just as Kant had been—that the claim to universal validity, though a necessary corollary of the provisional insufficiency of judgement and its constitutive appeal to others, was not only inescapably normative; it was also impossible to guarantee. It was required by reason, but this did not prevent it, however paradoxically, from being dependent on a series of ungrounded, unfounded arbitrary decisions which nothing could mitigate, and which, like the wilful acts of Azdak, had force of law not because of their obedience to established norms but because of the institutional authority invested in the adjudicator and because, in a given context, at a specific time, they made a—critical—difference.

What this meant was that Barthes's position in *S/Z* was uncomfortably divided: between criticism as act and criticism as legislation, between singular judgement and institutional code. Though Barthes the theorist proposed a rational, universalising typology, the strategy of reading on which his structural edifice was grounded was ultimately reliant on an idiosyncratic gesture, as witnessed by Barthes's crucial assertion that there is, he put it, "on the one hand, that which it is possible to write, and, on the other, that which it is no longer possible to write." For what is the status of such a claim? At first sight, and perhaps for most readers, Barthes's words are an uncontroversial, disarmingly naive, even self-evident statement of historical fact. In the margins of *S/Z*, however, though less explicitly in the book itself, Barthes offers two slightly different, not to say contradictory glosses on this crucial claim. From the first of these, it is quickly apparent that Barthes's assertion is anything but an unproblematic statement of empirical fact. It functions more as a supra- or metahistorical judgement that has more to do with what, by way of a coinage borrowed from Bachelard under the influence of Althusser's philosophical reworking of Marx in the early 1960s, came to be described by Barthes's friends on the editorial board of the journal *Tel Quel* (Julia Kristeva, Philippe Sollers, Marcelin Pleynet) as an epistemological break (or *coupure épistémologique*) affecting not only the work of Marx, as it moved from post-Hegelian philosophy to the critique of political economy, as Althusser had it, but, in a bold and arguably ill-considered, not to say dogmatic extrapolation, avant-garde writing too, as it abandoned established literary forms towards the end of the nineteenth century and entered into an intense phase of experimental innovation.[71] Between the so-called realist writing of Balzac and the modernist poetics of Mallarmé and Lautréamont produced around 1870 and after, the argument ran, there was a radical, unbridgeable gap, in every sense analogous with what, in relation to *Das Kapital*, Althusser had formulated as Marx's breakthrough from ideology to science. That it was within this framework that Barthes also sought to articulate the concepts of the *lisible* and the *scriptible* is clear from a lengthy interview given to *Les Nouvelles littéraires* in March 1970 to coincide with publication of *S/Z*. Invited to explain the antiquity, as he put it, of Balzac's writing, Barthes commented as follows:

There are some of us who are of the view that in the nineteenth century there was a break [*une coupure*] . . . which is what is described today rather grandly as the "epistemological break." On the world stage, it is marked by the name of Marx, while in literary terms it may be thought to correspond to the explorations of Mallarmé. From this break what may be thought to emerge was a new age of language, in the earliest beginnings of which we currently find ourselves, and which could be called modernity. For some of us, this notion of modernity is very precise, important, absolutely heterogeneous with the past. There really is a break. So, when I say that Balzac is a very ancient author [*un auteur très ancien*], this is obviously something of a provocative paradox, I acknowledge that, but it is a justifiable one, since Balzac is situated before the break. He is not part of modernity.[72]

On the basis of remarks such as these, whatever the status of the parallel between the modern literary text and Marxist political theory that Barthes describes, it would not be difficult to see in *S/Z* a continuation of the proto-Marxist discourse on history present in *Le Degré zéro de l'écriture*. This is not to say nothing had changed; between Barthes's two books, the failed revolution of 1848 had been replaced for instance by the Paris Commune of 1870, Sartre by Althusser, and writing as moral choice by writing as the play of the signifier. But in other ways, in both 1953 and 1970, the function of Marxism within Barthes's discourse remained largely the same. On the one hand, it served as a general statement of political principle, and allowed Barthes to keep faith with the Brechtian poetics and politics that had been so important for his own writing practice, while also enabling him to retain the allegiance of his left-leaning or leftist readership. More importantly, however, as far as *S/Z* was concerned, it provided Barthes with an acceptable teleological, eschatological narrative that gave external theoretical legitimacy to the attempt to subtract the *lisible* from the *scriptible* and contrast the writable future (and present) with the readable past. It thus made it possible for Barthes to portray *S/Z*'s would-be founding typology not as an idiosyncratic expression of desire, but a theoretical proposition grounded in universalising theory and Marxist metahistory. No doubt this discreet recourse to Marxism as a legitimating discourse explains why the otherwise problematic concept of (textual) production, borrowed from Marxist economics via the work of Kristeva and others, plays such a prominent role in Barthes's analysis, and how it is that Barthes declares the transformation of the reader into a producer to be the key criterion that underpins the typology of the *lisible* and the *scriptible*.[73]

But elsewhere in *S/Z*, aside from a suggestive account of the political economy of story-telling, the reference to Marxism is largely implicit, and this is one reason for thinking that, though the opposition between the *lisible* and the *scriptible*, in so far as it is taken transcendentally, is absolutely reliant on the concept of the epistemological break, Barthes himself was increasingly sceptical about its status as historical occurrence. This much is already clear from the interview with *Les Nouvelles littéraires*, where Barthes is more conspicuously engaged in reporting and defending the views of others than in speaking for himself, and it is not surprising, when revisiting the opposition between the *lisible* and the *scriptible* the following year, and taking the opportunity to reformulate it, in less manichean terms, as the difference between work and text (with Barthes now conceding the important possibility that "there may be 'a measure of Text' ['*du Texte*'] even in a very ancient work [*une œuvre très ancienne*]"), that he should refer not to a clean epistemological break but merely to a slippage.[74] The revision was a significant one, for it removed from Barthes's founding typology any metahistorical guarantee, with the result that, in retrospect, the opposition between the *lisible* and *scriptible* appeared increasingly less of a calculated theoretical move claiming universal validity than a tactical, pragmatic gesture, designed primarily as a kind of dispensable methodological overture, whose purpose was get the show underway (which is how Barthes goes on to present it, together with other binary contrasts, in *Roland Barthes par Roland Barthes*).[75]

There was of course a second, wholly different way of understanding Barthes's claim about the possibility of reading or writing texts. On this interpretation, Barthes's original assertion did not gesture at all in the direction of transcendental conditions, even historical ones. It was best understood elliptically, as a condensation of the claim that, for any given singular reader, there was that which it was possible—and impossible—for him (or her) to write. The question to which Barthes's assertion was an answer, then, was not a Kantian one about the conditions of possibility of the existence of a given text, which the critic had answered by positing a transcendental historical order manifesting itself in a regulated economy of signs and text, but its radical Nietz-schean counterpart, which did away with all reference to historical ground, legislation, or economy, and happily dispensed with the need for any morally responsible, constituted or constitutive subjectivity, in order to inquire instead: "what is the sense, the function, the use of this text *for me?*" Read in these terms, Barthes's assertion of value no longer claimed even universal validity, and was simply left to fend for itself as a transient singular gesture having its only proper purpose in itself. *Le Plaisir du texte,* published some three years after *S/Z,* put the case for such a reading as follows:

> If I agree to judge a text on the basis of pleasure, I simply cannot allow myself to say: this is good and that's bad. No league-tables, then, no criticism, for this always implies some tactical purpose, social conventions, and quite often an imaginary veneer [*une couverture imaginaire:* Barthes is most likely using *imaginaire* in its Lacanian sense of deceptive miscognition]. I cannot add or subtract things, and imagine that the text can be improved, or readily enter into the repertoire of normative predicates: it is too *this,* not enough *that,* the text (the same is true of the singing voice) can only prompt a verdict from me that is not adjectival at all: *that's it!* Or even: *for me that's it!* This "for-me" is neither subjective nor existential, but Nietzschean (" . . . deep down, the question is always the same: what is it *for me? . . .* ").[76]

Barthes, then, in two very different contexts, there a serious interview, here a dissident fragment, offers two disparate accounts of his initial founding gesture, attributing it on the one hand to the effects of class struggle in philosophy and on the other to philosophical perspectivism. But despite their considerable differences, the gap between these two interpretations is narrower than it seems. For however Barthes endeavours to justify his original decision, the outcome is largely the same. In neither case is the difference between reading and writing properly founded; it is merely displaced elsewhere, in the direction of another system or body of thought. Finally, Barthes's attempt at a founding typology is forced to yield to the realisation that it is a fragile, precarious, and uncertain edict, a contestable verbal decree, which no theory can absolutely guarantee, and which, as a result, is radically unable to found anything, including itself. But in the absence of a proper foundation, it still stages an interruption, appeals to an addressee, and practises an opening. It performs therefore an event, the event of Barthes's own writing, which in due course signs itself, as Barthes acknowledges, both in his title and in the course of the text, with the help of a monogram on which the book performs a series of variations, doublings, and inversions: SarraSine/Zambinella, BartheS/BalZac, BartheZ/BalSSa.[77] And in so far as it is an event, *S/Z* does not underwrite any system of values. Both the value of values and the value of value are left in suspense. Barthes's writing, however, affirms. Without accrediting any prior subject or identity, what it affirms is—affirmation. It affirms, intransitively, impersonally, aneconomically: without origin, goal, or justification.[78]

One of the more surprising effects of this self-deconstructive event or event of self-deconstruction opening like an abyss beneath Barthes's reading and writing is that much of what is advanced towards the beginning of the book as fulfilling a foundational role is gradually but systematically revoked as *S/Z* unfolds. Even the distinction between the *lisible* and the *scriptible,* arguably the cornerstone of Barthes's opening remarks, does not survive for long. For one, as many readers have observed, it is undermined by the theatrical performativity of *S/Z* itself, with its fragmentary inscription, its proliferating codes, its multiple levels of reading, its digressions and detours, all of which intervene to transform "Sarrasine," this so-called paradigmatically readable text, into a mobile production without product. At strategic moments too, *S/Z* evokes the perversely aberrant writing of Flaubert, in particular, the unfinished text of *Bouvard et Pécuchet,* in which the author's two retired clerks, two long syllables there, and three short ones here, same but different, different but same, undertake the endless task of citing and reciting, performing and re-enacting—much like Barthes himself—the endless discourse of worldly knowledge. By copying out this vast text, Flaubert's twin protagonists suspend, interrupt, fragment it. Its status is decisively transformed. Losing its normative consistency, the so-called readable text transcribed by Flaubert's protagonists is turned into an infinitely rewritable text that begins to unfold, in Flaubert's novel, as an endless movement of post-narrative, post-historical copying.

What is apparent here, as Barthes suggests (and as Blanchot and Derrida will agree, with far-reaching implications), is that anything and everything can be quoted, recycled, transformed. Everything I read can be rewritten, without restriction, by another or by myself. All textuality, whether it is deemed readable or writable by me or by another, is by definition beyond the control of whoever lays claim to it. There are, Barthes insists, no hierarchies, no privileges, no stable oppositions that the infinite text that is literature does not undermine or overturn: "literature itself," he writes, "is never anything but a single text."[79] If this is the force of the *scriptible*, as Barthes articulates it, it can only have one consequence, which is that the very opposition between the virtual text of the *scriptible* and the actual text of the *lisible* is in the end untenable. The readable is already the infinitely desirable text that the writable promises for tomorrow, if only because the time of reading is never now, but always infinitely deferred. The only opposition that may be said to exist between what I can or cannot write is a conventional, normative one. This is hardly surprising. For what is a writing that is not already a reading, and what is a reading that is not already a beginning to write? Barthes knew this of course; and it explains why, in 1975, in another palinodial gesture, he proposed adding to his original pairing, sabotaging it in the process, a third term, *le recevable*, corresponding to that which I can neither read nor write, but which lies in wait for me in the guise of "that unreadability that catches you unawares, burning brightly and produced without interruption beyond all concessions to plausibility, whose function—visibly assumed by its scriptor—might be to challenge the mercantile constraints of the written; such a text, guided, armed by the thought of *unpublishability*, would prompt the following response: I can neither read nor write what you are producing, but I can *receive* it, like a fire, a drug, an enigmatic chaos."[80]

Every antithesis, it seems, both requires and produces its own surplus, for which a third term proves necessary, not to reconcile its predecessors, but to supplement and displace them, overwhelming the simplicity of binary opposition with something excessive, exceptional, and exorbitant, like the singular, differentiated neutrality of the body, whether male or female, but always otherwise, and thus, like textuality itself, never reducible to the polarity of generic or gendered meaning, and which for that very reason demands to be narrated, yet narrated without end. "It is by virtue of the *excess* [*ce trop*] affecting discourse after rhetoric has decently saturated it," writes Barthes, "that something can be told and the story therefore begin."[81] This too is the lesson of *S/Z*, not only for its writer, but also its reader—not only the writer of its reading, but also the reader of its writing. For just as "Sarrasine" tells the story of a disastrous error, so Barthes's own interpretation, as it reads and rewrites Balzac's story, is necessarily drawn, by dint of the text's own seductive power, towards those catastrophic moments where differences are no sooner articulated than they are erased, where the oppositional paradigm is suspended, where letter and symbol coincide, where subject and object fuse, where what is offered to the reader as a task for reading demands henceforth to be (re)written, and where literary theory, singing its swan-song, is replaced by an endless scene of reading, writing, writing, reading.

In the process, reading-writing becomes inseparable from what, from the early 1970s onwards, reframing and reaffirming what he had sought to address under the rubric of the zero degree twenty years before, Barthes began to describe as an exemption of sense: not the unadulterated primacy of a world without meaning, but its release from meaning, manifested in the apocalyptic afterglow of what remained, at the end, in the end, and could be neither assimilated nor eliminated. As Barthes puts it, writing about himself in the third person, in *Roland Barthes par Roland Barthes*:

> For him, the point is not to return to some kind of pre-meaning [*un pré-sens*], an origin to the world, life, things, prior to meaning, but rather to imagine a sort of post-meaning [*un après-sens*]: what is needed, as in a journey of initiation, is to pass through the whole of meaning [*tout le sens*], in order to extenuate it, and exempt it. Whence a dual tactic: against the Doxa, it is necessary to protest in the name of meaning, since meaning is the product of History, not Nature; but against Science (paranoid discourse), it is necessary to maintain the utopia of meaning annulled [*l'utopie du sens aboli*].[82]

The exemption of meaning to which *S/Z* is finally dedicated is neither the presence nor the absence of meaning; it is something other, without unity or self-identity, traversing language as an interruption, attributable neither to a subject nor to an object, but to their reciprocal suspension or dissolution. As such, it is an occurrence, an event, an incident, elliptical, interruptive, and infinitely interpretable, that marks reading and writing with a singular kind of indecision, beyond activity or passivity, and which comes to language not as withdrawal or paralysis but as affirmation: not the affirmation of value or values, however, but the affirmation of affirmation, an affirmation that, interrupting all transitivity, both affirms its suspension and suspends its affirmation.

What arrives here, catching the writer unawares, defeating all expectation, and thus eluding, or so it would seem, the possibility of critical discourse as such, is less an interpretation than an exclamation or ejaculation, an affirmation empty of any content other than the convulsive, performative character of its own occurrence, announced impersonally, anaphorically, and addressed, without rejoinder, to a necessary, but unidentifiable, futural other: "*That's right, that's how it is* [*C'est cela, c'est ainsi*]," Barthes famously put it in *L'Empire des signes*, verbalising his response to the immediacy and ellipsis of the seventeen-syllable Japanese haiku, "*that's exactly it* [*c'est tel*]. Or even better: *Yes!* [*Tel!*], it says, with such a brief, immediate touch (without vibration or repetition) that the verb *to be* still seems excessive, like the lingering regret of an impossible definition, removed for ever."[83] At the extreme limit of language, then, interpretation, codification, rhetoric all yield to a moment of ravishing, almost mute intensity.

How to speak such affirmation, how to give it words, how to translate it into the language of criticism? How to pass from epiphany to discourse, from ecstasy to exposition? How, then, to theorise the untheorisable?

To questions such as these, from the mid-1970s onwards, and in particular in the three final lecture series at the Collège de France, devoted in 1977–78 to *Le Neutre* (*The Neutral*) and in 1978–79 and 1979–80 to what he mysteriously announced as *La Préparation du roman* (*Preparation for the Novel*), Barthes was to seek an answer in a perhaps surprising place: not in philosophy, theory, or critical discourse, but in literature itself, the haiku, and the texts of Joyce, then Proust.

V

Neither the one nor the other

> Figures of the Neuter: blank writing [*écriture blanche*], free of all literary
> theatricality—primeval language—delicious insignificance—
> smoothness—emptiness, seamlessness—Prose (a political category
> described by Michelet)—discretion—the vacancy of "personality," which, if
> not abolished, is at least made undetectable—an absence of *imago*—the
> suspension of judgement, of litigiousness—displacement—(refusing "to
> put on airs," refusing any airs whatsoever)—the principle of delicacy—
> drift—intense pleasure [*jouissance*]: anything that dodges, thwarts, derides
> ostentatiousness, mastery, intimidation.
>
> Roland Barthes, *Roland Barthes par Roland Barthes*[84]

The disruptive, undecidable event that echoes so powerfully through
S/Z was no single epiphany, entire and sufficient in itself. It was one in
a repetitive and proliferating series of similarly insistent, equally intractable interruptions of meaning, reported or staged by Barthes elsewhere
in his work, and finding oblique expression in a number of theoretical
and other languages Barthes had at his disposal. One such language,
for instance, was Zen Buddhism, which Barthes first explored in 1970
in *L'Empire des signes,* and which supplied both the necessary cultural
displacement and an alternative vocabulary with which to affirm the
elliptical intensity of an experience that otherwise, he wrote, might be
formulated only in "vaguely Christian terms such as illumination, revelation, or intuition."[85] Barthes's nodding familiarity with other coun-
tries such as Morocco or China extended this repertoire of extraneous
cultural discourses.

Elsewhere, it was Freudian and Lacanian psychoanalysis, exploited
in suitably piecemeal and eclectic fashion, that provided the framework—more temporary scaffolding than secure edifice—in which to address the pleasure or *jouissance* provoked by the ecstatic irruption of the
event. Barthes was also able to look to psychoanalysis as a source of jus-

tification for his abandonment of customary—fetishistic—attachment to critical objectivity and his willingness to give voice to the perverse pleasures of the amateur, rather than of the professional critic. But just as his relationship to Japan, on Barthes's own submission, was anything but objective, and served mainly to stage a desire for otherness as far removed as possible from the nauseous stereotypes of petty-bourgeois France, so his use of psychoanalysis was similarly dictated less by an obedience to theory than by an awareness of its potential for countertemporal cross-talk, which he demonstrated by turning his attention not to the Symbolic or the Real, those Lacanian concepts widely thought at the time (and since) to be at the cutting edge of theoretical inquiry, but to their poor relation, the Imaginary, deemed by Lacan to embody the very dimension of introspective error, but under whose deceptive authority, in more ways than one, Barthes was able to explore with greater theoretical legitimacy and not a little humour of his own the complex ironies governing the relationship between introspection and the exteriority of writing. The critic adopted a similar strategy in other areas too. Bringing together in a fresh setting in the early 1970s, in *Sade Fourier Loyola* or the *Nouveaux Essais critiques*, some of the articles on literary texts he had written during the latter half of the previous decade, the ambition was much the same: to affirm in literature, in writing, in his own textual practice, the timely untimeliness of the event, its incisiveness as intervention, interruption, and interregnum.

There was however nothing straightforward or simple about a responsiveness to the exemption of sense. It necessitated a dual approach, and Barthes was bound by a twofold imperative: by the requirement to traverse the whole of meaning, but also, and at the same time, to attend to the singular events that occurred at its various points of interruption, to maintain the rule, so to speak, but only in so far as it made it possible to affirm the exception. More specifically, as far as Barthes was concerned, this meant diligently exploiting all possible or available discourses not merely in the name of theoretical exhaustivity but also with a view to affirming the exhaustion of all discourse in general, an approach Barthes glossed, in one of his Collège de France lectures on the Neuter, by referring his audience to a series of passages by Blanchot in *L'Entretien infini* on the topic of fatigue. "It would appear," wrote Blanchot, attributing these words to one of two anonymous interlocutors, "that, however great your fatigue, you nevertheless complete your task, exactly as you should. Not only does fatigue not get in the way of work, it is as though work demands it, fatigue without measure," from which it followed, for Barthes as for Blanchot, that the burden or chance of writing was always double: for if it was the fate of writing to exist within limits and its responsibility to reach as far as possible towards those limits, what writing then necessarily encountered, as the paradoxical sign of its own exhaustion, and in the form of an event grounded in impossibility, was its own inexhaustibility as something always already traversed by the boundless, the limitless, the infinite.[86] "That is how we can say," Barthes went on, "that fatigue is not an empirical time, a crisis, something that happens organically, an episode affecting the muscles—but a quasi-metaphysical dimension, a kind of bodily (i.e. non-conceptual) idea, a mental cœnæsthesis: the touch or tact of infinitude: I accompany my work with its own infinity. What is then apparent is that fatigue: in a sense the opposite of death, because death = the definitive, and unthinkable ≠ fatigue, the infinitude livable in the body."[87]

The ramifications of this logic of exhaustion are many. As far as Barthes's own writing was concerned, it was plain that the purpose was no longer, if it ever had been, to enforce anything resembling an exhaustive methodology; it was on the contrary to address the inexhaustibility of the present by exploring alternative ways in which it might be put into words. Rather than to continue developing a verifiable account of some external theoretical object, Barthes's greater concern was to deploy a distinctive style or manner of thinking, less a theoretical discourse as such than a shifting, mobile series of paradigms, which he used to chart possibilities of meaning, but which he promptly suspended, lest the meanings they authorised become tyrannical in their turn. The point, however, was not to withdraw from the world; it was to find a new way of engaging with it. In the opening session of the lecture series on the Neuter in 1978 he explained that "reflecting upon the Neuter, for me, [is] a way of searching—in an uninhibited way—for my own style of involvement [*présence:* presence] in the struggles of my time."[88]

This simultaneous and dual commitment to writing as both system and syncope is no doubt what gives Barthes's texts at times their deliberate, speculative, almost theatrical manner, as though there was something faintly improvised about the articulation of the writer's theoretical discourse. It was of course no coincidence that, during the 1960s and 1970s, Barthes chose to pay particularly fulsome tribute to Emile Benveniste, whom he once identified as his favourite linguist, on the grounds that Benveniste, as Barthes put it, rather than a believer in innate grammatical structures or binding communicational norms, was the author of a linguistics of enunciation. In 1956 Benveniste published a brief but highly influential article on personal pronouns, in which, following Jakobson's work on linguistic shifters, he examined the question of personal pronouns and referentiality. Benveniste's conclusions are well known. The pronoun "I," he argued, did not refer to anything outside of language; its only reality was discursive. Personal pronouns had a kind of perverse circularity: "The pronoun *I*," Benveniste went on to explain, "signifies 'the person uttering the present instance of discourse containing *I*.'" "This is the key point," he added. "*I* can only be identified by the instance of discourse that contains it, and by it alone. It is only valid in the instance in which it is produced."[89]

Gone—and happily so, in Barthes's eyes—was a reliance on the subject as possessing any extralinguistic substance, essence, or nature. In its place stood a contingent, performative speaking self owing its existence to an event of language which was by definition both singular (in so far as it referred only to itself) and multiple (to the extent that it belonged to an infinite series). Subjectivity, then, was like an empty costume, which might be put on and then taken off by whoever lifted it from the basket of dressing-up clothes. Identity, meaning, subjectivity: all was linguistic performance, dramatisation, simulation, like in an endless Brechtian play where each performer would demonstrate who or what they were in the play by quoting their character's words. This was how meaning was produced, and how it might be disaggregated: as an infinite and mobile repertoire of scenes, structures, gestures, traits, and topoi, as Barthes shows in *Fragments d'un discours amoureux* (*A Lover's Discourse: Fragments*) by adopting a "'dramatic' method" of exposition, "eschewing examples and relying only on the activity of a first-level language (no metalanguage)."[90] But though meaning was performative, this did not prevent it from being real, sometimes painfully so. For the body too, according to Barthes, was similarly part of the show ("which body?" asks Barthes, "we have several");[91] and there would always be a moment when words would fail, the mask slip, and the play freeze, as in some infinitely suspended Brechtian tableau, and in that hiatus of indecision, that fissure of intractability, the body would intervene, as it had in *S/Z*, and something like an event occur.

Among the many shifts in emphasis that occurred in Barthes's writing in the early 1970s, this return of the body was arguably the most emblematic. There were however risks involved. In terms of the argument put forward in *Le Degré zéro*, for instance, it represented a retreat from History in favour of Nature (though this re-emergence of the body was also proof of the tendentious character of Barthes's earlier position). There was another danger too. It was that no two bodies were alike; each was irreducible. To opt for intractable difference was to risk abandoning universal intelligibility and forfeiting that appeal to a (future) audience that for Kant, and the Barthes of *S/Z*, at least in principle, was still an essential requirement for the practice of criticism. Admittedly, Barthes's point was that universal intelligibility was in fact anything but universal, but there was the reverse possibility that the attempt to address the body directly might lead to solipsism. "*My likes and dislikes* [*J'aime, je n'aime pas*]," he wrote in *Roland Barthes par Roland Barthes*, wistfully concluding, at least provisionally, not without feigned or simulated petulance, that Kant was probably right, and that "none of this is of any importance to anybody, it is all devoid of meaning apparently." Barthes nevertheless went on to explain how the prospect of transforming criticism into a list of idiosyncratic desires was an intensely appealing one, if only because what it implied was the singularity of this body as such, that is, that "*my body is not the same as your body.*"[92] But paradoxically, it was only by accentuating the distinctiveness of the body that Barthes was able to affirm its multiplicity. It was not that the same body was shared by all; it was rather that what was shared by all was the singularity of the body. There was no identification of the body with any prior model, exemplum, or type (which is why, among other things, Barthes was unwilling to have his body typecast, as he saw it, as that of an upstanding French white male homosexual). The body, in this respect, was exactly analogous with language: it was infinitely variable (according to culture, religion, history, class, sex, age, health, other factors too), but in its variability participated in a general, collective human reality. All humans are possessed of a body; but the body itself (including its relationship to other bodies) is irremediably various. "The body is irreducible difference," Barthes wrote, "and at the same time it is the principle of all structuration (since structuration is what is Unique in any structure)."[93]

In much the same way, then, that there was a rhetoric of figures reaching back to Quintilian to which Barthes had long been indebted, there was also a rhetoric of bodies, comprising a vast repertoire of corporeal gestures, postures, movements, or affects, each with its own textual realisation or translation, and it would not be hard to see much of Barthes's later output as contributing to the development of that discipline. The Barthesian body was not however a mere catalogue of tropes. Its status was at least threefold. It was an object of investigation, in so far as to write about a text, for Barthes, was not to judge it according to given criteria but to respond to its body. The body was also, so to speak, the subject (of pleasure) performing that inquiry. "The pleasure of the text," Barthes suggested, "is that moment when my body pursues its own ideas—for my body does not have the same ideas as me."[94] Thirdly, the body was what differentiated text from stereotype; it was therefore a name for what Barthes persisted in calling value: "the stereotype," he explained, "is that position [*emplacement*] in discourse *where the body is missing*, where one is sure the body is not."[95] The body, then, was what made writing occur, about which it occurred, and in whose name it occurred. It was affected with a vertiginous circularity symptomatic of the extent to which Barthes's thinking of the body had left behind the subject-object relation of traditional aesthetics, and which implied a relationship with textuality that, rather than being devoted to the recapitulation of meaning, was premised instead on this three-fold attention to otherness.

The effects of this radical transformation of the critical act in Barthes's work are everywhere apparent. Writing in a text dedicated to Benveniste on the subject of Schumann's *Kreisleriana*, for instance, Barthes was explicit: the topic of his essay was not the intelligibility of the artwork but a series of "beats [*des coups:* blows, strikes, thuds, thumps]," "what beats in the body, beats the body, or rather the body beating [*ce corps qui bat*]," as heard, played, acted, or performed by the essayist's own body, which was therefore as much the object of the essay as that of Schumann, the whole movement serving to dramatise and differentiate Schumann's writing for piano as the singular encounter that it was. In the process, in so far as it reactualised unconscious desires and affects on the part of the listener, Barthes's relationship to Schumann's music was less a theoretical than a transferential one, and it was rigorous logic rather than vaulting hubris that, in a later piece on the composer, allowed Barthes to voice the impression that "the true Schumannian pianist is me [*le vrai pianiste schumannien, c'est moi*]."[96] But if Barthes's account of Schumann was coloured by intense personal memories—of being taught piano by his aunt, of the singing lessons he pursued later in life, and of the maternal presence that figured so strongly, for Barthes, in Schumann's music—his engagement with Schumann was no mere exercise in narcissism. What occurred in response to Schumann's music was less an autobiographical experience in the literal sense, on the critic's part, than a heterobiographical one: for the intensity which it embodied did not belong to the subject as selfsame ego, but to the body as that which, being singular, is always other. In this respect it was far from indifferent that Schumann the Romantic was also the author of numerous fragmentary *intermezzi*, inserted between pieces that were similarly neither one thing nor another, resulting in what Barthes calls "a pure sequence of interruptions."[97]

The turn to fragmentary writing was another notable feature of Barthes's work after *S/Z*. True enough, much of Barthes's earlier output, as the critic was himself wont to observe, had already displayed a preference for the contingent brevity of the punctual intervention, whether in the guise of the short essay, magazine article, or book review.[98] From *Le Plaisir du texte* onwards, however, Barthes's use of fragmentary forms became more persistent and more self-conscious. First, the fragment was a way of expressing his opposition to academic orthodoxy, as embodied in the authoritative (and authoritarian) magisterial edict. As Barthes told Jacques Chancel in a primetime radio interview, "I wanted to draw the obvious consequences from a certain intolerance I have towards what I call the 'formal essay' [*la 'dissertation'*], i.e., that linear, heavily coded discourse that unfurls in a continuous, uniform manner [*comme une nappe*]."[99] But as Barthes was also aware, there was a lengthy historical tradition of fragmentary writing, occupied among others by Pascal, by the Jena Romantics, and later by Nietzsche, and there is little doubt that Barthes, like these predecessors, but also like Blanchot, who had begun writing in fragments in the late 1950s, found in the fragment a way of responding to an age in turmoil, where assertions of value could no longer be taken for granted and generic distinctions—between philosophy and literature, theory and fiction—could no longer be properly policed.[100] This was not to say there was not also a powerful canonic rhetoric governing the fragmentary. "A fragment," Friedrich Schlegel famously wrote in 1798, "must be like a small art work entirely separate from the surrounding world, and as complete in itself as a hedgehog."[101] The verdict was an influential one, and it would not be difficult to find evidence of a similar taste for rhetorical closure in many of Barthes's own fragments, which display an evident pleasure in oblique but still reliable titles, in definitions and examples, in antithesis and dialectical resolution, with the signature flourish or pointed remark arriving by way of conclusion; and even when, with playful irreverence, Barthes decided—or rather refrained from deciding—the sequence of fragments by a range of arbitrary or aleatory methods, each fragment would still stand apart, detached, articulate, and replete, a microcosm in itself, always with the air of having exhausted the topic in question.

But the desire to exhaust, Barthes had already discovered elsewhere, only produces inexhaustibility, and the Barthesian fragment also had other, more critical effects at its disposal. Notwithstanding Schlegel's recommendation, it was not self-evident that fragmentary writing might ever reach the finality to which it secretly aspired; what it created instead was a multiplicity of interruptive, suspensive events. At times, these would be scenes of yearning, like the fragmentary sketch of Barthes the young boy waiting for his mother at the bus stop, delicately given in an aside in *Fragments d'un discours amoureux* as an illustration—but more than an illustration—of that figure of love's discourse entitled Absence or the Absent.[102] But at others, separation would be affirmed with alacrity, and the fragment, no longer lamenting unbridgeable distance, would be allowed to take delight in its mortal dispersion. "Writing in fragments," Barthes notes, and offers the following scene by way of definition: "the fragments are then so many stones along the circumference of a circle: I am scattered all about: my whole little universe in scraps; at the centre, what?"[103] Here, Barthes's words announce another characteristic of fragmentary writing. Whatever theme the fragment

ostensibly addresses, it is that implicitly or explicitly each fragment necessarily also refers to itself as a fragment of fragmentary writing. By
staging or naming itself as a force or form of disruption, each fragment
in Barthes both implies and exceeds the totality against which it protests. The space it opens is that "perilous chasm" of self-reflexivity—
danger, gulf, abyss—which, self-consciously self-conscious, Barthes in
Roland Barthes par Roland Barthes claims to have been forecast by the
I-Ching.[104] It was in any case hardly by coincidence that Barthes's first
two sustained works of fragmentary writing, *Le Plaisir du texte* and
Roland Barthes par Roland Barthes, different though they were, devoted
themselves to introspection, subjective self-scrutiny, and self-reflexivity;
nor was it by coincidence that, as they embarked on that course, both
texts chose to do so in fragmentary writing. From Schlegel onwards,
though not unproblematically, fragmentary writing implied subjectivity, and vice versa. Not for nothing had the future of poetry been
announced in the *Athenäums-Fragmente* as turning on what Schlegel
called *Transzendentalpoesie,* poetry, that is, that was in itself an infinitely
regressive reflection upon its own possibility, poetry that was by definition the poetry of poetry, or, as Barthes would put it, the writing of writing, writing as the intransitivity of the absolute and the absolute as the
intransitivity of writing.[105]

But if writing was an absolute, it also followed that fragmentary
writing, being necessarily finite, could as yet only gesture towards itself.
Writing for Barthes, it seems, had still not yet properly occurred. It
belonged to a future that manifested itself in the present only as irrepressible desire. At any event, this is how he redeployed the Romantic
concept of the will and continued to do in the second lecture series on
La Préparation du roman, subtitled *L'Œuvre comme Volonté,* the Work as
Will. Here, fragmentary writing revealed its debt to that doubleness
inherent in textuality Barthes had attempted to theorise, provisionally,
under the rubric of the *lisible* and the *scriptible.* For while each fragment
(like the *lisible*) was necessarily finite, its address (like the *scriptible*) was
infinite. It was therefore at one and the same time both product and
production, structure and structuration, and its status as a text complete
in itself was inseparable from the incompletion to which it bore witness. And from now on, this double characteristic was to be shared by
all Barthes's favoured texts which were to occupy him in the last years

of his life: Chateaubriand's *Mémoires d'outre-tombe,* the aphorisms of Nietzsche, and Proust's *A la recherche du temps perdu.*

Being neither finite nor infinite, but both and neither, fragmentary writing belonged, so to speak, to the regime of the in-between, to what Barthes in the 1970s reverted to calling the figure of the Neuter or the Neutral, or more specifically, desire for the Neuter (*le désir de Neutre*).[106] The Neuter (occasionally capitalised by Barthes, occasionally not) was in part something of a throwback to earlier times, as Barthes freely acknowledged, at one stage wryly describing his Collège de France lectures on the topic as a kind of *remake* (as Barthes called it, using the English loan-word to self-mocking effect) of *Le Degré zéro de l'écriture.*[107] But like the zero degree of a quarter century before, the Neuter was far from simple or straightforward. It belonged in the first instance to the linguistic paradigm, and was part of the system of cultural meaning, but it did so in perversely negative fashion, to the extent that it corresponded to no identifiable position, but served instead to confuse the network of binary oppositions that allowed meaning to take place. This was Barthes's argument for the 1977–78 lecture course: "I define the Neuter," he began, "as that which outplays [*déjoue:* frustrates, foils, evades, outmanoeuvres, undermines] the paradigm, or rather I call Neuter anything which outplays the paradigm. For I am not defining a word, but naming a thing, gathering material under a heading: here, the Neuter."[108] "The paradigm," he added later, "is the law against which the Neuter rebels [*s'insurge*]."[109] Even as such, however, the Neuter was again double; for as in the case of so much else in Barthes's work, the Neuter had two contradictory faces. Its first, unhappy manifestation Barthes had denounced long ago in *Mythologies:* it was that rhetoric of the middle or third way (neither-nor-ism, *ni-nisme,* as Barthes called it), used by various powerful organs of opinion (such as Barthes's original target, the centre-left daily *L'Express*) to maintain the sham or pretence of balance, impartiality, and independence.[110] In 1978 Barthes conceded as much, but went on to argue that the Neuter, in its current, affirmative embodiment, though not unrelated to the rhetoric of the third way, was nevertheless "absolutely different from it"; neither-nor-ism, he said, was merely its farcical parody, its shadow, its grimace.[111] What Barthes sought to defend here was the pivotal but seemingly paper-thin distinction between a position of non-positionality, synonymous with ideological manipulation, and the non-positionality of all position, subversive of all ideology, and it was indeed as the latter of the two that, in the lecture course of that name, he proceeded to unfold the Neuter, fully acknowledging that it corresponded perhaps more to a desire, even a fantasy, than to any stable or universally applicable concept.

Just like the zero degree before it, the Neuter, reserving the paradigm of meaning, did not thereby simply denote the finite possibility of judgement, it also embodied, in the name of justice, the infinite deferral of judgement. And what was implied by the Neuter necessarily had to be applied to it. It was therefore imperative for Barthes, while still deploying the Neuter, to postpone any final definition of its conceptual content and frustrate the always imminent threat of theoretical closure. To this end, Barthes had recourse to two alternative strategies of exposition. The first may be found at work in the fragment entitled "The neuter [*Le neutre*]" (without capitalisation) in *Roland Barthes par Roland Barthes*.[112] This page-long, rhapsodic text consists of three paragraphs, each existing in counterpoint with the others, and each following a different discursive tack or tactic. In the first paragraph, Barthes begins by defining the Neuter abyssally, in terms of its figural mobility (a "to-ing and fro-ing [*un va-et-vient*]," "amoral oscillation"), then in terms of what it is not, then, with the help of a quotation from Marx's 1844 Manuscripts, on the dialectical reconciliation of opposites, recycled from *Sur Racine*, in terms of what it might be (i.e., if it were a value, archly deferring the question whether it *is* a value or not). In the second paragraph, countering the expectation (seemingly endorsed by the title of the fragment) that the neuter is a unified entity at all, he supplies a motley list of helpful-unhelpful paradigmatic examples (reproduced at the beginning of this section) that largely serve to derail the progress of the exposition. Finally, in the third paragraph, instead of the attempt at dialectical resolution promised by the reference to Marx, the reader is given an autobiographical narrative which culminates once more in an account of what the neuter is not—albeit what the Neuter is now *not*, paradoxically, is what in the first instance it would most likely have been seen to resemble, that is, the zero degree of old. But in this fragment Barthes explicitly rejects the assimilation of the one to the other, and goes on to position the Neuter not as a third, synthesising term in a dialectic but as the other term, or term of otherness in a fresh binary, of which the dominant term is violence, that is, not just violence as an isolated occurrence, but the paradigm of violence in general, in other words, as Barthes does not tire from arguing, the violence of the paradigm as such. This leaves the Neuter in a strangely paradoxical place or non-place: as one element among others in a dialectic that is not a dialectic, the member of a paradigm that is not a paradigm, part of a definition that is no longer a definition, and inscribed, so to speak, as a kind of irenic interval in Barthes's own discourse, like one of those islands of peace amidst a society at war that feature intermittently in Brecht's *Mutter Courage,* but not as a moment of contemplative stasis, but a plurality of incongruous, dissociated events.[113]

If in *Roland Barthes par Roland Barthes* the writer uses a strategy of purposeful misdirection or ellipsis to fend off the demand of the concept, so in the lecture series devoted to the Neuter Barthes strives in the course of thirteen two-hour sessions to reach a similar goal by the opposite route. To this end, in deadpan descriptive mode, he provides a kind of exhaustive, but always already exhausted catalogue of some twenty-three quasi-phenomenological instances or figures of discourse which all prove to be variations on the Neuter: kindness, fatigue, silence, delicacy, sleep, affirmation, colour, the adjective, images of the neuter, anger, the active side to the Neuter, what Barthes calls ideospheres, consciousness, responding, rites, conflict, oscillation, withdrawal, arrogance, panorama, *kairos, wou-wei,* and androgyny. As in the earlier fragment, dispersion rules, and it becomes hard to decide whether it is the Neuter that serves as a convenient pretext for this enumeration, or vice versa. Matters were aggravated, so to speak, by the lecturer's genial refusal to synthesise any of these figures, or impose on this increasingly heteroclite paradigm any syntagmatic order. What Barthes's audience therefore got to hear from February to June is less a conceptual exposition of the Neuter than a prolonged, indefatigable, perpetually oblique hesitation, a vast, virtual scenography of digressions and detours, of undecided and undecidable moments, which, by endlessly deferring the Neuter, dissolve it into an infinite series of life-affirming differences and singularities, named and caressed by the lecturer like so many subtle nuances (from the verb *nuer,* which names the shifting colour of clouds) or otherwise shimmering attributes or *scintillations,* as Barthes calls them (from the Latin *scintillatio:* a spark). To the grimace of the blandly oppressive stereotype, which seeks to flatten difference, the Neuter replies, says Barthes, not with indifference, far from it, but with the reserve, discretion, and indecision of the infinite, and the eternal ambiguity of a smile. (But how to tell the difference, many will ask, between a grimace and a smile?) And these are Barthes's closing words, announced mysteriously at least twice over in advance of the final session, and which are in the form of a moving encomium to the Neuter as trace, as slippage, as both a figure and an object of desire, not to say a signature, inscribed upon the body, in response to the binary paradigm of meaning governing language, criticism, and sexuality alike, which it evokes, but only to exceed it, annul it, and disperse it: memory without memory, difference without difference, both promise and wound:

> On that basis (and I shall finish here), following on from Freud and Leonardo, we might then perhaps say that the Neuter has its figure [*sa figure:* both its figure and its face], its gesture [*son geste:* gesture or gestus], its figured inflection in the fact that it is inimitable: the smile, the Mona Lisa smile analysed by Freud: Mona Lisa herself, St Anne, Leda, St John, Bacchus: men's and women's smiles alike, smiles or figures of smiles upon which the mark of exclusion or separation has been abolished, a smile that circulates from one sex to another: "a smile of ecstatic bliss, similar to that playing on his mother's (Caterina's) lips as she fondled him." Even if the biographical reference strikes me as being too precise, too rooted in anecdote, there is, it seems to me, this truth: the idea that the genital paradigm is outplayed (transcended, displaced), not in a figure of indifference, imperviousness, or dullness [*matité*], but of ecstasy, enigma, gentle radiance, and the Sovereign Good. The gesture of the paradigm, of conflict, of the arrogance of meaning, of castrating laughter, has its counterpoint in this gesture of the Neuter: the smile. *Exit* the Neuter.[114]

Barthes, of course, was not alone in addressing the Neuter as a radical alternative for thought. Its relevance for an understanding of the tasks facing literary criticism, philosophy, and politics had already been amply deployed in a number of ways by Blanchot whom Barthes began to reread—on the Neuter, on Proust—in the second half of the 1970s. There were many points of convergence between the two writers. For Blanchot too the Neuter—"the neuter the fragmentary [*le neutre le frag- mentaire*]," as he called it in *L'Entretien infini*—was inseparable from an exploration of fragmentary writing.[115] And the attention of both writ- ers was similarly drawn to the distancing effects of visible or invisible parentheses, frames, or quotation marks, first explored by Blanchot in the work of Kafka, as well as in a number of his own fictional texts, and likewise observed on numerous occasions by Barthes in Flaubert or Brecht, prompting both writers, in their distinctive idioms, alongside their commitment to the Neuter, to consider the implications for litera- ture and criticism of such important motifs as the death of the author, the irreducible ambiguity of literary language and its deferral or sus- pension of meaning, and the exposure of writing to excess and radical otherness.[116] These shared emphases were not coincidental; they had a common origin in phenomenology, which Blanchot had first studied alongside his friend Emmanuel Levinas in the late 1920s, and which Barthes was to encounter, more diffusely, in the intellectual exchanges dominating the post-war years that saw his emergence as a literary critic.

But it is also in their relationship to phenomenology that the dif- ferences between the two writers may be most readily discerned. For Blanchot, one of the earliest intuitions of what would later be explicitly addressed by him as the Neuter (now using the noun rather than the adjective), in texts collected for the most part in *L'Entretien infini*, was that infinitely regressive, pre-ontological principle of the *il y a*, the *there is*, which plays such an important role not only in Blanchot's early think- ing but also that of Levinas.[117] The *il y a* was a simple, yet immeasurably powerful, sovereign thought: it was that, prior to being or non-being, there was that which was necessarily always already affirmed in the alternative between being and non-being, which could belong in fact to neither, and which it was impossible to negate, if only because to negate it was implicitly to have always already presupposed and affirmed it. The implications of this modest insight were surprisingly radical. It fol- lowed, for instance, that any dialectic that conceived of its objects as a series of contradictions—between being and non-being, between what was and what was not, between the positive and the negative—was fatally flawed since, though it claimed to explain all, it also found itself unable to account for its own origin, which was irreducible to the concepts it proposed. Indeed, the origin of being or non-being, to the extent that it was conceivable at all, was in itself by definition inaccessible, since it was only possible to name or think it by employing words or concepts posterior to it, and which were thereby forced to take as given that which it was seeking to name or think. Any theoretical system that aimed to construct a total, totalising object and account for itself was logically impossible; it always owed its possibility to something other, prior or exterior to it, ineliminable and ineffaceable, on which it was dependent and which it could not make its own. And a similar paradox governed the thought of ending, as Bataille discovered when he grappled with the Hegelian—or, better, Kojèvian—concept of the end of history, since here too the very possibility of such a thought undermined that which was being thought, and vice versa, with the result that in the end the end could only be thought in terms of its own endlessness.

In the early work of both Blanchot and Levinas, the *il y a* comes to thinking in a number of exemplary concrete guises: in the experience of insomnia, as I lie awake at night, aware of the heavy presence of absence around me; in the experience of anguish, horror, suffering, fatigue, when I withdraw from the world, but am aware that my withdrawal is only ever a reminder of the world's irreducible strangeness; or in the approach to death, as I realise that what I am experiencing cannot be death itself, but merely death's impossibility. At a more fundamental level, even before the possibility of such experiences, the *il y a*, for Blanchot and Levinas alike, was also what necessarily preceded and exceeded all phenomenological manifestation as such, all worldliness, all meaning, all subjecthood or subjectivity. The suspension of the world that then followed was but a further logical step; indeed it was this exteriority of the *il y a* with regard to the world of experience that allowed the phenomenological *epoché* to take place at all, that famous reduction, bracketing, and putting into parenthesis of the world on the basis of which Husserl had embarked on the project of describing philosophically how the world exists and makes sense—to any "me." Blanchot too, in a way, had undertaken a similar project in literary form in *Thomas l'obscur*, his first novel, published in 1941—with the crucial and radical difference that what the novel uncovered was not the transcendental ego, as the phenomenological *epoché* had done for Husserl, but a vertiginous absence of foundation, an exteriority and an abyss that was necessarily without name, but which may plausibly be seen as a precursor to what, in Blanchot's writing, later became the Neuter. This in turn was why the Neuter was such an important name, figure, or concept (while also being none of these things) for Blanchot's literary criticism. Among others, it made it possible to understand how Kafka, say, as Blanchot famously puts it in *L'Espace littéraire*, might be drawn, not to construct a fictional other world, but to be exposed instead to the other of all world, that otherness Blanchot called the outside and which, taking his cue from Levinas's *Totalité et infini* (*Totality and Infinity*), he would later also call the Other: Autrui.[118] And this was also why, unlike Barthes, who persisted in the attempt to the very last (as the lecture course on the Neuter testifies), Blanchot realised that the question of the essence of art could not be answered within the world, by recourse to such ontological, metaphysical questions as: what is literature, what is writing? which always already presupposed their own answers.[119]

Although Barthes nowhere responds to this debate, he was, it seems, no foreigner to the thought of the *il y a*. It found immediate confirmation in the structure of language. Before words can negate anything, as Barthes would have learned from his reading of Benveniste, the state of affairs to which they refer must first of all be asserted. Whenever language says no, in other words, it must always already have said yes. As in the case of the *il y a*, negation could not be absolute; there were limits it could not exceed, which it could paradoxically only reaffirm. The point is one that Barthes made repeatedly, and was the basis for the notorious and provocative claim, made in his Inaugural Lecture to the Collège de France, that language, in so far as it was irremediably assertive and imposed on the speaker a binding code that could not be renounced, except at the cost of being deemed mad, bad, or worse, was "neither reactionary nor progressive, but quite simply fascistic," because fascism, Barthes explained, consisted not in preventing people from talking but rather in forcing them to speak in the first place: in normative manner.[120]

The contrast with Blanchot could not, however, be more striking. Where Blanchot discovered the radical gaiety of affirmation, prior to assertiveness and negativity alike, interrupting the world and the totalising power of its dialectic, Barthes for his part found the nauseous self-evidence of the incontrovertible stereotype. "In language," he concluded,

> it is always possible, without fail, to draw up two separate headings: the authority of assertiveness and the gregariousness of repetition. On the one hand, language is immediately assertive: negation, doubt, possibility, the suspension of judgement all require particular operators which themselves act as a series of linguistic masks; what linguistics calls modalities are only ever a kind of afterthought of language [*le supplément de la langue*], with which, like a supplicant, I endeavour to mitigate its implacable, constative power. On the other hand, the signs that go to make up language exist only in so far as they are recognised, i.e. in so far as they are repeated; signs are conformist, gregarious; and in each sign a monster lies dormant: the stereotype; I can only speak by taking on board whatever is *dragging around* [*ce qui traîne*] in language. As soon as I utter a word, the two headings come together, and I am both a master and a slave; it is not enough that I should repeat what has been said before, and settle down comfortably in the servitude of signs: as I speak, I also affirm, I also assert with brute force [*j'assène*] what I am repeating.[121]

Little wonder, then, that the experience of the impossibility of dying that so overwhelmed Blanchot, filling him with "a feeling of extraordinary lightness, a kind of beatitude (nothing happy, however),—sovereign joy [*allégresse souveraine*]?" should have served Barthes, referring to Edgar Allan Poe's story, "The Facts in the Case of M. Valdemar," as a compelling metaphor for the self-evidence of the stereotype. "The stereotype," he wrote, "is this nauseous impossibility of dying [*cette impossibilité nauséeuse de mourir*]."[122] Little wonder too that while for Blanchot the Neuter was what preceded all manifestation, challenging the privilege of the visual, for Barthes it was the opposite, as the infinite detail of the figures described in *Le Neutre* testifies; it was what manifested itself without end within the interstices and discontinuities of the paradigm.

What this meant too was that to the double evil of assertiveness and gregariousness poisoning language there was nevertheless an antidote, a *pharmakon,* operating like a form of radical homeopathy: it was of course the Neuter, in the guise of that which gave it voice and might be addressed indifferently as literature, writing, or text.[123] But the danger remained, so long as the Neuter was understood as the anti-stereotype par excellence, in much the same way that the fragment for Barthes was *l'anti-dissertatif,* the anti-formal-essay, that Barthes's engagement with literature, as threatened to be the case in *Le Degré zéro de l'écriture,* would become locked within a stance of oppositional negativity. This, however, was a fate Barthes was determined to resist; using as a foil what he took (mistakenly) to be Blanchot's effort to return to a world before meaning, he now embarked on a lengthy journey through the whole of meaning in the desire to reach beyond it—and touch, so to speak, the outside.

How better to do this than by finding a work of literature, finished-unfinished, finite yet endless, generically uncertain, and belonging equally to the past and to the future, in which life merged with writing and writing with life, which would not be content with the whole of a life, but would carry on into its own afterlife, marrying meaning with non-meaning, pleasure with pain, disappointment with revelation?

Happily, that work of literature existed, and Barthes already knew what it was: *A la recherche du temps perdu,* by Marcel Proust.

VI

Parallel lives

> I realise that the work of Proust, at least for me, is the major point of reference, the general *mathesis,* the *mandala* of the entire cosmogony of literature—just as Mme de Sévigné's letters were for the narrator's grandmother, tales of chivalry for Don Quixote, etc; that does not mean I am in any way a Proustian "specialist": Proust is what comes to me [*ce qui me vient*], not what I call up· not an "authority"; simply *a circular memory.* This is what the inter-text is: the impossibility of living outside the infinite text—whether that text is Proust, the morning paper, or the TV screen: the book makes meaning, meaning makes life.
>
> Roland Barthes, *Le Plaisir du texte*[124]

Midway through the seemingly interminable lecture course on the undecidability of the Neuter, to everyone's surprise, including perhaps his
own, on 15 April 1978 to be precise, in surroundings coloured with the
melancholy of his recent bereavement, Barthes had an illumination,
and formed a decision: his life would change, he would abandon his day
job, enter, so to speak, into literature, and undertake a Grand Project.[125]

Roughly sixteen months later, in mid-August and early September
1979, some three months before he was due to embark upon the second
of the two lecture courses devoted to *La Préparation du roman*, Barthes
sketched out a tentative plan for a new, perhaps fictional, semi-fictional,
even metafictional work, to be entitled *Vita nova*, suggesting at least to
some contemporaries that Barthes the semiologist, theorist, and critic
was intending to embark upon a new career as a novelist.[126] The notes
the writer left behind, however, tell an uncertain story. Their resonant
opening title, borrowed for the occasion from Dante and from Michelet,
one of Barthes's more illustrious predecessors at the Collège de France,
is immediately followed by more sober, even disenchanted words:
"Meditation. Summing up. Morality without hope of application [*Médi-
tation. Bilan. Morale sans espoir d'application*]." Barthes's draft then goes
on to outline, as far as it is possible to judge, in five or seven episodes,
depending on the version, framed with a prologue and an epilogue,
something resembling a story of initiation: of loss, temptation, decision, temporary disappointment, and discovery—culminating, so to
speak, in a revelation of "Pure Idleness [*Oisiveté Pure*]," captured emblematically in one of Barthes's favourite haikus and the memory of a
young Moroccan boy sitting by the roadside doing nothing.[127] The decisiveness of Barthes's project at some stage, then, seems to have given
way to deferral, inertia, and the peaceful neutrality of indecision; and it
is even possible, according to Barthes's own lecture notes, that the entire drama of *Vita nova*, this crucial turning point in the writer's personal, creative, and professional life, with its scenario of valediction,
change, and renewal, was no more than an absorbing if attractive mid-
life fantasy.[128]

As far as *La Préparation du roman* was concerned, Barthes's decision also proved unexpectedly dilatory. For long hours, from December
1978 till March 1979, and again from December 1979 till February 1980,

shortly before his fatal accident, Barthes lingered on his topic, as the subtitles of the two lecture series suggest (1: From Life to Work [*De la vie à l'œuvre*]; 2: The Work as Will [*L'Œuvre comme Volonté*]), preparing himself and his audience for a forthcoming event, the creation of a work, but which, by that very token, became ever more remote, ever less graspable. As Barthes freely admitted, the irony was that to prepare for the work was precisely *not* to write it; it was to approach the writing of the work by putting it off; it was thus to do the opposite of what was announced, and, instead of reaching a familiar destination, to follow a detour, both a digression and a deviation, with no guarantee that reader and writer would not simply end up losing their way. But that was Barthes's challenge to himself and to his audience; for if preparing for the novel involved a lengthy and unpredictable detour, it was because such a detour was itself the only possible form of preparation for what might or might not be in the form of a novel. In this regard, Barthes's procrastination was anything but a moment of aestheticising evasiveness. It was a mode of affirmative and decisive engagement with the undecided and undecidable demand of writing. It was therefore with purpose rather than preterition that Barthes opted to entertain his audience, for the bulk of the first year's lectures, not with the prospect of a novel at all, but with the delicate indecision of the seventeen-syllable Japanese haiku, and then move on, in the second year of the series, to supply a vision of the novel, not as an identifiable literary genre, but as "a form of writing capable of transcending writing itself," a "Pro-ject" or "work in progress [*œuvre en avant*]."[129]

True enough, what Barthes rediscovered in this way was the legacy of the German Romantic novel (the absolute Novel, as he also terms it), as described or envisioned by Novalis, and distinguished by its self-reflexive heterogeneity as a literary form incorporating all other literary forms, including itself.[130] And in the same way that Barthes's seminar on the metaphor of the labyrinth, which ran alongside the first lecture course, in the end turned into an exploration of the labyrinth of metaphor, so too Barthes's lectures on *La Préparation du roman* became a possible instance of that towards which they were groping. In the absence of any external critical object to which they might be subordinated, Barthes's lectures became a kind of proleptic commentary on their own inquiry. Indeed, they too were not only a kind of self-conscious performance, populated with a vast range of sometimes mysterious and improbable texts; they also followed an explicit narrative structure, which, after the lengthy prologue on the haiku, moved through a sequence of recognisable moments, not dissimilar in structure to that explored in the sketches for *Vita nova*: the desire to write, a first ordeal (choice, doubt), a second ordeal (patience), a third ordeal (separation), in order to culminate, finally, in a conclusion that was not a conclusion, the effect of which was to prompt writer and reader, under the affirmative sign of Nietzschean eternal return, to begin again, in order perhaps to experience anew the aporetic interruption that had left the first ordeal unresolved (and unresolvable) by Barthes at the moment of his writing, as silent testimony to the risk and unpredictability of the future. "I want a Work [*une Œuvre*]," says Barthes, "but do not know how to choose or programme it (and even if I had chosen the work I wanted, I would not say what it was)."[131] Barthes's diffidence is hardly surprising; for this had been the point of his project from the outset: not to write a theory of the novel, nor to produce a critique of this or that novel, nor in fact, contrary to rumour, to write a novel at all; but to *pretend* to write a novel, to act *as though* he were going to write it, to write it therefore without writing it: "Will I *really* write a Novel?" he asked in an early session, and, deploying a structure mingling with the theoretical the indecision of the virtual, replied: "I will say this, and this alone. I will act *as though* I were going to write one I shall take up residence within this *as if:* this whole lecture course could have been called: '*As if.*'"[132]

Barthes's lectures, then, were addressed to a work that did not exist, except as the promise of a future event, albeit a promise that might not be fulfilled and a future that might not arrive, and which, for the moment, survived only as a virtuality, a provisional model, or a figment of the writer's imagination. As for Barthes's methodology, such as it was, it seemed less reliant on secure theoretical knowledge than on a speculative fictional hypothesis. Barthes called it: a simulation. "I simulate someone who wishes to write a work [*qui veut écrire une œuvre*]," he declared.[133]

But whose desire, and to what end?

During the opening session of *La Préparation du roman*, on 2 December 1978, following the first mention of the pivotal decision of 15 April 1978, Barthes's most immediate gesture, his prime association, so to speak, was to recall Proust: "This 15 April," he explained: "all in all a kind of Satori, a sort of dazzling vision, analogous (no matter if the analogy is a naïve one) to the illumination felt by Proust's Narrator at the end of *Le Temps retrouvé* (his book, however, is *already written!*)."[134] Barthes quickly shrugs off any hint of immodesty by making it clear that the point is less to compare himself with Proust or Proust's narrator than to provide a didactic parallel. All the more surprising, therefore, is Barthes's confusion between Proust's Narrator, who, by the end of *A la recherche du temps perdu,* has yet to begin the novel he has long dreamed of writing but hitherto failed to write, and Proust himself, who, in the closing volume, according to the logic of the work, if not the chronology of its actual composition, was indeed reaching the end. It may be that Barthes's mistake was a momentary lapse, a passing distraction; it is at any event one he is careful to avoid elsewhere in order to emphasise the inverse relationship between Proust the author of *A la recherche,* carefully laying trails to be understood, misunderstood, and understood again, and the book's Narrator, whose task it is in his turn to follow those trails, understanding, misunderstanding, and understanding them anew as the narrative unfolds.[135]

Barthes's misreading is nevertheless revealing. For what it suggests is that, on this occasion, in remembering *A la recherche,* Barthes was no longer able or willing to decide between Proust and his Narrator, in other words, between a real-life writing that was a reading and a fictional reading that might one day become a writing, or between a reading that had already become a writing and a future writing that was still a simulation. From life to work and work to life, it seems, was no longer a straightforward one-way journey. And in a sense Barthes was right: as Proust's Narrator famously asserts, in a much-cited passage from *Le Temps retrouvé,* his life had indeed already been written, in the form of an "inner book of unknown signs . . . for the reading of which nobody else could provide me with any rules," and which it was therefore now his singular, lonely task to decipher and translate into text. "That book, the most painful of all to decipher," writes the Narrator, "is also the only one dictated to us by reality, the only one whose 'impression' has been made in us by reality itself." And he famously adds: "The book with figured characters, not traced by us [*aux caractères figurés, non tracés par nous*], is our only book."[136]

Reading, writing, the past, the future, completion, incompletion, life, the literary work—these are not distinct entities, then, but the multiple aspects of a single event, without subject or object, origin or term, simply called: writing. Writing for Barthes was never something that had already taken place, always something about to happen: as both a desire and a promise, in the future. The work of Proust was far from indifferent to this conception of textuality, and was perhaps even responsible for suggesting it to Barthes in the first place. Indeed, as long ago as 1954, when Barthes had first begun to write, intermittently, on Proust, it was in precisely those terms that he did so. Proust, he wrote, "throughout his vast work, is always on the point of writing; what he has in view is a traditional literary act, but he defers it endlessly, and it is at the end of this wait which is *never honoured* that the work finds itself constructed in spite of itself: it is the waiting that forms the density of a work whose *suspended* character was enough to found the writer's language."[137] Indecision, deferral, suspension: these were motifs that Barthes was to deploy later both in reading Proust and in writing about his work, but also, just as emblematically, in deferring writing about his work. For the texts by Barthes explicitly devoted to Proust are relatively few in number. And when he next had occasion to return to *A la recherche du temps perdu*, it was to retrace a familiar arborescent, retrocessive structure in seven or so moments: the initial desire to write, stalled and interrupted by a threefold disillusionment with literature (witness the Narrator's dispiriting discussions with Norpois, his disappointment upon reading a diary extract from the Goncourt brothers, his indifference at the sight of trees in the countryside in *Le Temps retrouvé*, all of which confirms him, provisionally, in the belief that "the new stage in life"—or *vita nova*—he has finally reached is an empty, arid one), redeemed by a similarly threefold series of illuminations: the ecstatic experience of memory, the rediscovery of the supreme revelatory power of literature, and the realisation that time, though past, was only ever suspended, and can therefore be regained, but only as a result of a final, determined, apocalyptic decision to write (in the absolute) which takes narrator and reader back to the beginning of the novel in order to begin again.[138]

What Barthes deploys again here is a story of initiation, of desire, disappointment, and redemption, the secret of which lies in the past, but whose only realisation is in the future; and it is indeed striking how far the inchoate sketches for *Vita nova* (in which Barthes toys at one stage with the idea of replacing Proust with Tolstoy), the vastly dilated lectures on *La Préparation du roman,* and Barthes's persistent if occasional reading of Proust—not necessarily in their content, so to speak, but in their discursive structure—each follow the same futural logic of deferral, transformation, and return, implicitly commenting on each other as they do so, displacing each other, like so many layers of a palimpsest, not because any one of these versions provides a definitive translation for any of the others, merely its abyssal re-enactment, its musical repetition, and constant propensity for variation. The story told in each of these texts is moreover both long and short; it embodies, in the form of a forever impending event, the drama of a decision, but also insists on the protracted postponement of indecision that alone makes decision necessary and possible: in the future. And this is why *A la recherche,* for author, narrator, and reader alike, Barthes observed, using a rare Latin future infinitive, is the novel of *scripturire,* of being-about-to-write, being-on-the-threshold-of-writing, desiring-to-write, writing-in-the-future.[139]

But how to address the futurity of desire, Barthes asks? Only by enacting it, replies Proust, and in enacting it, suspending it, and in suspending it, enacting it again. That is, by addressing it in literature, to literature.

But how, then, to write on or about literature?

This was one of the questions which Barthes, returning once more to Proust, sought to answer. He did so in three closely related texts, published over a twelve-year period.[140] The first, from 1967, entitled "Proust et les noms [Proust and Names]," deals with the all-important catalytic repertoire of fictional names devised by Proust, in what, for Barthes, was a decisive gesture, in so far as it on the one hand supplied the future novel with infinite possibilities of transformation while on the other serving to suspend meaning entirely, and for much the same reason, which was that proper names denote or connote, but do not signify. In the second, shorter piece, published in January 1979 under the culinary title "Ça prend [It's Taking]," drawing on material taken from *La Préparation du roman* lecture course, Barthes again focused attention

on the aesthetic (rather than biographical) transformation which, allegedly in the space of a single month, in September 1909, took Proust
from the prospective, failed author of a fragmentary critical essay on
Sainte-Beuve to the irrepressibly prolific author of a future novel without end.[141] This was a process, according to Barthes, that, alongside the
invention of a gallery of names, also involved a rediscovery of the multi-
valent performativity of the first-person narrative voice, the shift from
fragmentary forms to a broader, novelistic canvas, and the adoption of
the device of recurring characters, all decisions that bore essentially on
Proust's mobile treatment of time and identity, and which, plainly
enough, were more than questions of literary critical interest, for they
were of signal relevance for Barthes the writer, in that he too, just like
Proust, in the aftermath of his mother's death, envisaged changing
from a writer of fragmentary texts to the author of—something else, as
announced, perhaps, in the drafts for *Vita nova*.[142]

It was in the third text on Proust, first delivered as a lecture in 1978
and published only after his death, that Barthes moved to address explicitly the issue of the critic's relationship with the work. He did so
under the immediately recognisable title, "'Longtemps, je me suis cou-
ché de bonne heure,'" which, reinscribing and endorsing the opening
words of Proust's novel, added to them a second, additional signature:
his own. And Barthes continued in the same modestly immodest vein.
The topic of his talk, he said, was quite simply: "Proust et moi [Proust
and I]." The premiss was simple enough, yet also unexpected. Rather
than approaching *A la recherche du temps perdu* as a finite critical object,
rather than identifying with one or other of the characters in the story,
he would put himself in the position of Proust, not the grandee of
French literary history, but the author of a still unwritten future work,
the "at times anguished, at times exalted, and in any case humble la-
bourer who desired to undertake a task that, from the very outset, as far
as he was concerned, had the status of an absolute."[143] In beginning his
talk, following the logic developed in the 1979–80 lecture course, the
perspective Barthes adopted was that of a reader simulating the production of the text being read. His critical account of Proust's text, to the
extent that this description of Barthes's project is still an appropriate
one, was to be in the form of an enactment or re-enactment of a desire
to write, not just any text, but that singular, irreplaceable textual event

known as *A la recherche du temps perdu*. Criticism here, then, had little if
anything to do with bringing the text before a tribunal of meaning, significance, or value; it corresponded instead, while adding nothing and
taking nothing away, to a desire to provide the text with a unique performative shadow, simultaneously internal and external to it, and reaffirm
it therefore not as the finite, complete, past entity it was, but as the infinite, incomplete, futural prospect it now became. "Become who you
are": Barthes quoted Nietzsche's famous words at the very end of the
1979–80 lecture course; it was an injunction that he now applied not
only to himself as writer but to the work of art too.

  Barthes's lecture was itself in two sections. In the first, the critic
reaffirmed the event of writing as a decision in favour of the undecidable Neuter. Proust, according to Barthes's presentation, not unlike
the lecturer himself, was faced with the dilemma of having to choose
between a literary critical essay (the unfinished project for *Contre Sainte-
Beuve*) and a narrative fiction (what eventually would become *A la recherche du temps perdu*), in much the same way that Proust's Narrator, in
turn, was similarly compelled to opt either for the dull oblivion of sleep
spent by his mother's side or for the potent memories of sleeplessness
experienced in her absence. In neither case was there any given method
available for overcoming or reconciling these divergent paths. What
Proust—Proust's writing—elected to do instead, however, was to affirm
the aporetic impossibility of choice, the undecidability that lay between
these mutually exclusive alternatives, which then became, like the two
sides of Méséglise and Guermantes that structure the Narrator's child-
hood experience, the complementary aspects, not of something else,
but of each other, and resulting, not in a coherent dialectical synthesis,
but in the unpredictable monstrosity of *A la recherche* itself, part novel,
part essay, part autobiography, part fiction, part valediction, part promise, and, arriving within the opening pages of Proust's text with the
impenetrable singularity of an incalculable event, in the self-cancelling
impossibility of the phrase: *je dors*, "I am sleeping." The formulation,
Barthes suggests, like the phrase "I am dead," encountered earlier in
Poe, was a crucial moment, a *hapax*, not only because it evoked referen-
tial impossibility, but also because it made available to Proust the writer
a new textual logic, of indecision and alterity, of wavering (*Vacillement*)
and opening to the outside (*Décloisonnement*), the effect of which was

dramatically to transform the relationship between these apparent polar opposites: life (and death) and writing. Proust, wrote Barthes, marked a key development in literary history: the entry into writing not of the autobiographer but of the biographologist (the *biographologue*); and, on Proust's part, it was no doubt this radical conflation of living and dying with writing, and writing with living and dying, that prompted Barthes's desire to engage in a critically uncritical simulation of Proust the writer, and made of that simulation the place without place of a decisive transformation.[144]

For in the course of Barthes's lecture a slippage occurs: the writing subject, both rhetorical performer and textual practitioner, with whom Barthes began by identifying himself, also radically changes. It is no longer Proust who is cast in that role, but his shadow, his double, *"another* Proust," writes Barthes, by the name of "Marcel," neither entirely biographical nor entirely literary (and not to be confused with the Narrator of *A la recherche,* who remains nameless virtually throughout Proust's text), who figures in Barthes's reading as a strange figure of indeterminacy, "a singular individual [*être singulier*], both child and adult, *puer senilis,* passionate and wise, beset by eccentric habits [*proie de manies excentriques*] and given to peerless insight [*lieu d'une réflexion souveraine*] into the world, love, art, time, and death."[145] At some stage, then, Barthes's object of identification ceased to be Proust the toiling *artifex,* but became other: singular, undecidable, irreducible to any position either inside or outside the text. At this point, a further slippage occurs. The author of the lecture, Barthes himself, who has hitherto acted *as if* he were the writer of the novel, also undergoes a transformation. He too becomes in turn, so to speak, *another* Barthes, who, confronted with the actuality of death, also desires some kind of resurrection (Proust's working title for *A la recherche* was: "perpetual adoration [*adoration perpétuelle*]," as required by the Eucharist), and to that end seeks an intimation of a new life or *vita nova* to redeem the fatal torpor or accidia (*acédie:* this unusual word, even in French, appears not only in the lecture on Proust but also in two of the drafts for *Vita nova*) that, under the auspices of the endlessly repetitive, has begun to vitiate his relationship with writing.

Here, in a sense, Barthes gives up pretending or writing *as if.* A limit is reached, and something occurs which abolishes all possibility of distinction between actuality and simulation, enactment and repetition, memory and experience. Performance turns into what, displaying a Nietzschean commitment to the untimely, yet cautiously surrounding the expression with quotation marks, Barthes describes as a series of "'moments of truth' [*'moments de vérité'*]."[46] But there is nothing abstract, disembodied, theoretical, universal, or spiritual about these moments, these "summits of the particular [*cimes du particulier*]," as Barthes calls them, making Proust's expression his own, which are far from expressing the nature of things as they necessarily are. Instead, Barthes's "moments of truth" are so many irreducible, extreme events, whose force derives from their status not as *episteme* but *pathos*, not as finite knowledge but boundless feeling, not from any general validity as a summation of the world, but their singular intensity as points of infinite dispersion. As Barthes explains:

> The "moment of truth," assuming we agree to treat it as an analytical notion, could be thought to imply an acknowledgement of *pathos*, in the simple, non-pejorative sense of the word, and the science of literature, oddly enough, finds it hard to acknowledge *pathos* as a force in reading [*comme force de lecture*]; Nietzsche, no doubt, might help us to ground [*fonder*] the notion, but we are still far from a theory or history of the Novel based on *pathos*; in order to go any further, we would have to agree to break up the "whole" of the universe of the novel [*émietter le "tout" de l'univers romanesque*], no longer to locate the essence of the book in its structure, but on the contrary to acknowledge that the work inspires emotion, lives and grows by a kind of "dilapidation" that leaves only certain moments standing, which are properly speaking its peaks, with that reading that is still alive, concerned, only following, so to speak, along this ridge line: moments of truth are like points of *surplus value* in the plot.[47]

Simulation, then, provokes an event which suspends simulation as such. What therefore arises or occurs is not a scene of narcissistic self-recognition, in the sense that Barthes as critic might be thought simply to be reducing Proust to little more than an extension of his own ego, much as those petty-bourgeois purveyors or consumers of myth, vigorously attacked in *Mythologies,* or those traditionally normative literary critics mocked elsewhere were accused of doing by Barthes himself. True enough, this is one of the dangers of Barthes's methodology. It is also however a necessary risk, and it is hard to see how, without some degree of sympathetic convergence, identification between critic and writer of the kind practised by Barthes would be possible at all. There are of course numerous points of contact or communication between the pair. As Barthes himself points out repeatedly, both men turned to writing, not for the first time, but with a renewed sense of urgency in the wake of the death of the mother. Both were also much exercised by the indirect uses, the mystifications, lies, and deceptions, to which language was put in society, and by the ways in which French society, while seeming homogeneous, was marked and traversed by a vast range of differentiated, conflictual, mutually incompatible, yet constantly overlapping cultural codes, affecting speech, dress, polite behaviour, much else besides; both were attracted, partly as a result, by what was socially marginal or semi-clandestine; both shared a love of French music and of the singing voice; both were conscious too of living between times, at the end of an epoch and the beginning of another, whose inevitability they foresaw, but whose limitations they regretted; both knew what it was like to suffer debilitating illness, tuberculosis here, asthma there, from a relatively young age; both were male and homosexual; and so on.

At the same time, between the two, between the critic desiring to write and the text of a writer having written, between reader and text, therefore, there was a gap, an interval, a constitutive dissymmetry, dissipating the lure of gelatinous ideological or imaginary consensus, what Lacan, in his 1960–61 seminar on transference, describes as structural oddity, oddness, or disparity,[148] which meant that the relation between the two, between Barthes and Proust, as between perhaps any reader and a text, was a transferential one: grounded not in narcissism but in repetition, reactualisation, and transformation. Between reader and text, there was an unbridgeable distance, a margin of discretion, irreducible to the infinite regress of self-reflexivity. In reading a text, then, it was always possible that, rather than perpetually rediscovering oneself in the other, one might instead encounter the other in oneself, and oneself *as* another. And it was this that made all the difference, according to Barthes, beginning the 1979–80 lecture series, between a copy and a simulation:

> The word simulation may seem surprising [he argued] since I was keen to reject *Imitation* as a notion that was too strict and too literal and because simulation is a reinforced imitation. What I take it to mean, however, on the basis of the figure of "Simulation" itself: to merge the "true" with the "false," the "same" with the "other." In a forthcoming book, Severo Sarduy examines (classical) Painting, and substitutes for the standard notion of a "copy" the concept of a "simulation drive [*pulsion de simulation*]": which is a drive that incites one not to be *an* other but to *be other* [*non pas à être un autre, mais à être autre*], irrespective of who one is: a drive to uncover [*dégager*] an Other in myself = a force of alterity on the basis of, and within Identity → To pass from a love of reading to Writing is to bring to light and detach from imaginary Identification with the text or with a favourite author (to whom one is attracted), not what is different from that author (= impasse of the *effort* to be original), but what in me is different from me: the adored foreigner [*l'étranger*] drives me, and leads me actively to affirm the foreigner [*l'étranger*] that is within me, the foreigner [*l'étranger*] that I am for myself.[149]

But how to know, how to tell the difference between myself as another and the other as myself? The question is one that Freud often had to confront within the transferential setting of the psychoanalytic session, as he explains in a late paper entitled "Konstruktionen in der Analyse [Constructions in Analysis]."[150] The analyst, writes Freud, not unlike Proust's Narrator, and perhaps not unlike Proust's reader also, is in the position of having to act like the archaeologist faced with an ancient historical site, that is, by interpreting the available remnants of evidence, on the basis of which an historically or theoretically coherent narrative can then be constructed. It is admittedly always possible, Freud concedes, for analysis to take a false turn, and for inaccurate constructions to be put forward to the analysand. But these have little effect, says Freud, precisely because they find no resonance in the patient, who says neither yes nor no, but remains indifferent. But the converse also occurs, and an accurate construction may equally well elicit either agreement or denial from the analysand, by way of recognition or resistance, in which case the only proof, so to speak, of the effectiveness of the construction will be found, not in the analysand's positive or negative response, but in the fact that further unconscious material can be produced, confirming, amplifying, or extending what was already acknowledged. From this it would follow that the only proof of any reading, and therefore of any critical intervention whatsoever, is the affirmative force of that reading—yet not because that reading is forcibly asserted, but only in so far as its affirmative force is in turn affirmed by the deployment of new material. Paradoxically, then, for Barthes, it is, in the end, the endless affirmation of affirmation that is the only strategy able to underwrite criticism's possible or impossible futurity.

"In the beginning," Lacan announced to his seminar in November 1960, "was love."[151] The words served to open the first of that year's sessions on the topic of transference and provided a key to what Lacan would slowly unfold, as was his custom, over the months to come. And if it is true that Barthes's relationship to Proust the writer, or to the Proustian text, can justly be termed a transferential one, then Lacan's remark explains perhaps how Barthes's simulation of Proust the writer drew from him the perhaps otherwise unexpected affirmation, which falls at the end of the 1978 lecture, that in the face of finitude, death, grief, loss, the only recourse is to affirm the infinity of an event—which Barthes, declining to name it as such, nevertheless in 1978 took to mean: speaking those he loved, uttering affect, refusing arrogance.

VII

Feeling good

Now (I am convinced of this) there is no writing without a decision of generosity towards the world. An ethics of writing does exist (by which I mean the whole range of refined values [*valeurs fines*] that give desire and reason to live [*qui donnent envie et raison de vivre*]); or, better, writing is from the outset [*d'emblée*] an ethical act: writing, on each occasion, has something of the "crisis of goodness" [*"crise de bonté"*] about it. This goodness, of course, is not something writing ever states openly; it is when we finish the text, and only then, that we turn what we have read into a sort of indeterminate whole [*une sorte de total indéfini*], and feel "good" ["*bien*"].

Roland Barthes, "Préface," in Jean Daniel, *Le Refuge et la source*[152]

Literature, writing, the neuter were inseparable, then, for Barthes, from a thought of the Sovereign Good. Associated, however, with the seductive otherness of a mother's smile, always other than any paradigmatically opposed other, this was no moral argument, but more simply, perhaps more radically, an affective one. But could affect or affectivity include what, for want of a better word, might be called an ethics of writing? Barthes thought so. But the nature of the ethical stance he adopted in this way was contradictory, paradoxical, aporetic. In so far as it was grounded in what Barthes suggests is an a priori decision in favour of generosity, expressive therefore not of universal moral principle but of refinement, selectivity, and differentiation, it was anything but prescriptive. Indeed, if writing from the outset was already an ethical act, as Barthes seemed to suggest, this could only mean either that there was in fact no such thing as *unethical* writing, making it impossible in fact to decide in what an ethics of writing might therefore consist, or, alternatively, as far as writing was concerned, that there were at the very least situations or circumstances, texts or contexts, where, in so far as the words retained their meaning, it was equally ethical to be *both* ethical *and* unethical. In other words, the divorce between the one and the other was impossible to finalise, not least, as Derrida had already argued in *De la grammatologie* (*Of Grammatology*), because the one could only proceed from the other, and remain marked, troubled, even scarred by that difficult and never definitive emergence.[153] The ethical realm, in other words, for Derrida as for Barthes, was a world not of decisions but of undecidability, not of unanswerable conclusions but of unanswered and unavoidable questions, which it was necessary to affirm. From which it then followed that, if there was an ethics of writing, it was not because literature was a bearer of ethical values, since by that logic it was always already marked by the unethical as well, but precisely because at one and the same time it affirmed the necessity and impossibility of appealing to what might be identifiable as the ethical.

As Barthes's enduring engagement with the zero degree, the plurality of reading, and the neuter served to attest, this was anything but a negative condition. It contained the only chance of criticism's longevity. For Barthes, the futurity of writing was intimately bound to desire—desire, as he put it, that was desire not for possession but for the elusive seductions of the neuter: perpetually unsatisfied, forever renascent, continually groping for what eluded any grasp, never attainable therefore in any present, but only ever deferred, different, other to what it was. "And now? [*Et après*]?" the writer asked himself, in singular manuscript characters, traced white on black inside the back cover of *Roland Barthes par Roland Barthes,* annexing this liminal last-ditch space of the book to the work, while already pointing beyond its present confines, and went on to answer as follows, declining in protean fashion each of the available second-, third-, and first-person pronouns as he did so: "'What to write now? Will you be able [*Pourrez-vous*] to write something more?'—'One writes [*On écrit*] with one's desire, and there is no end to my desire [*je n'en finis pas de désirer*].'"[154]

Desire, for Barthes, was subject to a strangely contrary, self-defeating, self-renewing logic: for while on the one hand it was bent on achieving satisfaction for itself, on the other hand, and for that selfsame reason, it was obliged to turn aside from achieving satisfaction, not least because if it were to succeed in reaching its goal, it would only be at the cost of destroying itself. Desire, for Barthes, in other words, was incompatible with anything that would bring reading to a premature end: truth, values, morality, dogmatic certainty of any sort. Its future was inseparable from the requirement *not* to decide. "Stupidity [*la bêtise*]," Flaubert famously wrote, "consists in wanting to conclude," and Barthes frequently echoed that sentiment. "People who are quick to understand," he once put it in a lecture at the Collège de France, "scare the wits out of me [*Les gens qui comprennent vite me font peur*]."[155] What this meant in sum was that the task of criticism could not be to impose itself upon a text by appealing to ideological criteria external to it, but only to seek to fulfil the work by extending, continuing, completing, and reaffirming it, in the certain-uncertain, yet happy knowledge that the project was impossible, and that reading, writing, like desire itself, were necessarily interminable.

What resurfaced here in the work of Barthes, as elsewhere in contemporary literary criticism and theory, were the exact same questions as those with which, in the work of Schlegel and Novalis, modern literary criticism had properly or improperly begun. That Romanticism should stage a return in Barthes's own later writing was therefore perhaps not surprising. It was a development Barthes both recognised and welcomed, not least because, rather than belonging to some earlier epoch, as Barthes was once minded to suggest, Romanticism corresponded to a vast historical period, whose boundaries were as broad as those of modernity itself, stretching in France, he suggested in *La Préparation du roman*, from Chateaubriand (1768–1848) at least, perhaps even Rousseau (1712–78), to Proust (1871–1922), and ultimately himself too. And as his attention turned to the continuities between living and writing, fiction and theory, bearing ever more clearly for Barthes the promise of an affirmative, if always paradoxical ethics, it was not by chance he should for instance describe himself, in an aside, as "merely someone recounting his decision to write in the 'Romantic' manner."[156] The legacy of Romanticism was apparent in other ways too: in Barthes's commitment to the effusiveness of the discourse of love, his enthusiasm for the music of Schumann and others, and his interest in the literary text as an infinite encounter with the finite, and in the prospect of the absolute, transgeneric, self-reflexive work, sometimes called the novel.

There was, of course, always the danger, as the example of the Jena Romantics showed, that to affirm writing in this way, however much its demand exceeded the narrow confines of literature or the literary in the received, institutional sense, would turn out to be a nostalgic retreat into aestheticism. For Barthes, however, the risk was worth taking; for it reinforced his belief that the essential task facing criticism now was not to promote or defend past value or values but, according to the untimely countertemporality of an interruption, interval, or interregnum, to carry on desiring to write, to read, and thus persist: in affirming, beyond negativity, whatever the consequences, the irreducibility of affirmation.

Chapter Three

MAURICE BLANCHOT
The Demand of the Unreadable

I

On reflection

> Literature [with the *Athenaeum*] (I mean all forms of expression, which is
> also to say all forces of dissolution) all of a sudden becomes aware of itself,
> manifests itself, and in this manifestation has no other task or definition
> than to announce itself [*se déclarer*]. In a word, literature proclaims that it
> is assuming power [*prend le pouvoir*]. The poet becomes humanity's future,
> at the very moment when, no longer being anything, anything other than
> the certainty of being a poet, and having intimate responsibility for that
> knowledge, the writer marks the place where poetry will no longer be
> content with producing beautiful, determinate works, but will produce
> itself [*se produira elle-même*] in a movement without term or determination.
> In other words, literature here comes face to face with its most dangerous
> sense—which is to question itself in declarative mode, at times trium-
> phantly, by discovering that it thereby contains everything, at times in
> distress, by discovering that it is empty of everything, since it can affirm
> itself only by default.
>
> Maurice Blanchot, *L'Entretien infini*[1]

Blanchot's diagnosis of the challenges facing literary criticism in the
late 1950s, as described in his response to the journal *Arguments,* was no
isolated or idiosyncratic gesture. As the work of Barthes in subsequent

decades amply confirms, it showed an acute and urgent awareness of the irreducible disjunction between literature or writing and any normative discourse of ideological, moral, or aesthetic value or values, together with an unyielding conviction that it was essential to affirm that disparity or dissymmetry as a necessary response to the futurity not only of literature but of literary criticism too.

Blanchot in 1959 was careful to refer his reflections on the future of criticism to the exigencies of what, in France, was an important historical and political turning point. But he was aware too that the crisis he was articulating had roots stretching back to the beginnings of modernity itself. For this was not the first time that literary criticism had been brought to the realisation of its simultaneous necessity and impossibility; nor was it the first time that it had faced the enigma of its dangerous but seductive proximity, even complicity or identification, with the event of literature itself. Nor indeed was it the first time that criticism had given way to the recognition that its own object, elusive and inaccessible, lay somewhere outside of the artwork while being nowhere present except within it. All three motifs had played a central role in the early thinking of the German Romantics—Friedrich Schlegel, Novalis—during that crucial period between 1798 and 1800 in Jena, when, as Lacoue-Labarthe and Nancy have argued, the modern concept of literature was in full process of elaboration, the implications of which, for the future of literary criticism itself, as Barthes began to discover in the 1970s, were far from exhausted.[2]

It was Schlegel for instance who had noted with relief, upon reading Goethe's *Wilhelm Meister* (1795–96), how such a work, by dint of its self-reflexive narrative, already contained within it its own judgement upon itself. "Indeed," he wrote in 1798, "it not only judges itself [*beurteilt sich*], it presents itself too [*stellt sich auch selbst dar*]."[3] External legislative criteria were henceforth inappropriate and redundant. The work of the critic lay not in prescribing, in negative fashion, what was—or, better, was *not*—acceptable, nor did it consist in articulating judgements of taste that had, in principle, to command the universal assent of all other readers. Criticism's role for the Jena Romantics was rather to counter the legacy of Kantian critique and in its place, in the words of Fr. 3 of the *Athenaeum* fragments, endeavour to "introduce the concept of the positive into philosophy."[4] In such circumstances it was no longer the task of literary criticism to refer the text to universal aesthetic or moral criteria outside the work; it was to spell out how the work had already pre-empted its own reception and, as in the case of *Wilhelm Meister,* somehow always "knew more than it said and willed more than it knew."[5] It followed not only that each poem was already the best possible critical commentary on itself, but that criticism in its turn, to fulfil its pledge to the work, now had to aspire to the condition of poetry. "All art should become knowledge, and all knowledge art; poetry and philosophy should be unified," Schlegel famously wrote in his "Critical Fragments" of 1797. "Poetry," he added, "can only be criticised in poetry. Any aesthetic judgement which is not itself a work of art . . . has no legitimacy in the realm of art."[6]

Any artwork was necessarily a finite object; but as such it belonged to a movement that, reaching beyond the work, was infinite process, perpetual reflexivity, a questing after the absolute. "A work is formed [*gebildet*]," Schlegel put it in another fragment, "when it is sharply de-limited [*begrenzt*] on every side, while remaining within those limits both limitless [*grenzenlos*] and inexhaustible, and when, being completely true to itself, it is everywhere in equilibrium, and yet rises sublimely above itself [*über sich selbst erhaben ist*]."[7] As this description suggests, the Romantic artwork was a site of constant paradox. It was forever double: infinite yet finite, total yet fragmentary, impetuous yet ironic, singular yet universal, profoundly effusive yet deeply knowing. Its favoured rhetoric was allegory and *Witz*, and its manner of self-presentation playful and oblique, as Schlegel went on to show in the influential and influentially programmatic "Dialogue on Poetry [*Gespräch über die Poesie*]" that appeared in two parts in the final two issues of the *Athenaeum* in 1800.[8] As the—poemless—poet Lothario (a thinly veiled portrait of Novalis) says at one point to the philosopher Ludovico (representing Schelling), "All the sacred games [*Spiele*] of art are but distant copies [*ferne Nachbildungen*] of the infinite game that is the world, that art work that is eternally forming itself [*dem ewig sich selbst bildenden Kunstwerk*]." To which his friend replies: "[I]n other words, all beauty is allegory. The most high, since it cannot be expressed as such, can only be referred to allegorically."[9]

This specular dialectic between the time-bound and the timeless, the relative and the absolute, the finite and the infinite did not only govern the artwork. It also accounted for the relationship between text and audience. Here was the site of another paradox. For while on the one hand the contribution of the reader or critic to the infinite unfolding of the work was a necessary and inevitable confirmation of the work's spiralling power, it was also, on the other hand, and for that very reason, entirely superfluous, since the work, albeit obliquely, had already spoken in the reader's place and already said everything that criticism might have to say in its turn. But the effect of this forestalling of criticism was not to reduce criticism to silence. It made the intervention of the critic even more crucial to the logic of the work. Forced to relinquish its dependence on extraneous criteria, criticism's task was now to realise the artwork, and bring it into full awareness of itself. At the same time, this also meant criticism would become no more than a moment in the dissolution of the work, a stage in its absorption into the infinite movement of the absolute. So, while criticism was necessary for the realisation of the work, what was required of it was merely that it affirm the work. The two dynamics, though seemingly working at cross purposes, in reality followed logically the one from the other, as Benjamin was to argue in his doctoral dissertation of 1920; together they account for the strangely paradoxical and uncertain status of literary criticism, true to itself only in so far as it realises its redundancy, true to its object only in so far as it is an essential moment in the aesthetic realisation of the artwork.

There is much here that finds a ready echo in more recent thinking. This is perhaps not surprising; what it emphasises is the foundational significance of the *Athenaeum* for modern literary criticism and for modern conceptions of the aesthetic autonomy of the work. But if modern criticism shares with the *Athenaeum* an apparent reluctance to impose normative criteria upon the work, this is arguably not because the values previously embodied in external aesthetic norms have been abandoned. On the contrary, it is merely the location of those values that has changed. They no longer belong to the political, religious, ideological, or philosophical discourses that legitimate the work from the outside. They now inhabit the work itself, and fulfil their purpose all the more effectively for doing so implicitly. To this extent—and the same is doubtless the case with much modern literary criticism—the work of the Romantics is as deeply informed by ideological and other values as is the thinking of more explicitly dogmatic critics. As far as the *Athenaeum* was concerned, as Benjamin makes plain, if the artwork was defined by its spiralling reflexivity, this was primarily because, like nature itself as far as the Romantics were concerned, it was grounded in a concept of absolute subjectivity, meaning that any encounter with the textual (sexual, political) other was only ever an opportunity for rediscovering what was already embodied in the organic whole of the self. Both the artwork itself and the criticism that was an indispensable feature of it shared a logic, which functioned as an aesthetic, moral, and political category: the logic of what the Romantics, as Lacoue-Labarthe and Nancy point out, termed *Bildung*, both process and product, that is, both the movement of forming, formation, or shaping and its end result, culture itself, and which therefore represented the aesthetic edification or education of humankind in general.[10]

The concept of *Bildung*, then, is wide-ranging. At times it operates in a narrowly aesthetic context; at others, it takes on much wider philosophical, moral, and political significance. Either way, the result is largely the same; it is to restore to the act of criticism a covert normative horizon and reassert the status of the work as an embodiment of cultural values. Admittedly, these had never been properly abandoned, and the break between the *Athenaeum* and its predecessors was in reality no doubt much less complete than it might appear.[11] In the "Gespräch über die Poesie," for instance, Marcus (Ludwig Tieck) remarks, innocently enough, it seems, that the separation between genres is a feature of all artistic production. "Without separation [*Absonderung*]," he says, "no creation of form [*Bildung*] takes place, and the creation of form [*Bildung*] is the essence of art."[12] But the valency of *Bildung* is such that the wider moral and political senses of the word soon take over from its restricted aesthetic usage. Description rapidly turns to prescription. "The greatest good, and only thing of benefit, is culture [*Bildung*]," writes Schlegel in a fragment from the "Ideen" of 1800. "Only through culture [*Bildung*]," he adds later, "does man [*Mensch*], who is entirely human, become human in every respect, and infused with humanity."[13] *Bildung*, states another fragment, is what resolves conflict and guarantees belief in the social whole: "Now we are at one because we are of one mind [*eines Sinnes sind*]; but now we are not, because one or other of us lacks understanding [*Sinn*]. Which of us is right, and how can we be at one? Only through culture [*Bildung*], which extends each particular understanding [*Sinn*] to the general and the infinite; and through our belief in this understanding [*Sinn*] or in religion, which is what we already are, even before it is what we become."[14]

Three years earlier, Fr. 214 of the *Athenaeum* fragments had argued in similar vein. "The perfect state [*die vollkommne Republik*]," wrote Schlegel, "would not merely have to be democratic, but also at the same time aristocratic and monarchic; within the legislation for freedom and equality, the cultured [*Gebildete*] ought to predominate over the uncultured [*Ungebildete*], lead them, and organise everything into an absolute whole [*zu einem absoluten Ganzen*]."[15] Criticism, then, for Schlegel, while claiming to be immanent in the work, was nevertheless a pedagogy, imbued with a dream of totalisation. The "Gespräch über die Poesie" had begun by implying much the same. Poetry, Schlegel conceded, like love or individual character, lay in each one of us as a singular and original effusion, and it was clearly not the task of criticism to change that response into a pallid and uniform copy of itself. Nevertheless, criticism still had an educational purpose: "the lofty discipline of genuine criticism [*die hohe Wissenschaft echter Kritik*] should teach [*lehren*] [the individual reader] how to develop [*sich bilden*] and above all how to grasp every other independent literary form in its classical force and abundance so that the bloom and the seed of other minds should nourish and impregnate his own imagination."[16] And if *Bildung* was tantamount to creative freedom, this was also because freedom itself, for the Jena Romantics, was inseparable from teleologically ordained, theocratic mastery. Indeed, as Sylvester explains to the eponymous apprentice poet in Novalis's *Heinrich von Ofterdingen*:

All culture [*Bildung*] leads to what can only be called freedom, which is no mere concept, but the creative foundation of all existence. Freedom here is mastery [*Diese Freiheit ist Meisterschaft*]. The master exercises power [*Gewalt*] freely, by intent, in a determined and considered manner. The objects of his art are his own and do his bidding, and he is neither bound nor impeded by them. And it is precisely this all-encompassing freedom, mastery, or dominion that is the very essence and impetus of conscience. Within it the sacred particularity and immediate creativity of 'personality are disclosed, and each action of the master is simultaneously a revelation of the lofty, simple and transparent world—of the Word of God.[17]

From which it followed that poetry was virtue, both authority and obedience, and subject to an all-embracing divine law, from the perspective of which, notwithstanding the commitment of Novalis or Schlegel to a poetics of the fragment, which it paradoxically served to illustrate, all was as one, and one was as all. The infinite regress of literary self-reflexivity, then, whatever its propensity for abyssal dissolution, was also, and by that very token, a tribute to the creative powers of divine Logos.

For this reason, if not for others, the legacy of German Romanticism for modern literary criticism remains an ambivalent one. Much depends, as Blanchot suggested in 1964, on whether the group's thinking is approached from the perspective of its beginnings or its endings.[18] Novalis of course died young, a victim of tuberculosis, at the age of twenty-eight, in 1801. Friedrich Schlegel was more long-lived; he died at the age of fifty-seven in 1829. By then, the choice had become particularly acute, and readers of Schlegel had therefore to decide whether to place the emphasis on the youthful radical, atheistic, and individualist firebrand, or whether it should favour instead the mature diplomat, journalist, and Catholic convert, better known for his association with the reactionary authoritarianism of Metternich.[19] But as Blanchot was aware, the dilemma was a false one; beginning and ending were of a piece, and literary criticism, by its very nature, was inseparable from the philosophical and political agenda it implied and often served to promote.

The fact remains, as the work of Lacoue-Labarthe and Nancy has shown, that the *Athenaeum* can nevertheless be credited with conceiving of literature as an absolute for the first time, and thus announcing literary modernity as such; and it is also fair to say, as literary history records, that the legacy of the German Romantics, albeit indirectly, and diffracted through the work of others, such as Madame de Staël's *De l'Allemagne* (1810), continued to exert significant if covert influence in France during the late nineteenth and the early twentieth century, in the writings of Mallarmé, Valéry, Proust, Giraudoux, the Surrealists, and various others too, up to and including Blanchot himself, who in 1983, alongside Goethe and Valéry, was moved to cite as one of only a few early literary influences the author Jean-Paul, who already in the "Gespräch über die Poesie" had been identified by Schlegel as one of the prime contemporary practitioners of that most romantic, self-reflexive, and ironically self-transcendent of all possible literary genres: the novel.[20]

II

A literary absolute

> And this is why, to all his publishers and critics, present as well as future, we cannot prevent ourselves from whispering these words: Ah, in Sade, at least, respect the scandal [*Ah, en Sade, du moins, respectez le scandale*].
> Maurice Blanchot, *Lautréamont et Sade*[21]

Blanchot's own relationship to the heritage of the early Romantics was far from simple. It was complicated by an acute awareness of other forces at work in history in the years preceding and following the brief interregnum marked by the *Athenaeum*. For was there not in France, at the very same time, asked Blanchot in 1947, another author, thinker, novelist, and sometime political activist, who also represented a literary absolute and shared a commitment to literature as a form of radical pedagogy?

That author did indeed exist. His name was: Donatien Alphonse François, Marquis de Sade. And his vast literary output, Blanchot suggested, though long consigned to the darker recesses of the library, nevertheless remained, if only for that very reason, required reading. The chances were, moreover, that writing such as Sade's, deeply suspicious as it was of cultural value or values in general, would prove less readily assimilable to *Bildung*, even as the barbarity of what had been committed in the name of at least a certain, brutally prescriptive definition of *Bildung* between 1933 and 1945 was at last being uncovered, and offer therefore a more probing perspective on the increasingly troubled and contested question of the relationship between literature, culture, art, and progress.

For how did things stand with literary criticism in the changed political circumstances following France's Liberation in 1944?

Blanchot began writing on Sade in 1946, continued to do so in the three years that followed, and returned to the task in 1965, and then again briefly in the early 1980s.[22] Throughout that period, Sade's work evidently remained crucial to the issues explored by Blanchot in his 1959 contribution to *Arguments;* indeed, when *Lautréamont et Sade,* the most immediate result of Blanchot's post-war engagement with Sade, was reissued in 1963, it came with a preface consisting of that response, which thus had the opportunity of asking again: how do matters stand with criticism, what is the task of criticism today? Other revisions to the book served to reinforce the exemplary character of Sade's challenge. For the 1963 version of Blanchot's text also reversed the chapter sequence of 1949, and began, unlike its predecessor, not with the essay on Lautréamont but with the discussion of Sade.[23] It now moved more promptly than before, then, to its evocation of Sade's status as a literary absolute, in whom literature was not only given the task of telling all—"tout dire," in the famous words of Sade's Juliette—but indeed constituted itself as "literature," in that very process. "Sade," Blanchot had written in 1947, "is the writer *par excellence,* who brings together [*a réuni*] each and every contradiction."[24]

What was true shortly after the Occupation for Blanchot evidently remained so for more than a decade and a half. Indeed, it would be hard not to see the enduring relevance and urgency of Sade's writing for a critic who, in 1959, had nailed his colours so provocatively to the idea that literature, and therefore criticism, might invoke a kind of affirmation that preceded any appeal to value or values. For what other literary author might appear so radically bereft of all forms of cultural edification than Sade, and what other body of text might it therefore seem so dangerously problematic to affirm?

Blanchot was not alone in treating Sade as a test case for the possibility of any critical discourse whatsoever. The terms of this debate had been set earlier in the century, when Sade's life and work were first being reliably documented by Maurice Heine, who had found among the Surrealists an attentive audience for his biographical and biblio-

graphical research. But it was Georges Bataille, as he broke off his association with the Surrealist group proper, who identified the most important issue relating to Sade's reception when, in the unpublished
manuscript of his novel, *Le Bleu du ciel*, written in 1935, he had the narrator, Troppmann, announce to his girlfriend Xénie that "people who
admire Sade are crooks [*des escrocs*]." "What did they do that to Sade
for?" Troppmann demanded to know, his voice becoming ever more
shrill. "Had they eaten shit or not?"[25] Belonging as it did to a series of
acerbic exchanges with André Breton in the wake of the Second Surrealist Manifesto of 1930, Bataille's point was in part no more than crude
provocation. It raised, however, an enduring and irreducible question.
As Bataille formulated it, using Marxist terminology for idiosyncratic
purposes of his own, it was the question of the use value of Sade's writing: that is, not what cultural value was invested in Sade's work as an
object of exchange, nor what benefit it might confer on its readers, since
in Bataille's view there was clearly neither, but what an audience might
actually *do* with Sade's writing.[26] Bataille's own conviction was that the
Surrealists' public enthusiasm for Sade was essentially hypocritical:
their desire to sanctify Sade, he argued, was in reality a way of avoiding
the unrepentant violence of his writing. To admire Sade was in this
sense to refuse to read him; the attitude of the Surrealists, Bataille complained, was little short of intellectual toilet training.

The question, however, remained: under what conditions might it
be possible to read Sade as the work demanded? Bataille's objection was
that to read Sade's texts as works of literature was wilfully to ignore the
extent of their author's assault on culture and the radical social and
political consequences that then followed. To read Sade as literature,
Bataille implied, meant in fact not reading him at all, which was also to
say that Sade was properly—or, better, *im*properly—unreadable as literature. Bataille's position was uncompromising. It remained, however, deeply problematic. For how might it be possible to declare any
text unreadable as literature except by reading it precisely as literature—
even if this seemingly also meant failing to read it at all? Reading Sade,
it seemed, could take place only on condition it did *not* take place. It
could hardly be a straightforward act of understanding. Sade, according
to Bataille, was owed a debt by the reader. But this was a debt that somehow could be neither accepted nor honoured, since to do so amounted

in either case to a failure to read. Reading was faced, then, with a puzzling predicament: of being exposed from the outset to the intractable violence of the unreadable, and somehow obliged to assume responsibility for that to which it was impossible to respond. Forced in the name of reading to abandon any belief in the value of reading, Sade's reader was therefore left in an impasse, not knowing whether to read or *not* to read, in any case no longer certain of the difference between these joint possibilities—or impossibilities.

Notwithstanding the radicality of Bataille's strictures, the decades that followed saw no shortage of attempts at reading Sade. For the most part these were exercises in philosophical rebuttal or recuperation. For Horkheimer and Adorno, for instance, writing in wartime exile in the United States, Sade was a revealing embodiment of bourgeois enlightenment rationalism, who, in his fiction, had pushed the calculating reason of Kant (and, later, Nietzsche) to a point where the dangerously totalitarian implications of Western metaphysics were plain to see.[27] In 1947, with a very different aim in mind, the essayist (and soon-to-be novelist) Pierre Klossowski brought together in a volume provocatively entitled *Sade mon prochain* (*Sade My Neighbor*) a number of articles written over the previous decade and a half, in which he endeavoured to save Sade for Catholicism on the dialectically persuasive if tendentious grounds that the writer's ferocious denunciations of God betrayed an enduring reliance on the necessity of divine presence.[28] For his part, in a series of essays written in the 1940s and 1950s, collected in *La Littérature et le mal* (*Literature and Evil*) and *L'Érotisme* (*Eroticism*), Bataille retreated from the aporetical abruptness of the position he had defended in the polemic with Breton in order to articulate a philosophical, anthropological account of Sade's writing, indebted to Hegel, Kojève, and Mauss, the effect of which was to rescue Sade for a better understanding of the obscure sacrificial propensities of the human animal. "Now," Bataille concluded in 1957, "normal humanity knows it should have been more receptive to the things it found most violently repulsive, since what we find most violently repulsive of all lies in fact within us."[29]

Six years earlier, not to be outdone, Simone de Beauvoir had supplied an existentialist perspective in an article bluffly entitled "Faut-il brûler Sade? [Should We Burn Sade?]," which undertook to examine Sade's career not on the basis of the writer's prolific literary output but from the point of view of the aberrant sexual pathology his life and work were deemed to exemplify, expressing as they did so the power relations of eighteenth-century class society. Beauvoir's personal distaste for Sade was everywhere in evidence, and there is little doubt she spoke for others when she observed of Sade's work that "even his admirers freely admit that [it] is for the most part unreadable, while philosophically it eludes banality only to lurch into incoherence."[30] Such resistance, though, was not unusual on the part of the intellectual left during the post-war years. It was also a feature of Jacques Lacan's essay "Kant avec Sade," written in 1962 as a preface to Sade's *La Philosophie dans le boudoir*.[31] Freudian psychoanalysis, which had done much to create an audience for Sade's idiosyncratic *scientia sexualis*, might have been expected to have welcomed the writer's transgressive endeavours. But far from it; in Lacan's estimation, Sade's work fell a long way short of (Freudian) truth. Despite its encyclopaedic ambitions, he argued, all Sade's writing revealed, symptomatically, was its violent hatred of the maternal body. "Of a treatise truly on desire," Lacan concluded, "there is little evidence here, if indeed any at all."[32]

Despite their many differences, what is striking about each of these philosophically inspired readings of Sade (and many others could be adduced) is the relative ease with which they pass judgement on Sade's work. Bataille's early challenge, by being everywhere overlooked, belatedly proved its point. Dialectical reason, theology, social anthropology, psychopathology, psychoanalysis—all claimed an ability to frame Sade's text while remaining oblivious to the risk of being framed by it, though the threat of this happening could by definition never be eliminated, as Bataille in particular was probably most keenly aware. Literary critical accounts of Sade's work, on the other hand, faced a greater challenge. While a philosophical reading could content itself, at least in principle, with traversing Sade's text in order to extract from the multitude of set-piece debates and disputes it contained any number of philosophical opinions, upon whose validity or consistency it could then arbitrate, a literary critical reading had to grapple with the more elusive problem of deciding upon the readability—or not—of Sade's texts as writing.

It was with this question of readability that Blanchot in *Lautréamont et Sade* began. What was it about Sade's work, the critic asked, that, in the all too relative world of literary achievement, gave it the quality of an absolute event? Sade's writing, Blanchot explained, displayed two major characteristics. The first was its aspiration to tell all. If Sade's work was tiring to read, the critic remarked, this was merely because it was tireless in its aspiration. What it offered, for the reader's enjoyment, was an exhaustive—and exhausting—catalogue of perverse, violent, lubricious sexual acts, each one of which had its source in nature (and was therefore radically indifferent to all cultural morality), interspersed with an unremitting procession of philosophical arguments, each of which, by invoking nature's own endless cycle of creation and destruction, sought to describe, explain, and justify the various singular proclivities of Sade's libertine protagonists. Sade's totalising ambitions were not only reflected in the scabrous inhumanity of much of what the author wrote; it also found expression in the undiminished and undiminishing energy of his writing. Sade's language itself, Blanchot suggested, was not difficult. It was lucid, abundant, and forthright. But the author's commitment to the work—witness the famous twelve-metre-long roll of the manuscript for *Les Cent Vingt Journées de Sodome* (*The 120 Days of Sodom*), the three successive versions of *Justine*, the six volumes of the *Histoire de Juliette* (*The Story of Juliette*), not to mention countless other texts and manuscripts preserved or destroyed—was such that each of these texts was inseparable from the infinitely repetitive nature of its unfolding. To tell all did not simply imply affronting the pious, virtuous reader who preferred to avert his or her gaze from the world; it also meant entrusting the work to a kind of perpetual motion in which writing and reading could never properly come to an end.

Sade's dedication to the totalising ambitions of the work, according to Blanchot, was founded on what the critic went on to describe, drawing on Hegel's *Phenomenology*, as a "transcendent power of negation: a power that is in no way dependent on the objects it destroys, which, in order to destroy them, does not even presuppose they already exist, because, at the point when it does destroy them, they were always already considered in advance as null and void."[33] Such unremitting negativity had two corollaries. First, it implied the prior annihilation of the object by language (not to be confused with a critique of linguistic reference, since this suppression of the object by language is an indispensable precondition of referentiality itself). This was a crucial move. For what it identified in negativity was the possibility of the literary work as such, not only in the case of Sade, but in general. This was the first reason for Sade's absolute status, and it is no surprise to see Blanchot's argument about Sadian negativity rehearsed in turn by virtually all subsequent critics of Sade. What it made possible was the realisation, which Blanchot was the first properly to articulate, that the essential aspect of Sade's career was the self-evident, yet all the more intractable, circumstance that his works belonged first and foremost not to psychopathology or to sociology but to literature. Sade, in other words, was not a case-history but a writer of literary fiction.

What Sade's work also illustrated, however, Blanchot argued, was not simply this annihilation and sublation of the real by language, as expounded by Hegelian dialectics, it was the supplementary, suspensive, or neutralising power of literature that derived from its capacity to negate the world not in particular, determinate fashion, that is, in order to improve or aggravate this or that specific aspect of the given world, but in indeterminate fashion, that is to say, in its absolute entirety. Sade's writing testified to the strange propensity of the literary work, instead of interacting in particular ways with the world at large, to release language from transitivity or effectivity, negating the world at a stroke, so to speak, and replacing it not with a possible alternative but with an exteriority irreducible to any constituted world. In other words, in Sade the power of language reversed itself, eschewing the ability to intervene directly in the world, and taking on the oblique and spectral form of that which escaped all possibility. Sade's works rightly found themselves in literary hell; but literary hell was simply the other side of literary utopia, whose only place was here and now, immediately, and without delay. And if literature was an act, as Sartre for instance continued to insist, it was only in so far as it was simultaneously anything but an act, more nearly akin to a citation or simulation of an act, an act committed countless times over, but to that extent hardly an act at all: an event, so to speak, that no sooner announced itself than it withdrew or effaced itself entirely.

Sade in his writing could therefore infringe the conditions and norms of human life with total impunity; the only limits to which he had to submit were those of his language and his fevered imagination. Few, then, as a result, are the cultural values that survive Sade's unrestrained assault on morality, decency, humanity. But the effects of this sustained campaign of negation remain strangely inconclusive. True,

Sade's literary world had many points of convergence with the social, political, and cultural realities of late-eighteenth-century France, and it is a simple task to read the former as offering a protracted commentary on the latter; but at the same time, and perhaps more importantly, as its abiding preference for obscure but oddly transparent secret locations and outrageously unworldly practices seems to suggest, the relationship between Sade's fiction and the society to which it appeared to refer was obliquely ironical. Sadian irony operated, however, as Bataille among others was quick to realise, according to a kind of radical undecidability. A reader for instance who wished to resist Sade's relentless proselytising in a novel like *Justine* would find her or his moral—some might say: moralistic—convictions already anticipated and pre-empted by Sade's heroine, and therefore, as the novel develops, which it does by continually repeating the same points, placed increasingly in the self-same position as Justine, perpetually obliged, that is, to deny the evidence of her own eyes in order to maintain a belief in human virtue. At the same time, in order for it to proceed in this way, it is almost as though Sade's writing also requires the reader precisely to adopt that moral or moralistic stance in order that the provocative power of the text may achieve its full effect. Sade's prolixity is counterproductive; the more it endeavours to convince its audience, the more it tends to produce an exhausted or indifferent reader who is increasingly unimpressed by what is being narrated.

A kind of inconclusive circularity arises here. Sade's writing is endlessly repetitive, but rarely does it advance. Plots, characters, descriptions, all are summary in the extreme. What this indicates, paradoxically enough, is that, whatever the violence it is so often minded to portray, Sade's work rarely leaves the written page. What the reader is given, in the end, is words: words, words, and more words. So even as it negates each and every received cultural value, Sade's writing is not simply an exercise in unflinching nihilistic violence. It is inseparable from the infinite necessity of its own language. Before it is anything else, then, Blanchot argues, Sade's text is a consummate and limitless affirmation of its own unending power or powerlessness as a work of literature. Indeterminate negation in Sade inverts itself to become an affirmation of the absolute. In Sade's literary world, everything is possible; culture counts for nothing; and nature is all. Freedom beckons: as absolute, indeterminate indifference. And this is the undoubted appeal of Sade's writing. For if, as Blanchot suggests, Sade's work is synonymous with the project of telling all, as Juliette's celebrated *cri de guerre* would have it, what reader could *not* endorse in his or her turn that requirement, since not to do so would imply abdicating one's very existence as a reader, even if it also commits that reader, willy-nilly, to the intimidating task of reading each and every page of Sade's compelling yet rebarbative text?

It is of course impossible to choose between reading or not reading. One can only decide not to read by reading already, in the same way that to decide to abandon reading is a decision that can only be taken while reading. To read or *not* to read, in either case, then, is to countersign, whether by commission or omission, the infinity of the text. Any text that, like Sade's, identifies itself with the project of telling all—and this is another reason why, for Blanchot, what comes to pass in Sade is "literature" itself—leaves the reader with no alternative other than to read, to continue reading, and read again, unceasingly. In the process, as by Sade, the reader is simultaneously obligated and undermined, put in the text's debt and deprived of autonomy. As a result, at some point (and in Sade's case the point generally comes sooner rather than later), the tables are turned on the reader. Rather than the reader reading the text, with consternation, fatigue, and disarray, it is the text itself, so to speak, that begins to read the reader, mirroring or mocking the values, beliefs, and assumptions that are among readers' most treasured possessions but which, in order to read at all, the reader has been forced to abandon, if perhaps only provisionally.

Reading, like literature itself, is necessarily irresponsible, and this is why it does not in itself embody determinate, decidable values, since the goal of all such values, as Sade's writing amply demonstrates, is to enjoin the reader precisely to stop reading: in the name of humanity, culture, morality, or good taste, irrespective of the disturbing paradox that it is reading itself that is a fundamental condition of possibility of: humanity, culture, morality, and good taste. In the end, culture, *Bildung*, is riven by contradictions it cannot resolve. And if it is true, as Blanchot suggests, that Sade's *Juliette* is best seen as a *Bildungsroman*, it is because *Bildung*, at the hands of literature, is exposed to the threat—or promise—of its perpetual dissolution.[34] In order to read, the reader cannot *not* continue reading. So whatever the reader's distaste for Sade (in some ways, Sade implies, the greater the better!), Sade's text itself, in its assault on taste, seems to have more to say than any reader about the boundaries of taste. The argument is one that, again, has become a standard crux in modern readings of Sade; and it is how Blanchot famously concludes his 1947 essay:

> We cannot claim that [Sade's] thinking is at all viable. But what it does show is that between normal humanity [*l'homme normal*] which locks Sadian humanity [*l'homme sadique*] within an impasse, and Sadian humanity for whom the impasse is a way out, it is the second of the two that knows more about the truth and logic of its situation and has the deeper understanding of it, to the point of being able to help normal humanity understand itself by assisting it in modifying the conditions of all understanding.[35]

But however boundless its ambitions, Sadian totality necessarily has its limits, and the totalising power embodied in Sade's work is not entirely what it seems. True, as Blanchot suggests, the indefatigable energy of Sade's writing has its basis in the infinite potential of negativity itself. But negativity, Blanchot also points out, is not all. It suffers from the limitation of always having to presuppose that which is necessary for it to begin, and which it can but name, retrospectively, as being, existence, or the world as such. It cannot account for itself in its own terms. The negative always comes second. Like Orpheus, negativity cannot turn round, except to glimpse the spectre of a disappearance and thus confront the vertiginous depths of what it cannot touch. It is separated from itself by an absence, in the form of that always prior affirmation, before being and non-being, before the constitution and population of any world, to which both Levinas and Blanchot, in numerous early writings, give the name the *il y a*, the *there is*, which shows itself, without showing itself, as an interval of necessary weakness or impotence on the part of the negative. As such, the *il y a* corresponds to a crucial, unspoken moment in Sade's writing, to which the work itself is forced to respond, without being able to formulate it as such, since it is what is always already presupposed by the work.

While saying all there is to say, then, the work necessarily leaves something unsaid. An unresolved tension, ambiguity, or contradiction, never susceptible of resolution, weaves its way like some ghostly remainder through all Sade's writing, prompting its every word and gesture, while itself remaining necessarily unspoken. It expresses itself at times in Sade's own hesitation or indecision between an avowed belief in civil and libidinal equality between humans, on the grounds that nature does not distinguish between human desires or rights, which famously made the writer an early ally of the French Revolution, and a no less fervent commitment to the social and libidinal hierarchies implicitly and explicitly endorsed by the author's numerous libertine protagonists. But it manifests itself even more clearly in the bizarre and ambivalent behaviour of the libertines themselves. For what they all have in common, over and above their various, and variously excessive, exotic, or esoteric sexual enthusiasms, is their furious pursuit of the object of pleasure, which they do not merely desire to possess, but must go further and seek to annihilate. As a result, sexual activity in Sade seems inseparable from murder or torture. The writer admittedly justifies this relationship between desire and violence by pointing to nature's own consummate disregard for human life. The fact that the relation with the other is always marked with violence is nevertheless revealing. What it demonstrates, perhaps surprisingly, is the extent to which the radical egoism practised by Sade's protagonists is in fact untenable. For if egoism in Sade only expresses itself, as it must, in the violence it inflicts upon the object it bends to its will, then, even as it wreaks havoc on that object, what it is forced to concede, perhaps unwittingly, is its insurmountable dependence on that object, which is why, from the point of view of Sade's libertines, it is never enough simply to take pleasure in the object, and why it must be negated absolutely—with the ironic proviso that, if the libertine were to succeed in this ambition, there would no longer be an object of desire to enjoy at all. Well might Sade's libertines have echoed the wistful comment of their contemporary, Novalis: "Everywhere we *search* for the absolute [*das Unbedingte*], and *find* only contingency [*Dinge*]."[36]

Sadian violence, in other words, like all negativity, is profoundly ambiguous. It is indicative of both the power of the libertine and the inescapable limits of that power. This is why, strangely but importantly, it is finally illogical on the part of the morally responsible reader to seek to condemn Sadian violence; and why to censor Sade's writing, in the name of this or that cultural value, far from demonstrating upright opposition to Sade's work, is to reveal a secret complicity with it and fulfil its deepest intent. Sadian violence nevertheless speaks volumes. The paradox to which it gives voice, as Blanchot points out, is that of the Master and the Slave in Hegel's *Phenomenology* as reread or, perhaps better, rewritten by Kojève in his celebrated seminar series held at the École Pratique des Hautes Études between 1933 and 1939.[37] For in that Kojèvian fable it is never the Master who has the upper hand, always the Slave. The supremacy or sovereignty of the subject is impossible. Many are the Sadian characters who implicitly concede as much. Witness the ferocious Bandole, for instance, in *La Nouvelle Justine,* whose preferred occupation is to impregnate one by one the women held captive in his harem, only then to drown each of his offspring once the infant reaches the age of eighteen months, and who, to Justine's naive question as to whether he thinks himself capable of being loved for his actions, protests vociferously: "What, me, loved! . . . I would be at my wit's end if it even occurred to a woman to do this: the man who wants delicious enjoyment will never go in search of a woman's heart; to do so would only mean becoming her slave, consequently a most unhappy creature."[38] And so on.

What is true of the world of the Sadian libertine is no doubt also true of Sade's own writing. There, too, the ineliminability of the other is a simultaneous condition both of the work's possibility and of its impossibility. Juliette's maxim about philosophy's obligation to tell all commits Sade's writing to finality, but only with regard to the future. The only immediate prospect is incompletion; and so long as there is a future, it is clear that incompletion cannot be overcome. Sade's totalising ambitions prove only the impossibility of all totalisation. Literature, in other words, in its finality, is a site of infinity. Finitude brings with it the infinite, the indefinite, the interminable. But the limitlessness at stake here is not at all the infinity of the absolute subject as speculated upon by the early Romantics. It was more like the bad infinity of Hegel's *Science of Logic,* that indefinite indeterminacy of repetitive recapitulation that finds expression in the term: *etc, ainsi de suite, und so weiter.* In that sense, Blanchot suggests in *L'Écriture du désastre,* it was testimony to writing's disastrous resistance to the ascensional movement of the dialectic, and confirmation of the fact that, whatever the energy spent in attempting to achieve such goals, the end could never be reached, alterity never eliminated, and Sadian sovereignty never attained.[39] And strangely enough, as commentators have often observed, Sade's own work ultimately concedes as much in its recourse to the figure of the libertine, tempted, like Dolmancé at the end of *La Philosophie dans le boudoir*, not by the evidence of his own supremacy but by the *apathie*, the lack of will, of his own libidinal exhaustion.[40] At the limit of libertine power, then, stands a ravaging lack of power. Sadian sovereignty, being in fact impossible, can only culminate in radical indifference. Oddly, then, pedagogue though he is, Sade does not prescribe what it may be good or bad to do. "No specific behaviour emerges with any privilege," observes Blanchot: "one can choose to do anything; what matters, in doing it, is to make the greatest possible destruction coincide with the greatest possible affirmation."[41]

Sade's reader, then, according to Blanchot, is not being asked to agree or disagree, approve or disapprove. What counts is energy—up to and including, and therefore beyond, that necessary moment when subjective will, in response to the disaster of *apathie*, loses the potency with which it begins, and dissolves into its own absence. The experience is one for jaded libertines, but it is also something shared by all readers, especially readers of Sade. A reader reading cannot *not* affirm the text. Either he or she carries on reading, in which case he or she is carried by the movement of the text up to and therefore already beyond the limit of will and desire; or else she or he turns aside, in which case what is necessarily being affirmed is the superior power or endurance of the text just abandoned.

III

An interregnum

> Affirmation can do without proof, just so long as it claims not to prove anything.
>
> Maurice Blanchot, *L'Écriture du désastre*[42]

But if Sade's writing—and perhaps all literature, if it exists—was the site of what might be called, by oxymoron, a necessary affirmation, what is it, then, that was being affirmed?

The debate is one that, since the early work of Bataille or Blanchot, has remained at the forefront of literary critical reception of Sade. In the 1960s and 1970s much work was done, notably on the part of the literary avant-garde, to develop a theory and practice of literature from the perspective of which Sade might finally, so to speak, become readable. Of the various critics involved in that enterprise, there is little doubt that the most significant and influential, as far as Sade was concerned, was Barthes, who in *Sade, Fourier, Loyola,* published in 1971, and a series of more fleeting developments elsewhere in his work, radically transformed perceptions of the writer as a literary figure.[43] For Barthes too Sade was not just any author, but the writer par excellence, and, in his writing on Sade, Barthes was obviously capitalising on Blanchot's inaugural work.[44] But his thinking developed in a distinctive direction of his own. Unlike Marcelin Pleynet, who, in the attempt to make Sade more accessible, emphasised in the writer the eighteenth-century atheistic materialist and disciple of d'Holbach, or Philippe Sollers, who claimed Sade was best read as a transgressive textual innovator, Barthes adopted a more oblique approach. Tackling Sade at a time of increasingly virulent political confrontation in the France of the mid-1960s and after, Barthes's main priority, as we have seen, was to avoid redoubling the textual violence of Sade's writing by imposing upon it a moralistic, dogmatic, or ideologically motivated discourse of his own. What he sought in Sade's writing instead was to rediscover literary textuality as an object of contestatory and affirmative sensual enjoyment. To do so, Barthes devised the archly countertemporal strategy of reading the Sadian text, not by responding to its violence, but, citing a note passed by Sade while in prison to his wife, according to a principle of *délicatesse:* attentiveness, refinement, perversity. "Once the basis of History changes [*dès lors que les assises de l'Histoire auront changé*]," Barthes argued, in unusually apocalyptic vein, "the *principle of delicacy,* as postulated by Sade, is the only one that can constitute an absolutely new language, an unprecedented upheaval [*mutation inouïe*], whose task will be to subvert (not invert, but rather fragment, pluralise, and pulverise) the very sense of enjoyment [*jouissance*]."[45]

Was it possible, then, after all, to like Sade, and affirm his writing as an object of pleasure?

Barthes's answer was unambiguous: to read Sade with *délicatesse* meant neutralising the violence of Sade's writing in order to affirm a promise of subversive, perverse, but non-aggressive desire. "Never separate behaviour from the way it is depicted, because language [*le verbe*] permeates the act entirely": this, according to Barthes, was what the principle of *délicatesse* demanded of the reader.[46] In the case of Sade, it implied that the devastation, carnage, and suffering represented in Sade's texts be disregarded, or at least viewed from a distance, in such a way that it then became possible to read Sade's writing primarily as a verbal performance, a kind of ritualised movement of language and rhetoric, the key to which lay in its deliberate unfolding of a fantasmatics, necessarily detached from any effective or (as Barthes put it) operative reality. In this perspective, the silence implicit in Sade's text, rather than as a memory of its unspeakable beginning or its unreachable ending, might be interpreted by Barthes as a sign of ascetic sovereignty, as for instance in the following fragment from *Sade, Fourier, Loyola.*

> Aside from the cries of victims, aside from blasphemings, which both form part of the efficiency of the ritual, a profound silence is imposed upon every scene of lewd excess. In the great reception organised by the Société des Amis du Crime, "one could have heard a pin drop." This, however, is the silence of the machinery of pleasure, which is so well-oiled, and runs so smoothly that only a few sighs and shudders are noticeable at all; chiefly, however, just like the sovereign restraint of a great ascetic discipline (like Zen), the creation of a pure acoustic space is testimony to the control of bodies, the mastery of figures, the order of the scene; it is in a word, a heroic, aristocratic value, a *virtue:* "Venus's rapt votaries were unwilling to interrupt their ceremonies with any of those disgusting shrieks that are the custom of pedants and imbeciles"; it is *in order not* to be like the sex "shows" of petty-bourgeois eroticism that the Sadian orgy is silent.[47]

Blanchot no doubt agreed that the Sadian text was indeed entirely written and not translatable into immediate reality. This had been his own starting point. But he was far from persuaded that the silence in Sade's writing might be treated as something extraneous to Sade's

work, the sign of its disdain for petty-bourgeois normality, the negative imprint, so to speak, of the many shocked or scandalised readings that have accompanied it down the centuries. For Blanchot, Sade's
silence was inseparable from its repetitive, infinitely redoubled, seemingly inescapable violence; and what it served to trace and retrace as
a mute limit within the text was the indelible presence of the other.
Between Blanchot and Barthes, on this point, there was a crucial difference, which had largely to do with the status and consequences of their
common, but divergent and perhaps, in the end, incompatible appeal
to the Neuter. The effect of the intervention of the Neuter, for Barthes,
in so far as it implied the principle or figure of *délicatesse,* was to suspend the violence of Sade's writing, but in what might be termed oppositional, adversarial manner. It will be remembered that the Neuter, for
Barthes, while corresponding within the paradigm of meaning to an
absence of position or positionality, was also part of a dialectic, in which
capacity its function, and its finality, in Barthesian terms, was to oppose
the arrogance and violence of discourse itself, from which it then followed for Barthes that Sade's writing might be affirmed primarily as a
kind of rebuttal of moral dogma on behalf of the fantasmatics of a subject of desire. From Blanchot's perspective, however, this was already
to construe the Neuter in too derivative a manner. For Blanchot, the
Neuter was what preceded and exceeded the possibility of the paradigm as such and was irreducible to position or opposition alike. There
could be no question in Blanchot's eyes of determining or arraigning
the Neuter as any kind of adversarial value within a dialectical strategy.
The Neuter, in Blanchot's sense, went much further. As far as reading
Sade was concerned, what it implied was not that what found embodiment in writing was imperious, desirous subjectivity but rather that
what Sade made it possible to affirm was writing as an event traversed
by otherness, an otherness it presupposed but could never reduce, overcome, or assimilate.

For was there not a danger, Blanchot asked, that, in suspending the
brutality of violence, Barthes's principle of delicacy was turning aside
from the necessity of responding to the ineliminability of the other?
Barthes, from Blanchot's perspective, in glossing the principle of *délicatesse,* raises the question of the futurity of Sade's writing, but only to

retreat into a poetics, or a rhetoric, of the fantasmatic, which is perhaps why in the end futurity in Barthes, as the *Fragments d'un discours amoureux* seem to testify, retains an irenical utopian quality which in turn derives from a yearning for untroubled, eudemonistic access to the other, as reflected in the ordered domesticity of the Fourierist *phalanstère*.[48] In this respect, it is not altogether by chance that, in articulating the principle of *délicatesse* as a reading strategy, Barthes chooses to borrow from a wistful, archly fetishistic exchange between the marquis and his wife on the topic of the writer's soiled underwear. And it is revealing too that, in developing his reading of Sade, purposefully and provocatively, Barthes chooses not to read, among numerous others, a characteristically violent remark such as this, taken from *La Nouvelle Justine*, reminding the reader that "delicacy [*délicatesse*] is the illusion [*chimère*] love produces, enjoyment [*jouissance*] its element." And the irrepressible Bandole went on to add, more brutally still: in his view, "all delicate lovers [*tous les amants délicats*] are miserable fuckers [*de pauvres fouteurs*]."[49]

Some ten years after *Sade, Fourier, Loyola*, Blanchot remained unconvinced by the transformation of the Sadian text into an object of pleasure. Indeed, Blanchot's understanding of the Neuter implied a very different response. "To say: I like Sade [*j'aime Sade*]," he wrote in *L'Écriture du désastre*, "is to have no relation to Sade. Sade can be neither liked nor tolerated, what he writes making us turn away absolutely while drawing us towards him absolutely: the drawing towards of a turning away [*attrait du détour*]." And Blanchot goes on, invoking *apathie* again, and drawing a somewhat different lesson from that of Barthes:

> It is however quite true that there is a Sadian form of irony (a power of corrosion); whoever fails to notice this ends up merely reading a banal system builder [*un auteur quelconque à système*]; nothing there that can be deemed serious, or rather his seriousness is seriousness derided, just as *passion* in Sade *passes* through an icy, secret, neutral phase, as apathy [*apathie*], infinite passivity. This is grand irony—not Socratic irony: feigned ignorance—but impropriety to the full (when nothing at all is appropriate any more), dissimulation at the extreme [*la grande dissimulation*] where all is said, said again, and finally silenced.[50]

Any relation to the Sadian text, then, proves problematic. It resists capture as an object—be it an object of contestatory sensual enjoyment. There is an otherness, Blanchot argues, perceptible in Sade's muted irony, silently moving through Sade's work, that outstrips all aestheticism, all possible fetishisation. Otherness, in Sade, is nowhere named. It is, however, everywhere present as an object of violence. For what violence reveals in Sade, by dint of the tireless infinity it induces in the author's writing, is the indestructibility of the other. And however numerous the attempts made to destroy the object, the trace of destruction remains as testimony to the enduring memory—memory without memory in Sade's case—of the act itself. The thought recurs in a number of different contexts in Blanchot's writing in the 1960s, where, in particular, it represents a key moment in his thinking about nihilism. Elsewhere, Blanchot puts it as follows: "Humankind is the indestructible that can be destroyed."[51] In this particular form, the phrase marks Blanchot's response to his reading of Robert Antelme's memoir of imprisonment in a German labour camp in 1944–45, *L'Espèce humaine* (*The Human Race*).[52] To associate Antelme with Blanchot's reading of Sade in this way may appear strange, but it is a measure of Blanchot's obstinate attention to the demand of the other that in reflecting on the consequences of naked egoism in the one, he is drawn to read the implications of a remorseless "egoism without ego" in the other, since what is at stake in both cases, incommensurable and incomparable as these texts are, is this relation without relation with the other.[53]

Blanchot insists that Sadian violence is inescapable. Any reader of Sade, he argues, is interpellated with the abruptness of an enduring silence. This was not to pass judgement on Sade's writing. It was to maintain Sade's text, in its loquacious silence, as an infinite confrontation with the irreducibility of the other that is the hallmark of any affirmative response. Rather than transforming Sade's text into an aesthetic object, this meant traversing Sade's writing, radicalising, accelerating, dissolving it, until the work itself—like Orpheus' image of Eurydice—began to turn on the fulcrum of its own impossibility. This relationship between the Orphic image and its inaccessible shadow is irreducibly dissymmetrical. What it imposes on the reader is a double strategy, which consists in affirming at one and the same time not only the limitlessness of the work, which no authority can restrict without itself becoming implicated in the work and displaced by it, but also the radical silence of the work, in which what finds mute expression is what the work cannot say, but to which, in its endless recapitulation, it is always already an infinite response. In reading Sade, then, what was it necessary to affirm? Absolute freedom, on the one hand; but, on the other, the radical ineliminability of the other. Or, as Blanchot phrased it in 1959, summing up his own critical strategy, in words I have already had occasion to cite: "name the possible, respond to the impossible."

Such doubleness, resisting as it does all dialectical unification, precludes any simplicity of judgement. In the face of a text, no single answer is ever possible. There is no decision without a residue such that it always has the power to revoke that decision, which is also to say that no decision can be taken which is not simultaneously an affirmation of the impossibility of decision. In such circumstances, there is no choice other than to affirm the radical indecision with which, and to which, the text binds its reader. If writing, in order to exist, is bound to be responsive to its own irresponsibility, and reading responsive to the unreadable, so criticism in its turn has to be responsive to that which it cannot judge. To decide, then, is to be responsive to the undecidable: to answer to it and for it.

Indecision, though, is not indecisiveness. For to affirm indecision, even when it is impossible to do otherwise, itself involves a decision, from which it is impossible to withdraw. What is demanded of the reader by a writing such as that of Sade, then, at one and the same time, is that the reader subscribe without reservation to the work, and respond to what lies unspoken in the text. Affirmation here does not mean slavish subservience. The boundless freedom Sade's writing claims for itself belongs also to the reader, and the obligation to tell all does not cease with the work. On the contrary, it means that there can never be any last word, for either work or reader, and that it is necessary, as Blanchot puts it, to continue both endlessly to name the work and endlessly to respond to the unnamable silence that constitutes it as such, but has the capacity to dissolve it. Radical indecision is responsibility not only to the possible, then, but also to the impossible. What it requires of the reader is not only that the reader obey the law of the text but also that the reader obey the law that prescribes that the law, being never enough, should be revoked in favour of the prior law to which it is itself a forever inadequate response.

This much became clear in 1965, when Blanchot returned to Sade's work in order to preface a new edition of the writer's famous brochure of 1795, "Français encore un effort si vous voulez être républicains . . . " ("Citizens of France, Try Harder If You Wish to Be Republicans . . . "), which forms an integral part of *La Philosophie dans le boudoir*, where it functions as a kind of foreign body, present in the text as the object of a redoubled act of reading.[54] In his preface, with some change of emphasis, Blanchot retraced much of the ground covered in "La Raison de Sade" and "La Littérature et le droit à la mort" in 1947. But as the occasion demanded, Blanchot now lingered in greater detail on Sade's radical involvement in the early part of the French Revolution. For Sade's writing, Blanchot argued, belonged to a strange moment in and beyond history, in which literature and politics, though speaking different languages and on occasion obeying opposing interests, nevertheless coincided, as it were, for the duration of a brief interregnum: a moment in time when time was suspended, when one body of law had already been annulled, and another yet to be constituted, and when, as a result, the only law in force was a kind of radical counter-law, a pure interval of silence in which destruction and affirmation spoke as one. Despite appearances, this was not a moment of lawlessness or anarchy, rebellion or disobedience, but one in which the law made its demand felt as an infinite question without answer, a requirement for law never to be satisfied. And this, Blanchot wrote, was the moment on which all else turned:

> What Sade calls a revolutionary regime is that pure moment in time when history, having been suspended, marks an epoch, a time of between-times [*ce temps de l'entre-temps*] when between the old laws and the new reigns the silence of the absence of laws, the interval which precisely corresponds to the gap in speaking [*l'entre-dire*, i.e., both speaking-between and inter-diction] when everything ceases and stops, including the eternal drive to speak [*l'éternelle pulsion parlante*], because, then, there is no longer any prohibition [*interdit*]. This is a moment of excess, dissolution, and energy, during which, as Hegel puts it some years later, being is nothing other than the movement of infinity annulling itself and being ceaselessly born in its very disappearance, in a "bac-

chanal of truth where no one remains sober." This forever impending instant [*cet instant, toujours en instance*] of silent frenzy is
also the moment when man, affirmed in this very cessation, at-
tains his true sovereignty, being no longer merely himself, being
not only nature—natural man—but that which nature never is,
the awareness of the infinite power of destruction—that is, of negation, through which it is unceasingly made and unmade.[55]

The hiatus in history and language that Blanchot addresses here
corresponds to a far-reaching crisis of judgement. For a brief moment,
albeit a moment which compromises the structure and authority of the
law in general, it has become impossible to pass judgement. There are
no established laws to which appeal might be made; and no recognised
authority that might validate or justify decisions. And yet, for each and
every one of these reasons, it has become urgent to decide, if only
because any failure to decide is itself already a decision. The predicament may resemble an impasse. What Blanchot describes, admittedly,
is a state of exception, in all senses of the word. Indeed, just as any constitution is grounded on a preceding act of constitution that itself is
without foundation, as Sade and his contemporaries had observed at
first hand in the aftermath of 1789, so the suspension of law is the hidden basis of any legality whatsoever, and necessarily inhabits all acts of
judgement as such. To this extent, the legal vacuum or juridical void
enacted in Sade's writing is a banal, everyday circumstance.

But it does have its counterpart, if not in everyday political experience, so then in relation to literature. For it is one that is faced continually by all readers of literature, whenever and wherever they read. And
what readers of literature do, in such circumstances, Blanchot argues,
is to respond doubly: in accordance with what is spoken in the work and
what is enigmatically left silent. Which is also to say that any critical response to a literary text is essentially contingent; it cannot not subscribe
to the necessity of chance. This in turn is the reason why, for Blanchot,
in responding to the singularity of any text, there can be no such thing
as a universally applicable literary critical method, since a method, by
definition, implies a regular, systematic, given path in approaching an
object. Literature, for Blanchot, if it exists, is however not an object; and

the only path it follows is a path of nomadic errancy. So if literature is prescription, it is prescription without prescription. What "literature," then, has to say—to criticism, to politics, to itself—is that any critical decision is inseparable from critical indecision, with the essential proviso that it is always necessary to decide, in respect both of the possible and the impossible: both liberty here and now and the infinite demand of the other.

Both requirements were no doubt uppermost in Blanchot's mind when the following year he was invited to contribute to a special issue of the periodical *L'Herne* devoted to the poet Henri Michaux, whom Blanchot had long admired. Earlier issues, in January 1963 and March 1965, in an effort at posthumous rehabilitation, had been devoted to Céline, at the time largely persona non grata in the literary world because of his pre-war and wartime anti-semitic texts and complicity, though still much contested, with the German Occupation. Blanchot's response to the invitation was double. It was to agree to have an earlier essay of his on Michaux reprinted, on condition that the journal add a brief epigraph, taken from an article by Blanchot touching on the relationship between literature and dictatorship, in the course of which he had had occasion to mention Michaux, and append the text of a brief letter addressed to the issue editor, Raymond Bellour. In the letter, Blanchot contented himself with reiterating his unconditional opposition to anti-semitism, even if it took the form, as it no doubt did in Céline, of paranoid delusion. "All anti-semitism is in the last resort a delusion," he wrote, "and anti-semitism, even if it is a delusion, remains *the capital error [la faute capitale]*."[56] While saying this, Blanchot was careful not to impugn Céline's writing as such, except in so far as it had provided a voice for virulent anti-semitism. Instead, it was Michaux's example that was entrusted with the task of criticising Céline's work, which it did indirectly, without implying or invoking positive norms of its own. Blanchot's critical strategy, in other words, was to comment on the political implications of one literary work by citing another comparable, yet incomparable text in whose capacity it was to contest, exceed, and revoke the possibility of the first. Blanchot's epigraph made this abundantly clear; for what the critic chose to celebrate in Michaux were the qualities of a "writer who, at his most faithful to himself, has aligned himself with the foreign voice [*la voix étrangère*]": that is to say, with the other voice, the voice of the other, the voice of the foreigner—which was no arbitrary gesture.[57]

As Blanchot had made plain in 1959, there is no easy separation between literary criticism and politics. The issues at stake in any affirmative account of literature, if it exists, extend far beyond the putative closure of the literary sphere, as Blanchot was aware. Indeed, his preface to Sade's pamphlet, when it first appeared, did so barely two months before the French presidential election. This was not just any presidential election. It was the first to be held under new constitutional arrangements pushed through by de Gaulle and adopted in a popular referendum in 1962, according to which the president of France would henceforth be elected not by an elite group of *notables* or prominent local politicians but by universal suffrage. The device was a populist one, its purpose being to short-circuit the National Assembly and reinforce the personal authority of the president as providential saviour of the nation. De Gaulle's campaign for the presidency was accordingly an aloof affair; it mainly consisted of the head of state reminding the populace, in paternalistic mode, that the choice was simple: it was "moi ou le déluge," the status quo or chaos.[58]

For many on the left, including Blanchot, it was dangerously reminiscent of a return to the politics of the popular plebiscite, long associated in France with the demagogic reactionary right. Even in 1965, Blanchot wrote, the day still belonged to the First Consul, not the Napoléon Bonaparte whom the author of *Justine* and *Juliette* had good reason to fear, but the retired General whom Blanchot had opposed vigorously in 1958 and did so again, in outspoken terms, in May 1968. Sade's words to his fellow citizens, "Citizens of France, Try Harder If You Wish to Be Republicans . . . ," no longer belonged to the past, then, but formulated a response to the present by addressing an injunction to the impending future. All acts of political constitution, by definition, were subject to question. And where Sade had challenged the revolutionaries of 1795, so Blanchot, in the selfsame terms, appealed to the citizens of France of 1965:

> The title of Sade's pamphlet says: it is not enough to live in a republic in order to be a republican; nor to have a constitution in order to live in a republic; nor to have laws in order that the

creative power that is the act of constitution may endure and keep us in a state of permanent constitution. It is necessary to try harder, and always harder still—that is the invisible irony.[59]

But how to try harder?

Introducing his 1965 essay in *La Nouvelle Revue française,* Blanchot made the following point. It was necessary, he said, when reading Sade, to read everything. In itself this was no mean proposition. But Blanchot also went further, responding as though in advance to what Pleynet, among others, would write only three years later. Reading everything, he said, also meant reading what was unreadable. "Whoever reads in Sade only what is readable," he wrote, "has read nothing."[60]

In other words, it was necessary not just to read the work but also that which exceeds the work and, while making the work possible, also belongs to the impossible—necessary not just to gaze upon the Orphic image but also to reach out towards the intangible shadow that silently precedes and accompanies the image.

Or to put it another way, literature, if such exists, necessarily outstrips its own possibilities of reading, and is carried by a secret futurity, promise as well as threat, which is irreducible to the discourse, language, or values of the present. In those circumstances, there can only be one task for what calls itself literary criticism, which is, to the fullest possible extent, and in response to the demand of the impossible, to affirm "literature"—literature without literature—in its imponderable, corrosive refusal of all values and value: past, present, and future.

IV

Last words

Writing, the demand of writing [*l'exigence d'écrire*]: no longer that writing which has always put itself—by a far from unavoidable necessity—in the service of so-called idealist, i.e. moralistic speech or thinking; but instead that writing which, as the force proper to it (the aleatory force of absence) is slowly released, seems to be concerned only with itself—which is without identity—and, little by little, opens up entirely other possibilities:

a nameless, wayward, deferred and dispersed way of being-in-relation [*une façon anonyme, distraite, différée et dispersée d'être en rapport*], by virtue of which everything is put into question, not only the idea of God, the Self [*Moi*], the Subject, but also Truth and Unity [*l'Un*], and the idea of the Book and the Work too, with the result that writing in this instance (understood in its enigmatic rigour), far from having the Book as its ultimate goal, might rather be thought to be signalling its demise, a writing that could therefore be said to be outside discourse and outside language.

Maurice Blanchot, *L'Entretien infini*[61]

But what was there to prevent Blanchot's affirmation of literature without literature from reverting, in spite of itself, to a kind of undeclared or unacknowledged aestheticism?

In other words, in thinking literature in this way, as withdrawal and affirmation, how might it be possible *not* to think it, at the very same time, as some sort of mystified, negative entity that was a source of value or values precisely to the extent it resisted all given forms of representation? In continuing to affirm something called "literature," how might Blanchot avoid the risk (or temptation) of simply providing the institution of literature or criticism with another foundational, legitimising discourse, which, as far as the future was concerned, might turn into an even worse form of obscurantism than the traditional appeal to established values? Was there not a danger that, whatever the claims to the contrary, Blanchot was simply reinventing literature as a kind of latter-day reincarnation of Romantic poetry, dependent on a belief in the idea of art as a self-reflexive process having its sole end in itself and bearing no relation to the outside?

And if this was what Blanchot's thought of "literature" promised or threatened, was it not therefore something to be refused, in the most uncompromising terms, in the name of "literature," in the resolute knowledge that "literature" was precisely what did not admit of any essential or essentialising definition?

These questions were not new ones. They had been implicit in much of Blanchot's post-war critical writing on Mallarmé, Kafka, Proust, Musil, Broch, Beckett, Bataille, and others, and were no doubt the reason for the author's experiments with dialogic or other fragmentary forms in certain of the critical essays collected in *L'Entretien infini* and, in some cases, substantially reworked for the occasion.[62] Since Mallarmé at least, Blanchot reminded readers in a brief preface to the book, generic distinctions between essay and fiction, novel and poetry had become increasingly fragile, and Blanchot in his own writing was searching for ways to exacerbate this still potent crisis. Indeed, to affirm literature's withdrawal from itself demanded nothing less. But this did not mean disregarding differences between texts. On the contrary, it was rather a case of multiplying those differences, at times internalising them, at times externalising them, at any event accentuating the undecidability they bore as both hallmark and signature. The effect, in the essays brought together in *L'Entretien infini,* as the book's title suggested, was to undermine the authority and self-assurance of critical writing as such.

Blanchot's exploration of textual heterogeneity took many forms. Its most striking emblem was the fact that *L'Entretien infini* opened, not only with a prefatory literary-critical note, but also with a preamble, in the form of a fragmentary fictional dialogue or *récit*, initially published in *La Nouvelle Revue française* in March 1966 under the title "L'Entretien infini." This meant that Blanchot's title—*L'Entretien infini* itself—now named two different texts, ostensibly belonging to two distinct genres, the earlier of which, three years after first publication, now found itself framed by a much longer text bearing its name, which accordingly was itself also framed by the shorter text, the *récit* entitled "L'Entretien infini," which now opened the book. That fragmentary *récit* in its turn, reappearing in a book to which it had relinquished its name, now found itself nameless, untitled, somehow illegitimate, fracturing the unity of the volume while serving somehow to gather it together.[63] The theme (or non-theme) of Blanchot's story, which, as we have seen, later so impressed Barthes, was not indifferent to this complicated set-up. For Blanchot's dialogue dealt mainly with the (atopical) topic of fatigue or weariness, the characteristic trait of which, it is suggested, lay in its paradoxical position at the fragile limit between work and worklessness, between exhaustive power and exhausted impotence. But such indeterminacy was not simply a psychological trait affecting Blanchot's two interlocutors. It pointed to a predicament that was inseparable from literary criticism as such. For it is both a consequence and a necessary condition of the authority of decision invested in the critical act that criticism, at some stage, will always be brought to the limit of its powers. As the example without example of Sade indicates, and as Blanchot was more than keenly aware, criticism, in other words, is perpetually haunted by the prospect of exhaustion: by its always impending incompetence.

By 1965, it seems, work on Blanchot's forthcoming volume of essays was largely complete. But the book remained in abeyance, from fatigue and disenchantment, faithful in this respect at least to its working title: "L'Absence de livre [The Absence of the Book]," which it retained until a relatively late stage in the revision process. Admittedly, this mention of the absence of the book—or, rather, one might suggest, the "absent*ing*" of the book, in so far as Blanchot's syntax deliberately neutralises the idea of the absence of any particular book, whether real or imaginary—was not abandoned in the final version of *L'Entretien infini*. Glossed with the double and doubly neuter subtitle: *"le neutre le fragmentaire,"* the expression "L'Absence de livre" served to present, or, better, perhaps, to postpone presenting, the third and final section of the book, containing essays mainly devoted to so-called literary texts, by Rimbaud, Artaud, Char, Jules Supervielle, Beckett, Thomas Mann, Kafka, Brecht, and André Breton. Prefacing the penultimate essay in the collection, first published in April 1967, shortly after Breton's death, Blanchot took care to make the point that what mattered in Surrealism, notwithstanding the movement's reluctant but unavoidable concessions to literary culture, was not its past achievement but "the future question [*la question d'avenir*: the futural question] evoked in its endless ending [*cette fin infinie*],"[64]—which was to make plain that, if literature or writing had a future in Blanchot's view, it did not consist in any rediscovered past or deferred present, and was not to be thought as a realisation of the Book (whether poem, political protocol, or philosophical programme), but as an interruption that escaped conceptualisation.

Placing his remarks on "literature" for "'safekeeping,'"as he put it, under the rubric of this "absent*ing*" of the book, withdrawing *"literature"* [*sic*] from "literature" as that which defies or disappoints identification, disperses unity, and persists in the absence of any subject, Blanchot brought his own volume almost to an end.[65] As he did so, it was not without evoking *in fine*, implicitly and as though in passing, a series of events that in every sense were destined to remain outside the covers of any book, and which, when they did arrive, as both promise (to some) and threat (to others), a year or so before *L'Entretien infini* was eventually published, did so to the astonishment of many—albeit perhaps less so of the author of "L'Absence de livre," who could legitimately claim they were in accordance with the thoughts that had concerned him during much of the preceding decade.

Those events were the events of May 1968.[66]

The ramifications of the Paris *événements*, as far as Blanchot was concerned, were considerable. Some measure of their impact on the writer's thinking may be gauged from the prefatory note in *L'Entretien infini*, which concludes by associating literature not only with the radical change of epoch which Blanchot had begun to address in his work as early as April 1960, but, more specifically, with "the ultimate affirmation" that was communism: communism, Blanchot put it, that (in much the same way that "literature" was irreducible to literature) was "always and forever beyond communism."[67] This was no pious statement of belief. Blanchot quickly realised the implications of May for his own quasi-institutional position as a resident contributor to France's still most prestigious literary monthly, *La Nouvelle Revue française*, a position that, by summer 1968, he had filled for some fifteen years. But in October that year, at the age of sixty-one, Blanchot brought to an end his involvement with the journal, invoking in a letter to Dominique Aury, the editorial secretary and a long-standing friend, his commitment to the movement that had emerged from May, with which, at that time, he was entirely in agreement and in which his responsibility was fully engaged. At the height of the May events, Blanchot put it more strongly than most: faced with de Gaulle's repressive, paternalist presidency, it was incumbent on all writers, he wrote, as between 1940 and 1944, to resist, with all possible means. "We can never be too aware," he argued in *Comité*, "of the fact that we are part of a society with which we are in a state of war; we are living under occupation."[68] No compromise was possible; and in the circumstances, he explained to his correspondent, it made little sense for him to enjoy the generous editorial impartiality that had long characterised the liberal ethos of *La Nouvelle Revue française*.[69]

It is true that Blanchot did contribute to the journal in the years that followed, but only on a very occasional basis, in response to the death of friends who had been associated with the magazine: Jean Paulhan, Brice Parain, André Dalmas; and in 1980 lengthy prepublication extracts from *L'Écriture du désastre* appeared there too. A decisive step had nevertheless been taken; and Blanchot's relationship with the institution of literary criticism was significantly changed. To an extent, this was already apparent in the period leading up to May. Perhaps by design, or by pure serendipity, Blanchot's last regular piece for the journal, which appeared in the issue dated May 1968, already evoked a kind of ultimate finality. Devoted to Kafka's letters to Felice, the review carried the title: "Le Tout Dernier Mot [The Very Last Word]." This was no haphazard choice. Blanchot's formula resonated with several earlier texts, each of which had marked an historical, philosophical, and personal turning point, where also what had been at issue was precisely the relationship between writing and events. First, Blanchot's 1968 essay reprised the title of one of his own earliest narrative fictions, the story "Le Dernier Mot [The Last Word]," published in 1952, but written, the reader is told, in 1936, that fateful year of the remilitarisation of the Rhineland which, as Blanchot the contemporary political commentator had forcefully argued in what was virtually his own last word on the matter, already marked the beginnings of what would soon turn into World War II. The words "Le Tout Dernier Mot" also no doubt contained an allusion to his *récit* of 1957, *Le Dernier Homme* (*The Last Man*), which had itself been much exercised by the debate on nihilism, the end(s) of man, and the demands of the present.[70] More explicitly still, the May 1968 article referred the reader to a previous essay on Kafka's correspondence ("Le Dernier Mot de Kafka [Kafka's Last Word]"), published ten years earlier in *La Nouvelle Revue française*, in February and March 1959, around the same time as Blanchot's response on contemporary criticism in *Arguments*, and only three months or so after his return to active politics, which he had announced, to any who might be listening, in a fiercely uncompromising polemic entitled "Le Refus [Refusal]" in the second issue of Dionys Mascolo and Jean Schuster's anti-Gaullist broadsheet, *Le 14 Juillet*.[71]

Might it be said that, on each of these occasions, writing—literature as well as criticism—found itself overtaken by events, events that belonged to history but also largely exceeded it, to which writing could respond only by interrupting itself in similarly abrupt fashion?

Blanchot's title of May 1968 was also, however, ironic. Indeed, when the writer came to republish "Le Tout Dernier Mot" in *L'Amitié* three years later, he no doubt purposely placed it in penultimate position, followed only, printed entirely in italics, by a very different kind of text, the writer's obituary homage to Bataille from 1962. Only death, it seemed, might properly have the absolutely last word; but, then again, there was nothing proper about death, and it was not by chance that Blanchot's own closing word in *L'Amitié* was *"l'oubli* [forgetting]," this event without event whose fate, outside of time, history, or meaning, was to endure forever. By thus concluding while not concluding the volume, the essay on Kafka and Felice served only to confirm what was already implicit in the possibility of its writing. For what it necessarily announced, by dint of its mere existence, seemingly in spite of itself, was that writing could never have any last word. Language, Blanchot argued, was itself necessarily without end, having neither term nor purpose. And it was this that was essentially at stake in the May 1968 essay, concerned as it was with the spectral return of ever fresh pieces of epistolary or biographical evidence in the Kafka saga. Had Kafka ever achieved the finality to which he seemed to aspire? Had it in the end ever been possible for him to write—that is, to die—a free man? Blanchot's answer was unambiguous: reaching the end, Kafka discovered there was no end. Already, in the end, writes Blanchot, "timelessness [*l'éternité*] was beginning: the posthumous purgatory [*l'enfer posthume*], the sarcasm of glory, the admiring but presumptuous exegeses, the great confinement of culture [*le grand renfermement de la culture*] and, in these pages too, once again this last word which offers itself only in order to simulate and dissimulate the waiting for the very last."[72]

As the closing of this (nearly) closing essay took leave of a certain kind of discourse on literature, this did not however mean that writing, even a certain kind of critical writing, had somehow reached its end. That end had always been impending from the outset; and it was not without already conceding the rightly wrong quality of the project of criticism itself that, in 1943, Blanchot had given his very first collection of essays the title *Faux Pas,* a turn of phrase that was explained in the insert accompanying the book as an admission that it was criticism itself that constituted a false move, albeit one that, by that very detour, might somehow reach its proper-improper destination.[73] But if what criticism only ever promised or threatened was the prospect of a standing still or loss of direction, it followed, paradoxically, that words neither could nor should be resisted. They might lead to an unintended or unexpected place; but this was also proof that words offered a chance, and that, whatever its exhaustion, criticism might still be able dimly to perceive, in the gloaming, in the shadowy twilight world of the in-between, "between day and night [*zwischen Tag und Nacht*]," as Hölderlin calls it, in lines Blanchot used for the epigraph in *La Part du feu*, something, possibly a truth, the poet suggested (though Blanchot was less sure), which will never be revealed as such—yet for that reason nevertheless persists in order that it may be affirmed: as perpetual deferral, epochal suspension, endless futurity.[74]

What this also implied, of course, was that, even when the last word had been uttered, the very last still had to be spoken. Exhaustion in itself was not enough; it had to be enacted repeatedly, again and again. Which was to say that the requirement, provisionally at least, to write in response to something called "literature" or, at the very least, to something that, traversing literature, was somehow synonymous with it while remaining irreducible to it—that requirement still remained.

V

Very last words

> The day of judgement in German: *der Jüngste Tag*, the youngest day, the day beyond days; not that judgement is reserved for the end of time; on the contrary, justice does not wait, it is at every moment to be fulfilled, carried out, pondered too (and learnt); each act of justice (do they exist?) makes this day into the last day or, as Kafka calls it, the very last day, which no longer belongs to the ordinary sequence of days but turns the most ordinary of ordinaries into something out of the ordinary. Whoever lived at the time of the death-camps is forever a survivor: and will not know death in dying.
>
> Maurice Blanchot, *L'Écriture du désastre*[75]

The injunction, while remaining, had however become more enigmatic than ever. Not least because, if a response to writing by a reader was still required, it was in the double sense of the reader, or critic, being necessary to the work *and* indebted to it.

Blanchot's discreet resignation from *La Nouvelle Revue française* in autumn 1968 marked a turning point. After that date, his explicit literary critical output was less regular, less prolific, less constant. The writer's voice became more fragile, more oblique, more personal, at times even overtly autobiographical. As Blanchot's health began to fail, he concentrated (or dissipated) his efforts on his two late fragmentary works, *Le Pas au-delà* and *L'Écriture du désastre,* in which literary critical concerns were admittedly far from absent, but where they played an increasingly elliptical and allusive part. The desire or need to write about so-called literary texts nevertheless lingered on; and during the years that followed, in a range of sometimes short-lived periodicals to which he was linked by bonds of friendship (such as *L'Éphémère, La Revue de Belles-Lettres,* or *Le Nouveau Commerce*), or in various special issues of journals devoted to authors to whom he owed particular allegiance (*L'Arc, Digraphe, Critique*), Blanchot continued to pay his dues to literary criticism, returning, so to speak, among others, to Bataille, Beckett, Celan, Des Forêts, Duras, Jabès, Leslie Kaplan, Klossowski, Vadim Kozovoï, Roger Laporte, Bernard Noël, Valéry.

May 1968 had not however been alone in evoking the promise or threat of epochal upheaval. It was a characteristic shared by all the key historical or political events Blanchot was wont to recall in the years that followed, not least, he argued, because they each challenged the explanatory competence of received modes of intelligibility. They belonged to history, but marked an interval in history; they were, he wrote, "greater than their meaning [*plus grands que leur signification*]."[76] Such events, in Blanchot's own recent times, he remarked, were essentially three. There was the struggle against de Gaulle's return to power, which then gave way to the campaign of resistance against the Algerian War. And there was May 1968. But also, marking an absolute caesura in the history of the West, continued Blanchot, there was the event of the Shoah, to which the writer, like others of his generation, began to give increasingly explicit attention in the period after 1968, even to the point that responsibility not to forget the Shoah demanded, as Blanchot saw it, that he withdraw his support from those erstwhile political allies who, in the early 1970s, in solidarity with the Palestinians, argued for the dissolution of the state of Israel, a step that Blanchot, for his part, refused outright.[77]

Such events as these were not part of any series, except to the extent that they were each turning points: singular, inexhaustible, and incommensurable. What they had in common, then, also radically separated them. In other words, each in its own way brought literature—meaning, narrative, value—to the brink of collapse, to a limit where its future survival or even possibility seemed in jeopardy.

This was not just because of the radical historical, political, or human implications of these events. Also at stake were the limitations of art as such. For were there not, Blanchot asked, writing in the margins of Hermann Langbein's account of the artistic and other activities that somehow went on in Auschwitz (concerts, film shows, football and boxing matches), experiences of such extreme distress or affliction in the face of which art, in so far as it implied pleasure and enjoyment, was little short of an affront?[78] Did it not follow, the writer added, glossing his own pre-war stories "L'Idylle [The Idyll]" and "Le Dernier Mot [The Last Word]" in *Après coup* (*Vicious Circles*), that, "at whatever the date they may be written," by dint of the "narrating voice [*voix narrative*]" they presupposed, all narratives belonged henceforth to a time "before Auschwitz"?[79]

In such circumstances, how to affirm even "literature" at all?

Perhaps, Blanchot implied, only by effacing it, by pursuing it, so to speak, beyond the limit of its possibility, to that point where it ceases to be art or culture at all, in any case no longer gives rise to works or monuments, and where, as in dying itself, the power to affirm or deny gave way to something more akin to the neutrality of silence. "Dying," says a fragment from *Le Pas au-delà*, "might be what, on each occasion, in that place where we speak, holds us back from affirmation, self-affirmation, or denial. We can hear it: we think we can hear it, but it is mute, even the hiss of anguish [*le bruissement de l'angoisse*] stops."[80]

But how, then, to listen to "literature," to honour it in its distress, to measure up to its silence?

The question is one Blanchot ponders at length in a number of late essays. He does so perhaps most explicitly in a tribute to Paul Celan that appeared in a memorial issue of *La Revue de Belles-Lettres* published two years after the poet's presumed suicide, his death by drowning during the night of 19–20 April 1970 not far from the Pont Mirabeau in Paris, once celebrated in verse by Apollinaire. Entitled "Le Dernier à parler [The Last to Speak]," and explicitly evoking the theme or *topos* of the end without end of language touched on in the May 1968 article, Blanchot's contribution frames its encounter with Celan's poems by offering two quotations. The first, at the start of the essay, is taken from the closing lines of Celan's "Aschenglorie [Ash-aureole]," which Blanchot sets alongside a famous remark from Plato's *Apology of Socrates,* and comments as follows:

> Plato: *For of death, no-one has knowledge,* and Paul Celan: *No-one bears witness for the witness.* And yet, always, we choose for ourselves a companion: not for our own sake, but for the sake of something within us, without us, that requires us to be absent from ourselves [*que nous manquions à nous-mêmes*] for us to cross the line we will not reach. A companion lost [*perdu*] from the outset, whose loss [*perte*] henceforth takes our place.
>
> Where to seek the witness [*le témoin*] for whom there is no witness [*pour lequel il n'est pas de témoin*]?[81]

Some twelve pages later, Blanchot concludes his reading with another quotation, also from Celan, the longest in the essay, which comprises many such quotations, from the poem "Sprich auch du [Speak You Too]," which Blanchot reproduces *in extenso,* together with his own parallel translation, the opening lines of which supply the title—both entitlement and heading—for this obituary essay. "Sprich auch du, / sprich als letzter, / sag deinen Spruch," Celan's poem begins, and Blanchot translates as follows: "Parle, toi aussi, / parle le dernier à parler, / dis ton dire."[82] In giving prominence to the poem, but which, for essential reasons, he refrained from subjecting to metalinguistic analysis, preferring to dramatise its challenge to the reader, Blanchot was not alone. In acknowledging it as an explicitly abyssal, poetological statement, he was most likely following Beda Allemann, who some four years earlier, in his editor's afterword to an anthology of Celan's poetry, had presented the poem as a defence on Celan's part of the poetic decision to affirm poetic *indecision*.[83]

These quotations, almost all given in the original German, with Blanchot's own French translation alongside, describe or inscribe a critical trajectory. Blanchot begins, using Celan's words, by posing an unanswerable question; he ends, however, again using Celan's words, by prescribing the necessity of a response. Countersigning Celan's sober but intractable positioning of the poem, what Blanchot identifies as the very crux of the critical relationship is a double bind, one that each reader or critic is constrained to confront, here and now, without delay, in a manner that is incumbent on no other, from which it is therefore impossible to withdraw, which the reader or critic has no alternative but to affirm, and which turns precisely on the demand voiced in Celan's poem and underwritten by Blanchot as the prior condition of his own text, which is the requirement that the critic respond, in words, to the words in the poem, that the critic, in other words, in responding to the poem, therefore bear witness to that for which there is no witness—which is the poem itself.

But how to speak of an event, of this event of the poem, of which I know nothing? How to address that which was never present to me? How to speak as last, when I know this to be impossible? How to read that which, by chance and by necessity, is destined to remain unreadable, but which it is nevertheless necessary to read?

While asking such questions, Blanchot, for obvious reasons, sought *not* to answer them, but rather to prolong them, to make them resonate in his own writing as in that of Celan.

He did so, first, not as any kind of judge or arbiter of poetic prowess. But, more discreetly, as occasion demanded, as a mourner. Reading Blanchot's opening paragraph, it is impossible not to be reminded of the writer's testimony upon the death of Bataille, written ten years earlier, and republished in autumn 1971, some months before "Le Dernier à parler." There too, following his tribute to Kafka's "very last word," Blanchot acknowledged "there is no witness [*il n'y a pas de témoin*]."[84] And he continued, apropos of this death of a friend: "Everything we say tends only to obscure this one affirmation: that everything is bound to be erased [*que tout doit s'effacer*] and that we can remain loyal only by keeping watch over this movement of erasure [*qu'en veillant sur ce mouvement qui s'efface*], to which something in us that refuses all memory already belongs."[85]

But Blanchot does more than simply attend to the necessary rituals of mourning, which are dependent on an ambition to overcome death by erecting a monument to the absent, and achieve what, with revealing incongruity, is sometimes known as closure. "We will not escape the melancholy of Minerva's owl, which Hegel was the first to experience, and which he subsequently overcame [*dont il a fait son deuil*, which he grieved over, then relinquished]," admits Blanchot, as he reflects on Des Forêts's *Poèmes de Samuel Wood* in an essay written some seventeen years later, only to ask immediately after: "But is mourning even possible?"[86] Blanchot's scepticism concerning the dialectic of mourning functions here as a necessary interruption. For what is at stake in Blanchot's necessarily inadequate and incomplete response to Celan's death is not the gesture of mourning as such; it is rather the attempt to be-in-relation with the event—event without event—of dying, which is also to say: the dying without dying—the *mourir*, as Blanchot terms it—of a singular voice, in this case a singular voice in or of poetry.[87] What occurs, is given voice, or speaks, in "Le Dernier à parler," in this place without place of the commentator's absence from himself, is not a reader's critical assessment of Celan's poetic achievement but rather Celan's poetry itself, not as funereal monument, but infinite inscription—cited, recited, underwritten, overwritten, and translated at length, in its exteriority and dispersion, its readability and unreadability, its clarity and secrecy, its articulation and fragmentation. "Gras, auseinandergeschrieben," "Grass, written asunder," wrote Celan in the poem "Engführung [Stretto]." Blanchot concurred, and wrote out the two words again at the start of his own text.[88]

On this singular occasion of Celan's dying—criticism too, Blanchot implies, is always a response to a singular occasion, an anniversary or a death, if not simply an event of reading—what counts, then, for Blanchot is not the finality of mourning but rather the eschatological futurity of poetry, placed alongside the poet's strangely unaccountable suicide: poetry's capacity or, better, its obligation (which, in the absence of any power inhabiting poetry or duty governing it, cannot in fact be thought either as capacity or as obligation, and could quite easily be described as the opposite of both) to speak of the end, at the end, and in accord with the end, which is also to say its "capacity" or "obligation" (again Blanchot invites us to read these terms as though under erasure) endlessly to defer the end. Which is where poetry, like death, like criticism, encounters its impossibility.

All the more pressing, then, perhaps, is the question Blanchot raises: how to speak as last? But the question admits of no answer; it too is grounded in impossibility. There are no methods, strategies, recipes, or formulas that are adequate to Celan's poems or Celan's dying. All responses are equally bereft of authority, legitimacy, decisiveness.

In which case the question changes. As the poem "Sprich auch du" suggests, it becomes necessary to ask not: how? but: who? To which the answer might be: anyone and everyone, but to which, here, now, in reality, the answer can only be: "me"—"me," that is, yet not "me," insofar as "I" could be anyone, rather anyone, therefore, insofar as anyone is "me," "me" as other than me, myself as an unnamed, nameless, substitute for myself. And what speaks here, affirmed only by way of the relation without relation with Celan's poem, though subsequently deployed at length in *L'Écriture du désastre,* is Blanchot's version of that strange structure of irreducible singularity and expropriating anonymity prior to cognition, volition, or choice, which Levinas in *Autrement qu'être* (*Otherwise than Being*) terms substitution, prefacing his discussion with a verse from Celan, from the poem "Lob der Ferne [Praise of Distance]," which enigmatically asserts: "Ich bin du, wenn ich ich bin [I am you whenever I am I]"[89]—which Levinas goes on to gloss in the following terms: "*My* substitution—it is in so far as it is *mine* that substitution for the next person occurs. Spirit is a multiplicity of individuals. It is in *me*—in me and not another, in me and not in an individuation of the concept Me—that communication opens. It is I who am integrally or absolutely Me, and the absolute is my affair. No one can substitute themselves for me, who substitute myself for all [*Personne ne peut se substituer à moi qui me substitue à tous*]."[90]

Who, then, is last to speak?

Blanchot's response is complex, oblique, and susceptible to several different readings. First, in so far as he is writing as both retrospective commentator and posthumous mourner, it is apparent that the last to speak, on this occasion, is none other than Blanchot himself. No doubt the very discretion adopted by the writer is evidence of the responsibility that falls to him as a survivor, just as it did after Bataille's death, not forgetting the numerous others that Blanchot was later to mourn in public and in private: Paulhan, Foucault, Antelme, Mascolo, Duras, Laporte, Des Forêts, others far less well known. The fact too that Blanchot himself is able to frame his reading of Celan by citing—and translating—two otherwise disconnected passages from the poet's work is indicative of his place as one who has the chance to speak after the event, but also, of course, has no alternative but to do so. Blanchot's belatedness, however, is also uncannily and uncontrollably reversible. For while his tribute to Celan may appear to frame Celan's poems, it is also forcibly framed by them; and as Blanchot ghosts the words of this poet, thirteen years his junior, who has inexplicably predeceased him, it is no longer entirely clear who is speaking: is it Blanchot, is it Celan? Blanchot's tribute, in this sense, belongs more to Celan than it does to Blanchot, and it would not be excessive, perhaps, to read it as little more than an appropriately discreet, modest, tactful, even inconclusive response to the injunction expressed in the title of Celan's poem, with which Blanchot concludes his contribution. "Speak You Too," says Celan to Blanchot, after the event, and Blanchot replies, as he must, by allowing the dead to speak. Last to speak, then, closing Blanchot's discourse, is none other than Celan himself.

Blanchot cites, summons, appeals to Celan; but Celan also cites, summons, appeals to Blanchot. Demanding Blanchot speak, and speaking in the critic's own words as well as between them, in French translation and in German, Celan's poem calls, eerily, from beyond the grave.[91] Blanchot's essay turns again, and it now appears that last to speak, in fact, is neither the critic nor the poet, but the poem itself. It is even as though the poem had somehow always already anticipated this shadowy encounter, for that of which it speaks is none other than the shadowy figure of the shadow, populating with its spectral presence or absence that uncertain interval between midnight, noontime, and midnight, offering a semblance of meaning, but at the same time withdrawing it. For this is how Celan's poem continues: "Sprich — / Doch scheide das Nein nicht vom Ja. / Gib deinem Spruch auch den Sinn: / gib ihm den Schatten. // Gib ihm Schatten genug / gib ihm so viel, / als du um dich verteilt weisst zwischen / Mittnacht und Mittag und Mittnacht." Which Blanchot faithfully-unfaithfully, albeit accurately enough, transposes into his own words as follows: "Parle — / Cependant ne sépare pas du Oui le Non. / Donne à ta parole aussi le sens: / lui donnant l'ombre. // Donne-lui assez d'ombre, / donne-lui autant d'ombre / qu'autour de toi tu en sais répandue entre / Minuit Midi Minuit."[92] And there is additional poignancy too to this evocation of poetic spectrality as it proliferates and suddenly shrinks upon itself. For even as Celan's poem, impossibly, bears witness to Blanchot as future reader, who in his turn is called upon, impossibly, to bear witness to the poem, so it is apparent in retrospect that the poem also somehow bears witness to the forever impending instant of Celan's still future death from drowning. For "Sprich auch du" concludes—and this is perhaps another reason why Blanchot gives it prominence—with an uncannily prophetic, eschatological reference to a star, perhaps an image of the poem and the redemption it no more than promises, seeing its reflection shimmering in the water, floating, says the poem, also referring to its own very last, dying words, "in der Dünung / wandernder Worte," "dans le mouvement de houle / des mots qui toujours vont," writes Blanchot: "in the swell / of wandering words." And as these words die away, it is apparent that the last to speak is no longer simply Blanchot, or Celan, or even Celan's poem. It is also the reader of the poem, and the reader of Blanchot's essay: that is, this reader, and the forever future other reader reading—or not—these lines, but in any case required by the writing of the poem.

The future may be past, then, as it is in death, but the past belongs to the future. Whoever has the last word never has the last word. The only truth—but, by that token, no longer a truth at all—is errancy. Blanchot knew this, of course, and, as though to pay further tribute to Celan's wandering words, he extended the circle of literary, critical allusions at play in his essay for the 1984 book version and subsequent editions. This he did, unusually, by dedicating the essay not at the beginning but in closing, that is, at the very end, to the poet Henri Michaux. Again, there was an occasion, a time for mourning, since Michaux himself died on the morning of 19 October 1984, a date that Blanchot discreetly memorialised by inscribing it in the *achevé d'imprimer*, that mention of the day it went to press that, by convention, like an official signature, usually appears as a tailpiece in French printed books. When it reached bookshops some weeks later, then, Blanchot's slim volume bore as a further mark of election or distress its memory of this other poet who, it will be remembered, had, in Blanchot's words, "aligned himself with the foreign voice [*la voix étrangère*]."[93] The connection with Celan was not an arbitrary one. For a collected edition of Michaux's work in 1966, Celan had translated into German some thirty or so poems taken from Michaux's *Qui je fus, Mes propriétés,* and *La Nuit remue,* and had also given a poem in homage to Michaux to the special issue of the *Cahiers de L'Herne* published that same year, to which Blanchot also contributed, in circumstances described earlier. During this period too, in 1963 and 1967, Michaux had done what he could to assist Celan in receiving the medical and psychiatric treatment he needed.[94] In turn, Blanchot's dedication did more than simply name Michaux, it credited him, as Blanchot puts it, with "invisibly hold[ing] out a hand in order to guide us towards another form of invisibility."[95] And Blanchot's parting words also cited the ending of Michaux's obituary tribute to Celan that appeared alongside Blanchot's own in *La Revue de Belles-Lettres* in 1972. This too evoked the manner of Celan's dying, while also affirming, as Michaux does elsewhere, the perpetual need for poetry or the poet to go, to wander, to leave, to depart: "Depart. / In any case depart. / The long knife of the watery deep will put a stop to speaking [*Partir. / De toute façon partir. / Le long couteau du flot de l'eau arrêtera la parole*]."[96]

But while he lingers on the relationship between writing and death, Blanchot's purpose is not to rediscover in poetry any aspiration to timeless aesthetic value. Something else is at stake in his words. More simply and more radically, by appealing to Celan (and to Michaux) as a witness to the invisible, the errant, and the non-manifest, the endeavour was to emphasise the vulnerability of the poem's relation with what Blanchot, here as elsewhere, calls the outside, *le dehors.* This insistence on poetry's exteriority to itself, its withdrawal of and from art, literature, or any other self-identical concept of aesthetic functioning, is a compelling indication of Blanchot's rejection of aestheticising or self-reflexive closure; but it should be remembered too that the outside in Blanchot is nothing self-identical, whether as presence or absence; for it comes to writing rather in the manner of a fleeting, yet irresistible interruption, and as a chance that, in so far as it is both promise and threat, is irreducible to anything graspable as such.

This relation or non-relation with the outside at any event provides Blanchot with the main thread of his reading of Celan. But while the critic studiously explores the motif of vision, of the eye, or the look in Celan's work, supplying no fewer than fourteen separate apposite examples, it is not at all, like some latter-day phenomenologist, in order to describe the material consciousness of the poet's experience and ground Celan's work within the realm of the visible. On the contrary, it is to insist on the wandering movement of Celan's writing as it appeals to the outside as lying beyond the immediacy of the visible, natural world, and to underline in Celan the complex motif of the withdrawal or absence of world. "Augen, weltblind, im Sterbegeklüft [Eyes, worldblind, in the fissure of dying]," Blanchot reads in the poem "Schneebett [Snow-bed]," and attentively translates Celan's words into an idiom recognisably his own: "Yeux, aveugles au monde, dans la suite des fissures du mourir."[97] The outside, here, is not an exteriorisation of a poetic project constantly striving to refind itself within the same perceptual parameters.[98] It is more the promise of an encounter with the resistance of things—words as well as objects—in their elemental, preworldly materiality (Blanchot cites recurrent references to stone, chalk, lime, gravel, and crystal in Celan), and with the irreducibility of others, who appear in their silent strangeness ("the *I* is not alone," says Blanchot, quoting from the poem "Schneebett," "it turns into *we,* and this falling of the one with the other joins together what is falling, even into the present tense").[99] "*Wir sind Fremde,*" "we are foreigners," writes Celan in "Sprachgitter [Speech-Grille]," and Blanchot replies: "foreigners, yes, but both of us foreigners, having still to bear in common this distraction of distance [*cet égarement de la distance*] which holds us absolutely apart [*nous tient absolument à l'écart*]. *We are foreigners.* Just as, if there is silence, two silences fill our mouths: *zwei/Mundvoll Schweigen.*" And he adds: "Let us remember this, if we can: *a double mouthful of silence.*"[100]

"But the poem *speaks!* [*Aber das Gedicht spricht ja!:* i.e., the poem indeed speaks, or, more literally, the poem speaks yes, i.e., affirms]," Celan famously declared in "Der Meridian," his speech accepting the Georg Büchner Prize in Darmstadt in 1960, thereby affirming poetic affirmation itself.[101] But it does so "only ever in its own singular cause [*in seiner eigenen, allereigensten Sache*]."[102] As a "singable remainder [*Singbarer Rest*]," it survives, lives on.[103] Not however as anything static, standing, or stationary, as a positing, positioning, or placing: only on the edge of itself, with a "strong tendency to silence [*eine starke Neigung zum Verstummen*],"[104] as a movement of departure, "lonely and underway [*einsam und unterwegs*]." This is what was entailed by writing in German, this language of oppression, Celan suggests in his earlier 1958 Bremen address: writing as "event, movement, journey [*Ereignis, Bewegung, Unterwegssein*]" ("événement, mouvement, cheminement," translates Blanchot, discreetly eliding, with a warning nod to Heidegger, the question of "Being" implicit, if only grammatically, in the expression *Unterwegssein*), as the "attempt to gain direction [*der Versuch, Richtung zu gewinnen*]."[105] For "whoever writes [the poem], stays bound to it [*bleibt ihm mitgegeben*]." "And just exactly so," adds Celan, "doesn't the poem stand, here and now, in the encounter—*in the mystery of the encounter?*"[106] Writing, reading—writing reading, reading writing—is to encounter another. "The poem," Celan tells his Darmstadt audience, "reaches out to an Other [*will zu einem Andern*], it needs this Other, it needs a Counterpart [*ein Gegenüber*]. It seeks it out, speaks towards it." "Each thing [*jedes Ding*], each person [*jeder Mensch*], to the poem that heads towards the Other [*das auf das Andere zuhält*], is a form of this Other [*eine Gestalt dieses Anderen*]."[107]

If the poem, then, is relation with the outside or with the other, as Celan provocatively puts it, echoing as he does so Blanchot's own formulation on the exteriority of writing to culture, so powerfully reaffirmed in May 1968, it is because poetry [*Dichtung*] is not art [*Kunst*].[108] Just like Lucile in Büchner's play *Dantons Tod* (*Danton's Death*)— perversely declaring allegiance to the King at the very moment when the heads of Danton and others, including that of her husband, Camille, are falling on the guillotine (Lucile, on the very last page of the play, according to Büchner's stage direction, stands "musing, and as though making a decision," at which point she exclaims "suddenly: 'Long live the King!'")—so poetry [*Dichtung*] does not confirm (or conform to) the world's current or present values; it decides otherwise, and stands aside, treating language, says Celan, as "something personal and perceptible [*etwas Personhaftes und Wahrnehmbares*]," interjecting a counter-word (*ein Gegenwort*) that interrupts and disrupts prevailing discourse.[109] In Büchner's play, Lucile's words are also her very last, in both senses: she speaks no more in the play and, carried off at the end by the revolutionary guards, pays for her verbal indiscretions with her death on the scaffold. But Lucile's intervention, Celan insists, embodied in these words that will be her very last, is "an act of freedom," "a step [*ein Schritt*]."[110] But this is not because of the ideological content of what she says; indeed, Celan observes that the language to which Lucile's parting shaft belongs cannot be taken for granted. Is she serious, or distracted? Full of herself, or overcome with grief? Does she really intend to profess belated support for the French monarch, or is she just being contrary? In the end, Celan suggests, do her words not rather pay homage "to the majesty of the absurd that testifies to the presence of the human [*der für die Gegenwart des Menschlichen zeugenden Majestät des Absurden*]"?[111] In which case, rather than to her state of mind, gender identity, or ideological convictions, it is to the relationship between language and the outside that we should turn our attention in order to grasp—without grasping—the complex import of Lucile's words.

Lucile's counter-word, affirms Celan, having no stable content or self-identity, has to do, not with art, *Kunst*, which implies recognition, but with poetry, *Dichtung*, which erases art. Poetry is not a statement of what is or may be thought to be the case, but an appeal to the other, to another, in the name of something other. The argument is one Celan himself associates with the poetic thinking of Mallarmé, which is also to say, in 1960, though this is nowhere explicit, with the work of Blanchot too, with whose writings on Mallarmé Celan, living in Paris at the time, must surely have been familiar. At any event, in Darmstadt this was Celan's question: "May we, as happens in many places nowadays, proceed from art [*Kunst*] as from something prescribed and always already to be presupposed [*als von einem Vorgegebenen und unbedingt Vorauszusetzenden*], should we, to put it concretely, before all else—let's say—be thinking Mallarmé to the logical end?"[112]

As Blanchot and Celan both realise, poetry, writing, is not an object to be grasped by a subject. It is not a thing to be evaluated critically, according to established norms, conventions, rules, or parameters. It is rather a turning and a turning point, a caesura, a disjunction, an interruption; what Celan, untranslatably, describes as "eine Atemwende," a change of breathing, a rhythmic turn, a reversal, or change of identity, which inscribes another way of being-in-relation thinkable only in terms of infinite finitude, the limitlessness of the limit: mortality, freedom, the abyss below and above.[113]

Condensing, perhaps, these many thoughts (and others) into one, Celan on 22 October 1960 put before his audience for the Büchner Prize a dense, elliptical, and enigmatic formula that asks to be set alongside Lucile's very last word as Celan's own poetic counter-word. This is what it said: "Die Dichtung, meine Damen und Herren—: diese Unendlichsprechung von lauter Sterblichkeit und Umsonst!"[114]

Many attempts have been made to render these words effectively into either French or English. The difficulties are formidable. They have to do not only with Celan's choice of words, but also the syntax, tone, rhythm of the sentence, if indeed it is a sentence at all. Is the courteous but overstated address to the audience ironically modest or modestly ironical? Is it designed to mock the poet, poetry, the audience, or all three? If the intention is to chide, criticise, or provoke, to whom and to what end are these remarks directed? There are other difficulties of interpretation too. Is the first part of the compound noun *Unendlichsprechung* to be construed adverbally, and the coinage taken to mean "endlessly-speaking," referring to a kind of interminable speaking, unable to reach any conclusion, and without hope or prospect of transcendence, as some translators have concluded? Or should it not rather be understood adjectivally, as others have proposed, that is, as an "endless-speaking," a "making-endless-through-speaking" which, by infinitising *Dichtung*, releases it from the burden of finite temporality, conferring upon it a transcendence that a moment ago seemed unthinkable? Or are perhaps both meanings simultaneously in play, in which case what is to be made of a relation to the infinite that is at once both limited and limitless, constrained and unrestrained, interminable and boundless, and what is to be done likewise with a transcendence that is simultaneously posited and negated, affirmed and denied, adumbrated only then to be neutralised? Along similar lines, is the word *lauter* to be understood adverbally, meaning: merely, nothing but . . . , with dismissive connotations, or adjectivally, meaning: pure or honest, with overtones of unalloyed simplicity? Finally, what inflection to give to the substantivised adverb, *Umsonst*, which also can be read positively, meaning: free of charge, or negatively, meaning: in vain, to no avail?

Translation is admittedly never simple. Often—and this is arguably the case here—it is brought to a point of impossibility by the idiomatic complexity, singularity, or idiosyncrasy of the source text. But this prospect of failure, as Derrida convincingly shows with respect to both Joyce and Benjamin, is not an external threat against which writing could or should be protected.[115] For if the multiplicity of tongues is what makes translation possible, by supplying that which demands to be translated, so, in the absence of any single universal tongue, it is what makes translation impossible too. "[W]hat remains *untranslatable* [*intraduisible*: i.e., impossible to render in any other single language]," observes Derrida, in words that themselves defy translation, "is at bottom the only thing there is to *translate*, the only thing *translatable* [*traductible*: i.e., which demands to be translated]. The to-be-translated [*l'à-traduire*] of that which is translatable [*du traductible*] can only be the untranslatable [*l'intraduisible*]."[116] If translation always implies a series of difficult, at times irresolvable dilemmas, then, this is because, from the outset, it takes place as a kind of unavoidable exposure to the undecidability of the future, with the result, as practising translators are all keenly aware, that it is often hard to tell the difference between translation's failures and its successes, or for translators to agree what these are.

How to explicate Celan's words? How to render the poetic counter-word put forward in Darmstadt into a language other than that of its writing? How to translate the untranslatable?

Some proof of the sheer difficulty of translating Celan's words adequately (and of their implicit challenge to the criterion of adequacy itself) is that there exist in print no fewer than six different attempts to render the phrase into French, and at least three into English, and no doubt many others too merely awaiting their opportunity. In a discussion of Celan's poetics from 1986, Philippe Lacoue-Labarthe lists some of the solutions proposed by translators into French. First among these was André Du Bouchet, a celebrated poet in his own right (some of whose works Celan was responsible for translating into German in 1967 and 1968), who also in 1967 suggested the following: "La poésie —: conversion en infini de la mortalité pure et la lettre morte! [Poetry —: a conversion into the infinite of pure mortality and the dead letter!]." Next, in 1979, more prosaically but perhaps more accurately, Jean Launay, another eminent translator, settled for the following: "La poésie,

Mesdames et Messieurs —: ces paroles à l'infini où il n'est question que du mortel et de l'inutile [Poetry, ladies and gentlemen —: these words reaching into the infinite and dealing only with the mortal and the useless]." To which Lacoue-Labarthe, some years later, with some trepidation, as he freely admits, adds a version of his own, which runs: "La poésie, Mesdames et Messieurs — : ce parler à l'infini de la mortalité pure et de l'en vain [Poetry, ladies and gentlemen —: this speaking into the infinite of pure mortality and the in vain]." To which in turn can be added a second attempt by Jean Launay, who in 2002 thought again as follows: "La poésie, Mesdames et Messieurs, —: cette parole qui recueille l'infini là où n'arrivent que du mortel et du pour rien [Poetry, ladies and gentlemen, —: this speaking that gathers up the infinite where there occur only something mortal and for nothing]."[117]

The efforts of Celan's English translators are no less diverse. Rosmarie Waldrop, for instance, cited by Joseph Simas, proposes the following: "Poetry, ladies and gentlemen: what an eternalization of nothing but mortality, and in vain," while John Felstiner opts for the more sober rendering: "Poetry, ladies and gentlemen —: this speaking endlessly of mere mortality and uselessness." Other possibilities of course exist; let me, for my part, *substitution oblige*, suggest: "Poetry, ladies and gentlemen — this speaking infinitely of pure finitude for no purpose!"

Naturally enough, all these versions have both their merits and their shortcomings, over which, since that is the nature of translation, translators will argue, some preferring one wording to another, others another, and so on. There is however one, or even two, further attempts at Celan's gnomic dictum that I have so far left aside. They are in French, and are Blanchot's own. In some respects, they are the simplest and yet most daring of all. The first is proposed by Blanchot towards the end of "Le Dernier à parler," shortly after a celebrated passage from Celan's 1958 Bremen address which Blanchot also cites in a translation of his own. In that passage, Celan explains how the event of poetry (*Ereignis,* says Celan; *événement,* translates Blanchot) enabled his "own" language, German, this language recently become the vehicle of "murderous speech [*totbringende Rede, parole meurtrière*]," somehow to survive the memory of the Event of the Shoah [*Geschehen,* according to Celan; *Événement,* Blanchot writes again, this time with a capital letter], which it did, eerily enough, "enriched" as a result (already in quotation marks, already remembering a more threatening meaning of *Reich* in German, Celan's word is: *"angereichert"*; Blanchot, literally enough, suggests: *"enrichie"*). Poetry, then, for Celan, is inseparable from the future, and from the vulnerability inseparable from exposure to the future. However much it is threatened by politics, by history, and by the fate of language, it still seems to promise a kind of spectral survival, divorced however from all triumphalism or monumentality. Blanchot plainly endorses this view; but by rendering both *Ereignis* and *Geschehen* in Celan's text as *événement* (albeit with a shift in capitalisation), he powerfully reaffirms the historical or linguistic irony at stake. "The reason is," Blanchot writes, "a poem . . . allows us to read, allows us to live [*nous donne à lire, nous donne à vivre*]." And it is here that he adduces his own version of Celan's counter-word, which runs as follows: "La poésie, Mesdames et Messieurs: cette parole d'infini, parole de la mort vaine et du seul Rien." Which Charlotte Mandell, adding another twist to this seemingly endless spiral, in her version of "The Last to Speak," translates as: "Poetry, Ladies and Gentlemen: that speech of the infinite, speech of hollow death and of Nothing alone," while Ann Smock, for her part, in her translation of *L'Écriture du désastre*, where the quotation from Celan reappears, ever so slightly amended by Blanchot, now reading: "La poésie, Mesdames, Messieurs: une parole d'infini, parole de la mort vaine et du seul Rien," finally or not so finally opts for: "Poetry: ladies and gentlemen: an expression of infinitude, an expression of vain death and of mere Nothing."[118]

Blanchot's translation from Celan invites, I think, three remarks.

The first concerns the relationship between speaking and the infinite evoked in highly elliptical fashion by the compound noun *Unendlichsprechung*, which, as mentioned earlier, is one major source of difficulty.[119] For what is most striking about Blanchot's proposed translation is the extent to which, unlike virtually all other versions cited, it refuses to decide as to the exact nature of that relationship. True, Blanchot's phrase *parole d'infini* does indicate relationship, but it does so in the weakest manner possible in French, with the result that the relationship is left largely indeterminate. It is even hard to say which of the two terms has grammatical priority: does "speaking" govern the "infinite" or the "infinite" govern "speaking"? It is also impossible to tell—this is already the case in Celan—whether the infinite, in Blanchot's wording, is best characterised as positive or as negative, as boundless perfection or as limitless imperfection, and whether it corresponds to what Hegel describes as "good" or "bad" infinity. Much the same concerted hesitation is visible in the decision to translate *lauter Sterblichkeit* as *la mort vaine*. Here too mortality is marked neither affirmatively or negatively. Is death a limit to be welcomed or to be lamented? Why is death in vain? Is it because death makes a mockery of human endeavour? Or because death itself is a mockery? In other words, is it because death is the only ultimate possibility, or because death itself is ultimately impossible? Readers of Blanchot will know that this is no arbitrary dilemma. For its part, Blanchot's translation refuses to decide, which is to say that these two versions of death, while remaining irreducible to one another, are also inseparable. Which is to imply in turn, on Blanchot's part, shared with Celan, a deep suspicion not only of transcendent values and transcendence in general, since death conquers all, but of the transcendence of death in particular, since death, failing to provide access even to itself, is thus emptied of any identity, propriety or impropriety, and positive or negative meaning.

The third step (*Schritt, pas*) in Blanchot's translation is perhaps less easily defendable. For there seems little warrant for his translation of *Umsonst* as "(parole) du seul Rien," "(expression) of mere Nothing": either for the transposition of vanity into nothingness or for the capitalisation of Nothing. True, with the expression *la mort vaine* Blanchot had already merged the idea of mortality contained in Celan's *Sterblichkeit* and the pointlessness or lack of purpose implied by *Umsonst*, with the result that for this final element in Celan's three-stage definition, which Blanchot is bound to retain if only for rhetorical reasons, the critic has little option other than to paraphrase what has gone before, which he does by reiterating and reaffirming the lack of transcendence already given in the phrase *la mort vaine*. Blanchot's syntax also has an important role in reorienting Celan's formula. For the use of the expression *cette parole d'infini*, which in turn forces Blanchot to repeat the word *parole*, this time in apposition with the first, in the phrase: *parole de la mort vaine*, implies that "vain death" and "mere Nothing," being placed on the same syntactic plane as the "infinite," are synonymous with it. And the converse is also true: it is the infinite or indefinite of *parole d'infini* that serves to explicate death's vanity and the mere Nothing.

Blanchot's translation, like each and every other version of Celan's phrase, is naturally enough already an interpretation. It is an intervention which embodies or enacts a decision.[120] Remarkably, though, what it decides is a refusal to decide, it decides *not* to decide. It reserves judgement. Not for later, but here and now. In rewording or rephrasing Celan, it seems Blanchot's overriding concern as translator is at the very least to maintain, even perhaps to accentuate the hesitation in Celan's words, and one of the salient features of the version proposed by Blanchot is the extent to which it carefully eschews the connotations of negativity customarily associated with such themes as endlessness, mortality, and lack of purpose, in order to emphasise instead the reciprocity of the finite and the infinite and thus affirm, as the groundless ground of all poetry, the infinite finitude—the neutrality—of language. Poetry knows no bounds other than those of language itself, to which it is bound without being bound. It disappoints transcendence and immanence alike, suspending or neutralising the hierarchical opposition between them in the name of the neuter, both unsurmountable weakness and unmasterable strength, and irreducible either to the one or to the other.[121] Rather than an aspiration to the complete, the closed, the monumental, it inscribes itself instead as wandering motion, as a stepping out, a step (not) beyond perhaps, which inscribes as it effaces, effaces as it inscribes—which is why, in reading and translating Celan's poetic counter-word about poetry, what Blanchot seeks most of all is to insist how far it is itself already a modest example of what it professes, a self-effacing trace, whose possibility as an assertion of what poetry "is" is inseparable from its own semantic and syntactic undecidability. (And it is worth emphasising that Celan, like Blanchot, is careful to elide any attribution of existence to poetry: "I am speaking," he says later, "about a poem that does not exist! [*das es nicht gibt*].")[122] That to which Blanchot's translation proves most responsive, then, is the complex manner in which Celan's formula, in affirming poetry, also withdraws it, and vice versa.

Blanchot, however, is also at pains not to take excessive liberties with Celan. While deferring judgement, Blanchot seeks justice for the text, for its idiomatic singularity, its resistance to interpretative authority, and its refusal to conform. To seek justice is not to rush to judgement, or be judgemental. On the contrary, it is to be attentive to the very last. Justice in this sense knows only its own weakness, which it is obliged to affirm. And here, faced with this singular case that is a fragment of speech or of a poem, justice can only occur in the form of a response to the prescription, already contained in Blanchot's citation from the poem "Sprich auch du," by which the reader—that is, this reader, here and now, since there is no other—was and is enjoined, in negative, but all the more indeterminate manner, as the poem puts it, not to "split off No from Yes [*scheide das Nein nicht vom Ja*]."

Acting on this injunction, in his reading, in his writing about that reading, what Blanchot does in "Le Dernier à parler," and by the writing of that essay, is to affirm or reaffirm the formula given by the poem. To the extent that he is necessarily bound, as a reader of the poem, by the boundless indeterminacy of what the poem prescribes, and prescribes by virtue of being read by the singular reader that he is, Blanchot has no alternative, so long as he reads the poem, other than to subscribe without reserve to the poem's radical indecision regarding both poetry in general and itself in particular. As a result, in so far as it continues through reading to hold itself and its reader in relation, a relation that is necessarily without relation, since the poem itself can only take place as what it "is," or "is" not, by simultaneously suspending all normative relationality, the poem ceases to be an object of possible positive or negative evaluation. Assuredly, Blanchot affirms Celan, in the same way that he seeks to be just towards Celan, without it being at all given in advance what either gesture might mean, or even how the writer might choose *not* to do either, except in so far as affirmation here, like the requirement of justice, is a kind of silent and ineluctable subscription, a being-made-hostage (in the sense these words have for Levinas) to the otherness of Celan's writing, a passivity (as Blanchot phrases it in *L'Écriture du désastre*) which, being neither passive nor active, is logically prior to affirmation or negation, and exceeds all established principle or statute.

In translating Celan and displaced in his reading by the poet's text, Blanchot necessarily displaces that text in turn. In other words, Blanchot takes Celan's epigram away from itself, away from its own language (whatever this language is thought to be), towards somewhere else, which may not even be a place at all. This movement is inescapable. But Blanchot in his writing exacerbates it, with little if any restraint. It is one of the reasons why "Le Dernier à parler" takes on the appearance of a reader's notebook, full of quotations and fragmentary or even tangential remarks, and why at times the essay also has the air of an interlinear translation, with every fragment of Celan's poems being given at least twice, once in German and once in French, with the poet's words filling the margins of Blanchot's commentary and interrupting its discursive continuity in the same way that Celan's poems are themselves dismembered and dispersed and left, by and large, with no indication of their provenance in the course of Blanchot's text. Caesuras, separations, disjunctions proliferate, as they already do in Celan's poems. New, unexpected constellations appear and disappear. "Yes," says Blanchot, "even when nothingness [*le rien*] rules, when separation does its work [*fait son œuvre*], relationality [*le rapport*], though interrupted, is not ruptured [*n'est pas rompu*]."[123] But this explosion of the poem ("*Il n'est d'explosion qu'un livre* [*There is no explosion except a book*]," writes Blanchot, citing Mallarmé, several times over in *L'Écriture du désastre*) is no act of critical force or authority; it is rather a kind of radical weakness, the very space to which Celan's poems appeal, the outside of an endless questioning that nowhere finds shelter and nowhere seeks to take root. "When we speak with things in this way," says the poet, referring to the poem's address to the here and now, "we are always dealing with the question of their Whence and Whither: with a question 'staying open,' 'coming to no end,' pointing into the open and void and free [*bei einer 'offenbleibenden,' 'zu keinem Ende kommenden,' ins Offene und Leere und Freie weisenden Frage*]—we are far outside [*weit draußen*]."[124]

The poem speaks, then, says Celan, to the outside, to the future, to singularity, to the other. To read, in return, Blanchot implies, can only be to respond to that injunction, in exactly those terms.

Celan's remark, then, becomes a site of infinite finitude. Each text, each poem, each fragment of writing marks a limit, but does so infinitely and indefinitely. This is another reason why writing for Blanchot obeys the same double logic as death or dying. And it comes as no surprise, then, that in *L'Écriture du désastre* the commentary which Blanchot provides on the quotation from Celan, of which he is now, so to speak, jointly an author, is concerned with the double vanity of death. Indeed, in explicating Celan's words, he provides an implicit, retrospective justification for his own translation, its decision to opt for a grammatically flattened ternary rendition of Celan's phrase, where what is precisely at stake for Blanchot is the relation of non-relation between its component elements. "Let me recall," Blanchot explains, "that [Celan] places together, in a relationship of enigmatic juxtaposition, speaking infinitude [*la parole l'infini*] and speaking vain death [*la parole la mort vaine*]—the latter reiterated by Nothing [*le Rien*] as decisive term [*terminaison décisive*]: the final nothing which is nevertheless on the same level (without preceding or succeeding it) as the speaking [*la parole*] which comes from the infinite, in which the infinite is given and resounds infinitely." Blanchot goes on, "[S]peaking infinitude [*parole d'infini*], speaking nothing [*parole de rien*]: do these go together? Together, yet without agreement, without agreement but without discord, for there is speaking on both sides [*parole de l'un et de l'autre*], which implies that there would not be poetic speaking if infinite understanding [*l'entente infinie*] did not give itself to be heard as the strictly determined resonance of death in its emptiness, in a proximity of absence that might be thought to be the essential trait of *giving all* [*de tout donner*]." And he adds, "I am led to suppose the following. Pronouncements such as 'God is dead,' 'man is dead,' by the presumptuous nature of the assertion they endeavour to make, which is that 'being dead' is a possibility that belongs to God and belongs to man, are perhaps merely the hallmark of a language that is still too powerful, in some sense sovereign, which falls short of speaking without riches, in vain, in the absence of memory, in weakness and indigence—in the dying of its breath, these *the only marks of poetry*. (But can one say the 'only' ones? In the attempt to exclude all else, the expression fails poverty, which cannot defend itself, and is bound to die away in its turn.)"[125]

Glossing Celan's text further, Blanchot comes to renounce the assertiveness of affirmation. Not because affirming a text is a sign of weakness, and is somehow not assertive enough, but because it is too assertive, that is to say, not weak enough, and therefore not affirmative enough of the poverty that inhabits the poem as a fading or dying away. Affirming the poem here gives way to a withdrawal of affirmation, to the radical poverty that is affirmation without affirmation, affirmation before affirmation: an affirmation, that is, that affirms nothing. The weakness of affirmation that Blanchot invokes here is not an assertion of weakness, a form of quiescence or acquiescence. On the contrary, as it refuses it affirms, as it affirms it refuses, withdraws the poem from literature's claim over it. To this extent, Blanchot's reading of Celan is barely a critical discourse on poetry at all, any more than Celan's speech in Darmstadt was a critical treatise on art. It was at most an invocation addressed to the singular voice of a late poet, a shade or spectre. "Wahr spricht, wer Schatten spricht," wrote Celan. "Dit vrai, qui parle d'ombre," translates Blanchot. "Speaks true who speaks shadow."[126]

Shadows are by nature fleeting and ungraspable; they belong not to the present but to an impossible past, one that is forever bound to return. And no sooner is an attempt made to speak to them than they retreat, are withdrawn, efface themselves. In this, shadows no doubt announce death: this death that is an always possible occurrence, yet will never be in my power as an event and will thus never occur to *me;* this death, then, this dying, that, like my shadow, is mine alone, yet is impossible, and forever bears witness to another, and speaks of another.

Writing too, for Blanchot, is an empty event, which is why it appeals, in the last, to radical absence, including the absence of absence itself. For what beckons in every shadow is also the promise or threat of return, a kind of futurity that, in its very inaccessibility, is the most obstinate hope yet encountered—of the futurity of an encounter.

As may be witnessed, in speech or in silence, or in a poem perhaps. Or in the critical act that, exhausted yet inexhaustible, shadows the poem from afar.

VI

An enigmatic proposition

> The dying [*le mourir*] of a book in all books is the appeal [*l'appel*] to which it is necessary to respond: not only by reflecting upon the circumstances of an epoch, the crisis it prefigures, the upheavals to which it testifies, great things, small things, even if they demand everything of us (as Hölderlin was already suggesting, ready to throw his pen under the table in order to devote himself entirely to the Revolution). To respond, however, also concerns time, a *different* time [*un autre temps*: an *other* time], a different mode of temporality that no longer leaves us quietly to be our

own contemporaries. And responding is necessarily silent, without presumption, always already intercepted, and deprived of all propriety and self-sufficiency: tacit in that it can only ever be the echo of words of explosion [*d'une parole d'explosion*]. Perhaps I should cite this still unprecedented warning, these enlivening words of a poet very close by: "Listen, lend your ears: even far in the distance [*même très à l'écart*], books we have loved, essential books, have begun to breathe their last [*râler*]" (René Char).

Maurice Blanchot, *L'Écriture du désastre*[127]

But if it falls to the critic, in his or her reading, and in her or his writing of that reading, to accompany a text in this way, it is not in order to reveal the text to itself. It is to respond to an event that is of the order of an encounter: unexpected, incalculable, enigmatic.

So it was, in spring 1983, to his own surprise and without quite knowing what to expect, as the writer freely admits, that, for the first time in nearly fifteen years, Blanchot responded—to a puzzling, violent sixty-page work by Marguerite Duras, half-way between prose narrative and playscript, with at least a partial basis in the author's autobiography, provocatively entitled: *La Maladie de la mort* (*The Malady of Death*).[128] And if Blanchot, in reading the text, was encountering Duras's work again, as though for the first time, and with some uncertainty, so the story, in not dissimilar fashion, likewise sought to address itself to an implausible and impossible encounter, also involving a man and a woman, separated by almost everything, and occupying no common space, who nevertheless come together: not in spite of their radical differences, but precisely because of them. But this abyssal, transferential doubling of Duras's already transferential text was not all. For this literary, yet anything but literary encounter also implied and perhaps secretly evoked a further, political dimension, which Blanchot countersigned, for his part, albeit obliquely, by framing his discussion of Duras's story with an account of the Paris *événements* of May 1968, in the course of which, as history records, Blanchot and Duras, in friendship, alongside numerous others, found themselves acting in common, as writers, in the struggle against injustice and paternalistic oppression.[129]

Yet if Blanchot's encounter with Duras somehow repeated, while displacing and transforming it, the encounter between Duras's two protagonists, and if this encounter in turn repeated what had been at stake in May 1968 for Blanchot, it was not because literature, love, sexual difference, and politics might therefore be presented to each other, and made the object of a single, homogeneous, mutually transparent critical discourse. On the contrary, it was because the relationship between them was impossible to delimit by recourse to any overarching legislative or juridical order. This in turn, Blanchot emphasised in his opening remarks, served only to reaffirm the enigmatic proposition performed and described by Duras's text. It was in any event a reminder to the reader that the place in which *La Maladie de la mort* occurred, as Duras's notes regarding a possible stage version suggest, had no inside and no outside. But if nothing was mediated, everything was somehow there: present, that is, not as something final or finite but according to a kind of disastrous imminence.

In the retrospective evocation of the events of May 1968 with which he begins his essay, Blanchot highlighted two recurrent motifs. The first had to do with what Blanchot termed explosive communication, the virtue of which was precisely that it took place with the "suddenness of a happy encounter," and allowed "each, without distinction of class, age, sex, or culture, to meet up with just anybody [*frayer avec le premier venu*, literally, to rub up against the first corner, the contingent, singular other], as if they were already loved, precisely because they were strange-familiar."[130] This openness or ease of access to others was no standard revolutionary utopianism. It was testimony to the exceptional character of the May *événements*, which belonged in this respect, for Blanchot, less to politics as such, understood as a desire to acquire and maintain power in society, than to a momentary, impermanent, but no less radical suspension in politics, where what was set aside was precisely the quest for power. May, Blanchot insists, was not about achieving a new political order but about discovering and affirming, in the uncalculating effervescence of the moment, a different way of speaking the political in so far as it referred to relations with others and the other in general, what, translating and radically reframing Heideggerian *Mitsein*, Blanchot called *being-together:*

Unlike "traditional revolutions," the point was not to take power in order simply to put another in its place, nor to storm the Bastille, Winter Palace, Élysée, or National Assembly, all objectives without significance, nor even to overthrow an old world, but to allow to become manifest, outside of all utilitarian self-interest, a possibility of *being-together* [*être-ensemble*] that restored to all the right to equality in fraternity by virtue of *the freedom to speak* [*la liberté de parole*] that inspired them. Everyone had something to say, and, at times, to write (on the walls); what exactly, was not important. Saying took precedence over the said [*Le Dire primait le dit*].[131]

As Blanchot goes on to stress, not without recalling his observations about the writings of Sade, in which, earlier, he had seen played out not only the politics of the French Revolution but also the ferment of protest following de Gaulle's return to power, May was an event that knew no bounds. It was an absolute, immeasurable occurrence rather than any delimited, contingent happening, an event that was perhaps also therefore more like a non-event, a simultaneous affirmation and erasure, that, like other experiences of the limit, was no sooner there than it had disappeared, its presence eclipsed, already returned to a past that had already gone and a future still to come. It was therefore void of the necessary militancy of an assault on power by a recognisable, already constituted subject of historical action, like the bourgeoisie, the nation, or proletariat of old. It was this, writes Blanchot, that was the profound singularity of the *événements:* if the People [*le Peuple*], as Blanchot rather oddly calls the collective student-worker-intellectual protagonists of the *événements,* was forcefully in evidence in what was an important moment in French post-war history, it was paradoxically not as a subject, nor as an agent of history, nor as a group bent on achieving power: it was as the fleeting trace of a possibility of interruption, which it was essential to affirm not in its gathering but its dispersion, before the temptation of power turned into something other than what it was.[132]

At first sight, there seems little common measure between the joyful ebullience and solidarity of the May *événements* and the grim desperation and isolation of *La Maladie de la mort*. Indeed, mirroring France's own several times repeated evolution from hope to disenchantment between 1968 and 1983, the distance between them could not be more vast. As Blanchot concedes, they were separated by a gulf, an abyss, and though his discussion of Duras's story was framed by memories of the *événements,* it was plain that between the two there was no visible relationship of continuity. The point was not to treat sexual desire as an outpost of politics, nor politics as a culmination of sexual desire, and Blanchot's purpose was not to bring together Marx and Freud in a bold new synthesis, as numerous others, in the wake of the *événements,* attempted to do. But this was not all. For in the abyss separating the *contestataires* of May from Duras's ill-matched lovers, what might be seen nevertheless to be shared by both was the dim, yet binding conviction that the authority exerted over them by the horizon of conventional expectations was fragile and tenuous, and that the world to which they belonged was in retreat from established meaning: world without world, presence without present, time without time. Just as May inscribed an interval in the politics of the state, so sexual difference, desire, love, in Duras's story, installed an interruption in which the possibility of narrative, sexual relations, even love, was put in jeopardy. The events of May and the relationship without relationship between Duras's lovers belonged to the time of an interregnum. The one was a silent gesture towards the other.

That which in writing appeals to politics, and vice versa, according to Blanchot, is not that which asserts ideological or other kinds of value; it is that which is without authority, without identity, consequently without power. And if writing suspends power, it is not because the aesthetic in itself is external to the political or to power, which would simply be a return to *l'art pour l'art,* but because writing, for Blanchot, as it was for Celan, always being inscribed within a particular, shifting conjuncture or context, and having no identity of its own, and thus always exposed to the otherness of the other, does not fall under the jurisdiction of any established aesthetic, political, or aesthetico-political order. Writing, for Blanchot, is by essence disobedient, contestatory, and subject to no authority, including its own. Its effect is also its non-effect, and its appeal is to the outside; it creates a gap, an interval, an interruption, a spacing. What it opens, however, is not a space of anarchy, in the sense of rebellion against the law, nor is it a space of lawlessness, in the sense of a radical absence of law. It is rather that what the interruption of the law exposes, for Blanchot, is the law of interruption, that which, as it unfolds, must also of course interrupt itself, in a movement of infinite referral, deferral, and retrocession, without origin or term, simultaneously inscribing and effacing itself, like that figure (without figure) of the law before the law, or counter-law, uncovered by Derrida in his reading of Kafka's "Vor dem Gesetz [Before the Law]."[133] And this law, from which it is not possible to withdraw, and which it is impossible to overcome, does not impose identity, but errancy, implies not the positionality of the same but its constant displacement as other than it is. It affirms itself, therefore, perpetually, without negativity, as contestation: as a shattering of all semblance of unity, an uprooting of all forms of aesthetico-political grounding, an address to the uncertain, impoverished many and not to the privileged, established few.

Was it still possible, in these circumstances, Blanchot was asked in 1981, to believe in commitment in literature, in that *littérature engagée*, under the banner of which, in the post-war years and since, Sartre and others hoped to defend progressive human or humanist values? The title of Blanchot's response, in the form of both prescription and description, was brief. It announced: "Refuser l'ordre établi [Refuse the established order]." And the writer explained:

> There is perhaps such a thing as the power of culture [*un pouvoir culturel*], but it is ambiguous and always runs the risk, in losing this ambiguity, of placing itself in the service of another power which enslaves it. Writing is, at the limit, that which cannot be done [*ce qui ne se peut pas:* that which is impossible], which is therefore always in search of a non-power [*un non-pouvoir*], refusing mastery, order, most of all established order, preferring silence to any speaking of absolute truth [*une parole d'absolue vérité*], thus contesting and contesting without cease.[134]

And Blanchot went on to cite a rather unexpected example of committed literature, the biblical story of Exodus:

> There we have everything: the journey out of slavery, the wandering in the wilderness, the wait for writing, that is, the legislative writing which one always fails, so that the only tablets received are broken ones, that cannot possibly constitute a complete an-

swer, except in their fracture [*brisure:* both breakage and articulation] or fragmentation even; finally, the necessity of dying without completing the work, without reaching the Promised Land which as such is inaccessible, yet always hoped for and, thereby, always given. If in the Passover ceremony it is traditional to reserve a cup of wine for whoever will precede and announce the messianic advent of the world of the just, one can understand why the vocation of the (committed) writer is not to see himself in the role of prophet or messiah, but to keep the place of the one to come [*de celui qui viendra*], to preserve that empty place against all usurpers, and to maintain the immemorial memory that reminds us we were all slaves once, and that, though we may be free, we remain and will remain slaves so long as others remain so, that there is therefore (to put it too simply) freedom only for others [*pour autrui*] and through others [*par autrui*]: a task which is admittedly an infinite one, and risks condemning the writer to a didactic, pedagogical role and thereby excluding him from the demand he bears within himself and which constrains him to have no place, no name, no role and no identity, that is, to be never yet a writer.[135]

Writing, then, says Blanchot, was not something that could unproblematically be made to serve a political or moral cause, however desirable or worthwhile, yet neither was it something that had its aesthetic end in itself—not because writing might be defined in opposition to politics, morality, or aesthetics, but because, on Blanchot's submission, its only characteristic was its essential non-essentiality, its non-coincidence with itself, its exteriority to itself, all of which implied that writing was hardly anything at all, and was assuredly *not* something. The law of interruption that, in its very anonymity, was synonymous with writing, commanding it without commanding, was in this respect absolutely crucial. For it testified to the fact that the poverty or weakness of writing, its impossibility of measuring up to the power of the world or in the world—this was also the source of its secret strength: strength without strength, force without force, power without power. And this was the burden, or, better, the chance, that the law of interruption imposed: prior to all subjective constitution or choice, came the resistance of the fragmentary, the necessity of incompletion and, by that token, the irreducible and ineliminable futurity of writing's appeal to the other, whose place could never be appropriated, and would always remain empty, as a sign both of hope and of the never-to-be-satisfied demand for justice.

This address to the future was necessarily double in status too, both singular and universal. It spoke not just to the unknown other who might come, but to every other first comer too, including everyone and no-one who might be the other, whose duty it was to be the other, and who, in a sense, by that very token, already was the other, without ever having a relationship of identity with the other.[136] Politics, morality, literature, these categories and names, for Blanchot, were secondary ones; and there were situations, as Hölderlin had testified in a letter to his brother on New Year's Day 1799, to which Blanchot refers in *L'Écriture du désastre,* when poetry, literature, even politics, not because of any overriding commitment to ideological, aesthetic, or other values, but by virtue of the law of interruption itself, was obliged to renounce itself in order to respond to the urgencies of the moment. Justice for the other was not a contingent object of charity as far as Blanchot was concerned. The law of interruption required it. Like writing, however, justice could not be made present to itself as such. Each had to confront its undecided and undecidable futurity. What this meant, in turn, importantly, was that indecision was not helpless paralysis but corresponded rather to an obligation to intercede or intervene, which Blanchot did increasingly in the early 1980s in order to affirm the law of interruption, which was also the law of the neuter, and to reiterate the aesthetico-political lessons of that "humanity freed from myth" that Blanchot, following Levinas, found inscribed in Judaism.[137]

The universal, then, not as totalising nature or origin, but as the necessary counterpart of the multiplicity of the singular. Here was the nub of Blanchot's disagreement with Lyotard who, responding in 1983 in the negative to appeals for help from the crisis-ridden Mitterrand presidency, famously announced the happy news, at least as far as he was concerned, of the demise of the classic intellectual whose authority and legitimacy had resided in the capacity to speak, as Lyotard put it, on behalf of the "universal victim-subject" of history, whose fate had been at stake in so many of the twentieth century's political struggles or crises.[138] But those times were over, according to Lyotard; the postmodern condition no longer allowed an appeal to universal values that was not tarnished with the spectre of totalisation and totalitarianism. Replying to Lyotard, Blanchot, however, demurred.[139] Not necessarily because he thought the opposite, but rather because he was exercised by a very different idea of universality, derived not from a teleological Hegelo-Marxian conception of history but based instead, in sober, minimalist fashion, on "the simple idea of justice, a justice as abstract and as formal as the idea of humanity [*l'homme*] in general can be."[140]

Intellectuals, Blanchot went on, had particular responsibility to the universal understood in this way, not because of the prestige their art gave them, nor because they were the personal embodiment of cultural value or values, but precisely for the opposite reasons: because their writing endowed them with no authority at all, and because the fragility of their social position forced them to look beyond the interests of powerful minorities in order to see the bare universal principle that, beyond any attempt at dialectical synthesis, in speaking of the universal, did so by addressing the irreducibly singular. And this was for him, Blanchot explained, drawing on a passage from Jean Halpérin written in appreciation of Levinas, the radical philosophical importance of Judaism: for what was "spoken or announced with Levinas," Halpérin wrote, and Blanchot concurred, "is a surplus, reaching beyond the universal, a singularity that may be called Jewish and *waits* still to be thought. Judaism as that which exceeds sempiternal thinking [*la pensée de toujours*] in so far as it has always already been thought, but nevertheless carries responsibility for the thinking to come: that is what we are *given* by this other philosophy which is that of Levinas: both burden and hope, and the burden of hope."[141]

It is here, so to speak, in the "arid solitude" of the world's interruption, that Blanchot's reading of *La Maladie de la mort* properly begins.[142] The main elements in Duras's story are well known. Written in part in the form of an anonymous, sometimes hypothetical second-person address to its unnamed protagonist, the text concerns a man who, it appears, without the reader being told why, has never known love or sexual intercourse with a woman. He nevertheless, for that very reason, hires the services of an unidentified young woman—not a prostitute— who agrees to spend several nights with him in order that he may fulfil his desire not only for knowledge of the other sex but also for love. This enigmatic proposition, to which both subscribe, leads to a number of indeterminate, yet intimate acts: the man sleeps, for instance, with his face on the woman's crotch; by distraction, he provokes an orgasm in her; he rouses her from sleep by touching her body, breasts, eyes; at times he even penetrates her and remains there, asleep, till morning. But in accordance with their contract or pact, there is little, if any, communication between them. Eventually, the woman makes an admission: if she agreed to the exchange, it was because she could already see her partner was affected by the malady of death, which is deathly, she explains, "in that whoever is affected by it doesn't know he's a carrier—of death, that is. And also in that he could be said to be dead without having had any previous life to die to, and without any knowledge whatsoever of dying to any life."[143]

Relations between the pair, such as they are, continue: the woman sleeping largely, the man approaching her body, then walking away, onto the balcony, for instance, separated still from his own tears, writes Duras, returning to the woman, looking at her as she sleeps. Outside, the crashing waves mirror the whiteness of the sheets, and what the man sees in her sleeping form is "its infernal power, its abominable fragility, its weakness, the invincible strength of its incomparable weakness."[144] When she awakes, they agree to prolong the contract for three more nights. The man confirms he has never desired a woman; she smiles and says, "It must be odd, being dead [*C'est curieux un mort*]."[145] The man looks at her body, and sees in it the evidence of the malady of death affecting him. He has fantasies of killing her, and realises it is in her body that the malady is at work. Fondling her crotch, he brings her to orgasm again, goes away, returns, lies upon her, and penetrates her. He again admits to having never loved. They talk about the possibility or impossibility of love. "You ask," Duras's narrative voice tells him, "how the feeling of love might occur. She answers: Perhaps a sudden fault [*faille:* fissure or fault line] in the logic of the universe. She says: by mistake, for instance. She says: Never through an act of will [*un vouloir*]."[146] She shows him the "dark night [*nuit noire*]" between her legs, and invites him in: "Come. Come now [*Viens. Vous venez*]." The act, we are then told, whatever it is, is over: "It is done [*Cela est fait*]."[147] The following morning, or some other morning, the woman is no longer there; her absence, says Blanchot, reinforces her absence, accentuating once more the gulf between the pair which has never been bridged. The story peters out. "But in the end," Duras's admonishing voice has it, "you were able to live this love in the only way that might be for you, by dissipating it [*perdant:* i.e., losing, wasting, ruining it] before it happened."[148]

On first reading, Blanchot suggests, Duras's story seems straightforward enough. It is a withering indictment of men's subjugation, exploitation, and ignorance of the female other, an unremitting critique of homosocial male power, the first casualties of whom, in the end, are men themselves, whose obsession with power makes them blind to their own impotence. Knowledge of the other may be what the male protagonist desires, but this is only because his relationship to himself, dominated by sameness, is one of mortal sterility. And this, says Blanchot, is arguably what is at stake here: "Lack of feeling, lack of love, this, then, is what may be thought to signify death, this deadly disease by which the one [*l'un:* i.e., in the masculine] is unjustly [*sans justice*] struck down, while the other [*l'autre:* i.e., the woman] is apparently unaffected, even though she is its messenger and, in that capacity, not without responsibility."[149] Blanchot points out that Duras's text seems positively to invite this kind of reading, which admittedly has the capacity to be further nuanced, as Blanchot's summary already implies. Reading, in other words, might be tempted at this stage simply to stop. And this has often been the fate of Duras's story, to be left at that stage by its readers, unsure whether what was being delivered here was diagnosis or verdict, and still searching for the moral argument of the text, debating for instance whether *La Maladie de la mort* is primarily a feminist attack on men in general, or a homophobic attack on male homosexuality in particular, or a combination of the two, and where the line may be drawn in the text, if at all, between homosociality and homosexuality, whether male homosexuality in the story is identified with disruptive femininity, or whether it is simply a continuation of misogynistic power by other means, whether what was being endorsed by the text was responsibility for the other or the teleological privilege of normative heterosexuality.[150]

But in just the same way that the May *événements* were not recuperable within ideology, according to Blanchot, so Duras's text, he argues, was irreducible to these debates. This is not to say that they were secondary or unimportant. On the contrary, in this essay and elsewhere, as the commitment to justice required, Blanchot was unambiguous not only in his defence of the rights of homosexuals but also in his conviction that there was no case to be made for treating homosexual relations any differently than heterosexual love or desire, "since it is difficult to deny," he pointed out, "that all nuances of feeling, from desire to love, are possible between people [*les êtres*], irrespective of whether they are the same or the other sex."[151] But Blanchot's public commitment in favour of the rights of gay people did not mean that, in commenting on Duras's text, he was necessarily obliged simply to reiterate those firmly held opinions. Justice demanded a surplus; it required of the reader, in affirming gender equality and the universality of sexual and other rights, that he or she, without abandoning them, step beyond statements of political principle in order to read in *La Maladie de la mort,* for instance, not only what was readable but that which was unreadable too, not only that which was attributable perhaps to this or that position of meaning but also that which was irreducible to positionality and spoke to the future.

Every text, Blanchot implies, to the extent it is readable, is haunted in this way by its secret, unreadable shadow, which a reader cannot *not* read, since it is what is at stake in reading, though there can be no confidence on any reader's part that this other text, which faithfully repeats the first, without entirely coinciding with it, will prove readable at all. The reader is nevertheless required to go on, not to linger with or within Durassian polemic, but to read again, to read anew, and to read otherwise—which Blanchot does, initially, by reconsidering the present-absent female protagonist, whom he describes as the very first, not only for her hypothetical partner, but for all, both men and women alike, which is why Blanchot, in an aside, finds himself murmuring the nameless name of Eve or Lilith.[152] (Later in the essay, Blanchot will efface this move, complaining to himself that there is something less than rigorous in trying to rid oneself of the female other by employing such facile symbolism.)[153] Blanchot's purpose in proposing a detour through these names is, of course, to address the other-worldly, apocalyptic density of Duras's writing, what other critics have described as the mythic quality of the writer's twin protagonists, but which Blanchot at this stage is careful to translate not into the familiar terms of Greek legend but those of the Jewish Bible and the Kabbala. The reason is clear; it was to put Duras's story in the context of a *différend* not about (Greek) power but (Jewish) law, not the force of arms but the irreducibility of justice.[154]

The emphasis shifts too, in Blanchot's reading, to the prohibition enacted in the Sixth Commandment, passed down to the children of Israel while in the wilderness; and what now distinguishes Duras's female protagonist in this, the critic's second response to the story, is less her status as an object of homosocial exchange, more the act of unaccountable generosity with which she entered into the pact, less her place as a victim of male desire, more the limitless resistance to negativity embodied in her mortal vulnerability, a paradoxical sign of her radical ineliminability. "Two traits," suggests Blanchot, "give her a reality that nothing real [*rien de réel*] would suffice to limit." The first is this: "it is that she is defenceless, the weakest and the most fragile of all, exposing her body which she offers up repeatedly, as if it were her face [*à la manière du visage*], a face which is, in its absolute visibility, its own invisible self-evidence—thus prompting the act of murder . . . , but, by virtue of her weakness and fragility, not *being able* to be killed [*ne pouvant être tuée*], preserved as she is by the prohibition which renders her untouchable in her constant nudity, the closest and the furthest, the intimacy of the inaccessible outside."[155]

The second important trait is that, being persistently asleep, the young woman in Duras's play without play, which is simultaneously staged and not staged, is herself present without being present, absent without being absent. The judgement she pronounces regarding her partner's disease is therefore not the simple words of female vitality, liveliness, or fecundity, confronted with male deathliness, morbidity, or sterility, but testify instead to something more obscure, more insidious, and in the end more deeply shared by the pair than they seem to realise, which is that death here, Blanchot puts it, is "not death in the future [*à venir*], but death always already in the past [*dépassée*: outstripped, overtaken], since it is the abandonment of a life that was never present." And Blanchot insists, boldly interrupting the text, setting aside what Duras's narrator seemed earlier to imply: "Let us make sure we understand this (if indeed it is a case of understanding [*comprendre*], rather than hearing it said [*entendre*] without us realising): we are not facing this (sadly) banal truth: that I am dying without having lived, having never done anything but die while staying alive, or other than to remain unaware of this death which is life reduced to me alone and already over before it even started, filled with an emptiness that goes unnoticed."[156] Blanchot's interpretative intervention here is decisive; doubling the readability of the text with an attention to its unreadability, to what it says but does not say, it divorces the text from itself, interrupts its authority, and marks or remarks in Duras's writing an otherness that risks remaining implicit. Indeed, just to make sure, Blanchot returns to the point later in the essay to insist again: "The answers that [the young woman] gives concerning this deadly malady, however precise, and which amount to saying: he is dying from not having lived, he is dying without his death being death to any life (he does not die therefore, or his death deprives him of an emptiness that he will never know), these answers have no definitive validity."[157]

As Blanchot steps beyond the initial reading of Duras's story, one he shares with numerous other commentators, what thereby comes to be rearticulated is the status of the unbridgeable chasm between Duras's two protagonists, which ceases providing an opportunity for moral, ideological, or polemical comment, and becomes instead an affirmative sign of irreconcilable otherness. Passing from one reading to the other, from that which has always already been read to that which always still remains to be read, Blanchot suspends or neutralises the horizon of intended or other meanings, and relinquishes critique as such. In the irreducible distance between the pair, which is also a form of radical proximity, what Blanchot now intuits in Duras's text, necessarily resisting translation into familiar social or other norms, is the absolute inaccessibility of the female other: Duras's young woman, he writes, "is forever set apart [*séparée:* both separate and separated] by reason of the suspect closeness [*la proximité suspecte*] with which she offers herself, her difference which is that of another species, another genus, or that of the absolutely other."[158]

A second interpretation, then, accompanying the first, interrupts the readability of Duras's text by evoking the shadow of the unreadability of the absolutely other. But, then, suddenly, prompted by a quotation from Duras, a third version intervenes, interrupting Blanchot's analysis in turn, compromising perhaps the very possibility of critical commentary. Matters become more enigmatic still. It now appears that the malady of death circulating through Duras's story is not a condition, fate, or privilege, even, that may be attributed to one protagonist rather than to the other, and that, writes Blanchot, "'the malady of death' is no longer the sole responsibility of the one—i.e. the man—who is ignorant of the feminine, or, being familiar with it, is not familiar with it. The malady is also (or first of all) at work in the one—i.e. the woman—who is there, and decrees it by virtue of her very existence."[159] The malady of death can therefore no longer be treated as the prerogative either of the masculine or the feminine as such, and as grounds for opposing one to the other. But if it belongs to neither sex, yet affects all without exception, it follows that the malady of death is perhaps nothing other than sexual difference itself, in so far as it is what deprives the protagonists of shared stage space, or even a shared theatrical language, dividing the one from the other, and consigning each to arid solitude. Nobody, it seems, escapes the possibility or impossibility of dying: least of all the female author, least of all the male critic. But this moment of greatest clarity is also a moment of greatest obscurity—which, just as it did Duras's own, now most radically imperils Blanchot's response. Indeed, from this point on, as though in sympathy, Blanchot's own critical commentary is increasingly given to oxymoron, becoming elusive, elliptical, and tortuous, as it seeks to address the secret (the secret without secret) of sexual difference which it knows it cannot uncover, for it was never present to language, resists all thematisation, and cannot therefore be an object of criticism—yet somehow still remains as an irreducible demand.

Textuality becomes impenetrable; reading is exposed to the unreadable; criticism confronts its own impossibility. Dissymmetry rules. And *La Maladie de la mort,* this staging of death without death, becomes an oblique commentary on the enigmatic proposition which is the exigency of writing itself.

Having accompanied Duras's text this far, Blanchot pauses, and turns to philosophy: the other philosophy of Levinas, already intermittently in evidence in a number of earlier formulations in Blanchot's essay. Is the dissymmetry at issue in *La Maladie de la mort* "the same," asks Blanchot, as that articulated by Levinas? "This is not certain," is his reply, "nor is it at all clear."[160] Philosophy, invited to arbitrate, remains undecided—not because literature, if it exists, necessarily lies outside philosophy's jurisdiction, but because love, sexual difference, this interruption of the law that also corresponds to a law of interruption, this inscription of the other at the heart of the same, exceeds all law, is irreducible to all ethical prescription, if only because, like the ethical, it too knows no bounds, and submits to no authority other than itself, and which would only serve to denature it entirely—which is not to say, Blanchot insists, that ethics, love is reducible to any single principle, but that, on the contrary, by always already interrupting the other, each shares in an originary turbulence that, from the outset, disrupts all linear, authoritative, or hierarchical narratives which can only ever impose the values to which they subscribe by recourse to original violence.

Blanchot illustrates this perpetual retrocession, division, and erasure of self-identical origin by recalling that, in the Book of Genesis, sexual difference is famously the subject of two contradictory stories or explanations. In the first, Genesis 1:27, it is reported that God created humans, male and female alike; while a chapter later, in Genesis 2:22, it appears that, on the contrary, the first woman was in reality fashioned from Adam's rib. This conundrum or inconsistency is emblematic, suggests Blanchot, of the impossibility of positing any undivided, self-identical origin which has not always already been split in two. The origin, in other words, is never unified, and the law has always already been broken. Indeed, more than this, says Blanchot, it is paradoxically, and aporetically, in that breach of the law, in the breaking of the tablets, and in the law's very interruption, that the origin, if it exists, occurs at all—and does not occur: as an event. Moreover, this detour through the Hebrew Bible also takes Blanchot back to the figure of Lilith, Adam's supposed first wife, promoted in part, it seems, according to Scholem, as a way of reconciling these two narratives of origin, but, if so, only at the cost of exacerbating the difficulty.[161] Lilith is no idealised figure of the mother of humanity. Formed like Adam from the dust of the earth, she is not only his partner but also his rival, who claims equality, yet only to be rebuffed, after which she flies away, embarking upon a career as a demon, in Scholem's words, inhabiting the night and threatening death to all children. This relationship between death's always impending occurrence and the separation between the sexes is perhaps no coincidence. For Blanchot is drawn to a similar motif in Greek myth too, in the disconcerting, three-fold figure he names, in relation to Duras's protagonist, not as celestial or terrestrial Aphrodite but her Chthonian or subterranean counterpart, this creature of the earth who also belongs to death, is the most feared and the most loved—and the most inaccessible.[162] But there is still something facile about the neatness of such symbolic identifications, the critic later concedes, and they are barely to be taken seriously.

As Duras's story intimates, death is nevertheless what lies not only at the end but also at the beginning. Is this to imply that Duras's story, in offering death or deathliness as the only outcome for either sex, seemingly cancelling the possibility of all relationship between them, merely returns the reader to the uncontrollability of destructive, mortal desire, to what Blanchot recalls Hölderlin describing, in the outline for *Der Tod des Empedokles* (*The Death of Empedocles*), as the "extreme of the aorgic, the incomprehensible, the insensible, and the limitless"?[163] Or is it not once more the case, wonders Blanchot, in the loss of all origin, in the mortal abyss that separates Duras's partners the one from the other, that apparent opposites, faithful to their own infidelity, as Hölderlin himself had put it, instead of repelling each other, finally touch without touching? And is it not proof of the necessity of this always futural exigency that, in *La Maladie de la mort,* in the end something cataclysmic occurs, defying all logic, issuing even from a fault or fissure in logic itself: an unpredictable event, event without event, that is the interruption of the interruption confining the sexes to their own. The homogeneity of the selfsame is not all. It cannot be. What, in spite of all, asks Blanchot, does *La Maladie de la mort* therefore affirm?

> That it is necessary [*il faut*] that, in the homogeneity [*l'homogénéité*]—the assertion of the Same—required by understanding, something heterogeneous should rear up [*surgisse*], the absolute Other with whom all relationship signifies an absence of relationship, and the impossibility for the will [*le vouloir*], perhaps even desire, to cross the uncrossable, in the sudden (timeless) clandestine encounter which cancels itself out with ravaging feeling, never certain to be experienced in whoever, deprived perhaps of all sense of "self," this movement intends for the other. A

ravaging feeling: in truth, beyond all feeling, unrelated to *pathos*, overwhelming consciousness, outside of all care for myself [*le souci de moi-même:* i.e., Heideggerian *Sorge*], and requiring imperiously [*sans droit*] that which is irreducible to all requirement, because, in my demand, there is not only the beyond of what might satisfy it, but the beyond of what is demanded. A reaching to the limit, an exacerbating of life that cannot be contained within life, and, therefore, interrupting the claim always to persevere in being, an exposure to the strangeness of an interminable dying [*mourir*] or endless "error."[164]

It is necessary: *il faut,* writes Blanchot, mindful of the strange etymology of this most familiar of impersonal verbs in modern French. Deriving in the first instance from the classical latin *fallere,* meaning: to lead astray, deceive, or escape someone's notice, the verb in the fifteenth and sixteenth centuries splits apart into two separate but related forms: *falloir,* meaning: to be lacking, needed, and therefore necessary, and *faillir,* meaning: to be lacking, fall short, and therefore fail, with the third-person present indicative *il faut,* like other forms, being common to both verbs.[165] *Il faut,* then, refers *both* to what is necessary *and* to what cannot be found. That which is imperative, in other words, is also that which fails. This is, however, no accidental paradox, deriving from a mere quirk of language. For it is plainly the possibility and prospect of failure that turns any injunction into what it is, which, if it is to succeed at all, must always risk failure, and always bear within itself the threat or promise of failure, in exactly the same way that any decision, critical or otherwise, if it is to occur at all, must always already have traversed the undecidability that makes the decision possible and necessary, but by that token always threatens or promises failure.

The law, then, is always already broken. It falters, falls, falsifies, fails. "When, following Nietzsche," writes Blanchot, "I say: *il faut,* i.e. that it is imperative, with the ambiguity between *falloir,* meaning: it is necessary, and *faillir,* meaning: it is needed, what I am also saying is: it is lacking, it is falling, it is deceiving, this is the beginning of the fall, the law commands by falling, and, by that token, still escapes [*se sauve:* i.e., saves itself *and* runs away] as law."[166]

But if the law is inseparable from its own failure, what, then, is the relationship, for instance, between literature and ethics? Asked this very question by Claire Nouvet for a special issue of *Yale French Studies* in 1991, Blanchot replied, citing Mallarmé, in terms that were lengthy, but which were also brief.[167] The only requirement to which literature was subject, he wrote, was the infinite demand of its own disappearance; and if poetry might be thought secretly to incorporate an ethic, it was something that was always already preceded by poetry itself, in that poetry could not do other than obey its own, always already prior law. Outside, inside, secondary, primary: the ethical as such had no place in relation to literature, itself already under erasure—which did not prevent this relationship of non-relationship between literature and the ethical from being an eternal challenge, an intractable subject, says Blanchot, and an enigma.

Blanchot's response to *La Maladie de la mort* had already said as much. For implicit in Blanchot's reading was the awareness that Duras's story, in so far as it fell subject to no law other than the interruption of all law, including the law of its own interruption, was properly neither ethical nor unethical, but otherwise than ethical—which is not to say that it does not pose questions to the ethical, just as ethical questions may be asked of the story, so long as it is also apparent that the ethical, proceeding as it does necessarily from the non-ethical, as Derrida argued in *De la grammatologie,* is always already marked by the violence of that emergence, and therefore cannot coincide with itself, in much the same way that Duras's story too may be deemed to belong to something called literature only to the extent that literature is only ever the trace of its own disappearance, eclipse, and exteriority to itself. But this, so to speak, was Blanchot's enigmatic proposition, one that knew no conclusion, and remained forever unreconciled: with itself and with the world.

And Blanchot's reading did not stop. With the announcement of the apocalyptic event separating *La Maladie de la mort* from itself, interrupting its baleful prognostications, Blanchot's commentary hesitated, but only to resume once more. Striving now, says Blanchot, to betray the story less, if such were possible, he makes the point that Duras's female protagonist is strangely present, fragile, and giving; but that she is also refusal, among others, the refusal to name, to be satisfied with little—and Blanchot too refuses, refuses to stop, and continues, without satisfaction, affirming and reaffirming the text, dividing it from itself, addressing it to an unthought and unthinkable end, which is the end without end, the *"always uncertain end"* of unavowable community, that community, if one may say it, of those who have no community, who speak, read, and write.[168]

"Writing," Blanchot told *Le Monde* in 1983, "is admittedly a kind of work, but one that is entirely lacking in reason, that demands nothing, cannot be justified, and cannot be crowned by any recompense. Writing: a singular exigency (call it bizarre), more ethical than aesthetic, since it responds to a prescription [*un 'il faut'*] without obligation or sanction."[169]

Literature without literature: event without event; ethics without ethics; decisions without decidability.

Chapter Four

JACQUES DERRIDA

Addressing the Future

I

Hapax

> For what [Artaud's] screams [*hurlements*] put before us, articulated
> through such words as *existence, flesh, life, theatre,* or *cruelty,* prior to both
> madness *and* the work, is the sense of an art which does not give rise to
> works, the existence of an artist who is no longer a vehicle or experience
> leading to something other than itself, and of an act of speaking that is a
> body, a body that is a theatre, a theatre that is a text in so far as it is no
> longer subordinate to any anterior writing, arch-text [*archi-texte*], or arch-
> speaking [*archi-parole*]. If Artaud resists all clinical or critical exegesis
> absolutely, in a way never attempted before, in our view, it is by virtue of
> that which in his whole adventure (using the term to indicate a totality
> prior to any separation between life and work) is protest *itself* against
> exemplification *itself.*
>
> Jacques Derrida, *L'Écriture et la différence*[1]

On 2 February 1947, some eight months after his release from the asylum in Rodez, the last in a series of mental institutions where he had
been held since October 1937, Antonin Artaud, now living in a nursing
home in Ivry, was prompted to visit an exhibition of paintings by van
Gogh that had recently opened at the Orangerie in Paris. The previous

week, Artaud had received from the gallery owner, Pierre Loeb, a letter urging him to consider writing a piece on van Gogh, and enclosing by way of encouragement a cutting from the magazine *Arts* that in its coverage of the exhibition had reproduced an extract from a recent monograph on the artist by the psychiatrist François-Joachim Beer, who had concluded, in no uncertain terms, that he was a diminished, pathologically unstable, violent and impulsive individual, given to excessive, eccentric behaviour, and displaying all the symptoms of a congenital mental condition, probably unrelated to his talents as a painter, but clearly exerting a deleterious effect upon them. Galvanised by this brutally reductive and dismissive assessment, only too reminiscent of the diagnoses with which he himself had to contend over the previous decade, and powerfully affected by his subsequent, albeit brief visit to the Orangerie, Artaud quickly set to work. By the end of February a contract for publication had been signed, and weeks later Artaud was already putting the finishing touches to his typescript. *Van Gogh le suicidé de la société* (*Van Gogh, Society's Suicide Victim*), as Artaud's slim volume was called, appeared in mid-December that year and, bizarrely enough, was duly fêted the following month for its contribution to art criticism with the award of the prix Sainte-Beuve.[2]

Like much of what Artaud wrote in the brief but intense period of activity between his transfer to Rodez in February 1943 and his death in March 1948, *Van Gogh le suicidé de la société* is a highly charged, fervently committed, rhapsodic mixture of querulous invective, tenacious affirmation, and gnomic insight, staged both on and off the page, in a relentless, insistent, and percussively theatrical, not to say histrionic manner, interrupted at crucial moments with densely enigmatic passages of incantatory glossolalia, as though to express the conviction that all language could not but strain towards the pure idiomaticity of an invented, gestural performance. Though hardly a work of criticism in any conventional sense, Artaud's book nevertheless sought to make an incisive critical intervention. As such, it belonged to a sequence of letters, articles, and other texts by Artaud, written in the mid-1940s, some published but many left unpublished at the time, which shared the same uncompromising gesture of rejection and reversal that challenged the authority or legitimacy of every alien interpretative grid imposed upon the work of poets or painters, and sought by dint of its own linguistic dynamism to disengage the properly irreducible, bodily, experiential force of the artwork, and release its insurgent potency from all attempts at social normalisation and the always imminent threat of being diverted, purloined, and appropriated for its own purposes by society itself.[3]

In this way, as Artaud's title suggests, *Van Gogh le suicidé de la société* was at least as much an indictment of Western culture in general as an attempt to describe the radical originality of van Gogh's paintings in particular. Admittedly, as far as Artaud was concerned, these two perspectives were anything but contradictory. Nobody commits suicide alone, he charged, and if van Gogh was brought to such an "unnatural gesture," it was not without having been forced to do so by "an army of evil creatures," prominent among whom were van Gogh's psychiatrist, Dr. Gachet, and the painter's brother, Théo, both accused by Artaud, whatever the appearances to the contrary, of having left the painter little alternative but to remove himself from the world.[4] It was not only that van Gogh himself was perfectly sane when compared to the rest of society—after all, quipped Artaud, his only extravagance had been to put his hand in the flame of a lamp and cut off part of his left ear—it was also that psychiatry, according to Artaud, was little more than a form of systematic erotomania which, in league with the vampire-like rapacity of the institution of the family, had largely been invented to protect a vitiated, defective society from "certain superior lucidities," such as van Gogh and others, "whose faculties of divination were an embarrassment to it."[5] Madness, Artaud went on, or what passes for such in modern Western society, was in the end less a deficiency than a kind of principled rebellion: "What is an authentic madman [*un aliéné authentique*]?" he asked, overcoming any doubts he may have had about the aporetic, abyssal, unanswerable nature of the question. "Someone," he replied, "who prefers to go mad [*devenir fou*], in the sense society understands it, rather than betray [*forfaire*] a certain superior idea of human honour."[6]

The price paid for such devotion to the cause, Artaud believed, pointing meaningfully to his experiences of the previous ten years, could not be greater. Society, the writer complained, was dedicated to expunging, by whatever means necessary, the rebellious singularity of those deemed to have infringed its debilitating rationalistic norms. This might involve internment, often in abject conditions, in this or that repressive institution, like the four different psychiatric units that

Artaud himself had been forced to endure since 1937. Even more darkly, offenders might also become the object of sinister magical spells issuing from society itself, as it sought to wreak further vengeance on those it had already excluded. Seen in this light, van Gogh's suicide was less a sign of defeat on the part of the painter than a jealous, noxious act of possession by society, and this was how in *Van Gogh le suicidé de la société* Artaud staged or restaged for himself the events leading up to van Gogh's death. "It happened with van Gogh as it usually always happens," he wrote, "on the occasion of an orgy [*partouse*], a mass, an absolution, or some other rite of consecration, possession, succubation or incubation. / It therefore infiltrated his body [*s'introduisit donc dans son corps*], / this society, / absolved, / consecrated, / sanctified / and possessed, / blotted out [*effaça*] the supernatural awareness he had just acquired, and, like a flood of black crows in the fibres of his inner tree [*son arbre interne*], / submerged him in a final wave, / and, stealing his place [*prenant sa place*], / killed him."⁷ Van Gogh's crime, in the eyes of society, Artaud explained, was to have sought, by his painting, to irradiate his life with the infinite, and it was for this reason he died, not because he failed in that quest, but because the infinite was stolen from him:

> For it was not by dint of searching for the infinite that van Gogh died, that he found himself forced to suffocate from poverty and asphyxia, it was by dint of seeing himself rejected by the rabble [*tourbe*] of all those who, even in his lifetime, believed infinity to be theirs, and theirs alone [*croyaient détenir l'infini contre lui*]; and van Gogh could have found enough infinity to live out his whole life if the bestial consciousness of the crowd [*la conscience bestiale de la masse*] had not wanted to have it for itself [*se l'approprier*] in order to feed its own sexual orgies, which never had anything to do with painting or poetry.

"And I believe," Artaud concluded, in ominous words, "that at the extreme point of death there is always someone else to strip us of the life that is our own [*pour nous dépouiller de notre propre vie*]."⁸

Artaud insisted, however, that in itself there was nothing pathological about van Gogh's paintings. On the contrary, society itself was sick and diseased, and it was not van Gogh's paintings that were in need of the world or the earth but precisely the opposite. "Which means," he went on, "that apocalypse, a consummate apocalypse, lies brewing at this very moment, within old, martyred van Gogh's canvases, and that the earth needs him in order to rush forth [*ruer*] upon its head and feet." "Nobody," Artaud maintained, "ever wrote or painted, sculpted, modeled, constructed, or invented, other than in fact to escape hell."[9] For van Gogh was not alone. Standing alongside were Baudelaire, Poe, Nerval, Nietzsche, Kierkegaard, Hölderlin, Coleridge, all of whom, according to Artaud, had similarly travelled beyond society's pale.[10] But at the same time, no other painter was like van Gogh, and an exhibition of his work was an event not merely in the history of painting, but in history itself. What van Gogh had been able to do, on Artaud's submission, overcoming all society's dualisms or dualities, was to infuse his painting with such intensity that reality and myth, the writer called them, here, now, at this present moment, were as one. And this is what van Gogh's painting announced: "What no painter before poor van Gogh had done, / what no painter will do after him, / for I believe that this time, / this very day, / now, / in this month of February 1947, / reality itself, / the myth of reality itself, mythic reality itself, is in the process of embodying itself [*en train de s'incorporer*]."[11]

There could be for Artaud no higher accolade. For what he sought to uncover in the recalcitrance and obstinacy of the paintings of van Gogh, especially those canvases produced shortly before the artist's death, was paradoxical proof of the bodily presence of his own existence. And what he saw realised by van Gogh belonged in this sense both to painting and to something beyond painting, was therefore fully immanent and yet transcendent too, a singular intensity that, using both the perfect and future perfect tense, Artaud articulated in the following terms:

> For van Gogh will indeed have been the most truly painter-like of painters [*le plus vraiment peintre de tous les peintres*], the only one not to have wanted to go beyond painting [*dépasser la peinture*] as the strict medium [*moyen*] of his work, and the strict framework of his means [*moyens*].
> And the only one, absolutely the only one, who, at the same time, absolutely went beyond painting [*dépassé la peinture*], the inert act

of representing nature in order, in this exclusive representation of nature, to give expression [*faire jaillir*] to a spinning force, an element torn from its very heart.

Beneath this representation, he made an air [*air*] blossom, and in it enclosed a sinew [*nerf*], neither of which are part of nature, which belong to a nature and to an air that are truer than the air and the sinew of true nature.[12]

And if it followed that van Gogh's paintings were endowed with extramundane mundanity, an otherworldly worldliness, beyond "philosophy, mysticism, ritual, psychurgy, and liturgy," as Artaud put it, having little, if anything, to do with "history, literature, or poetry,"[13] this was confirmation of the fact that to encounter van Gogh's work was not to look at an obedient corner of reality but to be looked at by the paintings, to suffer their penetrating gaze, their radical propensity, according to Artaud, which perhaps only the work of Nietzsche had similarly displayed, to "lay bare the soul, release the body from the soul, strip the human body naked, beyond the subterfuges of the mind."[14] For in those paintings, says Artaud, "Van Gogh grasped the moment when the apple of the eye is about to tip into the void, / when this gaze, dispatched in our direction, [bursts through] like some explosive meteor, taking on the expressionless colour of the void and of the absence that fills it."[15]

But, if such is the piercing look enacted or embodied by van Gogh's paintings, how is a viewer to respond? How, for instance, does Artaud respond to van Gogh, and how, in turn, might Artaud's reader respond to Artaud?

For Artaud, the relationship between van Gogh's painting and his so-called madness was an essential one. What lay at the heart of van Gogh's work, as it did Artaud's own, was not only the inseparability between painting or poetry and that superior knowledge called madness but also painting's or poetry's resistance to all separation, alienation, or difference. "Van Gogh did not die from a state of delirium of his own [*un état de délire propre*] / ," Artaud claimed, "but from having been bodily the site of a problem with which the iniquitous spirit of humanity, as we know it, has been struggling since the dawn of time. / That of the predominance of the flesh [*chair*] over the spirit [*esprit*], or the body [*corps*] over the flesh, or spirit over the one or the other. / And where in this madness [*ce délire*] is the place of the human self [*moi humain*]?"[16] Such was the crux of Artaud's challenge, traversing, while also inverting, Platonism, Christianity, not to say the entirety of Western metaphysics. The stakes, then, could not be higher. But Artaud's question also raised many further questions, more than it could even undertake to answer. For one thing, Artaud's response to van Gogh was marked by a fundamental contradiction. It was that the purity of the painter's vision, which Artaud sought powerfully to reaffirm, had always already been appropriated by a jealous and vengeful society which had declared the painter mad, and manipulated and murdered him for his pains, and that, however much Artaud sought to reverse that process by honouring in van Gogh the spectre of society's martyred victim, rather than the recipient of its care and understanding, so the writer, in claiming access to a more authoritative or authentic interpretation of van Gogh's so-called madness, could not *not* repeat that selfsame gesture in his turn. Even as he prepared radically to challenge society's verdict of madness, the danger was that Artaud would end up inadvertently endorsing the violence of exclusion implied in that diagnosis, and, stealing van Gogh's place, deprive him once again of the infinity embodied in his paintings.

This left Artaud facing a difficult double bind. Plainly, as far as Artaud was concerned, no response to van Gogh that declared an allegiance, explicit or implicit, to the oppressive social norms represented by psychiatry could be thought to provide a legitimate basis for understanding the painter's work, for it would merely replicate the murderous jealousy inherent in psychiatric discourse in general. But equally, to disregard van Gogh's experience of "madness" would be tantamount to neutralising or negating the subversive charge of his paintings, and fail to honour van Gogh's honourable revolt against society's alienating violence. In such circumstances, as Artaud admits, even to attempt to describe one of van Gogh's canvases is to realise the inadequacy of the available forms of critical discourse. "To describe one of van Gogh's paintings, what is the point!" he wrote, before resorting to the expedient of citing three extracts from van Gogh's letters to Théo. "No description attempted by someone else [*par un autre*] could ever be the same as van Gogh's own simple alignment of natural objects and shades, / van Gogh who is as much a great writer as a great painter and who, on the subject of the work described, gives the impression of the most stunning authenticity [*la plus abasourdissante authenticité*]."[17]

Confronted with this impossible dilemma, Artaud's strategy was simple enough. As his tribute to the painter suggests, it was to identify van Gogh's cause wholly with his own, or vice versa, and thereby claim privileged insight into the facts of the case. Artaud's gesture of sympathy was not without its knowing black humour, and in a passage deleted from the final version of *Van Gogh le suicidé de la société*, he made it clear that the reason he knew what had really occurred between van Gogh and Dr. Gachet, and possessed documents to prove it, was that he, too, Antonin Artaud, was also suffering from "so-called persecution mania [*un délire caractérisé de persécution*]."[18] This gave Artaud's relationship with van Gogh its particular visionary insight. For it was no longer grounded, if it ever had been, in any kind of critical appreciation. Instead, it was vehemently autobiographical, with the result that the protagonist of Artaud's text quickly made more plausible sense to both reader and writer alike once understood as a meeker, more compliant, and in any case less militant version of Artaud himself. "I too am like poor van Gogh [*le pauvre van Gogh*]," Artaud admitted, and added to what he took to be the patronising philistinism of Dr. Gachet a powerfully felt grudge of his own, directed at the figure of Gaston Ferdière who had been responsible for treating him in Rodez: "I cannot think any more, but each day that goes by I am directing this extraordinary internal ferment ever more closely, and I'd like to see the day when any kind of medicine comes telling me off for tiring myself out."[19]

But identification too was not unproblematic. The only basis on which it might occur was necessarily a presumptive or presumptuous one, and there was always the risk that readers might take Artaud's own critical account and vehement defence of van Gogh to be little more than a continuation of his own paranoia by other means. True enough, van Gogh's predicament, according to Artaud, was not a solitary but a universal one. "For it is not for the sake of this world / ," Artaud claimed, "it is never for the sake of this earth that we have all always laboured, / struggled, / wailed in horror, hunger, poverty, hatred, scandal, and disgust, / that we were all poisoned, / though it may have put us all under its spell [*envoûtés*], / and that we in the end committed suicide, / for are we not all, like poor van Gogh himself, society's suicide victims [*des suicidés de la société*]!"[20] But if van Gogh's fate was therefore shared by all, it was even less apparent from what place, or with what language, it might be possible to address the recalcitrant singularity or uniqueness embodied in those selfsame paintings, and in so far as Artaud's own febrile, restlessly digressive and recursive intervention voiced radical doubts concerning the existence of any such stable place or language, then it followed that, whatever the committee awarding the prix Sainte-Beuve may have believed, Artaud's contestatory outpourings were anything but receivable as art criticism. Indeed, a more likely reaction was that, by denouncing society's judgements as at once plagiarised, perverted, and pernicious, they sought to force the very possibility of criticism into a radical impasse from which it was likely never to return, other than as a perpetual re-enactment of society's exclusionary violence. In this respect, Artaud's project was simple enough. It consisted, in the famous title of Artaud's banned 1948 radio broadcast, in "putting an end to the judgement of god": *Pour en finir avec le jugement de dieu.*[21]

In *Van Gogh le suicidé de la société*, then, Artaud inscribed a limit, both within critical discourse and beyond it. It divorced criticism from itself by challenging and interrupting its objectivity, equanimity, and authority, and gestured impatiently and passionately towards an exteriority that critical discourse was necessarily incapable of addressing. This raised at least two important issues. There was the matter of the complex collusion between psychiatric and aesthetic judgements, between the values embodied in clinical and critical discourse in relation to van Gogh, as well as other artists, like Artaud himself, where the artwork, as Foucault among others, explicitly evoking Artaud, once put it, was synonymous with its own absence, defection, or engulfment.[22] And there was the matter too of the enigmatic singularity of the work, its impenetrable obscurity, its resistance to assimilation by criticism as such; for if, on Artaud's submission, criticism was little more than a form of prejudiced or prejudicial reading, blind to its own inability or refusal to read, it followed that any writing that ventured beyond the pale of discursive normality was destined to remain unreadable by criticism.

These were not abstract questions but fundamentally practical ones, on which hangs the future viability of any act of interpretation or criticism as such. For how might it be possible, if at all, for a viewer to avoid subjecting the work to his or her spectator's normative, reductive, and appropriating gaze, and how might it be possible instead, as Artaud contends, to let the work stare back at the viewer, challenging, piercing, searing her or his understanding? And if these were questions that remained everywhere unanswered or unanswerable in Artaud's resolutely projective commentary on van Gogh, it was also no doubt because they were even less susceptible of resolution when it came to envisaging any possible future reading of Artaud's own stridently embodied poetical texts.

This question of the relationship between literature and madness, unreason and inspiration, discursive rationality and its poetic transgression, was admittedly not a new one. It had already featured importantly throughout the nineteenth century, as the fate of Hölderlin, Nerval, Nietzsche, and others served to testify, and it had been an abiding concern in the early twentieth century too, ever since poets such as André Breton and Paul Éluard, at the height of Surrealism, had begun experimenting with the simulation of clinical madness in their jointly authored collection, *L'Immaculée Conception,* prompting some interest at the time on the part of Jacques Lacan, who had also briefly treated Artaud, as it happens, at the Hôpital Sainte-Anne in 1938, and whose earliest documented case-history, the patient known as Aimée, on whom his 1932 thesis was largely based, was an aspiring historical novelist suffering from psychotic delusions.[23] But between the discourse of psychiatric or psychoanalytic knowledge and the discourse of literary criticism there remained considerable problems of articulation, which a writing such as that of Artaud, and the nature of Artaud's response to van Gogh, threw sharply into relief. How far might literary criticism rely on clinical diagnoses, and how far was it necessary for clinical judgements to take account of literary factors? These were not questions that were solely relevant to Artaud. They arose with equal urgency in respect of many other modern and not so modern writers and thinkers, with the important and telling difference that, more than any other, as he was to emphasise himself in the opening section of his epic 1946 poem, *Artaud Le Mômo,* which he entitled "Le Retour d'Artaud, Le Mômo [The Return of Madcap Artaud],"[24] Artaud had come back from the brink, as experienced by him in Rodez, if not necessarily from something that may properly be described as madness, in order to continue or resume writing, in an effort that was not without considerable heroism, and deserving of honour in its turn, and which conferred upon Artaud's writing the singular capacity to bear witness, here and now, as few others could, to a properly unique experience of a profoundly alien world, a world that was emphatically *this* world—but experienced otherwise.

But how, then, to speak to the extremity of what was now embodied in this signature and signature text: Artaud Mômo? This was the abrupt, even brutal, in any case urgent question that Artaud's writing posed in the mid-1940s, and continues to pose, to each of his friends, admirers, and would-be commentators in turn.

How, in other words, to address the case—not the case in general, but *this* case, here, now, as it offers itself to this encounter with the other, otherwise known as reading?

But what would be implied, in spite of all, by treating Artaud as a case? It would be to decide, inevitably, that Artaud, together with Hölderlin, Nerval, Nietzsche, van Gogh, and all the others, was, in the end, merely a passing instance of a general rule. It would deny him the bodily presence he craved, and thus prove him right *and* prove him wrong, and in either case to repeat the violence to which Artaud, as a casebook example of mental alienation, was seemingly destined to fall victim. Poor Monsieur Antonin Artaud!

Artaud, however, Roland Barthes once wrote, was neither a universal state of affairs nor a mere contingency. He was a *hapax,* a *hapax legomenon,* a word, form, or idiom of which only one occurrence has been recorded or exists, a trace or mark that is part of language while also standing outside the corpus of established meanings; which testifies to a limit therefore that is no sooner inscribed than effaced; where the difference between text and context is fragile to the point of imponderability; whose intended meaning has been mysteriously voided, by inscrutable accident or inexplicable design, and resists interpretation; which, though read, also remains unreadable; whose meaning or value cannot therefore be finally decided; but which nevertheless persists, demanding to be read again and again, lying in wait for an ever future reader as both an imminent promise and an impending threat, and, in either case, as an enigma: the enigma of that which, being unique, bears a single, singular, exceptional name which, by that token, is also, for the moment, if not forever, an absence of name.[25]

This question of the singular or the unique, of the margin it implies, the interruption it enacts, and the exteriority it invokes, unsurprisingly enough, traverses all writing on, or around, or after Artaud. It does so, for instance, two influential essays on Artaud by Blanchot, from 1956 and 1958, subsequently incorporated into *Le Livre à venir* and *L'Entretien infini*. It does so too the numerous emblematic references to Artaud to be found both in and alongside Foucault's *Histoire de la folie* (*History of Madness*) of 1961.[26] And it does so again, this time in more explicitly problematic fashion, what is without doubt one of the most influential and most probing responses to Artaud's work, or absence of work, Derrida's 1965 essay, first published in the journal *Tel Quel*, "La Parole soufflée."[27]

Derrida's intervention in that essay was radical and incisive. He framed his account of Artaud by considering two examples: that of Blanchot, who, before turning to Artaud, had explored at some length the relationship between poetry and so-called madness in relation to Hölderlin, and that of the philosopher and, latterly, psychiatrist and psychoanalyst Jean Laplanche, the author of a recent doctoral thesis on Hölderlin, which Foucault had reviewed for the journal *Critique*.[28] What Blanchot and Laplanche shared, according to Derrida, notwithstanding their divergent professional backgrounds, was a joint commitment to the task of bringing the experience of madness and the possibility or impossibility of the artwork into closer communication, and thus explore the common ground between clinical and critical understanding, notwithstanding that in both instances, as Derrida points out, any such synthesis or integration was in fact very far from reaching fruition: in the one case, because what was primarily at stake was the futural destiny of poetry, and, in the other, because what finally counted was the insight into schizophrenia as human possibility, and because between these two endeavours there stretched an inevitable and unbridgeable chasm.

These two examples were not of course selected at random. But the argument Derrida sought to make was not limited to these two cases. It was more general, both more fundamental and more wideranging. Writing some years later, for instance, he might easily have chosen instead a number of other influential critics or commentators for whom the prospect of marrying clinical and critical perspectives was an attractive one—like Gilles Deleuze, say, who enlisted the support of Artaud's violent invective against the family as part of his own project to overthrow the manipulative, dialectical negativism of Oedipal psycho-analysis, and yet was happy enough portraying Artaud's 1943 reworking of Lewis Carroll's "Jabberwocky" as evidence of a paradigmatic encounter between the language of schizophrenia (Artaud) and that of perversity (Carroll), and indeed, shortly after, remained sufficiently confident in the possibility of the articulation between the critical and the clinical to use that very expression as the title for a subsequent collection of literary and philosophical essays—or like Julia Kristeva, who, in similar vein, in July 1972, added Artaud's name to the repertoire of transgressive, anally regressive subversives entrusted with the task of hastening the arrival of radical cultural revolution—and both of whom, Deleuze and Kristeva alike, implausibly enough for anyone familiar with their work, were united, if by nothing else, by a shared belief in psychiatric classifications in general and in the clinico-critical diagnosis of Artaud as a schizophrenic.[29]

But to Derrida such strange convergences came as no surprise. For as he observed in 1965, whatever the yawning differences between these divergent, sometimes irreconcilable approaches to Artaud, one shared but troubling assumption seemed nevertheless to survive. It was that, for all concerned, "poor Artaud" was an example, an instance, a case, governed by an inescapable dialectic of the particular and the general, the contingent and the essential, such that Artaud's singular body was in fact always already secondary, always already incidental to the universal structure his recalcitrant writing, *volens nolens*, was deemed to illustrate—with troubling consequences that serve to underscore, even in their apparent antagonism, not only the common horizon of critical and clinical language, but also, more radically, the covert solidarity between them. As Derrida goes on to explain:

> It is perfectly apparent that, in fact [*en fait*], even as clinical commentary and critical commentary everywhere claim their autonomy, and demand by each other to be recognised and respected, they are nevertheless complicit—by virtue of a unity that refers,

via mediations that remain unthought, to the mediation [between the empirical and the transcendental, that which holds *de facto* and that which holds *de jure*] for which we were searching a moment ago—in the same abstraction, the same blindness [*méconnaissance*], and the same violence. Criticism itself, whether aesthetic, literary, philosophical, or so on, at the very moment that it claims to be protecting the sense of a thought or the value of a work against psychomedical reductiveness, reaches the exact same end by the opposite route: *it makes an example of it* [*elle fait un exemple:* i.e., treats it both as an instance and as a warning]. In other words: it turns it into a *case* or *case-history* [*un cas*]. The work or adventure of thought is called as a witness, to serve as an example or a case of martyrdom, to testify to a structure whose essential permanence becomes the main preoccupation of analysis. To take something seriously, as far as criticism is concerned, and make the case [*faire cas:* to attach importance to something] for its meaning and value, is to read an essence in the example which then falls between phenomenological parentheses. And this occurs according to the most irresistible gesture of even that style of commentary that is most respectful of the rampant singularity of its theme. Although they are radically opposed, for the entirely sensible reasons that we know, here, faced with the problem of the work and of madness, *psychological reduction* and the *eidetic reduction* function in the same way, and without realising serve the same end. The authority that psychopathology, whatever its tendency, might exert over Artaud's case, even supposing it were to achieve in its reading the sure profundity of Blanchot, would basically lead to the same *neutralisation* of "that poor Monsieur Antonin Artaud."[30]

Derrida's verdict was nothing if not severe.[31] His rigour was not, however, gratuitous; it was a necessary sign of the reading strategy of faithful infidelity practised by Derrida in so many of the early essays in *L'Écriture et la différence* (*Writing and Difference*). For it was clearly not enough (which is not to say: unnecessary), as Derrida explained in *De la grammatologie* (*Of Grammatology*), to "reproduce, by the self-effacing, respectful doubling of commentary, the conscious, voluntary, intentional relationship that the writer institutes in his exchanges with the

history to which he or she belongs by the element of language."[32] Indeed, it was only by pushing matters to a critical limit, by remaining attentive to that which was exorbitant in writing, and irreducible to any
self-identical theme, motif, or intentional structure, and which refused
to obey the convenient but always ominous opposition between madness and work, between the contingent and the essential, between inside and outside, that it might be possible to re-mark that limit in the
double sense of noticing it or making it legible *and* questioning or displacing it. This was not to say it was necessarily desirable, or even possible, to have done with the economy of exemplification. Indeed, examples are unavoidable, if only because it is part of the structure of any
trace, Derrida argues in *De la grammatologie,* to be repeatable, and, as a
consequence of this repeatability, to allow itself to be divided from itself
and re-marked, so that any trace, even as it necessarily refers to another,
thereby always already has the capacity of referring to itself, and thus
putting itself forward as an instance of what it is. This much is of course
clearly apparent in Derrida's essay, as its author is plainly aware. For it
is not for nothing that Derrida begins by citing Blanchot and Laplanche,
in the sense of both quoting and calling them to account, in order to put
to them the posthumous complaint lodged by or on behalf of Artaud's
writing, and thus adduces them as examples, as cases, as instances, of
the very rhetoric of exemplification that is the object of the writer's suspicion and scrutiny. And, in turn, like Blanchot before him, Derrida
was also prompted, at least up to a point, to consider Artaud's own writing about himself as exemplary.[33]

But there was more, which was a function of Derrida's affirmative, albeit no less vigilant response to Artaud's fiercely embodied resistance to being turned into a case-history, that is, to being deprived of the
presence of his body by paternalistic clinical or critical authority. True
enough, as Derrida demonstrates, Artaud's protests against the theft of
his own, proper body, or that of "poor van Gogh," Artaud's own, abyssal
proxy, were absolutely and entirely in vain, for it was part of the structure
of all that Artaud desired to claim back from god, society, the world, the
other—that is, the property, properness, and propriety of his own bodily
presence—that, even for it to appear as such, it was necessarily always
already marked by an inescapable prior act of expropriation. Appropriation here *was* expropriation under another name, and Artaud's quest
was both impossible and necessarily infinite. The conundrum was not

of course specific to Artaud. It affects, for instance, by definition, all proper names—which are thus always improper. For as Derrida shows in *De la grammatologie,* one can lay claim to a proper name only in so far as that name, no matter whether it is present or absent, invented or assumed, imposed or bestowed by another, is repeatable as such, which is to say: always already separated from what it names, always already other than itself, subject to *différance,* and part of the boundless, signifying and asignifying movement of language and text.[34]

Derrida insists, however, that Artaud's concern was not to pay tribute to the invincibility of this structure and serve merely to exemplify it. Artaud, he notes, wanted instead to shatter it, "to blow it to pieces [*la faire sauter*]."[35] In turn, Derrida's own project was not simply to produce a better, more coherent, more comprehensive reading of Artaud; it was also to speak to the singularity and irreducibility of Artaud's writing, its force, intensity, or presence as something other than an instance. To this end, it was essential not only to resist reading Artaud as an illustration of that confusion between poetry and paranoia that he himself most resisted but also, equally, to decline to read his work, as Artaud might have wanted, as an intact embodiment of his own pure presence. Both were tantamount to a refusal to read, and properly to attend to Artaud's writing meant reaching beyond the thematic horizon of his texts, and adopting the same suspicion towards Artaud's work as he himself did towards the inherited dualisms of Western metaphysics. As far as Derrida was concerned, rather than an example, Artaud more plausibly had the status of what might best be termed a counter-example: not in the sense that Artaud might serve as the exception that confirmed the rule, the mad poet, in other words, whose work proved the wisdom of poetic extravagance as such, but in the sense that Artaud, in so far as he remained, inevitably, an example of sorts, rather than merely exhibiting the law, served instead to expose it, that is, both reveal it and denounce it, and thus demand of the reader that he or she envisage an entirely different logic binding the singular to the universal, and vice versa. For the fact remained, the one was unthinkable without the other.

There are, of course, other resources to be found within the structure of exemplarity. For while, plainly enough, every example implicitly endorses the subjection and subjectivation of the singular to the universal, from which it derives its essence, identity, and status, there is also the fact that each trace, being repeatable, and thus always already part of a series, is never reducible to the series it may be held to instantiate.[36] It can always be detached or separated from that class, and institute an always possible other series, without end, a series which, provisionally, it may serve to instantiate, but whose continuity it interrupts, whose closure it revokes, and whose limits it exceeds. Examples, in this way, are always divided, heterogeneous, and disruptive. Here, the logic of exemplification proves once more to be a case not of subordination but of insubordination, with exemplarity providing evidence not of the supremacy of the law but of the obstinately irreducible singularity that, in both the temporal and the spatial sense, comes or arrives before the law, and without which it would not be possible to invoke or apply legal or legalistic norms at all.[37] If Artaud is a counter-example, then, it is because he calls into question the dialectic of exemplification not by negating and thus paradoxically confirming it but by outrageously supplanting it, reformulating and rewriting its familialist, Oedipal, trinitarian law under his own reappropriated signature. "I, Antonin Artaud," he famously declared, "I am my son, my father, my mother, / and me; / the leveller of that doltish circuit in which procreation is ensnared, / the circuit of daddy-mummy / and the child, / black soot of grandma's arse, / much more than of father-mother. [*Moi, Antonin Artaud, je suis mon fils, mon père, ma mère, / et moi; / niveleur du périple imbécile où s'enferre l'engendrement, / le périple papa-maman / et l'enfant, / suie du cu de la grand-maman, / beaucoup plus que du père-mère.*"[38]

For Derrida, then, Artaud was less example than limit. As such, his position was at least double. On the one hand, it was true, Artaud's protests highlighted with graphic violence the alienation and decadence that was the product of two millennia of Platonism, Christianity, spiritualism, and rationalism, and which were synonymous with modern European culture. In a word, Artaud was right. Signification *was* division, divorce, dispossession, silent proof that the body had always already been separated from its own presence and colonised by another: by language, society, god, the body's own organs. Difference, repetition ruled supreme. In affirming as much, however, Artaud was not being delusional but giving voice, in dramatically impassioned terms, to a moment of incontrovertible and necessary understanding. But it was impossible for it to be otherwise, as Derrida explains. This was the obverse of Artaud's stance. For Artaud was only able to articulate the stinging criticisms that he launched in the direction of psychiatry, religion, society, and much else besides, by fulfilling, albeit unwittingly, some of the most insistent motifs of metaphysics, most notably its—hypocritical or mendacious—privileging of presence, properness, and property. In this respect, the limit exposed by Artaud was indeed a limit, beyond which there lay, not uncharted virgin territory, as Artaud perhaps hoped, but the reverse image, the photographic negative of what it circumscribed. This was the cruel irony of Artaud's writing: at one and the same time it railed against the closure of metaphysics and yet sought to take seriously some of its most consistently declared principles. Even as he grappled with the burden of metaphysics, the themes, ideas, and demands of Artaud, Derrida argues, were indelibly marked by the history of metaphysics:

> Artaud *assails* [*sollicite*] metaphysics, *shakes* it [*l'ébranle*] by its foundations when it lies to itself and makes it a condition of the phenomenon of the proper [*propre*] that one depart properly from what is proper [*qu'on se départisse proprement de son propre*] (in what is an alienation of alienation); still *makes demands* upon it, draws on its fund of values, and wants to be more faithful to them than metaphysics itself, by restoring absolutely the proper, prior to all separation [*à la veille de toute discession*].[39]

The implications of this subtly bifocal account of Artaud's writing were several. It allowed Derrida, rather than treating Artaud as an object to be understood, to turn the writer's own understanding to creative, affirmative effect. Indeed, the drama of Artaud's thinking was far closer than it might seem to the dismantling of metaphysics being elaborated, in vastly different context and register, by Derrida himself, and in this respect it was just as much a case of the poet reading the philosopher as of the philosopher reading the poet. In addition, while Artaud's work was testimony to what might be called the inherent violence of metaphysics, it was also a warning to those who in the mid-1960s naively thought that it was possible, in one simple gesture, to pass beyond metaphysics or even philosophy.[40] Yet if it was not within

Artaud's power to escape the closure of metaphysics, this was not to say his work reverted simply to being an unfortunate casualty of metaphysical tradition.

On the contrary, Artaud, in so far as he touched the limit, remained on the edge, where possibility and impossibility met, and divided. Artaud, as Derrida later puts it, in a discussion of the writer's tense, dual relationship with the stage and the strange institution called the theatre, "cleaved as close as can be to the limit: to the possibility and impossibility of pure theatre."[41] This was a dangerous place to be, and the risks were considerable. Which is also to say there remained something excessive, extravagant, and exorbitant about Artaud's enterprise that could not be so easily written off. Artaud's writing, in a word, was irreducible to the themes, the motifs, the ideas from which it was made. It retained a bodily singularity that it was impossible to set aside, which could not be dismissed by appealing to this or that hermeneutic grid, and which defied translation and analysis alike. It was that thinking, at the limit, as Artaud put it, had still not yet begun. "Die [*Crève*], old bag of bones [*os de chien*]," he wrote, addressing himself under the auspices of an imaginary other. "Everybody knows that your thinking is not complete or finished, and that, whichever way you turn, you have still not even *begun* to think."[42] The injunction spoke, no doubt, not only to Artaud, but to all readers, present and future, and it was a measure of the demands Artaud made on those readers that the terms in which to begin thinking about his writing were not given in the present but belonged, if at all, to the future—a future without present.

In the meantime, so to speak, Derrida argued, it was imperative, rather than seeking to derive Artaud's writing from any one exemplary, self-identical origin, to affirm instead its double status, its double inscription, and its double appurtenance. For if Artaud indeed marked a limit, it meant that Artaud's writing, properly, or improperly, lay neither inside nor outside any given system, and was answerable to no single jurisdiction, which it necessarily exceeded. The gesture it enacted, then, was irreducible to any position other than an absence of position. Nothing might be determined in advance regarding the lived, thought, written, embodied adventure it inscribed. And this indecision, or undecidability, of Artaud was decisive. It was no longer a matter of subjecting Artaud's case to valuation, validation, or verification, but seeking justice, according to criteria still to be found, for the poet's screams or cries. To be done with the judgement of god required nothing less.

Derrida's response to this challenge was both tactical and strategic, idiomatic and economic, localised and general. It found its own emblem or signature in a verbal cluster, less semantic unit than syntactic operator, formed by the series: *souffle, pneuma, spiritus, ruah, breath*, together with its many ramifying connections with expressions referring to language (*glossa, lingua, langue, langage, language*) and to being (*ontos, esse, être, to be*).[43] In Derrida's account, Artaud's *souffle* was the site of a three-fold divergence, dilemma, and *différend:* first, it named the act by which all that was mine was stolen, taken, purloined, or lifted from me; second, it referred to the movement by which the words of others were whispered, murmured, breathed into my ear (*souffleur,* in French, is the theatrical prompt or prompter who reminds me of what I must say at given moments). But, thirdly, *souffle* (from Latin *sufflare,* meaning: to fill with breath) was a reminder that Artaud the man of theatre was primarily an actor, whose principal organ was his body, propelling, charging, inscribing, effacing, and affirming itself across space and time, in a movement that was itself already writing, and described as such by Artaud himself in numerous appeals to the ever future, possible-impossible theatre he sought to envision in the mid-1930s, and the promise of which, provisionally and momentarily, he encountered in the theatre from Bali glimpsed at the Colonial Exhibition of 1931. "One can sense in Balinese theatre," he wrote, "a state prior to language [*un état d'avant le langage*], which can choose its language [*langage*]: music, gesture, movement, words."[44]

But as Artaud's description implies, this state before language was neither a presence nor an absence of language in any received sense. It was more accurately a kind of writing or *écriture* in Derrida's sense, a kind of radical textuality, if one will, albeit having nothing to do with what is customarily called text, a movement of inscription that, preceding and exceeding, enabling and disabling all given signifying forms, was without essence or identity, had neither inside nor outside, but occurred nevertheless as a repetitive, differentiated, deferred event. And it was this that Derrida, in his commentary, sought to address and affirm, and why what was most incisive about the three-fold, untranslatable, abyssal title of his essay, "La Parole soufflée," as inspired or prompted simultaneously and in turn by each of the three meanings indicated above, was not its undoubted elegance, or economy, but the fact that it responded to the undecidability of Artaud's writing with an undecidability of its own. For Derrida too, like Artaud, like all commentators of Artaud, was ensnared within a system of thought and a language over which no writer had control, but which, in a devious, supplementary tactic of its own, had always already exceeded not only the horizon of intended meanings but also the unity and self-identity of the word. Writing, in a word, was itself the best available supplement or antidote to the dialectic of critical exemplification that Artaud, and Derrida, had cogently denounced, and which Derrida, affirming Artaud, sought in his own manner to displace.

But how far was Derrida able to elude his own critique of aesthetic, literary, and philosophical criticism? To what extent was Derrida's essay on Artaud itself reducible in the end to an act of literary criticism? And how to begin to think the inescapable relation between singularity and universality that was at the heart of Derrida's encounter with Artaud and which touched on the very future possibility of literary criticism itself, whenever it was required, as it necessarily was, to confront the unreadability of "poor Artaud"?

For the moment, Derrida concluded as he had begun, by evoking a question: a "question that still and forever will be secretly at issue [*encore et toujours enveloppée*] whenever a form of address [*une parole*], within the protection of a limited field of inquiry, allows itself from a distance to be provoked by the flesh-and-blood enigma [*l'énigme de chair*] who wanted properly to call himself Antonin Artaud [*qui voulut s'appeler proprement Antonin Artaud*]."[45] And as the word order of his final sentence insists, Derrida's closing gesture was to inscribe at the end of his essay, not only by way of homage, and in recognition of the debt incurred in respect of this other flesh, but also to reaffirm the singularity upon which his own discourse was itself suspended, Artaud's own proper-improper personal name.

But in subsequent editions of *L'Écriture et la différence*, from September 1969 onwards, "long after writing this essay," as Derrida put it, the commentator added a final footnote, comprising a further brief quotation from Artaud first published in 1958, and which he duly dated,

countersigning his text once again in the double sense of both endorsing and overwriting it, as though to remind himself and his readers that
no closure was ever an ending, and to make a promise to himself, and
to the future of Artaud's ghost, that he would one day return.

Before doing so, however, Derrida would embark on a long detour.

II

A mime

> Literature in its limitlessness cancels itself out [*s'annule*]. If this short
> treatise on literature [by Mallarmé] *meant* [*voulait-dire*, i.e., signified and
> intended] anything, which there is reason to doubt at this stage, it would
> begin by stating that there is no—or hardly any, very little—literature;
> that there is at any event no essence of literature, no truth of literature,
> no being-literary [*être-littéraire*] of literature.
>
> Jacques Derrida, *La Dissémination*[46]

At 9.00 P.M. on Wednesday, 26 February 1969, at an address in the rue
de Rennes in Paris, Jacques Derrida sat down—ready to deliver a paper
to the Groupe d'études théoriques that had recently been set up, in the
wake of May 1968, by the journal *Tel Quel*.[47] Before Derrida began speaking, each audience member had been handed a single sheet of paper, on
which there stood two quotations, in differing typefaces: the first, much
the longer, was an extract from Plato's *Philebus*, running across the
upper third of the handout, and continuing down the left-hand side; the
second, slotted into the bottom right-hand corner, "dividing or completing" the other, as Derrida put it, consisted of a brief, little-known prose
text by Mallarmé from the volume *Divagations*. A number of additional
quotations from Mallarmé were chalked up on the blackboard, and an
old-fashioned chandelier illuminated proceedings. Derrida's talk was
untitled, for strategic reasons he would shortly explain; and a second
session, similarly untitled, had been scheduled for the following week.

There were many reasons for this elaborate scenography. First, Derrida's own gesture, as he took his seat in the lecture hall, was calculated in such a way as to recall, repeat, or mime Mallarmé's own actions, also replicated in his own text, some seventy-nine years earlier, when at the Cercle artistique et littéraire in Brussels, and subsequently at a series of other venues, including, finally, on 27 February 1890, in Berthe Morisot's salon in Paris, before an audience composed of Degas, Monet, Redon, Renoir, Cazalis, Dujardin, Marras, Régnier, Vielé-Griffin, Wyzewa, and others, the poet had paid tribute to the memory of the late Villiers de l'Isle-Adam. Mallarmé had begun with this announcement: "A man accustomed to dreaming [*au rêve habitué*] comes here to speak of another, who is dead." "Ladies and Gentlemen," he continued, before adding, in an aside, by way of a fictional or non-fictional, at any event detached and already half-ironic stage direction that would furnish Derrida in 1969 with a belated or deferred epigraph, the following words, cited as though under glass: "(the speaker sits down [*le causeur s'assied*])." Mallarmé then turned to the topic of the day, which would similarly preoccupy Derrida two generations later, when he too would sit down to speak of the non-presence of a spectral other:

> Is it at all sure what it is to write [*Sait-on ce que c'est qu'écrire*]? An ancient and very vague but jealous practice [*une ancienne et très vague mais jalouse pratique*], whose meaning lies in the mystery of the heart. Whoever accomplishes it, integrally, retrenches himself [*se retrenche*]. Tantamount, by hearsay [*par ouï-dire*], to nothing existing and, specially, the self, in the reflection of sparse divinity: this senseless game of writing [*ce jeu insensé d'écrire*] is to assume, by virtue of a doubt—the drop of ink that resembles the sublime dark—a kind of duty to recreate everything, with reminiscences, to make sure we really are where we are meant to be [*qu'on est bien là où l'on doit être*] (because, allow me to express this apprehension, an uncertainty remains).[48]

There were several further remarkable traits alluding to his celebrated predecessor that Derrida took care to underline. For his deferred suspended heading not only evoked Mallarmé's own reluctance to grant special privilege to the commanding and intrusive authority of the title "that would speak too loud"; it was also a reflection on the chandeliers (or *lustres*) illuminating the stage in several texts by Mallarmé about the theatre, and which also had their counterpart in the rue de Rennes, casting its shimmering, multi-faceted light upon this two-fold verbal scene. Even the timetabling of Derrida's own double session, and the iterative structure it embodied, not to mention the distribution of the single sheet of paper to participants, derived some logistical inspiration from the arrangements studied by Mallarmé in his preparatory work for *Le Livre*, that poem—in the form of a semi-liturgical, theatrical event—that was to be the culmination of his life's work, but, left unfinished when he died, was largely destroyed by his heirs following the poet's instructions. And the blackboard too, with its emblematic quotations from the surviving notes for *Le Livre* and elsewhere ("Le Mystère dans les Lettres," "Solitude," and a drama review from *La Dernière Mode,* the fashion magazine which Mallarmé edited single-handedly during the latter part of 1874), repeating, reversing, shadowing with its white characters on a black background the black-on-white of writing ("You noticed [*remarquas*]," wrote Mallarmé, "one does not write, luminously, on a dark background, only the alphabet of the stars shows itself thus, sketched or interrupted; humanity [*l'homme*] pursues black on white"), drew the audience's attention not only to the differential play of language and writing but also to the structural and thematic importance of spacing or spatialisation in Mallarmé. "The 'blanks' [*'blancs'*], indeed," he wrote, in a prefatory note, later to be abandoned, for the poem "Un coup de dés," "grow in importance and are what is immediately most striking [*frappent d'abord*]."[49]

But Mallarme's text was more than a convenient fund of self-reflexive figures or tropes waiting to be exploited with wit and ingenuity by the commentator, and Derrida's artful restaging of these texts in the course of his protracted exordium was anything but an act of fetishistic preciosity. What was at stake went much further; it implied a radical rethinking of the whole relationship between literature and philosophy: a questioning of philosophy's downgrading or repression of writing in general, a renewed attention to the philosophical implications, in Mallarmé's famous words, of the question whether "[s]omething like literature [*quelque chose comme les Lettres*] exists" at all,[50] a suspicion, therefore, as to the deep-seated complicity between metaphysics, literary theory, and modern literary criticism, and an examination of the strategies of reading and writing that Mallarmé's work made not only possible, but necessary, and had a crucial bearing not only on any future understanding of the structure of textuality in general and on reception of this singular poet but also the challenge, infinitely repeated, yet always unique, of responding, in writing, to the writing of others, not in order to enforce the law of value and values, but according to the more compelling demand of a commitment to justice—in this moment of "exquisite crisis" which for the first time, Mallarmé put it, made it possible not only to express oneself in words, but modulate too, "in one's own manner [*à son gré*]."[51]

Replying to the occasion implicitly as well as explicitly, Derrida's citational preamble accentuated at least four decisive points. The first was that no origin in fact ever came first; any beginning was inseparable from a possibility of repetition, preceding, traversing, and surviving it. Derrida's own beginning, then, was not present to itself as such but was necessarily written belatedly in the margins of many preceding texts, notably those of Plato and Mallarmé. But though repetition was indispensable for any beginning to begin, and for identity to be secured, it also had the unavoidably contrary effect, even as it served to confirm or underwrite identity, of supplementing it, affecting it with a mark of irreducible difference or otherness, irrevocably dividing it from itself—without it being possible to bring this trace of difference, deferral, and return, in so far as it remained a fundamental component of all identity rather than a mere contingent external circumstance, under the dominance of the selfsame, or to control its always potentially reckless proliferation, or to confine its necessarily unpredictable divagations, as Mallarmé's title had it. As far as identity was concerned, repetition, then, was a condition both of possibility and of impossibility; identity could become identical with itself only to the extent that it departed from itself, and was by that very token non-identical with itself. No text, no experience, no event, therefore, was entirely what it was or considered itself to be. In so far as it bore a mark of identity, it was also inhabited by a mark, or re-mark, of its alteration, otherness, exteriority.

But repetition did not only, by enabling it, disable the self identity of any mark; it bound it to an always singular context or circumstance, to which it remained attached, albeit provisionally, and from which it was therefore, at the same time, always already detached. Text and context, as Derrida emphasised in the essay "Signature événement contexte [Signature Event Context]," written soon after, were inseparable; but while the one was unique, the other was necessarily infinite, and there was no end to the number of possible other contexts to which a text might belong, which had the effect, among others, of perpetually deferring, transforming, corrupting its address.[52] And this was already Derrida's second point: it was that any text, precisely in so far as it occurred, here and now, in a given context, and carried a date or signature to prove it, was by that very token not fully present to itself at all ("there is no Present [*il n'est pas de Présent*]," Mallarmé famously remarked, "no—a present does not exist"[53]); indeed, it was thinkable as a singular, unique event only on the basis of a movement of spatialisation and temporisation, of separation, differentiation, articulation, and repetition, that preceded both presence and absence, and was not recuperable within being or ontology, and reducible to those dominant values of presence, immediacy, originality, liveliness, authenticity, veracity, and truthfulness (no matter whether truth was interpreted in traditional terms as *adaequatio,* or according to that more originary Heideggerian dispensation as *aletheia*) that in all their various forms, as Derrida went on to show, have been privileged down the centuries, not only by the metaphysical tradition itself, but also, more insistently or emphatically still, by that minor branch of philosophical speculation called literary criticism. (And textuality, it also followed, was similarly irreducible to those more recently promoted, diametrically opposed criteria, which so-called postmodernist or neo-formalist theory has brought to the fore: absence, negativity, secondariness, inauthenticity, parody, and falsity, in so far as they prove simply to be the reverse of the traditional values they claim to replace.)

This critical dislocation of textual self-identity and presence had a further corollary. For what was also implicit in Derrida's citational mime-play was that each interpretative or other frame which philosophy or literary criticism might endeavour to draw around a text in order to position it as an object of reading and put it in its alleged proper context, and decide upon its meaning or meanings—which still today is how the task of reading is most commonly understood—was always already preceded by the possibility of another frame, be it in the form of an apparent absence of frame. Each and every frame was therefore necessarily partial and incomplete, which both enabled and required the intervention of yet another frame, while also making it superfluous and inadequate in its turn, without it ever being possible to set a term to this irresistible movement of addition or subtraction. But there was nothing negative about this dispersion of each and every text beyond itself. For it was an indispensable condition of possibility of reading—albeit one that could not do other than spell the end of reading understood as the positioning of the text as a clearly circumscribed object, interpretable only within its own given, so-called proper (historical, formal, biographical, or other) horizon of intentional meanings. Moreover, if no text could be deemed to be fully present to itself or entirely identical with itself (and it is hard to see how literary criticism or any other form of commentary might otherwise be possible), it followed that every text was indelibly marked by an irreducible, unavowable silence: an interruption, erasure, or withdrawal. The mastery to which philosophy or literary criticism aspired was simply impossible; for there was in every text an unmeasurable measure of secrecy, a secret whose fate was to remain unspeakable, and of which it might not even be possible to decide whether it was a secret at all. As far as textuality was concerned, something always escaped, resisted, remained at a distance without distance, while continually demanding a response.

This much, among other things, was already apparent from Derrida's handout. This single, singular sheet comprised two texts, one from philosophy, one from literature, both seemingly inhabiting the same rectangular space. But this semblance of unity or complementarity harboured a remarkable dissymmetry, in provenance, history, language, mode, genre, and layout. These two texts, by Plato, by Mallarmé, were not positioned side by side, with the one confronting the other, as in French legal proceedings, for instance, when the two parties are brought face to face in order that the one be proved right and the other wrong, and truth established. Admittedly, the passage from Plato came first, so to speak, occupying the head of the page, and enclosing, at least in part, the text of Mallarmé's "Mimique." But the significance of this spacing was uncertain: was it an indication of philosophy's ambition to dominate literature, or testimony to the fact that Mallarmé's writing had already begun to erode that dominance? Derrida's point, however, was not that either literature or philosophy had an advantage over the other, that the one might be able to decide reliably as to the truth or untruth of the other, in such a way, for instance, that philosophy might henceforth be deemed a branch of literature, or, conversely, that literature might be taken to be a continuation of philosophy by other means, nor even that either text, authored by Plato and by Mallarmé, might be properly or adequately named by such labels as philosophy or literature.[54] It was rather that, on the sheet where both figured, the two passages were simultaneously joined and disjoined in such a way that each framed, cited, or referenced the other, while being simultaneously framed, cited, or referenced by it. And by the very fact of its inscription or reinscription, each quotation was exposed to something contained within it but which it could not itself contain. Each was divided from itself; it had its place, but no place within that place.

The opposition between margin and text, centre and periphery, inside and outside, began to give way, within Derrida's own exposition, to an infinite continuous-discontinuous textual space in which every move was already both a deferral and a referral, and every point a vanishing point; if, in the end, as Derrida famously argued in *De la grammatologie*, there was nothing outside the text, it was because there was nothing inside it either. "Nothing," Mallarmé observed in "Un coup de dés," "will have taken place but the place [*Rien n'aura eu lieu que le lieu*]."[55] But this was not in itself proof of the presence, ideality, and closure of Mallarmean poetic space. It was rather a sign of its radical dispersion, its irreducibility to any horizon of intended meanings, a thought the poem dramatised in its own way by glossing the shipwreck of its own occurrence—occurrence without occurrence—with the help of the enigmatic final affirmation: "Every Thought emits a Throw of the Dice [*Toute Pensée émet un Coup de Dés*]."[56]

This much too was at stake that evening in February 1969. For what Derrida's opening remarks emphasised, following Mallarmé's precariously abyssal, circular proposition, disseminated through the poem to which it lent a title, that "a throw of the dice will never abolish chance [*un coup de dés jamais n'abolira le hasard*]," was that, if chance was necessity, as Mallarmé's poem implied, then, by another turn of the wheel, necessity itself was also chance. From the perspective of the poet's "anglish words," the opposition between essence and contingency, stance and circumstance, text and context, together with the dialectic of exemplification it held in place, could not be sustained.[57] From the outset it was impossible to avoid gambling on this or that gesture, phoneme, grapheme, or word. To do so, however, was not to conform to some prior dispensation that had always already subordinated to truth or un-truth what Mallarmé insisted was writing's perilous experience but to affirm the risk of language itself as unpremeditated, unprecedented, and futural occurrence. In this respect, the many quotations, allusions, and word-games that characterise Derrida's opening were more than a series of playful gestures of self-conscious reflection: they were a risk taken, and calculated as such, for in yielding the initiative to words what Derrida sought to do—though it would have happened in any case—was to expose the workings of his own discourse in such a way that it would be seen to have already supplied in advance, by way of oblique tribute to the logic of Mallarmean mimickry, or in fulfilment of a prom-ise or an oath on the part of the speaker, a confirmation of the discourse he was about to deliver. To stage his own reading in citational, idiomatic terms was at any rate to insist that there was no theoretical or critical language other than marked by idiom, and no event that was not an ef-fect of repetition, deferral, and difference.[58]

The angle adopted by Derrida in 1969, for reasons that were prop-erly neither contingent nor essential, was resolutely four-square. This commitment to the sign of four corresponded to both strategy and op-portunity. It affirmed the abyssal excess of doubles, doublings, repeti-tions, and replications over ternary dialectics, and it also allowed Derrida to mobilise considerable resources of language and idiom, including among others such coinages as the French word *coin* (from the Latin, *cuneus*), meaning a wedge (whence the English *quoin*), a die for stamp-ing money (whence the English *coin*), a corner or extremity, a remote location or locality, and such cognate expressions as *marqué au coin*, bearing a trademark imprint, or *celu m'en bouche un coin*, to be speech-less with surprise, or *regarder en coin*, to look askance at something, all of which are terms that, directly or indirectly, feature specifically in Der-rida's analysis. Derrida's interest in corners and angles, frames and wedges, is also part of a more general consideration of the joins, joints, and articulations, the fractures, breaks, and disjunctions inherent in writing, and one that finds a technical counterpart in the extensive rep-ertoire of types of graft or other kinds of prosthesis that Derrida ex-plores later in the essay, where what is precisely at issue, as in writing, is the problematisation of any opposition between nature and culture, essence and contingency, the self-identical and the hybrid. And by that very token, the purpose of Derrida's appeal to words, sustained at times by recourse to Littré's canonic dictionary, was not to uncover any original, hidden kernel of truth, surviving historical degeneration or erasure like a memory of authenticity, but beyond any restriction to theme, positionality, or intention, to chart the inexhaustible movement of Mallarmé's writing. Rather than seeking to translate Mallarmé's poems into intelligible prose, as more than one commentator had been tempted to do, it was more a matter of allowing the language of philosophical or literary commentary to be itself transformed by its exposure to the language of the poem—not in order to imitate Mallarmé, were it to be possible, but rather to render justice to Mallarmé's own language not as aestheticising affectation, but a necessary and rigorous style of writing and thinking.

As elsewhere, the ostensible topic, topos, or theme of Derrida's exposition, which was properly neither topic, nor topos, nor theme, was something disarmingly simple, yet capable of infinite expansion: it was, among others, the peculiar status of the (French) word *entre,* which was most readily to be understood as the syncategorematic conjunction or adverb *entre,* meaning: between, though it was also possible, or at least never impossible, that the word, in Mallarmé or elsewhere, might also turn out to be a form of the verb *entrer,* meaning: to enter, like perhaps the imperative: *enter!* or the first- or third-person singular of the indicative: *I enter* or *he/she/it enters,* or even a ghostly instance of the homophonic French noun, *antre:* den, lair, secret cave, or bodily cavity. Conjunction, adverb, verb, noun: it is true that readers of Mallarmé are often unable to decide to which part of speech certain words are to be attributed, and they can hardly ever be extracted from the complex syntactic chain to which, provisionally, they belong. This was on one level a simple literary critical point on Derrida's part. The implications were, however, far-reaching. That such hesitation could occur at all alluded to something like an opening of the possibility of language, prior and irreducible to the division between syntax and semantics. In other words, there necessarily had to be, both in language and, as it were, before language in the restricted sense, an ineradicable indecision deriving from the differential status of the trace itself, an undecidability that did not simply hesitate between meanings, or between syntactic or rhetorical forms, but hovered at the limit of language itself, irreducible to words, moving instead in the space or spacing between words and manifesting itself, for instance, albeit always as something other than itself, in the blank, white space of deferral that enabled signs to be inscribed, repeated, effaced, recognised, and interpreted at all. As Derrida later notes apropos of Mallarmé's use of the word *blanc* to refer to the blank space between words, the word *entre* was already an instance of what it signified, which was also to say that, framed by itself and folded upon itself, it was not reducible to that signification, which remained at a distance from itself, as though in parentheses. It not only meant: between; it also fell into a gap between meanings. Even as it cited or exposed its meaning, it outstripped or fell short of itself, and occupied only the space between.[59]

Here, then, was a humble, even banal word that was not only a mark of connection and disconnection, of junction and disjunction, of suspension, withdrawal, and iteration, but also stated as much, and did so from a distance: it was both itself and more or less than itself, itself and other than itself, divided from itself, therefore, between use and mention, simultaneously and without distinction.[60] As such, however, it described a path or passageway, albeit one whose direction could not be determined in advance, but which Derrida, for his part, followed in the rest of his paper, which by now, by the same iterative logic of the re-mark, had come to be entitled "La Double Séance [The Double Session]," in order to draw the necessary philosophical, literary, and other consequences regarding the space or spacing between what called itself philosophy and what, albeit not by itself but by convention, law, or mere institutional habit, was called literature. As he did so, Derrida put in train a textual machine whose implications were soon to be boundless.

What was it, then, that happened between—literature and philosophy? Faced with such a question, literature, if it exists, can always choose to turn aside, professing ignorance, incompetence, frivolity. Philosophy, however, has no such luxury. It is required to ask the primordial, opening, philosophical question. What is literature? *Qu'est-ce que la littérature?* These words tell, of course, a story, and not necessarily a philosophical one. For in French, if not in all other languages which name or conceptualise something called literature, they are already a quotation. As such, they are anything but primordial, but already second. They belong to a millennial tradition, one that persists to the present, encountering (among others) Sartre, whose question to this effect: *What Is Literature?* was soon, if not already, part of literature, confirming what Mallarmé had suspected: that everything—including all questions as to what literature might be—is already part of literature, in which case the question would merely be an instance of what it sought to explain, which it cannot do except at the cost of plunging into a movement of infinite, abyssal regress. Endeavouring to frame literature, the ontological question could not *not* end up being framed by it. If there was anything to be called literature, then, it was certainly not a thing or a something that was, more a space of limitless redefinition: perpetually (re)framing the frame.

This explains why Blanchot, taking up Sartre's challenge in "La Littérature et le droit à la mort [Literature and the Right to Death]" in 1948, as mentioned earlier, concluded in the end that all answers to the question of literary being, or the being of literature, were disappointing ones: they merely proved to be examples of what they sought to circumscribe. But if this meant literature could not be subordinated to anything other than itself, this was not to attribute aesthetic autonomy to literature but, on the contrary, to undermine its possible self-coincidence, its actual or potential boundaries, and its reduction to any essence whatsoever, except perhaps, as Blanchot puts it, its essential non-essentiality. Literature was as vast as language itself, even more vast, perhaps, in that it included not just words themselves but their silence too, and the gesture of their inscription and effacement, together with their infinite, perpetual re-mark as always different from what they were. And it was this excess of movement over position, of writing over theme, according to Derrida, that was so vertiginously in evidence in Mallarmé's unassuming and hitherto little noticed text.

For this restaging of Pierrot by Pierrot, doing all the parts himself, and retelling in mime, in a kind of pseudo-present resembling a simultaneously prospective and retrospective anamnesis, the tale of how he planned (in the past) to rid himself (in the future) of his cruel and unfaithful wife by killing her, and in a dream, after miming out various possibilities (rope, knife, poison), chanced or chances upon the notion of tickling her to death, which he then acts out, both as himself and as his intended or remembered victim, till death ensues, in mime, on Colombine's part, only for Pierrot, now miming himself, to be over-taken in turn by deathly convulsions of his own, in the course of which he sees, perhaps in a vision, the painting of Colombine with which the mime-play began to become alive once more, at which stage, to his wife's undying hilarity, he himself is tickled (or tickles himself) to death, rendering null and void this whole speculative performance— this whole story, then, not presented, but cited, so to speak, by Mallarmé, and retold only by allusion (without any attempt at illusion), had no positionality other than a vastly shifting horizon—horizon without horizon—of writings, literary and non-literary, vocal and gestural, ver-bal and non-verbal, spoken and unspoken; it therefore had no inside and no outside, no present and no present past or present future; in-stead, there was a proliferation of roles and doubles, and slippages from the one to the other, with the result that, while not being present to it-self as pure performance, the mime-play nevertheless referred beyond itself as though in memory or anticipation of an absent event that had always already (not) occurred. As such, its movement was citational; it referred obliquely and without end towards a perpetually deferred, ab-sent referent, putting the scene at a distance without distance, suspend-ing, detaching it, putting all effectivity into parentheses. Mallarmé's own text, displaying a phantom (non-)quotation at its own spectral cen-tre, referring not simply to textuality in general but also both to the sin-gular (non-)occurrence of the mime-play just witnessed and to itself as a commentary and deferred, oblique re-enactment of that mime-play, folded these many layers together in the following abyssal remark: "Here then [*Voici*]—'The scene illustrates but the idea, not an effective action, in a hymen [*hymen*] (from which proceeds the Dream), dissolute but sacred, between [*entre*] desire and fulfilment, perpetration and its memory: here preceding, there remembering, in the future, in the past, *under the false appearance of a present* [*sous une apparence fausse de pré-sence*]. Thus operates the Mime, whose acting is limited to a perpetual allusion [*une allusion perpétuelle*] without breaking the glass [*sans briser la glace*]: it installs, thus, a medium, pure, of fiction.'"[61]

In Mallarmé's text, this absence of hierarchy between textual levels, the impossibility of determining secure borders, the unavailability of any point of anchorage, all this was crucial for Derrida's reading. It

betokened, not a problematic overturning or inversion (the lesson of
Artaud was more salient than ever in this regard), but a displacement,
suspension, and interruption of the law of mimesis articulated by at
least a certain Plato and implicit in the whole tradition of thought issuing from Plato, at the core of which, Derrida argues, lay a belief in the
absolute discernibility of the imitated and the imitator, of that which is,
reality, the thing itself, and its image, copy, reproduction, together with
the unchallenged priority of the former over the latter.[62] This privilege
had a name: the *ontological*. Derrida explains:

> For what is it that "Platonism," i.e., more or less without media-
> tion, the whole history of Western philosophy, including all the
> anti-Platonisms that are regularly part of it, thereby decides and
> maintains? What is it that is decided and maintained in ontology
> or in dialectics through all the mutations or upheavals that sub-
> sequently followed? Precisely the *ontological:* the presumed pos-
> sibility of a discourse on what *is,* a *logos* that decides and can be
> decided, on or of the *on* (present-being [*l'étant-présent*]). That
> which is, present-being [*l'étant-présent*] (the underlying matrix
> for all substance and all reality, for each and every opposition
> between matter and form, essence and existence, objectivity and
> subjectivity, etc.), may be distinguished from all semblance [*appa-
> rence*], image, or phenomenon, etc., that is, from that which, pre-
> senting it as present being [*l'étant-présent*], doubles it, re-presents
> it, and thence replaces and de-presents it. In other words, there
> is the 1 and the 2, the simple and the double. The double comes
> *after* the simple; it multiplies it *as an afterthought* [*par suite*].[63]

In "Mimique," however, as Derrida's own mime-play showed, it was
readily apparent that the number two—as captured by the two-fold
hymen, gathering and dividing the two—had always already come first.
Which meant that Mallarmé's writing was irreducible to the dialectic of
the original and the copy, did not fall subject therefore to ontological
decision, and could not be addressed or arraigned by a discourse committed to refinding in writing the truth of present-being, whether as
presence, or being, or truth. Accordingly, if there was an entity such as
literature, and if Mallarmé's writing might be said to belong to it, then
it could only follow that literature was in fact not an entity at all, and that

any discourse that sought to determine the essence of that entity—which would in principle include not only all modern literary theory seeking to determine the autonomy of literature as such but also all literary criticism devoted to uncovering the truth of the artwork, would by that gesture merely confirm its reliance on the metaphysical tradition that, on Derrida's submission, Mallarmé in his writing had decisively interrupted.

The consequences, here, are not hard to measure.

Derrida indicated as much himself in a characteristically bold extended footnote that both tabulated and dispatched the philosophical legacy of Platonism in so far as it bore on the thinking of art and literature, as though to suggest in passing that the long history of literary criticism, together with the concept of literature on which it relied and which it promoted, though not necessarily the thing called literature itself, if it existed, was itself little more than a footnote to that even longer history of metaphysics. "This schema," Derrida concluded, "with its two propositions and six possible corollaries, forms a kind of logical machine: it programmes the prototypes of all the propositions inscribed in the discourse of Plato and those of the whole tradition. In accordance with a complex but implacable law, this machine supplies the critics of the future with their each and every cliché."[64]

But if literary criticism, in its underlying purpose, if not the detail of its analyses, had therefore always already preceded itself, how then might it be possible to respond, here and now, and in the future, to the writing of Mallarmé? Derrida insisted, however, from the start that there could be no standardised, regulated, literary critical or literary theoretical method that might measure up to Mallarmé's writing, for instance, not because of the aesthetic power, density, or quality of the poet's work, but more simply, if more radically, because the poet's writing failed to provide either criticism or theory with what they required, that is, an ontologically present, self-identical object that might be positioned and appropriated as such within critical or theoretical discourse. Mallarmé's writing nevertheless still required a reader and exacted from that reader a response, one that could not *not* be written.

But how?

In the precise context of "La Double Séance," Derrida for his part advances an intricately woven string or sequence of proto-concepts: the fold, the mime, the blank (or *blanc*), dissemination, the hymen, and so on, each of which is remarkable for the fact that it does not belong to any pre-established theoretical discourse of Derrida's devising but is extracted from Mallarmé's text and reinserted into it, the differential movement of its own singular, repetitive trajectory traced and retraced both in relation to its own displacements and the general discourse within which it is inscribed. Among these proto-concepts, there is one, the hymen, which, privileged on provisional, tactical grounds, is the occasion for an important discussion bearing on the concept of the undecidable or undecidability, which has done much to influence reception of Derrida's thinking of so-called literary texts. The term undecidable too, however, as Derrida points out, emphasising its provisional and analogical status in the discussion, is a quotation, not from Mallarmé, but from Gödel's famous theorem of 1931, according to which, Derrida notes, may be deemed undecidable "any proposition which, given a system of axioms governing a multiplicity, is neither an analytical nor deductive consequence of those axioms, nor in contradiction with them, neither true nor false with respect to those axioms. *Tertium datur,* without synthesis."[65]

Beyond the *caveat* (which Derrida does not specify further, but no doubt has to do with the fact that, though its operation may be formalised in logical terms, Mallarmé's writing is not reducible to a set of logical propositions), what is most importantly at stake here, and flagged as such by the concept of the undecidable, is Derrida's insistence that Mallarmé's writing is unresponsive to any criterion of *either* truth (however defined) *or* falsity. It is not therefore that Mallarmé's high modernism, avant-gardism, or precocious postmodernism leads him to prefer the trickery of the superficial copy over the essential radiance of the original, which would be at best little more than a back-handed compliment to truth. But nor is it that the poet, in the name of aestheticism, has merely opted for sybilline mystery and rich poetic suggestiveness at the cost of prosaic clarity or plain speaking. Equally, the undecidable does not correspond to a logic of negativity, nor to any kind of aesthetic autonomy (two principal areas of disagreement between Derrida and his erstwhile associates in the *Tel Quel* group). But nor is it a kind of semantic agnosticism, reflecting something that may or may not be true, according to opinion, that may be true for some readers, for instance, but not others, or true only at certain times of the day or month, or true without being true in so far as it voices some apophatic revelation, of which nothing may be said without betraying it. And neither is it evidence of aesthetic reclusiveness, on the part of either poet or philosopher, indicative of a lack of moral courage or commitment, or a sign of ideological or moral permissiveness, laxity, or tolerance, or proof of a fainthearted unwillingness to take decisions. The undecidable does not defer, then, to the conviviality of liberal consensus.

What is more radically at issue in Derrida's thinking of the undecidable is writing as inscription, an inscription that precedes and exceeds all horizons of meaning, intended, communicated, or revealed, which is therefore closer to a syntax than a semantics, and closer still to that opening of language that is neither a syntax nor a semantics, but their—undecidable—point of common possibility. What occurs, then, in Mallarmé's writing is not primarily that meaning is inexhaustible, though it is, but that writing is inexhaustible by meaning. And it is for this reason, contends Derrida, that the contradictory double meanings of a word such as hymen are possible at all: they are but an effect of the syntactic or pre-syntactic logic of between, *entre:*

> The word "between," whether it is a case of confusion *between* or of the interval *between,* thus bears the brunt of the operation. It is imperative to determine the hymen on the basis of the between, and not the reverse. The hymen in the text (as crime, sexual act, incest, suicide, simulacrum) may be put at the tip [*à la pointe*] of this indecision. The tip advances according to the irreducible excess of the syntactic over the semantic. The word "between" has no full meaning in itself. *Between,* opened [*Entre ouvert:* Derrida's formula may also be read as *entr'ouvert:* half open *and* half closed], is a syntactic hinge [*cheville:* ankle, pin, plug], not a categorem, but a syncategorem, what philosophers from the Middle Ages to Husserl's *Logical Investigations* have called incomplete meaning. What holds for "hymen" also applies, *mutatis mutandis,* to all those other signs that, like *pharmakon, supplément, différance,* and various others, have double, contradictory, undecidable status, always hinging on their syntax, whether "internal," so to speak, articulating and combining under the same yoke, *huph'hen,* two incompatible meanings, or "external," in so far as it is dependent on the code in which the word is put to work. But the syntactical composition and decomposition of a sign makes

this alternative between internal and external null and void [*cadu-que:* obsolete]. We are dealing simply with greater or lesser syntactic units at work, and with economically different degrees of condensation. Without reducing all these to the same, far from it, it is possible to recognise a persistent law [*loi de série*] at each of these indefinite pivot points [*lieux de pivotement indéfini:* i.e., the pivoting is indefinite, not the points]: they mark the edge [*points*] of what cannot ever be mediated, mastered, sublated, or integrated dialectically through *Erinnerung* and *Aufhebung*.[66]

The undecidable, then, for Derrida, is not primarily, if at all, a semantic value, though it may manifest itself as such. It is rather a radical interruption in sense, that cannot be interiorised or recuperated within dialectical unity, which is thus neither true nor untrue, more akin to a divided, deferred, non-identical, performative act. Resisting the presence of the present, the undecidable, in the text, signs a remainder, one that does not hark back to the present, either present past or present future but promises an irreducible future—always to come—that will never become present. In turn, as Derrida will stress in later texts, without conferring any particular privilege on the word itself, too often the target of wilful misunderstanding, this is why the undecidable is a necessary condition of possibility of all decision-making, and the reason it also makes all decisions impossible—in so far as to make any decision it is necessary to gamble on what is not within the power or capacity to predict of any deciding subject, and because no decision can ever overcome or exhaust the dilemma to which it is a response, since in that case it would no longer be a decision at all, but merely a mechanical application of what has already been determined in advance.

The undecidable, imposing itself on Derrida's reading of Mallarmé in this way, prompted by the poet's writing, yet not limited to it, soon came to be associated with many of the other so-called literary texts Derrida was to address in ensuing years. To this extent, it was hardly surprising that, in Derrida's own work, or in that of others, it should encounter, in due course, that other name for the more-than-one or the no-longer-one, the in-between, the irreducible, and the futural: the neuter or *neutre*, as explored and exploited in their differing idioms, by Barthes and by Blanchot.

What, then, happens between—the undecidable and the neuter?

Already the neuter, in Barthes, in Blanchot, is not self-identical. Neither the one nor the other, neither one nor other, it too divides against itself, punctures the semantic horizon, affirms the excess of syntax over semantics. Here too, then, all is hesitation, suspension, displacement, singularity, and this is at least one feature that the neuter in both Barthes and Blanchot shares with the Derridean undecidable. Most markedly, however, in Barthes, the neuter cleaves nonetheless to something resembling a position, albeit a negative one—position without position, position in excess of position, position as absence of position—within what Barthes describes, somewhat oddly, in the opening page of *S/Z*, as "the infinite paradigm of difference [*le paradigme infini de la différence*]," which, from Derrida's perspective, was inevitably to privilege, by taking it as already given, the vertical, semantic axis of language, rather than the horizontal, syntactic dimension, or, even more to the point, rather than rethinking the syntactico-semantic divide itself that Mallarmé had thrown into question. Barthes, admittedly, was no doubt prompted to restrict difference to the semantic axis by his reading of Saussure (and Jakobson) which gave priority, as far as linguistic or textual analysis was concerned, to differential semantics (and phonology), treating syntax as a series of agreed, conventional combinatory rules.[67] A similar presumption prevails too in the work of Barthes, with the result that, consistently if paradoxically, the neuter in Barthes is determined as aesthetic indeterminacy, as a moment of peace, he calls it, in the war of words—which would later, as we have seen, provide the writer with the basis for an ethics of critical suspension, ideological distraction, and textual pleasure, an excluded middle, so to speak, whose prime virtue lay in its capacity to abolish dualistic oppositions. Thus, for instance, in *Le Plaisir du texte*:

> The text, for its part, is atopical [*atopique*], if not as far as consumption is concerned, at any rate as regards production. It is not a way of speaking, a fiction, the system it contains is overwhelmed, undone (this overwhelming, this undoing, is what is called signifying [*signifiance*]). From this atopia it takes and communicates to its reader a bizarre state: simultaneously excluded [*exclu*] and at peace [*paisible*]. In the war of languages, there may

be quiet moments, and these moments are texts ("War," says a character in Brecht, "does not exclude peace. . . . War has its peaceful moments. . . . Between two skirmishes, it is perfectly possible to down a pint").[68]

Though from Barthes to Blanchot, and Blanchot to Barthes, the word *neuter* remains ostensibly the same, much else shifts and is transformed. For Blanchot, for instance, the *neutre* is initially a grammatical rather than semantic category, and is observed at work as such in the Greek of Heraclitus and the French of René Char.[69] It also is an abyssal term, simultaneously discrete and discreet, able by dint of its own modest reserve (or distance without distance) to reserve (defer, postpone, withdraw, divide) each and every other word and concept, including itself. The neuter in Blanchot is an unassuming term, yet it challenges all philosophical or theoretical assumptions. Withdrawing, it withdraws; retiring, it retires; retracting, it retracts. The neuter in Blanchot is an always supplementary mark that, like the use of invisible (or visible) quotation marks, neutralises (suspects, suspends, challenges, effaces, overwrites) all meaning, but in so doing only manifests (without manifesting) the essential non-coincidence of all words, the possibility of erasure and reinscription that always already inhabits each trace, all language, all writing. In this respect, the neuter in Blanchot is neither an addition nor a subtraction but simultaneously both: putting words at a distance, it affirms the distance that is inseparable from all words. It no more belongs to any paradigm than it does to any syntagm, but occupies instead the spacing between. Like *différance*, then, of which the undecidable is an effect, the neuter in Blanchot also has something resembling quasi-transcendental status: it denotes the inscription and erasure of difference—of inscription as already an erasure and erasure as already an inscription—while nevertheless remaining one discreetly discrete, modest word among others, soon to be quietly erased, reinscribed, or overwritten in its turn by an always supplementary, other mark that cannot be circumscribed or contained within any horizon, since it is itself nothing other than the possibility and impossibility of the horizon itself as differentiating trace.[70]

The neuter in Blanchot, then, far from naming an eirenic interval or moment of peace in the on-going war of words, more nearly designates its opposite: a kind of perpetually nomadic process of displacement, framing and reframing, decontextualising and recontextualising all words, language, and writing. This, in turn, explains why the neuter, in Blanchot's sense, without being exclusive to literature or in any way identical with it, is nevertheless inseparable from its possibility. "What Kafka shows us," writes Blanchot, for instance, in "La Voix narrative [The Narrative Voice]" of October 1964, "even if the formula cannot be attributed to him directly, is that story-telling [*raconter*] puts the neuter into play [*met en jeu le neutre:* i.e., risks, gambles with the neuter]."[71] Here, the convergence between the neuter in Blanchot and what Derrida for his part sought to address under the rubric of the undecidable is readily apparent, as is the kinship—the growing together as well as apart—between the Mallarmé of "La Double Séance," silently re-marking the spaces between all words with the unspoken blankness from which they came, and removing from the scene all semblance of ontological foundation, supplementing writing with an invisible, spectral gesture testifying neither to presence nor to absence, neither to an inside nor an outside, neither to the self-evidence of semantics nor the autonomy of the syntactic, and the Kafka of "La Voix narrative," realising in his writing, says Blanchot, that "[t]he narrating voice that is inside only to the extent that it is outside, at a distance without distance, cannot embody itself: whether it takes on the voice of a judiciously chosen character, or even (this voice that ruins all mediation) creates the hybrid function of mediator, it is always different from whoever or whatever utters it: it is the indifferent-difference that disrupts the personal voice." "Let us (for amusement)," Blanchot adds, "call it spectral, ghostlike."[72]

And it was not by chance that, as part of his demonstration, Derrida was drawn to lay particular emphasis on that movement of infinite referral—referentiality without referent—characterising Mallarmé's Pierrot performing, the poet wrote, "without breaking the glass [*sans briser la glace*]." Indeed, some ten years later, in 1979, in a ground-breaking essay devoted to Blanchot's *récit*, *L'Arrêt de mort*, which, as Derrida was quick to point out, was itself also given over to a singularly inconclusive *hymen*— a relation without relation between history and text, narrator and narrated, protagonist and heroine, living and dying—Derrida made a similar remark about Blanchot's own writing, emphasising the importance of a certain persistent motif of the *sous-verre:* that is, that which appeared under glass, at a distance without distance, within a frame that was also an absence of frame, and, Blanchot's story implied, had a mysterious connection with the boundlessness of desire: "Someone who has completely disappeared and who, suddenly, is standing in front of you, behind a pane of glass [*derrière une glace*], becomes a sovereign figure (unless one is bothered by it)."[73] But this hidden pact with Blanchot was not unqualified. Just like Levinas, among others, as far as the term *neuter* (or *neutrality*) was concerned, Derrida remained suspicious, as another of the footnotes in "La Double Séance" made plain, in so far as the word might be taken to imply an effacement of difference and a kind of unavowed negativity, at least in its formulation, albeit that for Blanchot, as indeed for Derrida, there was nothing negative about the step beyond truth (and falsity) at stake in the Blanchotian *neutre* and in the Derridean undecidable.[74]

But how to read affirmatively a text that does not obey the demands of either truth or falsity? In the guise of arbitrariness, fictionality, or playfulness, this did not necessarily consign the discourse of the commentator to blatant untruth, any more than it guaranteed the possibility of discursive truth either. But it placed criticism, in so far as any was still possible at all, before a demanding dilemma. For how far, Derrida asked, was the undecidability of the undecidable at all compatible with what had hitherto been the task, the duty, the responsibility of literary and other criticism, which was, quite simply: to decide?

But how *not* to decide—and to do so affirmatively? What might it be, in other words, following in Mallarmé's footsteps, for a commentator *not* to repeat, rephrase, or translate whatever the text might be thought to be wanting to say, convey, or communicate, but, overstepping the boundary between inside and outside, essence and contingency, truth and untruth, to begin instead to mime writing's infinite movement of deferral and referral: to write in turn, so to speak, in broken anglish?

III

"Coward, traitor, thief, and queer"[75]

Between the two effects of this so-called literature of theft, betrayal, and denunciation, is there room to decide [*y a-t-il à décider*]? Expropriation or reappropriation? Decapitation or recapitation? Dissemination or recapitulation, recapitalisation? How to cut the knot [*comment trancher:* i.e., how to arrive at a decision]?

Jacques Derrida, *Glas*[76]

Some five years after his Mallarmean "Double Session" of 1969, Derrida went on to publish another famously double text, *Glas*, nominally devoted to the question of love, the (holy) family, the signature, and the proper name—which on this occasion exhibited its doubleness or duplicity not just sequentially or horizontally but simultaneously or vertically too, in the form of two independent but juxtaposed columns of print, interrupted at appropriate or inappropriate, not to say inappropriable moments, by a series of notes, interpolations, or digressions, opening in what Derrida calls peepholes (or *judas*). Featured on the left-hand side of each pointedly square 25-by-25-centimeter page, exploring the double status of the family as both constituent part and overarching whole of the Hegelian system, was a detailed reading of the numerous halting or limping transitions and moments of passage affecting the thought of Hegel as it strained, inexorably, towards the pinnacle of Absolute Knowledge; and on the right-hand side of each page Derrida's claudicant, bastard progress through Hegel (what the book itself, in words to be read at least twice over, describes as its "démarche bâtarde") was countered, that is, redoubled, supplemented, and displaced by a similarly patient trawl (which Derrida at one point compares metaphorically to the workings of a kind of dredging—or cruising—machine)[77] through the novels, plays, and other texts of Jean Genet, starting (while necessarily having always already begun elsewhere) with that writer's own double, squint-eyed text of 1967, "Ce qui est resté d'un Rembrandt déchiré en petits carrés bien réguliers, et foutu aux chiottes [What remains of a Rembrandt torn into small rectangular pieces, and flushed down the toilet]," itself, like *Glas*, made up of two dissymmetrical texts of uneven length, printed in facing columns.[78]

By any measure, *Glas* is an exceptional tour de force: of erudition, understanding, inventiveness, imagination, wit, and style. It is, however, a work that is largely invoked from a distance by Derrida's readers,

rather than examined by them in its strict detail, and more often portrayed as a clever, but loosely improvised, largely playful literary or
aesthetic performance, rather than as an instance of philosophical or
theoretical rigour—which is not to say that it should necessarily be
classed as the one rather than the other.[79] Indeed, for essential reasons,
Derrida argues, it is to some extent both—while also being neither; and
it is perhaps one of the most striking trademark or signature effects of
Glas that it is itself a colossal work, but one whose brief is to stage the
reversibility of the colossus as such,[80] and to affirm the *restance* or resistance of what remains: its irreducibility to all ontological, that is, philosophical, aesthetic, or literary appropriation.

But why Hegel, why Genet?

Partly by chance, but also by necessity. True, the differences between the pair were hard to underestimate: on the left stood philosophy,
religion, family, property, heterosexuality, the law, while on the right
was literature, impiety, illegitimacy, theft, queerness, crime. But despite appearances, Derrida's odd couple had more in common than
might be expected. Few other bodies of work posed with such exceptional acuity the whole question of the one and the other; few other texts
too sought to the same extraordinary degree to totalise their own event,
incorporate their own unfolding, command their own destiny, and capi-
talise on their own potency (*potence*, this word deriving from power,
observes Derrida, in both English and French, is also a word for the
scaffold or gallows, an erection, so to speak, whose secret purpose is to
shorten, by a head, and vice versa).[81] And it was not only that both texts
thereby privileged the speculative or the specular—the reflection of the
one in the other, and the other in the one—it was that specularity had
become the dominant theme not only as far as the reception of Hegelian phenomenology was concerned, but of the prose and theatre writings of Genet too.[82]

Of this strange conjuncture, in France at any rate, there was one
powerful and eloquent symptom: the imperious, imposing six hundred
and ninety pages of Sartre's *Saint Genet, comédien et martyr* (*Saint Genet,
Actor and Martyr*), published in 1952, and a monument to the application of latter-day dialectical method to literary writing.[83] For though it
came out belatedly, after Genet's *Œuvres complètes* had started appearing in print—itself already a peculiar notion on the part of a writer

who was still only forty at the time—Sartre's influential presentation of Genet somehow contrived, and said as much on its title page, to occupy the entirety of the so-called first volume of Genet's complete works, which at the time comprised works that, because of the scandal they provoked, had so far circulated discreetly and fitfully, if not clandestinely, and were to that extent still largely unread, some would say unreadable (*Notre-Dame-des-Fleurs*, *Le Condamné à mort*, *Miracle de la rose*, *Un Chant d'amour*, *Pompes funèbres*, *Le Pêcheur du Suquet*, *Querelle de Brest*). By presenting Genet in this way, Sartre's *Saint Genet* no doubt sought to defend its subject by making his writing intelligible to its audience, but only at the risk and cost of defending Genet's work against itself. For while speaking on Genet's behalf, Sartre's essay could not *not* present itself, in advance of other, future writing by Genet, under the auspices of a comprehensive, exhaustive, and authoritative synthesis of Genet's texts as a whole. To this end, in his long and patient exposition, what Sartre undertook was to explain to his readers—including Genet, who was given sight of the manuscript before publication—who it was that Genet the writer took himself to be, which involved, so to speak, not only reading but also rewriting Genet's name, the story of his birth, adolescence, adulthood, and authorship, which Sartre did by elaborating, rather like a kind of well-made play, a carefully staged four-part scenario, portraying his sexually deviant, criminal protagonist in a series of ascending or descending roles: as bastard, thief, gay aesthete, and writer.[84]

Genet's dilemma, according to Sartre, was that he was unable to lay claim to his name other than as a series of judgements imposed upon him by others. Genet, Sartre argued, on the basis of a bold but tendentious synthesis of Genet's personal mythology on the one hand and existentialist doctrine on the other, was witness from the outset to a fatal event: the constitution of his self as other, and that other as himself. "This, then, is the key to Genet," asserts Sartre. "This is where we should begin: Genet is a child whom someone has convinced that, in the very depths of his being, he is *an Other than Self* [*un Autre que soi*]."[85] This ferocious dialectic was as irresistible as it was devastating. Genet became who he was, Sartre contended, only by being always already alienated from himself. His own attempt, through writing, to become his own name and embody his own singular identity, in

Sartre's perspective, was therefore doomed to fail. A name—this was Sartre's Hegelian hypothesis—could only be what it was in so far as it was mediated, raised, and dignified by universality, without which it would not stand up; and it was thus the purpose of literature, as Sartre consistently argued throughout this period, to communicate universal values, in a universally accessible manner, to an audience that was itself, in principle—though not always in reality—universal. This was the basis for the Sartrean theory of *littérature engagée* everywhere implicit in his reading. Genet, however, being other than self, was unable to respect this communicative contract and the dialogue it enabled. "Genet," Sartre put it, "is an object to which a name has been given, not someone who has given an object a name."[86] This explained, according to Sartre, why Genet, as a thief, was a loner, but also why homosexuals in general are similarly bereft of reciprocity.[87] Genet, the outcast, the thief and homosexual, could not therefore claim a universal audience; his fate was to miss his vocation, and be perpetually unable to overcome the words that singularised him as other, as coward, traitor, thief, and queer. Just like woman, or women [*la femme*], in *Le Deuxième Sexe* (*The Second Sex*), Sartre added, Genet the homosexual thief was always positioned not as a free subject but as somebody else's other, including his own.[88]

True enough, even if this potent dialectic, being limitless, knew no outside, it did provide Genet with the opportunity to relieve his fate, that is, overcoming or, better, interiorising it, by negating it, but only in so far as it was now Genet's failure to achieve universality that became the basis of his appeal to the universal, with the implication that whatever act or gesture Genet claimed as his own was irretrievably marked as a negative value. *Qui perd gagne, loser wins,* Sartre was fond of repeating; and though Genet's failure might therefore become reason for his success, this still meant that what made him a failure in the eyes of bourgeois society—his treachery, criminality, and homosexuality—rather than corresponding to an affirmative act, represented a purely negative gesture, which, for Sartre, was little different from a kind of passive acquiescence, an acceptance of sterility. "The objective essence of the lad [*du gosse*] being the No," Sartre concluded, "Genet gave himself a personality by giving himself the subjectivity of the No; he is the absolute opponent [*opposant*], for he opposes Being and all integration."[89] In the end, Genet's imagination, like his homosexuality, says Sartre, was an essentialism,[90] and his singular enterprise was merely the subjective face of what was indifferently a failed act of freedom and an act of failed freedom. In concluding *Saint Genet,* Sartre therefore felt able to portray Genet as a martyr to history, a counterpart to Bukharin, best known to Sartre's generation for having testified vehemently against himself in the Moscow show trials, laying claim to acts of treachery which empirically he had never committed, but which the savage dialectic of history judged him capable of committing, and thus, in the jargon of the period, to have objectively already committed. Unlike the enemies of Stalin, however, Genet's failure was not objective but subjective; but just like Bukharin, as far as Sartre was concerned, Genet had no future. His writing belonged only to the recessive past, where it had already been deflated by the limpness, nostalgia, and narcissism from which it was indistinguishable.

Throughout *Saint Genet,* like Baudelaire, Mallarmé, or Flaubert, in other critical essays, or even the boyhood Sartre in *Les Mots* (*Words*), from whom the writer would also endeavour forcibly to distance himself, Genet's main function, as he was later to observe, grudgingly and with little real conviction, was that of an illustration, an instance or case-study, for Sartre's dialectic of freedom.[91] In a word, Sartre's project was to make an example of Genet; and rarely can there have been a better example of that exact logic of exemplification, so often employed by philosophy and literary criticism in their dealings with the literary text, which, like Sartre does Genet, they routinely seek on the one hand to celebrate and raise up—while in the process in fact celebrating only themselves, mummifying and embalming the writing of their quarry, appropriating and purloining the singularity of a signature as proof and confirmation of their own potent authority over the text.[92] But the verbal and rhetorical inflation of Sartre's discourse, not to mention its sheer size, cut both ways. It also had the irresistible effect of making an example of Sartre's own reading. Set alongside Genet's writing, Sartre's treatise found itself exposed to unremitting ironical scrutiny, at which point what became more readily apparent was less the synthesising strength of Sartre's diagnosis, more its moral dogmatism, its teleological prescriptiveness, its normative violence.[93] "One *has* to decide [*Il faut décider*]," Sartre rightly says.[94] But the rush to judgement has a habit of backfiring, and even as he endeavoured from the outside to provide a secure, authoritative, not to say authoritarian frame for Genet's Complete Works, so Sartre's discourse necessarily became absorbed into what were already the writer's forthcoming Incomplete Works, including the remains of a Rembrandt, by which, as we shall see, Sartre's analysis itself ended up being framed. The frame, in other words, was about to fall into the picture, which had already begun to exceed its own contours.

Presentation, then, was of the essence.

For any reader newly arrived from Sartre's *Saint Genet,* with its indefatigable rhetoric, its infinitely recapitulated demonstrations, its over-reaching commitment to itself, the eccentric page layout adopted by *Glas* represents a remarkable change in tone. In economy and in organisation. *Wechsel der Töne,* Hölderlin called it. So, why two counterposed columns—the one nominally given over to philosophical discussion, framing, citing, enfolding, or arraigning the other, for its part nominally given over to literary analysis, while by that very token allowing itself simultaneously to be framed, cited, enfolded, or arraigned by it—without either discourse or either party to this odd coupling being in a position fully to contain or comprehend the other, while being simultaneously traversed, infiltrated, or penetrated by it, haunted, in order to be what it took itself to be, by what it was driven to banish, exclude, or repress?

Two reasons, no doubt, at least.

First, because literature, philosophy, these two hugely inflated institutions, though an abyssal divide set them apart, were anything but identical with themselves, and stood anything other than in opposition with one another. True, the one, Hegel insisted, in so far as its term was absolute knowledge, necessarily began by raising its game above the contingency of a mere signature. Philosophy's goal was truth, and since truth was universal, philosophy neither required nor tolerated any endorsement by a singular proper name.[95] Terms such as *here, now,* Hegel famously argued, from the threshold of *The Phenomenology of Spirit,* as Sartre would duly remember, and Derrida recall in his turn in the course of his own opening gambit, might preserve the meaning of the particular towards which they gestured only by destroying that particular, replacing contingent singularity with the monumental universality of the concept, without which, Hegel maintained, it would be impossible to name anything particular or actual at all. Pure singularity was in itself impossible; it could only be retained—but by that token already destroyed—by being elevated to (and with) the power of the concept. All of which, by happy chance, Hegel summed up in a single word: *Aufhebung* (which Derrida, in *Glas*, as elsewhere, translates as *relève:* a relieving of the guard, a pick-me-up, or an erection).

But what happens, asks Derrida, no longer at the beginning but towards the putative end of the infinite circle that is the Hegelian system, when within conceptuality it is a matter of facilitating the transition, say, from absolute religion, rooted in representation, to absolute knowledge, revelling in pure presence, and it then, now, becomes necessary to articulate absolute presence, the absoluteness of presence and the presence of the absolute, in philosophy, discourse, language, text? Oddly enough, the absolute, it seems, is still in need of time for it to be achieved or manifested—a time that, paradoxically, cannot be arraigned or addressed within presence. From the perspective of the absolute, Derrida argues, and on Hegel's own admission, that necessary but nonpresent temporal trace remains, but cannot be read—except as tautological repetition or empty verbiage:

> For example, when it [i.e., Hegel's text] describes the approach to *Sa* [i.e., Absolute Knowledge], can the adverb of time (*yet* [*encore*]) be read, semantically accomplished, from the perspective [*depuis:* in both spatial and temporal senses] of the absolute concept? Or without it? In the first case, the adverb disappears, forfeits its temporal sense, and, in a certain manner, is not read. In the other case, it is denied absolute conceptuality and does not let itself be truly understood. It is still [*toujours*] not read. In both cases, it is read only on condition of not being read. The fact is, *reading* [*lecture;* Derrida's emphasis] is defined simultaneously as a semantic filler [*remplissement*] and a semantically empty remainder [*reste de vide sémantique*].[96]

Derrida goes on:

> What can follow which does not precede already—subsequently— this next-to-last not yet [*cet avant-dernier pas encore*]? In the chapter of *Sa*, i.e. the last, what remains of time—of not-yet—finds

itself reduced, but suspended between relief (*Aufhebung*) and annulment (*Tilgen*). If so, to what "time," then, does the "text" of *Sa*, about *Sa*, now belong, and the time of its repetition, and readability—whether full or empty? Who reads it? Who writes it? Who frames it? Who signs it?[97]

In the end, spacing—iterability, *différance*, temporisation—without which thinking cannot begin and which it always already presupposes, cannot be erased, cannot be overcome, and cannot be subordinated to presence; its tell-tale signature always remains, infinitely repeated, reinscribed, and reaffirmed, even at the heart of the system that would negate, incorporate, and raise it up, but to which, not belonging to the present or to presence, it remains irreducible. And in so far as spacing precedes absolute knowledge, it must therefore be thought to be its precondition, which is also to say that, if it makes it possible, it must serve to render it impossible too. The circle cannot close; the debt cannot be cancelled; and the frame never fits—for if it did, it would no longer be a frame. Even as it carries on, as it must, and in order that it carry on, as it must, the dialectic still falters, gags: discourse, language, *glossa* allow that passage only in so far as the passage is also a constriction, hold out the promise of apocalyptic finality only in so far as that very finality is also a kind of aporetic suspension, of interruption, hiatus, and arrest, hanging on what Derrida calls a *reste de temps*, a temporal remainder (or "a remain(s) of time," as Leavey has it), that, having neither arisen nor fallen, (being) neither present nor absent, (being) neither positive nor negative, (is) irreducible to the movement of that dialectic, or even to time itself.

A temporal remainder, then, suspends Hegel's flight as, like some soaring eagle or *aigle*, he rises towards the absolute. But what of Jean Genet, his counterpart and double, this other dashing thoroughbred and delicate flower? For such was the hidden freight, the writer no doubt quickly discovered, that was secretly stored within his name, this name that was also only his mother's. "His mother's name," writes Derrida, taking his cue from *Journal du voleur* (*The Thief's Journal*) and gathering together his own floral tribute to this name of the mother that was the writer's name, "is allegedly—commonly—the name of a plant or a flower, from which it differs by a single letter, the dropped *s*, or by a circumflex, scarring over its loss [*pour en cicatriser la chute*]. Covering the gap between the parted lips or letters—in *s*'s place—with a piece of fabric extended to form a point, a tent, or a pyramid-like missing monument [*monumanque:* a portmanteau word that collapses together *monument*, monument, and *manque*, lack]." "*Genêt*," Derrida adds, "names a bush—with yellow flowers (*sarothamnus scoparius, genista;* broom, *genette, genêt-à-balais*, with poisonous and medicinal properties, and distinct from dyer's broom, *genistra tinctoria* or *genestrolle*, used for making yellow dye); *genet* is also a kind of horse. From Spain, a country of great importance in the text."[98]

This was not all. Genet too, just like his imperial philosophical predecessor, had begun by pledging himself, in binding fashion, to a project of sacralisation, magnification, and glorification, albeit one that involved the author not in renouncing his signature, the better to redeploy it elsewhere, but, conversely, in taking it upon himself to sign everything in sight and mark it, patently and ubiquitously, secretly and cryptically—the one because of the other, the other because of the one—with his own inimitable, fragrantly or flagrantly malodorous monogram. "In which case," Derrida explains,

> Genet may be thought to belong to that powerful, occulted tradition that had long been plotting its revenge [*préparait son coup*], its reverse jolt into consciousness [*son sursaut à l'envers*], while concealing its labours from itself by itself [*d'elle-même*], anagrammatising proper names, anamorphosing signatures and all that ensues. Genet, in one of these movements in *ana*, wittingly or unwittingly (I have my views on this, but no matter), silently, laboriously, minutely, obsessionally, compulsively, passing like a thief in the night, may be said to have left his signature behind where all the missing objects used to be. In the morning, expecting to recognise the things you know, you keep coming across his name everywhere, writ large, writ small, in full or in short [*en morceaux*], distorted or reinvented. He is no longer there, but you are living in his mausoleum or toilet [*chiottes*]. You thought you were doing the deciphering, sniffing out, following up [*Vous croyiez déchiffrer, dépister, poursuivre*], but you are the one caught out comprehensively [*vous êtes compris*]. He has affected [*affecté:*

touched, modified, appointed] everything with his signature. He has affected his signature. He has affected it with everything. He is affected by it (later on, he will even adorn himself with a circumflex). His task, his alone, was to write, properly, what happens between affect and seal [*seing:* a legal signature; the word is indistinguishable, to the ear, from *saint,* saint or saintly, or *sein,* the maternal breast].[99]

Here, too, there was a rub. To leave one's name everywhere, in whatever form, meant leaving it behind for others to read; it meant losing ownership over the name, forfeiting it, and running the risk of never retrieving it. But how to avoid this turn of events? What Genet wanted to write as his own was always translatable into something else, without which he would not have been able to write it; so what he wanted to claim as most proper to him could only be proper because it was already improper, and already belonged to others and to another. Genet's task, then, was not just to inscribe his own name everywhere, it was, by that very gesture, to efface that name, and forever to accuse himself in his own language, as he put it, this language not his own. But there was no escape. In the end, the pyramid was a pit, crime innocence, and erection detumescence. And vice versa.

Hegel, Genet: each, then, was the name for a strange reversibility by which the one, like a glove, a sheath, or envelope, irretrievably, undecidably, turned itself inside out, and, predictably-unpredictably, always ended up passing into the opposite. But this was no dialectical unity between contradictories. It proceeded without mediation, negativity, or *telos.* Its effects were nevertheless impressive. Stilitano's sectioned hand, for instance, in *Journal du voleur,* immediately becomes an intensive repotentialisation of his sexual member.[100] But in the place of his crotch (Genet offers this by way of a deferred commentary on the medieval tapestry of the "Lady and the Unicorn," this celebrated depiction of phallic desire restrained, and female chastity seduced), he sports an imitation bunch of grapes, made from cellulose, to attract and to ward off punters in a Barcelona gay bar.[101] Nothing, then, is what it seems; everything is a supplement or a prosthesis. In another famous episode, in the course of a parenthesis within a narrative digression (Derrida is intensely mindful throughout of Genet's concerted yet loosely bound writing), Genet's narrator describes, in the form of an image that suddenly occurs to him while writing, an encounter (did it ever happen in any present moment?) with an old woman, seemingly a thief, just released from prison, who is "perhaps [*peut-être*]" the narrator's mother whom he has never met. "Ah! If it was her," he writes, "I'd cover her with flowers, with gladioli and roses, and kisses!"—only then, thinking better, or worse, of it, and knowingly substituting *"gob of spit [glaviaux]"* for *"gladiolus [glaïeul:* Derrida points out that the word is a diminutive *gladius,* a miniature (phallic) sword]," to counter his own words by retorting, "I'd be glad to slobber [*baver:* both to drool and to suffer] all over her, overflowing with love," to which he adds: "To slobber [*baver*] over her hair or vomit [*vomir*] in her hands."[102]

Presence, then, turns to absence, and absence to presence, with neither retaining its identity, in a vertiginous round of reinscription. The more the one is affirmed, so the other is affirmed also, without reconciliation or progress. Famously, the head of the Medusa turned to stone whoever gazed upon the writhing multitude it held aloft, combining together as one both the increase and the reduction, both rampant virility and numbing castration, displaying the one under the auspices of the other, and vice versa. To guard against danger was already to succumb, and to reinforce one's defences to admit defeat. Derrida provides in *Glas* many instances of such self-averting apotropaic logic, where the turn to one side is always a turn to the other, by which the one exacerbates the other while being simultaneously exacerbated by it, plucking from his repertoire, by way of illustration, and only partly tongue-in-cheek, the decorous nonce-word: *anthérection,* formed from *anth-,* meaning *flower,* that is, that which by definition is cut before it goes to seed, and *érection,* referring to male sexual arousal—effecting a duplicity or double bind whose site of predilection, in Genet, was the *bagne* or penal colony: "the place," says Derrida, "of what from now on we shall call *antherection [anthérection]*: the time of erection countered, intersected [*recoupée:* cut again] by its contrary—in place of the flower." *"Enanthiosis [sic],"* he quips, slyly agglutinating *anthos,* the flower, and the term *enantiosis,* that figure of speech—or flower of rhetoric—in which what is meant is the opposite to what is said.[103]

In such cases, what counts, however, is not the conceptual power of the portmanteau coinage or neologism, not the virtuoso handling of words in general, but, more radically, the spacing that always already traverses the word or words, and which Derrida's writing boldly unleashes—or, rather, boldly unleashes Derrida's writing—across the two columns of the text of *Glas*, as they check out their erectile prowess—and penile malfunction—on either side of the page. It is by irresistible agglutinative necessity, then, rather than as a result of any showy aesthetic conceit, that Derrida's two columns, as though under glass, engage in such cross-talk, which will often pass from one side of the page to the other and later return, amplified or diminished, in any case dispersed and disseminated into the bargain. As Derrida points out, early on in the right-hand column, announcing, in abyssal manner, not only Genet's "Ce qui est resté d'un Rembrandt . . . ," but *Glas* itself: "Two unequal columns, they say [*disent-ils:* which may also be heard as *di-style,* i.e., as double style or stylus], each of which—envelops or sheaths [*enveloppe ou gaine:* both words can be read interchangeably as verbs or as nouns], incalculably reverses, turns inside out [*retourne*], replaces, remarks, intersects [*recoupe:* cuts again] with the other."[104]

Importantly, this was not to say that philosophy, literature were somehow one and the same. On the contrary, a gulf separated Derrida's two columns, which manifested itself in significant differences in typeface, style, tone, affect, much else besides. Indeed, as Derrida insists, the columns were unequal. This did not just mean they were unequal to each other, for they were also unequal to themselves, and numerous internal displacements or slippages came to affect the writing of Hegel and Genet both, if only because the one and the other, by dint of their silent dialogue on the page, thereby placed, so to speak, invisible quotation marks around their own text and that of the other, making it unsure, in the end, as Derrida copied out lengthy extracts from their work, whether Hegel was busily striving to overcome the stuttering movement of the dialectic or simply describing it, or whether Genet, in writing, was jealously stealing from others, as he had often wanted, or making generous gift of his writing to whoever cared to read.[105] Both parts of the equation were equally true, of course, were it not that, in the process, truth (and falsity) ran the risk of being gravely compromised. Whatever the intentions, conscious or unconscious, of the protagonists, it remained that neither project, whether undertaken in the realm of philosophy, so called, or that of literature, if it exists, could be main-

tained; it was the necessary but uncalculable fate of every tower, building, or erection, in order that it might rise, simultaneously to fall and
fall again, without ever coinciding with itself; and there remained in the
text, as themselves but always other than themselves, as proof of the
irreducible fissure or interval or interruption of spacing, the signatures
of all concerned, whose place was neither wholly in the frame (for if it
was, it would already have become something else), nor entirely outside
it (since, if so, it would have already lost whatever authority it enjoyed),
but only in the space between, the *entre-deux,* the point of intersection
between what might be thought to be intrinsic and extrinsic to any text,
which it simultaneously enabled and disabled. "Let us space [*Espaçons*],"
writes Derrida, referring at one and the same time, without term, to
Genet's text, *Glas* itself, all texts, and textuality in general.

> The art of this text is the air [*air:* both space and tune] it causes to
> circulate between its screens [*paravents:* as in Genet's play of that
> name]. The transitions [*enchaînements*] are invisible, everything
> seems improvised or juxtaposed. It induces by agglutination
> rather than by demonstration, by association [*en accolant:* em-
> bracing, and—by verbal association—gluing] and dissociation [*en
> décollant:* detaching, ungluing, taking off], rather than by exhibit-
> ing the continuous analogical, didactic [*enseignante*], stifling ne-
> cessity of discursive rhetoric.[106]

"Only I can do the layouts," Genet told his friend, Leila Shahid, in 1985,
shortly before his death, as he painfully went through the page proofs
for *Un captif amoureux* (*Prisoner of Love*), carefully inserting blank spaces
between the different sections of the text.[107]

This, then, was the second important question at stake in the page
presentation of *Glas.* For Derrida's attention to apotropaic reversibility
was no merely habitual literary critical predilection. More fundamentally, it had to do with what Derrida, eschewing the word structure,
called the stricture of the signature, that is, not the universalising dialectic that, raising the singular to the status of a concept, retains it only
by obliterating it, but the singular binding and counterbinding that governs the event, or non-event, of the signature. The signature, however,
was no point of origin, revelling in proximity with itself. Well might it

function, no doubt, in literary criticism, as in law, as a guarantee of aesthetic or moral value, of authorial responsibility, property, propriety, and authenticity—but this did not prevent it from the very outset, not as some external threat to its functioning, but as the very condition of its possibility, from being exposed to inauthenticity, falsification, and irresponsibility. For as any credit card owner knows, it is a necessary and indispensable feature of any signature that it be repeatable—and that each repeated instance of the signature should be different enough from the one that came before for it to be recognised as being the same. But by that very logic, as any fraudster will confirm, it can always be falsified. Conversely, if the signature were not repeatable, the risk of forgery would disappear—but so would the signature itself, and the possibility of it serving as a legal guarantee of any credit card, and the same would apply to whatever login codes, passwords, or numbers that, in more recent digital times, have been pressed into service as signatures. Credit cards, and many other things besides, would no longer exist.

Derrida had already argued as much in 1971 in "Signature événement contexte." And more was to come. It was not only that the signature was not identical with itself, it did not even provide a proper guarantee, contrary to reputation, of the living presence of whoever signed. On the contrary. Signatures are, of course, routinely used as proof of the assent of the person deemed to have performed the signature. This, however, is not the same; for any signature, if it is to continue to bear witness to the agreement of the person who has signed, it must do so in the absence and eventuality of the death of that named individual, in which case, if the possibility is a necessary one, as it is, then the signer's absence and death may be deemed in fact, structurally, if not empirically, to have always already occurred—without occurring. Whoever signs is never present to the act, not in the present or in the past. "When I sign," writes Derrida, "I am already dead [*je suis déjà mort*]," a formulation whose self-evidence and poignancy, already in 1974, were underscored by the fact that what resounds in those words, properly-improperly, is the event without event of the writer's death—this writer whose name, already, *déjà*, is none other than De[rrida] Ja[cques]. And who continues: "I barely have the time to sign than [*que:* than or that] I am already dead. I have to abbreviate the script [*l'écriture*], hence the acronym [*sigle*], because the structure of the event of 'signature' is such that with the event comes my death—which is why it is not an 'event' and perhaps signifies nothing, written from [*depuis*] a past that never was present and the death of one who never was alive."[108] And if the signature is that which (is) already, it is because the signature, before all else, (is) that which (is) already given, already gifted, *da*, there, both legacy and charge, a temporal remainder without presence, in the spacing without term that there is, that "il y a," or, writes Derrida, that "il lia"—that it—in the impersonal third person—banded, bonded, bound, or bounded.[109]

But that which is bounded, as the case of Genet amply shows, is also that which is unbounded. Law is exercised, stretched, bent by counter-law. The signature, in other words, does not correspond to any stable positioning, but inscribes a site of passage, a spacing between, implying both constriction and release, between inside and outside, proper and improper, proper and common, appropriation and expropriation—what Derrida terms *ex-appropriation*—the logic of which is in the form of a double bind, a double binding, bounding, and banding, by which the one and the other, rather than gathered together under the mediating control of the concept, are in a relationship of hyperbolic mutual intensification. This was Derrida's argument too, in 1975, apropos of the poet Francis Ponge, whose singular writing project, he suggested, in aiming to capture in improper, because human, words that which was proper to common things, was by that token silently to inscribe upon the world's surface, by dint of his own unmistake-able words, his own inimitable signature—which, necessarily and in-evitably, then itself became another improper, common thing, given over to others, and which it was essential for it to remain if it was to remain proper at all: improperly proper, properly improper. If Ponge succeeded in tracing his own name, then, it was only by effacing it. The more proper Ponge's response, the more improper it necessarily became; and the more improper it was, the more proper it was also. As Derrida explained:

> It is imperative [*Il faut:* i.e., it is both necessary and wanting], therefore, at one and the same time, that the signature both remain and disappear, that it remain to disappear, that it disap-pear to remain. *This is an imperative* [*Il faut*], that is what is impor-tant. It is imperative [*Il faut*] that the signature *remain to disappear*

[*reste à disparaître:* remain in order to disappear, remain by disappearing], obeying a simultaneous double requirement, a double contradictory postulate, a double obligation, and double bind. . . . It is imperative [*Il faut*] for there to be a signature so that it can remain-to-disappear [*reste-à-disparaître*]. It is wanting [*elle manque*], which is why it is necessary [*il la faut*], but it is necessary that it be wanting [*il faut qu'elle manque*], which is why it should not be [*il ne la faut pas*].¹¹⁰

"At the limit," says Derrida, returning to Genet's *Miracle de la rose* (*The Miracle of the Rose*), "of the text, of the world, there would remain only an enormous signature, heavy [*grosse*] with everything it will have engulfed in advance, pregnant [*enceinte:* girded] however with itself alone." But, he adds, "the signature keeps [*garde:* retains, protects] nothing at all of all that it signs."¹¹¹ A signature is its own necessary ruination; (being) the one, it (is) always already the other; and its necessary fate is to remain—radically undecidable.

The signature, then, is a case of the remainder, of which there are, Derrida reminds his reader, always at least two functions. The first is dialectical: it retains, idealises, interiorises, raises up. The other lets drop—beyond retrieval, recuperation, or restoration, beyond the exemplifying powers of any dialectic of the general and the particular.

Something of this strange oscillation, in its dumbfounding complexity, was no doubt already legible or illegible, in abyssal manner, in the title of the essay by Genet with which Derrida in part began, and which, like all titles, was already itself by way of a cryptic signature: "What remains of a Rembrandt torn into small rectangular pieces, and flushed down the toilet." Admittedly, the title was a provocation. As such, it was also the place without place of a series of singular, undecidable slippages. What, for instance, was the status of the name: Rembrandt? Did it refer, metonymically, to an actual—real or fictional—painting by Rembrandt Harmenszoon van Rijn? Or did it refer, by a kind of double metonymy, to a failed—real or imaginary—text, essay, article, or even book, devoted to the painter by some other, like, for instance, Jean Genet, whose signature also stood on the masthead of the journal where the text first appeared? But if Rembrandt's name might migrate in this fashion, from museum to toilet, so to speak, and have the status of a common noun, what was the implication for Genet's own name, which, even as the writer was endeavouring to appropriate Rembrandt's name for a piece of writing authored perhaps by himself, would by the same logic be denied him, rendering him illegitimate, and in effect nameless—which, in another paradoxical loop, by effacing his name, was to rebaptise him, all the more surely, more properly, by providing him with a given name—that was not his?

What, in any case, was the nature or status of the remainder announced in the title? Was it single, double, or neither? And if Genet's words referred to the ten or so rectangular pages of text that followed, to what absent or non-existent whole did those two unequal columns in fact belong, given, it seems, that they were all that remained? If so, had they too been flushed down the toilet? Did this make them more readable or less readable, or both? At any event, why had Genet's "Rembrandt" ended up, of all places, in the toilet, this prosthetic extension to human cleanliness and uncleanliness, token of propriety and impropriety alike, which, though it might serve quite properly as a means of disposing of unwanted paper, particularly if it was in the form of a pile of small rectangular sheets, was perhaps just as likely to become inappropriately clogged by an excess of waste? Of this last possibility Genet was doubtless aware: writing from Antwerp in 1957 to his agent and translator, Bernard Frechtman, he expressed his irritation at the fact that his friend Abdallah ("that arsehole [*ce con*]") had forgotten to burn the papers, including "bits of torn-up manuscript [*des morceaux de manuscrits déchirés*]," that were "in the toilet [*dans les chiottes*]"; Genet closed by urging his correspondent to put a match to any further manuscript remnants that might come his way."[12]

Moreover, at least one of Genet's columns was the site of a bizarre illumination, experienced on a train by its narrator, while meditating intently on the gaze of the man opposite, as a result of which he was filled with an increasingly dismal sense of disintegration, and which he describes as follows:

> Behind what one could see of the man, or further away—further away yet at the same time miraculously and distressingly near in this man—his body and face awkward and ugly, in some details, even disgusting: the dirty moustache, which in itself

would not amount to much, but with stiff bristling tufts growing out almost horizontally above the tiny, rotting mouth, and the gobs of spit he aimed between his knees at the carriage floor, already filthy with cigarette ends, bits of paper, and crusts of bread, in a word everything that in those days went to make up the dirt of a third-class compartment, as his gaze stumbled [*buta*] against mine, I discovered, and felt with a shock, a kind of universal identity common to all men [*une sorte d'identité universelle à tous les hommes*].

A few lines later, Genet carries on:

What I was feeling I could but translate into the following terms: I was leaching away [*je m'écoulais*] out of my body, and through my eyes [*par les yeux*], into the body of the man on the train, *at the same time the man was leaching away* [*s'écoulait*] *into mine.* Or rather: *I had leached away* [*je m'étais écoulé*], for the look was so quick that I can only remember it with the help of a pluperfect.[113]

Somehow, then, each man, however repellent, was the same as all men. But this was no belated conversion to cod humanism. It was much rather a calculated, sexually explicit, yet forcibly oblique response to Sartre's denunciation of Genet as an alienated solitarian, ignorant of all reciprocity. For Genet's account of the traveller's revelation pointedly echoes the very terms of Sartre's diagnosis, which, in *Saint Genet*, depicted a self sluggishly "leach[ing] away into the eyes of others [*qui s'écoule dans les yeux d'autrui*]."[114] But what for Sartre transfixed, and relegated irreconcilably to the sterile margin, for Genet was more in the manner of an eternal return, in which what returned was not alienation, but a simultaneous binding and counterbinding of the same and the different. For the dislocation experienced by Genet's traveller derailed him in more ways than one. On the one hand, it implied a kind of radical exchangeability between men, and meant that henceforth the traveller was merely one point of passage in a fluid homosexual economy in which each man was identical with every other. But this preliminary conviction, without apparent transition or explanation, then gave way to something more disorientating still, which was not that each man was the same as every other but that each man, writes Genet, *was* all other men, so that what Genet's text found itself affirming now was not that all men shared an identity but that each was a fragment—a remainder—irreducible to all others. The one, then, passes, undecidably, into the other. And Genet's narrator presented his conclusions in a kind of dramatic monologue that was already a kind of abyssal proof of what it advanced.

> How, this I couldn't say, how did I move from the knowledge that every man resembles every other [*tout homme est semblable à tout autre*] to the notion that every man is all other men [*est tous les autres hommes*]? But the idea was now part of me. It had become a certainty. More clearly—but I shall be robbing it of some of its bloom [*je vais un peu la déflorer*]—it might have been expressed in the following aphorism: "In the world there exists and has only ever existed but one man [*un seul homme*]. He is wholly in each one of us, so he is us [*nous-même:* Genet uses the singular, not the plural]. Everyone is the other [*l'autre*] and the others [*les autres*]. In the quiet of evening, a bright exchange of looks—deliberate or fleeting, not something I was much good at—made us realise. Save that some phenomenon, which I do not even have a name for, seems to divide this one man up infinitely, fragments him apparently in accident and in form, and makes each fragment foreign to us [*étranger à nous-même*]."[115]

The economy of the same, then, meets irreducible difference, unrelievedly, without opposition, contradiction, or mediation, and without recourse to a dialectic of exemplification. For it is not the negation of singularity, its elevation and idealisation, that gives access to the universal but the insistent materiality, the always affirmative reiterative movement of the singular itself. In so far as it is inseparable from a law of repetition, which is but another name for irreducible difference, the singular is always already universal, in its perpetual reinscription, its departure from itself, and its resistance to itself—as that which is never what it is "as such" or indeed "in itself." As Derrida famously put it in 1992, exploring a similar notion of plural singularity, "Tout autre est tout autre": "Every other is every other; every other is entirely other;

entirely other is every other; entirely other is the entirely other," and so on, according to whether *tout* is read as adjective or adverb, *autre* as adjective or noun.[116] The ring and the interruption. The circle and the wound. Law and address. Bind and counterbind. Stricture, without negativity. The signature joins, but also cuts. Circumcision, says Derrida, naming that unique, exemplary cut that was anything but an example.[117] Genet's first book, published at his own expense in 1943, was the poem, "Le Condamné à mort [The Man Condemned to Death]," written to celebrate his friend the murderer Maurice Pilorge—whom Genet had in fact never met—as he waited upon the guillotine in his prison cell in Saint-Brieuc.[118] "Beauty," Genet wrote elsewhere, paying tribute to Giacometti, for whom he sat for long hours in 1955, "has no other origin than the wound [*blessure*], singular [*singulière*] and different [*différente*] for each, hidden or visible, that every man keeps within himself and preserves, into which he retreats whenever he wants to leave the world behind for a temporary but profound solitude."[119] But there was no position, no place that did not shudder or vibrate with the movement right to left, left to right, around and back. "What troubles me most [*mon émoi*: agitation, turmoil, confusion]," wrote Genet, withdrawing into a footnote as he signed off the opening sentences of *Journal du voleur,* remembering the fragility and delicacy of flowers and the brutal insensitivity of convicts, "is the oscillation from the one to the other."[120]

But what was the truth value, or otherwise, of the illumination experienced by Genet's traveller? The essay had already replied without replying in an opening fragment already detached from what followed, and thus, so to speak, already a remnant of what was itself already a remnant. "Only those kinds of truths," it wrote, "that are not demonstrable and are even *'false'* [*'fausses'*: Genet's emphasis and quotation marks, the one cancelling out the other], that cannot without absurdity be taken to the limit without encountering their own negation and one's own, those are the ones that should be exalted by the work of art. They will never have the good or bad fortune one day to be applied. May they live by the song they have become and to which they give rise [*suscitent*]." Cue the sounding of bells, to which Genet's right-hand column, reaching without reaching its end, replies without replying, in turn: "And it goes without saying that the whole of Rembrandt's work has no meaning—at least for me—except if I know that what I have just writ-ten was false [*faux*]."[121]

Truth and falsity, then, but the one as the hyperbolic intensification of the other.

There remained, however, the (un)readability of a proper name. "Illegible [*Illisible*]," Bulkaen signs his first note to the narrator in *Miracle de la rose*, who, naming him without naming him, addresses him as such: "My Illegible [*Mon Illisible*]."[122] "A text," Derrida com-ments, "only 'exists,' resists, consists, represses, or lets itself be read or written, if it is beset [*travaillé:* worked upon, over, with] by the illegi-bility of a proper name." He adds, however, by way of caution, "I have not—not yet—said the proper name exists, or that it becomes illegible when it falls [*tombe:* audible too as a noun: tomb] into the signature. The proper name only resounds, immediately losing itself in the process, at the instant of its *debris,* when it breaks, gets scrambled [*se brouille:* clouds over, falls out with itself, is scrambled like an egg], or jams in touching [*en touchant:* touch or tamper with] the seal [*seing:* signature, breast, saint or saintly]."[123]

In such circumstances, what is it to read? What is it that may be called reading? Or what is it that enjoins reading?

At the Wallraf-Richartz-Museum in Cologne one day, studying one of Rembrandt's most famous self-portraits, Genet perhaps found an answer: by retreating to a corner of the exhibition room, and squinting diagonally, with his head upside down, at this picture of the painter laughing, which was so red, says Genet, that "the whole canvas reminds you of placenta drying in the sun."[124]

A sideways glance, a skewed angle, a glistening scene: a cryptic memory.

A *gl.*

Dangling above Derrida's two columns, swaying to and fro, tin-kling in the breeze, forming or forcing an opening and closing of the *glottis,* there was already—*déjà*—another title to read, another signature, another name, under the strange word of which ("The strange word of . . . [*L'étrange mot d'* . . .]" was the title given by Genet to a series of notes on the theatre as funeral mime),[125] undecidably singular or plural, with a silent, half-fallen *s,* announcing both the end of the beginning and the beginning of the end, the day of judgement or decision, when things, it seems, will be ready to pass each into their opposite. That title was: *Glas*, which could not *not* chime with Genet's meditation on the train.

Like many of Derrida's titles, *Glas* marries, condenses, agglutinates a vast range of unsuspecting and often unsuspected allusions and references, belonging not just to philosophical, mythological, scientific, and literary culture but also to the derivation and history of so-called ordinary words, and the multiple singularities of linguistic idiom. And in so far as it was a signature, *Glas* (was) a remainder both of itself and of everything other than itself, and by that token identical with neither: provisional gathering, infinite dissemination; economic inscription, fugitive trace.

Glas, it followed, was many things. It echoed, for instance, in the left-hand column, with the vibrations of that *Klang* that, in Hegel (or Hgl, as the eagle-eyed philosopher liked to sign himself), recalls Derrida, was not yet the voice proper, nor proper speech, but their recalcitrant conjoined possibility, and it also referenced all those tight bottlenecks (or *goulots*) in the Hegelian system that simultaneously, albeit without contradiction, both facilitate and impede the movement of *Geist*, testifying to its funeral rites and perpetual resurrection.[126] By that detour, on the right-hand side, it alluded too, for example, to the title of a funereal novel by Genet (*Pompes funèbres* [*Funeral Rites*]), and encrypted the given name of Genet's birth-mother, Gabrielle, whose family name was precisely not the name of the (writer's) father. Following this ever widening orbit, *glas* added to its repertoire of associations a vast galaxy of lactic and other references to the mother and the gift (and *Gift*) of life she had imparted to the writer, while also resonating, anagrammatically and otherwise, with numerous further agglutinative networks having to do, unclassifiably, with the intricate ramifications of the golden fleece, various other bushes and plants, yellow and other flowers, from the broom or gorse displayed in the words *genet* and *genêt* to the gladioli mentioned by Genet's narrator as he ungallantly imagines gobbing into his mother's hands (yellow, in French, is the colour of betrayal and treachery: of the son, of the mother). But there was no stopping the visible or invisible, interpretable and uninterpretable, readable and unreadable effects of *gl*. Which is to say, perhaps, that one of its most potent, if deflating epitaphs, as far as readers are concerned, might be its radically discontinuous continuity with itself, alongside it-self, countering itself, at a distance without distance from itself, and so on. Or, as Derrida was once tempted, emphatically, to title an essay on the deconstructive potential of the word "and": "Et cetera . . . (and so on, und so weiter, and so forth et ainsi de suite, und so überall, etc)."[127] For the repertoire of motifs trailed and dispersed by *glas* were literally with-out end: unsaturatable, unstoppable, indiscernible. A veritable glut.

Gl was, moreover, far from restricted to thematic or other effects of this kind—or, rather, its stricture was far less easily containable within any thematic or semantic horizon than even a cursory, indicative listing of this kind might imply. Rather than any theme, *gl* more resembled what might be called a gestural rhythm. As such, in so far as it can be determined as a recognisable unit at all, and in so far as its movement was a swaying to-and-fro, it performed a double movement in one: it was simultaneously a gurgling and a gargling, a gagging and a glug-ging, a clogging and a clearing, a clenching and an unclenching, a rock-ing to and fro from constriction to release and back again. And if it traversed a whole gallery of philosophical, literary texts, if such labels have any pertinence at this juncture, from Hegel to Kant, to Genet, Poe, Mallarmé, Freud, Heidegger, Bataille, and numerous others explicitly mentioned or only implied, it also traversed as many languages and more: French, English, German, Greek, Latin . . .

In this, no longer identifiable as a word, only a kind of futural, undecidable trace, midway between onomatopoeia and convention, and irreducible to either, *gl* raised, abyssally, the question of the boundaries of language, and, countering at least a certain received version of Saus-sure, dramatised the impossibility of securely demarcating inside from out, outside from in. For if it is the case, Derrida writes, anagrammatis-ing or acrosticating *glas*, that "the glue of chance makes sense [*la glu de l'aléa fait sens*],"[128] this is not to say that *gl* was a unit of meaning (or even meaninglessness). It not only fell below the threshold of what might be thought to occur within the horizon of intended or unintended mean-ing, it was not even a self-identical unit, but always already an agglutina-tive prosthesis or graft, traversed by constant reversion, conversion, or diversion. It was to this extent entirely irreducible to any established repertoire of linguistic or other marks. It was in other words neither a signifier, nor a phoneme, nor even a grapheme. Perhaps it might be thought simply as a mark (*marque*), suggests Derrida, but then again, perhaps not—for there was nothing material (or even immaterial) about *gl*, which was in any case without identity, sex, gender, or meaning, and belonged neither as whole or as part to any prior entity.[129] Which is also to say that, in Derrida's text, it is anything but privileged: it remains a remainder, without presence, without substance, without negativity. And without without.

But it is a foolish reader, in the end, who attempts to enumerate the machinations of *gl* in this way, not because Derrida's *Glas* is necessarily a particularly intimidating colossus of a work, but because in order to do justice to *gl* it would be necessary to cite, and recite, over and over again, not just *Glas* itself, and its two columns, their crossings, and recrossings, curious contiguities, and remarkable metastases, but also a veritable glut of other texts, including *Glas* itself, to which *Glas* refers, and defers, and which reverberate throughout, and again and again, in the multiple inferences and transferences of Derrida's text. Even then, it would be necessary to find a place where it might be possible to capture these resonances, a seat on the train, so to speak, from which to study the network. But any such place, as Genet had been quick to point out, could not *not* be part of the infinite circulation of traffic, and it would not take long for any confident, metalinguistic position to be rerouted by the unforeseeable workings of the text, indeed, as Derrida's text showed insistently, reading, like writing, was always already affected by such displacements, detours, and redirections, without which it would not occur at all. Errancy was not an accident that somehow befell purposeful communication; it was simply another name for the possibility of writing in general—which could therefore never pose or position itself "as such."

To the extent there was one, this was the burden, itself always already abyssal, of Derrida's demonstration: that every thesis, including this one, (is) a prosthesis. Or as *Glas* itself puts it, reinscribing *Journal du voleur* and addressing itself to its readers in ironically provocative, apotropaic mode:

> For the benefit of those who might not however regard gl as a satisfactory response, having expected it to be a response in the first place, for those to whom gl says nothing, having first believed it

to be saying something, and who, one wonders for what repast, might still be standing there slobbering [*baver*], let us suggest that the theoretical question, elaborated, slowly but surely (meta-language [*métalangue:* also audible as *mets ta langue,* put your tongue]—always reconstituting itself—in the tastiest spot) by this intervention, no other word for it today, a victim—even before it happens—of the censorship of the remainder in the ideological field, will produce [*produira*], that's the term to use, the follow-ing thesis: every thesis is (binds, erects [*bande*]) a prosthesis; what offers itself to reading [*se donne à lire*] offers itself to be read by necessarily truncated quotations (cuts, repetitions, suctions, sections, suspensions, selections, stitchings, grafts, postiches, organs without proper body [*corps propre:* i.e., a proper, clean body of one's own], or a proper body covered with bruises [*couverts de coups*], crawling with lice [*parcouru de poux*]).[30]

There was therefore no position or positioning, no posing or positing, that was not already exceeded by an originary supplementarity that de-posed, displaced, deferred, and divided it from itself, such that, no lon-ger coinciding with itself, it forfeited all propriety, property, and identity, and was always liable, without contradiction or mediation, to reverse it-self, and turn into its own contrary. Textuality, on this submission, was perpetually irreducible to any finite thematic, semantic, ethico-moral decisions, which would always end up being returned to their relative senders. As Derrida remarks, referring both to Genet's text and texts in general:

The rare force of the text is that you cannot catch it [*le surprendre*] saying (and therefore limit it to saying): *this is that,* or, what amounts to the same thing, this is in a relationship of apophatic or apocalyptic unveiling, or has a determinable semiotic or rhe-torical relationship with that, this is the subject, or is not the subject, this is the same, this is the other, that this is this text, and not that one, this corpus rather than that. There is still something else, something still other, always at issue [*Il est toujours question d'autre chose encore*]. A rare force. At the limit, equal to zero [*nulle*]. What ought to be called the potency [*puissance*] of the text. As

with the musculature of a tongue [*langue:* tongue or language].
And mathematical expansion [*développement*], too. Including the
enveloping [*enveloppement*] of what remains potential. At the limit,
equal to zero. Non-existent by dint of remaining infinitely potential. From being condemned to potency [*condamné à la puissance*]
and losing it [*d'y rester:* remain there, come a cropper].[131]

What singularised the remainder in *Glas* was its resistance to ontological determination. From this it followed that *Glas* was decidedly not:
a work of thematic criticism, or formalist criticism, or biographical criticism, or psychoanalytic criticism, or any other kind of literary criticism,
busying itself, say, with the task of positing, analysing, and illustrating
the conscious or unconscious meanings of a given, finite corpus. But
neither was it a work of structuralist, parastructuralist, or poststructur-
alist literary theory, semiology, or semiotics, purposefully attempting
to grasp, articulate, and explain the ontological status of the object arraigned under the heading of the literary text, literature, or poetic discourse. And *Glas* was irreducible too to a work of philosophy, to the
extent that its object was not truth, however this might be understood,
but something far stranger still, inseparable from the double banding
of Genet's "What remains . . . "—what "remains," writes Derrida, "beyond true and false, neither entirely true nor entirely false."[132]

In no sense, then, was *Glas* a playful textual performance or an
exercise in aestheticisation. It was not a tribute to the sensuous, signifying plurality of Genet's text, nor was it an attempt to confirm the heroic,
transgressive outsider status of the author's work. It remained nevertheless a critical intervention, a coming between, a separating, an interrupting, that both thought and practised, in affirmative style, writing's
resistance to ontologisation. It broke conclusively, therefore, with that
dialectic of exemplification inseparable from literary criticism as such,
declined its temptations of mastery in order to speak to what Derrida
rightly invokes as a radically preliminary question: the question of the
threshold—and, on that threshold, to address Genet's writing as a self-
possessed, yet necessarily always already spoliated inscription of the
possible-impossible signature the author claimed as his own.[133] In this,
Glas enforced no norms, policed no values, defended no final interpretative positioning of the text, its morality or lack of morality, its ethics or

counter-ethics. What it sought instead was to affirm a singularly irreducible event of writing, of *ex-appropriation*. It was an opening and closing that was radically prior to all meaning or thematisation, which it preceded, exceeded, and made both possible and impossible. As *Glas* explains:

> Even if we were able to reconstitute, bit by bit, the emblem or signature of a proper name, it would only be to release the very thing, just like pulling someone from a grave [*tombe*] buried alive, that neither Genet nor I would ever have succeeded in signing, or in reattaching to the lines of a paraph [*parafe:* an initial or official signature], and which speaks by and of that very fact. The text designated [*dénommé:* named, but also, literally, de-named, anonymised, unmarked] as Genet's is not something we are comprehending [*comprenons:* understand *and* include] here, nor is it exhausted in the pouch [*poche:* pocket] I am cutting, sewing, tying back. It is the text that makes a hole in it, first harpooning, then regarding it; but which also sees it escape, and carry its dart [*flèche:* arrow] to unknown parts. This very text (or *glas*) is no more reducible to a reading of Genet—who forms neither its example nor its essence, neither its case-history nor its truth—than it allows itself to be gathered together or pointed in some direction [*flécher*], along with others, by my paraph. And everything in it that might be related [*tiendrait:* to hold, or have to do with, or be keen on) to the singular form of the signature, of either the one or the other, keeps an altogether abnormal value. It is subject [*relève*] to no rule, nor does it supply one. The operation must each time be singular, and uniquely take its chances [*courir uniquement sa chance*].[134]

Glas traverses and re-traverses in meticulous detail both the philosophical legacy of the past and the contemporary challenge of one of the most gloriously singular literary events of the present. As it does so, it turns aside, knowingly, from all the great literary, critical, and theoretical orthodoxies of its time, not in the name of the irreducible negativity sometimes claimed to be inherent in literary discourse, nor under the aegis of any new theoretical beginning, but, invoking the "vast and boundless Yes[-saying]" of Zarathustra,[135] all the more urgently to face in the other direction, and address itself to the more pressing question, both possibility and impossibility, of the future—of writing, reading, and what, for want of a better word, might still be called criticism.

But what, then, to say, in the future, to the future, about the future?

IV

Countersignatures

> What then is at issue in this *yes* which names, describes, designates nothing, and which has no reference outside the mark [*hors marque*], though not outside language, since the *yes* can do without words or in any case without the word *yes*? In its radically non-constative or non-descriptive dimension, even if it says "yes" to a description or narration, *yes* is through and through [*de part en part*], and par excellence, a performative. But this characterisation seems to me inadequate. First, because a performative must be a *sentence* [*une phrase*], and a sentence sufficiently endowed with meaning in itself, within a given conventional context, to produce a determinate event. Now I believe, yes, I believe, that *yes*, to adopt a classic philosophical code, is the transcendental condition of any performative dimension whatever. A promise, an oath, an order, a commitment [*engagement*] always implies a *yes, I sign* [*oui, je signe*]. The *I* of the *I sign* says *yes*, and says *yes* in and to itself even if it is signing a simulacrum. Any event produced by a performative mark [*marque performative*], any writing in the broad sense of the word, binds itself [*engage*] to a *yes*, whether or not the *yes* is phenomenalised, that is, verbalised or adverbalised as such.
>
> Jacques Derrida, *Ulysse gramophone*[136]

It was not until some twenty-six years later, in August 2000, at a conference at Cerisy, that Derrida had occasion to revisit his encounter, textual as well as personal, with Genet, and address again not only the subsequent course of the writer's work but also the logic of futurity, or *obséquence,* as he called it, implicit, and at times explicit, in his own earlier reading.[37] For since 1974 much had happened. Derrida himself had continued to publish extensively on so-called literary texts, by Blanchot, Joyce, Kafka, Poe, Celan, Laporte, Baudelaire, Shakespeare, Artaud, Cixous, and others. And Genet too, after a lengthy silence, had produced a substantial, additional body of writing, rather different in manner, purpose, and tone from his earlier work, including notably, alongside articles and interviews in defence of the Black Panthers (1970–71) and the Baader-Meinhof Red Army Fraction (1977), an equally controversial eye-witness account of the Sabra and Chatila massacres in Beirut in September 1982, which in summer 1986 was followed by Genet's last, posthumous book, *Un captif amoureux,* a series of memories and reflections recounting his time with the Palestinians in 1970–71, 1982, and 1984, completed shortly before his death.

This late, more explicitly political phase in Genet's writing career represented a turning point in reception of his work. For some, as Genet would himself on occasion suggest, it testified to an apparent abandonment of the self-consciously fantasmatic, illusionist world of his earlier prison texts and plays in favour of a renewed appreciation of the need for decisive, political involvement.[38] As such, it was an evolution that, as well as fresh enemies, brought Genet new friends. Among these, in addition to those who sympathised politically with the causes with which Genet now identified himself, were numbers of other critics and commentators who particularly welcomed Genet's apparent ethico-political turn, chiming as it did, at least at first sight, with a parallel shift in French thought during the 1980s and after, and the subordination of textuality to ethical or political objectives it seemed to announce. In this context, the significance of Genet's later work for readers of Derrida was immediately apparent, and Simon Critchley was not alone, for instance, in an essay first published in 1990, in implying that Genet's re-emergence or reinvention as a committed writer provocatively gave the lie to Derrida's emphasis, in *Glas,* on the undecidable, and represented a significant challenge to the adequacy of Derrida's thinking of the literary. *Un captif amoureux,* wrote Critchley, as he went on to develop this argument, "enacts a profound inversion of the ethically privileged terms of Genet's earlier writing: homosexuality, betrayal, theft, solitude, alterity, abjection, and, most importantly, saintliness."[139] "[W]hat takes place," he continued, "is a collapse in Genet's ethical vocabulary which produces an inversion of values, from an ethic of saintliness which respects the other's alterity through an experience of aestheticised abjection, to an ethic of family and community, where the other is my mother or brother and is recognised as an object of loving cognition to which I am captive. With characteristic irony, it appears that Genet had the last laugh against both Derrida and Sartre."[140]

Admittedly, this account of Genet's conversion is not without its difficulties. Few readers, first of all, might be willing to recognise in *Pompes funèbres*, say, with its scenes of sexual domination, degradation, exploitation, its intermittent gratuitous cruelty to animals and to humans, and its ambivalent, yet still shocking encomium to the much-reviled, collaborationist French *milice*, the work of an ethically engaged writer respectful of alterity. And it is arguably a sentimental or nostalgic critic too who is willing to disregard the complex, corrosive ironies and slippages of Genet's writing in order to conclude, in explicitly Hegelian terms, that "the political truth that transcends Genet's writing is the dream of a *polis* of Palestinian *Sittlichkeit*, that is to say, a free ethical life rooted in the substantial *Sitten* of the community: family, marriage, love, heterosexuality, fecundity, property, and divinity."[141] The fact is, both here and there, as *Glas* persistently demonstrates, Genet's writing is far from easily reducible to any identifiable ontologico-ethical stance, and it is a brutal simplification to consider *Un captif amoureux* even as an elegaic, failed attempt to accredit, endorse, or impose a set of overriding ethico-political imperatives.

Much of Critchley's reading hinges on an interpretation of the writer's quest, in July 1984, forming the main, albeit tenuous thread of Genet's narrative, for the Palestinian couple, mother and son, who once offered him a bed for the night in Aljoun some fourteen years earlier. But the significance of this encounter was anything but anecdotal. According to the narrator of *Un captif amoureux*, named, but thereby denamed throughout the book (as Derrida has it), as a certain—uncertain—Jean Genet, the group formed by Hamza and his mother, disregarding their other family members, not only bore the mysterious seal, signature, or imprint of the Palestinian Revolution; they were, as far as the writer was concerned, not so much the public symbol as the private raison d'être of the Palestinian Resistance, which seemed only to have taken place, Genet explains, with extraordinary, yet knowing hubris, and hardly believing it himself, "in order that this couple should haunt me [*afin que me hantât ce couple*]."[142] Crucial to the haunting of the narrator by this explicitly Christological mother-and-son relationship is a scene, to which *Un captif amoureux* returns obsessively, nominally in an endeavour to verify it, but only to achieve the opposite effect, in which Genet's narrator-protagonist, fully clothed, finds himself occupying Hamza's bed overnight, while Hamza himself is absent, carrying out a dangerous terrorist mission over the border. Late in the evening, or early in the morning, as battle rages in the distance, there are two theatrical taps at the bedroom door, and as Genet lies half-awake, Hamza's mother silently enters, as she regularly does for her son, it seems, in order to serve her guest a night-time cup of Turkish coffee and glass of water, simultaneously bidding him to sleep and yet to stay awake, and thus protect him, and herself, from the Jordanian military. Shortly after, there are two more taps, and Hamza's mother returns to remove the tray left earlier.[143] And Genet's narrator comments:

> Since he was away that night fighting, in his room and on his bed I took the place and perhaps the role of her son. For one night and the duration of a simple yet multiple act, an old man more aged than she became [*devenait*: the use of imperfect tense emphasises an unfinished process] the mother's son for "I was before she was." Younger than me, during this familiar—familial?—action, she was, while remaining Hamza's, my mother. It was in that night, which was my own personal and portable night, that the door to my bedroom had opened and closed again.[144]

The writer finally falls asleep; Hamza returns at dawn; and Genet leaves.

For Critchley, this scene operates a four-fold movement of symbolic reconciliation: between writer and fedayee; between Genet the orphan and Hamza's mother, now standing in for the writer's absent mother, Gabrielle; between Palestinian roots and European rootlessness; between Genet and God, father and son.[145] On this reading, the ending of Genet's book marks an important breakthrough. "The economy of betrayal within which the writing of [*Un captif amoureux*] circulates," Critchley concludes, as he reads Genet's closing page, "is broken by a redemptive moment of transcendence that cannot be comprehended in writing and, precisely because of this, is able to comprehend the truth of the Palestinian Revolution. Writing the truth of the revolution is a writing of the truth of what lies outside writing: redemption, reconciliation."[146] But it is hard to see how this is so. For Genet's book ends on a more nuanced, ambivalent note than these words suggest. It does defend itself, admittedly, as an act of truthful witnessing; but the truth of the witness, it insists, is anything but something already grasped, thematised, and positioned as such. It is necessarily embodied, subject to error, distraction, or partiality, both because the witness is by definition a solitary, surviving, perhaps inarticulate voice and because of the possible inadequacy of the words on which testimony relies, from which it follows that, if one of the responsibilities of writing is to remember and cast light on the past, then, by that very token it cannot *not* also be traversed—threatened as well as enabled—by oblivion, and by darkness, such as finds expression, most particularly for Genet, in an impenetrable, mysteriously atemporal night once spent in Irbid. Genet's final page, in other words, may indeed be transparent to the narrator, as his closing, signature sentence claims; but that transparency is dense and opaque, like much of Genet's writing. There is therefore no finality to the writer's quest, other than the certain prospect of his own imminent dying.[147] And even as Genet seems to reach his goal towards the end of his narrative, and is able, perhaps, to seek confirmation from Hamza's mother of the existence of that scene long ago, it is apparent that much is irretrievably lost. Hamza is now in Germany, married, it seems, to a German woman; his mother is prematurely aged, and seems older now than the narrator; and much else is shrouded in conjecture, save for the fiercely affirmative eyes of Hamza's mother, demanding the past be forgotten, and with the exception of a standpipe or hydrant, still standing at a fork in the way, a quizzical vestige of what may or may not remain.[148] The enigma of that night remains unresolved, its memory surviving dimly in the mind of the narrator (much less so in the minds of the other participants) as a kind of hallucinatory prophecy, engulfing or replacing all else, a trace or remainder, that having never been properly present, cannot be identified with itself, resurrected, or made present again.

For nothing here is quite what it seems. As Derrida shows in *Glas*, positionality in Genet is rarely, if ever, given as such. It is always separated from itself, deferred, distanced, prosthetic. Interferences and discontinuities are many; and much information is withheld. This extends to Genet's syntax, which is often irregular, uncertain, improvisational. Narrative development too is rarely linear, always fractured, elliptical, and digressive, marked with countless achronological disjunctions or displacements, exhibiting a vast network of idiosyncratic connections and disconnections, like so many unexpected couplings and uncouplings. The encounter with Hamza and his mother is a case in point. The sequence is not described or recounted once but several times over, proleptically, retrospectively, and by preterition. Even the most detailed report of the night spent in Irbid is relatively brief, detached from its context like some singularity of time and space, in which nothing is given except as a series of undecidable substitutions or reversals. It casts the narrator, for instance, as he sleeps upon (but not in) Hamza's bed, in the role of the son, though his age, some forty years older than his absent host, more properly qualifies him to be Hamza's father, not to say his grandfather. Or is he perhaps Hamza's prosthetic lover, warming his bed in his absence, already mourning his impending loss?

Temporal continuity is disrupted here, and gender roles are subject to further turbulence. For Hamza's mother, in so far as she is her son's only surviving parent, is already his father, which is no doubt why her first, incongruous appearance in the book, by dint of another elliptical displacement, is as the phallic Virgin mother, exhibiting her infant son, says Genet, as a ruffian might brandish his virile member.[49] If so, the only position left for the narrator to occupy would be that of an ageing, sexless castrato, left blind, like Homer, to tell this epic story of long ago, whose own mother, who likewise was never present as such, is embodied in effigy by this woman at least ten years younger than he. As for Hamza himself, not only is he his mother's son, he is also the paternal head of the household, in which capacity he offers Genet his bed, thus turning the writer into something resembling his—Hamza's—son, a visitor who, as a result of this hospitality, comes to be reborn as a writer, but one whose story does not tell of fertile victory but dispossession, and hangs on an obsessive memory, congruously-incongruously acted out in Muslim Palestine, presenting without presenting, Genet himself explains, something resembling that age-old Christological—yet more than Christological—scene, its origins lost in time, of the Mother who comes after the Son while preceding her own Father, and reminding Genet of nothing so much as his quest for his own mother, *the* mother, who, at thirty weeks old, entrusted him to the French Republic, and disappeared, leaving her son to contemplate the strange series of circumstances that belatedly provided him with a replacement father in the figure of the State, giving him a name while also effacing it, and separating him from the birth-mother whose irretrievable existence henceforth lay always in a past that had never been present.

This explains, perhaps, why there is nothing linear or teleological about *Un captif amoureux*, which describes instead an often haphazard geographical, personal, political journey, in which nothing is final other than death: death, not as sacrifice, power, or victory, writes Genet, recalling the 1982 massacres in Lebanon, but "the phenomenon that destroys the world."[150] The singularity of the Palestinian Revolution, Genet contends, was to have understood this, which is why its ambitions were not in the first instance territorial, and reached far beyond the objective of the nation-state.[151] In this sense, he claims, albeit with potentially troubling implications, its nature was less political than metaphysical.[152] In the end, for Genet, this was perhaps also why, even as it clung desperately to its possible or impossible future, the Palestinian Resistance found itself betrayed, not only by its enemies but by its supposed friends too: "not so much a revolt," the writer concluded, "as a drowning [*une noyade*], even as the hope for a radiant outcome [*l'espoir d'une sortie lumineuse*] remains indestructible."[153]

Genet, in turn, albeit for different reasons, was no stranger to this predicament. While he pledged his fidelity to the cause, and campaigned whole-heartedly on its behalf, he was well aware that the Palestinian Revolution was not so easily grasped. "Did the Palestinian Revolution elude me?" he asks at the outset, and answers: "Completely."[154] This came as no surprise. Invited to write a book about the Palestinians by none other than Yasser Arafat, who in return facilitated the author's access to both people and places, Genet in *Un captif amoureux* barely takes the proposition seriously, and responds with surprising diffidence, comparing Arafat in passing, in a typically elliptical displacement, with the celebrated French actor-manager Louis Jouvet, who first directed *Les Bonnes* in 1947, and with whom Genet, as with other erstwhile collaborators, enjoyed a fraught, irritated, and suspicious relationship.[55] It is as though, as with Jouvet, the verbal contract with Arafat was simultaneously evoked and revoked, accepted and rejected, announced and denounced. Did Genet keep his side of this uncertain bargain, or was it in the nature of the agreement without agreement with Arafat that it would be betrayed? Betrayal, for Genet, was a notorious subject of fascination. "Betrayal," he wrote, "belongs at one and the same time both to curiosity and to dizziness [*vertige*]"[56]—perhaps nowhere more irremediably than when what is at stake is writing itself, which knows fidelity only because it is already familiar with infidelity too.

The politics of *Un captif amoureux*, then, are anything but founded on a mysteriously unspeakable, yet self-evident transcendent truth, embodied in some latter-day ethics of dialectical reconciliation, as Critchley's remarks suggest. This is not to deny that politics are indeed everywhere in Genet's book. It is rather that, in writing the memories that make up *Un captif amoureux*, for reasons of honour, Genet is constrained—and Genet's reader too—*not* to honour the platitudinous verities that are so often associated with political involvement but to betray them in the search for a more demanding, inconsistent, and less easily decidable relationship with the political. Far from being outside writing, the political in this sense is in fact nothing other than writing, not in the spurious sense that politics are only words, but because that which is inscribed in writing, as Genet's work testifies, is the enigmatic, two-fold possibility and impossibility of a signature.

The image of Genet the pro-Palestinian, anti-Zionist campaigner, reaching in his later work beyond the logic of reversibility to embrace progressive, not to say revolutionary political change, though far from unproblematic, achieved considerable currency in the 1970s and after.[57] It was not, however, the only available interpretation of Genet's ideological evolution. Indeed, other, politically less sympathetic critics soon began to question in a rather different way the relationship between the sombre rituals of *Pompes funèbres*, say, and the political agenda implicit in *Un captif amoureux*, drawing attention to what, it was claimed, lay deeply buried in both texts: Genet's covert, but enduring anti-semitism. True, there is, on the one hand, in Edmund White's assessment, little concrete evidence regarding Genet's alleged hatred of Jews, notwithstanding a number of worrying personal testimonies.[58] Some readers may nevertheless tend to the view that, at the very least, certain remarks in *Un captif amoureux* tread and sometimes even cross the thin line between Genet's anti-Zionism and anti-semitism. The charge of anti-semitism was not, however, a new one. Already in 1952, in *Saint Genet: comédien et martyr*, albeit rather oddly in a footnote, Sartre was making the case that Genet, as he put it, "is anti-semitic; or rather, feigns to be [*Ou plutôt, il joue à l'être*]."[159] And fifty years later, Sartre's remark returned as the point of departure for a more severe indictment of what, in the course of a provocative examination of Genet's later as well as some of his earlier work, the critic Éric Marty termed his "metaphysical anti-semitism," a position Marty defined, drawing on an eclectic mixture of theology, textual analysis, psychoanalytic theory, anthropology, and philosophy, from Kierkegaard to Lacan and René Girard, as a kind of "anxiety at the Good [*angoisse du Bien*] and in the face of Good [*angoisse devant le Bien*]," and which, in a later article, he described as a form of castration anxiety.[160]

Crucial to Marty's argument, following Sartre's lead, was the identification of Genet with the figure of Cain.[161] Cain, it will be remembered, in the Book of Genesis, is the murderer, responsible for killing his own brother, condemned as a result to remain a fugitive and a vagabond. Genet, in the role of Cain, argues Sartre, is the traitor par excellence, with no future other than his own past, consumed in a gesture of refusal, destruction, negation, and Marty agrees: Genet's moral stance, he asserts, in a fierce burst of invective, is "a morality [*une morale*] of deception [*trucage*], lying [*mensonge*], irreality [*irréalisation*], and fraud [*faux*], of loser wins, homosexuality [*inversion*], violence, theft, and nothingness [*néant*], all of which may be brought together and summed up in a single word that transcends them all: betrayal [*la trahison:* treachery]."[162] In Genet's private, manichean mythology, according to Marty, Cain has, however, a rival, of whom he is intensely jealous: the figure of Abraham. Between the two, the difference is infinite; for it is the difference between an act of sacrifice, forever tormented by the thought that it may be unwittingly committing evil, and an act of murder, intent on carrying out evil, fearful only that goodness may prove insuperable. Once more in a footnote Marty explains his point:

By interiorising the anxiety of Evil [*l'angoisse du Mal*] taken to its furthermost limit, by pursuing the simulation of the murder of

Isaac, his own son, to a point of extreme reversal, Abraham delivers both himself and humanity from human sacrifice and from sacrificial debt, and in return inscribes care [*le souci*] and anxiety within human consciousness as its most proper being [*son être le plus propre*]. This interiorisation, which takes Abraham to the core of deepest silence where he no longer utters [*profère*] anything, is the greatest possible experience of language, an experience that models all the great Jewish metaphysical ordeals from Moses to Job. Indeed, Abraham's attitude—like that of Jacob, Moses, or Job—is synonymous with an absolute confidence in the promise made to him, the promise of paternity and filiality, that is, an absolute confidence in language. Conversely, that which defines Genet's metaphysics presupposes a suspicion [*suspicion: suspiciousness*] cast on any speech [*toute parole*], address [*toute parole adressée*], or appeal [*tout appel*]; the point is to place oneself within treachery for perpetuity [*se situer à perpétuité dans la trahison*]: "Treachery, meaning to breach the laws of love [*rompre les lois de l'amour*]," as Genet puts it in *Journal du voleur*.[163]

Treachery, then, has a limit; for there is something it must strain to overcome, but which, in truth, it cannot defeat, which is the promise, the gift, the transcendence of speech. The reaction of both violence and frustration provoked in Genet by this manichean clash of values is what Marty understands by the writer's anxiety before the Good, which explains, among others, he argues, his phobic relationship to the state of Israel, as witnessed by the controversial charge, made in *Un captif amoureux*, of it being the self-styled expression of the Origin and the embodiment of Power in the world, which, according to Marty, rather than spontaneous sympathy with the fate of the dispossessed, was the main motivation for Genet's commitment to the Palestinians.[164] It is in fact the Jews, Marty goes so far as to say, rather than the Palestinians, in that they are Cain's most resilient opponents and as a result cast in the role of absolute Good [*le Bien absolu*], who are the major, not to say only protagonists in Genet's book.[165] Upon the Middle East of the 1970s and 1980s, then, in Genet's narrative, the history of the Nazi Third Reich comes to be superimposed, which is how Marty interprets the news that Hamza the fedayee is now living in Germany, at which point, in Marty's at times nuanced, but heavily dogmatic reading, *Un captif amoureux* trembles with the spectral presence of that figure of Hitler for whom the Genet of *Pompes funèbres,* it is claimed, displayed such deep fascination. But by now, the sense of Marty's polemic is clear enough: it is that Genet's avowed anti-Zionism is a façade, concealing a more profoundly rooted, aggressive anxiety directed at Israel in so far as it embodies, for the critic, all that Cain-Genet is driven to negate: the law, election, communal identity, the innocence and transparency of language, truthfulness in discourse, the possibility of filiation, the promise of the future.

As he approaches this conclusion, Marty undertakes a minor detour in order to consider other readings of Genet's work. He pauses briefly on *Glas,* taking time only to despatch a few polemical, albeit unconvincing and inconclusive remarks in the direction of Derrida. Derrida's reading of Genet, he writes, is secret, enigmatic, hard to judge, old-fashioned, irritating, boring, trivial, even childish, with Derrida, in the end, according to Marty, under cover of a partial identification with the homosexual Genet, exchanging one form of exclusion for another, merely taking the opportunity to indulge his memories of growing up a Jew in Algeria.[166] Marty, then, is unimpressed. "[I]s it necessary," he asks, quickly moving on, "still to read Genet in order to betray oneself?"[167] But as he addresses Derrida in this way, acknowledging *Glas* only in order to dismiss it, it is apparent that Marty's strategy is one of attempted exorcism. But exorcism is a double-edged sword, and even as Marty attempts to ward off the threat of undecidability, his reading all the more surely invites it. For as the critic moves to conclude, he abandons the manicheism attributed to Genet (more saliently a feature of his own reading) to suggest that Genet-Cain, despite his best efforts— and necessarily so, if its transcendent status is to be maintained—is ultimately unable to defeat the dialectic of the Good bequeathed by Abraham's decision. "In which case," remarks Marty, "if Jacques Lacan might say of Sade, in a choice paradox, that the end result was the systematic triumph of virtue, so, provided one preserves the wit of Lacan's formula, it might also be said of Genet that the same is true, and that, in a way, the end result is always the systematic triumph of the Jews, and the triumph of Israel."[168] Genet, then, because he was deeply wrong, was right after all, in spite of himself, even as, forever unrepentant, his treachery persisted.

But how might such a radical conversion—not unlike, in its own way, the reversal of Genet the saint of abjection into the proponent of Hegelian *Sittlichkeit*—be indeed possible? How might Genet's writing, in other words (at least on Marty's submission), be susceptible to betraying its own deepest motivations? Alternatively, how might it be seen to overturn one so-called ethical stance, grounded in the figure of the outcast, to replace it with its almost exact, conformist opposite? A sceptical reader might reply, of course, that what is decisive in such cases is merely the virtuosity, not to say the ideological predispositions of the individual critic. But other, more important factors are at issue. Such conversions in reading that are a striking feature of the reception of Genet's earlier and later work are no doubt only possible in so far as writing, from the outset, is irreducible to the positing of a single, self-identical, politico-ethico-ontological position—which is precisely the point made by Derrida in the passage from *Glas* which Marty cites, only to dismiss it as an embarrassing autobiographical digression.[169] For in that four-page peephole (or *judas*), which opens in the middle of a word (the word is *moignon*, stump, referring to Stilitano's amputated hand), separating *moi-* (ego, or self) from *-gnon* (a bruise, or swelling on the skin), and begins with the statement: "you can always keep looking for the subject [*vous pouvez toujours chercher le sujet:* i.e., the search is both endless and in vain]," what Derrida does is to interweave and overlay a sequence of texts, starting with a series of variations on the bandaged, severed extremity as a sign of phallic potency (in *Pompes funèbres* and *Miracle de la rose*), followed by an allusion to circumcision as a release of speech in Luke's Gospel, which then segues into an abyssal quotation from Genet's *Notre-Dame-Des-Fleurs* (*Our Lady of the Flowers*) devoted, precisely, to the similarities between three forms of inscription: the intricate pictorial tattoos which the inmates busy themselves tracing on their skin, the epidermic thrill at the rabbi's unrolling of the Torah (which Genet compares to the sexual excitement at seeing a fellow prisoner undress), and the chiselling of hieroglyphs upon a sacred column reminiscent of the passage from Hegel's *Lectures on Aesthetics* quoted in *Glas*.[170] In its turn, the quotation prompts a brief third-person narrative dealing with the ritual of the Torah: its two columns or rollers, the bands in which it is wrapped, which, undone, are given to a boy to take up to the women, sitting apart in an upper gallery, who will roll them up again, while the body of the Torah itself is laid out on a table, with the attendant male faithful covering themselves in veils, bearing fragments of the sacred text about their bodies; after which Derrida's *judas* ends with a fable, drawn from Jean-Paul's novel, *Leben Fibels* [*The Life of Fibel*], telling the story of the Anabaptist convert Jude (*Judas* in German), who, undergoing baptism fifteen times over and more, as his new-found faith demands, relinquishes his Jewish name Judas (*Judas* in German), that of the traitor Iscariot, only to be reborn into Christianity as his own exact homonym, as though to suggest that all conversions are always circular, and all forms of identity potential acts of treachery, and that any one Judas or *judas* is not only never the same as any other, but only ever gives itself as what it is in so far as it is marked or inscribed with heterogeneity and otherness.[171]

Rather than simply an autobiographical transposition of Genet's text, what Derrida provides here, then, is an abyssal meditation— between both description and performance—on the palimpsest-like structure of textuality, by which texts of different provenance, status, and material complexion, while preserving their contextual singularity, are drawn to interiorise each other and exteriorise themselves in the process, tracing a movement without origin that is always at least double: two texts, two columns, two bodies, two sexes, and, finally, two names, none of which is self-identical, each of which was implied, welcomed, and outstripped by the other, in a constant motion of inscription and erasure. "What is it that am I doing here? [*Qu'est-ce que je fais ici?*]," asks Derrida, not necessarily speaking in his own name, and without specifying what place it is to which the phrase refers, since it is always already everywhere (as Hegel, albeit in a different sense, had argued earlier). In his polemic against Derrida, Marty cites these words, but fails to see their relevance. "Let's put it," repeats the text, making matters doubly apparent, "that I am working at the origin of literature while miming it [*Mettons que je travaille à l'origine de la littérature en la mimant*]. Between the two [*Entre les deux*]."[172] For literature is what happens, occurs, transpires, without ever presenting itself as such, between the two: between the one and the other, like a bell swinging to and fro in the breeze, shuttling back and forth, tolling the end, announcing the beginning, always ahead of itself or just behind, never what it seemed, undecided, duplicitous, excessive. In a word: treacherous.

Everything, then, not for the first time, turns on this possibility of betrayal.

Can the threat of treachery be resisted, marginalised, excluded? Critchley and Marty, though they approach Genet from opposing perspectives, nevertheless both appear to think so, appealing in the one case to the redemptive transcendence of ethico-political truth, invoking in the other the transcendental absoluteness of language as beneficent promise.

But what is a promise that cannot be betrayed, asks Derrida, and what is a truth that is not exposed to error? For treachery and error are not contingent mishaps but ineradicable virtualities inseparable from the possibility of fidelity and truth, which are traversed by the threat or hope of what lies beyond their control, and without which they would not occur at all. For without the possibility of treachery, there would be no fidelity; and without the possibility of falsehood, there would be no truth.

In such circumstances, to what or to whom does a reader, critic, writer—owe responsibility?

Returning to Genet in August 2000, it was here, pointedly, that Derrida chose to begin—to begin, he put it, even before beginning to begin again.[173] For betrayal, *la trahison,* was itself a treacherous word, not unlike the word *revelation,* Genet himself suggests at one stage, which spoke both one thing and its opposite.[174] The phrase: betrayal of truth, *trahison de la vérité,* in similar fashion, Derrida continued, testified to an essential complication. For it could be understood in at least three, mutually incompatible ways. First, it might refer to the betrayal of truth by such enemies of truth as lying, falsity, disloyalty, inadequacy of memory, and other failures of understanding. But second, it might also imply, in Nietzschean vein, that truth itself was a treacherous value, and already from the outset a misleading travesty, a forgery, a false idol, constitutively untrue to the transparent self-coincidence it promised. As readers of *Un captif amoureux* will recall, both motifs circulate constantly throughout Genet's text, simultaneously authenticating and undermining its status as a reliable document, without it being possible in the end accurately to measure the extent of the book's veracity or mendacity.[175] It was not for nothing, in this regard, as many subsequent readers have noted, that Genet should describe himself in 1970 as seeking not a friend but an enemy. "No friends," he wrote. "Especially no friends: an enemy declared, but not divided [*un ennemi déclaré mais non déchiré*]."[76] But how to tell the difference between friend and enemy: between treachery as a betrayal of truth and truth as a betrayal of treachery? For there was a third understanding of the phrase, turning on the fact that the verb *to betray, trahir,* not only meant to be false, cheat, or lead astray, but also to disclose, show, or reveal, in which case it might be said after all that it was precisely the task of truth to betray, and the effect of betrayal to tell the truth.[77]

These were no playful or empty paradoxes. As Derrida suggests, they rather open up a series of terrible and terrifyingly unanswerable questions, which, as such, were nevertheless inescapable, and testified to the binding yet aporetic structure of what Derrida addressed at Cerisy under the heading of the concept of the countersignature.

In Derrida's exposition, the word gathered together a number of traits. First, in its own right, on the speaker's part, it was itself already a signature, which not only recalled to the listener's attention a number of earlier texts by Derrida on the logic of iterability commanding the possibility of signatures in general but also pointed in abyssal fashion to Derrida's own presentation which, as it unfolded, drew extensively on *Glas* and quoted from it at length. At times seeming almost excessively recapitulatory, didactic, and digressive, the text of "Contresignature" was itself, in this respect, both a signature and a countersignature, binding in a common seal both testimony and promise, both the call to memory and a commitment to the always future necessity of re-reading. And what Derrida sought to emphasise in particular was the shifting relationship of convergence and divergence between the texts of Hegel and Genet which the two columns of *Glas* had served to articulate. This was not, then, a case of dialectical opposition, which is why it is misleading to portray Derrida's Genet, as one critic puts it, as "the hero of dissemination whose texts and actions signal the overcoming of Hegelian Absolute Knowledge."[78] And this was readily demonstrable from the attention paid by Derrida to the two writers' respective treatment of Judaism, with Hegel's analysis or critique of Abraham, as found in *Der Geist des Christentums und sein Schicksal* of 1798–1800, mirroring Genet's lapsed but still powerful investment in Catholicism, and anticipating the writer's polemical remarks, in *Un captif amoureux,* regarding Israel's overweening attachment to its origins.[179] But so far as Derrida was concerned, the question of the continuity between Genet's anti-Zionism and his alleged anti-semitism, which had been a focus of debate since the early 1980s, was anything but resolved, either in one direction or in the other, and was hardly likely to be reducible to any single, unqualified verdict. This was not to say it should be ignored, but treated as an object of endless re-reading.

This was the second crucial feature in Derrida's account of the logic of signatures and countersignatures. The fact was, as he had previously argued, in so far as every signature was necessarily repeatable, rather than marking a point of primary, authorial origin, it was only ever a secondary replication of what, as a consequence, had no verifiable origin. Each proto-signature, in other words, as Derrida's own paper testified, was already its own countersignature. It might authorise, endorse, ratify, sanction, and declare responsibility for that to which it was attached, but it might equally be a forgery, a counterfeit, a reappropriation, or a fraudulent parody of the text, with these two opposing manifestations sharing in the structure of iterability a common condition of possibility, without it being possible ever definitively to distinguish the one from the other, or immunise it against its counterpart. And as Derrida went on, much turned here on the necessary ambivalence of the prefix, preposition, or adverb: *counter-* [*contre-*], which, like the two columns of *Glas*, and as in such signature concepts as countertime [*contretemps*], counterpart [*contre-partie*], counter-example [*contre-exemple*], conjugated proximity with opposition, crossed supplementarity as a kind of necessary binding (by which each word always appealed to another) with supplementarity as a kind of necessary unbinding (by which each word always gave way to another). Too much was always too little, and too little always too much. And this was why, above and beyond the extensive thematic treatment of treachery and betrayal in *Un captif amoureux*, it followed that this text, like any text, could not only never control its own reading, but also that no reader might ever fully exhaust it, in so far as, both aged and youthful, like Janus and like Genet, it necessarily faced two ways: towards the past and towards the future, without the security of a self-identical present. These were not, however, negative conditions but an essential and indispensable requirement if reading, writing, reading about writing, writing about reading, were to occur at all: in the future.

To sign and countersign, then, was a performative act, the outcome of which was necessarily uncertain, but which, by that token, always enacted an affirmation. Any signature or countersignature, Derrida insisted, always offered up and offered itself up to a redoubled yes—yes, yes—that, in so far as it was repeatable, was not in itself a stable position, attributable as such to a moral subject, but was always already a singular response to the priority of another and the other.[180] This, in turn, meant that the affirmation enacted in signing or countersigning, before it might be thought as properly active or passive, was more essentially governed by a radical passivity—inscribing itself as submission, subscription, and substitution—void of all presence. "'Yes' ['Oui']," Derrida argued, "is always a response, and structurally it is the response to a question from the other [*une question de l'autre*], a response that falls subject to the law of the other [*la loi de l'autre*], just like the countersignature itself."[181] And what was affirmed in this way was not the thematic content or ideological or other implications of the text, however interpreted, since these remained (and would always remain) to be decided, but its event-like occurrence as a text, which required of each and every reader, in so far as she or he was a reader, that he or she affirm and underwrite the text, even though what might then happen was by essence always futural: unpredictable, incalculable, and irreducible to totalisation.

To affirm the text in its non-coincidence with itself did not imply a belief in the abiding value or values of literature. On the contrary, its intervention preceded all positionality and thematisation and had nothing therefore to do with the meaning or meanings that might be attributed to any given artwork. But the radical, imperative, and imperious affirmation to which Derrida refers might nevertheless, he suggested, provide the ground without ground of what, cautiously, in "Contresignature," he formulated as the ethics of his own writing, an expression he glosses in a discussion of Ponge by distinguishing clearly between the ethics, politics, or philosophical position that might be attributed to a writer or a writer's work and the manner in which the instance of ethics, as he terms it, is materially implicated in literature, not because literature is necessarily subject to the prescriptions of morality, but rather because "the petition of the ethical [*la requête de l'éthique*], ethical concern [*souci*], or negotiation [*explication*] with the law, is at the origin of literature: one does not enter into literature without negotiating [*explication*] with commitment, with a promise [*la promesse*], and with an oath [*la foi jurée*]. For literature to be an-ethical or immoral, or for it to take on the challenge of being transgressive, is already for it to make an appearance [*comparaît:* to appear in court] before something that occupies the position of morality [*la morale*], and to be presented to it." "It is perhaps necessary here," he added, "to distinguish between ethics [*l'éthique*] and morality [*la morale*]: it is necessary to sign, and to answer, even in order to object [*récuser*] to the law."[182]

In "Contresignature," Derrida went on to explain further:

> What I have called the ethics of my writing [*l'éthique de mon écriture*], using a word that leaves me a little dissatisfied because it can so easily be misunderstood [*équivoque*], but by which I mean the law which it is inconceivable I should try to evade [*que je me dérobe*], is to say *yes* to the work that comes before me and will have occurred without me, a work that was affirmed and signed already with a "yes" from the other, with the result that my own "yes" is a "yes" in response to the other's "yes," a kind of blessing [*bénédiction*] and mutual pact [*alliance:* an alliance, wedding band, or ring].

But what, then, is this strangely implicit pact that binds the reader so mysteriously and so irrevocably to the writing of another and of the other? It is a prescription which it is impossible to elude, but which prescribes, it seems, only the impossible. As Derrida writes:

> Not to evade [*Ne pas se dérober*] this law is therefore to do everything possible in order not to commit treachery, and betray either the law or the other. But, first of all, the possibility of betrayal is part of respect for the law. It must be constitutive of respect for the law. It must be *possible* [*Il faut pouvoir*] to betray something or someone in order to obey or to be faithful. Whoever *could* not be treacherous *could* not be faithful either. Second, there is also a terrible law of betrayal, as in the declared enemy-friend discussed

earlier, a terrifying law that demands that the more I betray someone or something (by writing differently, or signing differently),
the less I betray them or it; and the less I betray them (by repeating the same "yes," by imitating, or counterfeiting it), the more
I betray them. Which means that perjury—or betrayal, if you
prefer—is lodged like a double bind [*double bande*] at the very
heart of the countersignature. That is what the betrayal of truth
as the truth of betrayal is. This too, however terrifying it may appear, is what faithfulness is. One has to recognise it faithfully and
be as faithful as possible to faithfulness. But in order for my
countersignature, that is, the law that comes before any literary
theory, before any critical methodology, before each and every
concept of exegesis or hermeneutics or criticism or commentary,
in order for this absolutely anterior, absolutely originary countersignature, which is subject to this law, to attest both to cognition
[*connaissance*], i.e. the best and most competent knowledge possible, and to the re-cognition [*re-connaissance*] that authenticates,
for it to both cognise and recognise at one and the same time—
and this "at one and the same time" is a double bind or, to revert
to the word that organises *Glas* in its entirety, a double band [*une
double bande*]—it is necessary to respect the absolute, absolutely
irreducible, untranslatable idiom of the other, i.e. what Ponge or
Genet did, and was only ever done once, and, at the very moment I recognise this singularity which is that of the other, to inscribe within my own "yes" the work of the other. It is necessary
that within my own "yes," in my own untranslatable, singular
idiom, I must countersign the text of the other without counterfeiting it, that is, without imitating it. Which is obviously impossible. It is necessary to imitate, but without imitating. It is necessary to recognise, countersign, and reproduce the signature of
the other, but without reproducing it, and without imitating it.[183]

The rigorously incontrovertible law Derrida articulates here culminates in an aporia. Writing imposes on who writes and who reads a burden, charge, or responsibility that cannot be evaded, if only because the
attempt at evasion is itself already a response to the demand. But if a
reader is thereby constrained to begin—to begin even before beginning

to begin, Derrida puts it—by affirming the event of the text, its read-ability or unreadability (necessarily prior, and irreducible to a reader's agreement or disagreement with what a text, in thematic or ideological terms, may be held to be saying), and in so far as the reader is therefore charged with the responsibility of responding faithfully to the singu-larity of the text, it is only to discover that to respond faithfully is already to respond unfaithfully, to attempt consciously to betray it is perversely to respect it, and that to betray it a little more or a little less is always at the same time to do precisely the reverse—without this paradox ever being mediated, pacified, or resolved. To countersign the writing of the other proves, then, to be as impossible as it is inescapable. And there is no end to the dilemma, which remains, continues to remain, in the future, without presence, as a perpetually unsatisfied, inconclu-sive demand laid on each reader, and by that token on all literary criti-cism, forced to confront the endless futurity of the task, its disappoint-ment, incompletion, failure—and longevity.

It follows from this, Derrida argued in *Glas,* and insisted again in "Contresignature," that there were no authoritative norms, values, rules, or procedures that might reliably be deployed in reading, other than the imperative demand of justice, but which, in the name of justice itself, was irreducible to any prescriptive methodology. And this, in the form of an endless questioning, was Derrida's conclusion—conclusion with-out conclusion—to the task of reading the singularity of the text signed Genet:

> How to act in order to ally [*allier:* marry] the singularity of a coun-tersignature without counterfeit and the equally irreducible sin-gularity of a protosignature, one that, as in the case of all language, let me reiterate this, is nevertheless already divided, repeating itself in a double "yes." In other words, how can my "yes, yes" at one and the same time attest to the singularity of the "yes" of the other, to which I say "yes" without imitating it? How is it possible to imitate without imitating, when the first "yes" of the other, the protosignature, already involves repetition, involves division and iterability, and thus in a way is already imitating itself? This makes for a strange kind of arithmetic. How to act? I may ask the question, but have no answer. Not only do I have no

answer, but I take the view that there must *not* be an answer in
the form of some general norm, rule, or prior criterion. By definition there can be no prior methodological or technical response.
Each time it is necessary to invent the singular law of what
remains [*ce qui reste*], and must remain a single event, caught in
this aporia or double bind.[184]

The future of reading, of writing, was unpredictable, out of reach, without term, and unreconciled with present or past, hanging as a challenge
that was simultaneously a prompt and an interruption: endlessly talka-
tive, but also deeply silent.

Long ago, in the mountains of Moriah, it was the fate of another to
experience without experiencing a similarly exacting, impossible conundrum: to be caught inexplicably between an absolute and intractable
duty to a singular, unique divine other and a no less absolute intractable
responsibility to another singular, unique human other, and to have to
choose between betraying his offspring, family, immediate community,
and human law in general or betraying the authority of his God, in the
withering knowledge that to obey God and sacrifice his son, as he was
commanded, would cast both the deity and himself in the role of mur-
derers, but that to disobey God would throw doubt on his very reasons
for not following the injunction, and that, conversely, to pay obedience
to God's edict would at the same time not only destroy his son's future
but compromise God's earthly survival too, while to disregard the command would result, perversely, in the same. The choice, then, was no
choice, and Abraham, since that was the man's name, bestowed on him
by God as a sign of his status as father of many nations, was left to pon-
der his responsibilities, neither assenting nor refusing, reluctant to lie,
yet unable to say what, if it existed at all, the truth of his predicament
was, lapsing therefore into the deep mutism of unavowable secrecy.

The story of Isaac has given rise, of course, to numerous famous
literary treatments, by Kierkegaard, Kafka, Blanchot, countless others.
And in December 1990, as he embarked on a detailed analysis of
the question of responsibility, decisions, sacrifice, and secrecy, Derrida too elected to linger on the endless aporetics of Abraham's dilemma.[185] However extreme, acute, and unfathomable, this was nonetheless no exceptional situation; what it dramatised were the conditions

of possibility and impossibility of decision-making in general. And this was why what announced itself in Abraham's predicament, observed Derrida, if not the institution of literature, which would have to wait for several centuries more before it might appear as such, was nevertheless its possibility—albeit a possibility that would never bring forth a self-identical, self-present object. In turn, this possibility—or impossibility—of a thing called literature was the topic of a second, shorter essay, adding itself to the first like a coda, codicil, or supplement, entitled appropriately enough: "La Littérature au secret [Literature in Secret]."[186]

Derrida's purpose in this epilogue, in glossing the suspended sacrifice of Isaac, was not, he put it, to supply merely another interpretation of this most undecidable of undecidable scenes. It was to offer a reading of Abraham's dilemma that insisted crucially on the silence that accompanied the protagonist's ordeal, and which, since it resisted all verbalisation, translation, or paraphrase, pointed to a secret that could not be unveiled, revealed, spoken, or otherwise made present, and which, paradoxically, therefore, was not properly a secret at all, while yet remaining the most impenetrable imaginable. Neither immanent, nor transcendent, such a secret—without secret—was nevertheless constitutive of the thing called literature, which thus came to be marked by six crucial traits that Derrida listed as so many implicit presuppositions, according to which it was—given that literature implied the right to say all, or conceal all, which was why it was inseparable from what Derrida addressed as futural democracy, *démocratie à venir;* given that the fictitious character of the artwork relieved the writer of civil responsibility in the face of the law, and replaced it with hyper-responsibility towards the work or what traversed the work; given that what was encrypted in the work operated (without operating) a suspension of worldly sense, position, theme; given that literature as the site of a secret without secrecy had no other law than the singularity of the event of the work; given that the right to literature presupposed a historical, institutional framework that made it possible to perform and reply to acts of language; and given that literature, divided between extreme autonomy and extreme heteronomy, having no identity or essence in itself, could be defined solely in terms of what it was not.[187]

But given all this, given this giving, and given this gift of literature, both donation and poisoned chalice, what was it, then, that followed? What followed, writes Derrida, is that literature was inseparable from the double logic of betrayal: from betrayal as truth, and truth as betrayal, for which literature asks forgiveness. As it does so, however, it accentuates simultaneously, and without end, both its responsibility and its irresponsibility, its burden and its gaiety, its complicity and its innocence.

As Abraham, then, stretches forth his hand, taking the knife, holding it suspended above the bound, yet unbound figure of Isaac, acting without acting, obeying without obeying, betraying without betraying, accepting without accepting, refusing without refusing, deciding without deciding, and exposing himself and his son both to the threat and the promise proffered by the deity, at this exact moment of radical indecision, as impossible to confront as it is impossible to evade, in the form of an event that is not an event, what then occurs, writes Derrida, is the possibility of literature, of that writing which, as it affirms itself, yes, yes, as a response to the impossible, is already, yes, yes, an impossible response in the affirmative.

And in that double movement lies, perhaps, literature's secret.

V

An interjection

Should one write like Artaud? This is not something of which I am capable, and in any case whoever might try to write *like* [*comme*] him, under the pretext of writing *towards* [*vers*] him, would even more surely pass him by, and, so derisory would be the mimetic contortion, forfeit even the slightest chance of crossing his path [*le croiser*]. But one should yield even less to the genre of summary judgements [*la sentence*] about [*sur*] Artaud who will never be, either as himself or his name, the subject, object, or even less the subjectile of some learned diagnosis. All the more so, since what is at issue here are his drawings and paintings, not merely his words or statements. Artaud himself, we shall see, never wrote *about* [*sur*: i.e., literally, on] his drawings and paintings, but only directly across their surface [*à même*: without distance, at the same level]. The relation is quite other, made of imprecation and altercation, particularly as relates to a subjectile, in other words, the dimension of a support [*la portée d'un support*].

One cannot, nor should one, write *like* [*comme*] Artaud *about* [*sur*] Artaud who himself never wrote *on-the-subject* [*au-sujet*] of his drawings and paintings. Who, then, could even claim to write *like* Artaud *about* [*sur*] his drawings and paintings?

One would have to invent an idiom, and cast [*jeter*] a signature otherwise. Yes or no, is it necessary to have done with the subjectile [*en finir avec le subjectile*], a mime might ask, and would not be wrong, for we shall see it unfold [*nous assisterons à la scène*]: in this whole business of the subjectile, what is at stake is a judgement of god. And the point is indeed *to have done with it* [*d'en finir*], interminably.

Jacques Derrida, "Forcener le subjectile"[88]

In 1986, and again in 1996, during the writer's centenary year, honouring a pact or alliance first contracted in 1965, countersigned and reaffirmed on several occasions since, it was to Artaud that Derrida also returned.[89]

Few writings, no doubt, are as enigmatically challenging as those of Artaud: unyielding, intractable, incandescent. And the questions raised by Derrida in his very first essay on Artaud, and asked of his own commentary just as much as of the contributions of others, remained as unanswerable as ever.

How to be just to Artaud? How to respond to Artaud's writing without betraying it? And if betrayal was inevitable, how to betray less, even if that meant betraying more, or how to betray more, if that somehow also meant betraying less?

How, in other words, to write—neither on, nor about, nor like, but somehow at the same level as, or across the very surface of—Artaud?

Derrida's initial move in 1986 was oblique, and involved a further detour. For the subject of the essay, written to accompany a catalogue of Artaud's drawings and portraits, thus reiterating in part Artaud's own gesture in *Van Gogh le suicidé de la société*, without, however, attempting to imitate it, assuming this to be possible, was not Artaud's writing

proper, so to speak, but his little-known surviving graphic work, con
sisting of some 116 pieces, in a variety of media, the majority of which,
numbering §§43–116 in the catalogue, dated from the last four years of
Artaud's life.[190]

But what might it mean to refer to Artaud's writing proper? True,
Artaud's own project, in so far as it might be gathered into a system,
philosophy, or ideology, was inseparable from a vehement rejection of
all forms of alienation and a corresponding desire for the reintegration,
repossession, and reappropriation of subjectivity or self. But as Derrida
argued in 1965, and continued to insist, discreetly but unrepentantly, in
his 1996 homage at the Museum of Modern Art, Artaud's emphasis on
the need to reclaim all that was proper to the self was anything but
unproblematic. For it represented a temptation, and a potentially disabling concession to the metaphysics of presence, which for Derrida it
was essential to resist, even as he was quick to acknowledge that it was
indeed the way in which Artaud took that risk and exposed his writing
to such dangers that constituted one of the most compelling and affirmative signature effects of his work.[191] At any event, notwithstanding
their technical accomplishment, to which Derrida in 1986 and 1996
payed ample tribute, and as even a cursory examination of Artaud's artwork confirms, there is little in the writer's output that might be deemed
proper in the sense of enjoying with itself a relation of familiarity,
immediacy, or proximity. On the contrary, many of Artaud's drawings
stage a scene (which in many respects, as Derrida points out, being traversed by invisible forces, is anything but a scene[192]) of forms and words
at war with themselves and with one another, deployed across the page
not only as ramifying figurative images but also as so many precarious
material objects, overlaid, overwritten, and overworked, sometimes
punctured, perforated, and scorched by the artist's own hand. As such,
their status was deliberately and purposefully unstable. As Artaud wrote
to Jean Paulhan in January 1945, referring to the coloured drawings he
had recently begun to produce, "[T]hey are written drawings [*des dessins
écrits*], with phrases inserted into the various forms in order to precipi-
tate them [*afin de les précipiter:* to push over the edge, plunge head first,
aggravate, accelerate]."[193]

Derrida's apparent detour, then, served only to exacerbate the difficulties facing any kind of discourse that aims or is required or is tempted

to measure itself against Artaud's text. Rather than allowing a commentator to approach Artaud with cautious circumspection, it led directly to an abyss. And the abyssal question that posed itself, to Artaud and Derrida alike, was no longer the question of the subject understood as theme, place, position, or self, as it was and continues to be for literary theory in general, but the enigma of that which, quoting Artaud, who was himself perhaps already quoting the critic Tristan Klingsor, Derrida termed: the *subjectile*.[194]

Subjectile: the word, in French, according to Derrida, was unusual, singular, esoteric, possibly barbarous, and untranslatable, not far removed from having the status of a *hapax*. Being quotable, however, and explicitly presented as such on at least one occasion by Artaud, and as Derrida's own title served to confirm, the word was not simple but at least double, indeed, as far as Artaud's published work was concerned, already triple.[195] Its associations, in Artaud, suggested Derrida, were many, ranging from *subjectif, subtile,* or *sublime* on the one hand, together with numerous other forms in *sub-*, through the many words derived from Latin *jacere:* to throw or cast, like abject, project, introject, reject, and so on (reminiscent of German *werfen,* so powerfully exploited by the Heidegger of *Sein und Zeit*), with its mysterious proximity with Latin *jacere:* to lie, as embodied in such terms as adjacent or subjacent, to other words still that shared the suffix *-ile,* such as *projectile, textile, tactile.* More specifically, *subjectile* was a technical term, and referred to the material surface (wall, panel, canvas, paper) on which a painting or drawing was traced or inscribed.

In Artaud, Derrida suggests, the three known occurrences of the term bound it (while thereby unbinding it) to three related, but distinct, and shifting contexts. In the first, a letter to André Rolland de Renéville from 23 September 1932, concerning the final version of the First Manifesto on the Theatre of Cruelty, which Artaud completed only at the page proof stage, the writer voiced his discontent with a poorly executed drawing, where, he wrote, "what's known as the subjectile betrayed me [*ce que l'on appelle le subjectile m'a trahi*]." In the second, dating from late January 1946, in a commentary of his own on the drawing entitled "La Machine de l'être ou Dessin à regarder de traviole [The Machine of Being, or Drawing to Be Looked at Askew]," already covered with various inscriptions, Artaud refers in more affirmative vein to "what until today has never been admitted [*reçu*] into art, the botching [*gâchage:* spoiling, and mixing mortar] of the subjectile, the pitiful clumsiness of forms collapsing around an idea after having for how many eternities panted [*ahané:* grunted, heaved] to reach it. The page is dirty [*salie*] and ruined [*manquée*], the paper crumpled, the characters drawn by the consciousness of a child." Finally, in the last known occurrence of the word *subjectile* in Artaud's work, from February 1947, just as he was writing *Van Gogh le suicidé de la société*, he observed in a series of notes about his own drawings: "The figures on the inert page conveyed nothing beneath my hand [*sous ma main*]. They offered themselves to me like millstones that would not inspire drawing at all, and that I could probe [*sonder*], prune [*tailler*], scrape [*gratter*], file [*limer*], stitch [*coudre*], unstitch [*découdre*], tear [*écharper*], shred [*déchiqueter*], and criss-cross [*couturer*] without ever by father or by mother the subjectile complaining."[196]

Inscription: as betrayal, decomposition, scarification—these were the coordinates of Derrida's reading, in which, resourceful as ever, Derrida examined and unpacked in detail, with discriminating and sympathetic attention, the many avatars of the Artaudian subjectile—the subjectile which was Artaud, which resisted Artaud, and which Artaud in turn resisted, and which betrayed, decomposed, and scarified the writer's body, as well as the body of his art, and the orphaned matrix of his (non-)being. And as the subjectile oscillated back and forth, occupying no positionality, as either subject or object,[197] but imposing and exposing itself in the manner of a unique signature, the effect was to invite or impel or require the commentator in turn, inescapably, to sign in his or her own idiom, which Derrida did here by attaching or detaching a second unusual, esoteric, perhaps barbarous, ancient word of his own (not of his own), another *hapax legomenon,* so to speak, in the form of the verb *forcener,* a word rarely, if ever, encountered as an infinitive in modern French, and existing residually at best only as the memory of an intransitive verb deriving from Old French *fors* (outside) and the root *sen* (sense or reason), and meaning: to find—or, better, lose—oneself outside of meaning.[198] *Forcener le subjectile,* then, in the abyssal indecision of its syntax (Is the verb transitive or intransitive? Does the infinitive form correspond to an injunction or a speculation? Is either word a word at all?), in so far as it titled or entitled a possible or impossible encounter, spoke of the chance or necessity of harassing or exasperating the subjectile, working it to a frenzy, pushing it beyond all meaning, reason, or sense, were it not that already it fell to the subjectile to work itself to a frenzy and put itself beyond sense, including whoever endeavoured to stand in relation to it. For that relation, in so far as it beckoned at all, only ever announced itself in the imminence of an incalculable future.

To address the futurity of Artaud's writing, then, if such an ambition were possible, was not to position Artaud's writings, drawings, or experience as an object of theoretical knowledge, diagnosis, and evaluation; it was to write, in turn, simultaneously with and without Artaud, inside and outside his writing, both alongside and far behind. In returning to Artaud in 1986, Derrida's wager was not that he might read Artaud now but rather that he might allow himself now to be read by Artaud, within whose texts he let his own signature circulate from passage to passage, place to place, in a movement without compromise, without truth, and without term. Rather than setting Artaud's drawings and paintings within a given frame, it was to allow his own writing to be framed by that of Artaud, in the knowledge that what crossed and crisscrossed Artaud's own writing was the fragile powerlessness of all framing, the realisation that while writing, like Artaud's drawing, may let itself be captured on occasion within the page, it was only to escape the confines of that place in order to reinscribe itself elsewhere: as both promise and threat.

Futurity's dual signature had for Artaud, as it had for others, a double consequence, and it was to this that Derrida turned his attention on 16 October 1996. The date was not without relevance; for it fell only six weeks or so after the centenary of Artaud's birth, and coincided with an inaugural exhibition of Artaud's drawings at MoMA, this indisputed progenitor or progenitrix of modern art as such. Accordingly, in his presentation, Derrida sought to acknowledge both the significance of Artaud's admission to the pantheon and the scandalous implications of such belated consecration. Artaud's birth was the occasion for a rebirth; but, as Artaud knew, whoever came to be born was only ever the other. Both parts of this strange equation were irreducible. On the one hand, as the logic of the subjectile implied, and with a rare extremity, intensity, and violence, Artaud's writings, including his drawings, paintings, and other works, sought to belong to themselves, to the singular place, date, and signature they held within themselves like an impenetrable and unspeakable secret. But by that very token, by dint of their singular inscription, they were nevertheless quotable, repeatable, and reproducible, according to the logic of iterability that inhabits all signatures and subjectiles as such, and therefore could not *not* invite their own incorporation, however alienating, within the institution of the museum, and thereby sanction the many consequences that followed, which had the effect of turning Artaud's writing into an object—of knowledge, desire, and criticism, notwithstanding that this annexation by others of the body of Artaud's writing did not prevent that writing, at every possible turn, from railing against this expropriation, and in so doing underwriting yet again, as Derrida tirelessly argued, the two-faced dilemma of the signature, by which a writer could write his or her name only in so far as that name was thereby hers or his no longer.

Of this intractable aporia, manifesting itself in the paradoxical form of a necessarily affirmative gesture, the occasion of Artaud's consecration by MoMA was only one ambiguous instance among many: an exemplification, so to speak, that, in every sense, could not but betray itself as such. This much, as already so often elsewhere, had been clearly signalled in the title Derrida gave to his talk, and which MoMA viewed with understandable suspicion, sensing no doubt the unpredictable reversibility of what Derrida's formula implied, that is, not only MoMA's attempted (mis)appropriation of Artaud and the institutionalisation of Artaud-Mômo the madcap simpleton, but at the same time Artaud's own attempted (mis)appropriation of MoMA and the release of the museum from itself by this intervention of Artaud-Mômo the grimacing jester.[199] But there was more. For to the threat or promise embodied in this already two-faced title, Derrida now added a subtitle, *Interjections d'appel* (which might roughly be translated, in both the verbal and the legal sense, as "Appeals"), already a partial quotation from Artaud, and itself susceptible to a double, if not triple reading.[200]

Among others, the term *interjections* drew attention to the siting of Derrida's own discourse at MoMA between two lengthy quotations from Artaud, drawn not from the writer's graphic work, nor even from his written texts as such, but from the archival tape recording of *Pour en finir avec le jugement de dieu*, made by Artaud and his collaborators for French radio in 1948, but never broadcast in Artaud's lifetime. To play the tape, this enduring trace, monument, or remainder of the almost fifty-year-old silencing of Artaud, within the hallowed confines of MoMA, was, on Derrida's part, towards the ghost of Artaud, a gesture, however belated, of generosity: of reconciliation, restitution, and redemption.

But the return of Artaud the Mômo, even as it spoke of recognition at last, also bore witness, not only to Artaud's continuing silence, but also to the affirmative, embodied intensity of the writer's voice, sardonic, vehement, and impassioned. "Of the body by the body with the body from the body and to the body," Artaud declaimed. "Life, and the soul, only come afterwards. They will no longer be born. Between the body and the body there is nothing."[201] In terms such as these, what Artaud's body and body of writing demanded above all was not acceptance, acknowledgement, or restoration but something more: justice. Here, the further implications of Derrida's intervention became audible. For the interjections mentioned in both Artaud's and Derrida's subtitle pointed not only to the former's vociferous interruption of the discourse of authority by recourse to the singular language of the scream and the cry, as the 1948 recording testified, but also, according to French idiom, to the process by which, in the legal system, against a given judgement, an appeal for justice is lodged. Artaud's interjections, then, demanded both an interruption of language and an interruption of judgement. It was necessary, in other words, as Artaud had insisted so many years before, now and interminably, in response to the singular event of writing, to have finished with judgement.

Shortly before handing over again to Artaud, with whose words and whose voice he wished to conclude, Derrida made the following closing submission:

> Let me briefly call a halt upon this word *interjection* to immobilise two of its three possible meanings. I first want to release it, however, since that is the bargain I made with myself, from everything that might draw it back into the semantic fold [*famille*] of *-ject* [*jet*], *-jection* [*jetée*], ejaculation, projection, or projectile— or even the subjectile eccentric [*du forcené subjectile:* in reversing standard word order, Derrida now suggests that *forcené* be read as a noun and *subjectile* as an adjective]. Although an interjection is a word or part of a word, i.e. that syllable or cry that is uttered as

an exclamation in order to interrupt meaning, or a sentence, or the other person, and although it is tempting to treat as interjections all Artaud's poems in that, coming from no identifiable tongue, they seem to raise up [*soulever*] the whole of his poetic work and drawings, let us instead allow the word to drift towards that which, in legal terminology, during a court case [*au cours d'une action:* Derrida underlines the word *action*], names the procedure for an appeal, lodged [*interjeté:* literally, thrown between] whenever a wrong [*le tort*], and therefore injustice, may have been allowed, then stabilised, and finally legitimised by an earlier judgement. When this occurs, an appeal is lodged [*on interjette appel*] to annul [*mettre fin*] the bad judgement [*la chose mal jugée*], with a view to challenging the judgement of all judges, belonging to the Court, the Church, the State, Family or Society, and the criteria of all those who swear an oath and pass judgement, all those conspirators [*conjurés,* who swear allegiance to one another] who criticise, evaluate, and diagnosticate: doctors, especially psychiatrists, art critics, literary critics, moralists and priests, professors, all of whom are secretly sanctioned by some judgement of god, with whom a final appeal [*une interjection finale*] would like to have finished. Through the counter-demonstration of a plea in the form of an indictment and the counter-initiatory counter-oath of an appeal, Artaud-Mômo, Artaud the madcap-child, Mômo the street urchin [*le môme*], in his own voice and with the whole of his body, will have made his protests heard, interposing and interjecting himself [*pour s'interposer, pour s'interjeter lui-même:* literally, to appeal by putting, or throwing himself between], in order to interrupt and rebut so many charges or counts of indictment: and thereby appealing to that other self [*un autre lui-même:* himself as another] whose wounds, electrocuted body, and barely cauterised scars we here hold before us.[202]

The only time for justice, it is well known, is the time that is now. But the task is interminable, and the present is never enough. Justice calls therefore to the future, a future always still to come.

Chapter **Five**

RADICAL INDECISION

Many pages ago, this book sought to identify the challenges facing literary criticism today by asking to what extent it is incumbent on criticism, confronted with the corrosive scepticism or antagonism of much
modern and not so modern literature, to defend literary value and the
accompanying aesthetic, moral, or ethico-political values literature is
sometimes held to embody, or whether criticism's more binding responsibility is not rather to affirm the recalcitrant otherness of writing
and its obstinate irreducibility to any economy of evaluation and exemplification. But between the one and the other of these alternatives,
between those who believe that literature has value because it embodies
values and those who tend to the view that literature, being anything
but coincident with itself, necessarily exceeds all normative assumptions, it is perhaps time to concede that no ultimate consensus or final
decision is ever likely to be reached.

This much is perhaps not surprising. The history of literary theory
and criticism provides ample evidence of the persistence of countless
long-running debates about the status of the artwork in general and the
interpretation of specific texts in particular. Numerous too are the acute
divisions and irreconcilable differences to which these debates have
given rise. This situation serves, however, only to confirm a paradox.
For if dissensus exists, as it plainly does, it can only be because something in the artwork resists the decisions readers feel required to take in
response to their reading. Between the alternatives adumbrated above,
in other words, there is fundamental dissymmetry. The first possibility
is given to criticism only because of the second possibility, and this
second possibility already contains within it the possibility of the first.
Value or values can only be posited in writing, imposed upon it, and

extracted or recovered from it, because writing from the outset makes evaluation difficult, if not impossible; were it otherwise, then all criticism committed to specifying the values allegedly embodied in an artwork would only ever be a sterile exercise in tautology, an unnecessary statement of the glaringly obvious.

The alternative announced at the beginning is therefore deceptive. Indecision is not the negative pole belonging to a simple binary opposition. It is not a refusal of interpretative responsibility, nor is it a covert form of contemplative aestheticism. On the contrary, as I have argued, it names at one and the same time the possibility and necessity of making critical decisions *and* the impossibility of finally ever having done with those decisions. Indecision, in other words, is both the condition and the limit of any critical decision whatsoever, and as such radically ineliminable. Each horn of every dilemma, as countless sleepless nights bear witness, is perpetually haunted by the possibility and the demand of the other. The predicament may seem at times an unhappy one, though some will be more sensitive to its protracted challenge. But in reality no reader can do other than affirm it: for as this book has repeatedly argued, it is not a condition susceptible to be overcome. Indecision, in other words, forever outlasts itself and endures beyond its limits as an infinitely intractable, implacable exigency, irreducible to any law, rule, regulation, or norm. What speaks in indecision, then, is not laziness, inertia, self-indulgence, but a demand that comes before, traverses, and exceeds any critical position whatever, simultaneously enabling and disabling, requiring and postponing the finality of decision. And what comes to be affirmed in this hyperbolic exposure to what resists all resolution is the demand of what here and there, following Derrida, for whom it was—using the word in the neuter—the indeconstructible, I have risked calling: justice. For justice too is both necessary and impossible: it is what must be achieved here and now without delay; but it is also what must forever be deferred. For what is justice that risks being mistaken for injustice? But what is justice that turns aside from all risk and opts for conformity? Such interference of the one by the other is no calamity: it is both essential and unavoidable. It is why justice, as Derrida goes on to insist, corresponds to no present moment, only to an infinite demand that cannot be satisfied.

But justice for whom, for what, and in what sense? In the sphere of literary criticism, as elsewhere, these are limitless questions, to which there are no formulaic, *passe-partout* answers. Justice always requires more than may be embodied in any civil code or statute book. Unlike the law or legal system, necessarily bound to an economy of instantiation, it does not require norms to be enforced, rules to be defended, examples to be made. Its demands exceed all aesthetic, moral, political, or ideological closure, to which it presents, insistently, critically, affirmatively, as an irreducible futural supplement, the singular spectral return of the unread, the unreadable, or the unwritten, lodged like a secret at the heart of every text. Rather than defining itself in terms of its conformity with received assumptions, justice, when it arrives, if it arrives, can only be in the form of singular and exorbitant exposure to an event: to the otherness of the other. There is nothing pious, moralising, or sentimental in this. For the other is not one but multiple, and irreducible to positionality, theme, or identity, which is why the response to the other cannot but be partial and provisional: hazardous, unreconciled, and inadequate.

The condition is one shared, as this book has argued, by literary criticism. Here too indecision is anything but complacent, comfortable, or reassuring, and can equally befall the reader as bewilderment, rapture, or violence. What it reveals, however, is that in all writing, in so far as its very possibility precedes the articulation, imposition, and enforcement of any law, as Blanchot suggests in the abyssal note that precedes and opens *L'Entretien infini*, there is something that exceeds all law, including that which is deemed to be its own.[1] This is not, however, as critics sometimes assume, to grant literature superior transgressive powers, but a direct consequence of the paradox that no law can ever found itself, is thus both legitimised and delegitimised by its own prior absence, and therefore, in so far as it is judged necessary, can only ever be found wanting. These may be grounds for scepticism, relativism, even despair. But what this strange aporia also implies, as in their different ways the remarkable texts of Barthes, Blanchot, and Derrida each confirm, is that at the heart of any law, enabling but interrupting its jurisdiction, under the auspices of the neuter, the neutral, or the undecidable, runs that which suspends the law, not because it disregards the law, but because, being what gives the law its necessary fragility and fragile necessity, it is more demanding than any law: the abrupt, unmediated, infinite encounter with the other, without which no writing, no artwork, no legislation would ever arrive, not as a body of norms, but as an event.

In their different, idiomatically diverse, at times philosophically incompatible ways, this, then, is what I believe the writing on literature by Barthes, Blanchot, and Derrida bequeaths to us who come after: that any sustained engagement with writing cannot but mutate, in the end, from prescriptive critique to an affirmative bodily or affective encounter with the other; that the readability of any text is made both possible and impossible only by the impenetrable shadow of the unreadable, to which reading is enjoined to respond as to an always futural demand; and that literature, if it exists, is the singular, affirmative trace of a signature: repetition and exposure, pact and risk, tomb and testimony. And to those of us who would still write about texts, what these three bodies of writing incisively demonstrate is that the singular event of reading is compatible only up to a certain point with institutional norms or conventions, however necessary or inevitable these are, and that, without abandoning them as such, but traversing, exceeding, and limiting them in turn, it is time now for criticism to begin to affirm anew the provocative intractability of reading as an experience of radical indecision.

In the face of planetary depredation, the vast exploitation of human and other populations, the proliferating spectacle of human and other suffering, the powers of literary criticism seem more limited and constrained than ever. But what I hope follows from this book is that, if there is a future for criticism, it consists not in laying down the law but in affirming the promise of justice, not in imposing value or values but in affirming the radical demand that comes from the other. For in the weakness of criticism speaks its strength, in its hesitation its appeal, and in its inability to reach its end the chance of its future: not as itself, but as perhaps always other than what it may be thought to be.

NOTES

Chapter One Instantiations

1. Immanuel Kant, "Kritik der Urteilskraft," *Werkausgabe*, ed. Wilhelm Weischedel, 12 vols. (Frankfurt: Suhrkamp, 1974), X, 247–48; *Critique of Judgement*, trans. Werner S. Pluhar (Indianapolis: Hackett, 1987), 180.

2. Samuel Beckett, *Watt* (London: Calder, 1963), 42–43; *Watt*, trans. Ludovic Janvier and Agnès Janvier in collaboration with the author (Paris: Minuit, 1968), 44–45. Earlier in the same paragraph, Beckett makes a rare and not inapposite reference to Kant when the speaker, Arsene, asserts: "I did not, need I add, see the thing happen, nor hear it, but I perceived it with a perception so sensuous that in comparison the impressions of a man buried alive in Lisbon on Lisbon's great day seem a frigid and artificial construction of the understanding." Beckett similarly recalls Kant's reaction to the 1755 earthquake in the poem, "ainsi a-t-on beau," in *Collected Poems in English and French* (London: Calder, 1977), 46. On the writer's familiarity with Kant, see James Knowlson, *Damned to Fame: The Life of Samuel Beckett* (London: Bloomsbury, 1996), 295.

3. Jacques Derrida, "Economimesis," in *Mimesis desarticulations* (Paris: Aubier-Flammarion, 1975), 89; "Economimesis," trans. R. Klein, *Diacritics* 11, no. 2 (Summer 1981): 22; translation slightly modified. Derrida's remarks comment explicitly on the passage from Kant cited in this epigraph.

4. The account given here is based on the following: Knowlson, *Damned to Fame*, 248–49, 295–96, 376–78, 396; Jérôme Lindon, "First Meeting with Samuel Beckett," in *Beckett at 60* (London: Calder & Boyars, 1967), 17–19; and Anne Simonin, *Les Editions de Minuit, 1942–1955: Le devoir d'insoumission* (Paris: IMEC Editions, 1994), 380–85. I am also grateful to Lois Overbeck for details about Beckett's early dealings with French publishers. The companies that rejected *Molloy*, according to Simonin (376–77), included Bordas (who had published the French translation of *Murphy* in 1947 and had an option on subsequent work by Beckett), the Surrealist K éditeur (who published some of Artaud's late texts), Gallimard (mainly, it seems, owing to the hostility of Albert Camus), Corréa (though, in this instance, it appears that non-receipt of the manuscript by Maurice Nadeau was at least partly to blame), and the Éditions du Seuil (because

of the opposition of Paul Flamand). Simonin also reports, on the basis of an interview with Lindon, that Beckett and Suzanne had by then decided that Minuit would be their last port of call (377). "Si cette fois-là il est édité," Beckett is said to have announced to his partner as they sat in the café facing the Minuit building, "je te paye un paquet de cigarettes. Mais promets-moi que ce sera ta dernière tentative" ["If it does get published this time, I'll buy you a pack of cigarettes. But promise me this will be your last attempt"].

5. As Knowlson records (390–91), *La Nouvelle Nouvelle Revue française* in February 1953 published a lengthy pre-publication extract from *L'Innommable*. A short passage on masturbation was silently excised from the text without the author's permission. (The passage omitted, from "La tuméfaction de la pine . . . " to " . . . Un percheron," appears in *L'Innommable* [Paris: Minuit, 1953], 93–94; and, in English, from "The tumefaction of the penis . . . " to "A Suffolk stallion," in Beckett, *Molloy, Malone Dies, The Unnamable* [London: Calder, 1959], 335.) Beckett was "livid" at this textual interference according to Knowlson, and vented his anger in an intemperate letter to Lindon (11 February 1953), cited by Simonin (450), in which he complained: "It's not just a few odd sentences that have gone, but a whole half page. . . . I'm too nauseated [*écœuré*] to read any further. . . . It literally makes me sick [*littéralement malade*]. Even a scathing letter doesn't go far enough. Can't I take him [Jean Paulhan, the editor] to court?" It appears, however, that, having taken legal advice, staff at the journal feared prosecution for indecency if they proceeded without at least minor cuts. It is more than likely that Beckett's failure to observe social niceties of this kind was a powerful contributory factor to his difficulties finding a publisher. As Lindon recalls, "[T]he printer [responsible for the first Minuit edition of *Molloy*], a Catholic from Alsace, worried that the book would be prosecuted for offending good morality, prudently omitted to put his name at the end of the volume" (*Beckett at 60*, 18). But why should Beckett be so exercised by the suppression of a passage on masturbation and horses? He can hardly have been surprised by the editors' reactions. Perhaps more was secretly at stake for Beckett. Readers may recall that the author's very first novel (still unpublished at the time) began with a somewhat similar evocation of an equine rump, glimpsed while astride a bicycle by Beckett's youthful protagonist, in a state of mock sexual, anal, masturbatory arousal: "Behold Belacqua an overfed child," the novel began, "pedalling, faster and faster, his mouth ajar and his nostrils dilated, down a frieze of hawthorn after Findlater's van, faster and faster till he cruise alongside of the hoss, the black fat wet rump of the hoss. Whip him up, vanman, flickem, flapem, collop-wallop fat Sambo. Stiffly, like a perturbation of feathers, the tail arches for a gush of mard. Ah . . . !" See Beckett, *Dream of Fair to middling Women*, ed. Eoin O'Brien and Edith Fournier (London: Calder, 1993), 1. Later in Beckett's work, in the radio play *All That Fall*, a similar "lifelong preoccupation with horses' buttocks" is attributed to Maddy

Rooney, with a dim but compelling connection to the story of the little girl who "had never really been born," borrowed from C. G. Jung; see Beckett, *Collected Shorter Plays* (London: Faber, 1984), 35–36. A complex subterranean association, then, connects the opening of Beckett's writing career with this recurring scene of masturbation, excretion, and botched parturition. On the relationship between bicycles, failed birth, and anality in the trilogy, see my *Beckett's Fiction: In Different Words* (Cambridge: Cambridge University Press, [1990] 2009), 87–92.

6. *Samuel Beckett: The Critical Heritage,* ed. Lawrence Graver and Raymond Federman (London: Routledge, 1979), 53.

7. Beckett, *Eleutheria* (Paris: Minuit, 1995), 136; *Eleutheria,* trans. Barbara Wright (London: Faber, 1996), 136. The *Dictionnaire Robert* glosses the adjective *groenlandais* with a quotation from Flaubert's *Madame Bovary* to mean "an unknown and incomprehensible language." Similar connotations attach to the reference to the Auvergne, the inhabitants of which, not unlike the Irish in England, are reputed for their allegedly impenetrable accent and surly manner. As for the term "Jew," it should be remembered that the name Samuel, taken from the Old Testament (where it has of course its Book), though exceedingly common in Protestant families elsewhere, was more than likely in anti-semitic Occupied France to be (mis)taken for a Jewish name. Evidence of Beckett's awareness of these implications may be found in *Molloy* in the author's use of the name *Youdi,* a word that belongs, in French, to anti-semitic slang, meaning a "Jew." I discuss these Old Testament, Jewish resonances in the trilogy in my *Beckett's Fiction: In Different Words,* 98, 107–11. See too Knowlson, *Damned to Fame,* 320.

8. Beckett, "Hommage à Jack B. Yeats," *Les Lettres nouvelles* 14 (April 1954): 619; *Disjecta,* ed. Ruby Cohn (London: Calder, 1983), 148–49.

9. See Simonin, *Les Editions de Minuit,* 376, 384; Knowlson, *Damned to Fame,* 377.

10. Some of these early reviews of *Molloy* are reprinted in *Samuel Beckett: The Critical Heritage,* 50–70.

11. On these early sales figures, see Simonin, *Les Editions de Minuit,* 379. As Simonin points out, these figures refer in fact to the numbers of copies distributed by Minuit; they do not include copies returned unsold by booksellers and therefore most likely overstate actual sales. Figures for *En attendant Godot,* though still modest, were somewhat better. Simonin (392) estimates 2,000 copies of the play were sold between October 1952 and the close of the following year. It was not until the late 1960s that sales significantly improved; in the wake of the Nobel Prize in 1969, sales of the French text of *Godot* reached an annual figure of around 25,000 copies. No doubt many more were sold in English.

12. Beckett, *Watt,* 43, 47; *Molloy* (Paris: Minuit, 1951), 252; *Molloy, Malone Dies, The Unnamable,* 163. On the motif of expulsion in general in Beckett's prose, see my *Beckett's Fiction: In Different Words,* 79–99.

13. On the use of the phonemes or graphemes /s/, /m/,/b/, and /k/ or /g/ as a textual signature in the trilogy, see my *Beckett's Fiction: In Different Words*, 113–20.

14. Lindon, "First Meeting with Samuel Beckett," 18.

15. For a philosophically informed critique of the assumptions of much Beckett criticism of the 1950s, 1960s, and after, and the sanitised view of the author's work they served to promote, see Thomas Trezise, *Into the Breach: Samuel Beckett and the Ends of Literature* (Princeton: Princeton University Press, 1990).

16. See *The Theatrical Notebooks of Samuel Beckett: Waiting for Godot*, ed. Dougald McMillan and James Knowlson (London: Faber, 1993), 69. The volume contains a revised English text of the play. As the editors point out, at the corresponding moment in the original French version of *Godot*, Beckett has Estragon cry, "architecte" (160), while in the German version he gives him the retort, "Ober . . . forstinspektor" (455–56)! In private, as Beckett's correspondence with Alan Schneider testifies, the author was even more outspoken in his condemnation of "these bastards of journalists" and "bastards of critics." "I feel the only line," Beckett wrote to Schneider (29 December 1957), "is to refuse to be involved in exegesis of any kind." See *No Author Better Served: The Correspondence of Samuel Beckett and Alan Schneider*, ed. Maurice Harmon (Cambridge, MA: Harvard University Press, 1998), 24.

17. Beckett, *L'Innommable* (Paris: Minuit, 1953), 124; *Molloy, Malone Dies, The Unnamable*, 350.

18. On the logic of auto-immunity, that paradoxical reaction by which an organism, in order to live longer, unwittingly provokes its own demise, see Derrida, "Foi et savoir," in *La Religion*, ed. Jacques Derrida and Gianni Vattimo (Paris: Seuil, 1996), 65–69; "Faith and Knowledge," trans. Samuel Weber, *Acts of Religion*, ed. Gil Anidjar (London: Routledge, 2002), 85–87; and Derrida, *Surtout pas de journalistes!* (Paris: L'Herne, 2005), 31. I have displaced Derrida's remarks, which in their original context (if these words have any meaning) were primarily addressed to the question of religion.

19. Beckett, *L'Innommable*, 25; *Molloy, Malone Dies, The Unnamable*, 301–2.

20. Beckett, *L'Innommable*, 106; *Molloy, Malone Dies, The Unnamable*, 342.

21. Maurice Blanchot, *L'Entretien infini* (Paris: Gallimard, 1969), 69; *The Infinite Conversation*, trans. Susan Hanson (Minneapolis: University of Minnesota Press, 1993), 48.

22. See Derrida, *Force de loi* (Paris: Galilée, 1994), 48; "Force of Law," trans. Mary Quaintance, in *Acts of Religion*, 250; translation slightly modified. Derrida is not referring here to literary criticism but to the law and justice as such. But can it be said with certainty or confidence where literature and the legal machine begin and end? After all, as Derrida suggests in his reading of Kafka's "Vor dem Gesetz" (*Before the Law*), literature as it is known today is inconceivable without

the law governing copyright, freedom of speech, civil responsibility, much else besides. "What if the law," asks Derrida, "without being penetrated by literature through and through [*transie de littérature*], were to share its conditions of possibility with the thing called literature [*la chose littéraire*]." See Derrida, "Préjugés," in *La Faculté de juger* (Paris: Minuit, 1985), 109; *Acts of Literature*, ed. Derek Attridge (London: Routledge, 1992), 191; translation modified.

    23. Blanchot, *L'Entretien infini*, 481; *The Infinite Conversation*, 329.

    24. Barbara Herrnstein Smith, *Contingencies of Value* (Cambridge, MA: Harvard University Press, 1988), 42. Does the phrase "responsive creature" imply that all creatures are responsive, or only some of them? If the latter, what is to be made of a creature that is deemed to be unresponsive? And what, in either case, is the status of the narrator of *L'Innommable*, for instance, who, being neither dead nor alive, is not a creature at all, responsive or not? What, then, of the relationship of a "responsive" reader to that which itself is not responsive? In other words, in reading *L'Innommable*, to what is it therefore necessary to respond, and how is it possible to do so? The questions quickly proliferate beyond the horizon of value and responsiveness: not because Beckett's text is beyond such questions, far from it, but because to decide in advance that reading such a text is indistinguishable from evaluating it is to limit peremptorily the questions that the text asks, among which is precisely the question of the possibility (and value) of any horizon of value as such. Similar issues arise with respect to Herrnstein Smith's sceptical reading of Bataille's influential 1933 essay, "La Notion de dépense [The Notion of Expenditure]," which the critic sees as trapped within precisely the dialectic of value that Bataille is seeking to overturn (134–44). True enough, it is soon apparent from any critical reading of Bataille's essay that what he is proposing is literally impossible, as Herrnstein Smith is able to show. But that, it might be said, is the point: the dialectic may be all-inclusive, but it still cannot include itself. The negativity of the dialectic has a limit, over which it has no power, since it is the source of the power of negativity as such. That limit has many names in Bataille's thinking: sacrifice, death, expenditure, poetry. Each of these terms is always already double. For while it is true that each may be integrated or incorporated, in one way or another, within the symbolic economy it claims to flout, it is also the case that each of Bataille's divided terms resists that economy. Even as death, for instance, constitutes the crux of the dialectic, enabling the economy of language, labour, and sacrifice to occur, it is also that which, for that very reason, is inassimilable to the exchange economy, for which it is a useless sham, an imposture, a pretence: "une comédie!" as Bataille famously calls it in the essay "Hegel, la mort et le sacrifice," in Georges Bataille, *Œuvres complètes*, 12 vols. (Paris: Gallimard, 1970–88), XII, 326–45 (336); "Hegel, Death and Sacrifice," trans. Jonathan Strauss, *YFS* 78 (1990), ed. Allan Stoekl, 9–28 (19); translation modified. Something of the same double logic also applies

to Bataille's thinking of literature. Literature too, for Bataille, was irreducible to the dialectic of work and the exchange economy constituted in, by, and for work; it was essentially irresponsible; and to write, for Bataille, was to have to respond to irresponsibility, not by transforming it into a superior kind of duty, which was always possible, but by confronting its essential worklessness. In 1962, shortly before his untimely death, Bataille wrote a preface for a volume that was republished soon after under the title *L'Impossible* (*The Impossible*). "Humankind," he wrote, "finds itself facing a dual prospect: on the one hand, violent pleasure, horror and death—exactly the prospect of poetry—and, on the other, that of science and the real world of usefulness. Only the useful, the real are thought to be serious. We are never entitled to prefer seductiveness: truth has a claim on us. It even has every claim on us. Yet we can, indeed we must respond to *something* which, not being God, is more powerful than any claim: that *impossible* to which we accede only by forgetting the truth of all these claims, and accepting our demise." See Georges Bataille, *Œuvres complètes*, III, 102; *The Impossible*, trans. Robert Hurley (San Francisco: City Lights Books, 1991), 10; translation modified. And in the unpublished notes for that preface, Bataille added, underscoring the phrase himself: "*the impossible is literature*" (III, 519). Responsiveness here, then, is not responsiveness to the economy of value, however contingent its terms or methods of circulation, but to something that, like time, death, or language itself, resists and escapes evaluation, not least because it is always already presupposed by it.

25. Steven Connor, *Theory and Cultural Value* (Oxford: Blackwell, 1992), 8.

26. On "bare life" and its investment by value and values, see Giorgio Agamben, *Homo Sacer: Sovereign Power and Bare Life*, trans. Daniel Heller-Roazen (Stanford: Stanford University Press, 1998), 119–25. For an important corrective to Agamben's account, see Andrew Benjamin, "Spacing as the Shared: Heraclitus, Pindar, Agamben," in *Politics, Metaphysics, and Death*, ed. Andrew Norris (Durham: Duke University Press, 2005), 145–72.

27. Beckett, *Molloy*, 34; *Molloy, Malone Dies, The Unnamable*, 24.

28. Connor, *Theory and Cultural Value*, 9.

29. Connor, *Theory and Cultural Value*, 32–33.

30. On the underlying complicity between humanism and nihilism (understood as boundless confidence in unlimited human possibility), see Blanchot, *L'Entretien infini*, 392–93; *The Infinite Conversation*, 262–63. I examine some of the implications of Blanchot's position in *A Change of Epoch: Blanchot, Writing, the Fragmentary*, forthcoming.

31. Beckett, *Worstward Ho* (London: Calder, 1983), 7. In *Theory and Cultural Value* (80–89), Connor offers a thoughtful and nuanced account of this almost final prose work of Beckett's career. He starts with describing the oscillating double movement of Beckett's writing, in which "the drive towards death consists

both in resisting forward movement and in surrendering to it, retarding and propelling it" (86), before going on to claim as follows: "In *Worstward Ho*, Beckett seeks to economise on time, to resist the waste of time by a procedure of remote control." (Connor is referring here to Beckett's strategy of verbal erasure, disqualification, and substitution.) "This technique of automated substitution," the critic continues, "attempts to keep a regulating hold over the text's future, controlling time at a distance and collapsing the lapse of time between affirmation and negation" (87). And Connor concludes: "Plainly, there is nothing to guarantee that [Beckett's] attempt to push negation to its limit will not itself be reconfigured as a form of critical or cultural value; indeed, it will be apparent that my own [i.e., Connor's] reading here evidently and inescapably predicates value in the play of value and non-value in *Worstward Ho*. . . . If Beckett's work suggests the metaphor of limit in the way it presses towards or transgresses accepted boundaries of possibility, this metaphor of the limit is itself a vehicle of the dialectical logic that alternates positivity and negativity as positive quantities, allowing one to constitute the denial or surpassing of limits as a heroic negation of a negation" (89). For Connor, then, it appears that, just as criticism is caught within a vicious circle, according to which it is always already impelled to attribute value even to that which appears to represent non-value, so too Beckett's writing falls subject to a similar dialectic, as exemplified by what Connor has to say here about Beckett's language and the treatment of time in *Worstward Ho*. But how certain is it that Beckett's writing is mere "automated" "technique," a mechanical procedure for the containment and production of expenditure, how certain is it that time—time that is always already the time of my dying, my "own" (i.e., *not* my own) impossibility—can ever be made subject to economic calculation, as Connor contends, and with what authority is the "metaphor of [the] limit" determined as always already belonging to a totalising, heroic dialectic? Are these not precisely the assumptions—interpretative decisions—that Beckett's writing throws into question and pushes beyond the limit? Does the inalienable belief in human possibility make it impossible, ironically enough, to envisage that Beckett's writing, even writing in general, might be without value?

32. Blanchot, *Le Pas au-delà* (Paris: Gallimard, 1973), 98; *The Step Not Beyond*, trans. Lycette Nelson (Albany: State University of New York Press, 1992), 70; translation modified.

33. Jean-François Lyotard, *Le Différend* (Paris: Minuit, 1983), 15; *The Différend*, trans. Georges Van Den Abbeele (Manchester: Manchester University Press, 1988), xvi; translation modified. As Lyotard indicates in *L'Inhumain* (Paris: Galilée, 1988), 102; *The Inhuman*, trans. Geoffrey Bennington and Rachel Bowlby (Stanford: Stanford University Press, 1991), 90; translation modified, "This is not a question about the sense or reality of *what* is happening or *what* it might

mean. Before we ask what it is and what it means, before the *quid*, it is necessary 'first,' so to speak, for it to 'happen,' *quod*. That it happens, as it were, 'comes before' the question about what is happening. In other words, the question comes before itself, because 'that it happens' is the question as event itself; it is 'afterwards' that it relates to the event that has just happened. The event happens as a question mark 'before' it happens as a question. *It happens 'in the first instance'* is more: *is it happening, is this it, is it possible?* Only 'afterwards' is the question mark determined by the question: is this or that happening, is it this or something else, is it possible that this or that?"

34. See Jacques Derrida, Gad Soussana, and Alexis Nouss, *Dire l'événement, est-ce possible?* (Paris: L'Harmattan, 2001), 81–112. On the event and the gift, see Derrida, *Donner le temps I: La Fausse Monnaie* (Paris: Galilée, 1991), 155–57; *Given Time I: Counterfeit Money,* trans. Peggy Kamuf (Chicago: University of Chicago Press, 1993), 121–23. It is worth pointing out that much of what is mobilised by Derrida in his account of the gift is closely linked to his reading of Blanchot's story *La Folie du jour* (*The Madness of the Day*).

35. See Lyotard, *L'Inhumain,* 70; *The Inhuman,* 59; translation modified: "That something happens [*que quelque chose arrive*], the occurrence, means that the mind is disappropriated. The expression 'it happens that . . . ' ['*Il arrive que . . .* '] is the very formula for the non-mastery of self over self. The event [*l'événement*] makes the self incapable of taking possession and control of what it is. It bears witness to the fact that the self is essentially subject to recurrent alterity." Compare Derrida, *Le Toucher, Jean-Luc Nancy* (Paris: Galilée, 2000), 71; *On Touching—Jean-Luc Nancy,* trans. Christine Irizarry (Stanford: Stanford University Press, 2005), 57: "Where the *possible* is all that happens, nothing happens, nothing except the meagre unfolding or predictable predicate of what, being already in place, or virtually so, produces nothing new, not even accidents worthy of the name of event"; translation modified.

36. On this always prior, always already repetitive, irreducibly affirmative structure of yes (yes, yes), see Derrida, *Ulysse gramophone* (Paris: Galilée, 1987); *Acts of Literature,* 256–309.

37. Blanchot, *Le Livre à venir* (Paris: Gallimard, 1959), 17; *The Book to Come,* trans. Charlotte Mandell (Stanford: Stanford University Press, 2003), 10; translation modified.

38. Blanchot, *Le Pas au-delà,* 100; *The Step Not Beyond,* 71; translation modified.

39. Beckett, *Molloy,* 53; *Molloy, Malone Dies, The Unnamable,* 36.

40. On reception of Beckett by recent French philosophy, see my "Post-structuralist Readings of Beckett," in *Palgrave Advances in Samuel Beckett Studies,* ed. Lois Oppenheim (New York: Palgrave Macmillan, 2004), 68–88. It goes without saying that there are significant and substantial differences between

these authors on the question of the event, which unfortunately cannot be explored further here.

41. See *Pourquoi écrivez-vous?* ed. Jean-François Fogel and Daniel Rondeau (Paris: Le Livre de poche, 1988), 232. Compare Blanchot, *Le Pas au-delà*, 170; *The Step Not Beyond*, 124; translation modified: "'Why write that [*avoir écrit cela*]?'—'I could not do otherwise.'—'Why does this necessity of writing give rise to nothing that does not appear superfluous, vain, and always excessive [*de trop*]?'—'The necessity was already excessive: in the constraint of 'I could not do otherwise,' there is the even more constraining sense [*sentiment*] that the constraint has no justification in itself.'"

42. Beckett, *Proust and Three Dialogues* (London: Calder, 1965), 125. On the structure of coming-and-going in the trilogy (and other Beckett texts), see my *Beckett's Fiction: In Different Words*, 59–78.

43. Kant, *Werkausgabe*, X, 155–56; *Critique of Judgement*, 85–86.

44. Beckett, "La Peinture des van Velde, ou le monde et le pantalon," *Disjecta*, 123; translation mine.

45. Lyotard, *Le Différend*, 11; *The Differend*, xiii; translation modified. The remarks that follow make no claim to originality. My discussion is most particularly indebted to Derrida's reading of the third *Critique* in "Economimesis," *Mimesis desarticulations*, 57–93; "Economimesis," *Diacritics* 11, no. 2 (Summer 1981): 3–25; and *La Vérité en peinture* (Paris: Flammarion, 1978); *The Truth in Painting*, trans. Geoff Bennington and Ian McLeod (Chicago: University of Chicago Press, 1987). I have also drawn on Lyotard's rethinking of Kant in *Le Différend, L'Inhumain, Leçons sur l'analytique du sublime* (Paris: Galilée, 1991); *Lessons on the Analytic of the Sublime*, trans. Elizabeth Rottenberg (Stanford: Stanford University Press, 1994); and *Misère de la philosophie* (Paris: Galilée, 2000). Other works I have also found helpful include Howard Caygill, *Art of Judgement* (Oxford: Blackwell, 1989); Paul De Man, *Aesthetic Ideology*, ed. Andrzej Warminski (Minneapolis: University of Minnesota Press, 1996); and Geoffrey Bennington, *Frontières kantiennes* (Paris: Galilée, 2000).

46. Kant, *Werkausgabe*, X, 125; *Critique of Judgement*, 54.

47. Kant, *Werkausgabe*, X, 117; *Critique of Judgement*, 46, translation modified.

48. Kant, *Werkausgabe*, X, 123; *Critique of Judgement*, 52, translation modified.

49. On this question of frames and framing in Kant, see Derrida, *La Vérité en peinture*, 21–168; *The Truth in Painting*, 17–147.

50. Kant, *Werkausgabe*, X, 83 ; *Critique of Judgement*, 14.

51. Kant, *Werkausgabe*, X, 85; *Critique of Judgement*, 16. On the distinction between *Feld* (area, field, realm), *Boden* (territory, ground), and *Gebiet* (domain, area of authority), see Kant, *Werkausgabe*, X, 81–82; *Critique of Judgement*, 12–13.

On analogy in the third *Critique*, see Derrida, *La Vérité en peinture*, 42–43; *The Truth in Painting*, 35–36.

52. Kant, *Werkausgabe*, X, 87; *Critique of Judgement*, 18–19.

53. Kant, *Werkausgabe*, X, 122; *Critique of Judgement*, 51.

54. Kant, *Werkausgabe*, X, 155; *Critique of Judgement*, 84.

55. Derrida, *La Vérité en peinture*, 101; *The Truth in Painting*, 88–89; translation slightly modified.

56. See Derrida, *La Vérité en peinture*, 113; *The Truth in Painting*, 98–100: "The *sans* of the *sans*-theme and the *sans*-text must be marked, without being either present or absent, in the thing to which it does not belong and which is no longer quite a thing, which one can no longer name, which is not, once charged with the mark, a material support or a form of what is to be found neither here nor there, and which one might indicate, given a certain displacement, by the name of text or trace [*Le sans du sans-thème et du sans-texte doit se marquer, sans être ni présent ni absent, dans la chose à laquelle il n'appartient pas et qui n'est plus tout à fait une chose, qu'on ne sait plus nommer, qui n'est pas, une fois affectée par la marque, un support matériel ni une forme de ce qui ne se trouve ni ici ni là, et qu'on pourrait indiquer, à la condition d'un certain déplacement, sous le nom de texte ou de trace*]."

57. Kant, *Werkausgabe*, X, 160; *Critique of Judgement*, 90.

58. See Kant, *Critique de la faculté de juger*, ed. Ferdinand Alquié (Paris: Gallimard, 1985), 176.

59. Kant, *Werkausgabe*, X, 158–59; *Critique of Judgement*, 89; translation slightly modified.

60. Derrida makes this point in *La Vérité en peinture*, 132; *The Truth in Painting*, 116. "What remains suspended here," he writes, "is whether the aesthetic principle of pure taste, in so far as it requires universal acceptance, has a specific place corresponding to a power of its own, or whether it is still an idea of (practical) reason, an idea of the unanimous universal community orienting its idealising process. As always, so long as such an idea is on the horizon, moral law allies itself with empirical culturalism to dominate the field"; translation modified.

61. See Lyotard, *Leçons sur l'analytique du sublime*, 30–33, and passim; *Lessons on the Analytic of the Sublime*, 16–19, and passim; and *Misère de la philosophie*, 15–41.

62. Kant, *Werkausgabe*, X, 212; *Critique of Judgement*, 146.

63. Kant, *Werkausgabe*, X, 212–13; *Critique of Judgement*, 146–47.

64. Kant makes the same point about the need or capacity of genius, this "nature's favourite [*Günstling der Natur*]," to distinguish between the imitating (*Nachahmung*) and aping (*Nachäffung*) of nature in art (*Werkausgabe*, X, 255; *Critique of Judgement*, 187).

65. Kant, *Werkausgabe*, X, 166; *Critique of Judgement*, 99.

66. Kant, *Werkausgabe*, X, 167; *Critique of Judgement*, 100.

67. See Derrida, *Force de loi*, 50–63, *Acts of Religion*, 251–58.

68. See G. W. F. Hegel, *Werke*, ed. Eva Moldenhauer and Karl Markus Michel, 20 vols. (Frankfurt: Suhrkamp, 1970), III, 87. Hegel makes a similar point in the introduction to his *Vorlesungen über die Ästhetik*, *Werke*, XIII, 88–89; *Aesthetics*, trans. T. M. Knox, 2 vols. (Oxford: Clarendon Press, 1975), I, 60.

69. As an example of the distortion and trivialisation of Derrida's thinking that sometimes passes for astute critical comment, see Terry Eagleton, *After Theory* (Harmondsworth: Penguin, 2003), 153–54. "For Jacques Derrida," Eagleton claims, "ethics is a matter of absolute decisions—decisions that are vital and necessary but also utterly 'impossible,' and which fall outside all given norms, forms of knowledge and modes of conceptualization. One can only hope that he is not on the jury when one's case comes up in court." On the contrary, what Derrida is addressing here are precisely the reasons why juries (rather than autocratic judges or computer programmes) are necessary at all for justice to occur. It might be reassuring to some to have Eagleton as one of their peers; but readers would be better advised to seek a jury member less given to self-serving polemic and more attentive to what Derrida actually wrote.

70. Derrida, *Force de loi*, 55–56; *Acts of Religion*, 254; translation modified.

71. Derrida, *Force de loi*, 60–61; *Acts of Religion*, 256–57; translation modified. On the idiosyncratic structure of *peut-être*, perhaps, compare Derrida, *Politiques de l'amitié* (Paris: Galilée, 1994), 43–66; *The Politics of Friendship*, trans. George Collins (London: Verso, 1997), 26–48.

72. Decisions are affected by the same temporal structure, which is why it is hard, says Derrida, to address the question of decision-making by relying on concepts of responsibility, conscience, intentionality, and propriety; see Derrida, *Force de loi*, 55; *Acts of Religion*, 253–54. The same no doubt could be said about interpretative decisions in general, notably those at issue in so-called aesthetic judgements.

73. See Jean-Luc Nancy, *Le Discours de la syncope: 1. Logodaedalus* (Paris: Aubier-Flammarion, 1976), 148; *The Discourse of the Syncope: Logodaedalus*, trans. Saul Anton (Stanford: Stanford University Press, 2007), 138–39. Nancy glosses this somewhat surprising remark (readers of Blanchot will recall that the writer hardly ever mentions Kant) by quoting from a tribute to Maurice Merleau-Ponty, in which Blanchot suggests, apropos of philosophy itself, as Kant's third *Critique* arguably shows, that "[p]hilosophical discourse always at a certain moment loses itself [*se perd*: i.e., both loses its way and fades away]: it may even be no more than a relentless process of losing and of losing oneself [*de perdre et de se perdre*]." See Blanchot, "Le 'Discours philosophique,'" *L'Arc* 46 (1971): 1–4 (4).

74. Blanchot, *L'Écriture du désastre* (Paris: Gallimard, 1980), 127; *The Writing of the Disaster*, trans. Ann Smock (Lincoln: University of Nebraska Press, 1986), 80; translation modified.

75. Blanchot, "Je juge votre questionnaire remarquable . . . ," from a response to a questionnaire on the critical method of Henri Guillemin, *Les Lettres nouvelles*, 24 June 1959, 9–10 (10).

76. Blanchot, "Qu'en est-il de la critique?" *Arguments* 12–13 (January–February–March 1959): 34–37. Another critic closely involved in the journal was Roland Barthes, who recalls his collaboration in a 1979 interview collected in Roland Barthes, *Œuvres complètes,* ed. Éric Marty, rev. ed., 5 vols. (Paris: Seuil, 2002), V, 774–78. Blanchot's contribution is reprinted, with modifications, as a preface to the revised edition of *Lautréamont et Sade* (Paris: Minuit, [1949] 1963), 9–14; and in English as "The Task of Criticism Today," trans. Leslie Hill, *Oxford Literary Review* 22 (Autumn 2000): 19–24; an alternative, not always reliable, version is given in Blanchot, *Lautréamont and Sade,* trans. Stuart Kendall and Michelle Kendall (Stanford: Stanford University Press, 2004), 1–6. For the allusion to Mallarmé, see Stéphane Mallarmé, *Œuvres complètes,* ed. Bertrand Marchal, 2 vols. (Paris: Gallimard, 1998–2003), II, 65. Blanchot comments: "When Mallarmé asks, 'Does something like Literature exist?,' this question is literature itself—literature when it has become the concern [*le souci*] for its own essence. The question is one that cannot be avoided. What happens [*Qu'arrive-t-il*] by virtue of the fact that we have literature? How do matters stand with regard to being [*qu'en est-il de l'être*], if one says that 'something like Literature exists'?"; see Blanchot, *L'Espace littéraire* (Paris: Gallimard, 1955), 35; *The Space of Literature*, trans. Ann Smock (Lincoln: University of Nebraska Press, 1982), 42–43; translation modified. Heidegger's preliminary question or *Vor-frage*, "How does it stand with Being? [*Wie steht es um das Sein?*]," is articulated in the opening chapter of the 1935 lecture course (first published in 1953), *Einführung in die Metaphysik* (Tübingen: Niemeyer, 1987), 25; *An Introduction to Metaphysics*, trans. Ralph Manheim (New Haven: Yale University Press, 1959), 32.

77. By the late 1950s Blanchot's institutional position as a critic had become increasingly uncertain. He had never been a member of the academic elite, unlike his co-respondents of 1959 and most of the influential thinkers of subsequent decades (Foucault, Barthes, Deleuze, Derrida, Lyotard, or Kristeva), though it is worth noting that some of these major figures occupied surprisingly modest positions in the French university system. After leaving university in the early 1930s, Blanchot was mainly active as a political journalist, and after the war derived his livelihood from his activities as a book reviewer and his association with the Gallimard publishing house. Admittedly, this was not an unfamiliar pattern in France during the first half of the century (Sartre is another prominent example of a writer and philosopher without university affiliation), as Régis

Debray shows in *Le Pouvoir intellectuel en France* (Paris: Ramsay, 1979). But by the late 1950s it had begun to be a thing of the past. By that time too, though it continued to appear regularly in *La Nouvelle Nouvelle Revue française* (or *La Nouvelle Revue française*, as it subsequently re-became) in (oblique) response to this or that recent publication, Blanchot's critical writing had largely left behind the usual constraints and methods of literary journalism. The writer's lack of enthusiasm for book-reviewing as such was the main reason for his withdrawal from *Critique*, the monthly journal he had been instrumental in helping Georges Bataille launch in 1946, but to which he ceased contributing after 1953.

78. Blanchot, "Qu'en est-il de la critique?" 35; "The Task of Criticism Today," 20.

79. See Jorge Luis Borges, *Labyrinths*, ed. Donald A. Yates and James E. Irby (Harmondsworth: Penguin, 1970), 62–71.

80. Blanchot, "Qu'en est-il de la critique?" 36; "The Task of Criticism Today," 22.

81. See Blanchot, *L'Espace littéraire*, 179–84; *The Space of Literature*, 171–76.

82. Ovid, *Metamorphoses*, trans. A. D. Melville (Oxford: Oxford University Press, 1985), 226.

83. Blanchot, *L'Espace littéraire*, 180; *The Space of Literature*, 172; translation modified. For a more detailed account of Blanchot's Orpheus story, see Chantal Michel, *Maurice Blanchot et le déplacement d'Orphée* (Saint-Genoulph: Nizet, 1997). Other critics have been less sympathetic. In a feminist reappraisal of Blanchot's retelling ("Blanchot's Mother," *Yale French Studies* 93 [1998]: 175–95), Lynne Huffer takes issue with what she takes to be the sexual politics of Blanchot's analysis. "Blanchot's description of a fragmented and dispersed Orphic voice," she writes, "in fact hides its own foundation in the binary and gendered structure of the origin and its loss." "That structure," she continues, "is the structure of nostalgia. The lost origin—Eurydice, the mother—is recuperated, as loss, into a form that is not only thoroughly human but, like humanism itself, decidedly masculine as well" (194). This is, however, to miss the point. It privileges the first part of Blanchot's presentation, where what indeed counts (as Blanchot agrees) is the abolition of the real object (in this case, the other person or other sex) as a precondition of the emergence of the work. But what motivates Blanchot's Orpheus above all else is *not* the work but rather the otherness or inaccessibility of Eurydice "in herself" (i.e., as an unreachable other), as she appears (without appearing) outside, beyond, or before the work. Here, the sexual and political implications of Blanchot's writing are indeed crucial. But far from conspiring in what Huffer calls "the homogenization of the feminine" (195), Blanchot does something infinitely more challenging, which is to confront and articulate in his writing the very question of the alterity of the other body. In fact Blanchot does not present the relation with the other primarily in terms of the

bipolarity of gender; indeed, as he makes clear in a number of places, gender, if it is to affirm the possibility of (sexual) difference, can only be articulated on the basis of a thought of alterity, which is why what Blanchot says about Eurydice in *L'Espace littéraire* reworks what he had already said about the raising of Lazarus in *La Part du feu* (Paris: Gallimard, 1949), 316; *The Work of Fire*, trans. Charlotte Mandell (Stanford: Stanford University Press, 1995), 327. But Blanchot's treatment of Orpheus and Eurydice ought not to be seen in isolation; it resonates with a number of other fictional or non-fictional texts where sexuality is at issue, as I have argued in *Bataille, Klossowski, Blanchot: Writing at the Limit* (Oxford: Oxford University Press, 2001), 200–205.

84. Blanchot, *L'Espace littéraire*, 181; *The Space of Literature*, 173; translation modified.

85. On "Abraham's eternal dilemma" in Kafka, see Blanchot, *L'Espace littéraire*, 57; *The Space of Literature*, 61. On myth and sacrifice in Blanchot, see Gisèle Berkman, "Le Sacrifice suspendu: à partir de *L'Écriture du désastre*," in *Maurice Blanchot, récits critiques*, ed. Christophe Bident and Pierre Vilar (Tours: Farrago, 2003), 357–75.

86. Blanchot, *L'Espace littéraire*, 182–83; *The Space of Literature*, 174; translation modified.

87. Walter Benjamin, "Der Begriff der Kunstkritik in der deutschen Romantik," in *Gesammelte Schriften*, ed. Rolf Tiedemann and Hermann Schweppenhäuser, 7 vols. (Frankfurt: Suhrkamp, 1974–89), I: 1, 78; "The Concept of Criticism in German Romanticism," trans. David Lachterman, Howard Eiland, and Ian Balfour, *Selected Writings*, ed. Marcus Bullock and Michael W. Jennings, 4 vols. (Cambridge, MA: Harvard University Press, 1996–2003), I, 159; translation modified.

88. Benjamin, *Gesammelte Schriften*, I: 1, 79; *Selected Writings*, I, 160; translation modified.

89. Daniel Payot, *Anachronies: de l'œuvre d'art* (Paris: Galilée, 1990), 120.

90. Blanchot, *L'Écriture du désastre*, 108; *The Writing of the Disaster*, 65; translation modified. On the relationship between the *il y a*, literature, and the promise, see Blanchot, "Notre compagne clandestine," in *Textes pour Emmanuel Lévinas*, ed. François Laruelle (Paris: Jean-Michel Place, 1980), 79–87 (86); *Face to Face with Levinas*, ed. Ralph A. Cohen (Albany: State University of New York Press, 1986), 41–50 (49). Already in 1948, in the famous essay "La Littérature et le droit à la mort [Literature and the Right to Death]," in *La Part du feu*, one of the prime effects of the *il y a* was to impede the forward march of the Hegelian dialectic. In later writings, the *il y a* comes to be treated rather differently by Blanchot and Levinas. In the case of the latter, it comes to provide the basis for an account of the ethical transcendence of the Other. In Blanchot, however, as Levinas was only too aware, it remains a decisive moment in the refusal of transcen-

dence. I examine the covert *différend* between the two friends in my *Blanchot: Extreme Contemporary* (London: Routledge, 1997), 167–84.

91. Blanchot, *La Part du feu*, 203; *The Work of Fire*, 207; translation modified.

92. Georges Bataille, *Œuvres complètes*, IX (1979), 182; *Literature and Evil*, trans. Alastair Hamilton (London: Calder & Boyars, 1973), 25; translation slightly modified.

93. Blanchot, *Le Pas au-delà*, 168; *The Step Not Beyond*, 123; translation modified.

94. See Derrida, "Préjugés," in *La Faculté de juger*, 115; *Acts of Literature*, 197. "Reading," writes Derrida, "can indeed reveal that a text is untouchable, properly intangible, *because it is readable*, and for that very reason unreadable, in so far as the presence within it of a perceptible, graspable meaning remains as withdrawn [*dérobée*] as its origin. Unreadability in this case is no longer the opposite of readability"; translation modified.

95. Blanchot, *Le Livre à venir*, 244; *The Book to Come*, 201; translation modified.

96. Blanchot, *L'Entretien infini*, viii; *The Infinite Conversation*, xii; translation modified.

97. See for instance Martin Heidegger, *Holzwege* (Frankfurt: Klostermann, 1950), 218. I discuss Blanchot's complex debate with Heidegger on the question of nihilism in my *Bataille, Klossowski, Blanchot: Writing at the Limit*, 237–43.

98. Blanchot, *Le Pas au-delà*, 91; *The Step Not Beyond*, 64; translation modified.

99. T. W. Adorno, *Ästhetische Theorie*, ed. Gretel Adorno and Rolf Tiedemann (Frankfurt: Suhrkamp, 1970), 9; *Aesthetic Theory*, trans. Robert Hullot-Kentor (London: Athlone, 1997), 1; translation modified. These are the opening words in Adorno's unfinished book.

100. On this motif of "a change of epoch," see Blanchot, *L'Entretien infini*, 394–418; *The Infinite Conversation*, 264–81; and *L'Écriture du désastre*, 158–60, 215; *The Writing of the Disaster*, 101–3, 142. Blanchot glosses the relationship between messianic time and the indecision of dying in a fragment from *Le Pas au-delà*, 149; *The Step Not Beyond*, 108; translation modified: "What is the meaning behind [Moses'] broken tablets?" asks Blanchot. "Perhaps the breaking apart of dying [*la brisure du mourir*], the interruption of the present that dying has always already [*toujours par avance*] introduced into time. 'Thou shalt not kill' evidently means: 'do not kill whoever in any case will die,' means: 'because of this, do not harm dying [*ne porte pas atteinte au mourir*], do not decide for what is undecided [*ne décide pas de l'indécis*], do not say: now it is done, thereby assuming a right over what is 'not yet' [*t'arrogeant un droit sur 'pas encore'*]: do not presume the last word has been said, time brought to an end, the Messiah come at last.'"

101. See Blanchot, *L'Amitié* (Paris: Gallimard, 1971), 139, 149; *Friendship*, trans. Elizabeth Rottenberg (Stanford: Stanford University Press, 1997), 119, 128. For a polemical misreading of Blanchot's essay on Des Forêts, which bizarrely presents it as a naive exercise in nihilistic textualism, see Yves Bonnefoy, *La Vérité de parole et autres essais* (Paris: Gallimard, 1988, 1992), 123–279. I have discussed Blanchot's essay on Des Forêts in a similar context elsewhere; see Leslie Hill, "D'un nihilisme presque infini," in *Maurice Blanchot: récits critiques*, 377–93.

102. Blanchot, *Une voix venue d'ailleurs* (Paris: Gallimard, folio, 2002), 57; "The Beast of Lascaux," trans. Leslie Hill, *Oxford Literary Review* 22 (2000): 12; *A Voice from Elsewhere*, trans. Charlotte Mandell (Albany: State University of New York Press, 2007), 41–42.

103. See Blanchot, *L'Arrêt de mort* (Paris: Gallimard, 1948), 127. On this recurrent "viens," "come," in Blanchot, see Derrida, *Parages*, rev. ed. (Paris: Galilée, [1986] 2003), 19–108.

104. See Blanchot, *Le Pas au-delà*, 104; *The Step Not Beyond*, 74.

105. Blanchot, *Le Pas au-delà*, 108; *The Step Not Beyond*, 77; translation modified.

106. Blanchot, *Le Pas au-delà*, 162; *The Step Not Beyond*, 118; translation modified.

107. Blanchot, "Qu'en est-il de la critique?" 36–37; "The Task of Criticism Today," 24.

108. Blanchot, "Qu'en est-il de la critique?" 37. Why does Blanchot delete this concluding passage in 1963? Did it seem rhetorically redundant, given the allusion to "unprecedented affirmation" in the preceding passage? Was Blanchot, four years later, unwilling, in the name of affirmation itself, to subscribe to such problematic values as the impersonality of *being* and the future as *communication*, both formulations Blanchot would abandon in subsequent texts?

Chapter Two   Roland Barthes

1. Barthes, *Œuvres complètes*, V, 437; "Inaugural Lecture," trans. Richard Howard, in *A Barthes Reader*, ed. Susan Sontag (London: Jonathan Cape, 1982), 467–68; original emphasis; translation modified. A detailed bibliography of all Barthes's publications is provided by Thierry Leguay in *Communications* 36 (1982): 131–73.

2. In this chapter, I shall not be giving a detailed exposition of Barthes's work or career, a task that has been more than ably carried out by earlier commentators to whom I am greatly indebted, including notably, Annette Lavers, *Roland Barthes: Structuralism and After* (London: Methuen, 1982); Jonathan Cul-

ler, *Barthes* (London: Fontana, 1983); Steven Ungar, *Roland Barthes: The Professor of Desire* (Lincoln: University of Nebraska Press, 1983); Vincent Jouve, *La Littéra-ture selon Barthes* (Paris: Minuit, 1986); Philippe Roger, *Roland Barthes, roman* (Paris: Grasset, 1986); Louis-Jean Calvet, *Roland Barthes 1915–1980* (Paris: Flam-marion, 1990); Michael Moriarty, *Roland Barthes* (Oxford: Polity, 1991); Andrew Brown, *Roland Barthes: The Figures of Writing* (Oxford: Oxford University Press, 1992); Andy Stafford, *Roland Barthes, Phenomenon and Myth* (Edinburgh: Edin-burgh University Press, 1998). *Critical Essays on Roland Barthes,* ed. Diana Knight (New York: G. K. Hall, 2000), provides a wide-ranging anthology of reviews and other responses to Barthes's work. Helpful accounts of particular aspects of Bar-thes's writing can also be found in the following: Ginette Michaud, *Lire le frag-ment: transfert et théorie de la lecture chez Roland Barthes* (Quebec: Hurtubise, 1989); Bernard Comment, *Roland Barthes, vers le neutre* (Paris: Christian Bour-gois, [1991] 2002); D. A. Miller, *Bringing out Roland Barthes* (Berkeley: University of California Press, 1992); Diana Knight, *Barthes and Utopia* (Oxford: Oxford University Press, 1997); "Roland Barthes," ed. Diana Knight, *Nottingham French Studies* 36, no. 1 (1997); "Sur Barthes," ed. Claude Coste, *Revue des sciences hu-maines* 268 (2002); Jean-Claude Milner, *Le Pas philosophique de Roland Barthes* (Paris: Verdier, 2003). Recent responses to Barthes, however, have not all been positive. Soon after Barthes's death, in his *Critique de la critique* (Paris: Seuil, 1984), 76; *Literature and Its Theorists,* trans. Catherine Porter (London: Rout-ledge, 1988), 64, Tzvetan Todorov, an early ally in developing a formalist and structuralist theory of narrative, was lamenting Barthes's cavalier attitude to-wards ideas: "It was enough," asserts Todorov, "for him to have formulated an idea to lose interest in it." A similar polemical stance, taken to an extreme of ob-fuscation, also informs Claude Bremond and Thomas Pavel's pedestrian and re-ductive diatribe, more specifically devoted to *S/Z, De Barthes à Balzac: Fictions d'un critique, critiques d'une fiction* (Paris: Albin Michel, 1998).

3. On the neuter in Barthes, see Barthes, *Le Neutre,* ed. Thomas Clerc (Paris: Seuil, 2002); *The Neutral,* trans. Rosalind E. Krauss and Denis Hollier (New York: Columbia University Press, 2005). Throughout this study, unlike Barthes's translators, I have preferred the grammatical or syntactic term "neu-ter" to the more politically charged and more contentious "neutral," if only on grounds of . . . neutrality. For a suggestive account of the consonances between Barthes's early and later thinking on the topic of the neuter, see Roger, *Roland Barthes, roman,* 318–40.

4. Barthes, *Œuvres complètes,* IV, 723, 745–46; *Roland Barthes by Roland Barthes,* trans. Richard Howard (New York: Hill and Wang, 1977), 149–50, 173–75. There is more at stake in this admission than simple procrastination; as we shall see, it is that, for Barthes, all writing is addressed to the future, and comes from the future.

5. See Barthes, *Œuvres complètes*, I, 840; *Mythologies*, selected and trans. Annette Lavers (London: Jonathan Cape, 1972), 128.

6. On the double-edged longevity of Barthes's example, see Knight, *Barthes and Utopia*, 102–3.

7. On *Bouvard et Pécuchet* as anti-mythological mythology, see Barthes, *Œuvres complètes*, I, 847–49; *Mythologies*, 135–37. Take for instance the scene in chapter 3 of Flaubert's novel (*Bouvard et Pécuchet*, ed. Claudine Gothot-Mersch [Paris: Gallimard: folio, 1979], 124–25; *Bouvard and Pécuchet*, trans. A. J. Krailsheimer [Harmondsworth: Penguin, 1976], 75), where Bouvard, having learnt from science that "body heat is developed by muscular contractions," endeavours to illustrate the fact, equipped with a thermometer, by exercising his limbs while sitting in a warm bath. At least as far as Flaubert's protagonists are concerned, the water should in principle get warmer; but to Bouvard's consternation, the water in the bath keeps getting colder, and what should have been an example of how nature is governed by verifiable scientific laws turns to impenetrable farce. The joke serves several purposes: it demonstrates the simplistic nature of received scientific knowledge and Bouvard's stupidity in believing otherwise; but, more significantly, by demonstrating their merely partial congruence with any complex slice of reality, it underlines the unreliability of examples as such.

8. Barthes, *Œuvres complètes*, I, 867; *Mythologies*, 157–58; original emphasis; translation modified.

9. Barthes, *Œuvres complètes*, I, 675; *Mythologies*, 11; translation modified.

10. Barthes, *Œuvres complètes*, I, 842; *Mythologies*, 129; translation modified.

11. Barthes, *Œuvres complètes*, I, 839; *Mythologies*, 126; translation modified.

12. Barthes, *Œuvres complètes*, I, 853; *Mythologies*, 142; translation modified.

13. Barthes, *Œuvres complètes*, I, 854; *Mythologies*, 142–43; translation modified.

14. Barthes, *Œuvres complètes*, I, 857; *Mythologies*, 146; translation modified. Compare Jean-Paul Sartre, *Réflexions sur la question juive* (Paris: Gallimard, 1954), 40–43; *Anti-Semite and Jew*, trans. George J. Becker (New York: Schocken Books, 1948), 35–37. Throughout the 1950s, while making no secret of his (anti-Stalinist) Marxist sympathies, Barthes was nevertheless reluctant to be pigeonholed as such, and it may well be that his knowledge of Marxist theory was in fact largely second-hand. In the early 1950s, his position might best be described as that of an attentist fellow traveller. This would seem to be the burden of Barthes's (historically rather naïve) 1951 *Combat* article replying to Roger Caillois, "'Scandale' du marxisme? [The 'Scandal' of Marxism?]," which concludes: "this is the

problem: the whole sociology of Marxism is premature, so long as the 'debate' about Marxism has not been exhausted by History, which is far from being the case." See Barthes, *Œuvres complètes*, I, 124–26 (125). By 1957, after Hungary, after Krushchev's speech denouncing Stalin at the XXth Party Congress, Barthes's political views had no doubt evolved, like those of many others sympathetic to the Marxist cause; at any event, the use of the word *production* in the closing pages of *Mythologies* carries not just semiotic but also economic, and traditionally political overtones, which the term was to retain in Barthes's writing for probably another decade and a half.

15. Barthes, *Œuvres complètes*, I, 673; *Mythologies*, 9.

16. See Barthes, *Œuvres complètes*, I, 676; *Mythologies*, 12.

17. See Barthes, *Œuvres complètes*, I, 846; *Mythologies*, 134.

18. See Barthes, *Œuvres complètes*, I, 862; *Mythologies*, 151; translation modified. "The petty bourgeois," writes Barthes, "is someone who is incapable of imagining the Other [*impuissant à imaginer l'Autre*]. If the Other comes into view, the petty bourgeois sees nothing, ignores and denies the Other, or transforms the Other into himself. Within the petty-bourgeois universe, all confrontations are like reflections in a mirror [*tous les faits de confrontation sont des faits réverbérants*], and all otherness is reduced to sameness."

19. Barthes, *Œuvres complètes*, I, 177; *Writing Degree Zero and Elements of Semiology*, trans. Annette Lavers and Colin Smith (London: Jonathan Cape, 1967), 11; translation modified.

20. Barthes, *Œuvres complètes*, I, 178; *Writing Degree Zero*, 12. No language, Derrida will later argue, to the extent that it is a language, is ever private. It must always be intelligible to at least one reader (who may be the same individual as the original speaker or writer); and if it is intelligible to one reader, it therefore in principle becomes intelligible to all possible readers. If style belongs to language (and Barthes describes it throughout in these terms), it cannot by definition be described as private.

21. Barthes, *Œuvres complètes*, I, 180; *Writing Degree Zero*, 16.

22. Barthes, *Œuvres complètes*, I, 179; *Writing Degree Zero*, 14; translation modified.

23. Barthes, *Œuvres complètes*, I, 205; *Writing Degree Zero*, 47–48; translation modified. "To return to the distinction between 'language' [*langue*] and 'writing' [*écriture*]," Barthes argues, "it may be said that until about 1650, French Literature had not yet gone beyond a problematics of language, and that as a result, it was entirely unaware of writing. For as long as a language hesitates as to its own structure, a morality of language [*une morale du langage*] is impossible; writing appears only when language, constituted nationally [*constituée nationalement*], becomes a kind of negativity, a horizon separating what is forbidden from what is allowed, without inquiring any further into the origins or justifications

for that taboo." This insensitivity to the role of French as the language of both Nation and Republic was soon remedied by others, for instance by Michel de Certeau, Dominique Julia, and Jacques Revel in *Une politique de la langue: La Révolution française et les patois* (Paris: Gallimard, 1975).

24. Barthes, *Œuvres complètes*, I, 205; *Writing Degree Zero*, 47; translation modified.

25. See Barthes, *Œuvres complètes*, I, 180; *Writing Degree Zero*, 15.

26. Barthes, *Œuvres complètes*, I, 202; *Writing Degree Zero*, 43. "But when poetic language radically questions Nature by dint of its very structure, without recourse to the content of discourse and without pausing within ideology, there is no more writing, only styles, through which humanity turns back upon itself to face the objective world without passing through any of the figures of History or of sociability"; translation modified.

27. On these debates, see for instance Georg Lukács, *Studies in European Realism* (London: Merlin, 1972); and Sartre, *Qu'est-ce que la littérature?* (Paris: Gallimard, 1948); *What Is Literature?* trans. Bernard Frechtman (London: Methuen, 1967).

28. Karl Marx, "Der achtzehnte Brumaire des Louis Bonaparte," in Karl Marx and Friedrich Engels, *Ausgewählte Schriften*, 2 vols. (Berlin: Dietz Verlag, 1970), I, 226; *The Eighteenth Brumaire of Louis Napoleon* (London: Lawrence and Wishart, 1954), 10; translation modified.

29. Lukács, *Wider den mißverstandenen Realismus* (Hamburg: Claassen, 1958), 31; *The Meaning of Contemporary Realism*, trans. John Mander and Necke Mander (London: Merlin, 1962), 31. The indirect target of this invective was also no doubt such Western Marxists as Adorno, whose admiration for Beckett was well known.

30. Sartre, *Un théâtre de situations*, ed. Michel Conta and Michel Rybalka (Paris: Gallimard, 1973), 75. The interview from which these comments are taken was first published in September 1955 in *Théâtre populaire*, which by then, partly as a result of Barthes's own influential support, was an enthusiastic advocate of Brecht in France.

31. Barthes, *Œuvres complètes*, I, 194; *Writing Degree Zero*, 33; translation modified.

32. Barthes, *Œuvres complètes*, I, 208; *Writing Degree Zero*, 51; translation modified.

33. Blanchot, *Le Livre à venir*, 249–50; *The Book to Come*, 205; translation modified. Blanchot's essay originally appeared under the rather more critical title, "Plus loin que le degré zéro [Further than Zero Degree]," in *La Nouvelle Nouvelle Revue française* 9 (September 1953): 485–94.

34. Blanchot, *Le Livre à venir*, 250; *The Book to Come*, 205. In the original review, Blanchot began in more reticent vein, remarking merely that Barthes's essay "would be interesting to consider" (489).

35. See Barthes, "La Mythologie aujourd'hui," in *Œuvres complètes*, III, 873–76. In the essay, Barthes amplifies some of the remarks made in the 1970 preface to *Mythologies* (I, 673). It is worth stressing that, if Barthes was unwilling in 1970 to resume his duties as official demythologiser of petty-bourgeois France, it was not merely because he found the prospect a tedious one, but, more importantly, because to do so in the same manner as in the early 1950s served merely to occlude the unpredictability of the future, which had so spectacularly made its mark only two years before, in the events of May 1968.

36. Barthes, *Œuvres complètes*, I, 673; *Mythologies*, 9; translation modified.

37. Barthes, *Œuvres complètes*, IV, 236; *The Pleasure of the Text*, trans. Richard Miller (London: Jonathan Cape, 1976), 29; original emphasis; translation modified.

38. See Barthes, "Racine est Racine," in *Œuvres complètes*, I, 745–46. Barthes introduces the piece with a similar tautology taken from chapter 5 of *Bouvard et Pécuchet*, which also sums up a certain influential current in modern and not-so-modern literary criticism: "le goût, c'est le goût [taste—is taste]." Unfortunately, like several other of Barthes's articles, the piece in question is omitted from the English version of *Mythologies*.

39. Barthes, *Œuvres complètes*, IV, 238; *The Pleasure of the Text*, 32; original emphasis.

40. See Barthes, *Œuvres complètes*, I, 173, 217–18, 223–24; *Writing Degree Zero*, 6, 64, 72.

41. On the background and genesis of *Le Degré zéro de l'écriture*, see Barthes's own account given in an interview with Jean Thibaudeau in 1971, *Œuvres complètes*, III, 1026–28; *The Tel Quel Reader*, ed. Patrick ffrench and Roland-François Lack (London: Routledge, 1998), 251–53. For a useful corrective to Barthes's expeditious and sometimes unreliable version of events, see Roger, *Roland Barthes, roman*, 237–61.

42. Barthes, *Œuvres complètes*, I, 217; *Writing Degree Zero*, 64; translation modified.

43. Barthes, *Œuvres complètes*, I, 223–24; *Writing Degree Zero*, 72; translation modified.

44. See Barthes, *Œuvres complètes*, I, 173; *Writing Degree Zero*, 6. "[I]n these instances of neutral writing [*ces écritures neutres*], here described as 'the zero degree of writing,'" writes Barthes in his introduction, "it is easy to discern a movement of negation [*le mouvement d'une négation*], yet an inability to bring it to a close within narrative duration [*dans une durée*], as though Literature, having tended for a century to transform its surface into a form without antecedents, was henceforth able only to find purity in the absence of signs, finally offering the realisation of the Orphic dream of a writer without Literature. Blank writing [*écriture blanche*], in Camus, Blanchot, or Cayrol, for example, or oral writing as in the work of Queneau, is the final episode in a Passion of writing marking step

by step the tragic division [*déchirement*] in bourgeois consciousness"; translation modified. When he wrote this in 1953, Barthes had already written, in 1944, on Camus's *L'Étranger* (*The Outsider*) (*Œuvres complètes*, I, 75–79), and, in 1950 and 1952, on the novels of Cayrol (*Œuvres complètes*, I, 105-6, 141–62), and would continue to do so again in the years that followed. In 1960 he reviewed Queneau's *Zazie dans le métro* in an essay collected in *Essais critiques* (*Œuvres complètes*, II, 382–88). Blanchot was a more troublesome case, admittedly not only for Barthes, and references to the writer in *Le Degré zéro* remain fleeting and insubstantial; and though it is true there is some convergence in language between the two, notably when Barthes claims for instance that "modernity begins with the quest for a Literature that is impossible" (*Œuvres complètes*, I, 194; *Writing Degree Zero*, 33), Roger is surely mistaken in claiming in *Roland Barthes, roman* (247–48) that *Le Degré zéro* is closer to Blanchot than it is to Sartre, and might even be deemed more Blanchotian than Blanchot! Indeed, it would not be hard to show that in *Le Degré zéro* and later, whenever Barthes cites Blanchot, he most often misconstrues or misunderstands him, attributing to him a conception of unrelenting negativity, even nihilism, that bears little relation to Blanchot's actual thinking. This misapprehension endured to the very end, and in an interview given in December 1979 on the failed *Revue internationale* project of the early 1960s (in which both men were involved, albeit in markedly different ways: Blanchot absolutely, Barthes with customary reserve), Barthes can be found referring somewhat bizarrely to Blanchot as "a leader of negativity with a capital N [*un leader de la négativité avec un grand N*]" (*Œuvres complètes*, V, 780). Admittedly, this did not prevent Barthes from continuing to read Blanchot, whose name or work is mentioned on nearly thirty separate occasions, more than any other living contemporary, in the last three lecture series given at the Collège de France before Barthes's death. Rarely, however, does he comment in any detail on the texts drawn from *L'Entretien infini* and *Le Livre à venir* that he quotes, and it is as though, while being profoundly attracted to Blanchot's writing, Barthes is also keen to distance himself from it. This relationship of fascination and resistance finds perhaps its most eloquent symptom in Barthes's final reference in print to a text by Blanchot. This occurs towards the end of *La Chambre claire* (*Œuvres complètes*, V, 873; *Camera Lucida*, trans. Richard Howard [London: Vintage, 1993], 106), where Barthes cites Blanchot at some length on the topic of the image (it is by far the longest quotation in the book). Barthes does not provide a source for the extract (which is from Blanchot's 1954 essay on Proust in *Le Livre à venir*, 22; *The Book to Come*, 14, and does not in fact deal with the photographic image at all, but with the Proustian literary image), and fails even to mention Blanchot's name either in a marginal note (unlike the vast majority of other sources) or in the bibliography (omitted from the English version), which nevertheless finds room for several other, less crucial items. Why this omission? The passage taken from Blanchot supplies an oddly abyssal clue. It runs as follows: "The essence of the image is to be entirely outside, without intimacy, and yet more inaccessible and more mysterious than the innermost thought; without signification, but calling upon the depth of every possible meaning; unrevealed and yet manifest, having that presence-absence that constitutes the attraction and the fascination of the Sirens"; translation slightly modified. For further discussion of Barthes's relationship to Blanchot, see Christophe Bident, "The Movements of the Neuter," trans. Michael FitzGerald and Leslie Hill, in *After Blanchot: Literature, Philosophy, Criticism*, ed. Leslie Hill, Brian Nelson, and Dimitris Vardoulakis (Newark: University of Delaware Press, 2005), 13–34; and "R/M, 1953," trans. Michael Holland, *Paragraph* 30, no. 3 (Autumn 2007): 67–83.

45. See Barthes, *Œuvres complètes*, I, 503–5. Barthes contributed a large number of reviews or essays on Brecht during the period up to 1965, and it would not be difficult to demonstrate Brecht's continuing relevance for Barthes, albeit in different ways, after this date. On the general significance of Brecht in 1950s France, see Bernard Dort, *Lecture de Brecht* (Paris: Seuil, 1960); and Daniel Mortier, *Celui qui dit oui, celui qui dit non, ou la réception de Brecht en France (1945–56)* (Paris-Geneva: Champion-Slatkine, 1986); on Barthes's response to Brecht, see Moriarty, *Roland Barthes*, 46–52; and Stafford, *Roland Barthes, Phenomenon and Myth*, 38–40, 69–70. It is worth noting that support for Brecht was far from universal, even on the part of those who were politically sympathetic. Sartre, for instance, even during his period of *rapprochement* with the French Communist Party and the Soviet bloc, had strong reservations about Brechtian distantiation. "For my part," he told *Théâtre populaire* in the interview from September 1955 cited earlier, "I firmly believe that all demystification should in a sense also be mystifying. Or rather that, faced with a partially mystified crowd, it is impossible to have confidence solely in the critical reactions of the crowd. It needs to be given a counter-mystification. And for that, the theatre should make full use of all its potential magic." See Sartre, *Un théâtre de situations*, 77.

46. Barthes, *Œuvres complètes*, I, 503.

47. Barthes, *Œuvres complètes*, I, 923.

48. Barthes, *Œuvres complètes*, I, 648.

49. Barthes, *Œuvres complètes*, I, 1076. On this figure of the *numen*, which refers, according to etymology, to a nod of the head indicating approval or disapproval on the part of the gods as they prepare to dispense justice, see Barthes's own commentary in *Roland Barthes par Roland Barthes*, in *Œuvres complètes*, IV, 709; *Roland Barthes by Roland Barthes*, 134.

50. Barthes reviewed the play in the left-wing monthly *Europe* for August–September, 1955; see Barthes, *Œuvres complètes*, I, 615–18.

51. Bertolt Brecht, *Berliner und Frankfurter Ausgabe*, ed. Werner Hecht, Jan Knopf, Werner Mittenzwei, and Klaus-Detlef Müller, 30 vols. (Berlin and

Frankfurt: Aufbau-Verlag and Suhrkamp, 1988–2000), VIII (1992), 162, where the phrase is as follows: "Immer war der Richter ein Lump, so soll jetzt ein Lump der Richter sein." See Brecht, *The Caucasian Chalk Circle*, trans. James and Tania Stern, with W. H. Auden (London: Methuen, 1963), 72; translation modified.

52. Barthes, *Œuvres complètes*, I, 617.

53. Brecht, *Berliner und Frankfurter Ausgabe*, VIII, 185; *The Caucasian Chalk Circle*, 96; translation modified.

54. See Barthes, *Œuvres complètes*, V, 634. "In an evil society, says Brecht," Barthes puts it, "the best judge is the judge who is a rogue: the failings of the one are counterbalanced by the failings of the other. I like this solution because it is a dialectical one: it puts immorality in the service of morality, and simultaneously excludes both evil violence and good conscience." It is worth noting here that, though he configured it at times in unusual ways, Barthes, unlike many of his contemporaries, never properly renounced the dialectic. Perhaps through nostalgia for the Marxism he felt able to profess in the mid-1950s, he continued till the end to exploit its conceptual resources. But how far, it may be wondered, do the actions of Azdak genuinely amount to that unification of contraries the dialectic represents? Is it not more plausibly the case that Azdak's intervention suspends any possibility of reconciliation?

55. Barthes, *Œuvres complètes*, III, 706–7; *Sade, Fourier, Loyola*, trans. Richard Miller (London: Jonathan Cape, 1976), 10; original emphasis; translation modified. Barthes makes a similar point in *S/Z* about Flaubert's *Bouvard et Pécuchet*, amplifying and extending what he already had said about it in *Mythologies*. "The only power the writer has," he wrote, "over the infinite regress of the stereotype (which is also the infinite regress of 'stupidity' or 'vulgarity') is to enter into it without quotation marks, producing a text, not a parody." Barthes, *Œuvres complètes*, III, 200; *S/Z*, trans. Richard Miller (London: Jonathan Cape, 1975), 98; translation modified.

56. See Barthes, *Œuvres complètes*, II, 711–14. Barthes reiterates the point in a piece titled "L'Éblouissement [A Dazzling Sight]," in Barthes, *Œuvres complètes*, III, 871–72, written on the occasion of the Berliner Ensemble's return visit to Paris in 1971, where it again performed *Die Mutter* alongside Brecht's *Die Tage der Commune* [*The Days of the Commune*].

57. See Barthes, *Œuvres complètes*, IV, 784–85.

58. See Brecht, *Berliner und Frankfurter Ausgabe*, III (1988), 235–60. Some slippage in the meaning of Brecht's phrase may be observed as it passes from the original German to its standard French translation. "L'exception et la règle," the exception and the rule, say both French and English versions; it is clear, however, from the play that what is principally at stake here are not the virtues of the exception in itself but the argument (as Barthes phrases it somewhat more faith-

fully elsewhere) that it is the exception that proves the rule, that, in other words, prevailing rules are themselves abusive, that is, exploitative, violent, and inhuman. And Brecht's play ends with its assembled chorus of actors addressing the audience in these terms: "Was die Regel ist, das erkennt als Mißbrauch / Und wo ihr den Mißbrauch erkannt habt / Da schafft Abhilfe!" (260); "What passes for the rule recognise as abuse / And where you have recognised abuse / Bring help!"

59. Barthes, *Œuvres complètes*, IV, 244; *The Pleasure of the Text*, 41; original emphasis; translation modified.

60. Barthes, *Œuvres complètes*, IV, 260; *The Pleasure of the Text*, 65; original emphasis; translation modified.

61. Barthes, *Œuvres complètes*, II, 788; *Criticism and Truth*, trans. Katrine Pilcher Keuneman (London: Athlone, 1987), 74; translation modified.

62. Barthes, *Œuvres complètes*, II, 788–89; *Criticism and Truth*, 74–75; original emphasis; translation modified.

63. Barthes, *Œuvres complètes*, II, 801; *Criticism and Truth*, 93–94; translation modified.

64. Barthes defends this shift from the historical to the transhistorical as a questioning of the monolithic authority of history—which was ultimately, he claimed, only another form of writing. See Barthes's remarks from 1968 commenting on his own 1965 review of Sollers's novel *Drame*, in *Œuvres complètes*, V, 585.

65. Barthes, *Œuvres complètes*, II, 505–6; *Critical Essays*, 259; original emphasis; translation modified. Barthes went on to address the question of the obstinately meaningless, entropic detail in 1968 in the essay "L'Effet de réel," in *Œuvres complètes*, III, 25–32; *The Rustle of Language*, trans. Richard Howard (Oxford: Blackwell, 1986), 141–48. On the detail in Barthes, see Naomi Shor, *Reading in Detail: Aesthetics and the Feminine* (London: Methuen, 1987), 79–97.

66. Barthes, *Œuvres complètes*, IV, 242; *The Pleasure of the Text*, 39; translation modified. Barthes's reprise of the figure of Moses as a figure of radical futurity, rather than melancholy exclusion, is no doubt indicative of the distance travelled by him since *Mythologies*.

67. Barthes, *Œuvres complètes*, III, 121–22; *S/Z*, 3–4; original emphasis; translation modified. For the key terms *lisible* and *scriptible* I have preferred throughout the more literal rendering, *readable* and *writable*, to the *readerly* and *writerly* proposed by Miller. *OED* defines the second of these terms as meaning: "appropriate to, characteristic or worthy of a professional writer or literary man; consciously literary." Here lies the difficulty: whatever else the *scriptible* may be, it is not anything "consciously literary"; indeed, it is hardly an object at all, certainly not one that corresponds to any pre-existing model of what is recognisable—or acceptable—as literary.

68. On this distinction between value and values, see Barthes, *Œuvres complètes*, IV, 239; *The Pleasure of the Text*, 34. In this fragment, where he toys for a moment with the possibility of collecting together all those texts that have given pleasure, only to realise that such an enterprise would defeat its own object, Barthes engages with the debate on the value of values in an oddly negative manner symptomatic of the precariousness of his position. "I can only approach a subject of this kind," he says, "by *going round in circles*—in which case it would make more sense to do it briefly and in private rather than in public and interminably; it makes more sense to give up [*renoncer*] moving from *value*, the cornerstone of affirmation, to *values*, which are cultural effects"; original emphasis; translation modified.

69. Barthes, *Œuvres complètes*, III, 122; *S/Z*, 5; original emphasis; translation modified.

70. See Barthes, *Œuvres complètes*, IV, 894.

71. On the theory of the epistemological break and the opposition between science and ideology derived from it, see Louis Althusser, *Pour Marx* (Paris: Maspero, 1965); *For Marx*, trans. Ben Brewster (London: Verso, 1990); and Louis Althusser and Etienne Balibar, *Lire Le Capital*, rev. ed., 2 vols. (Paris: Maspero, 1968); *Reading Capital*, trans. Ben Brewster (London: New Left Books, 1970). Its application to literary history was a prominent feature in the *Tel Quel* group's endeavour in the late 1960s to bind avant-garde textual experiment to a heady mixture of Marxism, structuralist theory, and psychoanalysis. On the use of the so-called epistemological break as a means of discriminating between those writers still mired in ideology from those (notably Mallarmé and Lautréamont, followed by Artaud and Bataille) who were thought to have broken through to a science of the text, see Philippe Sollers, *Logiques* (Paris: Seuil, 1968), 9–14; Julia Kristeva, *Séméiotikè* (Paris: Seuil, 1969); and Marcelin Pleynet, *Lautréamont par lui-même* (Paris: Seuil, 1967). On the *Tel Quel* group's relationship to Althusserianism more generally, see Patrick ffrench, *The Time of Theory: A History of Tel Quel (1960–1983)* (Oxford: Oxford University Press, 1995).

72. Barthes, *Œuvres complètes*, III, 642.

73. On the concept of textual production, see Kristeva, *Séméiotikè*, 208–45. Barthes paid enthusiastic tribute to Kristeva's work in a review that appeared at much the same time as *S/Z*. See Barthes, *Œuvres complètes*, III, 477–80; *The Rustle of Language*, 168–71. The concept of productivity, applied to textuality, is problematic for many reasons, not least because it reduces the text to a manufactured object having a pre-emptive, already specified function. In January 1968 in "La Différance [*Differance*]," Derrida was already drawing attention to these difficulties; see Derrida, *Marges: de la philosophie* (Paris: Minuit, 1972), 13; *Margins of Philosophy*, trans. Alan Bass (Chicago: University of Chicago Press, 1982), 12. Increasingly, during the 1970s, at least in Barthes, Kristeva, and others, it tended to

be replaced by the psychoanalytically charged term *dépense*, expenditure, derived initially from Bataille, albeit also by way of an idiosyncratic rereading of Marxian political economy.

74. On this relationship between work and text, see Barthes, *Œuvres complètes*, III, 908–16 (909); *The Rustle of Language*, 56–64 (56). Barthes explains in his opening remarks that "the mutation that seems to have taken hold of the idea of the work [*l'œuvre*] should not however be overestimated; it is part of an epistemological slippage [*glissement épistémologique*] rather than a proper break [*une véritable coupure*], which, it has often been suggested, may be said to have occurred in the course of the last [i.e., nineteenth] century, with the appearance of Marxism and Freudian psychoanalysis; no fresh break is thought to have taken place since then, and it can be said that, in a sense, for a hundred years [i.e., since 1870] we have been caught up in its repetition." Eight years later, deploying the analogous opposition between *studium* and *punctum* in *La Chambre claire*, Barthes was less prescriptive still, cheerfully entertaining the notion that these two regimes might for a given viewer coexist at any one time, or vary from one viewer to the next. By the late 1970s any pretence that the *lisible* and *scriptible* (or their cognates) were anything other than possible responses to a text by a given reader or viewer seems largely to have been abandoned.

75. See Barthes, *Œuvres complètes*, IV, 669; *Roland Barthes by Roland Barthes*, 91–92.

76. Barthes, *Œuvres complètes*, IV, 225–26; *The Pleasure of the Text*, 13; original emphasis; translation modified. Oddly enough, much later, in March 1979, as *La Préparation du roman* records, during the final session of a seminar series devoted to the metaphor of the labyrinth, Barthes rehearses this same Nietzschean point ("what is the meaning of this *for me*"), only then to ask, as though the thought had never occurred to him before, but had remained in abeyance in some dark labyrinthine recess, as follows: "This, then, is the question: where does readability begin [*où commence la lisibilité*]? This, for me, opens up the question of the labyrinth [*la question labyrinthique:* the question of the labyrinth and labyrinthine question]. Not: what is it, how many of them exist, nor even how to escape from one? But: *where does a Labyrinth begin* [*où commence un Labyrinthe*]?" See *La Préparation du roman*, ed. Nathalie Léger (Paris: Seuil, 2003), 179. Remarks made during the same lecture course on 23 February 1980 are even more striking. "I do not wish to get into this whole debate about *readability* [*lisibilité*]," he says, "which is very complex, to the extent that any text, even the most classical, I am thinking here of Pascal, or the most modern, say, like Rimbaud, can be felt [*senti*] simultaneously to be both readable and unreadable: everything depends on the *level of perception* of the text, the *rhythm of reading,* and its *intentionality*" (378–79; original emphasis). What this belated return to the question of the readable proves more than anything else perhaps is that nothing

in Barthes is ever definitive, everything is always already undecided: both as a question and as an answer.

77. See Barthes, *Œuvres complètes*, III, 207; *S/Z*, 106–7. Barthez is a common alternative form (and, in the critic's case, misspelling) of Barthes; Balssa was the novelist's original family name, changed to Balzac by the author's father.

78. In a passage from an essay written in 1962, in memory of Georges Bataille, Blanchot wrote as follows: "Inner experience affirms, it is pure affirmation, and does nothing but affirm. It does not even affirm itself, for then it would be subordinate to itself: what it affirms is affirmation. This is why, having devalued all possible forms of authority and dissolved the very idea of authority, Bataille can accept that affirmation holds within itself the moment of authority. This is the decisive Yes." See Blanchot, *L'Entretien infini*, 310; *The Infinite Conversation*, 209; translation modified. Barthes's own writing, committed as it is to the task of criticism, no doubt falls short of the radicalism described here by Blanchot. But what was at stake for both writers, as they pursued their divergent careers, was the challenge embodied in Bataille's work: how to reconcile literary criticism, reading, writing, with radical affirmation?

79. See Barthes, *Œuvres complètes*, III, 128; *S/Z*, 12.

80. See Barthes, *Œuvres complètes*, IV, 694; *Roland Barthes by Roland Barthes*, 118; original emphasis; translation modified.

81. Barthes, *Œuvres complètes*, III, 141; *S/Z*, 28; original emphasis; translation modified.

82. Barthes, *Œuvres complètes*, IV, 664; *Roland Barthes by Roland Barthes*, 87; translation modified. Compare Barthes, *Œuvres complètes*, III, 407–9; *The Empire of Signs*, trans. Richard Howard (London: Jonathan Cape, 1983), 73–76. In *Roland Barthes, roman*, 338–39, Roger makes the interesting suggestion that the unnamed counter-example evoked in this fragment is none other than Blanchot. Nowhere, however, does Blanchot suggest that it is possible to return to this presumed origin of the world before meaning. Indeed, when he considers the question, in a famous passage from the essay "La Littérature et le droit à la mort [Literature and the Right to Death]," it is to argue that any such return is impossible. What he does go on to suggest, however, is that this impossibility of return, this necessary failure of the Orphic gesture, is inseparable from the (im)possibility of literature. "The language of literature," he writes, "is a search for the moment that precedes it. Generally, it calls this existence; it wants the cat as it is, the pebble seen *from the side of things*, not man in general, but this man and, in this man, what man rejects in order to say it, which is the founding of speech and which speech excludes in order to speak, the abyss, Lazarus in the tomb and not Lazarus returned to the light, the one already beginning to smell, who is Evil, Lazarus lost and not Lazarus saved and raised from the dead" (original empha-

sis). See Blanchot, *La Part du feu*, 316; *The Work of Fire*, 327; translation modified. What is at issue for Blanchot is not the primal simplicity of the origin but the simultaneous necessity and impossibility of reaching beyond the dialectic of the concept. Barthes's strategy is, by contrast, more modest, perhaps even naïve: it is to attempt to suspend the dialectic of the concept by appealing to the dialectic itself.

83. Barthes, *Œuvres complètes*, III, 415; *The Empire of Signs*, 83; original emphasis; translation modified. Barthes returns several times, particularly in the late 1970s, to this question of how to voice the singular event, often addressing his remarks either to non-literary pieces (paintings, drawings, photographs) or to elliptically fragmentary texts (like the haiku). See Barthes, *Œuvres complètes*, V, 688; *The Responsibility of Forms*, trans. Richard Howard (Oxford: Blackwell, 1986), 177; *Œuvres complètes*, V, 792; *Camera Lucida*, 4–5; and *Le Neutre*, 220–21; *The Neutral*, 174–75. It is also important to stress the role of the other or otherness in the event, which prevents it from turning into an autotelic, solipsistic, arbitrary occurrence. In 1976, in a letter to Philippe Roger (in *Œuvres complètes*, IV, 942), Barthes insists on this address to the other. "The critic, indeed," he writes, "cannot say 'anything whatever' ['*n'importe quoi*'], because one writes with a reader's desire [*le désir du lecteur*: the desire *of* a reader and desire *for* a reader] (take the expression either way), and there is no such thing as 'anything whatever' in desire."

84. Barthes, *Œuvres complètes*, IV, 707; *Roland Barthes by Roland Barthes*, 132–33; original emphasis; translation modified.

85. Barthes, *Œuvres complètes*, III, 408; *The Empire of Signs*, 75.

86. Blanchot, *L'Entretien infini*, xvi; *The Infinite Conversation*, xvii; translation modified. I examine the figure of the limitlessness of the limit in Blanchot, in my *Blanchot: Extreme Contemporary*, 91–102.

87. Barthes, *Le Neutre*, 47–48; *The Neutral*, 20; translation modified. What is noticeable here is the extent to which Barthes persists in reading Blanchot as a phenomenologist, as though the neutrality of what Blanchot articulates here as fatigue were still subordinated to a logic of manifestation, appearance, perception: subject, in a word, to the metaphysical concept of the subject.

88. Barthes, *Le Neutre*, 33; *The Neutral*, 8; translation modified.

89. Emile Benveniste, *Problèmes de linguistique générale I* (Paris: Gallimard, 1966), 252; *Problems in General Linguistics*, trans. Mary Elizabeth Meek (Coral Gables: University of Miami Press, 1971), 218; translation slightly modified. For Barthes's tributes to Benveniste, see Barthes, *Œuvres complètes*, II, 814–16; IV, 513–15; *The Rustle of Language*, 162–67.

90. Barthes, *Œuvres complètes*, V, 29; *A Lover's Discourse: Fragments*, trans. Richard Howard (Harmondsworth: Penguin, 1990), 3; translation modified.

91. Barthes, *Œuvres complètes*, IV, 228; *The Pleasure of the Text*, 16; translation modified. Barthes explains: "the body of anatomists and physiologists, as seen or spoken by science: the text of grammarians, critics, commentators, philologists (the phenotext). But we also have a body of enjoyment [*corps de jouissance*] solely made up of erotic relations, quite separate from the first." Barthes returns several times later to this multiplicity of the body; see for instance Barthes, *Œuvres complètes*, IV, 640; *Roland Barthes by Roland Barthes*, 60–61.

92. Barthes, *Œuvres complètes*, IV, 692; *Roland Barthes by Roland Barthes*, 117; original emphasis; translation modified.

93. Barthes, *Œuvres complètes*, IV, 747; *Roland Barthes by Roland Barthes*, 175; translation modified.

94. Barthes, *Œuvres complètes*, IV, 228; *The Pleasure of the Text*, 17; translation modified. The *me* to which Barthes refers is not the self in general but the Lacanian Imaginary or Freudian ego.

95. Barthes, *Œuvres complètes*, IV, 667; *Roland Barthes by Roland Barthes*, 90; original emphasis; translation modified.

96. Barthes, *Œuvres complètes*, IV, 827; V, 722; *The Responsibility of Forms*, 299, 295; translation modified. Barthes's use of the term *beating* also recalls Freud's famous essay on the mutability of subject and object positions in fantasy, "Ein Kind wird geschlagen [A Child Is Being Beaten]," the standard title of which in French is "On bat un enfant." See Sigmund Freud, *Gesammelte Werke*, 18 vols. (London: Hogarth Press, 1940–52), XII, 197–226; *Standard Edition of the Complete Psychological Works of Sigmund Freud*, ed. James Strachey, 24 vols. (London: Hogarth Press, 1953–74), XVII, 177–204. For a helpful account of the uses to which the concept of transference may be put in this context, see Jean Laplanche and J.-B. Pontalis, *Vocabulaire de la psychanalyse* (Paris: P. U. F., 1967), 492–99; *The Language of Psycho-analysis*, trans. Donald Nicholson-Smith (London: Karnac Books, 1988), 455–62.

97. Barthes, *Œuvres complètes*, IV, 671; *Roland Barthes by Roland Barthes*, 94.

98. See Barthes, *Œuvres complètes*, IV, 670; *Roland Barthes by Roland Barthes*, 93.

99. Barthes, *Œuvres complètes*, IV, 896; translation mine.

100. On the fragmentary in Blanchot, see my *A Change of Epoch: Blanchot, Writing, the Fragmentary*, forthcoming.

101. Friedrich Schlegel, *Kritische Schriften und Fragmente*, ed. Ernst Behler and Hans Eichner, 6 vols. (Paderborn: Ferdinand Schöningh, 1988), II, 123; *Dialogue on Poetry and Literary Aphorisms*, trans. Ernst Behler and Roman Struc (University Park: Pennsylvania State University Press, 1968), 143; translation modified.

102. Barthes, *Œuvres complètes*, V, 42; *A Lover's Discourse*, 14–15.

103. Barthes, *Œuvres complètes*, IV, 670; *Roland Barthes by Roland Barthes*, 92–93.

104. Barthes, *Œuvres complètes*, IV, 637; *Roland Barthes by Roland Barthes*, 56. The fragment to which this allusion belongs, naturally enough, is entitled: "La Coïncidence [Coincidence]."

105. See Schlegel, *Kritische Schriften und Fragmente*, II, 127; *Dialogue on Poetry and Literary Aphorisms*, 145. In Fr. 238, Schlegel explains: "There is a poetry [*Poesie*] whose One and All is the relationship of the ideal and the real: it should thus be called transcendental poetry [*Transzendentalpoesie*] according to the analogy with the technical language of philosophy. It begins in the form of satire with the absolute disparity of the ideal and the real, hovers in their midst in the form of the elegy, and it ends in the form of the idyll with the absolute identity of both. But we should not care for a transcendental philosophy unless it were critical, unless it presented the process of production [*das Produzierende*] along with the product, unless it embraced within the system of transcendental thoughts a characterisation of transcendental thinking: in the same way, that poetry which is not infrequently encountered in modern poets should combine those transcendental materials and preliminary exercises for a poetic theory of the poetic faculty with the artistic reflection and beautiful self-mirroring, which is present in Pindar, the lyric fragments of the Greeks, and ancient elegy: and among the moderns, in Goethe: thus this poetry, in each of its presentations, should present itself, and everywhere at the same time be both poetry and the poetry of poetry"; translation modified. On the complex philosophical and literary legacy of the *Athenaeum*, see Philippe Lacoue-Labarthe and Jean-Luc Nancy, *L'Absolu littéraire* (Paris: Seuil, 1978); *The Literary Absolute*, trans. Philip Barnard and Cheryl Lester (Albany: State University of New York Press, 1988). That Barthes was familiar with the book is apparent from *La Préparation du roman*, 195; Barthes also refers in the course of those lectures to several other texts by Schlegel and Novalis. Barthes's rediscovery of Jena Romanticism in these late texts should not, however, be taken as proof, as is sometimes alleged, that the whole of French literary theory can be reduced to a ghostly return of German Romanticism. The reality, as always, is far more complex.

106. See Barthes, *Le Neutre*, 38; *The Neutral*, 12; translation slightly modified.

107. See Barthes, *Le Neutre*, 222; *The Neutral*, 176.

108. Barthes, *Le Neutre*, 31; *The Neutral*, 6; translation modified.

109. Barthes, *Le Neutre*, 72; *The Neutral*, 42; translation slightly modified.

110. See Barthes, *Œuvres complètes*, I, 783–85; *Mythologies*, 81–83.

111. Barthes, *Le Neutre*, 115–16; *The Neutral*, 80. Rather oddly, Barthes goes on to contrast the two faces of the Neuter with the help of two pairs of Nietzschean terms borrowed from Gilles Deleuze as follows: "neither-nor-ism [*le*

ni-nisme] is affirmative-reactive ≠ the Neuter is negative-active." In the terms of the current argument, and those proposed by Deleuze, it would be more logical to describe the Neuter as affirmative-active, and neither-nor-ism as the reverse. This signals a curious idiosyncrasy in Barthes's account of the Neuter, which is responsible for at least some of the disagreement with Blanchot, viz., Barthes's assimilation of the affirmative to the assertive. For Blanchot, the distinction between the two is an absolutely crucial one, even though it can barely be made in French, which has at its disposal, for both meanings, only the one word: *affirmer*.

112. Barthes, *Œuvres complètes*, IV, 706–7; *Roland Barthes by Roland Barthes*, 132–33; translation modified.

113. Barthes, *Œuvres complètes*, IV, 236; *The Pleasure of the Text*, 29–30.

114. Barthes, *Le Neutre*, 243–44; *The Neutral*, 195; original emphasis; translation modified. The biographical anecdote is no doubt abyssal. As Barthes makes clear from the outset, the movement and direction of the lecture course itself were powerfully inflected by the death of his own mother, which occurred 25 October 1977, that is, midway between the writing of the lectures in summer 1977 and their delivery in 1978.

115. See Blanchot, *L'Entretien infini*, 419; *The Infinite Conversation*, 283. The phrase (to which Susan Hanson adds an intrusive comma) is used by Blanchot as the subtitle for Section III in the book. Some pages later, in an essay on fragmentary writing in René Char, no doubt in order to avoid the impression of hierarchy, Blanchot writes the phrase otherwise: *le fragmentaire le neutre* (451, 307).

116. On shifting frames in Kafka, see Blanchot, *La Part du feu*, 79–89; *The Work of Fire*, 74–84; and *L'Entretien infini*, 556–67; *The Infinite Conversation*, 379–87. The impossibility of finally determining the position of any frame (just as it was in his account of Kant's third *Critique*) is a major emphasis in Derrida's readings of Blanchot contained in *Parages*, new ed. (Paris: Galilée, [1998] 2003). Barthes exploits much of the same argument, of course, in his numerous references to Flaubert's *Bouvard et Pécuchet*.

117. On the *il y a* in Blanchot or Levinas, and the debate surrounding the Neuter, see my *Blanchot: Extreme Contemporary*, 103–57.

118. See Blanchot, *L'Espace littéraire*, 72; *The Space of Literature*, 75. "The 'poet,'" Blanchot adds a few pages later, "is someone for whom there exists not even one world, for there exists for the writer only the outside, the glistening flow of the eternal outside"; translation modified.

119. From a very early stage, Blanchot had set aside such questions, notably in response to Sartre's famous essay: *Qu'est-ce que la littérature?* (*What Is Literature?*); see Blanchot, *La Part du feu*, 294, *The Work of Fire*, 302. "It has already been noted with some surprise," says Blanchot, silently quoting Jean Paulhan, "that to the question: 'What is literature?,' there have only ever been insignifi-

cant answers"; translation modified. That Blanchot had already refused it in 1948 did not however prevent Barthes, thirty years later, in answer to the question: "Can writing be arrogant?," from confessing to his Collège de France audience: "I do not have (or do not yet have) the conceptual means to theorise this position (which would suppose a 'What Is Writing?' [*un 'qu'est-ce que l'écriture?'*])." See *Le Neutre*, 206; *The Neutral*, 162; translation modified.

120. Barthes, *Œuvres complètes*, V, 432; *A Barthes Reader*, 461; translation modified. The idea is one Barthes probably first encountered in an influential essay by Benveniste on language in Freud, published in 1956; see Benveniste, *Problèmes de linguistique générale I*, 84; *Problems in General Linguistics*, 73. "The characteristic trait of negation in language," Benveniste argues, "is that it can deny [*annuler*] only what has already been uttered, which it must explicitly posit in order then to suppress [*supprimer*] it, and that a judgement of non-existence has necessarily the same formal status as a judgement of existence"; translation modified.

121. Barthes, *Œuvres complètes*, V, 432; *A Barthes Reader*, 461; original emphasis; translation modified.

122. Blanchot, *L'Instant de ma mort* (Paris: Gallimard, [1994] 2002), 11; "The Instant of My Death," in Maurice Blanchot and Jacques Derrida, *The Instant of My Death / Demeure: Fiction and Testimony*, trans. Elizabeth Rottenberg (Stanford: Stanford University Press, 2000), 5; translation slightly modified. Barthes, *Œuvres complètes*, IV, 246; *The Pleasure of the Text*, 43; translation slightly modified. Barthes published a textual analysis of Poe's story, utilising some of the same methodology as in *S/Z*, later the same year; see Barthes, *Œuvres complètes*, IV, 413–42; *The Semiotic Challenge*, trans. Richard Howard (Oxford: Blackwell, 1988), 261–93. Oddly enough, in Barthes's actual analysis on the story there is little evidence of the sense of repulsion apparent in the remark cited here. Indeed, it is as though M. Valdemar's dramatic (and dramatically undecided) declaration: "Yes; — no; — I *have been* sleeping — and now — now — I *am dead*" (in Edgar Allan Poe, *The Complete Tales and Poems* [Harmondsworth: Penguin, 1982], 101; original emphasis), is more powerfully reminiscent of the impossible suspension of meaning enacted by the Neuter than it is of the stereotype. Perhaps this is simply another indication of the strange reversibility of the one into the other, which is the principle without principle of the Neuter.

123. Barthes, *Œuvres complètes*, V, 433; *A Barthes Reader*, 462.

124. Barthes, *Œuvres complètes*, IV, 240–41; *The Pleasure of the Text*, 36; original emphasis; translation modified.

125. See Barthes, *La Préparation du roman*, 31-32. The date indicated by Barthes corresponds to the brief interval in the lecture series on the Neuter, that is, both its mid-point and its own neutral fulcrum, occasioned by the Easter vacation, which fell after the first seven sessions in the series and preceded the closing six. Barthes was visiting Casablanca at the time.

126. See Barthes, *Œuvres complètes*, V, 994–1001, where the various plans for *Vita nova* are reproduced in facsimile (a transcription is given, 1007–18). Barthes died 26 March 1980 without completing the project and without providing any clarification as to its status or likely final form. For an assessment of Barthes's plans and their relationship to other late or posthumous texts, see Diana Knight, "Idle Thoughts: Barthes's *Vita nova*," *Nottingham French Studies* 36, no. 1 (Spring 1997): 88–98.

127. The haiku in question, as Knight points out, was also cited at the end of *Fragments d'un discours amoureux* (*Œuvres complètes*, V, 287; *A Lover's Discourse: Fragments*, 233); it is also mentioned by Barthes in an interview given in September 1979 (*Œuvres complètes*, V, 763), and also appears alongside a description of the young Moroccan in the posthumous "Incidents." See Barthes, *Œuvres complètes*, V, 974: "A young lad, sitting on a low wall by the side of a road, but paying no attention—sitting there as though for all time, sitting for the sake of sitting, *without dithering:* 'Sitting peacefully, doing nothing, / Spring is coming and the grass grows of its own accord.'"

128. See Barthes, *La Préparation du roman*, 282.

129. Barthes, *La Préparation du roman*, 227.

130. Barthes, *La Préparation du roman*, 201–2. This motif of the Romantic Novel or Absolute Novel recurs in the drafts for *Vita nova;* see Barthes, *Œuvres complètes*, V, 999, 1015.

131. Barthes, *La Préparation du roman*, 266.

132. Barthes, *La Préparation du roman*, 48.

133. Barthes, *La Préparation du roman*, 230; original emphasis.

134. Barthes, *La Préparation du roman*, 32.

135. See Barthes, *Œuvres complètes*, IV, 68. "The two discourses, that of the narrator and that of Proust," Barthes wrote in 1967, "are bound by homology, not by analogy. The narrator is *about to* write [*va écrire*], and this future tense keeps him in an order of existence, not language; his struggle is with psychology, not technique. Marcel Proust, on the other hand, writes; and has to deal with categories of language, not of behaviour" (original emphasis).

136. Marcel Proust, *A la recherche du temps perdu*, ed. Jean-Yves Tadié, 4 vols. (Paris: Gallimard, 1989), IV, 458; *In Search of Lost Time*, trans. Carol Clark, Peter Collier, Lydia Davis, James Grieve, Ian Patterson, John Sturrock, and Mark Treharne, ed. Christopher Prendergast, 6 vols. (Harmondsworth: Penguin, 2002), VI, 187–88; translation modified.

137. Barthes, *Œuvres complètes*, I, 500; original emphasis.

138. See Barthes, *Œuvres complètes*, IV, 66–77.

139. See Barthes, *La Préparation du roman*, 32–33, 198.

140. See Barthes, *Œuvres complètes*, IV, 66–77; V, 459–70, 654–66.

141. In the notes for *La Préparation du roman*, 329–30, Barthes concedes that there is something largely mythical (i.e., resonating powerfully in the sensi-

bility of the critic rather than necessarily corresponding to literary historical fact) about his presentation of the "mysterious hiatus," "chicane," or "suspense" of September 1909. In reality, as Jean-Yves Tadié demonstrates in his *Marcel Proust* (Paris: Gallimard, 1996), 603–69; *Marcel Proust,* trans. Euan Cameron (London: Viking, 2000), 504–62, the transition from Essay to Novel, from *Contre Sainte-Beuve* to *A la recherche,* was far more complex than Barthes's summary account indicates. The crucial turning point for Barthes was nevertheless Proust's decision in favour of the (generically) undecidable.

142. Proust's mother died in 1905, and on several occasions, albeit in passing, Barthes notes its likely significance for the transition of September 1909. For understandable reasons, Barthes was reluctant to draw the reader's attention to his own recent personal loss, but it is hard to believe that it was not responsible, at least in part, for Barthes's return to Proust in the wake of his own bereavement in October 1977. Barthes was no doubt right, however, in the suggestion that the shift to first-person narrative in Proust was at least equally important. It recalls a similar if converse point once made by Blanchot about Kafka, whose novel writing came into its own (notably in the case of *Der Prozeß*) with the change from the first-person to the third-person narrative voice. See Blanchot, *L'Espace littéraire,* 70; *The Space of Literature,* 73; and *L'Entretien infini,* 558; *The Infinite Conversation,* 380. In both instances, what was essential is the discovery of otherness at the heart of the selfsame, and it is worth recalling that, as Barthes began rereading Blanchot in the late 1970s, one of the texts to which he returned, and to which he refers on several occasions, was Blanchot's essay on Proust in *Le Livre à venir,* which explores the question of writing as relation without relation with the outside.

143. Barthes, *Œuvres complètes,* V, 459; *The Rustle of Language,* 277–78; translation modified. Elsewhere, Barthes explains that the object of his identification was not the author as such but the practice of writing for which the author merely provided a name. See Barthes, *La Préparation du roman,* 234–35. Barthes was ready to take many risks in pursuit of this methodology: witness for instance, in *La Préparation du roman,* 298–201, his interest in the food preferred by various writers he admired, including Nietzsche, Joubert, Chateaubriand, and Proust.

144. Barthes, *La Préparation du roman,* 278. As Proust famously writes in "Le Temps retrouvé [Finding Time Again]," fusing the two together in an infinite circle, "true life [*la vraie vie*], life finally uncovered and clarified, the only life consequently lived to the full is literature." See Proust, *A la recherche du temps perdu,* IV, 474; *In Search of Lost Time,* VI, 204; translation modified.

145. Barthes, *Œuvres complètes,* V, 465. Discreetly but provocatively, Barthes illustrates this figure of "Marcel" by referring his listeners to George D. Painter's still controversial *Marcel Proust: A Biography,* 2 vols. (London: Chatto and Windus, 1959–65), the first volume of which he reviewed in 1966 under the title "Les

Vies parallèles [Parallel Lives]," in *Œuvres complètes*, II, 811–13. In similar vein, Barthes also cites the photographic material illustrating Proust's life (and identifying numerous alleged sources for *A la recherche*) contained in the Pléiade *Album Proust*.

146. Barthes, *Œuvres complètes*, V, 468.

147. Barthes, *Œuvres complètes*, V, 468; original emphasis. Barthes's remark about the need to "break up the universe" of the novel is based on a famous passage in Nietzsche's posthumous papers, from 1886–87, in Friedrich Nietzsche, *Kritische Studienausgabe*, 2nd ed., ed. Giorgio Colli and Mazzino Montinari, 15 vols. (Berlin: de Gruyter/dtv, 1988), XII, 317: "The whole needs to be split apart, respect for the whole unlearned, and whatever we have given to the unknown and what is whole should be reclaimed for that which is close at hand, and ours alone [*Man muß das All zersplittern; den Respekt vor dem All verlernen; das, was wir dem Unbekannten und Ganzen gegeben haben, zurücknehmen für das Nächste, Unsre*]."

148. See Jacques Lacan, *Le Séminaire. Livre VIII : Le Transfert*, ed. Jacques-Alain Miller (Paris: Seuil, 1991), 11.

149. Barthes, *La Préparation du roman*, 194–95; original emphasis.

150. See Freud, *Gesammelte Werke*, XVI, 43–56; *Standard Edition*, XXIII, 257–69.

151. Lacan, *Le Séminaire. Livre VIII : Le Transfert*, 11–26.

152. Barthes, *Œuvres complètes*, V, 313.

153. On this "non-ethical opening of the ethical [*ouverture non-éthique de l'éthique*]," see Derrida, *De la grammatologie* (Paris: Minuit, 1967), 202; *Of Grammatology*, trans. Gayatri Chakravorty Spivak, corrected ed. (Baltimore: Johns Hopkins University Press, [1976] 1997), 140; translation slightly modified.

154. Barthes, *Œuvres complètes*, IV, 771; *Roland Barthes by Roland Barthes*, 188; translation modified. For the original page presentation of this closing fragment, see *Roland Barthes par Roland Barthes* (Paris: Seuil, 1975), 193.

155. Barthes, *Le Neutre*, 67; The *Neutral*, 37; translation modified.

156. Barthes, *La Préparation du roman*, 206.

Chapter Three   Maurice Blanchot

1. Blanchot, *L'Entretien infini*, 520; *The Infinite Conversation*, 354–55; translation modified. Blanchot's essay was first published as "L'Athenaeum," in *La Nouvelle Revue française* 140 (August 1964): 301–13. The reference to "forces of dissolution" is an addition from 1969.

2. See Lacoue-Labarthe and Nancy, *L'Absolu littéraire*; *The Literary Absolute*. The "concept" of literature here is to be distinguished from both the word

and the thing of that name, as Lacoue-Labarthe makes clear in an essay on Schlegel's *Lucinde;* see Philippe Lacoue-Labarthe, "L'Avortement de la littérature," in *Du féminin,* ed. Mireille Calle (Saintefoy: Quebec, 1992), 3–19 (3).

3. Schlegel, *Kritische Schriften und Fragmente,* II, 162.

4. Schlegel, *Kritische Schriften und Fragmente,* II, 105; *Dialogue on Poetry and Literary Aphorisms,* 133. Unfortunately this English edition translates only a selection of Schlegel's early fragments.

5. Schlegel, *Kritische Schriften und Fragmente,* II, 166.

6. Schlegel, *Kritische Schriften und Fragmente,* I, 249.

7. Schlegel, *Kritische Schriften und Fragmente,* II, 133.

8. See *Athenäum, eine Zeitschrift von August Wilhelm Schlegel und Friedrich Schlegel,* facsimile ed., 3 vols. (Darmstadt: Wissenschaftliche Buchgesellschaft, 1992), III, 58–128, 169–87; *Dialogue on Poetry and Literary Aphorisms,* 53–117.

9. Schlegel, *Kritische Schriften und Fragmente,* II, 206; *Dialogue on Poetry and Literary Aphorisms,* 89–90; translation modified.

10. On the various meanings of *Bildung,* see Lacoue-Labarthe and Nancy, *L'Absolu littéraire,* 371–93; *The Literary Absolute,* 101–19.

11. See Lacoue-Labarthe and Nancy, *L'Absolu littéraire,* 376–78; *The Literary Absolute,* 105–7.

12. Schlegel, *Kritische Schriften und Fragmente,* II, 199; *Dialogue on Poetry and Literary Aphorisms,* 77; translation modified.

13. Schlegel, *Kritische Schriften und Fragmente,* II, 225, 227; *Dialogue on Poetry and Literary Aphorisms,* 152; translation modified. Behler and Struc translate *Bildung* as "liberal education."

14. Schlegel, *Kritische Schriften und Fragmente,* II, 228.

15. Schlegel, *Kritische Schriften und Fragmente,* II, 123.

16. Schlegel, *Kritische Schriften und Fragmente,* II, 186; *Dialogue on Poetry and Literary Aphorisms,* 53; translation modified.

17. Novalis, *Werke,* ed. Gerhard Schulz (Munich: Verlag C. H. Beck, 1981), 274.

18. See Blanchot, *L'Entretien infini,* 516–17; *The Infinite Conversation,* 352.

19. For a succinct account of Schlegel's career, see Ernst Behler, *Friedrich Schlegel* (Hamburg: Rowohlt, 1966).

20. See Blanchot, *Après coup, précédé par Le Ressassement éternel* (Paris: Minuit, 1983), 92; *The Station Hill Blanchot Reader* (Barrytown, NY: Station Hill Press, 1998), 491. For an account of the life and work of Jean-Paul [Richter] (1763–1825), see Hanns-Josef Ortheil, *Jean Paul* (Hamburg: Rowohlt, 1984); for Blanchot's early interest in the writer, see Blanchot, *Chroniques littéraires du Journal des débats,* ed. Christophe Bident (Paris: Gallimard, 2007), 548–52. In 1964 Blanchot ended his essay on the *Athenaeum,* in a note omitted from *L'Entretien infini,* by inviting publishers, in addition to recent translations of

Siebenkäs (1796–97) and *Hesperus* (1795), to consider Jean-Paul's other works, notably *Die unsichtbare Loge* (1793) and *Titan* (1800–1803), last translated into French a century before. On the presence of Jean-Paul in Blanchot's fiction, see Dimitris Vardoulakis, "'What terrifying complicity': Jean Paul as Collocutor in *Death Sentence*," in *After Blanchot: Literature, Philosophy, Criticism*, 168–88.

21. Blanchot, *Lautréamont et Sade*, 18; *Lautréamont und Sade*, 8; translation modified.

22. Blanchot's essays dealing principally with Sade are as follows: "Quelques remarques sur Sade," *Critique* 3–4 (August–September 1946): 239–49; "A la rencontre de Sade," *Les Temps modernes* 25 (October 1947): 577–612; "Français, encore un effort . . . ," *La Nouvelle Revue française* 154 (October 1965): 600–618. The second of these texts is collected in *Lautréamont et Sade*, the third in *L'Entretien infini*, 323–42; *The Infinite Conversation*, 217–29. There are, in addition, a number of important, if fleeting references to Sade in *L'Écriture du désastre*, 18, 77; *The Writing of the Disaster*, 8, 45; and *La Communauté inavouable* (Paris: Minuit, 1983), 12, 79, 81–82; *The Unavowable Community*, trans. Pierre Joris (New York: Station Hill Press, 1988), 3, 47, 49. Blanchot's early reading of Sade was also taking place, it should be noted, in the margins of his work on the novel *Le Très-Haut* (*The Most High*), completed in May 1947, and Blanchot's most explicitly political work of fiction. On the politics of the novel, see Georges Préli, *La Force du dehors: extériorité, limite et non-pouvoir à partir de Maurice Blanchot* (Paris: Recherches, 1977) ; and my *Bataille, Klossowski, Blanchot: Writing at the Limit*, 181–206. For an account of Blanchot's reading of Sade in the context of the work of Paulhan, Bataille, and Lacan, see Christophe Halsberghe, "Au prix de la béance," in *Maurice Blanchot, récits critiques*, ed. Bident and Vilar, 339–56.

23. The 1949 version of *Lautréamont et Sade*, published by Minuit in the *Propositions* series, consists of two essays, headed "Lautréamont" (9–213) and "Sade" (217–65) respectively, in the order announced in the title of the book, which, oddly enough, carries as a running head throughout the reverse mention: *Sade et Lautréamont*, as though to suggest that from the outset the sequence of the two essays was the object of some indecision. The 1963 version of the book, reassigned by Minuit to its *Arguments* series, linked to the journal of the same name, added as a preface the text of "Qu'en est-il de la critique?" (9–14), slightly modified for the occasion, and, together with other minor changes, retitled the two essays, which now appeared, in this order, as "La Raison de Sade" (17–49) and "L'Expérience de Lautréamont" (243–380). The 1963 printing, unusually, also gave the complete 1874 text of Lautréamont's *Les Chants de Maldoror* (51–242), which it sandwiched between the two essays; when Blanchot's book was reissued in 1973, the text of *Maldoror*, which had in the interim become more readily accessible elsewhere, was duly excised. All page references here, unless otherwise indicated, are to this most recent version of the book.

24. Blanchot, *La Part du feu*, 311; *The Work of Fire*, 321; translation modified. Juliette's celebrated dictum: "philosophy should tell all [*la philosophie doit tout dire*]" appears in the closing pages of the *Histoire de Juliette*; see Sade, *Œuvres*, ed. Michel Delon in collaboration with Jean Deprun, 3 vols. (Paris: Gallimard, 1990–98), III, 1261.

25. Bataille, *Œuvres complètes*, III, 428. *Le Bleu du ciel* was not published until 1957, but there is little doubt that Blanchot, like other friends of Bataille, had read the novel well before that date.

26. See Bataille, *Œuvres complètes*, II, 51–109. Bataille's letter on the use value of Sade is collected, together with later material, in *Sade and the Narrative of Transgression*, ed. David B. Allison, Mark S. Roberts, and Allen S. Weiss (Cambridge: Cambridge University Press, 1995), 16–32. The aporetic nature of the question finds a provocative answer of sorts in the would-be event-like non-event that is Guy Debord's 1952 film or anti-film, *Hurlements en faveur de Sade*, in which lengthy sequences of silence, accompanied by a totally dark screen, alternate with brief sequences of fragmentary dialogue, drawn from a variety of readymade sources (news items in the local paper, quotations from the *Code civil*, letters, other unidentified documents), accompanied by a totally white screen. First shown under the auspices of the ciné-club d'Avant-Garde at the Musée de L'Homme in Paris in June 1952, at least until the screening was violently interrupted by the audience, the film was screened for a second time, in full, at an alternative venue in the Quartier latin later the same year. For the final script of the film, see Guy Debord, *Œuvres*, ed. Jean-Louis Rançon in collaboration with Alice Debord (Paris: Gallimard, 2006), 60–68. As a girl's voice rightly interjects (63): "[T]his film isn't about Sade at all [*Mais on ne parle pas de Sade dans ce film*]." The only way of speaking about Sade, the film suggests, is in fact to speak of something entirely other.

27. See Max Horkheimer and T. W. Adorno, *Dialektik der Aufklärung* (Frankfurt: Fischer, 1969), 93; *Dialectic of Enlightenment*, trans. John Cumming (London: Verso, 1997), 86. "The work of the Marquis de Sade," the authors claim, quoting Kant's essay "What Is Enlightenment?" "portrays 'understanding without the guidance of another person [*den Verstand ohne Leitung eines anderen*]': that is, the bourgeois individual freed from tutelage."

28. See Pierre Klossowski, *Sade mon prochain* (Paris: Seuil, 1947). In 1967, in a substantially reworked version of the book, retitled *Sade mon prochain, précédé de Le Philosophe scélérat* (Paris: Seuil, 1967); *Sade My Neighbor*, trans. Alphonso Lingis (Evanston: Northwestern University Press, 1991), Klossowski dramatically reversed this earlier interpretation, and now insisted on Sade's irreducible atheism, arguing that Sadian perversion was no longer based in psychopathology but instead conspired to bring about a radical dismantling of all subjective unity whatsoever. On these opposing versions of Sade in Klossowski's

work, see *Traversées de Pierre Klossowski*, ed. Laurent Jenny and Andreas Pfersmann (Geneva: Droz, 1999), 25–56; and my *Bataille, Klossowski, Blanchot: Writing at the Limit*, 116–30.

29. Bataille, *Œuvres complètes*, X, 195; *Eroticism*, trans. Mary Dalwood (London: Boyars, 1987), 196; translation modified. It is revealing that, when he appeared for the defence at the famous Sade censorship trial in 1957, Bataille described himself in court as representing "philosophy." See Bataille, *Œuvres complètes*, XII, 454.

30. Simone de Beauvoir, *Faut-il brûler Sade?* (Paris: Gallimard, folio, 1955), 50.

31. See Lacan, *Écrits* (Paris: Seuil, 1966), 765–90; "Kant with Sade," trans. James B. Swenson Jr., *October* 51 (1989): 55–75.

32. Lacan, *Écrits*, 790. It is worth noting that, as far back as 1933, because of his interest in Sade, Klossowski had been dismissed from his position as secretary to the psychoanalyst René Laforgue. See Alain Arnaud, *Pierre Klossowski* (Paris: Seuil, 1990), 186.

33. Blanchot, *Lautréamont et Sade*, 36; *Lautréamont and Sade*, 28; translation modified.

34. Blanchot, *Lautréamont et Sade*, 45; *Lautréamont and Sade*, 38.

35. Blanchot, *Lautréamont et Sade*, 48–49; *Lautréamont and Sade*, 41; translation modified. This is the argument which Bataille is invoking in the passage from *L'Érotisme* cited earlier, to which he gives an anthropological twist of his own.

36. Novalis, *Werke*, 323; author's emphasis. The aphorism was first published in the opening issue of *Athenaeum* in 1798. On this secret convergence between Sade and Novalis on the *apathie* of the subject, see Blanchot, *L'Écriture du désastre*, 18; *The Writing of the Disaster*, 8.

37. See Alexandre Kojève, *Introduction à la lecture de Hegel*, ed. Raymond Queneau, 2nd ed. (Paris: Gallimard, [1947] 1968). Unlike Bataille, Blanchot did not attend the seminar, but there is little doubt that discussion of Hegel's work figured importantly in the almost daily conversations Blanchot reports the pair had during the Occupation.

38. Sade, *Œuvres*, II, 587.

39. See Blanchot, *L'Écriture du désastre*, 161; *The Writing of the Disaster*, 103–4. Blanchot explains: "The terms good and bad infinity, which we owe to Hegel, makes one wonder, by their very use of the adjectives 'good' and 'bad.' Bad infinity—the *etcetera* of the finite—is needed by the understanding (which in itself is in no sense bad) which freezes, fixes, immobilises one of its moments, whereas the truth of reason suppresses the finite: infinity, or the finite suppressed, 'sublated' ['*relevé*'], is deemed 'positive' to the extent that it reintroduces the qualitative and reconciles quality with quantum. But what, then, of bad infinity? Having been consigned to repetition without return [*le répétitif sans*

retour], does it not clash with the Hegelian system in the manner of a disaster [*désastre*]? This would suggest that, were infinity to be decided upon as that which is given first, only subsequently giving rise to the finite, then this immediate infinity would disturb the whole system, albeit in the manner Hegel always rejected in advance, with his ironic comments on the infinity of the night"; translation modified. It is not difficult to recognise here a variation on Blanchot's description of the other night [*l'autre nuit*] that is such a key feature of "The Gaze of Orpheus" from *L'Espace littéraire*.

40. See for instance Sade, *Œuvres*, III, 156. On Sadian *apathie*, see Klossowski, *Sade mon prochain* (1967 text), 37–49; *Sade My Neighbor*, 28–38. *Apathie* is also the main point of reference of Blanchot's remarks on Sade in *L'Écriture du désastre* and *La Communauté inavouable*, where it functions as an extenuation of the subject as such.

41. Blanchot, *Lautréamont et Sade*, 43; *Lautréamont and Sade*, 35; translation modified.

42. Blanchot, *L'Écriture du désastre*, 102; *The Writing of the Disaster*, 62; translation modified.

43. See Barthes, *Œuvres complètes*, III, 699–868. For an overview of Barthes's writings on Sade, see Philippe Roger, "Traitement de faveur (Barthes lecteur de Sade)," *Nottingham French Studies* 36, no. 1 (1997): 34–44. During the 1960s and 1970s (and since), a number of other writers and critics associated with the journal *Tel Quel* were also actively involved, in the words of a 1968 article by Marcelin Pleynet, in making "Sade readable [*Sade lisible*]"; see Marcelin Pleynet, *Art et littérature* (Paris: Seuil, 1977), 147–60; *The Tel Quel Reader*, 109–22. Sollers too is another who has written extensively and repeatedly on Sade; see Sollers, *Logiques*, 78–96; *La Guerre du goût* (Paris: Gallimard, 1996), passim; *Sade contre l'Être suprême* (Paris: Gallimard, 1996); and *Éloge de l'infini* (Paris: Gallimard, 2003), passim. I should note here the violent antipathy displayed by Sollers (and other members of the ex–*Tel Quel* group) towards Blanchot, who is rather oddly accused in *Sade contre l'Être suprême* (13) of treating Sade as a "negative theologian." Even more bizarrely, in *La Guerre du goût* (10) and again in *Éloge de l'infini* (1056), Sollers goes on to attack Blanchot (admittedly alongside Breton, Sartre, Lacan, Barthes, Foucault, Althusser, Derrida, Deleuze, and Guy Debord) for a failure to read . . . Heidegger's *Nietzsche!* The charge is not only demonstrably false (as any reader of *L'Entretien infini* can verify); it is also part of a concerted strategy on the part of Sollers and others to discredit Blanchot (in particular, by casting doubt on his friendship with Bataille) on the more than questionable grounds that Blanchot is a nihilist. Not for the first time, one suspects, the accusation makes more plausible sense when applied to its originator. For a broader contextualisation of *Tel Quel*'s strategy with regard to Sade, see ffrench, *The Time of Theory*, passim.

44. On the special status of Sade for Barthes, see the letter to Philippe Roger published in 1976 as a review of the latter's *Sade: La Philosophie dans le pressoir* (Paris: Grasset, 1976), in Barthes, *Œuvres complètes*, IV, 942–43. "Sade," writes Barthes, "is not a writer like any other, and yet he is a writer—perhaps the writer as such [*peut-être l'écrivain même*], since he disregards all law (whether philosophical or political, as you show), except precisely for the law, which is both very secret and very self-evident (the purloined letter again), of the Sentence: and what Sentences!" Earlier in the letter, perhaps surprisingly, Barthes argues that, like Brecht, Sade is one of those "very rare" authors who limit criticism's constitutive freedom by imposing on the critic the requirement to be "just [*juste:* fair, fitting]." "What is unbending [*ne peut être fléchi* in Sade," says Barthes, "is that he wishes to show something, and does so obstinately. What is this? A virtue: the virtue of fantasy [*la vertu du fantasme*]." Psychoanalytical language aside, it is apparent how much this formulation owes to Blanchot. However, in a interview with Jean-Jacques Brochier given the same month (in *Œuvres complètes*, IV, 1003–7), in which he acknowledges the status of Sade as a "kind of absolute writer [*une sorte d'écrivain absolu*]" for a critical tradition running from Léon Bloy, through Apollinaire and Klossowski, to Bataille and *Tel Quel*, Barthes is noticeably reluctant to confirm any debt he might have contracted towards Blanchot, in what is no doubt another instance of Barthes's ambivalence.

45. See Barthes, *Œuvres complètes*, III, 850; *Sade, Fourier, Loyola*, 171; original emphasis; translation modified. Richard Miller unfortunately translates *délicatesse* here as "tact." *Délicatesse*, however, is a more sensual, affirmative quality, less to do with observing proprieties than with respecting perversity. Barthes further glosses the idea of *délicatesse* in two interviews from the same period: see Barthes, *Œuvres complètes*, III, 1000; IV, 211–12. He returns to it again in the 1977–78 Collège de France lecture series as a key figure of the *Neutre*, taking the quotation from Sade used in *Sade, Fourier, Loyola* as his starting point, but going on to analyse the stylisation of the Japanese tea ceremony, the haiku, and related cultural practices; see Barthes, *Le Neutre*, 58–66; *The Neutral*, 29–36 (where it is again translated as "tact").

46. Barthes, *Le Neutre*, 58; *The Neutral*, 29; translation modified.

47. See Barthes, *Œuvres complètes*, III, 845–46; *Sade, Fourier, Loyola*, 166; original emphasis; translation modified.

48. On Barthesian utopia, and some of the difficulties it raises, see Knight, *Barthes and Utopia: Space, Travel, Writing*.

49. Sade, *Œuvres*, II, 587.

50. Blanchot, *L'Écriture du désastre*, 77; *The Writing of the Disaster*, 45; original emphasis; translation modified.

51. Blanchot, *L'Entretien infini*, 192; *The Infinite Conversation*, 130; translation modified.

52. See Robert Antelme, *L'Espèce humaine* (Paris: Gallimard, [1947] 1957); *The Human Race*, trans. Jeffery Haight and Annie Mahler (Marlboro, VT: Marlboro Press, 1992). Blanchot's first mention of Antelme's memoir, separating the two major phases of Blanchot's engagement with Sade, comes in a note signalling its re-publication appended to the essay "L'Expérience de Simone Weil," in *La Nouvelle Nouvelle Revue française* 56 (August 1957): 297–310 (306), reprinted in *L'Entretien infini*, 175; *The Infinite Conversation*, 446–47.

53. See Blanchot, *L'Entretien infini*, 196; *The Infinite Conversation*, 133. I am reminded here of a remark by the novelist and critic Roger Laporte. There were only two books, says Laporte, a voracious reader, that he found impossible to read to the very end: Antelme's memoir and Sade's *Les Cent Vingt Journées de Sodome;* see Roger Laporte, "L'Interruption—l'interminable," *Lignes* 21 (January 1994): 152–53.

54. Blanchot's essay was first published under the title "L'Inconvenance majeure" ("Irreducible Impropriety"), as a preface to a reprint of Sade's pamphlet in J.-J. Pauvert's *Libertés* series, dedicated to "campaigning literature [*littérature de combat*] of all times and all tendencies," and edited by the journalist and polemicist Jean-François Revel, who, in 1961, following the lead of Blanchot and others, had been a signatory of the *Manifeste des 121*, protesting at France's continuing war in Algeria. Blanchot's essay reappeared almost immediately as "Français, encore un effort . . . " ("Citizens of France, Try Harder . . . "), in *La Nouvelle Revue française* 154 (October 1965), 600–618. It was published for a third time under the heading "L'Insurrection, la folie d'écrire," in *L'Entretien infini* (323–42) ("Insurrection, the Madness of Writing," in *The Infinite Conversation*, 217–29). These shifting titles are not without significance; they frame and reframe the text according to different political circumstances.

55. Blanchot, *L'Entretien infini*, 336–37; *The Infinite Conversation*, 226; translation modified. For a commentary on this passage that intersects with my own, see Thomas Keenan, *Fables of Responsibility* (Stanford: Stanford University Press, 1997), 70–96. It is worth noting that the expression "drive to speak [*pulsion parlante*]" that Blanchot uses in this passage, which first appeared two months after his essay on the *Athenaeum* mentioned earlier, is a direct borrowing from Novalis's famous short text "Monolog," in Novalis, *Werke*, 426–27. Readers of Blanchot's *L'Instant de ma mort* will recognise the expression, this "forever impending instant [*cet instant, toujours en instance*]," of which this is probably the first occurrence in Blanchot, and which returns, to powerful effect, in Blanchot's testamentary narrative; see *L'Instant de ma mort*, 18; *The Instant of My Death*, 11; translation modified.

56. See Blanchot, letter to Raymond Bellour, *L'Herne*, 1966, special issue on Henri Michaux, 88; original emphasis. The article itself, on Borges and Michaux, and entitled "L'Infini et l'infini," first appeared in *La Nouvelle Nouvelle*

Revue française for January 1958. For a recent assessment of Céline's politics, see Nicholas Hewitt, *The Life of Céline* (Oxford: Blackwell, 1999). A year earlier, in January 1965, Barthes replied to a survey in *Le Nouvel Observateur* regarding Céline's status in rather different terms. "Céline," he wrote, "belongs to everybody. He made mistakes only because he viewed reality through literary spectacles. He was in the process of transforming reality with his language. Many writers are in his debt. Starting with Sartre. Sartre's writing, or, if you will, his 'verbalised vision,' beats to the same sort of pulse as Céline's. Céline's work seems to me at any rate less dubious, more healthy than that of a Claudel. But what does commitment [*l'engagement*] amount to these days? During the Algerian war, it was not out of the question for writers to commit themselves publicly to the hilt, and at exactly the same time write entirely uncommitted works"; see Barthes, *Œuvres complètes*, V, 1024. Claudel, of course, was France's most prominent Catholic playwright and poet, and a career diplomat to boot. As for those writers who opposed the Algerian War, to the point of risking jail by signing a petition supporting French conscripts who refused the draft (a petition Barthes for his part failed or refused to sign), and who wrote notoriously disengaged works, there was in reality only one prominent candidate, whom Barthes clearly had in mind: Blanchot. One may deduce from this that, at times, the difference (or *différend*) between Barthes's Neuter and that of Blanchot could become sharpened to the point of radical incompatibility. The reasons why Barthes refused to sign the *Manifeste des 121* are not entirely clear. A partial account is given in Calvet, *Roland Barthes 1915–1980*, 168–69; further detail may be found in Christophe Bident, *Maurice Blanchot: partenaire invisible* (Seyssel: Champ Vallon, 1998).

57. For the epigraph, see Blanchot, *Le Livre à venir*, 270; *The Book to Come*, 222; translation modified. Some years later, Blanchot brought together his four essays on Michaux in *Henri Michaux ou le refus de l'enfermement* (Tours: Farrago, 1999).

58. See Maurice Larkin, *France since the Popular Front*, 2nd ed. (Oxford: Oxford University Press, 1997), 300.

59. Blanchot, *L'Entretien infini*, 330; *The Infinite Conversation*, 222; translation modified.

60. Blanchot, "Français, encore un effort . . . ," *La Nouvelle Revue française* 154 (October 1965): 600; the note was excised from the version given in *L'Entretien infini*. There was no doubt also a subtext to this remark. It amounted in part to a plea in favour of the publisher Jean-Jacques Pauvert, who had been taken to court in 1957 for bringing out a pioneering edition of Sade's complete works, which remained largely under embargo. It also served to draw the reader's attention to Blanchot's own unambiguous, if oblique, intervention into the unfolding election campaign, which de Gaulle was to win only on a second ballot. This was in any case not the first time Blanchot had discreetly used *La Nouvelle Revue française* as something akin to a political platform. (It should be remembered that

Jean Paulhan, the journal's influential editor, was a supporter of de Gaulle.) He had done the same to express his opposition to de Gaulle's return to power as "un homme épisodique," or man of providence, in a postscript to the article "Passage de la ligne" in *La Nouvelle Nouvelle Revue française* 69 (September 1958): 479, in which he replied to an unsigned opinion piece published in the journal the previous month (*La Nouvelle Nouvelle Revue française* 68 [August 1958]: 346), in which Paulhan asked: "What, in 1940, could one hold against Drieu La Rochelle [the Fascist novelist and polemicist who became the collaborationist editor of the journal under the Occupation], who was otherwise so sophisticated, so ardent? That he was too ready to despair of France. Despair has changed sides. Today, its name is Sartre, Domenach, Nadeau [all prominent left-wing intellectuals opposed to de Gaulle]?"

61. Blanchot, *L'Entretien infini*, vii; *The Infinite Conversation*, xii; translation modified.

62. On Blanchot's revisions for *L'Entretien infini*, see my *Blanchot: Extreme Contemporary*, 127–42.

63. For more detail on the relationship between the two texts, see my "Weary Words," in *Clandestine Encounters*, ed. Kevin Hart, forthcoming.

64. Blanchot, *L'Entretien infini*, 596; *The Infinite Conversation*, 406; translation modified.

65. See Blanchot, *L'Entretien infini*, 596; *The Infinite Conversation*, 406.

66. In a piece published in *Comité*, the *samizdat* magazine that brought together many of the texts circulated in the course of the summer by the Comité d'action écrivains-étudiants [Writers-Students Action Committee], the majority of which, it later transpired, were written by Blanchot, the writer commented on the absence of books about May 68 as follows: "In May, there were no books about May: not because time was lacking or because it was more urgent to 'do something,' but because of an unforeseen difficulty that was more decisive; things were being written elsewhere, in a world without publishing, things were being disseminated in the confrontation with the police and, in a sense, with their help, violence facing up to violence. This pausing of the book [*cet arrêt du livre*] which was also a pausing of history [*de l'histoire:* history and narrative] and which, far from leading us back prior to culture, points somewhere far beyond culture: that is what above all else provoked the authorities, the powers-that-be, the law. Let this missive itself [*ce bulletin*] prolong the pause [*prolonge cet arrêt*], even while preventing it from stopping [*tout en l'empêchant de s'arrêter*]. No more books, no more books ever [*Plus de livre, plus jamais de livre*], so long as we remain in relation with the upheaval of the breach [*en rapport avec l'ébranlement de la rupture*]." See Blanchot, *Écrits politiques 1958–1993* (Paris: Léo Scheer, 2003), 119–20. Readers should not be surprised to find here echoes of some of Blanchot's best-known literary narratives, notably *L'Arrêt de mort* (*Death Sentence*) and *La Folie du jour* (*The Madness of the Day*).

67. See Blanchot, *L'Entretien infini*, vii–viii; *The Infinite Conversation*, xii; translation modified. The "Entretien sur un changement d'époque" ("On a Change of Epoch") that closes the second section of *L'Entretien infini* (394–418) (*The Infinite Conversation*, 264–81) first appeared in an earlier form in *La Nouvelle Revue française* 88 (April 1960): 724–34. On this motif of a change of epoch, see my *A Change of Epoch: Blanchot, Writing, the Fragmentary*, forthcoming.

68. Blanchot, *Écrits politiques 1958–1993*, 100.

69. Blanchot, letter to Dominique Aury, 7 October 1968. Blanchot concluded by underlining the discreet, private nature of his decision. The date marked the end of an era in more ways than one. Two days later, Jean Paulhan, the long-standing editor of *La Nouvelle Revue française*, who admittedly, for reasons both of ill health and disenchantment, had had little to do with the journal from 1965, was dead. Blanchot's letter, together with other unpublished correspondence with Aury, is quoted by Angie David, *Dominique Aury* (Paris: Léo Scheer, 2006), 378. Blanchot and his correspondent (who had enjoyed a long-standing love affair with Paulhan) were close friends from long ago. They had worked together in the mid-1930s as reviewers for *L'Insurgé*, the short-lived extreme nationalist-syndicalist weekly broadsheet launched in 1937 by the critic and polemicist, Thierry Maulnier, a close associate of Blanchot's at the time, and with whom Aury from 1933 onwards, according to her biographer, was "madly in love" (203). There was another reason too. Blanchot and Aury almost shared a birthday. Blanchot was born 22 September 1907, Anne Desclos (as Aury then was) one day later.

70. On Blanchot's *Le Dernier Homme*, see my *Bataille, Klossowski, Blanchot: Writing at the Limit*, 226–55.

71. Together with the text of "Le Refus," these two essays on Kafka were later republished side by side. See Blanchot, *L'Amitié*, 130–31, 285–325; *Friendship*, 111–12, 252–88.

72. Maurice Blanchot, *L'Amitié*, 321; *Friendship*, 284; translation modified. As though to reinforce the point, Blanchot's essay does not cease with these (final) words; two unusual, and unusually long footnotes extend the text for four more pages, before these give way to the book's concluding memorial tribute to Bataille. Already in 1964, in the essay "La Voix narrative [The Narrative Voice]" (in *L'Entretien infini*, 556–67; *The Infinite Conversation*, 379–87), an unattributed passage from Kafka's *Das Schloß* (*The Castle*) had allowed Blanchot to explore the perverse logic of the limitlessness of the limit, as I show in my *Bataille, Klossowski, Blanchot: Writing at the Limit*, 219–26.

73. The text inserted by Gallimard into *Faux Pas* in December 1943, which is more than likely to have been written by Blanchot himself, concludes as follows: "Each and every book of some significance conceals a secret that makes it better than what it may be [*supérieur à ce qu'il peut être*]. This secret is what every

critic aims to approach but always misses, distracted by the need to inform readers of books about to appear. The critic advances, but goes nowhere, and remains rooted to the spot. And if the journey sometimes reaches its goal, it does so only by taking a false step [*un faux pas*]." At the other end of his writing life, remembering his friendship with Dionys Mascolo, who was given the task, it seems, of bringing together (physically) the essays published in *Faux Pas*, he made a similar point. See Blanchot, *Pour l'amitié* (Paris: Farrago, [1996] 2000), 10; "For Friendship," trans. Leslie Hill, *Oxford Literary Review* 22 (2000): 26.

74. For the epigraph from Hölderlin, which is taken from the poem "Germanien," see Blanchot, *La Part du feu*, 7; *The Work of Fire*, xi. Blanchot comments in more detail on the implications of Hölderlin's words later in the book as part of his sustained *Auseinandersetzung* with Heidegger; see *La Part du feu*, 129–31; *The Work of Fire*, 127–29. On Blanchot's reading of Heidegger's Hölderlin commentaries, see my *Blanchot: Extreme Contemporary*, 77–91. The phrase *zwischen Tag und Nacht* is rendered idiomatically in Blanchot's text as "entre chien et loup"; it is apparent from early printings of *Le Très-Haut*, published shortly before, that the original title of the forthcoming collection was based on the same expression: *Entre chiens et loups*.

75. Blanchot, *L'Écriture du désastre*, 216–17; *The Writing of the Disaster*, 143; translation modified.

76. Blanchot, "N'oubliez pas!," *La Quinzaine littéraire* 459 (16–31 March 1986): 11–12; "Do Not Forget!" trans. Leslie Hill, *Paragraph* 30, no. 3 (November 2007): 34–37.

77. On Blanchot's criticisms of the anti-semitism of sections of the extreme left after May, which he concedes was in some cases unwitting, see the 1969 letter cited by Emmanuel Levinas in *Du sacré au saint* (Paris: Minuit, 1977), 48–49; *Nine Talmudic Readings*, trans. Annette Aronowicz (Bloomington: Indiana University Press, 1990), 115–16.

78. Blanchot, *L'Écriture du désastre*, 132; *The Writing of the Disaster*, 83. See Hermann Langbein, *Menschen in Auschwitz* (Vienna: Europaverlag, [1972] 1989), 150–57; *People in Auschwitz*, trans. Harry Zohn (Chapel Hill: University of North Carolina Press, 2004), 125–32. Blanchot himself was drawing on the abridged French version of the book, *Hommes et femmes à Auschwitz*, trans. Denise Meunier, ed. Jacques Branchu (Paris: Fayard, 1974). "Football, boxing matches, Zarah Leander [a contemporary Swedish film star with a significant following in Nazi Germany] behind electrified barbed wire fences," writes Langbein, "Beethoven concerts put on by prisoners for the benefit of other prisoners in the extermination camp—it is entirely possible that, reading this, some will find it hard to comprehend that victims were willing to listen to music and watch movies in Auschwitz. Whoever thinks that wrong would logically have to criticise inmates for not committing suicide. The instinct for survival makes you seek distraction

wherever you can." Langbein adds, however, a rider which, ever so slightly re-phrasing it, Blanchot makes his own: "To be sure, for the grey mass of pariahs there was neither cinema nor sport nor concerts" (157; 132; translation modified). This failure of art—narrative—to respond adequately to Auschwitz raises the vast question of the nature and reach of Blanchot's own thinking of the Shoah in such texts as *L'Écriture du désastre*. I discuss what is at stake in more detail in *A Change of Epoch: Blanchot, Writing, the Fragmentary*, forthcoming.

79. See Blanchot, *Après coup, précédé par Le Ressassement éternel*, 99; *The Station Hill Blanchot Reader*, 495. On the "voix narrative" or narrating voice, see Blanchot, *L'Entretien infini*, 556–67; *The Infinite Conversation*, 379–87; and my *Bataille, Klossowski, Blanchot: Writing at the Limit*, 219–26.

80. Blanchot, *Le Pas au-delà*, 94; *The Step Not Beyond*, 66; translation modified.

81. Blanchot, "Le Dernier à parler," *La Revue de Belles-Lettres* 96 no. 2–3 (1972): 171–83 (171); *A Voice from Elsewhere*, 55–93 (55; original emphasis; transla-tion modified). I examine Blanchot's essay in a slightly different context in my "'Distrust of Poetry': Levinas, Blanchot, Celan," *MLN* 120, no. 5 (Winter 2005): 986–1008. In its original French, the essay has been reprinted three times: first, in 1984, in a single volume by Fata morgana, using the 1972 text, but incorporat-ing a number of typographical and other errors in the quotations from Celan; second, in 1986, again by Fata morgana, in a corrected version (subtitled *édition définitive, corrigée*) checked for accuracy against Celan's 1983 *Gesammelte Werke* (but incorporating a number of new errors); and thirdly, in the collection *Une voix venue d'ailleurs* (Paris: Gallimard, folio, 2002), 71–107, this most recent ver-sion being based on the 1984 Fata morgana text. Admittedly, from one version to the other, Blanchot's own text remains unchanged; what does alter, however, is the accuracy (more specifically, the page layout) of the numerous quotations from Celan. In what follows, for convenience, reference will be made to the 2002 text. It is worth noting in passing that in 1996, following the publication by Fata morgana of a book by the fascist ideologue Alain de Benoist, Blanchot broke off all relations with the press; after some litigation, rights for the texts concerned were transferred to Gallimard. On the dispute, see Blanchot's open letter to Bruno Roy, the proprietor of Fata morgana, published in *La Quinzaine littéraire*, 1–15 November 1996, 5. Blanchot's opening quotation from Celan is from the collection *Atemwende* (1967), and reads: "Niemand / zeugt für den / Zeugen"; see Paul Celan, *Gesammelte Werke*, ed. Beda Allemann and Stefan Re-ichert in collaboration with Rudolf Bücher, 7 vols. (Frankfurt: Suhrkamp, [1983] 2000), II, 72; *Selected Poems and Prose of Paul Celan*, trans. John Felstiner (Lon-don: W. W. Norton, 2001), 261. It may be remembered that Derrida also draws on this enigmatic, densely overdetermined quotation in his reading of Celan in *Schibboleth* (Paris: Galilée, 1986), 60–62; *Sovereignties in Question: The Poetics of*

Paul Celan, ed. Thomas Dutoit and Outi Pasanen (New York: Fordham University Press, 2005), 32–33; and comments on it further in *Poétique et politique du témoignage* (Paris: L'Herne, 2005); *Sovereignties in Question*, 65–96. The context of Blanchot's quotation from Plato's Socrates, from the *Apology* 29b, is not unimportant, serving as it does to pay tribute to Celan in his moment of dying, and thus place the possibility or impossibility of death at the core of both literature and philosophy. For in his submission to the court, Socrates points out that what makes a life worth living is not the fear of death but whether or not one does one's duty. Socrates defends himself against the charge of corrupting Athenian youth by maintaining that his duty as a philosopher is to do right by philosophy whatever the consequences, even though this may make his own death inevitable. Shortly after Celan's death, Henri Michaux, some of whose work Celan had translated into German, remembered him in a brief poem published in *Études germaniques* 25, no. 3 (July–September 1970): 250, where he wrote: "He took his leave. He chose to, was still able to do so . . . [*Il s'en est allé. Choisir, il pouvait encore choisir* . . .]." When Blanchot's essay on Celan was brought together with other later texts in *Une voix venue d'ailleurs* in 2002, the collection also reprinted "La Bête de Lascaux [The Beast of Lascaux]," Blanchot's much earlier 1953 essay on René Char (whom Celan had also translated). It too included various references to Socrates. Blanchot concluded his discussion of the voice of poetry in Plato as follows: "Strange wisdom: too ancient for Socrates but also too new, from which, despite the uneasiness that made him spurn it, it must nevertheless be assumed Socrates was not excluded either, Socrates who accepted the only guarantee for speech was the living presence of a human being and yet went as far as to die in order to keep his word." See Blanchot, *Une voix venue d'ailleurs*, 67; "The Beast of Lascaux," trans. Leslie Hill, *Oxford Literary Review* 22 (2000): 38; *A Voice from Elsewhere*, 51.

82. Celan, *Gesammelte Werke*, I, 135; Blanchot, *Une voix venue d'ailleurs*, 103; *A Voice from Elsewhere*, 89. Felstiner, in *Selected Poems and Prose of Paul Celan*, 77, translates: "Speak you too / speak as the last / say out your say." An earlier French translation by Jean-Claude Schneider, with which Blanchot was probably familiar, published in *La Nouvelle Revue française* 168 (December 1966): 1012–13, offers this clumsy alternative: "Énonce toi aussi / énonce, le dernier, / ton verdict."

83. See Beda Allemann, "Nachwort," in Celan, *Ausgewählte Gedichte* (Frankfurt: Suhrkamp, 1968), 151–63. What Allemann says about the poem (and Celan's work in general) might almost have been written with Blanchot in mind: "To the not-yet-decisiveness [*Noch-nicht-Entschiedenheit*]," Allemann writes, "that hesitates in the face of the fundamental decision between Yes and No, there corresponds a no-longer-decisiveness [*eine Nicht-mehr-Entschiedenheit*] that has moved beyond each and every conceivable contradiction, without however disowning any. In this way Celan's poetry is able to explore unreservedly the paradoxes of its

own language. It does not founder on them, for its indecision [*Unentschiedenheit*] in respect of any unambiguous 'statements' (whether affirmative or negative ones) makes it aware of its own form of purely poetical decisiveness [*Entschieden-heit*]" (152–53). On the initial context of the poem, written in response to a hostile review of Celan's work by the influential critic Hans Egon Holthusen in the journal *Merkur*, see John Felstiner, *Paul Celan: Poet, Survivor, Jew* (New Haven: Yale University Press, 1995), 78–81. "What happens here, with the fighting, drinking, and making of wreaths," Holthusen had written, referring to Celan's early poem "Ein Lied in der Wüste [A Song in the Wilderness]," systematically overlooking in the process the poem's biblical references, "is not to be taken 'literally,' but as a metaphorical, or, better, symbolic, ceremonial operation which is meant to represent certain basic impulses and emotions. We do have to say, however, in another sense, that these procedures are to be taken utterly and entirely 'literally': as a pure play of language, concerned only with itself. When everything becomes metaphor, it no longer seems permissible to look for the 'meaning' [*Sinn*] of the poem, as it were, *behind* the metaphors." See Hans Egon Holthusen, "Fünf Junge Lyriker," *Merkur* 8, no. 3 (March 1954): 284–94; and 8, no. 4 (April 1954): 378–90 (386–87). What Celan sought to challenge in this reading was the simplistic assumption that meaning could be located in univocal manner somewhere behind the poem, rather than within it, and the implication that, if such meaning was not readily available to the reader, this could only be because the poem had nothing to say and wanted merely to explore its own quasi-musical verbal textures.

    84. Blanchot, *L'Amitié*, 327; *Friendship*, 289; translation modified.

    85. Blanchot, *L'Amitié*, 327; *Friendship*, 289; translation modified.

    86. See Blanchot, *Une voix venue d'ailleurs*, 30; *A Voice from Elsewhere*, 16; translation modified. On Blanchot's reading of Des Forêts in this context, see my "D'un nihilisme presque infini," in *Maurice Blanchot: récits critiques*, ed. Bident and Vilar, 249–65.

    87. On this motif of *le mourir* in Celan, see Blanchot, *Une voix venue d'ailleurs*, 99; *A Voice from Elsewhere*, 85.

    88. Celan, *Gesammelte Werke*, I, 197; *Selected Poems and Prose of Paul Celan*, 119; Blanchot, *Une voix venue d'ailleurs*, 74; *A Voice from Elsewhere*, 58.

    89. See Emmanuel Levinas, *Autrement qu'être ou au-delà de l'essence* (Paris: Le Livre de poche, [1974] 1990), 156–205 (156); *Otherwise than Being, or, Beyond Essence*, trans. Alphonso Lingis (The Hague: Nijhoff, 1981), 99–129 (99); Celan, *Gesammelte Werke*, I, 33.

    90. Levinas, *Autrement qu'être ou au-delà de l'essence*, 200; *Otherwise than Being*, 126; original emphasis; translation modified.

    91. This silent presence of Celan's poems in Blanchot's writing is not a feature exclusive to "Le Dernier à parler." It may also be observed in other texts of

the same period, notably in several fragments from *Le Pas au-delà*, which I have discussed elsewhere. See Leslie Hill, "De seuil en seuil," *Maurice Blanchot, la singularité d'une écriture*, ed. Arthur Cools, Nausicaa Dewez, Christophe Halsberghe, and Michel Lisse, *Les Lettres romanes*, hors série (2005): 205–16.

92. Celan, *Gesammelte Werke*, I, 135; Blanchot, *Une voix venue d'ailleurs*, 102–3; *A Voice from Elsewhere*, 88–90. Felstiner gives: "Speak — / But don't split off No from Yes. / Give your say this meaning too: / give it the shadow. // Give it shadow enough, / give it as much / as you see spread round you from / midnight to midday and midnight" (*Selected Poems and Prose of Paul Celan*, 77). Allemann, in his afterword, cited above (157), suggests that the more likely primary meaning of *Sinn* is "direction" (rather than "sense"). French *sens*, like the German, can maintain both possibilities without deciding between them.

93. Blanchot, *Le Livre à venir*, 270; *The Book to Come*, 222. Coincidently, earlier in 1984 and for the first and only time, Michaux's and Blanchot's names had appeared within the covers of the same book: Vadim Kozovoï's *Hors de la colline*, trans. by the author, in collaboration with Michel Deguy and Jacques Dupin (Paris: Hermann, 1984), for which Michaux supplied the artwork, and Blanchot an afterword entitled "La Parole ascendante, ou: Sommes-nous encore dignes de la poésie? (notes éparses)."

94. For Celan's translations from Michaux, see Celan, *Gesammelte Werke*, IV, 598–712; the poem published in *L'Herne* is reproduced in *Gesammelte Werke*, III, 135. On Michaux's personal dealings with Celan, see Paul Celan and Gisèle Celan-Lestrange, *Correspondance*, ed. Bertrand Badiou and Eric Celan, 2 vols. (Paris, Seuil, 2001), passim; and Henri Michaux, *Œuvres complètes*, ed. Raymond Bellour with Ysé Tran, 3 vols. (Paris: Gallimard, 1998–2004), II, xlix–l; III, xvi–xviii, xxii, xxx–xxxii, xxxiii–iv, xxxix, xliv. Michaux had personal contacts in French psychiatric circles and sought to be of assistance to Celan in finding appropriate treatment for the severe bouts of depression from which he suffered increasingly during the years before his death.

95. This reference to the invisible can be explained in at least two ways. First, it was because Michaux, like Blanchot, was profoundly allergic to the idea of being photographed or otherwise represented and insisted on remaining the anonymous, unseen author of his texts or paintings. But why was Michaux's invisibility different from that associated with Celan? *L'Écriture du désastre* supplies an answer, that had to do with the manner of Celan's death. "To kill oneself," Blanchot wrote, ostensibly in the margins of a famous passage from Novalis, but also, more pertinently, in memory of Celan, "is to put oneself in a space to which nobody is allowed access [*interdit à tous*], including oneself: the *clandestine*, *non-phenomenal* character of relations between humans is the essence of 'suicide,' which is always hidden, not so much because it involves death [*la mort y est en jeu*] than because dying [*mourir*]—passivity itself—is thereby turned into action

and shown in the very act of receding beyond phenomena [*hors phénomène*]. Whoever is tempted by suicide is tempted by the invisible, this faceless secret." Blanchot, *L'Écriture du désastre*, 56; *The Writing of the Disaster*, 32; original emphasis; translation modified.

96. Michaux's text in memory of Celan is entitled "The Days, the Day, the End of Days [Les Jours, le jour, la fin des jours]" and appears in *La Revue de Belles-Lettres* 96, no. 2–3 (1972): 113. In reproducing Michaux's conclusion as he does, Blanchot forces the poet's syntax. Michaux had originally written: "Je vois des hommes immobiles / couchés dans des chalands // Partir . . . [I see motionless men / lying in barges // Departing . . .]." For an overview of Celan's dealings with Michaux that also translates Michaux's 1972 homage, see Bernhard Böschenstein, "Paul Celan and French Poetry," trans. Joel Golb, *ACTS: A Journal of New Writing* 8–9 (1988): 181–98.

97. Celan, *Gesammelte Werke*, I, 168; Celan, *Poems*, trans. Michael Hamburger (Manchester: Carcanet, 1980), 107; Blanchot, *Une voix venue d'ailleurs*, 97; *A Voice from Elsewhere*, 83.

98. The point is powerfully made by Peter Szondi in an important article on Celan that Blanchot (a member of the advisory committee of the journal in which it first appeared) is almost certain to have read before completing his own; see Peter Szondi, "Lecture de Strette: essai sur la poésie de Paul Celan," *Critique* 288 (May 1971): 387–420 (387–89 and 419).

99. Blanchot, *Une voix venue d'ailleurs*, 87; *A Voice from Elsewhere*, 71, translation modified; compare Celan, *Gesammelte Werke*, I, 168; *Paul Celan: Poems*, trans. Michael Hamburger, 107.

100. Blanchot, *Une voix venue d'ailleurs*, 89–91; *A Voice from Elsewhere*, 75–77; translation modified; compare Celan, *Gesammelte Werke*, I, 167; *Selected Poems and Prose of Paul Celan*, 107; translation modified. "Between silence and silence," says a later fragment of Blanchot's, "an exchange of words—an innocent murmur [*parole échangée—murmure innocent*]." See Blanchot, *Le Pas au-delà*, 93; *The Step Not Beyond*, 66; translation modified.

101. Celan, *Gesammelte Werke*, III, 196; *Selected Poems and Prose of Paul Celan*, 408; translation modified.

102. Celan, *Gesammelte Werke*, III, 196; *Selected Poems and Prose of Paul Celan*, 408.

103. Celan, *Gesammelte Werke*, II, 36. Blanchot translates: "Reste (résidu) chantable," *Une voix venue d'ailleurs*, 93; *A Voice from Elsewhere*, 79.

104. Celan, *Gesammelte Werke*, III, 197; *Selected Poems and Prose of Paul Celan*, 409; translation modified.

105. Celan, *Gesammelte Werke*, III, 186; *Selected Poems and Prose of Paul Celan*, 396, translation modified; Blanchot, *Une voix venue d'ailleurs*, 101; *A Voice from Elsewhere*, 89.

106. Celan, *Gesammelte Werke*, III, 198; *Selected Poems and Prose of Paul Celan*, 409; translation modified.

107. Celan, *Gesammelte Werke*, III, 198; *Selected Poems and Prose of Paul Celan*, 409; translation modified.

108. It may be wondered how far Celan, in making this claim, was himself familiar with Blanchot's writing. It is hard to believe that, living in Paris from 1948, Celan had not encountered at least some of Blanchot's regular essays in *Critique* or *La Nouvelle Revue française*. Esther Cameron, who visited the poet in Paris in August 1969, reports that Celan recommended Blanchot's writings to her, as well as those of Michaux. See "Erinnerungen an Paul Celan," in *Paul Celan*, ed. Werner Hamacher and Winfried Menninghaus (Frankfurt: Suhrkamp, 1988), 339. There were no doubt other convergences too. Celan, it seems, just like Blanchot, read Kafka's diaries with an acute awareness of the talismanic relevance of certain dates for his own life; and one of Celan's first major book purchases, in May 1948, in Vienna, shortly before his migration to Paris, was a complete seventeen-volume set of the collected works of Jean Paul, as Andréa Lauterwein reports in her *Paul Celan* (Paris: Belin, 2005), 15, 17. And there are at least two places in Celan's writing where Blanchot's name is mentioned explicitly. It does so first in a series of unpublished notes from the mid-1950s, apparently in relation to an anthology of French poetic writing that Celan was considering editing at the time, but subsequently abandoned. Celan's note, underlined once, then twice, is enigmatic, yet somehow heavy with the futurity of a possible or impossible encounter. It reads: *"Blanchot: weil: [Blanchot: because:],"* and is followed almost immediately after with these words: " . . . since a poem can make a claim to universality only when it finds a way to affirm its place in the poetic perspective of its own language." See Celan, *Mikrolithen sinds, Steinchen: Die Prosa aus dem Nachlaß*, ed. Barbara Wiedemann and Bertrand Badiou (Frankfurt: Suhrkamp, 2005), 103. Celan's editors add that there is no evidence the two writers ever corresponded. Blanchot's name also occurs in some of the notes related to the Meridian, from which it transpires that Celan had taken a particular interest in Blanchot's reading of Hölderlin, and more particularly in his remarks on poetic rhythm, as witnessed by Blanchot's essay "La Folie par excellence," reprinted as a preface to Karl Jaspers, *Strindberg et Van Gogh, Swedenborg–Hölderlin* (Paris: Minuit, 1953), which Celan purchased on 12 June 1962. See Celan, *Der Meridian: Endfassung, Entwürfe, Materialien*, ed. Bernhard Böschenstein and Heino Schmull in collaboration with Michael Schwarzkopf and Christiane Wittkopp (Frankfurt: Suhrkamp, 1999), 198; the same fragment is also given in Celan, *Mikrolithen sinds, Steinchen*, 114. Blanchot for his part prolongs his remarks on rhythm in Hölderlin in *L'Entretien infini*, 42; *The Infinite Conversation*, 30; and in *L'Écriture du désastre*, 173; *The Writing of the Disaster*, 112.

109. Celan, *Gesammelte Werke*, III, 189; *Selected Poems and Prose of Paul Celan*, 402.

110. Celan, *Gesammelte Werke*, III, 189; *Selected Poems and Prose of Paul Celan*, 403.

111. Celan, *Gesammelte Werke*, III, 190; *Selected Poems and Prose of Paul Celan*, 403; translation modified. On the complex political and poetical implications of Lucile's counter-word, see Derrida, *Séminaire: La Bête et le souverain I*, ed. Michel Lisse, Marie-Louise Mallet, and Ginette Michaud (Paris: Galilée, 2008), 289–313; *Sovereignties in Question*, 108–34.

112. Celan, *Gesammelte Werke*, III, 193; *Selected Poems and Prose of Paul Celan*, 405; translation modified.

113. For more detailed discussion of the philosophical implications of Celan's poetics, see Philippe Lacoue-Labarthe, *La Poésie comme expérience* (Paris: Christian Bourgois, [1986] 1997); *Word Traces: Readings of Paul Celan*, ed. Aris Fioretos (Baltimore: Johns Hopkins University Press, 1994); and Christopher Fynsk, *Language and Relation: . . . that there is language* (Stanford: Stanford University Press, 1996), 135–58. In all these studies, and Blanchot's essay too, the historical presence of Heidegger looms large. For a detailed, if dispiritingly one-sided account of relations between philosopher and poet, see Hadrien France-Lanord, *Paul Celan et Martin Heidegger: le sens d'un dialogue* (Paris: Fayard, 2004).

114. Celan, *Gesammelte Werke*, III, 200. Celan's working drafts for "Der Meridian" reveal that an earlier version of this formula was first used by him in a letter to Hermann Kasack, dated 16 May 1960, in which he indicated his formal acceptance of the Büchner Prize. In the letter Celan wrote: "Worte, zumal im Gedicht—sind das nicht werdende—und vergehende Namen? Sind Gedichte nicht dies: die ihrer Endlichkeit eingedenk bleibende Unendlichsprechung von Sterblichkeit und Umsonst?" ("Words, especially in a poem—are these not names being born—and dying away? Is this not what poems are: the speaking infinitely of mortality and pointlessness, ever mindful of its own finitude?") See Celan, *Der Meridian: Endfassung, Entwürfe, Materialien*, 222.

115. See Derrida, *Ulysse gramophone;* "Two Words for Joyce," trans. Geoff Bennington, in *Post-Structuralist Joyce*, ed. Derek Attridge and Daniel Ferrer (Cambridge: Cambridge University Press, 1984), 145–59; and *Acts of Literature*, 253–309; see too Jacques Derrida, *Psyché* (Paris: Galilée, 1987), 203–35; *Acts of Religion*, 104–33.

116. Derrida, *Ulysse gramophone*, 59–60; *Acts of Literature*, 257–58; original emphasis; translation modified.

117. The first three versions are reproduced in Lacoue-Labarthe, *La Poésie comme expérience*, 146. The last appears in Celan, *Le Méridien et autres proses*, trans. Jean Launay (Paris: Seuil, 2002), 81. I have supplied in parentheses as far as possible a literal English translation of these different French versions.

118. For this first occurrence of Blanchot's version of Celan's definition, see *Une voix venue d'ailleurs*, 103; *A Voice from Elsewhere*, 89. In "Le Dernier à parler" Blanchot adopts the policy of citing the original German of all Celan's poems alongside his own French versions; but in the case of Celan's prose writing Blanchot gives only his own French text. Blanchot quotes Celan's definition a second time in a contribution to a special issue of the journal *Givre*, devoted to the poet Bernard Noël, where it appears slightly amended; see Blanchot, "La poésie, mesdames, messieurs," *Givre* 2–3 (1977): 176–77; this corrected (or simply mistranscribed) version is the one that appears in *L'Écriture du désastre*, 143; *The Writing of the Disaster*, 90.

119. Jean Launay, in a note to his 2002 translation (114), makes the plausible suggestion that Celan's coinage be treated by analogy with a noun like *Seligsprechung*, meaning: a declaring-holy, or beatification. Ambiguity, however, remains; and it is worth noting that the indeterminacy of compound words is a recurrent feature of Celan's writing, as Peter Szondi observes in his "Lecture de Strette," *Critique* 288 (May 1971): "[Celan's] compound words, by the very fact that they are a result of syntagmatic condensation, do not require the question to be settled as to which of the (two or more) components of the word governs the other, and in what way" (411). Again, there is every reason to believe that Blanchot was familiar with this article before undertaking his own essay on Celan.

120. It is not, however, the first time that Blanchot uses translation in an idiosyncratic manner to make a powerful critical point. In *L'Écriture du désastre*, for instance, in the course of a discussion of fragmentary writing in Schlegel, redeploying and radicalising the version cited in 1969 (in *L'Entretien infini*, 526; *The Infinite Conversation*, 358–59), Blanchot proposes the following revised translation of Fr. 53 from the *Athenaeum*: "To have a system, this is what is fatal for the mind; not to have one, this too is fatal. Whence the necessity to maintain, while ruining them [*en les perdant*], the two requirements at once" (*L'Écriture du désastre*, 101; *The Writing of the Disaster*, 61; translation modified). What Schlegel in fact wrote was this: "Es ist gleich tödlich für den Geist, ein System zu haben, und keins zu haben. Er wird sich also wohl entschließen müssen, beides zu verbinden" (Schlegel, *Kritische Schriften und Fragmente*, II, 109; see *Dialogue on Poetry and Literary Aphorisms*, 136). A more literal version might run as follows: "It is equally fatal for the mind to have a system and to have none. It will therefore have to decide to combine the two." It is not that Blanchot is a casual translator from German; it is rather that, as a translator, Blanchot is sensitive not just to the letter of the text, but what might be termed its futural, self-deconstructive tendencies.

121. On the neuter in Blanchot (notably in dialogue with Levinas) as a withdrawal and a recasting of the opposition between transcendence and immanence, see my *Blanchot: Extreme Contemporary*, 167–84.

122. Celan, *Gesammelte Werke*, III, 199; *Selected Poems and Prose of Paul Celan*, 410.

123. Blanchot, *Une voix venue d'ailleurs*, 95; *A Voice from Elsewhere*, 81; translation modified. This is why the arrangement of the quotations from Celan that fill the margins of Blanchot's essay is an essential part of Blanchot's writing strategy.

124. Celan, *Gesammelte Werke*, III, 199; *Selected Poems and Prose of Paul Celan*, 410.

125. Blanchot, "La Poésie, mesdames, messieurs," *Givre* 2–3 (1977): 177; *L'Écriture du désastre*, 143–44; *The Writing of the Disaster*, 91–92; translation modified.

126. Celan, *Gesammelte Werke*, I, 135; *Selected Poems and Prose of Paul Celan*, 77; Blanchot, *Une voix venue d'ailleurs*, 103; *A Voice from Elsewhere*, 91; translation modified.

127. Blanchot, *L'Écriture du désastre*, 191; *The Writing of the Disaster*, 124; original emphasis; translation modified. *Parole d'explosion* is of course a reference to Mallarmé's famous phrase which recurs several times in Blanchot's book: "There is no explosion, save a book [*Il n'est d'explosion qu'un livre*]." For Mallarmé's original text and an account of the circumstances surrounding its first publication, see Mallarmé, *Œuvres complètes*, II, 660 and 1722–23. The quotation from René Char is taken from the 1977 collection *Chants de la Ballandrane*, in René Char, *Œuvres complètes* (Paris: Gallimard, [1983] 1995), 539.

128. See Marguerite Duras, *La Maladie de la mort* (Paris: Minuit, 1982); *The Malady of Death*, trans. Barbara Bray (New York: Grove, 1986). In a note, Duras explains how it might be possible to envisage a theatrical reading or film of the text: with regard to the first, Duras stipulates "the man the story is about would not be represented [on stage]; even when he speaks to the young woman he would do so only through the man reading his story." For an insight into the extraordinary circumstances in which the text was written, see Laure Adler, *Marguerite Duras* (Paris: Gallimard, 1998), 503–9. For Blanchot's essay on the story, see Blanchot, *La Communauté inavouable*, 51–93; *The Unavowable Community*, 29–56. Early in 1983, part of Blanchot's response to Duras appeared under the title "La Maladie de la mort (éthique et amour)" in the journal *Le Nouveau Commerce* 55 (Spring 1983): 31–46. In a preamble not retained in the book version, Blanchot notes: "It is some considerable time since I last read a book by Marguerite Duras, perhaps because the ability to do so was denied me, or because I wanted to linger with books by her that I had loved so perfectly that I lacked the capacity to go further. For other reasons, too: there is never any shortage of reasons."

129. For an overview of Duras's political itinerary and her involvement in May 1968, see my *Marguerite Duras: Apocalyptic Desires* (London: Routledge,

1993), 1–39; and Adler, *Marguerite Duras*. Why did Blanchot after all these years feel moved to write about Duras's text? First of all, because Blanchot admired Duras's work as a writer. "Whenever I am able to see how much I am in agreement with your books," he wrote to her at some stage (the letter is undated), "my response is one of happiness. It seems to me it is there, truly, I could meet you, such as you are, and in the space of a truth that is close to us both. But the truth is a painful one, and my response of happiness also belongs to this pain"; see *Duras, l'œuvre matérielle* (Paris: IMEC, 2006), 118. Then, no doubt because Blanchot and Duras were friends; because Duras was going through a difficult period; because, after several years spent making films, this was Duras's first "literary" text since *L'Amour* (1971), but also since *Abahn Sabana David* (1970), which Duras had dedicated to Blanchot and Antelme; because already in an earlier essay on Duras's *Le Square* (in *Le Livre à venir*, 185–94; *The Book to Come*, 150–58), Blanchot had been interested in the writer's examination of a relationship without relationship between a man and a woman; and, finally, because Blanchot himself was no foreigner to unorthodox relations between men and women, as may be seen from his own story, *Au moment voulu* (*When the Time Comes*), which itself begins with a strangely expected-unexpected encounter between the (male) narrator and another woman.

130. Blanchot, *La Communauté inavouable*, 52; *The Unavowable Community*, 29–30; translation modified.

131. Blanchot, *La Communauté inavouable*, 52–53; *The Unavowable Community*, 30; original emphases; translation modified. *Le Dire* and *le dit* are terms borrowed here by Blanchot, as elsewhere, from Levinas. The reference to fraternity, implying as it does a primarily male community, is no doubt problematic, as Derrida suggests in a long footnote in *Politiques de l'amitié*, 56–57; *The Politics of Friendship*, 46–48; though Derrida seems to ignore the relevance of Blanchot's engagement with Duras in the book, and the role played by sexual difference in his reading of *La Maladie de la mort*.

132. I explore the wider implications of this argument in Blanchot in my "'Not in Our Name': Blanchot, Politics, the Neuter," *Paragraph* 30, no. 3 (November 2007): 141–59.

133. See Derrida, "Préjugés," in *La Faculté de juger*, 87–139; *Acts of Literature*, 183–220.

134. Blanchot, *Les Écrits politiques 1958–1993*, 152; "Refuse the Established Order," trans. Leslie Hill, *Paragraph* 30, no. 3 (November 2007): 20–22 (21). This reply to a questionnaire was first published in *Le Nouvel Observateur*, 8 May 1981.

135. Blanchot, *Les Écrits politiques 1958–1993*, 152–53; "Refuse the Established Order," 21–22. In *La Communauté inavouable*, 57; *The Unavowable Community*, 33, Blanchot returns to the story of Exodus, where "the gathering of the children

of Israel in preparation for the Exodus, if at the same time they had somehow assembled while forgetting to leave," provides Blanchot with a point of comparison with the actors of 1968. The figure of Moses is prominent in other later texts too. See for instance Blanchot, "L'Ecriture consacrée au silence," *Instants* 1 (1989): 239–41; and "Grâce (soit rendue) à Jacques Derrida," *Revue philosophique* 2 (April–June 1990): 167–73; "Thanks (Be Given) to Jacques Derrida," trans. Leslie Hill, in *The Blanchot Reader*, ed. Michael Holland (Oxford: Blackwell, 1995), 317–23. It is closely related too, also during the Feast of the Passover, to Derrida's invocation of the prophet Elijah in relation to Joyce. See Derrida, *Ulysse gramophone*, 91–122; *Acts of Literature*, 277–96.

136. On the complex treatment of Jewish messianic thought in Blanchot, see *L'Écriture du désastre*, 214–16; *The Writing of the Disaster*, 141–42.

137. Blanchot, *Les Intellectuels en question* (Tours: Farrago, 2000), 48; "Intellectuals under Scrutiny," trans. Michael Holland, in *The Blanchot Reader*, 221; translation modified. Blanchot's essay was first published in *Le Débat* 29 (March 1984): 3–24. It responds indirectly, among others, to Lacoue-Labarthe and Nancy's 1980 essay, *Le Mythe nazi* (Paris: éditions de l'Aube, 1991); "The Nazi Myth," trans. Brian Holmes, *Critical Inquiry* 16 (1990): 291–312.

138. Lyotard, *Tombeau de l'intellectuel et autres papiers* (Paris: Galilée, 1984), 20. Lyotard's article was first published in *Le Monde* in October 1983, in reply to a call from Max Gallo, the novelist and official spokesman for Pierre Mauroy's Socialist government, urging left-leaning intellectuals to be more explicit in their support of the two-year-old Mitterrand presidency.

139. See Blanchot, *Les Intellectuels en question*, 29–30; *The Blanchot Reader*, 215. Blanchot's counter-example was a politically conservative, socially privileged officer in the French Armed Forces, a certain Alfred Dreyfus...

140. Blanchot, *Les Intellectuels en question*, 31; *The Blanchot Reader*, 215; original emphases; translation slightly modified.

141. Blanchot, *Les Écrits politiques 1958–1993*, 169; "Do Not Forget," trans. Michael Holland, in *The Blanchot Reader*, 246; translation modified. Blanchot's letter to Salomon Malka from which this passage is taken first appeared in *L'Arche*, May 1988, 68–71.

142. Blanchot, *La Communauté inavouable*, 57–58; *The Unavowable Community*, 33–34. Blanchot's phrase—"the arid solitude of nameless forces"—is borrowed from Régis Debray.

143. Duras, *La Maladie de la mort*, 24; *The Malady of Death*, 19; translation modified.

144. Duras, *La Maladie de la mort*, 31; *The Malady of Death*, 27; translation modified.

145. Duras, *La Maladie de la mort*, 35; *The Malady of Death*, 31; translation modified.

146. Duras, *La Maladie de la mort*, 52; *The Malady of Death*, 49–50; translation modified.

147. Duras, *La Maladie de la mort*, 53; *The Malady of Death*, 51; translation modified. The sacrificial or Christological phrase "C'est fait," or "Cela est fait" [It is done], denoting, as here, a kind of apocalyptic narrative accomplishment, is a recurrent feature in Duras's work, as I indicate in *Marguerite Duras, Apocalyptic Desires*, 56–57.

148. Duras, *La Maladie de la mort*, 57; *The Malady of Death*, 55; translation modified.

149. Blanchot, *La Communauté inavouable*, 61–62; *The Unavowable Community*, 36; translation modified.

150. For an absorbing and intricate exploration of the divergent, equivocal, and antagonistic readings that *La Maladie de la mort* can sustain, see Martin Crowley, *Duras, Writing and the Ethical* (Oxford: Oxford University Press, 2000), 207–32. As Crowley demonstrates, Duras's numerous interviews or other writings from the 1980s provide support for readers who take the view that Duras is directing her text, in challenging feminist vein, at the economy of oppressive homosociality *and* for readers who take the story, wittingly or not, to be directed, in normative homophobic manner, at male homosexuality in general as a (far from unproblematic) embodiment of the homosocial order. Crowley, for his part, rather hastily, aligns Blanchot's reading with the first of these two interpretations. Much hinges on the extent to which the male protagonist is identified by the reader as "homosexual." As Crowley points out, Blanchot in his reading resists that identification, which is nowhere made explicit in Duras's text, and retains a degree of scepticism about the theme of homosexuality as such, whose relevance to the story he dismisses as "somewhat contrived [*un peu factice*]," preferring to some extent to read Duras's text against (some of) its author's recorded opinions. Crowley, on the other hand, while acknowledging that the protagonist's sexual orientation is indeed never explicit in *La Maladie de la mort*, nonetheless feels able to conclude, "resting on a weight of implication," as he puts it, that "the text nudges the reader towards the realisation of the man's homosexuality" (220). On this reading, Duras's text, in its unresolved equivocation, is necessarily and exhaustively engaged, albeit to uncertain effect, in critique or polemic, and in so far as Crowley's interpretation is primarily concerned with constructing or reconstructing the reversals of meaning of which Duras's story seems capable, the same also goes for his reading of the story, which is itself exclusively mobilised and exercised by Duras's supposed ethico-moral critical or polemical stance. But how far, Blanchot asks, is any text, and notably *La Maladie de la mort*, reducible to critique or polemic? How far may Duras's protagonists be treated as exemplary, mythic, representative figures? And how far is it the purpose of reading to identify and realise (as Crowley contends) the

positionality, meaning, and ideological inscription of any text? Everything here, it seems, turns on the power of decision embodied in the act of naming—and on the consequences of the irreducible disjunction between the universality of law and the singularity of justice.

151. Blanchot, *La Communauté inavouable*, 84; *The Unavowable Community*, 51; translation modified. In 1996 Blanchot was one of over two hundred writers and intellectuals who declared their support for the legal recognition of gay and lesbian couples; see "Pour une reconnaissance légale du couple homosexuel," *Le Nouvel Observateur*, 9–15 May 1996.

152. Blanchot, *La Communauté inavouable*, 62; *The Unavowable Community*, 37.

153. Blanchot, *La Communauté inavouable*, 88; *The Unavowable Community*, 54.

154. On apocalyptic motifs in Duras, see my *Marguerite Duras, Apocalyptic Desires*. The debate between Athens and Jerusalem is a recurrent motif in Blanchot's response to Levinas. The (not unproblematic) distinction between Greek power and Jewish law Blanchot may also have found in Benjamin's famous essay, "Zur Kritik der Gewalt [Critique of Violence]," which appeared in French in the volume of *Œuvres choisies*, trans. Maurice de Gandillac (Paris: Julliard, 1959), that Blanchot reviewed in an article for *La Nouvelle Revue française* 93 (September 1960): 475–83, reproduced in part in *L'Amitié*, 69–73; *Friendship*, 57–61. For Benjamin's original text, see Walter Benjamin, *Gesammelte Schriften*, II: 1, 179–203; *Selected Writings*, I, 236–52.

155. Blanchot, *La Communauté inavouable*, 63; *The Unavowable Community*, 37; translation modified. This reference to the woman's face or *visage* is clearly to be taken in a Levinasian sense, as a token of the woman's status as Other.

156. Blanchot, *La Communauté inavouable*, 63–64; *The Unavowable Community*, 37; translation modified.

157. Blanchot, *La Communauté inavouable*, 85; *The Unavowable Community*, 51; translation modified.

158. Blanchot, *La Communauté inavouable*, 65; *The Unavowable Community*, 38; translation modified.

159. Blanchot, *La Communauté inavouable*, 65; *The Unavowable Community*, 38–39; translation modified.

160. Blanchot, *La Communauté inavouable*, 68; *The Unavowable Community*, 40; translation modified. On Blanchot's substitution of "dissymmetry [*dissymétrie*]" for what Levinas himself describes as "asymmetry [*asymétrie*]," see my *Blanchot, Extreme Contemporary*, 167–84.

161. On the figure of Lilith, see Gershom Scholem, *Zur Kabbala und ihrer Symbolik* (Frankfurt: Suhrkamp, 1973), 215–16; *On the Kabbalah and Its Symbolism*, trans. Ralph Manheim (New York: Schocken Books, 1969), 163.

162. See Blanchot, *La Communauté inavouable*, 76–77; *The Unavowable Community*, 45–46.

163. Friedrich Hölderlin, *Werke und Briefe*, ed. Friedrich Beißner and Jochen Schmidt, 3 vols. (Frankfurt: Insel, 1969), II, 574.

164. Blanchot, *La Communauté inavouable*, 68–69; *The Unavowable Community*, 41; original emphasis; translation modified.

165. See the articles *falloir* and *faillir* in *Le Grand Robert de la langue française*, 2005.

166. Blanchot, *L'Écriture du désastre*, 75; *The Writing of the Disaster*, 44; translation modified.

167. See Blanchot, "Enigme," *Yale French Studies* 79 (1991): 5–7. For the Mallarmé text on which Blanchot draws, see Mallarmé, *Œuvres complètes*, I, 623.

168. Blanchot, *La Communauté inavouable*, 92; *The Unavowable Community*, 56; original emphasis.

169. Blanchot, "Nous travaillons dans les ténèbres," *Le Monde*, 22 July 1983, 9; "We Work in the Dark," trans. Leslie Hill, *Paragraph* 30, no. 3 (November 2007): 25–27 (26–27).

Chapter Four   Jacques Derrida

1. Derrida, *L'Écriture et la différence* (Paris: Seuil, 1967), 260–61; *Writing and Difference*, trans. Alan Bass (London: Routledge, 1978), 219; original emphasis; translation modified.

2. See Antonin Artaud, *Œuvres complètes*, 26 vols. (Paris: Gallimard, 1956–), XIII (1974), 11–64. In her editorial notes, Paule Thévenin, to whom much of Artaud's text was originally dictated, supplies the factual background to its composition, and reproduces the extract, printed in *Arts*, from François-Joachim Beer's *Du démon de van Gogh* (Nice: A.D.I.A., 1945).

3. See for instance Artaud's draft letter to Georges Le Breton, dated 7 March 1946, in *Œuvres complètes*, XI (1974), 184–201, protesting at the critic's mechanical attempt to decode the notoriously hermetic allusions of Gérard de Nerval's sonnet cycle, *Les Chimères*, on the basis of symbolic motifs taken from alchemy, the Tarot, or the Kabbala, and the similar letter, from the same period, about Lautréamont in *Suppôts et Suppliciations*, in *Œuvres complètes*, XIV: 1 (1978), 32–37.

4. Artaud, *Œuvres complètes*, XIII, 61.

5. Artaud, *Œuvres complètes*, XIII, 14.

6. Artaud, *Œuvres complètes*, XIII, 17.

7. Artaud, *Œuvres complètes*, XIII, 21. The reference is to the painting *Crows in the Wheatfield*, the last to be finished by van Gogh, days before his death.

This account of van Gogh's demise is no doubt coloured by Artaud's painful experience of electric shock treatment which at Rodez, in the course of 1943 and 1944, was administered to him, it appears, no fewer than fifty-one times, leaving him in a coma, unable to work for weeks at a time, and provoking severe memory loss. On this, and Artaud's physical condition at the time, see Paule Thévenin, *Antonin Artaud, ce Désespéré qui vous parle* (Paris: Seuil, 1993), 147–54. Artaud's death on 4 March 1948 was caused by an overdose of chloral hydrate, prescribed as an analgesic to treat the pain from what had been diagnosed as inoperable cancer of the rectum. In March 2000, save in exceptional cases, chloral hydrate was withdrawn from the list of approved medications by the French Ministry of Health because of its dangerous side-effects.

8. Artaud, *Œuvres complètes*, XIII, 61.

9. Artaud, *Œuvres complètes*, XIII, 38.

10. Artaud, *Œuvres complètes*, XIII, 18.

11. Artaud, *Œuvres complètes*, XIII, 29–30.

12. Artaud, *Œuvres complètes*, XIII, 46.

13. Artaud, *Œuvres complètes*, XIII, 47.

14. Artaud, *Œuvres complètes*, XIII, 59.

15. Artaud, *Œuvres complètes*, XIII, 60.

16. Artaud, *Œuvres complètes*, XIII, 20.

17. Artaud, *Œuvres complètes*, XIII, 39.

18. Artaud, *Œuvres complètes*, XIII, 177. "I never knew Dr. Gachet," Artaud adds, "but I am familiar enough now with psychiatry and psychiatrists to know what went on between van Gogh and Dr. Gachet. And in any case I have had in my possession, relating to van Gogh's death, certain incontrovertible documents whose authenticity I defy anyone to challenge." Artaud does not of course specify what these documents are.

19. Artaud, *Œuvres complètes*, XIII, 35. Artaud's complaint, on both van Gogh's behalf and his own, was that Dr. Gachet had told the painter to concentrate on working with set motifs. Elsewhere, Artaud presents himself, half-ironically, as "that poor Monsieur Antonin Artaud [*ce pauvre Mr Antonin Artaud*]." See Artaud's letter to Peter Watson, begun 27 July and completed 13 September 1946, in *Œuvres complètes*, XII (1974), 230–39 (231). The letter was originally intended for *Horizon*, but never published by the magazine; it first appeared in *Critique* in October 1948, where it would have been seen by many more French readers, possibly including Blanchot, Foucault, and Derrida.

20. Artaud, *Œuvres complètes*, XIII, 49–50.

21. See Artaud, *Œuvres complètes*, XIII, 67–104. Artaud's text, performed by Maria Casarès, Roger Blin, Paule Thévenin, and himself, was originally scheduled for 2 February 1948, but prevented from being broadcast by the last-minute intervention of the director-general of French Radio, Wladimir Porché, who de-

creed its language too violent. The recording survived, however, and has been re-issued as a commercially available CD from the archives of Radio France/INA.

22. See Michel Foucault, *Histoire de la folie à l'âge classique*, rev. ed. (Paris: Gallimard, 1972), 555; *History of Madness*, trans. Jonathan Murphy, ed. Jean Khalfa (London: Routledge, 2005), 536. Foucault writes, "Artaud's madness does not slip away into the interstices of the work; it is precisely the *absence of any work* [*l'absence d'œuvre*], the presence, repeated over and again, of this absence, its central void, explored and measured out in each of its unending dimensions"; translation modified. "What you mistook to be my works [*mes œuvres*]," Artaud announced to his friends in 1925, "were only the left-over remnants of myself [*les déchets de moi-même*], these scrapings of the soul that normal people will not accept." See Artaud, *Œuvres complètes*, I (1970), 114.

23. See André Breton, *Œuvres complètes*, ed. Marguerite Bonnet, 4 vols. (Paris: Gallimard, 1988–2008), I, 879–84. For Lacan's early interest in this relationship between the poetical output and clinical investigation, see Jacques Lacan, *De la psychose paranoïaque dans ses rapports avec la personnalité, suivi de Premiers écrits sur la paranoïa* (Paris: Seuil, [1932] 1975), 365–98. According to Roger Blin, cited by Évelyne Grossman, Lacan's assessment of Artaud at the time was as follows: "definitively fixated, lost to literature [*définitivement fixé, perdu pour la littérature*]"; see Artaud, *Œuvres*, ed. Évelyne Grossman (Paris: Gallimard, 2004), 1753. According to Thévenin and Grossman, Lacan, encountered by Artaud in 1938, is the psychiatrist named as "Doctor L. [*docteur L.*]" in the introduction to *Van Gogh le suicidé de la société* (*Œuvres complètes*, XIII, 15), and the only one to object to the writer's claim that all psychiatrists were erotomaniacs.

24. See Artaud, *Œuvres complètes*, XII, 13–20. In *Antonin Artaud, ce Désespéré qui vous parle*, 238–39, Thévenin glosses the word *mômo* as follows: "In Provence, more particularly in Marseille, le *mômo* (related to the Spanish *momero*: jester, and *momo*: grimace) is a fool, in the sense of an innocent, a village idiot, a simpleton, a loon. (Mistral, who derives *momo* from the Catalan *moma*: money, loose change, provides two different meanings for the Provençal term according to gender. He defines la *momo*, in the feminine, as a childish term for sweet or delicacy, whereas le *momo*, in the masculine, is Marseille slang for child or brat.) This colloquial usage gives the title its primary meaning: the return of Artaud the simpleton, the madcap from Marseille, from the asylum in Rodez, his return to so-called normal life."

25. See Barthes, *Œuvres complètes*, III, 877. In this piece, intended as a preface to a book on Artaud by Bernard Lamarche-Vadel that was subsequently abandoned by its author, Barthes asks: "How to speak about Artaud? This question is not only specific (it could be asked about any author at all), but, so to speak, semelfactive (whatever the scientific aura of the word): the impossibility of speaking about Artaud is more or less unique; Artaud is what in philology is

called a *hapax legomenon*, a form or error that is encountered only once in a whole text." After writing this chapter, I came across Jean-Luc Steinmetz's book, *Signets: essais critiques sur la poésie du XVIIIe au XXe siècle* (Paris: Corti, 1995), which includes (275–88) a thoughtful, if largely descriptive chapter on Artaud's *Cahiers du retour à Paris*, entitled . . . "Hapax" ("a Greek term," explains Steinmetz, without going further, "meaning an expression that appears only once in a language"), as though to remind me that nothing is unique or singular without necessarily also being repeatable—and repeated.

26. See Blanchot, "Artaud," *La Nouvelle Nouvelle Revue française* 47 (November 1956): 873–81, collected in *Le Livre à venir*, 45–52; *The Book to Come*, 34–40; and "La Cruelle Raison poétique," *Cahiers de la compagnie Madeleine Renaud–Jean-Louis Barrault* 22–23 (May 1958): 66–73, republished as "La Cruelle Raison poétique: rapace besoin d'envol," in *L'Entretien infini*, 432–38; *The Infinite Conversation*, 293–97. See also Foucault, *Histoire de la folie à l'âge classique*, 554–57, 575–82; *History of Madness*, 535–38, 541–49; *Dits et écrits 1954–1988*, 4 vols. (Paris: Gallimard, 1994), I, passim.

27. See Derrida, *L'Écriture et la différence*, 253–92; *Writing and Difference*, 212–45. The volume also contains a later essay (1966) by Derrida on Artaud, dedicated to Paule Thévenin, "Le Théâtre de la cruauté et la clôture de la représentation [The Theatre of Cruelty and the Closure of Representation]."

28. The texts to which Derrida refers are as follows: Blanchot, "La Folie par excellence," *Critique* 45 (February 1951): 99–118, republished in 1953 and in 1970 (with a supplementary note) as a preface to Karl Jaspers, *Strindberg et Van Gogh, Swedenborg–Hölderlin, étude psychiatrique comparative*, trans. Hélène Naef in collaboration with M.-L. Solms-Naef and Dr. M. Solms (Paris: Minuit, [1953] 1970), 9–32; "Madness par excellence," trans. Ann Smock, in *The Blanchot Reader*, ed. Michael Holland, 110–28; Jean Laplanche, *Hölderlin et la question du père* (Paris: Presses universitaires de France, 1961); and Foucault, "Le 'non' du père," in *Dits et écrits 1954–1988*, I, 189–203. The respective careers of all three writers demonstrate the complex interrelationship, common in France at the time, between the clinical and the philosophical or critical. As Christophe Bident records in *Maurice Blanchot: partenaire invisible*, 35–56, Blanchot first of all studied philosophy at university, turning his attention briefly to a career in neurology and psychiatry, completing perhaps no more than a year's training at the Hôpital Sainte-Anne, before devoting himself to journalism, writing, and literary criticism. Laplanche, similarly, like many in his generation, began as a student of philosophy at the École Normale Supérieure (E.N.S.) before embarking on a career in medecine and psychoanalysis; while Foucault, after studying concurrently at the E.N.S. for the *licence* in philosophy and in psychology, maintained a foothold within philosophy only to undertake a two-part thesis (as was usual in France at the time) on the history of medicine and psychiatry, the first of which, *Histoire de la folie*,

was published in 1961 by Plon, partly as a result of Blanchot's support, with the second, *Naissance de la clinique* (Paris: Presses universitaires de France, 1963), appearing two years later. And though they apparently never met, Blanchot and Foucault shared a strong mutual admiration, as witnessed by the essays they devoted to one another.

29. For Artaud's reworking of "Jabberwocky," see *Œuvres complètes*, IX (1971), 156–74. Deleuze's essay on Artaud and Carroll first appeared in 1968, and, under the heading "Du Schizophrène et de la petite fille," was subsequently incorporated into *Logique du sens* (Paris: Minuit, 1969), 101–14; *The Logic of Sense*, trans. Mark Lester with Charles Stivale, ed. Constantin V. Boundas (New York: Columbia University Press, 1990), 82–93. For Deleuze's enduring commitment to the articulation of psychiatry with literary criticism, see his *Critique et clinique* (Paris: Minuit, 1993); *Essays Critical and Clinical*, trans. Daniel W. Smith, Michael A. Greco, and Anthony Uhlmann (London: Verso, 1998). Kristeva's paper, "Le Sujet en procès [The Subject in Process]," chiefly focussed on Artaud as an exemplary test case, was first presented at the 1972 *Tel Quel* Cerisy conference entitled, in explicitly Maoist terms, "Vers une révolution culturelle [Towards Cultural Revolution]: Artaud, Bataille," and is reproduced in Kristeva, *Polylogue* (Paris: Seuil, 1977), 55–106; *The Tel Quel Reader*, 133–78. For a particularly vehement reaction to the use of clinical terminology as a way of reading Artaud, see Thévenin, *Antonin Artaud, ce Désespéré qui vous parle*, 197–210.

30. Derrida, *L'Écriture et la différence*, 254–55; *Writing and Difference*, 214; original emphasis; translation modified.

31. Treated with particular severity in Derrida's discussion of critical responses to Artaud, surprisingly enough, was Blanchot, whose essays and *récits* Derrida would later read with perhaps greater sympathy. Derrida's criticism of Blanchot is that he announces the irreducibility of that which is "proper" to Artaud, but fails to go further, no doubt because in doing so, as Derrida suggests, Blanchot had already begun to touch one of the limits of critical discourse in general and the assumptions with regard to the self-identity of the poet and the work by which it is governed. Dividing sameness from the self-identical, and the singular from the original, these are Blanchot's concluding words: "Each poet says the same [*le même*], yet it is not the same, we can sense it is the unique [*l'unique*]." The phrase is taken from Blanchot, *Le Livre à venir*, 52; *The Book to Come*, 40, and cited by Derrida in *L'Écriture et la différence*, 256; *Writing and Difference*, 215. Interestingly, Derrida in 1967 does not comment on the fact that in the original version of Blanchot's essay in *La Nouvelle Nouvelle Revue française* for November 1956, the main body of the article was preceded by four fragments in the third person, in which Artaud is not mentioned, but which bear a close resemblance to several passages in Blanchot's 1957 *récit*, *Le Dernier Homme* (*The Last Man*), published shortly after, which perhaps explains their omission from

the version given in *Le Livre à venir*. This unusual textual convergence between so-called fictional and critical texts is testimony to the extent to which Blanchot was increasingly conscious of the limits to which Artaud forced both modes of writing, each having to contend here, as Blanchot puts it, with "[a] thought, in the present, always already past [*Une pensée, dans le présent, toujours déjà passée*]." On the proximity between Blanchot's deletions and *Le Dernier Homme*, see Bident, *Maurice Blanchot: partenaire invisible*, 360–61; and Évelyne Grossman, *Artaud, "l'aliéné authentique"* (Tours: Farrago, 2003), 157–67. Immediately after the discussion of Blanchot's article on Artaud, Derrida goes on to take issue with the writer's earlier essay on Hölderlin, "La Folie par excellence," suggesting that it too makes the same contentious essentialising moves. When his Hölderlin essay was republished in 1970, however, Blanchot added a postscript, which it is difficult not to read as an oblique response to Derrida's strictures. It was in two parts. First, Blanchot maintained his text unaltered, claiming, as he put it, without explaining further, that his pages resisted any desire to modify them, but "obviously not," Blanchot went on, "because they might be deemed to be true, nor even untrue (even if this is what they are), nor because they may be thought to constitute a closed discourse unaffected by judgements as to their truth or value. Why, then? I shall not pursue this issue [*Je laisse là la question*]." But even as he left this question dangling, Blanchot carried on for two more pages replying to a query of his own about the use of the word *mad* or *madness*, arguing that it might only ever correspond to an open, abyssal question: "To say: Hölderlin is mad [*fou*]," replied Blanchot, "is to say: is he mad? But, on that basis, it is to make madness so utterly foreign to all assertiveness that madness would be quite incapable of finding any language in which to assert itself without in turn threatening language with madness: language, as such, always already gone mad. Language gone mad would then be, in every act of speech, not only the possibility that allows it to speak, at the risk of turning it into something non-speaking (a risk without which it would not speak at all), but also the limit enclosing all language, which, never fixed in advance or determinable theoretically, even less in such a way that it might be possible to write: 'there is a limit [*il y a une limite*],' and thus outside of all 'there is [*il y a*],' might only be inscribed in so far as it had already been crossed—a crossing of the uncrossable [*le franchissement de l'infranchissable*]—and on that basis prohibited [*interdite*: i.e., both banned and, literally, spoken-between]." See Jaspers, *Strindberg et Van Gogh*, 30–31; *The Blanchot Reader*, 126; translation modified. On Blanchot's part, notwithstanding his apparent diffidence earlier in the same note, this was to reaffirm what had already been at stake in his twenty- or fifteen-year-old readings of Hölderlin and Artaud, that is, that it is not possible to found a literary critical discourse, indeed perhaps any discourse at all, on clinical judgement, except at the cost of acknowledging that the limits of discourse were not outside language, but at its very centre, disabling and undermining its authority, exposing it, as Blanchot adds a paragraph later, to "the presence of the outside that has always already suspended [*suspendu*] and prohibited [*interdit*] presence," as witnessed by Nietzsche's—and, wonders Blanchot, Hölderlin's?—experience of Eternal Return. What is at issue, then, for Blanchot, far from the *neutralisation* against which Derrida rightly cautions, here and elsewhere, is the affirmation of the *neuter* as a thought of non-identity, difference, and alterity.

32. Derrida, *De la grammatologie*, 227; *Of Grammatology*, 158; translation slightly modified. On the whole question of reading in Derrida, see Michel Lisse, *L'Expérience de la lecture*, 2 vols. (Paris: Galilée, 1998, 2001).

33. See Derrida, *L'Écriture et la différence*, 264; *Writing and Difference*, 222. Quoting from Artaud's famous early correspondence with Jacques Rivière, Derrida notes that "it would be tempting, easy, and *up to a certain point legitimate* to underline the exemplarity of this description" [emphasis mine]; translation slightly modified.

34. See Derrida, *De la grammatologie*, 159; *Of Grammatology*, 109.

35. Derrida, *L'Écriture et la différence*, 266; *Writing and Difference*, 224; translation modified.

36. This is why, as Derrida puts it, if nothing is ever properly an example, it is because everything and everybody, even Artaud, is already improperly an example of something—if only of itself. "The example itself, as such [*en tant que tel*]," he argues in *Passions*, "exceeds [*déborde*] its singularity as much as it does its identity. This is why there is no such thing as an example just as, at the selfsame time, examples are all there are. . . . The exemplarity of the example is obviously never the exemplarity of the example." See Derrida, *Passions* (Paris: Galilée, 1993), 43; *On the Name*, ed. Thomas Dutoit, trans. David Wood, John P. Leavey Jr., and Ian McLeod (Stanford: Stanford University Press, 1995), 17–18; translation modified.

37. On this double sense, both spatial and temporal, of standing before the law, see Derrida, "Prejugés," in *La Faculté de juger*, 87–139; *Acts of Literature*, 183–220.

38. Artaud, *Œuvres complètes*, XII, 77.

39. Derrida, *L'Écriture et la différence*, 272; *Writing and Difference*, 230; original emphasis; translation modified. Derrida's positioning of Artaud in this way, within metaphysics but at the extreme limit of metaphysics, is not without recalling Heidegger's reading of Nietzsche as similarly embodying the end of metaphysics: as the very last in a long line of metaphysicians and as the philosopher in whom metaphysics reached its final avatar. This is not to say, however, that Derrida subscribed without reservation to Heidegger's analysis; on the contrary, he was obviously concerned to develop a different conception of metaphysics and of the logic of the limit, margin, or frame. See Derrida, *De la*

grammatologie, 31–34; *On Grammatology*, 18–21. Blanchot too, while equally attentive to Heidegger's reading, was also rather sceptical. "Philosophy trembles in Nietzsche," he wrote in 1969, agreeing with Derrida, and continued as follows: "But is it merely because he may be called the last philosopher (each one being always the last)? Or was it because, required [*appelé*] by an entirely other language, the disruptive writing [*l'écriture d'effraction*], which is destined to accept 'words' only in so far as they have been crossed out [*barrés*], spaced out [*espacés*], put under erasure [*mis en croix*] by the very movement that sets them apart, but in that distance holds them back as a place of difference, he had to contend with a fractious demand [*une exigence de rupture*] which constantly diverts them from what he has the *power* to think?" See Blanchot, *L'Entretien infini*, 226–27; *The Infinite Conversation*, 150–51; translation modified. These remarks in response to Heidegger's reading of Nietzsche give the lie to the flippant claim advanced by Philippe Sollers in a 1994 interview to the effect that, unlike Hölderlin, Artaud, as he put it, "still awaits his Heidegger"—who, says Sollers, would have to be a Catholic. "There's a great book to be written," he goes on, "and I'm surprised nobody has ever done it, but that's not my job, which would be to show how much Heidegger was misunderstood, and to show how no major thinker of the twentieth century ever understood Heidegger. He's far ahead of them all. Neither Sartre, nor Merleau-Ponty, nor Husserl, nor Foucault, nor Deleuze, nor Derrida, nor Lacan, nor Althusser ever got the message." See Sollers, *Eloge de l'infini*, 881, 888–89.

40. The point is one that Derrida reiterates in numerous other texts from this period. See for instance Derrida, *La Dissémination* (Paris: Seuil, 1972), 234–35; *Dissemination*, trans. Barbara Johnson (Chicago: University of Chicago Press, 1981), 206–7.

41. Derrida, *L'Écriture et la différence*, 366; *Writing and Difference*, 314; translation modified.

42. Artaud, *Œuvres complètes*, I, 148; original emphasis. Blanchot quotes this passage from "L'Art et la mort" (1929) in *Le Livre à venir*, 48; *The Book to Come*, 36.

43. Readers will remember that Derrida follows a similar trail in reading Heidegger in *De l'esprit: Heidegger et la question* (Paris: Galilée, 1987); *Of Spirit: Heidegger and the Question*, trans. Geoffrey Bennington and Rachel Bowlby (Chicago: University of Chicago Press, 1989).

44. Artaud, *Œuvres complètes*, IV (1964), 74.

45. Derrida, *L'Écriture et la différence*, 292; *Writing and Difference*, 245; translation modified.

46. Derrida, *La Dissémination*, 252–53; *Dissemination*, 223; original emphasis; translation modified.

47. On the activities of the Groupe d'études théoriques, see Philippe Forest, *Histoire de Tel Quel 1960–1982* (Paris: Seuil, 1995), 338–41. The Group was first

launched in October 1968 and continued meeting until 1971. By that time, critical of the increasingly theatrical and dogmatic political turn taken by members of the *Tel Quel* editorial committee, notably the self-styled *mouvement de juin 71*, Derrida had clearly distanced himself from the journal, and although *La Dissémination* was eventually published in 1972 by the éditions du Seuil in the Tel Quel series edited by Sollers, it was on both sides more a sign of imminent rupture than of lingering solidarity. Something of *Tel Quel*'s jealous rivalry at the time is apparent from Kristeva's subsequent attack on Derrida in her autobiographical novel, *Les Samouraïs* (Paris: Grasset, 1990); *The Samurai: A Novel*, trans. Barbara Bray (New York: Columbia University Press, 1992), in which, less than ten years after AIDS in French became known as *le sida*, the philosopher found himself portrayed as the voguish guru (and architect of "condestruction") Saïda. For Derrida's relatively mild response to this extraordinary free association, see Derrida, *Résistances de la psychanalyse* (Paris: Galilée, 1996), 68–69; *Resistances of Psychoanalysis*, trans. Peggy Kamuf, Pascale-Anne Brault, and Michael Naas (Stanford: Stanford University Press, 1998), 49–50. That Derrida was reluctant to follow the *Tel Quel* group's short march into Maoism was less an expression of apoliticism than the result of his friendship with the eminent Sinologist Lucien Bianco, who gave him a more nuanced perspective on events in China at the time; see Derrida, "Signé l'ami d'un 'ami de la Chine,'" in *Aux origines de la Chine contemporaine,* ed. Marie-Claire Bergère (Paris: L'Harmattan, 2002), i–xv.

48. Mallarmé, *Œuvres complètes*, II, 23. For an account of the shifting importance of Mallarmé's work for a number of twentieth-century French philosophers, critics, and other writers, including Derrida, see *Meetings with Mallarmé in Contemporary French Culture,* ed. Michael Temple (Exeter: University of Exeter Press, 1998).

49. Mallarmé, *Œuvres complètes*, II, 215; I, 391; *Selected Poetry and Prose,* ed. Mary Ann Caws (New York: New Directions, 1982), 77; *Collected Poems*, trans. Henry Weinfield (Berkeley: University of California Press, 1994), 121; translations modified. It will be remembered that Derrida uses a fragment from Mallarmé's preface (*Œuvres complètes*, I, 391) as an epigraph for *L'Écriture et la différence:* "all without novelty other than a spacing of reading [*le tout sans nouveauté qu'un espacement de la lecture*]."

50. Mallarmé, *Œuvres complètes*, II, 65. Mallarmé's query features in another lecture, delivered by him in Oxford and Cambridge in March 1894.

51. See Mallarmé, *Œuvres complètes*, II, 208.

52. See Derrida, *Marges: de la philosophie*, 365–93; *Margins of Philosophy*, 309–30.

53. Mallarmé, *Œuvres complètes*, II, 217; *Selected Poetry and Prose,* 79.

54. To press the point, it would no doubt be possible to claim that of the two texts selected by Derrida it is the extract from Plato's dialogue that is more "literary" than the passage from Mallarmé, which, beginning as it did as a theatre

review, might plausibly be seen to belong to that (minor) branch of philosophical discourse known as literary criticism rather than to poetry. But beyond or before any such attributions of genre, what is at play in both texts, on Derrida's submission, that is, both in Plato and in Mallarmé, is a scene of writing that is not subject to that mimetic division between inside and outside, performance and text, stage and auditorium, that Derrida shows to be always already unhinged by writing.

55. Mallarmé, *Œuvres complètes*, I, 384–85; *Collected Poems*, 143.

56. Mallarmé, *Œuvres complètes*, I, 387; *Collected Poems*, 144; translation modified.

57. Mallarmé, who earned a living as a secondary school teacher of English, was also the author of an idiosyncratic, pre-Saussurian linguistic treatise entitled *Les Mots anglais* (*English Words*), which gave him the opportunity to indulge an interest in the graphic and phonetic similarity between letters, sounds, and words. See Mallarmé, *Œuvres complètes*, II, 939–1345. Paying tribute in 1976 to the psychoanalytic explorations of his friends Nicolas Abraham and Maria Torok into the private language of Freud's Wolfman, Derrida gave his preface to their work ("Fors") the homophonic subtitle: "Les Mots anglés [Anglish Words]." See Nicolas Abraham and Maria Torok, *Cryptonymie: Le Verbier de l'homme aux loups* (Paris: Aubier-Flammarion, 1976), 7–73; *The Wolf Man's Magic Word: A Cryptonomy*, trans. Nicholas Rand (Minneapolis: University of Minnesota Press, 1986).

58. In addressing the writings of Mallarmé, Derrida was entering a much-ploughed field, already the subject of a significant amount of commentary on the part of philosophers and critics alike, including most recently Jean-Pierre Richard, whose pioneering phenomenologically inspired thesis, *L'Univers imaginaire de Mallarmé* (Paris: Seuil, 1961), Derrida subjects to detailed scrutiny in the second of his two untitled sessions. The other important figure he was bound to encounter in reading Mallarmé was Blanchot, the author of several influential essays on Mallarmé from the 1940s and 1950s (collected in *Faux Pas, La Part du feu, L'Espace littéraire*, and *Le Livre à venir*). Admittedly, Blanchot's name is nowhere mentioned in "La Double Séance," but the influence of his thinking on Derrida—though the word does little justice to the complex dialogue taking place between the pair from the mid-1960s onwards—is hard to miss, and may be seen to inform much of Derrida's 1969 opening strategy in at least four ways. First, already in 1952 for Blanchot the only beginning is an impossibility of beginning: "Rebeginning," he writes, "repetition, the fatality of return, everything that is alluded to in those experiences where the sense of strangeness is coupled with a sense of *déjà vu*, where the irremediable takes the form of endless repetition, where the same is given in the infinite regress of duplication, where there is no cognition but only *recognition*—all of this alludes to that initial error which may be expressed as follows: what is first is not the beginning, but rebeginning,

and being is precisely the *impossibility* of being for the first time." See *L'Espace lit-téraire*, 255–56; *The Space of Literature*, 243; translation modified. Second, some pages earlier, Blanchot had already drawn the conclusion, replying covertly to Heidegger, that the artwork was neither true nor untrue, but otherwise: "As soon as the truth which it is thought to yield is brought into the light of day and be-comes the life and labour of the day, the work closes upon itself as something that is alien to this truth and without meaning, for not only in relation to estab-lished and reliable truths does the work seem alien, the very scandal of what is monstrous and un-true, but always it refutes the true: whatever it is, and even though it may come from the work itself, the work overturns it, takes it back, buries it, and hides it away." See *L'Espace littéraire*, 239; *The Space of Literature*, 228–89; translation modified. Third, by 1963, under the rubric of the neuter, Blanchot had similarly begun to address writing, albeit not necessarily in these terms, as a citational movement of referral without referent, irreducible to any horizon of meaning. "I may represent things, roughly speaking, as follows," he writes, "narrative could be said to be like a circle neutralising life, which does not mean not having any relation with it, but relating to it in the neuter. Inside this circle, the meaning of what is and of what is said is still given, but on the basis of a withdrawal, at a distance from which all meaning and lack of meaning are neutralised in advance: a reserve that exceeds all meaning that has already been signified, without it being considered either as abundance or as pure and simple privation. It is like a speaking that neither illuminates nor obscures." See *L'En-tretien infini*, 557; *The Infinite Conversation*, 379–80; translation modified. Fourth, and finally, Blanchot had insisted from the outset that what literature sought to touch, perhaps impossibly, was not the concept but the unique, the singular, the contingent in so far as they resisted conceptual assimilation; whence, for in-stance, the famous declaration from 1948, dramatising the cataclysmic emer-gence of language in the world: "[S]omething was there, which has now gone. Something has disappeared. How can I retrieve it, and can I rediscover what comes *before*, if all my power consists in turning it into what comes *after*? The language of literature is a quest for the moment that precedes it. Generally, it calls this existence; it wants the cat as it is, the pebble seen *from the side of things*, not man in general, but this man and, in this man, what man rejects in order to say it, which is the founding of speech and which speech excludes in order to speak, the abyss, Lazarus in the tomb and not Lazarus returned to the light, the one already beginning to smell, who is Evil, Lazarus lost and not Lazarus saved and raised from the dead." See *La Part du feu*, 316; *The Work of Fire*, 327; original emphasis; translation modified.

59. As elsewhere, there is in "La Double Séance" an ongoing debate be-tween Derrida and Heidegger. In the latter's famous 1936 essay, "Hölderlin und das Wesen der Dichtung [Hölderlin and the Essence of Poetry]," it is the motif or

theme—rather than the abyssal syncategorem—of "between" (suitably substantivised as *das Zwischen*), referring to that—poetry—which separates and joins the signs that come from the gods [*Winke der Götter*] and the voice of the people [*Stimme des Volkes*], which is privileged in overwhelming fashion, with significant consequences for the relationship not only between poetry and Being, according to Heidegger, but also between poetry and the political. On Hölderlin and the *Zwischen*, see Martin Heidegger, *Erläuterungen zu Hölderlins Dichtung* (Frankfurt: Klostermann, 1981), 46–49.

60. On iterability as simultaneous repetition *and* alteration, and the instability between use and mention, see Derrida, *Marges: de la philosophie*, 374–76; *Margins of Philosophy*, 315–16.

61. Mallarmé, *Œuvres complètes*, II, 178–79; original emphasis. It is important to stress the extent to which this sentence, and Derrida's remarking of it, does not serve to accredit a global theory of textual self-reflexivity. On the question of reflexivity in Derrida, Rodolphe Gasché provides an authoritative account in *The Tain of the Mirror* (Cambridge, MA: Harvard University Press, 1986). In the context of "La Double Séance" what is paramount is less the fact that Mallarmé's text refers to itself than that it simultaneously refers to all other texts, including and exceeding itself, and to itself as an irreplaceable singularity, without contradiction. On this point, see Geoffrey Bennington, *Interrupting Derrida* (London: Routledge, 2000), 47–58.

62. See Derrida, *La Dissémination*, 218; *Dissemination*, 192.

63. Derrida, *La Dissémination*, 217; *Dissemination*, 191; original emphasis; translation modified. On this anteriority of the 2 over the 1, of repetition over identity, running through Derrida's book, and necessarily already at work in Plato, see Derrida, *La Dissémination*, 194–97; *Dissemination*, 168–71.

64. Derrida, *La Dissémination*, 211–13 n. 8; *Dissemination*, 186–87 n. 14; translation modified.

65. Derrida, *La Dissémination*, 248–49; *Dissemination*, 219.

66. Derrida, *La Dissémination*, 250; *Dissemination*, 220–21; original emphasis; translation modified.

67. This is perhaps most clearly apparent from Saussure's recourse to the metaphor of the game of chess to describe language as a synchronic series of states of play. See Ferdinand de Saussure, *Cours de linguistique générale*, ed. Tullio de Mauro (Paris: Payot, 1972), 124–27; *Course in General Linguistics*, trans. Wade Baskin (New York: McGraw-Hill, 1966), 87–89.

68. See Barthes, *Œuvres complètes*, IV, 236; *The Pleasure of the Text*, 29–30; translation modified. Compare Brecht, *Berliner und Frankfurter Ausgabe*, VI, 56; *Mother Courage and Her Children*, trans. Eric Bentley (London: Methuen, 1962), 50. In his reading, Barthes appropriates the cheerful cynicism of Brecht's Chap-

lain and turns it into something more subversive or contestatory than in the play, where it serves mainly to confirm the continuity between warfare and business as usual.

69. See Blanchot, *L'Entretien infini*, 119–31, 439–46; *The Infinite Conversation*, 85–92, 298–302.

70. On the precariousness that affects all horizons, see Blanchot, *L'Écriture du désastre*, 158–60; *The Writing of the Disaster*, 101–3. This necessary capacity of writing to exceed all horizons is one reason why Blanchot resists the reduction of fragmentary writing to the aphorism. See Blanchot, *L'Entretien infini*, 526–27; *The Infinite Conversation*, 359. Elsewhere, in the preparatory material for the abortive *Revue internationale* in the early 1960s, Blanchot rightly points out that "[e]tymologically, aphorism means horizon, a horizon that limits and closes off [*qui borne et qui n'ouvre pas*]." See Blanchot, "Cours des choses," in *Écrits politiques 1958–1993*, 63. I discuss Blanchot's distinction between the aphorism and the fragmentary in more detail in my *A Change of Epoch: Maurice Blanchot, Writing, the Fragmentary*, forthcoming.

71. Blanchot, *L'Entretien infini*, 563; *The Infinite Conversation*, 384; translation modified. I have discussed this essay at greater length in the context of Blanchot's reading of Kafka, in my *Bataille, Klossowski, Blanchot: Writing at the Limit*, 206–26.

72. Blanchot, *L'Entretien infini*, 565–66; *The Infinite Conversation*, 386; translation modified. Derrida quotes this passage in *Parages*, 141.

73. Blanchot, *L'Arrêt de mort* (Paris: Gallimard, 1948), 72–73; *Death Sentence*, trans. Lydia Davis (New York: Station Hill Press, 1978), 43; translation modified. For Derrida's commentary, see *Parages*, 171–74 (in the footnote strip).

74. See Derrida, *La Dissémination*, 235; *Dissemination*, 207. On the disagreement or difference of emphasis between Blanchot and Levinas on the topic of the neuter, see my *Blanchot: Extreme Contemporary*, 136–37.

75. Jean Genet, *Journal du voleur* (Paris: Gallimard, 1949), 186; *The Thief's Journal*, trans. Bernard Frechtman (London: Anthony Blond, 1965), 156; translation slightly modified.

76. Derrida, *Glas* (Paris: Galilée, 1974), 19b; *Glas*, trans. John P. Leavey Jr. and Richard Rand (Lincoln: University of Nebraska Press, 1986), 12b; translation modified. In referring to *Glas*, quotations from the left-hand and right-hand columns are indicated with the use of *a* and *b* respectively; page numbers given first refer to the 1974 Galilée edition, and those given second relate to the Leavey-Rand translation; references to the various passages inserted into the text are indicated by the letter *i*. Also worth noting here is the informative commentary on Derrida's text provided by John P. Leavey Jr. and Gregory L. Ulmer in *Glassary* (Lincoln: University of Nebraska Press, 1986), which, among others, sources all the quotations used by Derrida, helpfully supplies an index to both French text

and translation, and includes a short foreword (or postscript) by Derrida, "Proverb: 'He that would pun . . . '" (17–20).

77. On Derrida's "démarche bâtarde" (meaning hybrid or mongrel manner *and* bastard manner of walking) in approaching Hegel, see *Glas*, 12a; 6a, where Derrida asks, with a visible wink (or *clin d'œil*) in the direction of the corresponding right-hand column, whether there is "any place for bastards [*le bâtard*: i.e., such as Genet, born to an unknown father] in onto-theology or in the Hegelian [or Hegel's] family"; translation slightly modified. On Derrida's "machine à draguer" (*draguer*, of course, in French, can have both a mechanical as well as a sexual meaning), see *Glas*, 228–30b, 204–5b.

78. See Jean Genet, *Œuvres complètes*, IV (Paris: Gallimard, 1968), 19–31; *Fragments of the Artwork*, trans. Charlotte Mandell (Stanford: Stanford University Press, 2003), 91–102; translation modified. From the mid-1950s onwards, it seems Genet was indeed hard at work on a text devoted to Rembrandt, whose paintings he much admired, but which, like many of Genet's other projects, as his 1967 title indicates, was eventually either destroyed or abandoned. A number of fragments belonging to the work on Rembrandt do however remain: the essay "Le Secret de Rembrandt" (1958) in *Œuvres complètes*, V (Paris: Gallimard, 1979), 31–38; *Fragments of the Artwork*, 84–90, together with two further pieces, "Il mio antico modo di vedere il mondo . . . " and "Il nostro sguardo . . . ," which first appeared in Italian, printed the one after the other, translated by Francesco Quadri in *Il menabò* 7 (1964): 35–45. On their first appearance in the original French, printed in two parallel columns, in *Tel Quel* 29 (Spring 1967): 3–11, it was these last two texts that took on the joint or additional title, "Ce qui est resté d'un Rembrandt . . . " The longer of the two also appeared on its own in English, in a translation by Bernard Frechtman, under the title "Something Which Seemed to Resemble Decay," in *Art and Literature: An International Review* 1 (March 1964): 77–86. When in 1966 Genet was invited by Philippe Sollers to contribute a text to *Tel Quel*, it was at Paule Thévenin's suggestion that the two Rembrandt fragments were brought together, though it was Genet who insisted they be printed in facing columns. During the same period it was also Thévenin who was responsible for introducing Derrida to Genet, and in the years that followed the two men were to see each other frequently, if not on a regular basis. On Genet's Rembrandt project and his friendship with Thévenin and Derrida, see Jean-Bernard Moraly, *Jean Genet: la vie écrite* (Paris: Éditions de la Différence, 1988); and Edmund White, *Genet* (London: Chatto and Windus, 1993). Moraly (298–99) also usefully reprints Genet's brief tribute to Derrida published in *Les Lettres françaises* in the 29 March–4 April issue, 1972.

79. To date, rather surprisingly, *Glas* has received relatively little detailed attention. The only sustained analysis of the book remains Geoffrey Hartman's *Saving the Text: Literature/Derrida/Philosophy* (Baltimore: Johns Hopkins Uni-

versity Press, 1981), which provides a responsive and well-documented account of *Glas,* though it takes the not unproblematic step of approaching the book, in Hartman's words, "as a work of art" and by "bracket[ing] specific philosophical concepts developed by Derrida, especially in the *Grammatology*" (90). Other readers have placed the emphasis more squarely on Derrida's interpretation of Hegel, as testified by the essays collected in *Hegel after Derrida,* ed. Stuart Barnett (London: Routledge, 1998). Other predominantly philosophical studies worth noting include François Laruelle, "Le Style di-phallique de Jacques Derrida," *Critique* 334 (March 1975): 320–39; Sarah Kofman, "Ça cloche," in *Lectures de Derrida* (Paris: Galilée, 1984), 115–51; Mark C. Taylor, *Altarity* (Chicago: University of Chicago Press, 1987), 255–303; Rodolphe Gasché, *Inventions of Difference* (Cambridge, MA: Harvard University Press, 1994), 171–98; Robert Smith, *Derrida and Autobiography* (Cambridge: Cambridge University Press, 1995); and David Farrell Krell, *The Purest of Bastards: Works of Mourning, Art, and Affirmation in the Thought of Jacques Derrida* (University Park: Pennsylvania State University Press, 2000), 149–73. More specific discussion of Derrida's reading of Genet (and of Sartre) may be found in the following: Juliette Simont, "Bel effet d'où jaillissent les roses . . . ," *Les Temps modernes* 510 (January 1989): 113–37; Colin Davis, "Genet's *Journal du voleur* and the Ethics of Reading," *French Studies* 48, no. 1 (January 1994): 50–62; Christina Howells, *Derrida: Deconstruction from Phenomenology to Ethics* (Cambridge: Polity, 1998), 84–95; Ian Magadera, "*Seing* Genet, Citation and Mourning: apropos *Glas* by Jacques Derrida," *Paragraph* 21, no. 1 (March 1998): 28–44; Simon Critchley, *Ethics, Politics, Subjectivity* (London: Verso, 1999), 30–50.

80. Witness for instance this short passage towards the end of *Glas*—without it being clear to whom it refers—which sparks a sequence of reflections on spontaneous, sacrificial combustion in Hegel, set alongside the minor ritual observed by Genet's narrator in *Pompes funèbres,* who carries a small matchbox in his pocket as a provisional, but empty coffin: "How does he do it? He is ready. He has always had his corpse on him, in his pocket, in a matchbox. Near at hand. It catches fire [*Ça s'allume:* as Derrida points out throughout *Glas, Ça* or *Sa* is code for *Savoir absolu,* Absolute Knowledge] all on its own. It would have to, truly [*Ça devrait*]. He feels himself obstructing his death, a tiny living soul obstructing the sublime, immeasurable, unconstricted [*sans taille:* both huge and uncut] erection [*surélévation*] of his colossus. He is only a detail [*détail:* a detached element] of his double, unless it is the reverse [*à moins que ce ne soit le contraire*]." See Derrida, *Glas,* 289b; 260b; translation modified.

81. On *Potenz* and *potence,* see Derrida, *Glas,* 120–22a, 104–6a; 223b, 199b.

82. There were no doubt further, strategic reasons for Derrida's choice of texts. That of Hegel was arguably self-evident, a self-evident moment in the questioning of self-evidence as such. The choice of Genet was equally far from

arbitrary. For Genet, the imprisoned vagrant, failed shoplifter, and purloiner of rare books, was also the obverse—which is also to say the continuation by other means—of the jealously possessive, yet always dispossessed, cruelly incarcerated figure of Artaud. "Property is theft," Proudhon famously observed; in Artaud and Genet, what Derrida explores is the circularity and solidarity of the two terms in that equation.

83. See Jean-Paul Sartre, *Saint Genet, comédien et martyr* (Paris: Gallimard, 1952); *Saint Genet, Actor and Martyr*, trans. Bernard Frechtman (London: W. H. Allen, 1963).

84. On Genet's reaction to the book, and the reason why he agreed publication should proceed, see the 1964 interview with Madeleine Cobeil in Jean Genet, *L'Ennemi déclaré*, ed. Albert Dichy (Paris: Gallimard, 1991), 21–22; *The Declared Enemy*, trans. Jeff Fort (Stanford: Stanford University Press, 2004), 11–12.

85. Sartre, *Saint Genet, comédien et martyr*, 47; *Saint Genet, Actor and Martyr*, 35; original emphasis; translation modified. Derrida cites this passage in *Glas*, 37b, 29b.

86. Sartre, *Saint Genet, comédien et martyr*, 52; *Saint Genet, Actor and Martyr*, 40; translation modified.

87. Sartre's crudely stereotypical argument continues as follows: "I am well aware that respectable people are also objects for each other. I am given names: I am this fair-haired man with glasses, this Frenchman, this teacher. But if I am named by someone else, I can name them in return. Both naming and named, I live in this reciprocity; words are thrown to me, I catch them, and pass them on to others, I understand from others what I am to them. *Genet is alone when he steals [Genet est seul à voler]*. Later on, he will become acquainted with other thieves, but he will remain alone. In the world of thieving, as we shall see, there is no reciprocity. This is not surprising, since these monsters have been designed [*on a fabriqué ces monstres*] in such a way that they are unable to express solidarity with one another. [At this point in Sartre's text, a lengthy footnote opens, which begins: "The same absence of reciprocity may be noted among homosexuals [*chez les pédérastes*]" and continues in similar vein for some seventeen lines in all.] Thus, when Genet is given this dizzying name [i.e., the name: thief], he cannot make out its meaning from those who have given him that name. It is as if a page in a book suddenly became conscious and felt itself being *read aloud* [*lue à haute voix*] without being able to *read itself [se lire]*. He is read, deciphered, pointed at: others take possession of his being; but this possession by others is experienced by him as if it were a hemorrhage, he leaches away into the eyes of others [*il s'écoule dans les yeux d'autrui*], he avoids himself, is emptied of all substance." See Sartre, *Saint Genet, comédien et martyr*, 52–53; *Saint Genet, Actor and Martyr*, 40–41; original emphasis; translation modified. Admittedly, this view of homosexuality was not far removed from one that Genet was also given to pro-

fess on occasion, notably in a prose sketch written in the wake of Sartre's study, and published in *Les Temps modernes* in August 1954, but by then already abandoned by its author, in which he declares that "homosexuality is not a given I could accept as such. Not only is there no tradition to come to the help of the pederast [*le pédéraste*], or to bequeath him a system of references—except by omission—or to instruct him in any convention of morality based solely on homosexuality, its nature, irrespective of whether it is acquired or given, is experienced on the theme of guilt [*thème de culpabilité*]. It isolates me, cuts me off from the rest of the world and from every other pederast. We hate ourselves and each other, both in ourselves and in each one of us. We tear ourselves and each other apart. Our relationships being shattered [*brisés*], homosexuality [*l'inversion*] is lived out in solitary fashion. As for language, which is the basis, constantly renewed, for ties between people [*d'un lien entre les hommes*], homosexuals vitiate it, parody it, dissolve it." See Jean Genet, *Fragments . . . et autres textes* (Paris: Gallimard, 1990), 77–78; *Fragments of the Artwork*, 23; translation modified. A more complex, albeit similarly speculative account of homosexuality by Genet is outlined in a 1952 letter to Sartre, cited by Edmund White in his *Genet*, 441–44. In this encounter between Sartre and Genet, it was nevertheless the straight existentialist philosopher rather than the perverse delinquent writer who desired the last word, making the astonishing claim, a hundred or so pages later, that "[w]hatever mistakes I may make about him, I am sure that I know him better than he knows me, for I have a passion for understanding men and he a passion for not knowing [*ignorer*: not to know, to ignore] them." See Sartre, *Saint Genet, comédien et martyr*, 158; *Saint Genet, Actor and Martyr*, 137; translation modified. In this encounter between philosophy and writing nothing, perhaps, could be further from the truth.

88. Again, the lofty—prescriptive—omniscience that informs Sartre's interpretation is breathtaking. "First and foremost an object—for others," he writes, "this is what Genet is in the depths of his being. It is too early to speak of his homosexuality, but we can at least indicate its origin. Simone de Beauvoir has shown that female sexuality derives its chief characteristics from the fact that woman [*la femme*] is an object for the other and for herself before being a subject. One can guess that Genet, who is an object par excellence, *will make himself an object* in sexual relations and that his eroticism will be similar to female eroticism." See Sartre, *Saint Genet, comédien et martyr*, 48; *Saint Genet, Actor and Martyr*, 37; original emphasis; translation modified.

89. Sartre, *Saint Genet, comédien et martyr*, 658; *Saint Genet, Actor and Martyr*, 596; translation modified.

90. See Sartre, *Saint Genet, comédien et martyr*, 521; *Saint Genet, Actor and Martyr*, 469.

91. Asked by Madeleine Cobeil why he thought Sartre had spent six hundred pages analysing his life and work, Genet replied with simple, but potentially devastating irony: "I am the illustration of one of his theories about freedom." See Genet, *L'Ennemi déclaré*, 21; *The Declared Enemy*, 11. In similar vein, shortly after the publication of Sartre's book, he reportedly observed, in conversation with Cocteau (who had a strong antipathy for *Saint Genet*), "You and Sartre turned me into a statue. I am another [*Je suis un autre*]. This other must now find something to say." See Jean Cocteau, *Le Passé défini I: 1951–1952*, ed. Pierre Chanel (Paris: Gallimard, 1983), 391. Both remarks, at least in part, were no doubt self-defensive, and this explains why Genet may be found elsewhere declaring the very opposite, albeit to the same end. In a later remark to Cocteau, for instance, he asserts that "[Sartre's] book about me is very clever [*d'une grande intelligence*], but it merely repeats what I say myself. It doesn't tell me anything new [*Il ne m'apporte rien de neuf*]." See Jean Cocteau, *Le Passé défini II: 1953*, ed. Pierre Chanel (Paris: Gallimard, 1985), 252.

92. Derrida makes a similar point about Sartre's interpretation of Genet in *Glas*, 37bi; 29bi.

93. Though Sartre's *Saint Genet* is not the main object of Derrida's reading, it is nevertheless the object of severe criticism at several points in *Glas*. See for instance Derrida, *Glas*, 20–21b; 13–14b; and 36–37b; 28–29b. Readers sympathetic to Sartre's *Saint Genet* have on occasion tried to rebut Derrida's analysis. Juliette Simont, in her article, "Bel effet d'où jaillissent les roses . . . ," published in the Sartrean house-journal *Les Temps modernes*, offers a laborious defence of Sartre's position in *Saint Genet* before going on to conclude that, contrary to appearances, as she puts it, it is Sartre rather than Hegel who is the privileged interlocutor of *Glas*, and as such destined in spite of all to make an unscheduled, spectral—Simont calls it "dialectical"—return (137). For his part, Colin Davis, in "Genet's *Journal du voleur* and the Ethics of Reading," also strains credibility, but in another way: after helpfully setting Derrida's commentary on a famous passage from *Journal du voleur* alongside that given by Sartre, Davis then takes issue with what he bizarrely calls Derrida's failure "to say *anything* about the moral shock [sic] occasioned by the image of the abandoned child dribbling and vomiting on his mother" (54). Christina Howells, in her *Derrida: Deconstruction from Phenomenology to Ethics*, takes a different approach, reminiscent of the Freudian logic of the borrowed kettle, suggesting that a key argument in Derrida's early work on Husserl was in fact anticipated over twenty years previously by Sartre (28), that in any case Derrida is guilty of misreading Sartre, albeit creatively (86), and that what Derrida has to say about Genet is profoundly indebted to Sartre anyway. "*Glas*," she concludes, "may be read as an unacknowledged response to Sartre's work, whether by opposing it, striking off obliquely from it, expanding it, or even imitating it" (87).

94. Sartre, *Saint Genet, comédien et martyr*, 63; *Saint Genet, Actor and Martyr*, 49; translation modified.

95. Compare Derrida, *Signéponge / Signsponge*, trans. Richard Rand (New York: Columbia University Press, 1984), 30–33; *Signéponge* (Paris: Seuil, 1988), 31.

96. Derrida, *Glas*, 254a, 227–28a; translation modified.

97. Derrida, *Glas*, 255a, 228a; translation modified.

98. Derrida, *Glas*, 43b, 34–35b; translation modified. Later, Genet identifies the wild or dog-rose, the *églantine*, as one of his own fondest personal emblems, and sole luxury once it came to pushing up his own gravestone. See Jean Genet, *Un captif amoureux* (Paris: Gallimard, 1986), 453–54, 486; *Prisoner of Love*, trans. Barbara Bray (New York: New York Review of Books, 2003), 386, 414–15.

99. Derrida, *Glas*, 50–51b, 41–42b; translation modified.

100. See Genet, *Journal du voleur*, 24; *The Thief's Journal*, 19. "When a limb [*membre*] is removed, I am told," Genet writes, "the one that is left grows stronger"; translation modified.

101. See Genet, *Journal du voleur*, 55; *The Thief's Journal*, 45–46. Derrida cites this sequence at some length in *Glas*, 235–39b, 210–14b.

102. Genet, *Journal du voleur*, 22; *The Thief's Journal*, 17; translation modified. Derrida quotes this passage and comments on it in *Glas*, 164–69b, 145–49b. This is the allegedly shocking episode to which Davis refers in the article cited earlier.

103. Derrida, *Glas*, 148b, 130b; translation modified. As Derrida points out, the *Journal du voleur* both begins and ends with a lament for the *bagne*, and the subject or theme of the penal colony was to haunt Genet for many years to come, culminating—but precisely not culminating—in the unfinished theatre project published after Genet's death under the title *Le Bagne*, the most complete version of which is given in Jean Genet, *Théâtre complet*, ed. Michel Corvin and Albert Dichy (Paris: Gallimard, 2002), 757–811. It should be noted that *antherection*, here, though owing more than something to the psychoanalytic concept of castration, is anything but reducible to it, as Derrida explains some pages later. "The logic of antherection," he writes, "ought not to be simplified. It [*Ça*: simultaneously the impersonal *it*, the psychoanalytic *id*, and the *Sa* of Absolute Knowledge] does not erect *against* or *in spite of* castration, *despite* the wound or infirmity, by castrating castration. It bands [*Ça bande*: from *bander*, to have an erection, to bend, and to bandage] erect, castration [*la castration*: Derrida's syntax leaves it open whether castration is subject or object of the clause]. Infirmity itself bandages itself [*se panse*: from *panser*, to bandage, but phonetically indistinguishable from *penser*, to think] by banding erect [*à bander*: i.e., bandages/thinks in the very act of bandaging or having an erection]. Infirmity is what (as still today the

old language has it) *produces* erection [I commented earlier on Derrida's criticisms of this concept of production]: a prosthesis [*prothèse:* both prosthesis and
pro-thesis] that no event of castration will have preceded. The structure of prosthesis belongs to intumescence. Nothing holds up [*Rien ne tient debout:* both literally and metaphorically] otherwise." See *Glas,* 157b, 138b; translation somewhat
modified.

104. Derrida, *Glas,* 7b, 1b; translation modified.

105. See Derrida, *Glas,* 222a, 198a; 19–20b, 12b.

106. Derrida, *Glas,* 88b, 75b; translation modified.

107. White, *Genet,* 726. Unfortunately for English-speaking readers, the
standard translation of the book tends, however, to normalise Genet's often idiosyncratic use (or non-use) of paragraph and section breaks. Compare "Entretien
avec Leila Shahid," *Genet à Chatila,* ed. Jérôme Hankins (Arles: Actes Sud, [1992]
1994), 23–78, where Genet explains as follows: "Because in this book the blanks
count a lot. And I would like to stage the book myself, and lay out the text as I
want. I would like to choose the places where I insert a gap between one paragraph and the next" (55).

108. Derrida, *Glas,* 26bi, 19bi; translation modified. Derrida himself draws
attention to the function of the words, *déjà* (already), *Derrière le rideau* (behind
the curtain) as cryptic signatures. As Geoffrey Hartman points out in *Saving the
Text* (94), Derrida even provides his readers with another extended epitaph in
the form of the following one line paragraph: "*Dionysos Erigone Eriopétal Ré-
séda*"; see *Glas,* 129b, 112b.

109. Derrida, *Glas,* 30b, 23b. It would not be too much of an exaggeration to
suggest perhaps that *Glas,* among others, might be read not only as a reworking
of the problematics of the *il y a* (and the *neutre*) in Blanchot and of the reading of
Hegel advanced in "La Littérature et le droit à la mort [Literature and the Right
to Death]" but also as a discreet commentary on Blanchot's *Le Très-Haut, L'Arrêt
de mort,* and *La Folie du jour.* Many similar motifs come into view: the recessive
movement of *Aufhebung,* undecidability, the figure of the sister (and particularly
of Antigone), the crypt, the apocalypse, the giving and taking of light, blindness
and vision, and the remainder of time. It would equally be possible to read
L'Écriture du désastre in turn as a commentary on *Glas.* It is perhaps not surprising in this respect that Derrida's very last paper on Blanchot, presented in March
2003 shortly after Blanchot's death, was an analysis of "La Litterature et le droit
à la mort" and the death penalty. See Derrida, *Parages,* 269–300.

110. Derrida, *Signéponge / Signsponge,* 56–57; original emphasis; translation
modified. A slightly different version appears in Derrida, *Signéponge,* 48–49. On
ex-appropriation with specific reference to Ponge, see Jacques Derrida and Gérard Farasse, *Déplier Ponge* (Villeneuve d'Ascq: Presses universitaires du Septen-
trion, 2005), 72–73.

111. Derrida, *Glas,* 48b, 39b; translation modified.

112. Genet, *Théâtre complet*, 912. The letter in question is dated 21 November 1957; it is quite likely therefore that among the torn-up manuscripts that Genet mentions was at least some of the material he had written on Rembrandt. (In August 1952, he similarly reported to Cocteau that he had burnt, or rather torn up all he had written in the preceding five years, i.e., since the publication of *Pompes funèbres;* see Cocteau, *Le Passé défini I*, 318. In 1982, Genet said much the same to Leila Shahid, referring to the presumed initial version of the article, "Quatre heures à Chatila," similarly torn to pieces and consigned to the toilet, with the caveat that, according to Genet, if what he had written was worth anything, it was preserved somewhere else than on paper; see *Genet à Chatila*, 46.)

113. Genet, *Œuvres complètes*, IV, 21–22, 22–23; *Fragments of the Artwork*, 92, 93; original emphasis; translation modified; author's emphasis. Readers of Sartre's *Les Mots* will recall the importance of the metaphor of the train journey for the author's account of responsibility and irresponsibility, innocence and guilt.

114. Sartre, *Saint Genet, comédien et martyr*, 53; *Saint Genet, Actor and Martyr*, 41; translation modified. Genet describes the same experience in a passage in the essay, "L'Atelier de Alberto Giacometti," *Œuvres complètes*, V, 50–51; *Fragments of the Artwork*, 49, where it is reported as having occurred in 1953, barely a year after the publication of Sartre's *Saint Genet*.

115. Genet, *Œuvres complètes*, IV, 26; *Fragments of the Artwork*, 96–97; translation modified.

116. Derrida, *Donner la mort* (Paris: Galilée, 1999), 114–16; *The Gift of Death*, 2nd ed., trans. David Wills (Chicago: University of Chicago Press, 2008), 82–84. Wills translates: "Every other (one) is every (bit) other."

117. See Derrida, "Circonfession [*Circumfession*]," in Geoffrey Bennington and Jacques Derrida, *Jacques Derrida* (Paris: Seuil, 1991), 70–73; *Jacques Derrida*, trans. Geoffrey Bennington (Chicago: University of Chicago Press, 1992), 70–74.

118. On Genet's strange relationship with Pilorge, see François Sentein, *L'Assassin et son bourreau: Jean Genet et l'affaire Pilorge* (Paris: Éditions de la Différence, 1999).

119. Genet, *Œuvres complètes*, V, 42; *Fragments of the Artwork*, 42; translation modified. Compare Derrida, *Glas*, 207bi, 184bi.

120. Genet, *Journal du voleur*, 9; *The Thief's Journal*, 7; translation modified. *Émoi* can also be read as the emotion most proper to me [*moi*] *and* as the one that has the effect of excluding me from myself [*é-moi*]. What Genet rightly calls: oscillation from one to the other.

121. Genet, *Œuvres complètes*, IV, 21, 28; *Fragments of the Artwork*, 91, 99; translation modified.

122. Genet, *Œuvres complètes*, II (Paris: Gallimard, 1951), 274; *The Miracle of the Rose*, trans. Bernard Frechtman (Harmondsworth: Penguin, 1971), 62; translation slightly modified. Some pages earlier, Genet's narrator had written: "I am

glad to have given the finest names and finest titles (archangel, sun-child, my Spanish night-time) to so many youngsters that I have none left with which to magnify Bulkaen." See Genet, *Œuvres complètes*, II, 248–49; *The Miracle of the Rose*, 33; translation modified. Bulkaen, accordingly, received the only remaining, the worst—which was also the best.

123. Derrida, *Glas*, 41b, 33b; translation modified. The word *debris* [*débris*], underlined by Derrida himself, is of course another signature, and recurs as such at the foot of the last page of *Glas*, on the right-hand side: see *Glas*, 291b, 262b.

124. See Genet, *Œuvres complètes*, IV, 27; *Fragments of the Artwork*, 98; translation modified.

125. See Genet, *Œuvres complètes*, IV, 9–18; *Théâtre complet*, 879–88; *Fragments of the Artwork*, 103–12.

126. See Derrida, *Glas*, 9a, 3a. "The *Klang*," Derrida explains, "announces the end of the religion of flowers and the phallic columns, but is not yet a voice or a language. This ringing, sonorous light reverberating as on a stone bell [*cloche*] is already no longer mute, but not yet speaking [*parlante*] (*nur Klang und nicht Sprache*)"; translation slightly modified. *Klang* echoes persistently at the beginning and ending of the left-hand column. "An affinity here," says Derrida, "between *Klang* and writing. In so far as it resists conception [*conception:* in the philosophical and gynecological sense], the *Klingen* of *Klang*, for the Hegelian logos, is cast in the role of its dumb player or fool [*joue le rôle de son muet ou de son fou*], a kind of mechanical automaton that sets itself going and operates itself without meaning, or meaning to say anything." See *Glas*, 16ai, 9–10ai; translation modified.

127. See Derrida, *Et cetera* . . . (Paris: L'Herne, 2005); "Et Cetera," in *Deconstructions: A User's Guide*, ed. Nicholas Royle (Houndmills: Palgrave, 2000), 282–305.

128. Derrida, *Glas*, 159b, 140b.

129. See Derrida, *Glas*, 137–39b, 119–21b.

130. Derrida, *Glas*, 189b, 168b; translation modified.

131. Derrida, *Glas*, 222–23b, 198–99b; original emphasis; translation modified.

132. Derrida, *Glas*, 54b, 44b; translation modified. For the various explicit gestures by which *Glas* turns aside from contemporary literary theory or literary criticism, see *Glas*, 50b, 40–41b; 56–57b, 47b.

133. See Derrida, *Glas*, 229b, 204b. "What he would tolerate with the greatest difficulty would be for me, whether for myself or for others, to gain mastery over his text. By supplying—they put it—the rules for production or generative grammar of all his statements. There is no risk of that. We are very far from it, this, I repeat, is barely preliminary [*à peine préliminaire*], and will remain so. No

more names [*plus de noms:* more names or nouns, no more names or nouns]. I shall have to go back to his text, which has this one under surveillance as it unfolds [*pendant son jeu*]"; translation modified. The principal target of these remarks, rather than literary criticism in general, was clearly the linguistics-based literary theory widely practised in France at the time, notably by Julia Kristeva and the *Tel Quel* group.

134. Derrida, *Glas*, 191–92b, 169–70b; translation modified.

135. Derrida, *Glas*, 291b, 262b. The quotation may be found in Friedrich Nietzsche, *Kritische Studienausgabe*, IV, 207–8; *Thus Spoke Zarathustra*, trans. R. J. Hollingdale (Harmondsworth: Penguin, 1961), 184–85.

136. Derrida, *Ulysse gramophone*, 125–26; *Acts of Literature*, 297–98; original emphases; translation modified. Though Derrida, albeit with an important caveat, does indeed characterise the *yes* in this instance as having transcendental status, this should not be taken to imply that yes is a single, self-identical point of origin. As Derrida goes on to argue, *yes* is always, yes, yes, always, traversed by repetition and necessarily redoubled, never self-identical, always a response or responding to the arrival of the other.

137. See Derrida, "Countersignature [*Contresignature*]," trans. Mairéad Hanrahan, *Paragraph* 27, no. 2 (2004): 7–42. I am grateful to Mairéad Hanrahan for allowing me sight of Derrida's French text. On *obséquence*, a coinage that condenses *séquence* (sequence, what follows), *obséquieux* (obsequious, deferential, even differential), and *obsèques* (funeral rites), compare Derrida, *Glas*, 134bi, 116–17bi, where Derrida writes: "I follow, I am [*je suis*, which may be construed as belonging either to the verb *suivre*, to follow, or *être*, to be] the mother. The text. The mother is *behind* [*derrière*: Derrida's emphasis, and signature]—everything I follow or am [*que je suis*], do [*fais*: do or make], and appear [*parais*: this may be the present tense of the verb *paraître*, meaning: I appear, or the imperfect tense of the verb *parer*, meaning: I adorned, or of its homonym, *parer*, meaning: I parried; needless to say, none of these possibilities can entirely be excluded]—the mother follows [*suit*]. As she follows absolutely, she always survives, in a future that will never have been presentable, that which she will have engendered, attending, impassive, fascinating and provocative, the burial [*la mise en terre*] of that of which she has foreseen the death. Logic of obsequence [*Logique de l'obséquence*]"; translation modified. Derrida's words, though they rehearse in the first instance the recurrent, central scene of Genet's *Pompes funèbres*, have particular resonance for readers of Genet's subsequent work, particularly the final sequences of *Un captif amoureux*. At the same time they constitute a coded allusion to the death of Derrida's father, Aimé Derrida, in 1970, and his survival by Derrida's mother, Georgette, who, thirty years earlier, in March 1940, had also found herself in the position of burying a son, Derrida's younger brother, Norbert, aged two; Derrida recalls his mother's own subsequent illness and death in

some detail in "Circonfession," in Bennington and Derrida, *Jacques Derrida*. There, Derrida reminds the reader that his mother's holy name was Esther (20); elsewhere he points out that the word *reste*, remainder, which is such a crucial resource in the whole of *Glas*, is a cryptic quasi-anagram of that maternal name; see Jacques Derrida, *La Carte postale* (Paris: Aubier-Flammarion, 1980), 79; *The Post Card*, trans. Alan Bass (Chicago: University of Chicago Press, 1987), 71.

138. Interviewed in 1983 in Vienna by Rüdiger Wischenbart and Layla Shahid Barrada, Genet declared, for instance, preaching very much to the converted, as follows: "When I wrote what I did, I was thirty years old, when I began writing. When I finished, I was thirty-four or thirty-five [i.e., 1944–45]. But it was all a dream [*du rêve*]; at any rate a day-dream [*une rêverie*]. I had done my writing in prison. Once I was released, I was lost. And I only rediscovered myself, and in the real world [*le monde réel*], with these two revolutionary movements, the Black Panthers and the Palestinians. Then I began to accept the real world for what it was [*me soumettais au monde réel*], meaning: this is what you've got to do today, don't do what you did yesterday, in a word, I began acting according to the real world and no longer the grammatical world. . . . In so far as the real world is thought to be the opposite of the world of daydreaming. Of course, if you go into it a bit further, you soon realise that daydreaming belongs to the real world. Dreams are reality. But you also know that you can act on daydreaming in an almost unlimited way. You can't act upon the real [*le réel*] in an unlimited way. You obviously need a different discipline, which is no longer grammatical discipline." See Genet, *L'Ennemi déclaré*, 269–96 (277); *The Declared Enemy*, 232–56 (239–40); translation modified. Genet's remarks seem forthright enough; but they are also deceptive. Though they seek to accredit the idea of a decisive shift or evolution in the author's relationship to writing, it is apparent that, as the explanation proceeds, Genet is driven to revise most of the terms of his original statement. Here, as earlier, the writer shows himself more than usually adept at giving his audience mixed messages.

139. Critchley, *Ethics, Politics, Subjectivity,* 48–49. Critchley it was, of course, who was one of the first to chart in English the so-called ethico-political turn in recent French thought in his book, *The Ethics of Deconstruction: Derrida and Levinas* (Oxford: Blackwell, 1992). For an early, contrary view of *Un captif amoureux* that firmly placed the emphasis on the poetical rather than political dimension of the book, see Patrice Bougon, "Un captif amoureux," *L'Infini* 22 (Summer 1988): 109–26.

140. Critchley, *Ethics, Politics, Subjectivity,* 49.

141. Critchley, *Ethics, Politics, Subjectivity,* 47. This is not to say that *Pompes funèbres* should necessarily be read as "a celebration of Nazism," the view taken, for instance, by Leo Bersani in *A Future for Astyanax* (Boston: Little, Brown, 1976), 287; it is to underline that the novel is nothing if not profoundly am-

biguous, as Patrice Bougon suggests in "Le Cliché, la métaphore et la digression dans *Pompes funèbres* et *Un captif amoureux*," *L'Esprit créateur* 35, no. 1 (Spring 1995): 70–78; and "Politique, ironie et mythe dans *Pompes funèbres*," *Europe*, no. 808–9 (August–September 1996): 65–77.

142. Genet, *Un captif amoureux*, 243; *Prisoner of Love*, 204; Genet's emphasis.

143. See Genet, *Un captif amoureux*, 229–31; *Prisoner of Love*, 192–93. Interestingly, in the precursor episode that prefigures the night-time scene in Irbid recounted in Genet's 1972 article, "Les Palestiniens," the mother brings a glass of tea as well as a cup of coffee to the narrator (who drinks the tea). See Genet, "Les Palestiniens," retranslated from the English by Valérie Cadet and Jérôme Hankins, *Genet à Chatila*, 116.

144. See Genet, *Un captif amoureux*, 230–31; *Prisoner of Love*, 193; translation modified.

145. See Critchley, *Ethics, Politics, Subjectivity*, 46.

146. Critchley, *Ethics, Politics, Subjectivity*, 47.

147. Genet, *Un captif amoureux*, 414; *Prisoner of Love*, 353. Genet's words are banal, yet prophetic and also true: "Literary illusion is not pointless, or not entirely, even if the reader knows all this better than I do, a book also has the ambition of showing, beneath the disguise of words, causes, clothes, even mourning dress, the skeleton and the skeleton dust lying in wait. The author too, like those of whom he speaks, is dead"; translation modified.

148. See Genet, *Un captif amoureux*, 476, 483; *Prisoner of Love*, 405–6, 412.

149. See Genet, *Un captif amoureux*, 51; *Prisoner of Love*, 40.

150. Genet, *Un captif amoureux*, 443–44; *Prisoner of Love*, 378; translation slightly modified.

151. See Genet, *Un captif amoureux*, 123; *Prisoner of Love*, 103. "Whenever I considered the broader perspective, the Palestinian Revolution was never a desire for territories, for so much derelict land, small-holdings, and unfenced orchards, but a vast movement of revolt about land rights reaching to the limits of the Islamic world, not only involving territorial boundaries but also calling for the revision, probably even the negation of a theology as numbing as a Breton cradle. It was clear the dream, not yet the decision, of the fedayeen was to overthrow the twenty-two Arab nations, to go beyond this and make everyone burst out in smiles, childlike ones at first, but quickly foolish ones after"; translation modified. Genet reinforces the point in the 1983 interview mentioned earlier. "Listen," he says, "the day the Palestinians turn into an institution, I will no longer be on their side. The day the Palestinians become a nation like any other, I won't be there any more"; Genet, *L'Ennemi déclaré*, 282; *The Declared Enemy*, 244; translation slightly modified.

152. See for instance Genet, *Un captif amoureux*, 448; *Prisoner of Love*, 381. "The metaphysical struggle, it is impossible to ignore it, is between Jewish morality [*les morales judaïques*] and the values [*valeurs*] of Fatah (using the word in its monetary sense as well, since it is true a few Palestinians have got rich) and of other elements in the PLO, the most reliable of whom smell of cash; between Judaic values [*les valeurs judaïques*], as I say, and living revolts [*les révoltes vivantes*]"; translation modified. Encountering passages such as these, readers are entitled to ask how far Genet's explicit anti-Zionism draws on the language of anti-semitism or at least serves to legitimise it. But if Genet's words are disturbingly ambiguous, is it because of what they say or what they leave unsaid, and how far is it possible, in reading, to reduce a text to any single ideological or other position that may circulate within it? This is of course not to say that to read is to ignore the ineliminable demand of the unspoken and the unreadable—the parameters of which it is impossible by definition to limit in advance. As Blanchot puts it apropros of Nietzsche, some of whose own provocative and controversial statements still give readers pause, "[I]t is true, the thought of Nietzsche is dangerous. But what he tells us before all else is this: if we think, no rest [*si nous pensons, pas de repos*]." See Blanchot, *L'Écriture du désastre*, 189; *The Writing of the Disaster*, 123; translation modified.

153. Genet, *Un captif amoureux*, 437; *Prisoner of Love*, 372; translation slightly modified.

154. Genet, *Un captif amoureux*, 12; *Prisoner of Love*, 6; translation modified.

155. See Genet, *Un captif amoureux*, 126; *Prisoner of Love*, 105–6. In this passage, Barbara Bray's translation unfortunately introduces a paragraph break before the reference to Jouvet, normalising the carefully calculated rhythm of Genet's text and diminishing its impact. On Genet's meeting with Arafat, see White, *Genet*, 637–38. Regarding Jouvet's part in the original staging of *Les Bonnes*, see White, *Genet*, 344–52; and for a detailed account of Genet's work on the play, which soon turned into two plays, the one staged by Jouvet and the one originally written by Genet, see the account given by Corvin and Dichy in Genet, *Théâtre complet*, 1039–79. When both texts were first published together in 1954 Genet added a preface, in the form of a letter to the publisher, Jean-Jacques Pauvert, in which he claimed erroneously and rather mischievously that "having been commissioned by an actor once famous in his day, my play was therefore written from vanity, but amidst great boredom. The publisher can therefore have it, in its two groping versions, but let it stand as proof of inspired stupidity [*une preuve de bêtise inspirée*]." See Genet, *Fragments . . . et autres textes*, 103; *Fragments of the Artwork*, 37; translation modified. In a later interview, given in 1969, Genet offers a slightly different, albeit still questionable account of his relations with the future director of *Les Bonnes*, suggesting that Jouvet "forced me to shorten

and condense the text, which originally was somewhat longer. I believe the end result of these observations was generally positive, though I disliked the production." See Genet, *Théâtre complet*, 1047. Whether the arrangement with Arafat was a further instance of inspired stupidity or represented a decisive positive intervention is a question Genet does not answer.

156. Genet, *Un captif amoureux*, 42; *Prisoner of Love*, 32; translation modified. Here too Bray's English version dispenses with Genet's careful layout, and annexes the sentence to the passage that follows, rather than abandoning it (like Genet) to its strange abyssal solitude as a simultaneously contextualised-decontextualised, stand-alone pronouncement.

157. The secondary literature dealing with the politics of Genet's late phase is now extensive. For a defence of Genet's position, with contributions from Leila Shahid, Jérôme Hankins, Tahar Ben Jelloun, Alain Milianti, Georges Banu, François Regnault, and Genet himself, see *Genet à Chatila*; for a wide-ranging, informative, yet disappointingly descriptive account of Genet's political and other activities after 1968, see Hadrien Laroche, *Le Dernier Genet* (Paris: Seuil, 1997).

158. See White, *Genet*, 641–44.

159. Sartre, *Saint Genet, comédien et martyr*, 230; *Saint Genet, Actor and Martyr*, 203; translation modified. Sartre continues, however: "It is not hard to imagine he would find it difficult to subscribe to most of anti-semitism's key propositions. Deny the Jews political rights? But he doesn't care a fig about politics. Exclude them from the professions, and prevent them from opening shops? That would amount to saying he wouldn't deign to rob them, since shopkeepers are his victims. An anti-semite defined by his reluctance to rob Jews would be a curious beast. Does he therefore want to kill them in their masses? But massacres are of no interest to Genet; the murders of which he dreams are individual ones. What then? When cornered, he declares that he 'couldn't sleep with a Jew [*ne pourrait pas coucher avec un Juif*].' Israel, then, can rest easy at night"; translation modified.

160. Éric Marty, *Bref séjour à Jérusalem* (Paris: Gallimard, 2003), 176. Marty's core chapter, "Jean Genet à Chatila," was first published six months earlier, amidst some controversy, in *Les Temps modernes* 622 (December 2002–January 2003): 2–72. On the denial or disavowal [*déni*] of good castration or the right sort of castration [*la bonne castration*] in Genet ("good," the author explains, "in that it represents for the subject the possibility of inscribing himself within the symbolic order, in the true order of language [*l'ordre vrai du langage*], that is, an order that allows the possibility of the true"), see Éric Marty, *Jean Genet, post-scriptum* (Lagrasse: Verdier, 2006), 100. Rather oddly, in a contemporary essay on Genet's theatre, "Jean Genet dramaturge ou l'expérience de l'Autre," in *Critique* 671 (April 2003): 252–65, not collected in this volume, Marty draws attention to the

mysterious fact (which might have prompted a lesser commentator to revise his or her initial interpretation) that "while [Genet's] whole narrative work aims to foreclose the figure of the Other, not only through a psychology of betrayal, but also through an ontology in which language itself is the bottomless pit from which speech, in its very appearance, draws treachery like some natural poison, his theatrical work by contrast presupposes, at multiple levels, an abandonment as real as it is imaginary, as passive as it is active, to otherness [*l'altérité*]" (254–55). Marty was not however alone in accusing Genet of covert rightist, fascist sympathies; following Marty's lead, Ivan Jablonka, in *Les Vérités inavouables de Jean Genet* (Paris: Seuil, 2004), puts forward a similar, sociologically grounded analysis, using some informative but inconclusive archival research into the writer's early life, and invoking some of his collaborationist friendships under the Occupation, together with the thematic evidence of *Pompes funèbres* and other texts, in order to present Genet as a writer motivated largely by *ressentiment* against the bourgeois state, and prey to a deep fascination for the Fascist cult of virility, not unlike, according to Jablonka, despite many appearances to the contrary, the notorious Fascist intellectual and collaborator, Drieu La Rochelle, who, in order to avoid arrest, committed suicide in March 1945. For an indication as to how the continuity between *Pompes funèbres* and *Un captif amoureux* may be understood differently, as a sustained critique of the fantasmatics of political allegiance, see Jean-Michel Rabaté, "Jean Genet: La Position du Franc-Tireur," *L'Esprit créateur* 35, no. 1 (Spring 1995): 30–39; and for a succinct rebuttal of the readings proposed by both Marty and Jablonka, René de Ceccatty, "Jean Genet antisémite? Sur une tenace rumeur," *Critique* 714 (November 2006): 895–911. For Marty's response to de Ceccatty, see "À propos de Jean Genet et de l'antisémitisme," *Critique* 718 (March 2007): 209–20.

161. See Sartre, *Saint Genet, comédien et martyr*, 282–394; *Saint Genet, Actor and Martyr*, 250–353.

162. Marty, *Bref séjour à Jérusalem*, 100.

163. Marty, *Bref séjour à Jérusalem*, 100. For the phrase from Genet (glossing the actions of the French Gestapo), see Genet, *Journal du voleur*, 158; *The Thief's Journal*, 133; translation slightly modified. Elsewhere in his essay Marty dismisses *Journal du voleur* as a work unduly influenced by Sartre and full of empty bravado (104), and Genet's "most contrived book [*son livre le plus factice*]" (125). In his foreword, Marty identifies what he describes here as the promise made to Abraham (and to Job, Noah, and Moses) as a salient characteristic of the philosophy of Husserl, intimately linked with the philosopher's Jewish legacy, in which, Marty writes, "there resounds an entire metaphysics of language that radically excludes the idea of originary treachery [*d'une trahison originaire*], but, on the contrary, makes language the site of a promise, the promise of a bond, the promise of the possibility of truthful discourse" (23–24). On Husserl as an antidote to Genet, see Marty, *Bref séjour à Jérusalem*, 22–25.

164. See Genet, *Un captif amoureux*, 198–99; *Prisoner of Love*, 166. The passage in question is this: after a brief evocation of the air of harmony reigning between the Palestinians and their environment, Genet writes: "These last few lines are intended to delay the moment when I shall ask myself the following question: were it not for the fact it was being waged against a people that seemed to me to be among the murkiest [*ténébreux*] of all, the people whose origin claimed itself to be *the* Origin [*l'Origine*], who proclaimed themselves to have been—and fully intend to remain—the Origin, who designated themselves as being the Depths of Time [*Nuit des Temps*], would the Palestinian Revolution have attracted me with such force? In asking myself the question, I believe I have already supplied the answer. In that it stood out against the backdrop of a Night of Beginnings [*Nuit des Commencements*]—and eternally so—the Palestinian Revolution ceased being an ordinary battle for appropriated land: it was a metaphysical struggle. Imposing its moral code [*sa morale*] and its myths [*mythes*] upon the whole world, Israel became inseparable from Power [*se confondait avec le Pouvoir*]. It *was* Power [*le Pouvoir*]. The mere sight of the meagre guns of the fedayeen showed the immeasurable gap between the equipment of the two armies: on the one hand, only a few dead or wounded, on the other, annihilation, accepted, even intended, by the nations of Europe and the Arab world"; original emphasis; translation modified.

165. See Marty, *Bref séjour à Jérusalem*, 94, 155.

166. See Marty, *Bref séjour à Jérusalem*, 183–84.

167. Marty, *Bref séjour à Jérusalem*, 186. Marty's barb drew from Derrida a swift, if indirect response that bore on the aftermath of the events of Sabra and Chatila. In a footnote to "Jean Genet à Chatila," addressing the issue of the Israeli army's involvement in the massacres, Marty had written as follows, referring to the Israeli defence minister, Ariel Sharon: "Certainly Sharon is not guilty [*Certes Sharon n'est pas coupable*], but he may be suspected of complicity. It is, shall we say, an ambiguous subject" (169). A few months later, in April 2003, interviewed for a special issue of *Le Magazine littéraire* devoted to Emmanuel Levinas, without naming Marty (mentioned merely in passing as some "Parisian author"), Derrida responded to the critic's footnote, which he contrasted sharply with Levinas's more forthright reaction to the massacres, as documented in an article by Alain Finkielkraut some years before ("Le risque du politique," in *Emmanuel Levinas*, ed. Catherine Chalier and Miguel Abensour [Paris: L'Herne, 1991], 468–76). These were the concluding words of Derrida's interview: "In this same article, Finkielkraut cites [these words by Levinas] that I hold to be a true lesson in politics, in Israel, Palestine or anywhere else: 'The person is more holy than any land, even when it is a holy land, for in the face of an offence against a person, this holy land, in its nudity, appears as stone and wood.'" See Derrida, "Entre lui et moi dans l'affection et la confiance partagée," interview by Alain David, *Le Magazine littéraire* 419 (April 2003). 30–34. (Derrida had already quoted

more or less these very same words at Levinas's graveside on 27 December 1995; see Derrida, *Adieu à Emmanuel Levinas* [Paris: Galilée, 1997], 15; *Adieu to Emmanuel Levinas*, trans. Pascale-Anne Brault and Michael Naas [Stanford: Stanford University Press, 1999], 4.) Two months later, exercising his right to reply, Marty sought to set the record straight (*Le Magazine littéraire* 421 [June 2003]: 5). But this did not prevent him in October 2003, in a piece republished in *Jean Genet, post-scriptum*, from again loftily dismissing Derrida, in yet another footnote, declaring his stupefaction [*sic*] at the treatment of perversion, castration, and the phallus in *Glas*, in a passage, Marty wrote, "designed, like a major part of [Derrida's] work, *not* to be read [*pour ne pas être lues*]" (99). But, as so often, the remark cannot do otherwise than rebound on its author, who, perhaps unwittingly, simply shows himself to be—incapable of reading. (In another, earlier footnote in *Bref séjour à Jérusalem*, 186, he had feigned surprise that a significant part of the left-hand column in *Glas* touched on Hegel's discussion of Judaism.)

168. Marty, *Bref séjour à Jérusalem*, 192. The reference is to Lacan's essay, "Kant avec Sade," in Lacan, *Écrits*, 765–90; "Kant with Sade," *October* 51 (1989): 55–75.

169. For the passage in question, see Derrida, *Glas*, 267–69b, 240–42b.

170. See Genet, *Œuvres complètes*, II, 133–34; *Our Lady of the Flowers*, trans. Bernard Frechtman (New York: Grove Press, 1963), 223–24. Compare Derrida, *Glas*, 9ai, 3ai.

171. See Jean-Paul, *Werke*, ed. Norbert Miller, 6 vols. (Munich: Hanser, 1963), VI, 374–75. Jean-Paul, it will be remembered, was one of Blanchot's favourite authors. On conversion as a spectral haunting of the one by the other, see Derrida, *Donner la mort*, 15–56; *The Gift of Death*, 3–35.

172. Derrida, *Glas*, 269b, 241–42b; translation slightly modified. On the *tallith*, or Jewish prayer shawl, which derives its importance from the fringes attached to its four corners, as that which precisely "does not veil or conceal anything, neither shows nor announces any Thing, nor promises the intuition of anything," see Derrida, "Un ver à soie," in Hélène Cixous and Jacques Derrida, *Voiles* (Paris: Galilée, 1998), 44–47; "A Silkworm of One's Own," trans. Geoffrey Bennington, in Derrida, *Acts of Religion*, 326–28; translation modified.

173. See Derrida, "Countersignature," 7.

174. See Genet, *Œuvres complètes*, III (Paris: Gallimard, 1953), 152–53. In this passage, Genet's *curé* has a sudden revelation; it is that the word *revelation* is ambiguous: "'God *reveals* himself to me, and I *reveal the sins of others*.' The word revelation [*révélation*] indicated simultaneously both glory and its precise opposite."

175. The effect of the uncertainty affecting Genet's memories is at times abyssal, as when he wonders in the course of writing *Un captif amoureux*, recalling the famous words of a certain Cretan liar: "what if it were true [*s'il était vrai*]

that writing is a lie"; see Genet, *Un captif amoureux*, 42; *Prisoner of Love*, 32. For Derrida's commentary on these problems in Genet's text, see Derrida, "Counter-signature," 11–12.

176. Genet, *L'Ennemi déclaré*, 9; *The Declared Enemy*, 1. As Derrida notes in "Contresignature," 16–17, Genet's statement belongs to that tradition of para-doxical remarks on friendship and enmity that Derrida explores in *Politiques de l'amitié; The Politics of Friendship*.

177. Derrida, "Countersignature," 7–8. For a different account of the be-trayal of truth, see Critchley, *Ethics, Politics, Subjectivity*, 38–44.

178. Colin Davis, "*Un captif amoureux* and the Commitment of Jean Genet," *French Studies Bulletin* 23 (Summer 1987): 16. If it were a matter of seeking to overcome Hegel, this would merely confirm the movement towards Absolute Knowledge.

179. See Derrida, "Countersignature," 8–10, where Derrida cites *Glas*, 50–51a, 41–42a; and, immediately after, *Glas*, 50–51b, 42–43b. Some pages later ("Countersignature," 19), he adds: "The Hegel and Genet columns are not only opposed, they sometimes confirm and countersign one another, in very strange, surprising ways, with slight displacements, and even on occasion go so far as to authenticate or betray themselves while betraying the truth of the other. That might be thought to be the case, for example, not in *Glas*, but in what I might think of Genet's politics in general in respect of a so-called 'Jewish question,' where a certain Hegel and a certain Genet put forward arguments that are strangely convergent [*concurrents*] or closely related [*proches l'un de l'autre*]"; trans-lation modified.

180. On the redoubled yes, see Derrida, *Ulysse gramophone*, 57–143; *Acts of Literature*, 256–309.

181. Derrida, "Countersignature," 22; translation modified.

182. Derrida and Farasse, *Déplier Ponge*, 107–8. Derrida is glossing here the statement made in *Signéponge / Signsponge*, 52–53, to the effect that "[Ponge's] lesson (his ethics and politics, in other words, his philosophy) interests me less (and in fact I do not always listen to it without a murmur) than the basis on which it is constituted, and which he shows better than anyone, thereby demon-strating (and this is something that is too readily put into doubt) that the in-stance of ethics [*l'instance éthique*] is materially implicated in literature [*travaille la littérature au corps*]. Which is why, rather than *listening* to the lesson he deliv-ers, I prefer to *read him*, that is, in so far as he delivers a lesson *about* morality [*une leçon sur la morale*], and not a moral lesson [*et non pas de morale*], about his genealogy of morals drawn . . . from a morals of genealogy"; original emphasis; translation modified.

183. Derrida, "Countersignature," 28–29; original emphasis; translation modified.

184. Derrida, "Countersignature," 29–30; translation modified.

185. See Derrida, *Donner la mort*, 79–114; *The Gift of Death*, 54–81. As readers will have noted, the figure of Abraham that emerges from these texts is
strongly at odds with the supremely confident patriarch described by Éric Marty
in his presentation of the authoritative power of the biblical promise. This no
doubt explains Marty's insensitivity to at least one element that is crucially at
stake in Derrida's account of Abraham, which is the extraordinarily complex,
often violent and bloody entanglement, the one within and alongside the other,
of which *Un captif amoureux* is itself a faithful-unfaithful dramatisation, of the
three so-called religions of the Book: Judaism, Christianity, and Islam. This is
what Derrida meant, as Simon Critchley seemingly fails to realise, glossing it
simply as a statement in favour of "the concrete actuality of revolution" (*Ethics,
Politics, Subjectivity*, 48), when, in response to the news that Genet was in Beirut,
"among the Palestinians at war," Derrida remarked in *Glas*, "I know that what interests me is taking place (and has its place) [*a (son) lieu*] over there"; see Derrida,
Glas, 45b, 36b. "These warring brothers, Jews, Christians, and Muslims," Derrida observes, "have no idea of what their unconscious gives them, they have no
inkling of the legacy their Father had lent them. A sacred heritage, spoils of war,
prayers without guarantee of address: so many poems for all eternity." See Derrida, "Lettres sur un aveugle," in Jacques Derrida and Safaa Fathy, *Tourner les
mots* (Paris: Galilée, 2000), 99. Some years before, in February–March 1994,
Derrida for similar reasons concluded his essay "Foi et savoir" ("Faith and Knowledge") by countersigning a sentence from Genet's recently published 1972 text
"Les Palestiniens," in which the writer remarked: "One of the questions that I
will not avoid [*que je n'éviterai pas*] is that of religion." See *Genet à Chatila*, 117; and
La Religion, ed. Jacques Derrida and Gianni Vattimo, 86; *Acts of Religion*, 101.

186. See Derrida, *Donner la mort*, 161–209; *The Gift of Death*, 119–58. The expression *au secret* means literally: in solitary confinement, in isolation, or kept
incommunicado.

187. See Derrida, *Donner la mort*, 206–8; *The Gift of Death*, 156–57. It would
not be hard, in each of these given clauses, to detect the overwhelming and unavoidable influence (both more and less than influence) of the work of Blanchot,
and, more specifically, of Blanchot's thought of the *neutre*. "There is secrecy [*Il y
a du secret*: i.e., secrecy and secret]," Derrida notes elsewhere, recalling Blanchot's earlier remarks on Heraclitus and the neuter, and explains: "But the secret
does not conceal itself [*ne se dissimule pas*]. Heterogeneous to the hidden, the obscure, the noctural, the invisible, that which may be concealed [*au dissimulable*],
or even the non-manifest in general, it cannot be unveiled [*dévoilable*: i.e., unveil-
able]. It remains inviolable even when it is believed to have been revealed. Not
that it is hidden forever in some indecipherable crypt or behind some absolute
veil. Simply, it exceeds the play of veiling/unveiling: concealment/revelation,

night/day, forgetting/remembering [*anamnèse*], earth/heaven, etc. It therefore does not belong to truth, neither to truth as homoiosis or adequation, nor to truth as memory (*Mnemosynè, aletheia*), nor to truth as given, nor to truth as promised, nor to truth as inaccessible. Its non-phenomenality is without relation (even a negative one) with phenomenality. Its reserve is no longer of the order of that intimacy fondly described as secret, that closeness or properness that soaks up or inspires so many deep discourses (on *Geheimnis* or, richer still, the inexhaustibility of the *Unheimlich*)"; Derrida, *Passions*, 60–61; *On the Name*, 26; translation modified. Compare Blanchot, *L'Entretien infini*, 44, 131; *The Infinite Conversation*, 31, 92.

188. Derrida, "Forcener le subjectile," in Paule Thévenin and Jacques Derrida, *Antonin Artaud: dessins et portraits* (Paris: Gallimard, 1986), 60; "To Unsense the Subjectile," in *The Secret Art of Antonin Artaud*, trans. Mary Ann Caws (Cambridge, MA: MIT Press, 1998), 70; original emphases; translation modified.

189. See Derrida, "Forcener le subjectile," in Thévenin and Derrida, *Antonin Artaud: dessins et portraits*, 55–108; *The Secret Art of Antonin Artaud*, 60–157; and Derrida, *Artaud le Moma* (Paris: Galilée, 2002), first delivered as a commemorative talk on the occasion of Artaud's centenary at the Museum of Modern Art (MoMA) in New York, 16 October 1996. On the pact with Artaud, and with Thévenin, see *Artaud le Moma*, 98–99.

190. See Thévenin and Derrida, *Antonin Artaud: dessins et portraits*, 142–251. Unfortunately, the English translation of the essays by Thévenin and Derrida was unable to reproduce the reproductions from Artaud that were an integral part of the original volume. A number of these are, however, also reproduced in *Antonin Artaud, dessins* (Paris: Centre Georges Pompidou, 1987), the catalogue of an exhibition held between 30 June and 11 October 1987 at the Centre Pompidou in Paris. The notebooks filled by Artaud during this last period of his life also contain many drawings, some of which Artaud was planning to publish shortly before he died. See Artaud, *50 dessins pour assassiner la magie*, ed. Évelyne Grossman (Paris: Gallimard, 2004). One of the last notebooks used by Artaud before he died has also recently been published in facsimile; see Artaud, *Cahier, Ivry, janvier 1948*, ed. Évelyne Grossman (Paris: Gallimard, 2006).

191. See Derrida, *Artaud le Moma*, 19–21.

192. See Derrida, "Forcener le subjectile," 55; "To Unsense the Subjectile," 61.

193. Artaud, *Œuvres complètes*, XI, 20.

194. See Derrida, "Forcener le subjectile," 56; "To Unsense the Subjectile," 64. Derrida also uses the word to refer to Ponge's *sponge* and *table* in the 1988 version of *Signéponge*, 56, 116. It is also worth noting that, according to the writer in 1964 (and again in 1975), Genet's first realisation of the possibilities of writing

was while in prison in 1939, when he sent a postcard to a German friend in America at the time (or, according to a different version, in Czechoslovakia). "I didn't really know what to say to her," comments Genet. "The side of the postcard I was meant to write on had a coarse bleached look to it [*un aspect grumeleux blanc:* Genet later describes it as *grenu,* grainy], a bit like snow, and the surface made me talk about snow, which you didn't see in prison obviously, and refer to Christmas, and instead of talking about nothing in particular, I spoke to her about the quality of the card. That was the trigger that got me writing. I don't suppose it was the motive, but it was what gave me the first taste of freedom." See Genet, *L'Ennemi déclaré,* 19; *The Declared Enemy,* 9–10; translation modified. It will be remembered that in 1980 Derrida published a book much concerned, among other things, with the readability or unreadability of writing, entitled *La Carte postale, The Post Card.*

195. According to *Le Dictionnaire Robert,* the word *subjectile,* in French, dates from the mid-twentieth century. Derrida speculates for his part whether it may have had earlier, more distant origins in French or Italian; see "Forcener le subjectile," 56; "To Unsense the Subjectile," 64. In English, according to the *OED,* the word was first introduced in 1859.

196. See Derrida, "Forcener le subjectile," 55, 89, 99; "To Unsense the Subjectile," 61, 122, 136–37; translations modified. For the three passages in Artaud, see Artaud, *Œuvres complètes,* V (1964) 171; XIX (1984), 259; and *Œuvres,* 1467. "La Machine de l'être ou Dessin à regarder de traviole" is reproduced in *Antonin Artaud: dessins et portraits,* 165; and in *Antonin Artaud, dessins,* 31.

197. On the subjectile as neutral *khora,* "a figure of the *khora,* if not the *khora* itself," see Derrida, "Forcener le subjectile," 89; "To Unsense the Subjectile," 123. On *khôra* as an indication of the undecidable logic of the namelessness of the name, see Derrida, *Khôra* (Paris: Galilée, 1993); *On the Name,* 87–127.

198. See Derrida, "Forcener le subjectile," 59–60; "To Unsense the Subjectile," 69–70.

199. See Derrida, *Artaud le Moma,* 11–12. As a consequence, Derrida's talk was advertised by way of a strange circumlocution: "Jacques Derrida . . . ," MoMA announced, "will present a lecture about Artaud's drawings."

200. "Interjections" is the title used by Artaud for one of the individual sections, and one of the longer discrete, incantatory, and radically untranslatable texts that make up *Suppôts et Suppliciations,* which begins: "**maloussi toumi / tapapouts hermafrot / emajouts pamafrot / toupi pissarot / rapajouts erkampfti** / It isn't the crushing [*concassement*] of language but the random pulverisation of the body by a bunch of ignoramuses [*des ignares*] which . . . "; see Artaud, *Œuvres complètes,* XIV: 2 (1978), 11; boldface in original. No doubt, the numerous **ar**'s and **ot**'s contained in these interjections are readable as so many cryptic attempts, both this way and that, at signing the name: Antonin Artaud.

201. Artaud, *Œuvres complètes*, XIV: 2, 12.
202. Derrida, *Artaud le Moma*, 102–3.

Chapter Five   Radical Indecision

1. Blanchot, *L'Entretien infini*, viii; *The Infinite Conversation*, xii; translation modified.

Index

LESLIE HILL

is professor of French studies at the University of Warwick.

He is the author or editor of several publications,

including *The Cambridge Introduction to Jacques Derrida*.